Computer Information
Systems with BASIC

Jerome S. Burstein

San José State University

Edward G. Martin

Kingsborough Community College
City University of New York

Computer Information Systems with BASIC

THE DRYDEN PRESS

Chicago•Fort Worth•San Francisco•Philadelphia•Montreal•Toronto•London•Sydney•Tokyo

To Lynne and Michael—Jerome
To Lesley, Elissa and Andrea—Edward

Acquisitions Editor: David Chodoff
Production Coordinator: Lila M. Gardner, Spectrum Publisher Services, Inc.
Production Manager: Roger Kasunic
Text and cover design: Gayle Jaeger
Cover, title and part-opening photographs: Longcore Maciel Studio
Illustrations: Scientific Illustrators
Photo Research: Teri Stratford
Composition: Science Press
Printing and Binding: R. R. Donnelley & Sons, Inc.

Library of Congress Cataloging-in-Publication Data

Burstein, Jerome S.
    Computer information systems with BASIC.

    Includes index.
    1. Electronic data processing.   2. Management
information systems.   3. BASIC (Computer program
language)   I. Martin, Edward G.   II. Title.
QA76.B86   1989   004   88-37352
ISBN 0-03-029379-0

Printed in the United States of America

ISBN 0-03-029379-0

9 0 1   0 4 1   9 8 7 6 5 4 3 2

Address editorial correspondence: 908 N. Elm Street, Hinsdale, IL 60521

The Dryden Press
Holt, Rinehart and Winston
Saunders College Publishing

brief contents

detailed contents

part three: Productivity software 236

8 *Software packages: programs off the shelf* 238

16 Distributed processing: linking the world 534

appendix: An introduction to programming in BASIC A-1

Glossary of key terms G-1

Credits C-1

Index I-1

Successful business people don't spend money on fads. When they invest in a computer information system, they expect it to contribute to the goals of their organization. To do so, it must serve the needs of the people in the organization and the clients the organization serves.

Computers, after all, are only tools, and like any tool, they exist to serve the people who use them. This simple fact, so easy to forget amid the hype of the high-stakes, high-tech, and rapidly changing world of the information industry, is the foundation of this book.

Our goal has been to create a text that stresses the role of people—users—in information systems. We wanted to provide students—the future users of information systems—with the basic technical resources they will need to make computers work for them. We wanted to be sure they understood the role of information systems in the organizations in which they are likely to work. And we wanted to provide them with a thorough understanding of the variety of software tools available to them.

Features of the text

The key features of *Computer Information Systems* were all developed with these goals in mind. They include readability, a stress on the role of people in information systems, exceptionally strong coverage of productivity software, currency, and a flexible organization.

Readability

The first and most important feature of this text is clear, direct, and lively writing. Without good writing even the simplest concepts can seem obscure. We use numerous examples to illustrate key points. The primary source of examples is the world of business, although many business problems, say, in accounting, are applicable in any area.

The role of people in information systems

The parts of an information system are people, rules and procedures, data, software, and hardware. The parts are not equal, however—people are more important than the other four.

To show how people interact with the other elements of an information system in an organizational setting, we have developed four fictional organizations. Most chapters start with a story that draws on one of these organizations or the people in them. The story presents the people in the organization with a problem that relates to the subject matter of the chapter. A wrap-up at the end of the chapter then shows how the problem is resolved.

Productivity software

Computer Information Systems includes five chapters on productivity software: Chapters 8, "Software Packages: Programs Off the Shelf;" Chapter 9, "Word Processing: Manipulating Text and Ideas;" Chapter 10, "Electronic Spreadsheets: Thinking in Rows and Columns;" Chapter 11, "Database Management: Harnessing the Power of Files;" and Chapter 12, "Desktop Publishing and Graphics: Art and Information Merge." These chapters give a thorough introduction to the capabilities of current applications software, using the most popular software in the business world as examples. They give students an overview of each type of software package, providing them the in-depth understanding they need to approach the computer lab or the workplace with confidence.

Currency

In a fast-changing field like that of information systems, currency is important. We have endeavored throughout to include material that is as up-to-date as possible.

Flexibility

Computer Information Systems is divided into five parts: Introduction, Hardware, Productivity Software, Creating Information Systems, and Social Issues. Hardware and Productivity Software were written to be independent modules. Depending on your preference, you can go from the introductory chapters directly to productivity software before covering hardware, or you can cover the material in the sequence in which it appears.

Other features

In addition to these key features, the book includes many other learning aids. For each chapter these include:

- A chapter outline.
- Learning objectives.
- An opening vignette or story and a closing wrap-up that are usually taken from one of the fictional organizations introduced in Chapter 1 and that present the subject matter for the chapter in a realistic setting.
- Key words set in boldface and defined when they are introduced.
- Case in point boxes that present real cases related to the chapter material.
- Career boxes that focus on a chapter-related career.
- Enhancement boxes with interesting supplementary examples and cases.
- A concise summary.
- A key terms list that gives the boldface terms in that chapter and the page on which they appear.
- A comprehensive set of review questions, including true-false, multiple-choice, fill-in, short answer, and essay questions. Answers to all except the short answer and essay questions appear at the end of the review questions. The short answer and essay question answers are found in the *Instructor's Manual*.

The text also features a Glossary with concise definitions of all of the key terms in the book.

Computer Information Systems is designed for a class in computers and information systems and meets or exceeds the suggested content for a first course in the Data Processing Management Association (DPMA) curriculum for the first course (CIS-1 Introduction to Computer-based Systems). It presents a firm foundation for information system majors, for business students with other majors who must be familiar with information systems, and for students in other disciplines who need a general introduction to computers. Most students who take the course for which this book is written are business majors, but we do not intend the book to be limited to business students. It can also serve students of diverse majors in a general service course. In fact, at both San José State and Kingsborough College our classes have many nonbusiness majors from the social sciences, aeronautics, engineering, and health science areas.

Programming in BASIC

Two versions of *Computer Information Systems* are available, one with an appendix on programming in BASIC, and one without. The appendix provides a comprehensive introduction to the BASIC programming language that stresses structured techniques.

The instructional package

Computer Information Systems comes with a complete package of ancillary materials for both student and instructor. The package includes a student *Study Guide*, an *Instructor's Manual*, a set of *Transparency Acetates*, a *Test Bank*, and a range of productivity software with accompanying workbooks available through The Dryden Press.

The Study Guide

The student *Study Guide*, written by Jerry Ralya and the authors of the textbook, uses self-testing to help students master the material in the textbook. For every chapter in the textbook the *Study Guide* provides an outline, a pretest, a list of objectives, a detailed summary, and extensive review questions (with the answers provided in an answer key). Each chapter also includes an expanded discussion of the vignette/wrap-up sections called "Information Systems at Work" to stimulate further student interest in the material.

The Instructor's Manual

The *Instructor's Manual* contains materials to help instructors organize lectures and class discussions. It also includes additional case studies, productivity software projects, and suggestions for using the *Transparency Acetates*, In preparing it we tried to provide material useful to the full range of people who teach about information systems: both full-time and part-time instructors, veterans and first timers.

For each chapter of the textbook the *Instructor's Manual* contains:

A brief summary of the chapter that stresses its major objectives; annotated learning objectives; a glossary with definitions of the key terms in the chapter; a lecture outline that reviews the key points of the chapter—the outline is keyed to teaching suggestions and transparency acetates, indicating when they should be used; teaching suggestions with ideas for enlivening lectures and discussions and pointers on how to make the most of the textbook and the other elements in the package; a script, or description, of each transparency acetate; case studies in a ready-to-duplicate format; answers to the end-of-chapter short answer and essay questions.

For the chapters on productivity software, the *Instructor's Manual* includes suggested projects that can be carried out on any major software package.

Transparency Acetates

Computer Information Systems comes with a set of ready-to-show *Transparency Acetates* for use with an overhead projector. All of the diagrams have been rendered especially for projection. They include both completely original diagrams and important figures from the book.

The Test Bank

The *Test Bank* contains over 3000 test questions including true-false, multiple-choice, fill-in, matching, and short answer questions. The questions were prepared by the authors. The *Test Bank* is available in printed form and on disk for the Apple II family and the IBM PC.

Productivity software

The Dryden Press has a variety of software packages and workbooks that can be combined with *Computer Information Systems* to support a productivity software lab. See your Dryden representative for details.

Dryden supports its software offerings with a free consulting service. The consultants, including Ed Martin, one of the authors of this text, are academic professionals who can offer you assistance by phone or in on-campus demonstrations by special arrangement. Your Dryden representative can provide you with consulting schedules and telephone numbers.

Journal Abstracts

Dryden periodically publishes a series called *Selected Abstracts in Data Processing and MIS* that contains abstracts of current articles from major journals in the information systems field.

Acknowledgments

A textbook like this could never be created without a variety of assistance. Our goal, after all, is to serve the instructors and students who will use this book. Thus we owe a special word of thanks to the people who reviewed this book in all its many drafts and kept us in touch with the user's perspective: Joyce H. Abler-Kaypen, Eastern Michigan University; Susan Brender, Boise State University; James Chalfant, Midwestern University; William Cornette, Southwest Missouri State University; Theodore R. Coyle, Arapahoe Community College; Pat Fenton, West Valley College; Carol Grimm, Palm Beach Junior College; Dennis Guster, Meramec Community College; Earl Halvas, Western Michigan University; Tom Harris, Ball State University; Richard Hatch, San Diego State University; Marvin Haas, Monmouth College; Joyce Little, Towson State College; Jean Melman, Mount Union College; Jeffrey Mock, Diablo Valley College; Garry Morris, Moorhead State University; Jan Olsen, North Hennepin Community College; Rod Southworth, Laramie County Community College; Evelyn Speiser, Glendale College; Venkat Subramanian, University of Wisconsin, Parkside; T. J. Surynt, Stetson University; Andrew Targowski, Western Michigan University; Anthony Tiona, Broward Community College; Paul Will, State University of New York, Oswego; Margaret Zinky, Phoenix College.

Special thanks are due to friends and colleagues for their contributions and for their willingness to share their expertise. At San José State: we would like to thank Susan Ashley, Larry Gerston, Larry Lapin, Edward Laurie, David Lee, and John Lehane. Marshall Burak, school dean, and David Smith, department chair, supported classroom release time without which it would have been difficult for us to finish the text on time. At Kingsborough Community College, City University of New York: we would like to thank André Montero, CPA and accounting professor; and Melvin Levine, department chair, for his support and encouragement. We would also like to thank Alan Friedenthal, a direct marketing consultant in New York City; George Lancer, software designer and principal at Bally Systems; and Warren Wolfsohn a dedicated Mac user.

A number of people assisted us in creating or evaluating the text. First, Lynn Burstein collated the glossary and index. She also provided valuable feedback on all phases of the project.

Lila M. Gardner, of Spectrum Publisher Services saw the book through production under an incredibly tight schedule. We are grateful for her efficiency, intelligence, tireless energy, and wry wit. She is as responsible as anyone for the handsome text you are reading.

We would like to thank Gayle Jaeger for the extremely attractive design of the text, and Teri Stratford for her work as photo researcher.

Many people at The Dryden Press and its sister division, Holt, Rinehart, and Winston helped make this book possible. David Chodoff, Acquisitions Editor at Holt, survived our countless questions, telephone calls, and reams of manuscript to help organize this textbook. Also to be thanked at Dryden and Holt are DeVilla Williams, Butch Gemin, Howard Weiner, Roger Kasunic, Doug Chilcott, and Elaine Pascal.

We also want to thank the software vendors who provided us with their newest software releases, helping to assure the timeliness of the text.

Finally, we have to thank our students at San José State and Kingsborough who used portions of this book over the past several years. Their comments—both critical and encouraging—helped make this book what it is.

Jerome Burstein　　　　　*Edward Martin*
San José　　　　　　　　　New York City

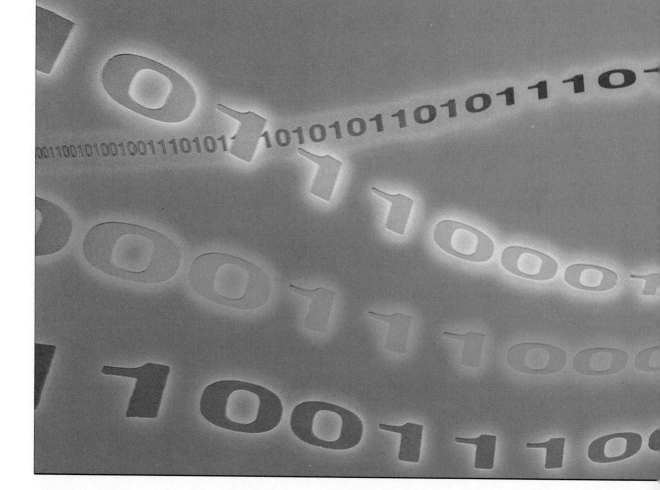

part one

Introduction

Welcome to this book on computers and information systems. Part One introduces you to basic concepts concerning the uses of computers found all around us.

We begin in Chapter 1 with an introduction to information systems and computers as tools for business. In Chapter 2 we see what makes information systems tick—the people, rules and procedures, data, software, and hardware. Chapter 3 examines management information systems, information resource management, and decision support systems. Chapter 4 discusses the historical evolution of computers and information systems.

1 Information systems and computers: tools for business
2 What makes information systems tick: from people to hardware
3 Information systems in business: functions and management
4 Why information systems were created: a bit of history

Information systems and computers: tools for business

After studying this chapter you should understand the following:

- *The importance of the computer in business.*
- *How computers affect your life.*
- *The difference between data and information.*
- *How information systems convert data into information.*
- *The wide use of information systems throughout industry and commerce.*

chapter 1

Enter the computer

Janis Roberts closed the door of her travel agency office for the day. She passed its window displays, which beckoned to vacation as well as business travelers. Janis had a lot on her mind. She walked to her car, got in, started it, and set off toward home.

After driving a few minutes, she stopped at a light near another Freddy Johnson's Travel Agency office. There were four Johnson offices scattered across Oakriver. Only a few months had passed since Janis had been promoted from an agent at the downtown office to the manager of the new branch. Though she was new at her job, the owner, Freddy Johnson, had asked her to lead the group that would select small computers for the four offices.

Janis parked her car, scooped the day's mail from the box, and entered her house while glancing at the envelopes. She held a letter from her mother, a mail-order catalog, a brochure from a local university, a telephone bill, and an unexpected letter from the Internal Revenue Service. She was already tired from a hard day of work and worried about the computer assignment her boss had given her. This stack of mail did not look like it was going to ease her mind.

Her mother's letter was the most important. Janis read that first. Her mother wrote that she had received the results of the hospital tests. One test employed a computerized body scan. Her mother assured her that there was no need to worry, since the doctor said the tests revealed no serious problems.

Janis next opened the phone bill. It seemed larger than usual. And what about those three long-distance calls to Anchorage? She didn't know anyone in Alaska! She decided to call her long-distance phone company tomorrow and give them a piece of her mind.

The mail-order catalog, a new one, caught her eye. She wondered why she kept receiving catalogs she hadn't requested. Placing the catalog aside, she saw the envelope from the IRS. Well, after dinner would be soon enough to open that one.

At any moment her family would arrive home. Her husband George, a quality-control supervisor, had picked up their daughter Meagan from school. George intended to treat Meagan to a science fiction movie filled with special visual effects. George and his co-workers used computers every day at the appliance factory. As quality control inspectors and supervisors, they relied on computers to check that goods were up to standards during all stages of production.

Meagan, 9 years old, loved to play video games at home with her friends, and she was learning how to program computers at school.

"Perhaps we should buy Meagan a home computer," Janis thought. In fact, it seemed to Janis that her life was becoming increasingly surrounded by computers. Still reflecting on her new assignment at the travel agency, she scanned the Oakriver University catalog again and decided to sign up for the introductory computer course.

Computers all around us

A large part of our lives

In a single day, Janis Roberts came into contact with computers used in office work, customer service, health care, education, government, and entertainment. Like her, we have all felt the impact of computers on our personal and work lives. Let's briefly review the uses of computers that Janis encountered.

■ *Office work.* The travel agents whom Janis managed already used a link to a computer to make reservations and help issue tickets (Figure 1-1a). Janis was faced with the challenge of leading a team to select the new small computers that would further smooth work at all four offices. Her husband George used computers at the factory to assure that materials, parts, and finished products were checked for quality (Figure 1-1b).

■ *Customer service.* The telephone company used computers to route calls (Figure 1-1c), as well as to create the bill from records of calls made by the Roberts family during the billing period. Janis wondered why she received so many mail-order catalogs. They were addressed from computerized mailing lists. Direct-mail companies and nonprofit organizations, such as churches and universities, often trade lists among themselves. Insurance companies, banks, brokerage houses, credit card companies, and many other businesses, also trade or buy lists.

(a)

(b)

(c)

■ *Health care.* The good news from the body scan—which allowed a physician to look inside the body of Janis's mother without surgery—was made possible by computers (Figure 1-1d). Such scans are only one example of many applications of computers in medicine. Among other uses, computers routinely monitor the heart and other vital signs, help in diagnostic work in the laboratory, and keep tabs on the condition of both mother and infant during childbirth.

■ *Education.* The computer age has affected all levels of education, from Meagan's elementary school classes all the way through to continuing education at colleges and universities for people like Janis (Figure 1-1e). As computers have become increasingly common in the workplace, more and more people have had to learn to use them. And computers are themselves used as teaching tools in a variety of subjects, from writing to mathematics.

■ *Government.* Of course the Internal Revenue Service is not the only computer user in government, but merely the tip of the iceberg. The IRS relies extensively on computers to process tax returns. Among other tasks, computers help verify that figures on a return add up and that formulas are applied correctly. And, what was in that letter? Just a note saying the Roberts family was entitled to a larger refund!

■ *Entertainment.* The special effects in the movie George and Meagan saw were produced by computers that create and manipulate animated images (Figure 1-1f). The video games Meagan loves to play with her friends also owe much of their rapid-paced entertainment value to the electronic speed of computers.

Figure 1-1
Ways that computers affect our lives. (a) Making reservations. (b) Quality control. (c) Computerized switching. (d) Science and medicine (a computer-generated image of a DNA molecule). (e) In school. (f) Entertainment.

(d)

(e)

(f)

*The computer:
what it is and
what it does*

A COMPUTER is a very-high-speed electronic device that can accept data and instructions, use the instructions to perform logical and mathematical operations, and report the results of the processing. Although a computer is only a machine, it can free people from laborious calculations, giving them time for more important creative tasks. It can help in problem solving and information management. Businesses use computers in thousands of ways. To businesspeople, the computer is a tool. With it, business managers can provide themselves with the information they need to manage their companies' resources.

To know how to use a computer well, you must know what it can do, how it operates, and how it might affect your life. Often, we hear computer terms bandied about as if they were magic cures for every problem. In fact computers must be used very thoughtfully. They are only as smart as their users, and they must always be directed toward specific goals. If garbage goes in, garbage comes out.

How much you need to know about computers depends on the tasks you want them to perform. For example, a marketing manager may only need to know how to request certain reports from the staff who run the company's computer system. On the other hand, a manager of computer operations will need to know in some detail how the computer works. Similarly, if you own a small computer, you may want to find out more about it than a person who simply uses one.

Getting to know how a computer works is much like learning any other skill. It does take a certain amount of time and organized study.

*Four model
organizations*

To help you understand computers, we will explore their roles in three private businesses and one nonprofit institution. Throughout this text, we will draw on these four organizations to illustrate many points about computer capabilities. Though these fictional organizations reside only in the invented city of Oakriver, they represent thousands of real-life workplaces across the country.

■ *Freddy Johnson's Travel Agency* is a service-oriented retail company. Medium-sized, it has four offices in Oakriver, with the main one downtown and the other three in major shopping centers.

■ *Global Electrical Equipment* is a large multinational manufacturing company with plants in 25 countries and sales offices in over 80. Global Electrical's home appliance design and manufacturing facility in Oakriver employs several thousand people.

■ *Paul's House of Electronic Wonders* is a wholesale distributor of electronic parts to retailers, wholesalers, and manufacturers. With customers across the country, the company faces many challenges in this ever-changing market.

■ *Oakriver University*, a nonprofit institution, offers undergraduate, graduate, and professional degree programs. With 22,000 full-time students, OU also offers its surrounding community programs for job enrichment and continuing education.

Each of these organizations must acquire and manage information to function. To do so more efficiently, they have turned increasingly to the computer.

The need for information

Data and information

Earlier we learned that Freddy Johnson wants to use computers to extract useful information that his managers can use to make better decisions. If they cannot get this information, Johnson's travel business could suffer from incorrect or poorly timed decisions. Putting the computer to work, however, could provide the agency with a competitive edge and prevent customers from defecting to a competitor.

The information Johnson seeks is drawn from data. DATA are facts. For a travel agent preparing a client's itinerary, relevant data are such facts as the client's name, account number, credit status, departure and return dates, and desired airlines. These facts must be accurate and timely. Accuracy is ensured through verification of the data. Incorrect data or data acquired too late can be damaging. For instance, if Freddy Johnson and his agents relied on outdated airline schedules or misentered customer billing numbers, they would soon have many disgruntled customers.

To a manufacturing company like Global Electrical Equipment, data are product types, their specifications, compatible subcomponents, the current number of units being produced, and suppliers by type. If the supplier of a switch can only supply Global for 30 more days, where else can Global buy the part? If the data on suppliers by type are up to date, Global should find its answer there.

Our recognition of the sources of data to aid in making decisions has broadened in recent years. Originally, decision makers were satisfied with computerized systems that focused on processing data gathered from internal operations. We now recognize that data for business decisions come from three major sources: transactions, text, and voice/image (see Figure 1-2).

■ TRANSACTION DATA come from facts gathered from routine day-to-day operations common to a business. Our transaction examples include purchasing an airplane ticket and ordering electronic parts. Usually these data are collected and maintained internally by the organization.

■ TEXT DATA are found in written sources—reports, documents, and articles or abstracts from magazines, journals, and other printed media. Much of this material may be generated from outside of the organization.

■ VOICE/IMAGE DATA are gleaned from various telecommunications media. Telephone messages (voice) and image transmissions from both inside and outside the organization must be considered.

In looking at information for organizations, we have assumed until recently that crucial data for business decisions came almost exclusively from internal data sources. Hence, the other two sources of data have not been integrated fully into business systems.

INFORMATION is knowledge communicated in a timely, accurate, and understandable fashion. Information is extracted, or distilled, from

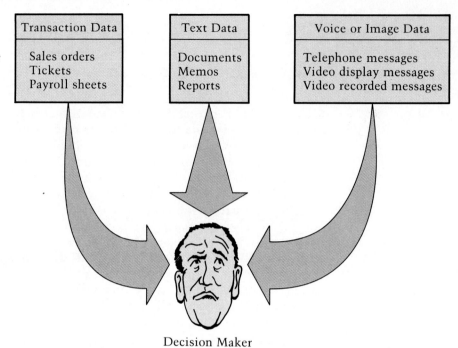

Figure 1-2
*Sources of data for deci-
sion makers include
transactions, text, voice/
image.*

data. As a manager at Johnson's Travel Agency, Janis Roberts might need a monthly report on her agents' performances. The report, extracted from data on each agent's *transactions*, would help her determine which agents were performing well and which needed help.

Sometimes all three types of data are needed to arrive at a decision. At Oakriver University, the financial aid director uses reports extracted from *transaction data* on student financial status and academic performance to allocate on-campus scholarships. The director needs access to current scholarship allocation rules set by private foundations and government agencies. These rules, *text data*, come from off-campus sources. Clarifying these rules may require a number of telephone calls over several days—*voice data*. Some messages can be transmitted to display screens as *image data*. Combining these data sources, the administrator (like many other decision makers) can acquire accurate, prompt, and readily understandable information to do an effective job.

At times, data and information seem identical, and often, *one person's information may be another's data.* Penny Helmsley is a sales manager at Paul's House of Electronic Wonders. Susan Paul is vice-president of sales and marketing. Every week Penny uses a report derived from sales records or data for the previous week. Penny considers the report information. Vice-President Paul treats these same weekly reports as data for quarterly and annual sales reports. To her, the reports covering a longer period are information.

**The value of
information**

Information is valuable. It is a resource to be managed and protected—just like more "physical" assets such as cash or inventory. Information's value declines over time (Figure 1-3), so speed in gathering and communicating information is essential.

Figure 1-3
The value of information
declines over time.

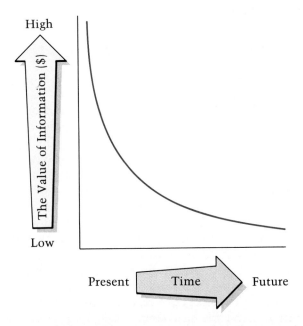

Freddy Johnson's agency managers need to know how to adjust their agents' schedules to fit peak travel periods. Therefore, managers must have information about expected demand soon enough to help shape their agents' schedules. Many customers pay for their tickets with credit cards. Credit card records must be adjusted for each transaction and checked against the customer's credit limit. If a credit card is stolen but the owner does not report the theft immediately, the computer credit card verification system may not have this information on hand. As a result, the card company risks losses because of illegal transactions.

A wholesaler needs to know the products that retail stores, manufacturers, and other wholesalers require. The type and volume of inventory needed are monitored so the wholesaler knows how much to order and when. Like the retail travel operation, wholesalers need up-to-date information to determine their customers' credit-worthiness.

Late or garbled information can cost time, money, and sometimes even lives. Minimizing these costs and maximizing the flow of information to the people who need it is the role of the information system.

The information system: converting data into information

An information system provides users with timely, accurate, understandable, and relevant information. Information systems are known by many names: data processing systems, business computer systems, electronic data processing systems, and information-processing systems. To avoid confusion, we will use only the term *information system* in this book.

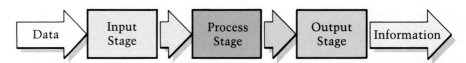

Figure 1-4
The input, processing, and output stages for converting data into information. To assist you in understanding the illustrations, a color-coding scheme is used throughout the text. The orange arrows show the flow from input to processing; the green tinted ones, from processing to output. Each box is also color-coded: input is tinted yellow; processing, blue; and output, green.

Figure 1-5
A computer and its peripherals. The arrow identifies the computer.

Meet the computer

A SYSTEM is a set of interrelated elements working together toward a goal. Therefore an INFORMATION SYSTEM is a set of interrelated elements working together to produce information. The elements in such a system must obtain data, process or convert the data into information, and then communicate the information to decision makers.

Creating information involves three stages: input, processing, and output. Figure 1-4 illustrates how the three stages in a typical information system interact. To assist you in understanding illustrations such as Figure 1-4, a color-coding scheme is used throughout the text. The orange arrows show the flow from input to processing; the green ones, from processing to output. Each box is also color-coded: input is tinted yellow; processing, blue; and output, green.

Ideally, if current, correct, and complete data are input to a system, processed data exit the system as timely, accurate, and useful information.

At the heart of today's information system lies the computer (shown by the arrow in Figure 1-5). It has tremendous capacity to accept, process, and retain data and information. It can perform calculations in billionths of a second and produce consistently accurate results. But it needs to be told exactly what to do.

This is where software comes into play. SOFTWARE is a general name for computer PROGRAMS—lists of precise instructions written in a language the computer can understand. These programs tell computers how to proceed step by step on particular processing jobs.

Computers cannot operate alone. They need additional hardware to function. Input, output, storage, and communication devices are called PERIPHERAL EQUIPMENT because they are attachments to the computer (surrounding the computer in Figure 1-5). Input devices present computers with data and programs in a form they can understand, and output devices transmit processed information in a form people can understand. Probably the most common input device today is the typewriter-like keyboard. Common output devices include printers and display screens or monitors. Keyboards and screens are usually linked together in a device called a display terminal that is used for both input and output.

The computer itself has a memory that stores data and programs during processing. Although this memory may be large, it cannot permanently hold all of the programs and data of an organization. Thus in addition to input and output devices, computers also need a way to store data and programs in a machine-readable form. Secondary storage devices, such as magnetic tape readers and disk drives, serve this purpose. Finally, peripherals may be located some distance from the computer linked to it or even to each other by communication devices.

In Chapter 2, we will explore systems in general and information systems in particular. But now let's look more closely at input, processing, and output.

Input

During the INPUT stage data are entered into the information system from the environment. With computerized information systems this means translating data in a machine-readable form. In most business settings transaction data are recorded on a SOURCE DOCUMENT and transferred to some machine-readable medium like magnetic tape or disk. Data from text and voice/image sources can also be converted into machine-readable form for processing. Figure 1-6 (page 14) shows some typical input data for Paul's House of Electronic Wonders.

Data from many sources do not require transfer from documents. Often data are recorded directly in machine-readable form. Whenever you use an automatic-teller machine at a bank, for example, you enter data directly into the bank's information system.

The most important requirement of the input stage is the collection of accurate, timely, and useful data. If incorrect, late, or irrelevant data enter the system the resulting information may be misleading or wrong.

Processing

In the PROCESSING stage, data are transformed into information. Processing can be performed either manually or by computer. When performed by a computer, processing usually takes one of three forms: batch, time-sharing, and real-time. Most larger computers are capable of running a program in any of the forms. With BATCH PROCESSING, data are collected over a period of time and processed as a group. The data accumulation

case in point

The user's view of information

Working with computers

Chief executive officers have often expressed a "can't work with them or without them" view of people involved in the information management field.[1] W. J. "Bill" Marriott Jr., CEO of Marriott Corporation, comments: "I asked for some information on a specific problem. In response they brought in a computer runout several inches high. I threw them out of the office. I said 'You're not running a business when you bring in something like that. You're not contributing.' "[2]

Marriot feels the best way to prevent such incidents is to put a person "in charge who is first and foremost a businessman. He has to share your values of tight cost control and doing things that are practical and not overly complex. Of course he needs to know systems but he also needs to understand people and how to manage them and their productivity."[3]

The knowledgeable user

Two factors have the greatest impact on the design of information systems: the increase of educated users as more consumers become aware of information-processing services; and the change in how businesspeople view data—coming not only from internal transaction records but also from internal and external text and voice/image sources.

Look at the increase in user-friendly output. Users have demanded the faster and less "computerlike" output available with laser printers—changing the types and capabilities of the hardware and software required. Users now require the incorporation of formalized exception procedures into information systems, such as systems that permit in-home booking of airline reservations or banking services.

Information systems can thus be used not only to maintain existing files but to attack and secure greater markets for the benefit of the whole company. One prime example is American Hospital Supply, which successfully fought to gain market share against Johnson & Johnson Corporation and other competitors in hospital purchasing departments.[4] AHS provided a terminal to the hospital for the on-line ordering of goods. The value per on-line order was higher than conventional methods, and orders could be filled more quickly—thus enabling hospitals to manage their inventories better.

The search for strategic business advantage—where information loses value quickly over time—has drawn on technologies once only used at the forefront of scientific research.[5] On Wall Street, stock market analysts are using supercomputers and programs (once reserved for esoteric research, such as antisubmarine warfare simulations) to look for patterns in past stock trading to predict the best times to buy and sell shares. The potential profits—for the firm that guesses right—are enormous.

From targeting stock options to targeting households, the information systems have an

period for a batch run may be an hour, a day, a week, or longer. A common example of batch processing is the creation of payroll checks for a company's employees.

With TIME-SHARING PROCESSING, the computer alternates between several operations. This allows several users to run programs at the same time, giving all users the illusion that they have the computer to themselves. Most time-sharing systems are terminal-based and interactive, with the requests a user makes and the responses a computer gives, taking place as a "dialogue" between the user and the computer.

impact. Using image-processing methods developed from NASA's space program, geographers are aiding the efforts of corporate marketing departments in selling products ranging from automobiles and grocery products to express package services and oil drilling equipment.[6] Detailed maps ranging in size from whole states or provinces down to city blocks are available to traveling salespeople and dispatch drivers on display terminals placed in their vehicles.

Of course information systems do not instantly guarantee success. Writing on the "puny payoff from office computers" William Bowen observes: "In upbeat stories that some managers tell about computers and productivity, two themes recur. One, work is done differently from the way it was done in precomputer days. Two, getting there took time."[7]

Bowen reinforces his position on office automation by sharing insights from a consultant in this area. "Nancy Bancroft, manager of office systems consulting at Digital Equipment Corp., advises prospective clients to scrutinize their procedures before they decide what to buy. 'If people are doing the wrong things when you automate,' she says, 'you get them to do the wrong things faster.' "[8]

Certainly we need people with more than a "hardware" or a "software" view of a business to assist the user in the quest for greater productivity.

The view toward tomorrow

As information systems continue to evolve, practitioners will extend the support given executives and people at other corporate levels. Efforts will be made to match the needs of users to the elements of information systems—the rules and procedures, data, software, and hardware. The point of these efforts is to aid managers in making corporate decisions.

[1]Portions of this discussion are based on Jerome S. Burstein, "Can IRM Break the Information Log-Jam," *Northern California Executive Review* (Fall 1986): 1–5.
[2]Cited in Stephanie K. Walter, "A CEO's Recipe for Mixing Management and Machines," *Management Technology* 2 (July 1984): 43.
[3]Ibid.
[4]"Information Power: How Companies Are Using New Technologies to Gain a Competitive Edge," *Business Week*, 14 October 1985, 108–114.
[5]John W. Verity, "Street Smarts: The Supercomputer Becomes a Stock Strategist," *Business Week*, 1 June 1987, 84–85.
[6]Mimi Bluestone and Evert Clark, "These Maps Can Almost Read People's Minds," *Business Week*, 11 May 1987, 138–139.
[7]Willian Bowen, "The Puny Payoff from Office Computers," *Fortune*, 26 May 1986, 22.
[8]Ibid.

In **REAL-TIME PROCESSING**, the computer processes data rapidly enough that the results can be used to influence a process that is still taking place. Real-time processing is interactive and usually involves more than one user of a computer. The principal difference between time-sharing and real-time processing is speed. With a real-time system the response must be immediate. With time-sharing, the loss of a few seconds is not so crucial.

The systems used in space navigation are real-time. Banks and credit card companies often use real-time systems to check customer balances

Figure 1-6
Where data come from.
(a) A sales order serves as
a source document. (b)
Text in a document. (c)
Voice/image data sent
via satellite from a dis-
tant sales office.

(a)

SALES ORDER

Paul's House of Electronic Wonders
1500 Commerce Way, Oakriver, California 90617-0012
Telephone (223) 555-2112

Customer: _____   **Ship to:** _____
_____   _____
_____   _____

Account Number: _____

Contact Person: _____   **Bill to:** _____
_____
_____

Item	Description	Unit Price	Quantity	Price

Terms [   ]

Salesperson: _____

Subtotal
Discount   _____
Post Discount Total
Tax
GRAND TOTAL   _____

Quarterly sales are . . .

(b)

Ms. Susan Paul
Marketing Vice-President
Paul's House of Electronic Wonders
1500 Commerce Way
Oakriver, CA 90617-0012

Dear Ms. Paul:

In response to your sales inquiry . . .

Great!

(c)

that may well be changing simultaneously because of another transaction. If you think about it for a moment, you can see that this level of service could never be offered with batch processing.

There is some overlap between these processing categories. For instance, one of the users of a time-sharing system might run a program that performs batch processing: he or she would be unaware that this program shared the machine with interactive programs being used by other people. The type of processing a computer can perform is regulated by its operating system, a topic we will cover in detail in Chapter 15.

Processing, whether batch, time-sharing, or real-time, can consist of one or more actions. These actions include:

- Calculating
- Comparing
- Classifying
- Communicating
- Sorting
- Summarizing
- Selecting
- Storing
- Recalling

CALCULATING involves performing mathematical functions on data. These include addition, subtraction, multiplication, division, and higher functions such as exponentiation. Figure 1-7 shows an example of calculating. A salesperson at Paul's House of Electronic Wonders has just closed a sale for 1500 microprocessors at $6.85 with a 15 percent discount (85 percent of the list price). The salesperson, following prompts from the computer system that appear on the display terminal, enters data about the sale on the terminal (input). The computer *calculates* the total cost (processing) and produces the invoice (output).

Data can be organized by using one of four methods: comparing, classifying, selecting, or sorting. **COMPARING** involves determining

Figure 1-7
Calculate. A salesperson enters data about a sale on a microcomputer. The computer calculates the total and a printer produces the printout.

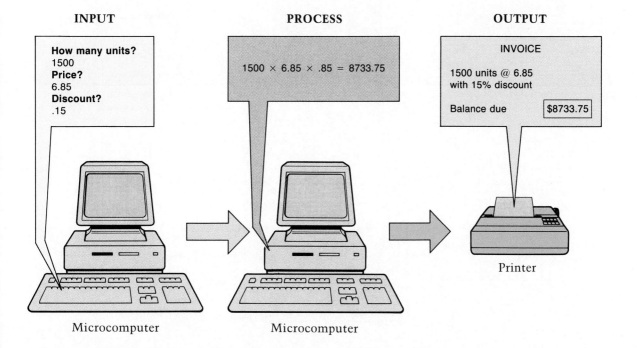

INPUT

How many units?
1500
Price?
6.85
Discount?
.15

Microcomputer

PROCESS

1500 × 6.85 × .85 = 8733.75

Microcomputer

OUTPUT

INVOICE

1500 units @ 6.85
with 15% discount

Balance due $8733.75

Printer

whether two items are the same or different. **COMMUNICATING** involves transmitting data or information from one place to another. Figure 1-8 shows how a credit verification system uses comparing and communicating to let a retailer know whether or not to allow a credit sale to a customer. The retailer enters data from the customer's credit card and the sale on a display terminal in the store. These data are *communicated* over the phone to the credit card company's computer system. The system then retrieves data about the customer's account balance and credit limit from a storage device (the beige unit), *compares* these with the data about the current sale to determine whether the customer will exceed the credit limit, and finally *communicates* the results back to the retailer's display terminal.

CLASSIFYING is a type of comparing that involves grouping data by various criteria. In Figure 1-9a, business accounts are *classified* by those with payments that are more than 60 days overdue, and those that are not. Sorting takes classifying a step further. **SORTING** refers to arranging data in some desired order—numerically from highest to lowest (as in the balance amount in Figure 1-9b), or alphabetically from "A" to "Z."

Figure 1-8
Communicate and Compare. A retailer enters data about a sale and a customer's credit card on a display screen. These data are communicated to the credit card company's computer system. The computer compares the sale amount to the customer's balance and credit limit (stored on magnetic disk—the beige unit) and communicates credit approval back to the retailer's display screen.

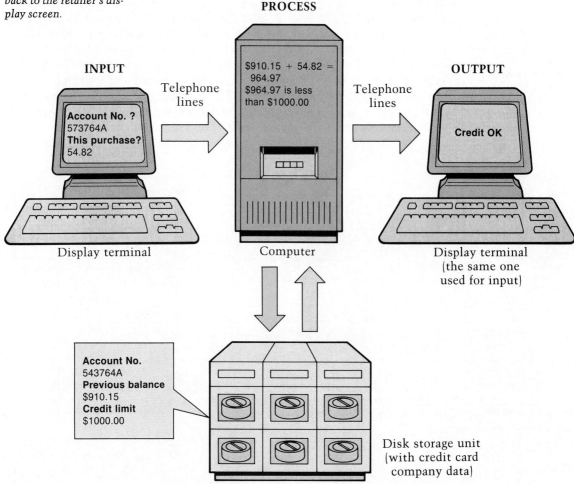

PROCESS

INPUT

Account No. ?
573764A
This purchase?
54.82

Display terminal

Telephone lines

$910.15 + 54.82 = 964.97
$964.97 is less than $1000.00

Computer

Telephone lines

OUTPUT

Credit OK

Display terminal (the same one used for input)

Account No.
543764A
Previous balance
$910.15
Credit limit
$1000.00

Disk storage unit (with credit card company data)

Figure 1-9
Classify, Sort, and Summarize. (a) A list of companies with their bal-
ances and 60-days-overdue balances are classified into those with
nonzero 60-days-overdue balances and those without. (b) The com-
puter then sorts those with nonzero overdue balances from highest to
lowest. Finally, the overdue balances are summarized by averaging
and the results are printed out.

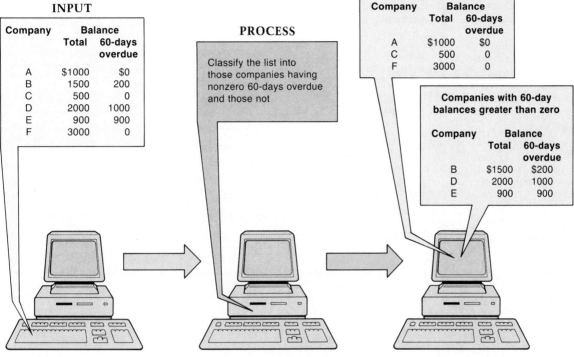

(a)   CLASSIFY

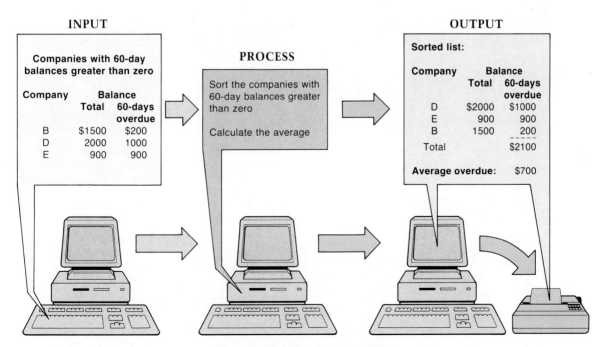

(b)   SORT AND SUMMARIZE

Figure 1-10
Store, Recall, and Select.
An administrator enters
a list of student names
and grades on a display
screen and a computer
records the names on
disk. Later the adminis-
trator requests the
names of "A" students.
The computer recalls the
list from storage, selects
the appropriate names,
and sends output to the
printer.

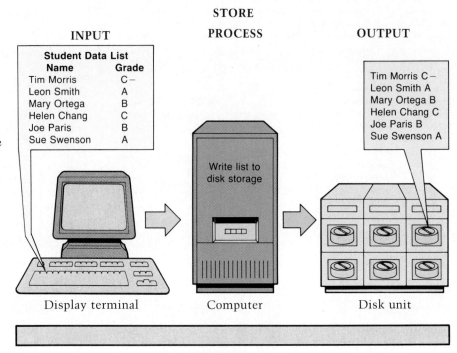

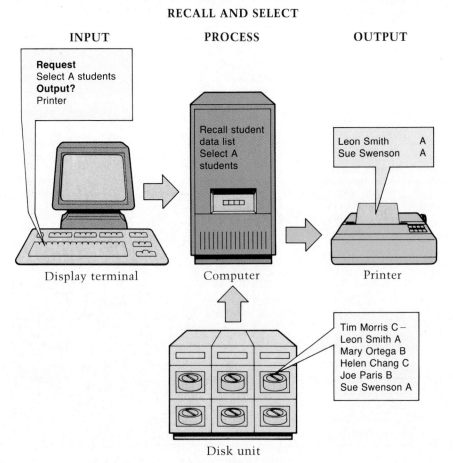

Data can also be sorted into chronological order (by date). **SUMMARIZING** involves reducing data into an easily understood format. In a business, properly summarized data can speed up the workflow—and "time is money." Calculating the averages of the *classified* and *sorted* balances in Figure 1-9 is an example of *summarizing*.

SELECTING involves extracting from data those items that have certain characteristics. If, for example, an administrator at Oakriver University wanted to identify the "A" students in a particular course, those students would be selected from a list of all the students in the class. Figure 1-10 shows how this selection might occur. It also illustrates **STORING** and **RECALLING** by placing the data into secondary storage and later recalling them. The names and grades of all students are entered on a display terminal. The computer then takes this list and *stores* it in machine-readable form on a disk system. When the data are needed again for processing, in this case to select the names of "A" students, they are *recalled* from the disk system. The computer *selects* the appropriate names and the resulting list appears as output on a printer.

Output

The **OUTPUT** stage conveys the results of processing. As the examples in Figure 1-11 show, output is often in a form people can read. As we saw in our discussion on processing, output can also be in a machine-read-

Figure 1-11
Examples of output readable to people. (a) A quality-control report summary on a display screen. (b) A printed sales report. (c) An airplane ticket printed on a specialized printer.

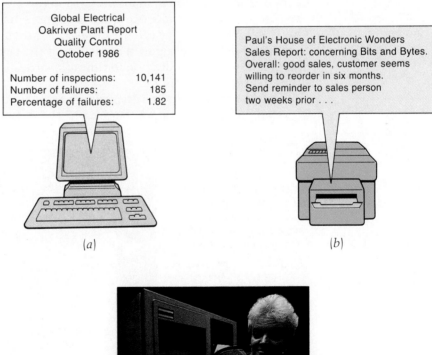

(a)

(b)

(c)

able form for *storage* for later use. Output can be "permanent," such as on paper, or "temporary," as on a display terminal or audio speaker. Paper output may be printed on blank pages or on preprinted forms such as purchase orders, airplane tickets, customer invoices, or grade reports. Output reports range from simple listings—all of the students at Oakriver University in alphabetical order—to highly condensed or summarized responses—a special report for the dean of students that shows, by department, the percentage of students who make OU's honor roll. Of course what is *output information* for the dean may become *input data* for the university's president.

From raw materials to the final user

Let's explore some of the many ways information systems are used outside of the regular business office. (Office-oriented applications, such as accounting, are discussed in Chapter 3.) Some of these applications may surprise you.

Design and manufacturing

Computer information systems are used in the design, testing, and manufacture of many products. When designers have ideas for new or improved products, they can use **COMPUTER-AIDED DESIGN (CAD)** systems to create and revise designs in a fraction of the time it would take with older methods. This reduction in time allows designers greater opportunities to exercise creativity.

The designer works at a display terminal (Figure 1-12) and draws on a special pad that transfers the data in the drawing to the computer,

Figure 1-12
Computer-aided design (CAD) system. The designer can create an initial design, modify it, look at it from different perspectives, and store it for later retrieval for production.

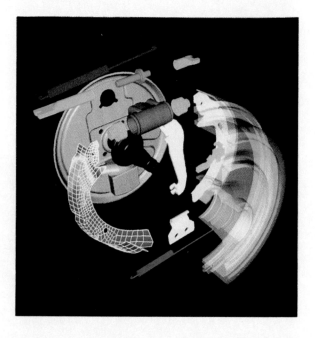

Figure 1-13
The computer-aided
manufacturing process—
an automated assembly
line.

which simultaneously shows the plans on the display screen. When the design is complete, it can be stored for later use. In addition, permanent copies of the design can be created.

Once a component or a product has been designed, it can be tested using computer simulation. COMPUTER SIMULATION programs model real-world events and attempt to predict the possible consequences of those events. Simulation programs can test the characteristics of a product for weaknesses before a prototype is even built.

If the decision is made to start manufacturing a product, computers can help here, too. Using simulation programs, engineers and managers can determine the optimal way to design the production process or assembly line to minimize costs. Once the line is set up, COMPUTER-AIDED MANUFACTURING (CAM) can use a computer to direct the actual production process (Figure 1-13). The machine tools—grinders, lathes, and drills—used to produce the product can be programmed to exact specifications, such as how deep to drill a hole.

Robots perform various production tasks today, ranging from welding or painting to final assembly. Quality-control systems use computerized methods to detect errors. The trend in manufacturing is toward greater use of computers, information systems, and robots to reduce costs further. Some factories in Europe, Japan, and North America have introduced the FLEXIBLE MANUFACTURING SYSTEMS (FMS) approach, which emphasizes the use of computer-directed machinery throughout the production process with the ability to quickly change what the line produces. With FMS, robots are not only used to produce and assemble the

Figure 1-14
Information systems in agriculture. A computerized dairy farm.

product, but to move it from one workstation to the next along the assembly line.

Agriculture

Agriculture is one of the largest industries in the United States, Canada, and other countries, and is a major source of export dollars. Information systems are available to today's farmer to help manage every aspect of farming (see Figure 1-14). Computer programs can determine the right feed mix to give animals. Microcomputers attached to sensing devices can determine how to adjust the level of fertilizer to be placed in the soil, and how deep the plow should cut into the earth. University and private researchers use information systems to analyze and develop new strains of plants and animals.

Weather forecasts based on computer predictions (Figure 1-15) can help farmers determine when to plant, water, fertilize, and harvest. To

Figure 1-15
A computer-enhanced satellite image of an oncoming storm.

give weather forecasters a better picture of the weather conditions, satellite photographs or radar images can be made clearer using computers.

By receiving up-to-the-minute information a farmer can determine the optimal time to sell animals, grain, and produce to wholesalers, slaughterhouses, and other merchants. Both before and after farmers deliver their goods to market, the use of information systems continues, as brokers and traders seek to buy and sell the commodities in the hopes of making a profit.

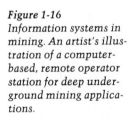

Natural resource management

Information systems can aid virtually every area of natural resource management. Consider the area of forestry. Computers assist foresters in selecting and breeding better trees for timber production. When trees are mature enough to cut, selecting the right area to log depends in part on the environmental impact of logging. Computer simulation programs can give a picture of the potential environmental effects specific logging operations may have. Even at the sawmill, computers are no strangers: they can be used to direct machinery to align the logs to minimize waste and maximize the usable timber obtained from the logs.

Information systems help locate and extract mineral resources (Figure 1-16). Computers can use satellite images to identify resources and give an idea of their value. Computers can also be used to help evaluate the best method for mining the minerals, testing the quality of the ore, monitoring antipollution controls, and other functions. Computer-directed robot mining machines can help detect and extract the ore.

Information systems are used in all phases of energy resource management: exploration, extraction, and production. Petroleum exploration teams use computer-based information systems to analyze poten-

Figure 1-16
Information systems in mining. An artist's illustration of a computer-based, remote operator station for deep underground mining applications.

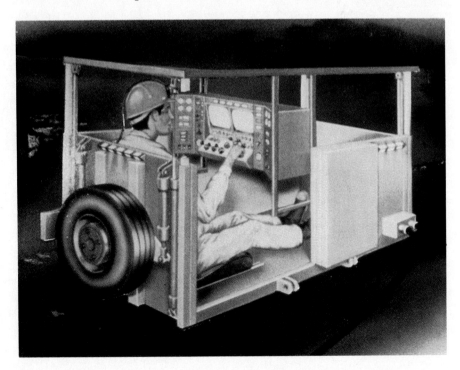

Figure 1-17
Information systems in electric power generation applications. (a) The control room of a large conventional power plant. (b) A solar energy system controlled by computers. (c) A computer-generated picture of a power grid.

(a)

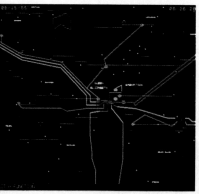

(c)

(b)

Figure 1-18
Information systems working on the railroad. (a) A computerized railroad switching yard. (b) Bay Area Rapid Transit system uses computers to control train movements.

tial oil or gas-bearing rock formations deep below the Earth's surface. Another application includes the use of submersible robots to repair off-shore undersea oil drilling rigs or wells.

Electrical utilities use information systems to determine how much power should be generated to meet the demands of consumers (Figure 1-17). Almost all generating facilities, from large power plants to wind farms, use computers to monitor energy consumption and power output. National power grids are protected from equipment failure by computers that will shut down or redirect portions of the electrical grid in order to protect expensive equipment from damage and to protect consumers from a resulting blackout.

Transportation

All forms of transportation use computers. Railroads rely on computerized switching facilities to guarantee safe uncoupling and redirecting of rail cars bound for various destinations (Figure 1-18). Freight and passenger trains on mainline tracks rely upon signals and switches set under the direction of traffic-management programs.

Trucking companies use information systems to determine schedules for drivers, for vehicle maintenance, and cargo shipping require-

(a)

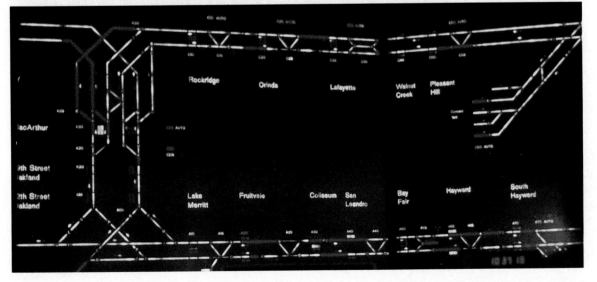

(b)

Figure 1-19
Information systems for safe air travel. (a) Ground-based air-traffic control systems depend heavily upon computers to maintain up-to-the-second track of airplanes in the air. (b) On-board computers can literally fly the modern aircraft to its destination.

(a)

(b)

ments. The cargo in a truck can also be arranged so that the first items in are the last to be delivered, using load-scheduling software programs. Car rental agencies and fleet dispatchers for bus and taxi companies often have access to computer-supplied address and driving route information to aid them in their jobs. *0*

At sea, ships use signals from satellites to on-board navigational computers to determine their positions. On-board computers assist in monitoring the engines, fire-protection devices, and other equipment. In areas of heavy shipping traffic, the U.S. Coast Guard staffs radar stations that use computer-enhanced images to locate and direct ship traffic.

The airline industry was one of the earliest and remains one of the heaviest users of information systems (Figure 1-19). Airlines utilize these systems to schedule aircraft, flight crews, and aircraft maintenance, and to track passenger reservations and air freight packages. Air-traffic control systems could not exist without computer-based information systems to monitor aircraft on the ground and in the air. On-board computers, in concert with airport-based systems, can even land aircraft with minimal pilot assistance.

Communications

The communications systems we have come to expect would be impossible to operate without the support of information systems. The switching of telephones, both local and long distance, is made possible by specialized computers used to select the proper transmission line. Many of the parts of our information systems depend upon fast communication of data within and between offices, factories, and other places of business. The information system hardware that makes all these communications "miracles" possible are discussed in Chapter 16.

All forms of communications media—print, television, radio, telex, and facsimile transmission—rely on information systems to manage the vast amounts of material they use. Newspapers, for instance, use computer-based methods to edit copy and compose page layouts.

Finally, the modern era of office automation systems is made possible through effective communications systems. Office automation is covered in detail in Chapter 3.

Wholesaling and warehousing

Information systems allow wholesalers more precise means of controlling their inventory levels. Many wholesalers are tied together through modern telecommunications networks. For example, auto-parts recyclers (formerly called junkyards) use communications links to trace hard-to-find parts. In many modern warehouses, cargo rolls into the building on automated pallets or platforms for holding cargo (see Figure 1-20). A scanner reads the product code on cartons, and an inventory program assigns cartons to specific locations. Cartons and containers no longer have to be stored alphabetically or by product type—the location of each item is recorded by the inventory programs. Computer-controlled machines can physically store and retrieve cartons. Manufacturers use similar systems to store parts and finished goods.

Retailing

Information systems are used at all stages of a customer's transaction. A common input device is a **POINT-OF-SALE (POS) TERMINAL**, which combines a cash register with a computer terminal linked to an information system. When the salesperson rings up the sale, many steps occur. First, the employee number is entered by the clerk. After the information system checks the validity of the number, the transaction proceeds. The clerk might use a laser scanner, a magnetic wand, or a keyboard to enter the

Figure 1-21
A laser scanner reads in sales data from a universal product code.

product code and other inventory information, such as size and color of the item being purchased (Figure 1-21).

For cash sales, the machine calculates the correct change. On a credit card transaction, the credit card company's data are accessed to determine the customer's credit status. Check-approval systems use similar methods so merchants may inquire about the customer's account. After the sale is approved, the POS terminal communicates data to the store computer for calculating changes in inventory level. Some POS terminals even keep a record of how quickly and accurately the clerk inputs the data.

Retailers frequently face problems in stocking the right amount of inventory for customers. Too much inventory entails heavy costs such as interest and taxes. On the other hand, if merchandise levels are kept too low and shortages develop, customers may become dissatisfied and take their business elsewhere. Poor stocking and ordering procedures can lead to severe cash-flow problems, and in extreme cases to bankruptcy. Inventory management systems help retailers determine when and how much of a product to order from a wholesaler or manufacturer.

summary

□ A computer is a very-high-speed electronic device that can accept data and instructions to perform logical and mathematical operations and report the results of the processing.

□ Computers have assumed a growing role in almost all aspects of our lives, from the home to the workplace. To use a computer well, you should know what it can do, how it operates, and how it might affect your life.

■ All organizations must acquire and manage information in order to function, and computers can help them do so efficiently.

■ Information is knowledge communicated in a timely, accurate, and understandable fashion. Information is derived from data, and data are, essentially, facts. Data can come from several different sources: transactions, text, and voice/image. The distinction between data and information is not always hard and fast. Often one person's information may be another person's facts.

■ Information is valuable, but its value declines over time. Late or garbled information can cost time, money, and sometimes even lives. The role of an information system is to minimize these costs and maximize the flow of information to the people who need it.

■ A system is a set of interrelated elements working together toward a goal. An information system is a system that converts data into information. This conversion process involves three stages: input, processing, and output.

■ The most prominent item in a computerized information system is the computer itself. Software, also known as programs, are detailed instructions that tell the computer exactly what to do. Peripheral equipment performs input, output, secondary storage, and communication functions to support the computer's processing effort.

■ Data enter an information system during the input stage. Often data are first recorded on a source document, or input directly into a machine-readable form.

■ Processing can be batch, time-sharing, or real-time. Processing tasks include calculating, comparing, communicating, classifying, sorting, summarizing, selecting, storing, and recalling.

■ The output stage conveys the results of processing. Output may take many forms, some readable, others decipherable only by machine.

■ Engineers design products using computer-aided design (CAD) systems, and test product characteristics with computer simulation programs. Computer-aided manufacturing (CAM) can then produce the actual product. Flexible manufacturing systems (FMS) use computer-directed machinery throughout the production process.

■ In agriculture, natural resource management, and transportation, information systems assist in a wide variety of planning and control functions.

■ The communications systems we have come to demand today would be impossible to operate without the support of information systems.

■ Information systems offer wholesalers, warehouses, manufacturers, and retailers more precise means of controlling levels of inventory. Sometimes goods are physically moved about under computer control as well.

■ In retailing, information systems are used at all stages of a customer's transaction. Clerks often use point-of-sale (POS) terminals to speed the transaction process.

Buying an airplane ticket

To illustrate the workings of an information system, let's see what happened when a customer phoned the branch of the travel agency that Janis Roberts ran. William Branscomb wanted to fly his parents from Los Angeles to Hong Kong to see his new business venture and enjoy a relaxing vacation. Mr. Branscomb called Freddy Johnson's Travel Agency, where he had an account. Janis herself took the call. Figure 1-22 shows what happened.

Mr. Branscomb's request for the Los Angeles to Hong Kong tickets comprised the raw data shown in step 1 of Figure 1-22. Janis entered his request on a keyboard (step 2). A communications link (slate blue) then transmitted the data to an airline reservation system computer (step 3). The computer compared Mr. Branscomb's request with available flights from Los Angeles to Hong Kong (step 4).

A flight with three seats open was available, and the computer sent a message stating this back to the travel agency. There the message appeared on Janis's screen (step 5). If the flight had been full, the computer would have sent a negative message, and Janis would then have had to try a different itinerary.

About a minute had now passed from Janis's initial "Hello" to step 6, asking Mr. Branscomb—still on the phone—to approve the flight reserved. Mr. Branscomb gave his OK, along with praise for Freddy Johnson's Travel Agency. Mr. Branscomb told Janis he would like to pay by credit card. Janis transmitted his approval and the billing data to the airline reservation computer (step 7).

The airline computer next recalled the data on the reservation that it had stored, and calculated Mr. Branscomb's bill. The computer also checked Mr. Branscomb's credit, and stored the traveler's data for future reference (step 8). Next the airline information-processing system communicated to the travel agency (step 9) the information to be printed on the actual tickets, as well as on the invoices for Mr. Branscomb and the agency. The tickets and invoices were then prepared by the printer in Janis's office (step 10).

Janis informed the delighted Mr. Branscomb that he could pick up his three Los Angeles to Hong Kong tickets whenever he liked, or that she could drop them in the mail.

Although this transaction was now complete, quite a bit of information could still be extracted that would be useful to Freddy Johnson, owner of the travel agency. It is to tap this potential information, that Mr. Johnson is considering installing a computer-based information system in his agency.

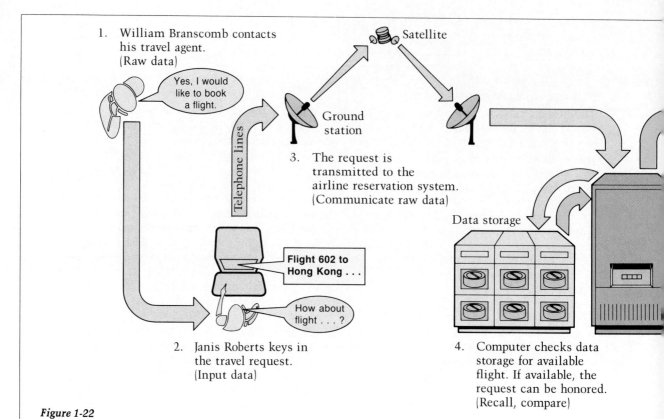

1. William Branscomb contacts his travel agent. (Raw data)

3. The request is transmitted to the airline reservation system. (Communicate raw data)

2. Janis Roberts keys in the travel request. (Input data)

4. Computer checks data storage for available flight. If available, the request can be honored. (Recall, compare)

Figure 1-22
The information system in action: Purchasing an airplane ticket.

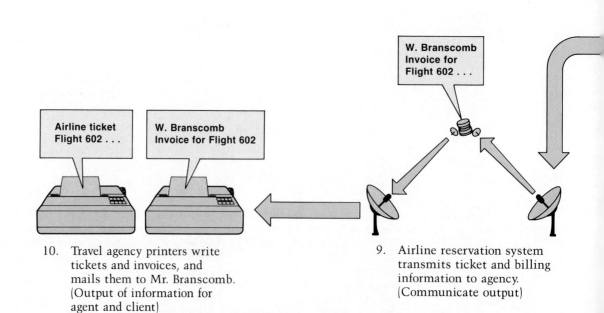

10. Travel agency printers write tickets and invoices, and mails them to Mr. Branscomb. (Output of information for agent and client)

9. Airline reservation system transmits ticket and billing information to agency. (Communicate output)

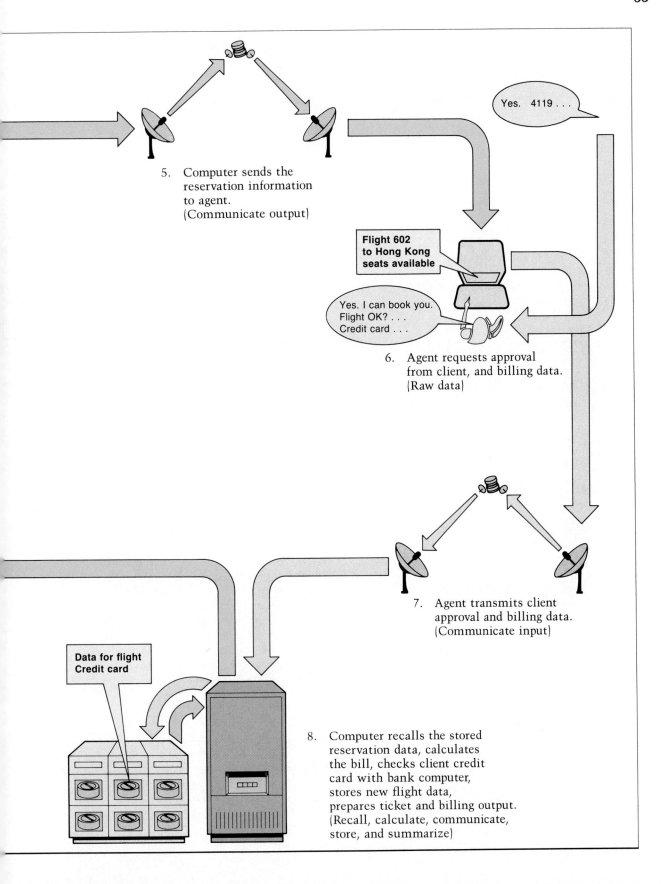

key terms

These are the key terms in alphabetical order. The number in parentheses refers to the page on which each term is defined.

Batch processing (11)
Calculating (15)
Classifying (16)
Communicating (16)
Comparing (15)
Computer (6)
Computer-aided design (CAD) (20)
Computer-aided manufacturing (CAM) (21)
Computer simulation (21)
Data (7)
Flexible manufacturing system (FMS) (21)
Information (7)
Information system (10)
Input (11)
Output (19)
Peripheral equipment (11)
Point-of-sale (POS) terminal (28)
Processing (11)
Programs (11)
Real-time processing (13)
Recalling (19)
Selecting (19)
Software (11)
Sorting (16)
Source document (11)
Storing (19)
Summarizing (19)
System (10)
Text data (7)
Time-sharing processing (12)
Transaction data (7)
Voice/image data (7)

review questions

objective questions

True/false. *Put the letter T or F on the line next to the question.*

1. A system is a set of interrelated elements.   1 ____

2. Source documents contain information to be converted into data.   2 ____

3. Data refers to the output from an information system.   3 ____

4. Point-of-sale (POS) terminals are used primarily in the wholesale business.   4 ____

5. Considerable human effort is required to make computers perform various processing operations.   5 ____

6. A credit card slip is an example of a source document.   6 ____

7. The value of information increases over time.   7 ____

8. Whatever comes out of the output end of an information-processing system must be considered information.   8 ____

9. Selection refers to extracting from a collection of data those items that meet certain characteristics.   9 ____

10. Input devices and computers are referred to as peripheral equipment.   10 ____

Multiple choice. *Put the letter of the correct answer on the line next to the question.*

1. To be considered information, output from an information system must be   1 ____
   (a) Timely.
   (b) Accurate.
   (c) Understandable to the user.
   (d) All of the above.

2. Hook-the-Resident, a large mail-order company, sends out hundreds of thousands of advertising mailers each day. The address labels are probably created using   2 ____
   (a) Batch processing.
   (b) Real-time processing.
   (c) Time-sharing processing.
   (d) Calculating processing.

3. In an information system the three basic operations for converting data into information are performed in the following order: 3 ____

(a) Processing, input, output.
(b) Input, processing, output.
(c) Output, processing, input.
(d) Input, output, processing.

4. Which of the following processing operations would be used to determine the sales tax a customer owes?
(a) Summarizing.
(b) Calculating.
(c) Sorting.
(d) Storing and recalling.

5. The use of computer-directed machinery throughout the production process is called
(a) Computer-aided design (CAD).
(b) Computer-aided manufacturing (CAM).
(c) Flexible manufacturing systems (FMS).
(d) Robot manufacturing systems (RMS).

Fill in the blank. *Write the correct word or words in the blank to complete the sentence.*

1. Knowledge communicated in a timely, accurate, and understandable fashion is _____.

2. A _____ is a set of interrelated elements working together toward a _____.

3. A _____ gives step-by-step directions to the computer.

4. During the _____ stage, _____ are transformed into information.

5. Computer applications in the product design and manufacturing process include _____, _____, and _____.

6. Arranging by city a list of customers with overdue payments from a complete list of customers involves both _____ and _____ processing steps.

7. The processing step, _____, permits the reduction of data into an easily understood form.

8. The _____ of _____ declines over time.

9. Data used in processing can come from _____, _____, and _____ or _____ sources.

10. A computer is a very-high-speed electronic device that can accept _____ and _____.

short answer questions

When answering these questions, think of concrete examples to illustrate your points.

1. What is a computer?
2. What is the difference between data and information?
3. What is a source document?
4. What is meant by the value of information?
5. Describe the input and output stages in relation to the information system.
6. Describe how information systems are used in wholesaling and retailing.
7. What are the operations involved in the processing stage of an information system?
8. What are the different sources of data decision makers use?
9. What purpose does an information-processing system serve?
10. What are the differences between real-time and time-sharing processing systems?

essay questions

1. It has been said, "One person's data is another's information." What is the difference between data and information? How can this statement be true? Provide examples from the chapter.
2. Consider how you might use data from source documents, text, and voice or image, input the data, perform processing steps, and then communicate the results for the following situations:
(a) Studying for an examination.
(b) Looking for an apartment to rent.
(c) Shopping for groceries.
3. How are computers used in your field?
4. If you are working, describe the ways computers are used in your workplace.

Answers to the objective questions
True/false: 1. T; 2. F; 3. F; 4. F; 5. F; 6. T; 7. F; 8. F; 9. T; 10. F
Multiple choice: 1. d; 2. a; 3. b; 4. b; 5. c
Fill in the blank: 1. information; 2. system, goal; 3. program; 4. processing, data; 5. computer-aided manufacturing (CAM), computer-aided design (CAD), flexible manufacturing systems (FMS); 6. sorting, selecting; 7. summarizing; 8. value, information; 9. transaction, text, voice, image; 10. data, instructions or programs

What makes information systems tick: from people to hardware

After studying this chapter you should understand the following:

- *The parts of a simple system.*
- *Which people are involved with an information system.*
- *How an information system incorporates rules and procedures.*
- *The hierarchy of data elements.*
- *How software fits into an information system.*
- *The general types of hardware used by information systems.*
- *The steps in the system development process.*

chapter 2

Determining information needs

Janis Roberts greeted each of the travel agents in the downtown office as she walked toward the conference room. There she took her place at the conference table with the other managers.

Freddy Johnson entered the room a few minutes later. "Good morning, everyone," Freddy said. "I called this meeting to discuss what we want our computer system to do. We must know our system needs before we buy any new hardware or software. Of course, it must be flexible enough to help us survive in the competitive travel industry environment."

"To help us, I hired a systems analyst," Freddy continued. "A consultant who specializes in the travel industry. Janis will serve as our liaison with the analyst."

"What's a systems analyst?" Steve Garber asked.

Janis was glad she'd been to several sessions of her new computer class at Oakriver University. She could answer questions that would have mystified her before.

"A systems analyst helps set up information systems," Janis said, "much like an architect who designs, say, a house. The architect finds out what is needed, and then designs it in detail. If the clients approve the design, she builds it—or rather, hires people to build it."

"The systems analyst will spend time watching how we work, and trying to figure out what we need a computer for," Janis continued. "Then the analyst will recommend the capabilities of the system we should have. This meeting is probably the last one we will have without the analyst. Now I'm going to listen to your ideas and take notes. What do *you* want a computer to do? Take a moment and let's come up with some ideas."

After a short time, Cynthia Brown spoke. "Obviously we will all want it to do some of our work for us—or at any rate make our work easier for us to do. Besides that, though, my main concern right now is to give more support to our corporate accounts."

"In what way?" Janis asked.

"Corporate clients have been asking me for reports on how effectively their funds are being spent. They need to know, for instance, if they are wasting money by booking too many flights on short notice."

"Good point," Freddy said. "We need summaries and perhaps other extra services for corporate clients. While I have the floor, I believe, first, we need to serve our clients more efficiently, as Cynthia said. Second, I want a method of linking the four offices electronically. I spend a lot of time driving back and forth now, and when we phone each other half the time we don't get the person we want."

"Another need is special information for people sitting in this room," Freddy said. "We need reports that give us market share, sales analyses, and show the quality of our travel agents. And all the accounting and billing should be done by computer, so it can be done faster and more efficiently." Freddy paused for a moment. "That's all I can think of," he said.

Janis smiled. "Well, it fills two pages," she said. "Can anyone else add anything Freddy missed?"

Tom Rivera spoke up. "I understand the need for everything Cynthia and Freddy talked about," Tom said. "But my office doesn't have many corporate accounts. Cynthia has most of them at the downtown office. My agents cater to individuals, and individuals don't want analytical reports, they want tips about hotels, cruises, and so on that make a big vacation or honeymoon worthwhile."

Janis thought for a moment. "Tom, I don't know enough about computers to say whether they can help with individual tips. At the least, a computer shouldn't *interfere* with catering to individual preferences. I'll write down your point as 'give individualized assistance to travelers taking advantage of recommendations, complaints, and other comments.' "

Janis glanced around the table. "Steve, do you have any additional points?"

"Yes," Steve Garber replied. "We're all experienced travel agents, so we know that there are rules and procedures that have to be followed—for instance, we have to account strictly for what we do with every blank airplane ticket."

"But as I understand it," Steve went on, "data about all kinds of things are going to pop up on a screen at us, at the touch of a button. How can we control our work with some machine rather than ourselves in charge?"

"Good question," Janis said. "One thing I've learned in the computer course I'm taking is that computers are approached differently now, as a result of the kinds of problems you mentioned Steve."

"How so?" Steve asked.

"Today computer systems are set up using structured systems development," Janis said. "That amounts to certain techniques and a philosophy that puts people first."

Freddy had been following this conversation with interest, and now he joined in. "I'm glad to hear that," he said. "I've seen the kind of mess some agencies got into trying to computerize, and I want to avoid that. *We* will still be running things, not some machine. The computer is going to help us in the way that *we* want to be helped, and it is going to have to prove it to us *first*, before we switch to it."

Freddy continued, "If anyone has additional ideas, please let Janis know as soon as possible."

Amid general agreement, the meeting adjourned.

What is a system?

In Chapter 1 we defined a *system* as a set of interrelated elements working together toward a goal. Systems surround us. A factory assembly line is a system, as is a subway network, or an automobile. Within a business, the accounting department, personnel department, and sales department are systems—and at a higher level so is the business itself.

A SUPERSYSTEM consists of two or more smaller systems, which are known as SUBSYSTEMS. Your body can be thought of as a supersystem, made up of circulatory, nervous, digestive, and other subsystems. In a business setting the company itself is the supersystem, made up of such subsystems as the manufacturing, accounting, marketing, and other divisions. Each subsystem can often be broken down into its own subsystems—such as dividing the manufacturing subsystem into assembly stations.

Parts of a simple system

Systems do not exist in isolation, but within an ENVIRONMENT, consisting of those external factors that affect the system. The environment is shown by the cloud-shaped line in Figure 2-1. The environment for a business system includes government regulations such as tax laws, competitors' sales prices, and the state of the economy.

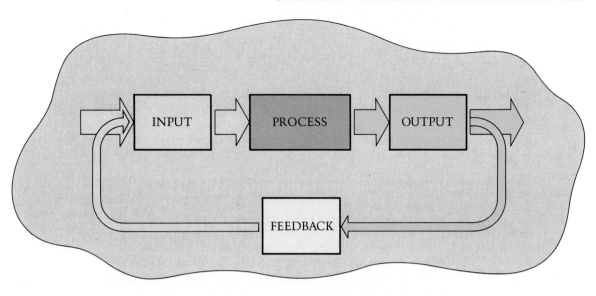

Figure 2-1
A simple system.

Environmental factors from another part of a company can also affect a business subsystem. Suppose you are developing a compensation package for your sales force. The personnel department may have certain companywide rules on such packages. These rules are environmental factors you must consider in your plans.

As Figure 2-1 shows, there are three stages in a system's operation: input, processing, and output. INPUT brings data into a system from the environment. Input can include business receipts, sales orders, data about personnel, or data about competitors. The emergency services system of a large city receives a flood of input daily from citizens calling for ambulances, and reporting accidents, crimes, and fires; from police officers investigating traffic or criminal offenses; and from other sources.

In the PROCESSING stage data are manipulated to produce the desired information. Processing creates order out of all the incoming data, which includes determining which data are important and which are not. In your body, the nervous system must screen out unnecessary facts and focus first on the most important incoming signals, for basic survival. These signals are analyzed, organized, and the correct course of action determined.

The OUTPUT stage communicates the results of the processing stage, and is the end product of a system. You see in Figure 2-1 that following output, some of the flow continues through a box called feedback, and returns to the input stage. FEEDBACK allows a system to regulate itself by treating the effect of its output on the environment as new input. Suppose, for example, that our electronics wholesale company, Paul's House of Electronic Wonders, after analyzing costs and expected demand, decides to sell superduper chips at $87.95 each. After a few weeks, they find the chips aren't selling well and they're losing money. Using this information as *feedback*, they lower the price to stimulate sales. If sales pick up, they will stick to the new lower price. If the chip sales are weak, they might reduce the price further (as long as they still make a profit), or they might tell their supplier that they're not interested in stocking the item any longer.

Elements of an information system

An **INFORMATION SYSTEM** is a set of interrelated elements working toward a common goal that provides users with timely, accurate, understandable, and relevant information. Viewed from the perspective of an organization—a supersystem—an information system is a subsystem.

Information systems do not themselves make decisions; nor do they guarantee that managers will make the right decisions every time. Instead, a well-run information system assists people in determining what choices or actions are available. Figure 2-2 shows how an information system fits into a business organization.

Figure 2-2
Relating the information system to a business organization. Data enter the information system from other parts of the organization. The information system produces useful information for the rest of the organization. Some of the information returns as feedback.

Five elements make up an information system: people, rules and procedures, data, software, and hardware. Note that in terms of the input-processing-output model, the five components of an information system are found throughout each of these stages (see Figure 2-3). For instance, in the input stage people gather data following various rules and procedures. Software helps to carry out these rules, and hardware physically transmits the data. All five elements need to work together if an information system is to be effective.

Let's look at some of the points touched upon in the example at the beginning of this chapter, in terms of the elements of an information system. In his little speech concluding the meeting, Freddy Johnson

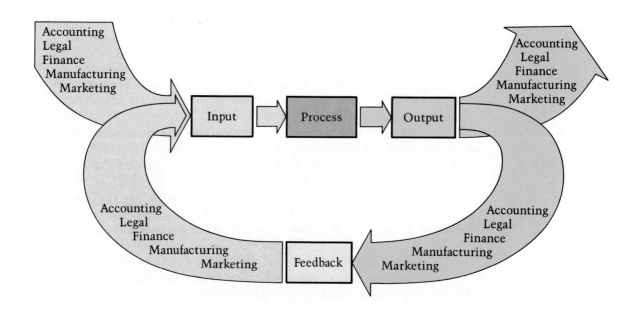

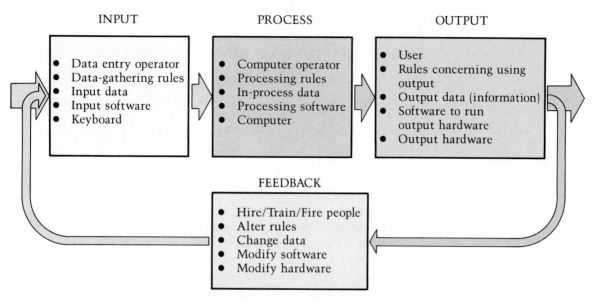

INPUT

- Data entry operator
- Data-gathering rules
- Input data
- Input software
- Keyboard

PROCESS

- Computer operator
- Processing rules
- In-process data
- Processing software
- Computer

OUTPUT

- User
- Rules concerning using output
- Output data (information)
- Software to run output hardware
- Output hardware

FEEDBACK

- Hire/Train/Fire people
- Alter rules
- Change data
- Modify software
- Modify hardware

Figure 2-3
Relating the information system elements to the model of a simple system.

stressed the importance of *people*. Steve Garber was worried about how the *rules and procedures* the agency followed would be retained and implemented under the new system. Janis also observed that one of the jobs of the systems analyst would be to watch how people worked, to learn how a computer could help them—again, relating to rules and procedures.

Data were the focus of many of the managers around the table. *Software*, although no one specifically mentioned it, will be intimately involved in handling all of the data and producing information. *Hardware* involves capital expense to the travel agency, as well as setting limits on how much the system can do and how fast it can do it. These will be items of most concern to Freddy Johnson and Janis Roberts. Although Freddy will not want to go broke financing the new system, he will also want hardware sophisticated enough so that the firm can stay competitive within a rapidly changing industry. Now let's take a more detailed look at each of the five elements of an information system.

People

People are the most important part of an information system. How people relate to the other elements directly affects the success or failure of the system. As obvious as this may seem, in the history of information systems this lesson has been learned the hard way. It is recognized today that people's needs must be paramount in any information system from its inception.

Three main categories of people are involved in any information system:

- Users
- Clients or clientele
- Information system staff

USERS employ the information system to provide services for their CLIENTS. INFORMATION SYSTEM STAFF support the users by providing assistance in developing and maintaining the system.

Users

Both management and nonmanagement personnel use information systems. Users generally are not concerned with the physical operations of the system. Rather, they make use of the system. A retail clerk uses an information system when checking the credit of a customer, and records transactions using POS terminals tied into the rest of the information system. The retail manager plays the role of user when analyzing the performance of employees, examining sales patterns, or evaluating future buying decisions.

Clients

Clients are those people for whom the users provide a service. The service may be either voluntary or involuntary. Note that a user and a client can sometimes be the same person. If you have ever used an automatic teller machine at a bank, you have been both a user of the bank's information system (the teller machine is tied in directly to the bank's computer) and a client of the bank. At Freddy Johnson's Travel Agency the clients are the customers who seek to make various travel arrangements. The travel agency also takes on the role of client when negotiating with the managers of the airline's reservation system, individual hotels, and tour operators.

Information system staff

The information system staff supports the users by developing, operating, and maintaining an effective information system. We can classify the information system staff by the component of the information sys-

Figure 2-4
Some of the occupations found in an information system. Note that some occupations may overlap among categories.

PEOPLE-ORIENTED
    User Representative
    Systems Analyst
    Information Resource Manager

RULES- AND PROCEDURES-ORIENTED
    User Representative
    Systems Analyst
    Information System Auditor
    Decision-Support Analyst

DATA-ORIENTED
    Data Entry Operator
    Data Administrator
    Database Manager
    Information Resource Manager

SOFTWARE-ORIENTED
    Computer Programmer
    Software Designer
    Systems Analyst

HARDWARE-ORIENTED
    Computer Operator
    Operations Administrator

tem with which they most interact. Figure 2-4 shows typical job categories in an information system.

In a small information system many of these tasks may be performed by one or two people. For instance, many hardware and software tasks fall on your shoulders when you use a small personal computer. At the other extreme, large corporate and government information systems sometimes have thousands of employees.

One common job category is the computer programmer. This person designs, writes, tests, and maintains some of the software that controls what a computer does. Another important job, at least in large information systems, is that of computer operator, who keeps the machine physically running.

Rules and procedures

All organizations have **RULES AND PROCEDURES** to guide their operations. These rules may be formal and clearly written, or they may be informal, vague, and unwritten. Understanding these rules is critical in examining an information system. The "generally accepted accounting principles" (GAAP) provide an example of formal rules used in setting up, working with, and auditing any business organization. Tom Rivera, in contrast, is applying an informal rule when he tries to reserve accommodations for his customers in Bangkok only in hotels that he himself has visited.

Whether formal or informal, rules and procedures fall into two categories: (1) those for normal conditions and (2) those for exceptions. In normal situations, decisions are usually made using **STANDARD OPERATING PROCEDURES (SOP)**. In some cases, for example when a manufacturer tests a product for electrical malfunctions, there can be no exceptions to SOP. In other situations, **EXCEPTION PROCEDURES** may be permitted. In a retail store, the normal check-approval procedures might not be followed if the customer is known to the clerk or store owner, or if the check is for a small amount.

Under certain conditions, exceptions may even be built into the rules. For example, if you become ill on vacation, you can often rearrange your airplane tickets without paying a penalty. A good information system should be able to handle exceptional conditions, as well as standard operating procedures.

Data

In an information system, data should be organized and protected. In Chapter 1 you learned that data can come from several different sources: *transactions*, such as sales orders or airline reservations; *text*, from newspapers, magazines or books; and *voice/image*, from telephone or graphics. One way to organize data, especially transaction data, is through the data hierarchy. The **DATA HIERARCHY** is a classification of data from the lowest or most basic level to the highest or most inclusive level. Moving from the lowest level to the highest, there are four main categories:

- Field
- Record
- File
- Database

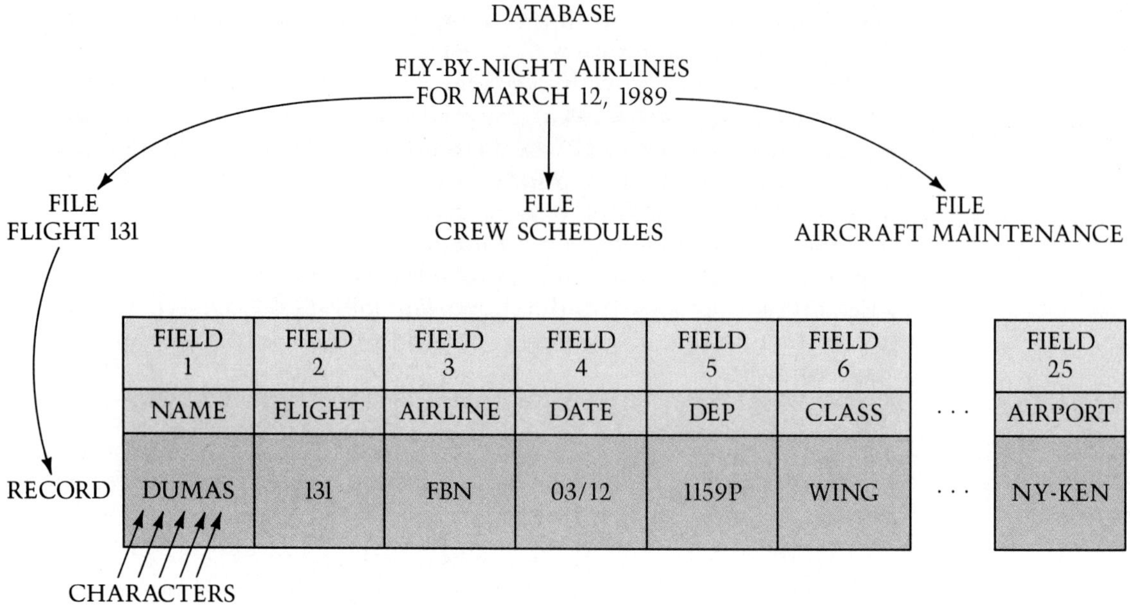

DATABASE

FLY-BY-NIGHT AIRLINES
—— FOR MARCH 12, 1989 ——

| FILE
FLIGHT 131 | | FILE
CREW SCHEDULES | | FILE
AIRCRAFT MAINTENANCE | |

FIELD 1	FIELD 2	FIELD 3	FIELD 4	FIELD 5	FIELD 6		FIELD 25
NAME	FLIGHT	AIRLINE	DATE	DEP	CLASS	...	AIRPORT
DUMAS	131	FBN	03/12	1159P	WING	...	NY-KEN

RECORD

CHARACTERS

Figure 2-5
The data hierarchy. Fly-By-Night's database consists of a collection of related files, including flight files, crew schedule files, and aircraft maintenance files. Each file consists of a collection of related records for all passengers on the flight. Each record in the flight file consists of related fields with data on each passenger. A field is a single data element and is made up of one or more characters.

These levels of the hierarchy are illustrated using airline transaction data in Figure 2-5.

A **FIELD** is a single data element that is treated as a unit, such as name, age, or social security number. Fields are made up of one or more **CHARACTERS** (individual letters, numbers, or symbols like "t", "5", or "@"). Figure 2-5 shows Fly-By-Night Airlines uses 25 fields to record data about each reservation. The fields contain data consisting of passenger name, flight number, airline code, date, and so on.

A **RECORD** is a set of related fields. Each record contains all the fields for a single case. The data for each customer's reservation make up a record in Figure 2-5.

A **FILE** is a set of related records. In Figure 2-5 the records for all of the passengers on Fly-By-Night Airlines flight 131 make up a file. That is, the entire grid shown represents the file: the horizontal rows are the records; the vertical columns are the fields.

The **DATABASE**, a set of interrelated files, is at the top of the data hierarchy. As Figure 2-5 shows, Fly-By-Night's database includes a file with data on passengers for each of its flights (including flight 131), a file on crew schedules, and a file on aircraft maintenance. Databases will be covered in detail in Chapter 11.

Text and voice/image data can be stored in similar fashion. Most libraries now allow users to access databases containing abstracts and full texts of major newspapers, professional journal articles, and even books. Modern telephone systems in many businesses can store messages and allow the proper user access to his or her messages from virtually anywhere in the world. Designers can fill databases with many types of design and color selection data. As a sales tool, Milliken Mills, a textile firm, converts photographs of a customer's residence or office into storable data. Then Milliken's own database of its products can be integrated and displayed on a video screen in the customer's office.

So far we have looked at data from the perspective of the user. How does the computer view data? Inside the computer and its peripherals each character is represented by a unique combination of binary digits called a byte. A single binary digit (a 1 or 0) is known as a BIT, a word derived from "*BINARY DIGIT*." A BYTE is a binary character made up of adjacent bits that the computer stores as a unit.

The BINARY (base 2) NUMBER SYSTEM is innate to digital computers—computers understand nothing other than binary. Binary utilizes only the numerals 1 and 0, with the 1 corresponding to the "on" state of an electrical component, and the 0 corresponding to the "off" state. *Binary* is derived from the Latin word for "two." The usual number of bits per byte is 8, although other sizes are used on some of today's computers. For example, using one of the more popular coding conventions, the letter *D* is coded under one method as the 8-bit byte, 11000100.

A single byte is a very small unit. For convenience most users of computers speak of bytes in multiples of a thousand (called a KILOBYTE or K) or a million (called a MEGABYTE or M), much the same way we give our ages in years instead of minutes or seconds. (A detailed discussion concerning binary numbers and coding systems is found in Chapter 5.)

Software

SOFTWARE, or PROGRAMS, provide the detailed instructions that the computer can interpret. These instructions tell the physical equipment what actions to perform and when to perform them. Software converts the rules and procedures of the organization into a form computers can understand. PROGRAMMING refers to the process of designing and writing programs. The two major categories of software are application software and system software.

APPLICATION SOFTWARE directs the actual input, processing, and output activities for users. The program that allows Freddy Johnson's agents to make airplane reservations for their clients is an example of application software.

Application programs cannot work without the proper systems software. SYSTEM SOFTWARE links the application software to the computer hardware (Figure 2-6). The most important type of system software, the OPERATING SYSTEM, supervises and directs all of the software components and the computer hardware. Other system software elements translate application software into a form the computer can understand. In fact the application program shown in Figure 2-7, running about 500 bytes (characters) in length, requires tens of thousands of bytes of system software programs. System software is covered in Chapter 15.

Application programs can be written by the user, developed within another part of the company, or purchased. The simple application program shown in Figure 2-7 is written in a programming language called BASIC (*Beginner's All-Purpose Symbolic Instruction Code*). Entering the program into the computer, and typing the system command RUN, executes the program. The results appear at the bottom of the figure. For a detailed examination of software and programming, turn to Chapters 14, 15, and the appendix.

Figure 2-6
The relationship among users, application software, system software, and hardware of an information system.

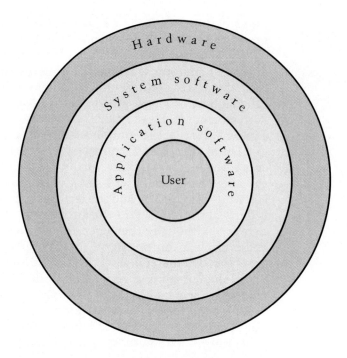

PRODUCTIVITY SOFTWARE are prewritten, pretested, ready-to-run software packages from outside suppliers. (See the box: Productivity Software for Problem Solving). Common business application packages can be purchased that meet a wide range of business needs. These include electronic spreadsheets (used for forecasting and managerial analysis), and word processing programs (used for writing reports, letters, and other printed output). Other packages include database management systems (for extracting data) and desktop publishing software (for office newsletters and reports). In Chapters 8 through 12 we will learn more about the general features of productivity software packages.

*Hardware:
the computer*

The term HARDWARE refers to the physical equipment used in an information system—the computer and the peripheral devices that support it. Peripheral devices include input, output, secondary storage, and communications devices. Later chapters will take a detailed look at hardware. Right now we'll limit ourselves to a brief overview.

The computer
The central piece of information system hardware is the COMPUTER. Recalling the definition in Chapter 1, this is the electronic machine that, under software control, does the actual processing of input data. The computers we have been talking about have a more general name—GENERAL-PURPOSE DIGITAL COMPUTERS. They are the main types of computer in use today. These computers can be used for a variety of large and small business, engineering, and scientific applications. Indeed, a single general-purpose digital computer can tackle all of these applications (even simultaneously), a situation common on college campuses.

Figure 2-7
A simple program written in BASIC. This program reads six numbers, accumulates them, and then prints out the numbers and the total.

```
LIST
100 REM   This program uses a loop tested with a trailer value
110 REM   to read six numbers, add them , and print out their sum.
120 REM   The variables are:
130 REM        X = The number to be added
140 REM        Y = The total of the numbers
150 REM **** Main Program ****
160 REM **** Initialize the Accumulator ****
170 LET Y = 0
180 REM **** Print Headings ****
190 PRINT "This program reads six numbers,"
200 PRINT "adds them, and prints out the sum."
210 PRINT
220 PRINT
230 PRINT "The numbers are:"
240 PRINT
250 REM **** Begin the Loop ****
260 READ X
270 IF X=-9999 THEN 340
280 PRINT X
290 REM  The next line accumulates the numbers
300 LET Y = Y + X
310 REM  The GOTO command returns the program flow
320 REM  to the READ statement in line 260
330 GOTO 260
340 REM **** Leave the Loop ****
350 REM **** Final Total and Closing ****
360 PRINT
370 PRINT
380 PRINT "The total of the numbers is:"; Y
390 PRINT
400 PRINT
410 PRINT "End of Program"
420 REM **** Data List ****
430 DATA 12.5, 10.27, 7, 15, 170.21, 99, -9999
440 END
RUN
This program reads six numbers,
adds them, and prints out the sum.

The numbers are:

 12.5
 10.27
 7
 15
 170.21
 99

The total of the numbers is: 313.98

End of Program
```

Digital computers represent data as discrete (meaning "separate and unconnected") values. Data are expressed by the "on" or "off" state of electrical components. Like a light switch on a wall, a component must be either on or off. In this text, our only concern will be with general-purpose digital computers—or for brevity—computers.

Inside the computer
In Chapter 5 we will discuss how the computer works in detail. For now, however, let us cautiously pry the lid off the "black box" and peer

Productivity software for problem solving

We all solve problems every day, often without being aware that we are doing so. When we want a computer to solve a problem for us, however, we have to tell it exactly, step by step, how to do so. We do this in a program. But rather than spending a great deal of time writing your own programs you can use programs others have written. We call these programs *productivity software* because they allow us to perform our jobs more efficiently. These software fall into two broad categories: (1) *General-purpose productivity software*, applicable to a wide variety of businesses and other applications, and (2) *Special-purpose productivity software*, used in specific application areas.

General-purpose productivity software packages include word processing packages, electronic spreadsheets, database management systems, graphics, and desktop publishing packages.

Word processing packages
These packages allow users to input text material to the computer—term papers, memos, legal documents, and even poetry. With a few simple keystrokes the user can edit and rearrange the document. The document can be stored and later retrieved for printing or further editing. Other features available to word processing users include the software packages that create "personalized" form letters and check for errors in spelling, grammar, style, and punctuation (see Chapter 9).

Electronic spreadsheets
Users can create tables containing rows and columns of numbers—for budgets, sales summaries, profit and loss statements, and other vital business documents—with electronic spreadsheets. These numbers can be entered from the keyboard or derived by the use of formulas ranging from simple addition and subtraction to rather complex algebraic expressions. For example, by changing one numeric value (say, the percentage discount offered to distributors of a product from 15 percent to 20 percent), any related numbers (such as gross profit) will be altered quickly (see Chapter 10).

Database management systems
These systems help users design a database—for retrieving crucial records. Data for files and records can be entered, checked and edited, and even deleted. Later, desired records can be retrieved and listed either as a group or individually. Further, summary statistics for these selected records can be output as a report to management. Some spreadsheet packages incorporate simple data retrieval procedures (see Chapter 11).

Graphics packages
Users can use graphics packages to present data in effective displays with understandable labels—a must for good business presentations. Graphs are available ranging from circle or pie graphs, to line graphs and multiple bar charts. Both black-and-white and color packages are available (see Chapter 12).

Desktop publishing packages
These packages help users design professional-quality documents for internal and external business use. The features of desktop publishing packages include choices of typestyle, layout, and graphics. A number of packages have canned illustrations and layout designs to help the novice user (see Chapter 12).

Integrated software packages
Many companies offer packages that integrate two or more of these general-purpose

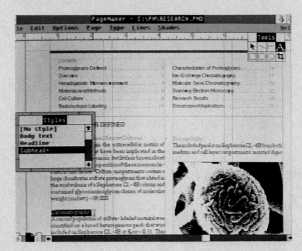

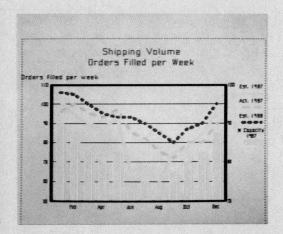

(a)

(b)

(c)

The power of general-purpose software. With a spreadsheet and a graphics package you can convert tables into colorful graphs (a and b), and with desktop publishing software you can combine text and graphics into finished, professional-looking documents (c).

elements. Consider using a database management system to extract the names and addresses of customers who are more than 60 days late in paying bills. The list can be transferred to the word processing package, where the customers are written "personalized" letters reminding them of their overdue payments.

Thousands of special-purpose productivity software packages are available for virtually every field of interest—accounting, financial management, market research, manufacturing management, statistics, and other business applications. Many of these special-purpose programs can link to general-purpose ones, such as transferring customer payment information that is calculated using an accounting package to the relevant customer records in the database.

Recreational computing packages include amateur astronomy, flight simulators, and one that helps you find your way through a fictional bureaucratic nightmare—where the first challenge is to properly fill out a form.

Packages in a wide range of prices and compatible with a number of different computers are available off the shelf, at a price and time savings competitive with writing the program yourself.

Figure 2-8
Parts of the computer.

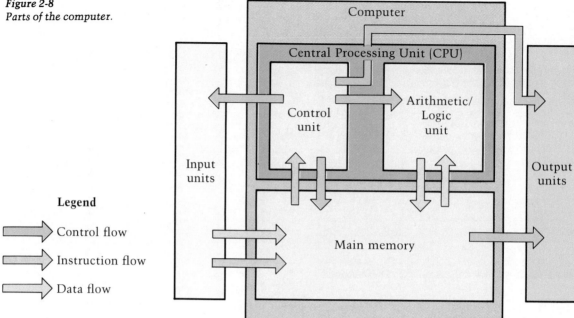

Legend

Control flow

Instruction flow

Data flow

inside. Figure 2-8 shows what we would see. The computer consists of two parts: the central processing unit or CPU which contains the control and arithmetic/logic units, and the main memory unit.

▫   The **CENTRAL PROCESSING UNIT (CPU)** carries out the instructions given to it by software to process the input data and produce the output information. Inside the CPU the **CONTROL UNIT** serves as the "manager" of the computer. Working under the direction of software, the control unit directs the input, processing, and output of data. The **ARITHMETIC/ LOGIC UNIT** performs calculations and logical operations with the data, as directed by the control unit.

▫   The **MAIN MEMORY** or **PRIMARY STORAGE UNIT** stores data and instructions that have been input and are waiting to be processed, and stores the results of processing until they are released to output devices. Although main memory is closely associated with the central processing unit, main memory is *not* considered part of the CPU.

For more about how the control, arithmetic/logic, and main memory units actually work see Chapter 5.

The pieces of the computer: chips for processing and storage
Packed into the central processing unit of today's computers are miniature electronic circuits etched onto small wafers of glass called **SILICON CHIPS**. Figure 2-9 shows some types of silicon chips used in modern computers. The chips are so tiny that many circuits can be squeezed into a small space. We find them in many places today, controlling appliances, automotive systems, watches, and much more. They are the brainchild of the computer industry, however. Today's silicon chips work faster

than earlier silicon chips, because they are so small that electricity has to travel only a short distance from one circuit path to the next.

Computers use silicon chips throughout the CPU. Chips are used in the control unit to monitor processing and decode instructions. The arithmetic/logic unit uses chips to perform mathematical and logical operations. The main memory unit consists of banks of chips devoted to storage.

In certain computers, the entire CPU is contained on a single silicon chip known as a **MICROPROCESSOR**. A microprocessor can contain the control unit, the arithmetic/logic unit, and some of the main memory. Further increases in processing speed can be obtained by combining microprocessors. In larger computers, the CPU may contain several microprocessors linked together.

It is in their role as main memory that silicon chips serve their most visible purpose—fast storage. Chips used for main memory have a variety of names reflecting their various functions.

The mainstay of main memory is the highly price-competitive **RANDOM-ACCESS MEMORY (RAM)** chip. It is called "random access" because the address of any memory location can be reached ("accessed") without the necessity of checking or referring to any adjacent locations. This is the part of main memory where users can store their programs and data.

RAM chips are *volatile*; that is, they immediately lose their data when the power is turned off. To avoid costly losses of instructions or data, backup power supplies such as batteries can be provided.

READ-ONLY MEMORY (ROM) chips are chips on which programs (or data) have been permanently encoded. A ROM can be read, but cannot be written onto by the user. Under normal conditions, ROMs provide *nonvolatile* storage—when the power is interrupted, instructions are not lost. ROMs are used for various purposes. In many microcomputers, for example, part of the system software is stored on ROM, as are the

Figure 2-9
The chips inside the computer. (a) A microprocessor. (b) A random-access memory (RAM) chip.

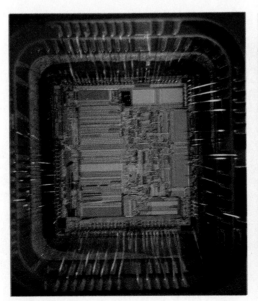

(a)

(b)

programs that allow the computer to run application software written in certain programming languages such as BASIC. ROM is also used to store instructions for frequently used procedures, for instance, how to calculate square roots. ROM can also be used to store entire database, word processing, and spreadsheet application programs. Software encoded on ROM chips is often called **FIRMWARE**, because, strictly speaking, it is neither "hard" nor "soft."

Sometimes users of an information system want to program and protect their own procedures on a read-only memory chip. **PROGRAMMABLE READ-ONLY MEMORY (PROM)** chips serve this purpose. Some PROMs, known as *EPROMs*, are erasable under special circumstances, so that they can be reprogrammed.

Types of computers

Computers are ranked by how fast they can process data, and by how much they can store in their memories. From smallest to largest, they are microcomputers, minicomputers, mainframe computers, and supercomputers. These four categories are not exclusive. Some larger microcomputers are more powerful than small minicomputers, and mainframes overlap with both minicomputers and supercomputers.

MICROCOMPUTERS (Figure 2-10), the smallest type, are frequently found in homes and offices. The actual processing element—the *microprocessor*—is extremely small. Because the computer is relatively small, most users apply the term *microcomputer* to both the computer itself and its built-in peripherals (display terminal and disk drives). Often called **PERSONAL COMPUTERS**, microcomputers can be used for thousands of applications in virtually every field. Smaller microcomputers are often used in the home, while larger systems are more likely to be assigned to business-oriented tasks. Microcomputers can be categorized by size and relative capabilities into: workstation, desktop, portable, and laptop. Microcomputers are often used in the classroom, from ele-

(a)

Figure 2-10
(a) A microcomputer. (b) The microprocessor for this microcomputer.

(b)

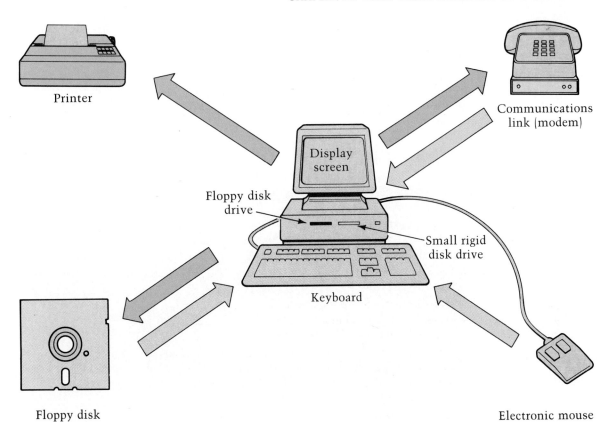

Printer

Communications
link (modem)

Display
screen

Floppy disk
drive

Small rigid
disk drive

Keyboard

Floppy disk

Electronic mouse

Figure 2-11
Hardware components of
a typical microcomputer
system.

mentary school through the university level. Figure 2-11 shows the
hardware components in a typical, small computer system associated
with a microcomputer.

MINICOMPUTERS (Figure 2-12) are larger, faster, and have more memory capacity than the typical microcomputer. These machines predate
microcomputers, and were often used to support time-sharing *computer networks*. In terms of capability, small minicomputers and large
microcomputers overlap. Minicomputers are frequently used to support
scientific and engineering tasks. Several microcomputers can be linked
to one or more minicomputers to form a network for more efficient processing. Many university teaching labs use such networks.

MAINFRAME COMPUTERS are large machines that range over a wide
spectrum of processing speeds and other capabilities (Figure 2-13). Used
in a great variety of applications in business, government, science, engineering, and education, these systems were for many years the basis of
the popular image of the computer. Mainframe computers are used by
wholesale and retail stores to manage inventories, check customer
credit levels, handle accounting, personnel, and payroll tasks, and perform forecasting calculations. Airline reservation systems use mainframe computers linked together for *multiprocessing* or simultaneous
processing of travelers' requests. Manufacturers have access to mainframe systems that process thousands of production inquiries each day.
Universities use such systems for supporting large student computer

labs, research, recordkeeping, and business-related procedures. Figure 2-14 shows hardware components commonly associated with large mainframe systems.

SUPERCOMPUTERS are the biggest and the fastest machines in the computer world (Figure 2-15). These machines can execute hundreds of millions of calculations a second. Multiprocessing methods allow these units to model extremely complex conditions, such as stock market activity, weather forecasts, and the in-flight behavior of aircraft and rocket prototypes.

Figure 2-12
A minicomputer.

Figure 2-13
A mainframe computer.

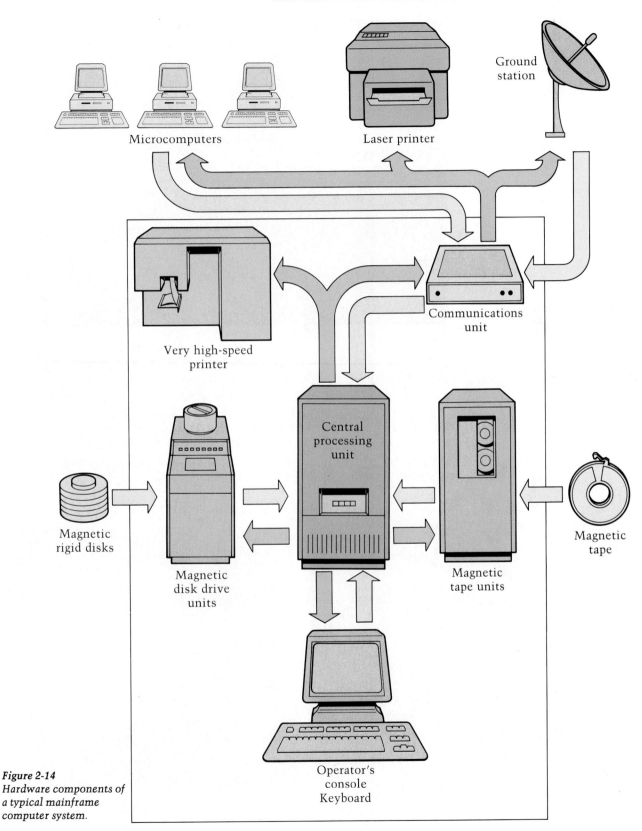

Microcomputers

Laser printer

Ground station

Very high-speed printer

Communications unit

Magnetic rigid disks

Magnetic disk drive units

Central processing unit

Magnetic tape units

Magnetic tape

Operator's console Keyboard

Figure 2-14
Hardware components of
a typical mainframe
computer system.

Figure 2-15
A supercomputer.

**Hardware:
peripheral devices**

Input and output devices
To place data and software into the central processing unit, you need input devices; and to make use of the processed information requires output devices. INPUT DEVICES (Figure 2-16) transmit data and instructions to a computer for processing. OUTPUT DEVICES (Figure 2-17) reverse the process, producing information in either a form that people can read or that is machine-readable.

(a)

Figure 2-16
Input devices. (a) A keyboard. (b) An optical scanner.

(b)

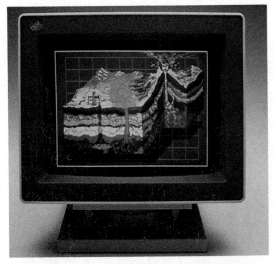

(b)

Figure 2-17
*Output devices. (a) Graphic output on a display
screen. (b) A laser printer.*

(a)

At Freddy Johnson's Travel Agency the agents use a **KEYBOARD** similar to an electric typewriter, with a few keys for special functions added.
They simply "key in" (or "type" or "input") the data concerning travel
arrangements.

Another common input device, the **OPTICAL SCANNER**, reads marks
or special characters printed on packages or paper forms. A common
type of scanner uses laser beams to read the product codes on grocery
items.

Output can appear on a televisionlike screen of a **DISPLAY SCREEN** or
it can be produced by a **PRINTER** on blank paper or preprinted forms
(such as invoices or airplane tickets). Output on a display screen is not
permanent, whereas printed output is. Permanent output from printers
is often called **HARD COPY**; nonpermanent displays, **SOFT COPY**. Output
for storage is recorded on a magnet-sensitive surface coated on a tape or
disk, usually the same device that will later read the data again for input.
Chapter 6 will examine input and output devices in greater detail.

Secondary storage devices
SECONDARY, or **EXTERNAL**, **STORAGE DEVICES** (Figure 2-18) record data and
programs on a machine-readable medium for later use. Figure 2-19
shows some of the most important storage media. **MAGNETIC DISK UNITS**
and **MAGNETIC TAPE UNITS** are the most common secondary storage
devices. They can read and write magnetic codes onto the storage surface. Magnetic devices send input data and receive output at high rates
of speed and are suitable for handling and storing large amounts of
data.

Secondary storage may be classified by its accessibility to the computer. The computer has direct control over **ON-LINE STORAGE** and can
access stored data and software without human intervention. On-line
storage systems generally use magnetic disk or magnetic tape as the storage medium. **OFF-LINE STORAGE** is not under the direct control of the
computer—as soon as an on-line device is turned off, it becomes off-
line. Similarly, when a reel of magnetic tape or a removable disk is taken

(a)

(c)

(b)

Figure 2-18
Secondary storage de-
vices. (a) A magnetic
tape unit. (b) A magnetic
disk unit for a large com-
puter system. (c) A mag-
netic disk unit for a mi-
crocomputer system.

out of the unit that reads and writes upon it, perhaps for storage in a library, the data on the tape or disk are off-line as far as the computer is concerned. In Chapter 7 we will take a more thorough look at secondary storage devices.

Communications devices

COMMUNICATIONS DEVICES link the information system together. They can be as simple as a series of wires or cables connecting the central processing unit to the various input, output, and secondary storage devices located a few feet away. Computers of all sizes can be linked together into NETWORKS. A large network can include special communications processors, transmission lines, and space satellite switching systems to link widely distributed components.

For the information system shown in Figure 2-20, the telephone lines are linked to the computer through a special modulating/demodulating device called a *modem* (to translate the signal patterns between the computer and the telephone lines). The signal is thus sent from a one-computer center to a satellite ground station, to a communications satellite, to a receiving ground station, and then to a large computer center.

Multinational firms use communications networks to tie far-flung offices and factories into their information systems. College students, faculty, and staff use a network of terminals in dormitories, offices, and labs to tie into the main computer system. In Chapter 16 we will describe the techniques and hardware used for communications and distributed processing.

Chrysler's information system

No more squeaks, shudders, stalling, surging, or misfiring that baffles mechanics time and again—that's the promise that Chrysler Motor Corp. is making to customers. While the reborn company spends millions to automate its manufacturing plants, it is also employing information technology in a classic way—using systems to lock in customers.

But there's more. If the system—Service Bay Diagnostics (SBD)—works, the mechanic can correctly repair any annoying misfire, stall, surge, hard starting, or any other auto problem the first time. For thousands of disgruntled drivers, such a system would be Nirvana on wheels.

Service Bay Diagnostics is the next key element to be implemented in Chrysler's long-term strategy to utilize information systems in the production and servicing of vehicles. While the rest of Detroit's Big Three auto makers have similar plans, none of them can match SBD. . . .

SBD will work like this: A mechanic will have a computerized analyzer at his workbench that he will plug into a diagnostic terminal in the car. This terminal will feed relevant information about the car's ailment into a diagnostic minicomputer housed at the dealership. The minicomputer will analyze the symptoms and flash to the mechanic a series of possible reasons for the failure, as well as a list of solutions ranked in order of likelihood.

Simultaneously, data transmitted from the vehicle to the minicomputer at the dealership is also fed to a mainframe at Chrysler headquarters in Detroit. That mainframe has a file on the model's service history and technical service bulletins (TSB). TSBs are up-to-date notices of modifications, procedures, and repairs. Dealerships receive hundreds of TSBs through the mail each year. . . .

SBD is only one aspect of Chrysler's MIS strategy. Another facet is evident to an observer walking through the Dodge City truck assembly plant in Warren, Mich. . . .

In 1986 Chrysler spent $500 million to update this 50-year-old plant.

The key aspects of the Chrysler plant modernization program are a just-in-time (JIT) inventory management system and the Performance Feedback System (PFS). The JIT system allows assembly plants to reduce the number of parts they must keep in inventory. Fewer parts in inventory translate into better cash flow, since companies buy only what they need; that maximizes the use of capital and also cuts storage costs. Today, 71 percent of Chrysler parts—equivalent to 1122 truckloads of parts per day—are delivered by the just-in-time system. . . .

With JIT, each assembly plant has a direct communications link to its suppliers, who are informed what parts are needed, at what time, at what gate, and in what sequence the parts must come off the trucks. . . .

Just-in-time inventory, which is now receiving industrywide attention, didn't evolve without headaches, including resistance by assembly-line veterans who feared that if the system developed glitches, production lines could shut down. They argued that it was taking a big chance to have parts delivered just minutes before they have to go into cars. . . .

The Performance Feedback System, which is unique to U.S. auto manufacturing, monitors the assembly of each vehicle to catch mechanical defects that would often go undetected using traditional quality-control inspection procedures. Performance feedback begins at the start of a car's production cycle and lasts until it is completed. . . .

PFS relies on many terminals—in some cases, several hundred—on plant floors that are tied into the manufacturing process. The system detects problems—often small ones—that would or could result in an on-the-road failure, such as settings that are misadjusted, parts that are defective, and parts which have been inadvertently left off. The information is fed back to a controller, who directs a mechanic to correct the defect.

Source: Mort Schultz from "Customer Satisfaction Drives Chrysler's IS," *InformationWEEK*, February 1, 1988 Issue 154 pp. 23–27. © 1988 by CMP Publication, Inc., 600 Community Drive, Manhasset, NY 11030. Reprinted with permission from InformationWEEK.

(a)

(b)

Figure 2-19
*Storage media. (a) A variety of magnetic media:
tape reels, floppy disks, cassette tapes, and
3½-inch diskettes. (b) A hard disk pack. Each pack
contains several disks.*

The system development process

All systems, including information systems, go through a cycle of birth,
growth, maturity, and decline. The owners of a rapidly expanding business, for example, may find that the informal information system that
served them well when they were operating out of their own homes and
had no employees, is inadequate now that they have a staff of fifty and
are approaching sales of $20 million. Information systems must adapt to
the changing needs of the organizations of which they are a part. The
SYSTEM DEVELOPMENT PROCESS provides a method for studying and
changing systems.

The structured approach to the system development process, which
Janis touched on in our opening story, will be explained in more detail in
Chapter 13. In general, this approach stresses that the more careful we
are in the early stages of a system's life, the easier the growth, maturity,
and even the decline stages will be to manage.

The system development process can be broken down into six
stages. These are:

1. *Problem recognition*—identifying a need or opportunity that a new
system could address.
2. *Systems analysis*—studying how the existing system works.
3. *System design*—determining in general and in detail how the new
system will work.
4. *System acquisition*—creating the new system based on the design.

(a)

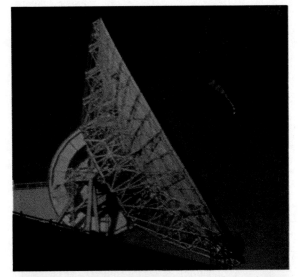

(b)

Figure 2-20
Hardware links in a communications network. A
user at a computer, linked to the telephone system
through a special device called a modem (a), can send
data to a satellite ground station (b), which bounces
microwave signals off a satellite (c), to another
ground station (d), that could be thousands of miles
away, which in turn transmits the data over phone
lines to a large computer center (e).

(c)

(d)

(e)

5. *System implementation*—changing from the old system to the new one.

6. *System maintenance*—a continuing process of keeping a system in good working order.

At each stage, the different components of the information system (people, rules and procedures, data, software, and hardware) must be contended with.

People called systems analysts assist users through the steps of the system development process. **SYSTEMS ANALYSTS** are responsible for studying and developing systems that meet the information needs of users and clients.

summary

▫ A system is a set of interrelated elements working together toward a goal. A supersystem consists of two or more smaller subsystems.

▫ Systems exist within an environment. Input enters the system from the environment, the system processes it and communicates the results to the environment as output. Feedback allows a system to regulate itself by treating the effect of its output as new input.

▫ An information system is a set of interrelated elements that provide users with timely, accurate, and relevant information. The five elements of an information system are people, rules and procedures, data, software, and hardware.

▫ People are the most important part of an information system. The people involved in an information system include users of the system, their clients, and the information system staff.

▫ Rules and procedures fall into two categories: standard operating procedures (SOP) for normal situations, and exception procedures for unusual conditions.

▫ The data hierarchy classifies data from the lowest, most basic level to the most inclusive. The categories are field, record, file, and database. A field is a single data element made up of one or more characters. A record is a set of related fields; a file a set of related records; and a database a set of related files.

▫ With a computer, all numbers, letters, and symbolic codes must be translated to a two-state, on or off, pattern of binary digits or bits. The binary number system allows the values 1 and 0.

▫ A byte is a binary character made up of adjacent bits that the computer stores as a unit. The usual number of bits per byte is 8. Often we refer to bytes in multiples of kilobytes or Ks (thousands) or megabytes or Ms (millions).

▫ Software, or programs, falls into two general categories: application software and system software. Application software performs the actual input, processing, and output activities for users. It can be written by the user or purchased as a productivity software package from a vendor. System software helps the application software use the computer. The most important type of system software is the operating system, which supervises and directs all of the other software components. Programming is the process of writing software.

career box
The systems analyst

The systems analyst plays a critical role in any information system. More than anyone else, the systems analyst deals with the most pressing problems in an organization—and provides the solutions, usually with a computer system.

Effective analysts are generalists who possess analytical skills suitable to a wide range of problems. They must be comfortable talking to top management about productivity issues, to specialists about hardware and software specifications, and to staff about the details of their day-to-day problems.

Systems analysts work singly or in teams, depending on the size of the problem. Firms of all sizes hire analysts as consultants. Other firms employ a number of analysts, generally within their information system department. In terms of hierarchy, the bottom of the pyramid of information-processing jobs is occupied by computer operators; above them, in varying gradations, come programmers; above them, systems analysts; and at the top, managers.

One can become a systems analyst either by advancing up the information system career ladder; or, by crossing over from the ranks of users of the information system. People who do cross over have the advantage of knowing user needs thoroughly; their training then consists of learning computer-related skills. According to a survey released by *Datamation*, average salaries in 1986 for lead systems analysts ranged from $33,211 at small firms to $39,787 at larger ones.[1]

Analysts need training in the areas of information systems, general management practices, programming techniques, statistics and research methods, and communications skills. Detailed knowledge of the user's requirements is an absolute necessity, but is often picked up as the first phase of a systems analysis assignment.

A good analyst needs above all to be familiar with the user's needs, which are not always the same as what users *say* they are. Through interviews, questionnaires, and direct observation the analyst finds out exactly how work is being done.

Once the analyst defines the problem, the task is to design an information system that solves the problem. Then, the analyst oversees implementing the design—guiding programmers or evaluating and purchasing appropriate packaged software, arranging for the purchase and installation of necessary hardware, vigorously testing the system, training people who will use the system, writing documentation, and arranging for conversion from the old system to the new. Even after the system is running well the job isn't done, as the system will require tuning. Like a good doctor who has performed major surgery, a systems analyst does not merely shake his or her user's hand and say goodbye—follow-up visits are in order.

All of these tasks require continuous communication with users and management, so a good systems analyst must possess excellent written and oral communications skills, as well as the ability to listen to others. Further, a systems analyst must be able to work independently, with little supervision. The systems analyst is the only person involved who possesses all the relevant facts and the knowledge necessary to solve the problem. Managers can only judge whether or not a proposed solution *sounds* as if it will work, and then whether it in fact *does* work. Managers will not fail to determine the latter.

[1]Parker Hodges, "What Are You Worth?" *Datamation*, 1 October 1987, pages 78–92.

■ Hardware consists of the physical equipment used in an information system. The central piece of hardware is the computer itself, which under software control, does the actual processing of data.

■ General-purpose digital computers can be used for a variety of applications. They represent data by the "on" and "off" states of electrical components, and treat data as discrete. The focus of this textbook is on general-purpose digital computers.

■ The two parts of the computer are the central processing unit (CPU) which consists of the control unit and the arithmetic/logic unit, and main memory or primary storage.

■ Today's mainframe computers and minicomputers use silicon chips throughout the CPU. In microcomputers, the entire CPU is etched onto a single chip known as a microprocessor. Main memory is contained on random-access memory (RAM) chips.

■ Read-only memory (ROM) is permanent memory that can be read from, but cannot be erased by being written over. ROM is often used on microcomputers to store parts of the system software, and instructions for frequently used or entire application programs. Software encoded on ROM is often called firmware. A variant on the ROM is the programmable read-only memory (PROM) chip.

■ Computers are ranked by how fast they process data and by how much they can store in their memory units. Microcomputers or personal computers are small computers used in homes and offices. Minicomputers are larger machines, often used for business, scientific, and engineering tasks. Mainframes are large computers commonly used in businesses that require considerable information processing. Supercomputers, the most powerful units, are used for complex scientific and business problem solving.

■ Input devices make data and software available to the CPU, output devices communicate the results of processing, and secondary, or external, storage devices record data and programs in a machine-readable form for later use. Communications devices link the hardware together. Some machines, such as magnetic tape and disk units, combine input, output, and storage functions.

■ Common input devices include keyboards and optical scanners. Common output devices are display screens and printers. Printers produce hard copy; display screens produce nonpermanent soft copy. Common storage devices include magnetic tape units and magnetic disk units.

■ If the computer has direct control over a storage device, it is on-line; otherwise it is off-line.

■ Communications devices link the parts of an information system, making it possible to join widely dispersed elements into networks.

■ All systems go through a system development process of six steps: problem recognition, systems analysis, system design, system acquisition, system implementation, and system maintenance.

■ Systems analysts are actively involved in systems development. Their job is to study systems, pinpoint problems, suggest solutions, and help guide the organization through design, acquisition, and implementation.

Developing the new information system

With Janis Roberts working hard as liaison, Ron Sloan—the systems analyst Freddy hired—was able to perform the systems analysis, system design, and system implementation for the new information system.

Ron studied people's work methods and needs, and proceeded to create a design for the new information system. At prearranged key points, Ron asked Freddy and the other managers for approval for what he had done so far and permission to continue. The final specifications and testing requirements for the equipment and software were at last developed by Ron and Janis. Among the alternatives offered, Freddy chose a computer that had proven reliable in other agencies, rather than a new machine potentially more exciting but also potentially more problematic.

At the insistence of everyone, Ron Sloan stressed proper training of the travel agents during the implementation stage. Apart from Ron, Janis was the most knowledgeable person about computers. Her branch was the first to implement the new system.

Ron and Janis installed the system at her office, ironed out the kinks, trained the other managers, and convinced doubters of the system's worth. When Freddy gave his permission, the system was then installed at the other branches.

Let's take a look at how the system worked after 3 months of operation.

People. The managers were adjusting to the new system, and were happy with the new reports and analyses that the system produced for them "automatically." Together with Ron Sloan and Janis, the managers trained the agents to use the system. Some caught on rapidly; others did not. Two agents moved to different—less automated—agencies. After 3 months, the average working speed of a travel agent had just about caught up to what it was before the new system was installed. Once the slower agents became fully accustomed to the new system, work efficiency would presumably increase.

Clients saw evidence of the new system only through the new information offered them. Cynthia Brown's corporate clients responded so well to the reports on travel costs that similar reports were being provided to individuals who did a lot of traveling.

Three people were hired to operate and manage the new equipment at the main office. Janis transferred to the main office, to head the new team and continue helping Freddy and the other managers productively utilize the new system. The systems analyst and Janis still met occasionally to iron out problems that accompanied the new system. To help broaden her background knowledge, she was taking additional courses at Oakriver University.

Rules and Procedures. With the new system, these actually stayed about the same. Standard operating procedures were put into manuals to assist in training personnel. One major rule change, however, was that managers were expected to use an electronic message system as much as possible to communicate from branch to branch. The other major change was the standardization of comments and complaints about travel arrangements. A traveler's advice file informed both travel agents and customers about the "best" places to stay and the ones to avoid. Agents were required to enter information of this sort as soon as they received and evaluated it. Tom Rivera was no longer concerned about sacrificing the tips he gave to customers because of having to use computers; on the contrary, he saw his tips being passed on to more people than ever.

Some managerial information—such as statistics on how well travel agents performed—was private, and the new system protected it in a way such that only managers could see it. This eased the mind of Steve Garber, as did a computerized tracking system for blank airline tickets that proved even tighter than the manual one had been.

Data. The data for the travel agency was stored in a database, to allow fast access to clients' records by the agents. In addition, managers alone could inspect the personnel file and other sensitive data concerning their workers. Freddy Johnson and one assistant were permitted access to data concerning the managers.

Messages also constituted a form of data. These were sent from one manager to another between offices, or sent from clients to the agency when the offices were closed, for retrieval when the offices opened again.

Software. System software supported the companywide database system and the interoffice message communication system. The application software design stressed programs that required as little keying as possible. ("By that I mean when feasible, one keystroke," analyst Ron Sloan said). Application software included programs to perform sales analyses, create reports of travel usage, perform financial planning, and handle accounting. The software supported the traveler's ad-

vice file, and was useful in selecting options with which an agent was not entirely familiar.

Hardware. A minicomputer was installed at the main office. To minimize equipment expenses, the old terminals in each office were retained and modified to communicate with the new minicomputer. In addition to the minicomputer, several inexpensive microcomputers were purchased for the four offices, for use by the managers and personnel concerned with marketing and accounting.

The database was stored in secondary storage at the main office. Three printers were purchased for each office: one just to produce airline tickets, and two to produce invoices, reports, and letters. Communications hardware was installed to allow the peripheral devices to communicate with the minicomputer, and to permit expansion should more devices be added later.

key terms

These are the key terms in alphabetical order. The numbers in parentheses refer to the page on which each term is defined.

Application software (45)
Arithmetic/logic unit (50)
Binary number system (45)
Bit or binary digit (45)
Byte (45)
Central processing unit (CPU) (50)
Character (44)
Client (41)
Communications device (58)
Computer (46)
Control unit (50)
Database (44)
Data hierarchy (43)
Display screen (57)
Environment (38)
Exception procedures (43)
Feedback (39)
Field (44)
File (44)
Firmware (52)
General-purpose digital computer (46)
Hard copy (57)
Hardware (46)
Information system (40)
Information system staff (41)
Input (39)
Input device (56)
Keyboard (57)
Kilobyte or K (45)
Magnetic disk unit (57)
Magnetic tape unit (57)
Mainframe computer (53)
Main memory or primary storage unit (50)
Megabyte or M (45)

Microcomputer (52)
Microprocessor (51)
Minicomputer (53)
Network (58)
Off-line storage (57)
On-line storage (57)
Operating system (45)
Optical scanner (57)
Output (39)
Output device (56)
Personal computer (52)
Printer (57)
Processing (39)
Productivity software (46)
Program (45)
Programmable read-only memory (PROM) (52)
Programming (45)
Random-access memory (RAM) (51)
Read-only memory (ROM) (51)
Record (44)
Rules and procedures (43)
Secondary or external storage device (57)
Silicon chips (50)
Soft copy (57)
Software (45)
Standard operating procedures (SOP) (43)
Subsystem (38)
Supercomputer (54)
Supersystem (38)
System development process (60)
Systems analyst (63)
System software (45)
User (41)

review questions

objective questions

True/false. *Put the letter T or F on the line next to the question.*

1 _____ 1. The database is the least inclusive part of the data hierarchy.

2 _____ 2. Clients are the people who operate the information system.

3 _____ 3. Input units include keyboards and optical scanners.

4 _____ 4. The operating system is a type of hardware.

5 _____ 5. The first stage in the system development process is problem recognition.

6 _____ 6. The most important part of the information system is the computer.

7 _____ 7. The roles of user and client can be combined in an area such as the use of automatic teller machines for making deposits and withdrawals.

8 _____ 8. Rules and procedures should not permit exception conditions.

9 _____ 9. The system development process generally does not involve the user.

10 _____ 10. People today must adapt their behavior to the other parts of the information system.

Multiple choice. *Put the letter of the correct answer on the line next to the question.*

1 _____ 1. In an information system the person who receives a service, such as a customer buying an airplane ticket from a travel agent, is a
(a) User.
(b) Client.
(c) Programmer.
(d) Systems analyst.

2 _____ 2. The data hierarchy, in order from broadest to narrowest, is
(a) Database, field, record, file.
(b) Database, file, record, field.
(c) File, record, field, database.
(d) Field, record, file, database.

3 _____ 3. The rules and procedures of an organization are
(a) Not affected by the environment in which a system exists.
(b) Developed by the information system staff.
(c) Developed by the users of the information system.
(d) Developed to apply only to standard operating conditions.

4 _____ 4. Software or programs
(a) Should only contain instructions to handle standard operations.
(b) Consist of two major categories: application and user programs.
(c) Should be developed or purchased by the information system staff without consulting the users of the system.
(d) Consist of two major categories: application and system software.

5 _____ 5. The largest and fastest computers are called
(a) Workstation microcomputers.
(b) Mainframe computers.
(c) Supercomputers.
(d) Personal computers.

Fill in the blank. *Write the correct word or words in the blank to complete the sentence.*

1. Rules and procedures must account for both _____ and _____ conditions.

2. A nonvolatile device to hold permanent instructions is called a _____ chip.

3. To link application programs to the hardware used in the information system requires _____.

4. Secondary storage is called _____ when it is directly accessible to the computer.

5. The two parts of the CPU are the _____, and _____ units.

6. The smallest or narrowest usable element of the data hierarchy is the _____.

7. When a computer reads a character it is reading a string of 8 _____ called a _____.

8. The _____ is often responsible for studying and developing systems that meet the needs of users and clients.

9. The five components of an information system are _____, _____, _____, _____, and _____.

10. The two parts of the computer are the _____, and the _____.

short answer questions

When answering these questions, think of concrete examples to illustrate your points.

1. Describe the five elements of an information system.

2. Describe the interrelationship between the users of an information system and their clients.

3. Describe the features of RAM, ROM, and PROM chips.

4. What are the functions of system software?

5. Give examples of application software that may be used by an airline.

6. For a microcomputer-based information system, what are the hardware requirements?

7. What is the purpose of communication units in an information system?

8. What is the difference between on-line and off-line external storage?

9. Describe the differences between microcomputers and minicomputers.

10. What is the function of the systems analyst?

essay questions

1. Consider how information systems might be used in your area of training or at your job.

2. Do you think government agencies should share information systems and databases with each other? Take a position pro or con.

3. It has often been stated that many purchasers of computers buy these machines without really knowing what to do with them. Comment on this statement.

4. How would this chapter help a decision maker, or you in your own job?

Answers to the objective questions

True/false: **1.** F; **2.** F; **3.** T; **4.** F; **5.** T; **6.** F; **7.** T; **8.** F; **9.** F; **10.** F
Multiple choice: **1.** b; **2.** b; **3.** c; **4.** d; **5.** c
Fill in the blank: **1.** standard, exception;
2. read-only memory (ROM) **3.** system software;
4. on-line; **5.** control, arithmetic/logic; **6.** field;
7. bits, byte; **8.** systems analyst; **9.** people, rules and procedures, data, software, hardware;
10. central processing unit (CPU), main memory unit

Information systems in business: functions and management

After studying this chapter you should understand the following:

- *The types of data needed to support decisions at the three management levels.*
- *Those functions common to any business.*
- *How a management information system helps managers make decisions.*
- *The features of decision support and expert systems.*
- *The features of an information resource management system.*
- *Trends in business management and office systems.*

chapter 3

Sales management with a difference

Penny Helmsley put down the phone. That had been a good conference call. Penny really liked her sales manager job at Paul's House of Electronic Wonders. With locations in four cities in North America, and customers across the world, Paul's House of Electronic Wonders faced many opportunities and challenges. The electronics market was changing rapidly and unpredictably, and was rife with competition. Paul's sold electronic parts to retailers, other wholesalers, and manufacturers.

Penny enjoyed the sales game immensely. She had learned how to negotiate over the phone. She was skilled at setting sales targets based on prices and delivery dates, and making sure the staff at Paul's gave clients the speedy and attentive service they demanded. This paid off in repeat sales and larger reorders.

Penny turned to her terminal, and began the sales analysis software package she used. The package was part of the company's decision support system. She was able to access the package by selecting various options from a menu. The program displayed information from the database about the sales representatives she had just talked to. Penny entered a note as a reminder to send each of them, through the electronic mail system, a follow-up memo confirming the outcome of the call.

The information system at Paul's was quite useful to Penny. She used it to maintain needed data, and also to keep track of company competitors and how to best counter their tactics. In fact there were so many uses for the information system that Penny almost forgot that her sales force used it to place orders, too. Penny spent a minute proofreading all of the messages on the screen, and then saved them for later reference.

"Does everything happen that fast around here?" Bonnie Meyer asked. Bonnie was a new member of the sales staff.

"Well it usually starts that way," Penny said. "Placing the sales order is fast, but now the accounting department has to approve credit and create an invoice. Shipping gets the data and has to act on it."

"That's our first training area, right?" Gene Tomaselli asked. Gene was the other trainee Penny was instructing. Their training program called for them to spend brief periods in accounting, marketing, finance, and warehouse operations. "Yes, the shipping department's your next stop," Penny said. "And to answer your original question, Bonnie, people do work hard here, but an order must go through a lot of steps. Consider shipping—if the item isn't in stock, the data are passed on to the purchasing people. Meanwhile, my customer is still waiting. And now," Penny said, standing up, "let's pass you two on to shipping and receiving. I'll check back later to see how you're doing."

Managers: charting a course over troubled seas

Our opening example illustrates how the elements of an information system play several important roles in managing a business. Stated briefly:

□ *People.* The users of an information system depend upon the system to perform their jobs properly. Penny Helmsley works with an information system to follow up on the progress of her contracts.

□ *Rules and procedures.* The rules of an organization help determine the nature of its information system. The accounting department's rules at Paul's House of Electronic Wonders are used to evaluate the credit-worthiness of a client.

□ *Data.* Data, like that found on a sales order form prepared by a sales representative, or on a shipping invoice prepared by the warehouse, are critical to the day-to-day functions of any business. These same transaction data can also be converted into useful information to help the higher management people at Paul's, in particular the owner Philip Paul, Jr., make informed decisions.

□ *Software.* The application programs at Paul's serve to process the data gathered, given the rules of the organization. It is possible that a credit sale negotiated by Penny would be disallowed, because the procedures written in the credit-approval software package found the client to be a poor risk.

□ *Hardware.* The equipment used will allow Bonnie and Gene to transmit the order details electronically from one part of the office to another. The computer and its peripherals process and print the sales order.

All five information system components must fit together and work together for a business to benefit fully from its information system.

Management principles

Many of you may have already taken a course in management; others have not. We will review those points that are relevant here. A *manager* organizes people and other resources to achieve some organizational goal. A manager's activities are known as "management"; sometimes "management" is also used loosely to mean "manager" or "managers."

An *organizational goal* refers to an organization's purpose or objective. Like most concepts, a goal should be stated in clear and measurable terms to be understood by others. Examples might be: "Achieve a 20 percent return on investment," or "Reach number one in beverage sales in northern Illinois by 1992." It helps to associate numbers or dates with a goal, to have something concrete to measure against. Unclear or conflicting goals hinder effective management.

A manager's job entails five activities: planning, organizing, staffing, directing, and controlling. *Planning* refers to the process of anticipating opportunities and selecting the best strategy to meet the organization's goal. Managers at Paul's House of Electronic Wonders, for instance, might decide to add a new branch location. Their planning would involve collecting information about possible locations, and estimating the sales that each location might generate.

Organizing concerns the gathering of resources—people, money, and materials—to achieve the goal. One of the most important tasks of a manager is *staffing*, which involves the selection and training of people to accomplish the goal.

Directing involves supervising personnel as they work. Organizing, staffing, and directing are the management activities that nonmanagerial employees see the most evidence of.

Controlling is a form of feedback that evaluates the organization's progress toward the achievement of its goal. If Paul's House of Electronic Wonders decided to add a new branch, the manager in charge of the expansion would carefully monitor the expense by comparing it against the original plan. Was land purchased on schedule, and for the budgeted amount? Is construction proceeding on schedule? How do sales at the new branch compare to anticipated figures?

All of these functions require managers to make decisions.

Making decisions

The first step in making a decision is to *define the problem and the decision criteria*. For example, the problem might be whether or not Paul's House of Electronic Wonders should upgrade their present sales analysis system with a new one. The criteria for making the decision would involve measurable costs and benefits: how much would the system cost, how long would it take to install, how much would installing it disrupt the organization, and what tangible benefits would the new system bring?

Once we know what the problem is, we need to *gather data* upon which to base an intelligent decision. We would seek quantitative data, consisting of numerical facts, such as how many sales are made per day. Qualitative data, which cannot be expressed as numbers, are also important. An example of qualitative data might be how people feel about having one of three regional warehouses closed.

When the data are in hand, the next step is to *process the data*. Management information systems and decision support systems provide managers with information upon which to base informed decisions. We will discuss these systems in detail later in the chapter.

Even though a state-of-the-art computer may have provided the information, managers still need to *evaluate the information* themselves. If the information indicates orders are being lost because of ineffective sales analysis, yet nine out of ten employees feel that changing systems would disrupt their work intolerably, the manager has to weigh these factors. Then comes the point of the whole process: managers must *make the decision*. No respectable information system relieves managers of this burden, nor provides a surefire formula to prevent managers from calling some shots wrong. Sometimes managers decide to follow the "null alternative," which means to leave things the way they are.

Once the decision has been made, the manager's next task is to *implement the decision*. If the decision is to install a new sales analysis system, this will mean managing the actual creation and installation of such a system, which may take many months. When the decision has been implemented, the manager then needs to *evaluate feedback* on whether or not the solution has in fact solved the problem. Is Paul's House of Electronic Wonders selling more with the new sales analysis system, or less?

Management levels

Managers can be arranged into a three-level hierarchy of top, middle, and supervisory. Figure 3-1 illustrates the three levels and their responsibilities. The figure is arranged into a triangular shape to reflect the fact that there are increasingly fewer managers as one moves from the bottom to the top.

Managers at each of the three levels make different types of decisions and require different information support from their computer systems. *Top-level managers* define organizational goals and make *strategic decisions* on overall plans, or the "big picture," to reach these goals (Figure 3-2). Such decisions may be effective for a period of 1 to 10 or more years. Of the five management activities outlined earlier, top-level managers are mainly concerned with planning and organizing.

Middle managers, such as department heads and plant managers, make *tactical decisions* necessary to carry out the overall plan devised by the top-level managers (Figure 3-3). Carrying out the plan entails developing budgets and acquiring and managing resources over a period ranging from about 3 months to 1 year. Middle managers spend about an equal amount of time at each of the five management activities— planning, organizing, staffing, directing, and controlling.

Supervisory managers (sometimes called *lower-level managers*), such as project leaders or factory floor managers, have the narrowest scope of all, making *operational decisions* that put into effect the details of the tactical decisions made by middle managers (Figure 3-4). Opera-

Figure 3-1
The three management levels and their responsibilities.

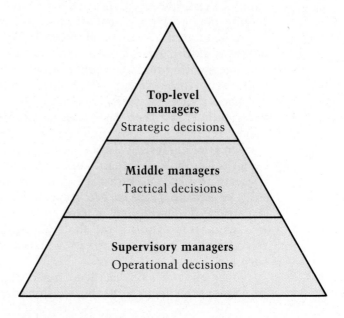

Figure 3-2
Top-level managers de-
termine a company's
overall strategy.

Figure 3-3
Middle managers de-
velop the tactics used to
bring about the "big pic-
ture" envisioned by top-
level managers.

Figure 3-4
Supervisory (lower-level)
managers direct the day-
to-day operations that
get the work done.

tional decisions involve the use of existing resources to carry out functions within a budget, and cover events that take place over a period
ranging from less than 1 day to about 3 months. The primary task for
supervisory managers is directing subordinates. Figure 3-5 summarizes
the activities carried out by the three levels of managers.

Figure 3-5
Management activities
by level.

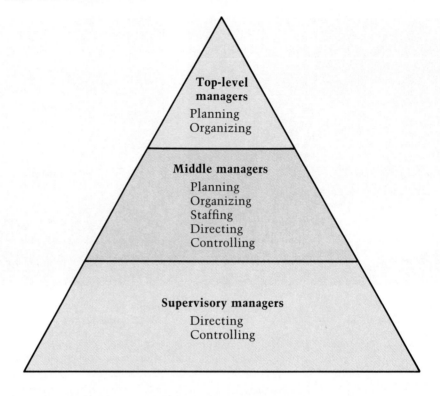

Top-level managers
Planning
Organizing

Middle managers
Planning
Organizing
Staffing
Directing
Controlling

Supervisory managers
Directing
Controlling

Reports managers need

Information systems provide decision support in the form of reports. The reports can be produced in "permanent" form by a printer or graphic output device, or "temporarily" displayed on a screen. Regardless of medium, the reports differ in terms of how often they are created, the degree of detail they show, and the level of analysis they reflect.

The most common type of report, the SCHEDULED LISTING, is created on a regular basis—daily, weekly, monthly, or yearly. Scheduled listings show as much detail as possible, and reflect very little analysis. An inventory report that simply lists the quantity of each item in stock is an example of a scheduled listing.

An EXCEPTION REPORT highlights significant changes from whatever conditions the business considers as normal. Such a report may be created at regular intervals, or when a special condition arises. Less detail is shown than with a scheduled listing. Since exception reports identify situations that may require action by mangers, they reflect more analysis than do scheduled listings. A list of out-of-stock inventory items is an example of an exception report.

A DEMAND REPORT is generated only on request, and usually concerns a specific topic of interest to a manager. Details are confined to the matter of interest, and the information can reflect some analysis. A purchasing manager may be concerned with the out-of-stock items and request a demand report that lists late suppliers.

PREDICTIVE REPORTS attempt to identify trends. These reports are based on specific data, such as those found in scheduled listings, exception reports, and demand reports. Predictive reports go beyond the data at hand, however, to project into the future. They do not show much detail, but reflect considerable analysis. Predictive reports often answer

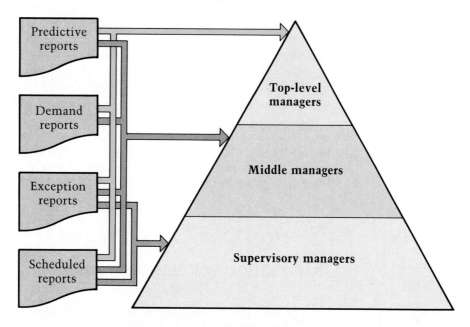

Figure 3-6
Management report needs by level.

"What if?" questions. A corporate vice-president might request a report on the effects on company market share 10 years in the future if the company grew 5 percent each of those years and competitors did not.

Different levels of managers require different reports (see Figure 3-6). Top-level managers require reports that show little detail and generally reflect a fair amount of analysis. The data are drawn from all parts of the company database, and even from outside of the company (Figure 3-7). Therefore these managers often use demand reports and predictive

Figure 3-7
Access to the company database. Each higher level has access to whatever data are accessible to the lower levels.

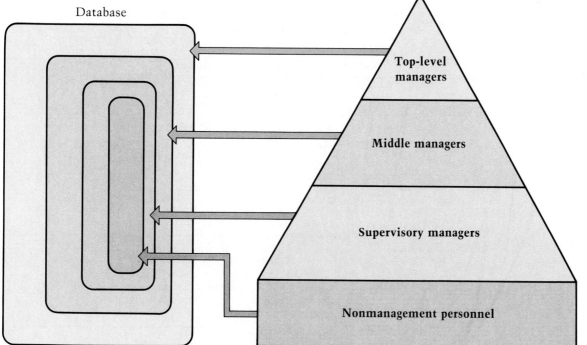

reports to help make planning decisions. In addition, top-level managers may refer to scheduled listings. Middle managers rely on scheduled listings supplemented by exception reports as necessary. Supervisory managers tend to work with scheduled listings exclusively.

Naturally we have simplified matters somewhat, and not all business organizations have managers, levels, and reports categorized this neatly. In fact these categories can blur together. For example, managers may find the information presented in demand and exception reports to be so valuable that they request them on a regular, scheduled basis. One task of the information system is *to supply different levels of managers with different types of information.*

Information systems in business

Business functions at the office

Let's look at the main business applications an organization's information system can handle. Our example with Penny Helmsley touched on some of these applications. No matter how big or small, all businesses deal in some way with the areas of accounting, marketing, finance, and personnel. (Nonoffice applications such as communications, manufacturing, retailing, transportation, and wholesaling were discussed in

Figure 3-8
The most important information system business applications.

Application	Brief Description
Accounting	Maintain financial records
Accounts Receivable	Money owed the company
Accounts Payable	Money the company owes
General Ledger	Summary of business accounts and to prepare balance sheets and income statements
Billing	Prepare statements for customers (part of accounts receivable)
Inventory	Manages items in stock (either finished or unfinished)
Payroll	Manages payroll records and issues paychecks
Marketing	Moving goods and services from producers to consumers
Order Processing	Order entry, processing status
Market Analysis	Market share analysis, sales-call analysis
Finance	Use and management of funds
Financial Analysis	Long- and short-term financial planning and budgeting
Credit Analysis	Client credit status
Personnel	Management of human resources
Hiring	Testing new personnel
Training	Training and evaluating personnel
Management	Handling personnel records and creating reports

Chapter 1.) Computer-based information systems can assist in carrying out each of these functions (Figure 3-8). Let's review the ways computers can help.

Accounting

Accounting is the maintenance of organized business and financial transaction records. These records are used to support a number of business-related functions. When a business computerizes its information system, accounting is one of the first areas to be automated. The accounting operations listed in Figure 3-8 typically occupy about 30 percent of the computer's time in a business information system. *Accounts receivable systems* keep track of money owed to a company. An accounts receivable report produced by the information system at Paul's House of Electronic Wonders is shown in Figure 3-9. It lists the amounts owed to Paul's by various customers for goods purchased.

Accounts payable systems show money a company owes others. When a wholesaler purchases goods from a manufacturer, money owed on the purchase is an accounts payable item until the bill is paid.

The *general ledger* contains a summary of all business accounts. It is used in preparing (1) balance sheets—statements of the financial position of a business at a particular time; and (2) income statements—summaries of the financial position of a business over a period of time. Paul's has the general ledger on its information system as well. Figure 3-10 shows an income statement.

Billing involves the preparation of statements of money owed by customers. Technically billing is part of the accounts receivable process.

Figure 3-9
Accounts receivable report showing the aging of various accounts.

Paul's House of Electronic Wonders

Accounts Receivable Report

as of September 1, 1989

Customer Number	Customer Name	Current Balance	Balance Over 60 Days Past Due	Balance Over 90 Days Past Due	Total Balance
19244	Bits and Bytes	$2535.34	$35.42	$0.00	$2570.76
24411	World of Computers	355.22	24.53	0.00	379.75
26331	Terminal Connection	3441.35	244.34	424.32	4110.01
29353	Consolidated Storage	1100.00	600.00	452.00	2152.00

Figure 3-10
Income statement.

Paul's House of Electronic Wonders Corporation Consolidated Statement of Earnings Year Ended December 31, 1989		
		Current Earnings (in thousands of dollars)
Gross Sales		$41,700
Returns and Discounts	$ 2,140	
Net Sales		39,560
Cost of Goods Sold	29,276	
Gross Profit		10,284
Selling and Administrative Expenses	6,172	
Operating Income		4,112
Other Income		340
Other Expenses	428	
Earnings Before Income Taxes		4,024
Income Taxes	2,052	
Net Income		$ 1,972

Inventory management systems are used to minimize the total cost of ordering and stocking various items sold or used by a company. *Payroll systems*—computerized by virtually any business of at least medium size—keep track of employee wages, taxes, and benefits, and issue paychecks.

Marketing

The second major application for a business information system is marketing. *Marketing* is the planning, pricing, promotion, and distribution of goods and services from producers to consumers. Penny Helmsley, through her sales efforts, promotes the product, offers it for a competitive price, and sets the distribution effort in motion.

Two marketing areas where computer information systems are used are order processing and market analysis. *Order processing* entails entering sales orders, processing these orders, and monitoring the status of the orders. *Market analysis* focuses on such matters as the product life cycle, sales strategies, market share of competitors, and sales-call strategies.

Finance

Finance refers to the acquisition and use of funds. Computerized information systems offer the thoroughness and speed to monitor the whereabouts and use of funds more efficiently than manual systems. *Finan-*

cial analysis involves examining and attempting to predict the best way to obtain funds for long- and short-term corporate financial needs. Two aspects of financial analysis are corporate planning and budgeting. Computerized information systems, with their ability to rapidly manipulate and summarize great quantities of data, give corporate planners the flexibility to explore the financial implications of alternate strategies.

Credit analysis refers to methods for determining the credit-worthiness of clients. Advancing credit is a classic method of stimulating sales, although it carries the risk of some clients defaulting. Information systems are used extensively today to analyze the credit risk posed by each customer.

Personnel

Personnel systems are concerned with recruiting and developing human resources. Information systems can aid in finding individuals to fill specific jobs, by searching the records of present personnel to locate individuals with the requisite skills. Reports concerning compensation, affirmative action, and security clearances can be created from data stored in the information system database.

Office systems

Many of the management and business functions discussed above, whether performed with a computerized information system or manually, are performed in an office. The office is the place where many of you will work. People meet and perform transactions, exchange money, provide services, and plan and manage business operations as well as engage in social activity at the office. Many modern offices have taken advantage of technology to help increase productivity. Three of these technologies are word processing systems, electronic mail/message systems (EMMS), and teleconferencing systems (Figure 3-11).

WORD PROCESSING SYSTEMS allow people to compose, edit, and store text using a computer. The text can be recalled, modified, printed, or transmitted electronically at a later date. Input is faster than with many electric typewriters and corrections are simpler to make. Standard paragraphs can be saved and spliced into documents during editing to further speed the writing task.

ELECTRONIC MAIL/MESSAGE SYSTEMS (EMMS)—sometimes called E-MAIL—allow people to send memos, messages, facsimiles or illustrations and photographs, and other materials electronically. The messages may be routed locally within an office, between branch locations, or around the world through satellite-based telecommunications.

TELECONFERENCING uses a computer network to link people in different locations in a meeting. Participants can talk to one another and can often see each other as well. Teleconferencing can save time and travel costs.

What effect the new technologies will have on people who work in information-age offices is not yet clear. Already people who understand how to use the new systems have an advantage. This has, however, always been true of office work. Clerks and their managers may find themselves with a greater number of responsibilities than in the past.

(a)

(b)

Figure 3-11
*Increasing productivity
in the modern office.
(a) Word processing.
(b) Electronic mail/mes-
sage systems (EMMS).
(c) Teleconferencing.*

(c)

The trend toward automation may continue to the point that offices become "paperless," with all records and documents created, stored, and
retrieved electronically—though this still seems to be some time off.

**The office at home
or on the road**

Today it is possible to take your office anywhere (Figure 3-12). Portable,
or laptop, personal computers can be linked up to regular or mobile telephone communications systems. You can transmit vital data to your
central office and receive responses without actually being there. A "vir-
tual office" is one that can follow you everywhere, unlike a regular
"physical office," which, of course, can't.

EMMS can reach almost anywhere. A sales representative can use
such a system to call up records on a client while en route to the sales
call. At the sales call, the representative can use EMMS to transmit questions and receive responses to customer inquiries, and to send in sales
orders and other messages. These messages can go to several destinations at the salesperson's office. One message might be sent to the word
processing center, requesting that a letter of thanks be sent to a customer for placing an order with the company.

Teleconferencing can also be arranged between a customer and the
home office to help answer questions. This information system can help
increase sales-call productivity. Similar applications abound in other
fields where quick responses are crucial to completing transactions. In
health care, such systems can be utilized to transmit diagnostic results
to specialists for quick response to medical difficulties.

Figure 3-12
You can take your office
anywhere.

Figure 3-13
Information systems for
your in-home office. The
in-home workstation has
certain advantages, such
as a short commute to
work and flexibility over
how you decorate your
office.

Working as an employee at your home through a telephone link between your microcomputer or display terminal and the company office computer, has come to be known as TELECOMMUTING (see Figure 3-13). EMMS can be used to communicate between the home workstation and the office. Most tasks can be done at home—writing memos, analyzing data, preparing reports, updating database information—and the results or data can be transmitted to coworkers or to other computers. Such in-home systems allow people greater flexibility over their personal schedules and, potentially, the opportunity to work with greater concentration than many office environments permit. It is estimated over one-half million workers telecommute all or part of the time. This figure is expected to grow in the future. From the employer's point of view, telecommuting can also offer a welcome flexibility. Advantages include less missed work because of bad weather or reduced office space requirements.

The managing of information requirements

To meet the evolving information requirements of business, *information system staff* have changed and enhanced how they organize and deliver services to managers and nonmanagers alike. We will look at several somewhat overlapping approaches developed for meeting business needs:

- Management Information Systems (MIS)
- Decision Support Systems (DSS)
- Expert Systems
- Information Resource Management Systems (IRMS)

In the evolution of information systems, MIS precedes decision support, expert, and information resource management systems.

Management information systems

A **MANAGEMENT INFORMATION SYSTEM (MIS)** is an information system designed to aid in the performance of management functions. It processes the transaction data of an organization's day-to-day operations, and creates information in the form of reports, in order to support a manager's tasks of planning, organizing, staffing, directing, and controlling.

Management information systems have their origins with unsatisfactory information computers produced in the 1960s. Managers got tired of flipping through scheduled listings that presented far too much detail and that reflected little of the types of analysis they really needed. Listings stressed bulk rather than quality. Printed reports that stood taller than the person that requested them were not unknown. It is very difficult to find the kernels of wisdom in such a printout fast enough to base correct decisions on them.

At the same time that managers were feeling frustrated, computers were getting faster and more powerful, and becoming cheaper and easier to use. Clearly they could handle time-sharing and real-time processing as well as the batch processing that produced those listings. Managers wanted to put this computing power to work for them. Management information systems were born.

An MIS processes data to create information for managers in the form of scheduled listings, exception reports, demand reports, and predictive reports. Some of these reports can be listings produced by batch processing programs. Other reports can be requested and received almost immediately at terminals served by time-sharing or real-time programs.

Figure 3-14
Accessing the transaction-oriented database. A nonmanagement person in a business might access a database to update a customer record. This person's supervisor could access more of the database to read a scheduled report. The middle manager could rely upon these reports and other data to analyze exceptional patterns over the past fiscal year. A high-level manager may make use of the same data plus vast amounts of additional data to project corporate plans over the next several years. Access is on a "need-to-know" basis and must be properly authorized.

Like any other information system, a management information system consists of people, rules and procedures, data, software, and hardware. The *people* are, of course, the managers. The *rules and procedures* concern the types of reports to be created and who is allowed to see them. Since an MIS can deliver highly distilled, powerful, sensitive information, care must be taken with distribution. For instance, reports generated for top managers that evaluate middle- and low-level managers should not be accessible to the people evaluated. Chapter 17 will cover the important topic of security.

Data for an MIS are extracted from accumulated *transaction data*, and generally contained in a database. Figure 3-14 shows one approach to using a database for different levels of management. Here a single database serves the whole organization, from the president down to nonmanagement personnel. For security, each level is only allowed to work with the portion of the database it actually needs. Security implies not only a mistrust of certain individuals, but the concern that someone might unintentionally cause irreparable damage to a database by simply hitting the wrong key. Chapter 11 will explore database design and use in depth.

The *software* for an MIS processes the data using an appropriate level of analysis for the particular management level, and outputs the right amount of detail. It manages the database and incorporates MIS rules and procedures such as security requirements.

Hardware is a computer of any size, together with the peripherals necessary to promptly and legibly create the desired quantity of output. All but the simplest management information systems require at least a display terminal or microcomputer for the managers served.

With an MIS supplying them with up-to-date and appropriate information, managers can spend more time planning and less time scouring files and printouts for information—or worse, guessing. Managers can move faster in response to the information. They can make decisions to correct problems or respond to opportunities that might not even have been recognized without an MIS. Graphic output from an MIS (Figure 3-15) can help a manager present his or her case for action to others in the organization.

Figure 3-15
Not only do modern sys-
tems provide vital infor-
mation, but they can also
express it as graphics
that can be used in a pre-
sentation or published.

Decision support and expert systems

Management information systems can do a lot, but are more effective for supervisory and middle managers than for top managers. They are difficult to use, and prove virtually impossible to change. It was only logical that the same concept would be developed further. The DECISION SUPPORT SYSTEM (DSS) is an information system that provides managers with highly refined information to help make nonroutine decisions. Decision support systems were originally used at some corporations to assist the highest management levels, the chief executive officers.

What are the features of a decision support system and how does it differ from a management information system? The features of a DSS provide for:

▫ A user-friendly environment.
▫ The processing of heterogeneous (dissimilar) data.
▫ The analyzing of the data using sophisticated techniques.

These three features allow users to access easily a wide variety of data, and to process the data using a range of methods not available in a traditional MIS environment.

A *user-friendly environment* in a DSS means managers can use it without much training. Skillfully designed display screens and clear documentation help managers determine which program functions they need (Figure 3-16). As we saw in the opening example, Penny Helmsley could easily get the decision support system to do its job by picking commands such as "DISPLAY REPORT" from a menu.

The *processing of heterogeneous data* using a decision support system is a major difference from the processing capabilities found in the typical MIS environment. Heterogeneous data means data are not all of the same type or format. (Compare data entered onto a sales order to that found in a report concerning a competitor's pricing policy.) Top-

Figure 3-16
Using a decision support system (DSS).

level managers need to analyze data from different sources to make strategic decisions; the sources may include the in-house database as well as external databases. A DSS is able to extract data from different locations.

The *analyzing of the data using sophisticated techniques* is possible because DSS software exists that can handle a whole range of analysis and modeling. Statistical studies can be made of the data, or mathematical models of a business can be built and differing data run through them to see the effects on the outcome.

Many of today's managers are accustomed to using electronic spreadsheets on their microcomputers to manipulate financial data and make projections into the future. Using a DSS, a manager can retrieve relevant data from the company database or an external database, and copy it to his or her microcomputer system to work on it with a spreadsheet.

Not every business has a DSS. Those that do, use them in such areas as budgeting, product planning, government policy analysis, personnel planning, managing research and development, sales planning, and developing overall corporate plans.

Expert systems

EXPERT SYSTEMS are software, or programs, that try to imitate human experts by giving technical advice in forms closely resembling the user's language.[1] Expert systems packages are subsets of a decision support system. The expert system software contains a particular subject area stored in the form of rules, as well as an inference engine that makes choices from the stored knowledge. Expert systems work best when fully integrated into a business's existing information system environment. This integration effort requires: training and supporting people in the use of the expert system, tapping into the business's transaction databases, linking with standard productivity software, and carrying out processing using hardware common to the business environment. (See Case in Point: Expert System Applications.)

[1] Adapted from Mohammad H. Qayoumi and Jerome S. Burstein, "HAL: The Expert System Is Here," *Northern California Executive Review* (Spring 1988), by permission of the authors.

Figure 3-17
The components of an
expert system.

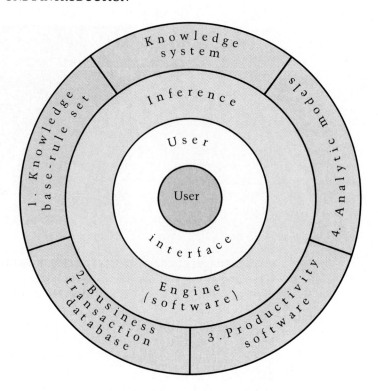

A typical expert system (Figure 3-17) is made up of three components:

■ A **USER INTERFACE** (software and hardware) that includes easy-to-follow menus, readable display screens, and high-quality printed output.

■ An **INFERENCE ENGINE**, which is a software package for carrying out the logical reasoning (as differentiated from data calculations).

■ A **KNOWLEDGE SYSTEM** that contains knowledge bases or rule sets, transaction databases, productivity software (spreadsheets, word processing, and graphics), and those analytical models commonly found in a decision support environment. The **KNOWLEDGE BASE** or **RULE SET** tells the inference engine how to reason in this particular business environment.

Potential benefits of expert systems
The potential benefits of this type of system include:

1. *Disseminating scarce knowledge.* Human expertise can be distributed across an organization efficiently and among a larger number of people. The organization's knowledge base can thus be accumulative, despite fluctuations in personnel. Thus, costs of acquiring, holding, and disseminating information can be steadily reduced.
2. *Training personnel.* The system can be an effective training resource for both new and experienced personnel. Individuals can test their knowledge in a safe, well-paced interactive manner, with constructive nonbiased feedback.
3. *Delivering optimal solutions.* Since the system uses a process that

Remember HAL, the humanized computer in the movie *2001: A Space Odyssey*?[1] He was a work of fiction, but his cousins are alive and well today, only a few years before his literary birth. These cousins can be experts in their various fields. Businesses rely constantly on expertise, but usually anticipate receiving it in human form. Nowadays, however, these skills can be available in other forms, as "expert system software packages," the "HALs" of the 1990s.

A bit of history

Expert systems try to imitate human experts by giving technical advice. They are a branch of computer science called artificial intelligence, and became available in the 1970s.

Artificial intelligence (AI) covers computer-based areas that try to mirror human abilities. These include manipulative skills in robotics, natural languages and speech recognition, aural and visual pattern recognition, locomotion, and expert systems.

Examples specific to expert systems include MYCIN, developed in 1976 to diagnose and prescribe medications for bacteriological infections, and PROSPECTOR, developed in 1978 to predict discovery of mineral deposits. In 1986, revenues from expert systems applications reached $35 million. Revenue for 1991 is projected at $900 million, an increase of 2500 percent in 5 years.

Today about half of the Fortune 500 companies have initiated research in expert systems with approximately fifty companies having developed applications. Most insurance companies are considering expert systems for underwriting: 47 percent for claim evaluation, and 22 percent for financial planning.[2] Federal agencies, including the Department of Defense, Securities & Exchange Commission, and Internal Revenue Service, are now experimenting with this technology.

In almost every case, expert systems have been helpful.

Current applications

Current industrial applications of the expert system to troubleshoot include: General Electric's CATS (computer-aided troubleshooting system), used to maintain diesel locomotives; AT&T Bell Lab's ACE (automated cable expertise), used to determine when deteriorating cables need repairs; and Westinghouse's Process Diagnosis System (PDS), used to monitor turbines and generators.

If faced with unfamiliar situations or incomplete information, a system might make obvious mistakes or come to erroneous conclusions. Current software, however, can deal with fuzzy information, handle perturbations of the knowledge base, and extrapolate from knowledge that does not fit the prior rules. Some systems, moreover, are not static but are able to modify a rule set or knowledge base over time, using new information that needs to be integrated or the feedback from consultative sessions.

Conclusions: HAL, 1990s style

It was only 20 years ago that HAL was portrayed in the science fiction motion picture, *2001*, as able to solve the most complex problems in an easy, straightforward manner. Today's expert system can only solve significantly smaller questions. Artificial intelligence scientists believe that expert systems will have a fundamental impact on the jobs of white-collar workers in the way that industrial automation had a tremendous impact on the blue-collar work environment.

Will expert systems be able to replace human expertise? It is unlikely, because the human mind is so complex. The expert system is a tool to help a manager augment human expertise. It is by no means a panacea, but it can be very useful.

[1] Adapted from Mohammad H. Qayoumi and Jerome S. Burstein, "HAL: The Expert System Is Here," *Northern California Executive Review* (Spring 1988), by permission of the authors.
[2] Ibid.

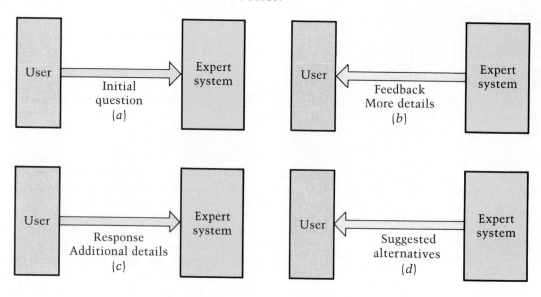

Figure 3-18
How an expert system works.

considers every detail in an iterative process, it will often deliver the best possible solution. (See Figure 3-18).

4. *Maintaining the knowledge base.* Knowledge bases in most disciplines are very large compared with the know-how of one person or a small group of people. In addition, if people do not constantly reuse data, the data may be quickly forgotten. In an expert system, stored knowledge will always be available.

5. *Reducing outside interference.* Negative operating conditions (fatigue, boredom, or hazardous situations) can affect human expertise, causing hasty conclusions or biased opinions. In an expert system, the knowledge base will be less "distracted" by outside interference.

6. *Increasing user efficiency.* An expert system can be operated to make the best use of the user's time. When it finds sufficient evidence to rule out a hypothesis, the system will cease asking questions about it.

Clearly expert systems bring data and decision criteria together, handle tedious but necessary tasks, and help users find solutions to both simple and complex problems in a perfectly consistent manner, in normal times as well as crisis situations.

Information resource management systems

An **INFORMATION RESOURCE MANAGEMENT SYSTEM (IRMS)** coordinates the total acquisition, flow, storage, and distribution of data and information in an organization. Data come from transactions generated by the firm, written text, and voice/image communications. This broad view of data sources differs from the transaction-data-only view of traditional MIS operations. (See Databases Reach Out to Text and Images, page 95.)

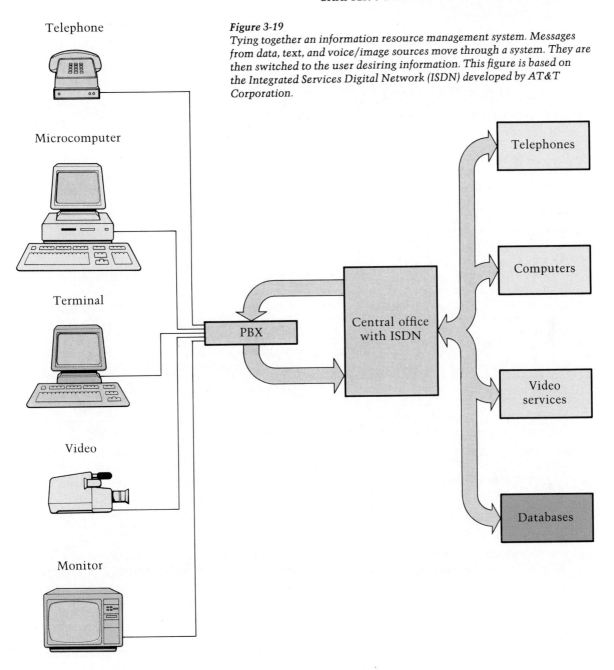

Telephone

Microcomputer

Terminal

Video

Monitor

Figure 3-19
Tying together an information resource management system. Messages from data, text, and voice/image sources move through a system. They are then switched to the user desiring information. This figure is based on the Integrated Services Digital Network (ISDN) developed by AT&T Corporation.

PBX

Central office with ISDN

Telephones

Computers

Video services

Databases

To support these expanded data-handling requirements an information resource management system does everything that a traditional MIS or DSS does, but in addition, has such capabilities as text- or word processing systems, electronic mail/message systems, digital telephone lines, and in some cases video channels (Figure 3-19). Thus an IRMS can serve as a means to properly manage the far more complex processing needs of today's business.

IRMS are a response to changes in the information-processing environment. The microcomputer was the main new type of hardware. Soft-

The recent trend to regard information as a companywide resource requires the creation of a suitable management position—the information resource manager. The information resource manager usually reports to the chief executive officer of the organization.

The information resource manager is responsible for the total flow and storage of information in an organization. He or she must see that managers get timely, appropriate information when they need it. While this is easily stated, carrying it out involves every possible aspect of information systems. The information must be obtainable by the managers without fuss or undue technical knowledge, must be refined enough to assist in making strategic, tactical, or operational decisions, and must sometimes be extracted from heterogeneous sources. The information systems must work smoothly to achieve these goals.

The information resource manager is responsible for more than just the computer center(s). All of the information-related technical facilities in an organization also come under his or her umbrella: word processing, electronic mail/message systems, and any other area of office management that has been automated. In sum the information resource manager is responsible for designing, implementing, and maintaining an information resource management system so thorough that no scrap of paper or telephone message is too small, and no statistical analysis of disparate data too complex, to merit handling in an expeditious manner.

Requirements for filling this job are extensive. As with the position of director of information systems, it is possible to join an organization in a low-level information-processing position and gradually work one's way up. This provides the opportunity to demonstrate technical competence, and ideally a stint as leader of some project—such as developing a system—can give experience in management as well as exposure to higher-level managers who can advance one's career.

Once the move to management is made, it is possible to ascend to the top and become information resource manager, with dozens or thousands of employees organized in an elaborate pyramid with subordinate managers and specialists. At some point in the ascent, interpersonal and administrative skills become more important than technical knowledge; accordingly, a degree in management or business administration and an extensive, impeccable track record are musts.

Salaries are high and the pressure is intense. Also, heads tend to roll when things don't work right. Nevertheless, for the aspiring manager who feels a sense of mission in grasping an organization's information needs in all their complexities, and crafting intricate systems to fill them, shooting for this position may be the best alternative.

ware became more user-friendly, and a host of prepackaged programs to manage databases, analyze data, and perform many other functions were created. The development of information resource management systems would not have been possible without this technical progress.

With an IRMS, managers and their assistants working at terminals or microcomputers can use software to retrieve data from a database, analyze them, and store the results of analysis for incorporation into documents produced by a word processing system. The document can then be output on a laser-xerographic printer right in the office, or electronically transmitted so that multiple copies can be produced and distributed. Besides documents, the electronic mail/message system can be used to send messages from one person to another in the network.

Exxon Corporation uses a large-scale IRMS run by its Communications and Computer Sciences Department. The network offers managers and other personnel access to decision support systems, office systems such as electronic mail/message systems and word processing systems, and sixteen "client support centers" that provide advice and training as well as the traditional computing power.

Fitting the information system into a business

MIS or IRMS can be incorporated into a business in various ways. One common method is to create a separate department headed by a vice-president for information systems. This person oversees all of the operations associated with computers, information systems, and MIS or IRMS. Figure 3-20 illustrates such an organizational structure. Reporting to the vice-president for IRMS are the top managers for computer operations, programming, database administration, and systems analysis.

An earlier, less effective approach placed control of all computer systems, including MIS, in the department that made heaviest use of its services—usually the accounting department. This organizational structure made it difficult for people in other areas, such as manufacturing and purchasing, to take advantage of the power of information systems.

Of course, mere cosmetic changes of the title of the department will not change how people will respond to requests. Information system staff used to working in a familiar area—such as accounting—may require time to adjust to the needs of the other departments.

Today's changing organizations

Regardless of their specific "spot" in the organization information system, managers in the system face the same pressures as those in other vital company functions, be it accounting or marketing. One major issue facing managers is how to survive the pressure brought on by the information-processing age. Over the years we have seen this tension in terms of how centralized or decentralized an organization should be. The elements of the information system seem to point in both directions simultaneously.

On the one hand, the use of widespread teleprocessing promotes centralization by allowing people to tie into a single information-processing center. Vast amounts of data can be entered, transmitted, processed, and retransmitted back as output to distant locations.

On the other hand, the microcomputer revolution has put undreamed-of processing power into the hands of millions of people. No longer need a manager wait days (or *months!*) to receive a financial analysis. The manager or an assistant can simply use a prepackaged software program, retrieve data from a local or distant database, and quickly perform quite complex financial modeling—models a centralized computer center might be unable or unwilling to provide.

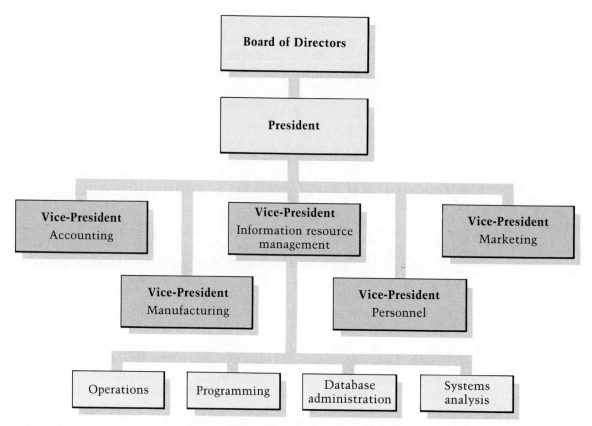

```
                    ┌─────────────────────┐
                    │  Board of Directors │
                    └─────────────────────┘
                              │
                    ┌─────────────────────┐
                    │      President       │
                    └─────────────────────┘
                              │
```

Vice-President
Accounting

Vice-President
Information resource
management

Vice-President
Marketing

Vice-President
Manufacturing

Vice-President
Personnel

Operations   Programming   Database administration   Systems analysis

Figure 3-20
A corporate organiza-
tional chart showing the
relationship between the
IRMS department and
the rest of the company.

The executive in charge (usually the vice-president for MIS, DSS, or IRMS) is caught in the middle of the dilemma of whether to encourage centralization or decentralization. Distributed data processing recognizes the fact of decentralization and ties all the computers, big and small, together into a network that can share tasks and data. In the present chapter, when we have spoken of using a DSS or IRMS to retrieve information from an organization's database and process it locally at a manager's microcomputer, this can only be done with distributed data processing. Distributed data processing appears to hold the most promise for the powerful management information systems, decision support systems, and information resource management systems of tomorrow.

Distributing information resources throughout an organization—whether within a building or scattered across a continent—both reflects that organization's philosophy and can ultimately cause the philosophy to change. There have been predictions that middle managers will disappear. Top-level managers at headquarters can take over the planning and organizing activities of middle managers, this argument runs, and the supervisory managers at local facilities can handle the day-to-day direction of their employees. Other observers have predicted the opposite, that middle managers will thrive as never before because of the availability of the new systems. As with any attempt to see what's coming around the corner, the only thing we can say with certainty is that we don't know what it will be.

Databases reach out to text and images

Four years ago, New Jersey Public Service Electric & Gas wrote a specialized database management system [DBMS] to track its vast real estate holdings.

If questions arise on specific land parcels, users can call up and view a map of any property on a computer screen. Text information about property acquisition, disposition, and easement rights can be called up as well. No commercial packages were available for this application when the utility first conducted its software search. Today, that software space is somewhat more filled, as the Centers for Disease Control in Atlanta recently discovered.

The CDC installed Information Dimension's Basis. . . . "We're building an on-line catalog to track the full text of articles about different scientific subjects," said Susan Wilkin, chief of the information center management and services section. The databases will include unlimited and fully indexed text information.

The two experiences exemplify a trend. Business users are increasingly asking database management systems to reach out beyond alphanumeric data to accommodate text and images. "There is going to be a demand for databases that do a whole lot more than alphanumerics," according to David Harris, president of Cucumber Information Systems in Rockville, Md. "That will eventually include pictures, voice, and music in addition to text."

A text/image DBMS offers standard database functions, in that it handles text and image in a structured manner, requiring users to locate information by fields. However, the fields can be of variable lengths and the products can usually handle huge volumes of data. . . .

Some observers define text/image database products simply as packages that allow users to quickly retrieve documents, books, photographs—whatever is stored in the system—by typing relevant keywords or strings of words. . . .

Joseph McGrath, vice president of office information systems at the Gartner Group, Stamford, Conn., feels... "At the workstation level you can structure things for yourself because, by setting up the structure, you know how it works. But at the department or enterprise level that structure isn't valid for everyone's way of doing things."

The common bond in all the text-related products is the ability to allow users to store and retrieve documents. But few packages allow those documents to be changed; only some of the products handle numbers—traditional data—as well as text; and very few handle image as well.

Within the industry, the lack of a standard term for a textual DBMS complicates matters. "You've got a very new market and a lot of different ways of approaching it," says Barry Frankel, director of marketing and sales for Advanced Data Management Inc., a software manufacturer in Kingston, N.J.

Text management systems, document-retrieval systems, text information management systems . . . are all labels applied to text management products. . . .

"Companies are using these products to track their competitors' new products, articles in the press, financial information, and other information," according to Harry Kaplowitz, executive vice-president of Infodata.

The need to manage the information glut is driving the increasing use of text-oriented databases. Professionals need help in navigating through the staggering number of documents and other information which can reside in computers anywhere within an organization.

Savvy top managers recognize that information is a valuable resource—once it is located.

Source: Johanna Ambrosio, "Databases Reach Out to Text and Images," *Software Magazine* (February 1988). Reprinted with permission from *Software Magazine*, February 1988. Copyright 1988, Sentry Publishing Company, Inc., Westborough, MA 01581.

summary

▪ A manager organizes people and other resources to achieve some organizational goal. A manager's work entails five activities: planning, organizing, staffing, directing, and controlling. To carry out these activities, a manager must make decisions. The steps in making a decision are defining the problem and the decision criteria, gathering data, processing the data, evaluating the information, making the decision, implementing the decision, and evaluating feedback.

▪ Managers can be arranged into a three-level hierarchy of top, middle, and low. Top-level managers make strategic decisions, middle managers make tactical decisions, and supervisory (low-level) managers make operational decisions. Top-level managers require reports that show little detail and generally reflect a fair amount of analysis. They, therefore, often use demand reports and predictive reports. Middle managers rely on the more detailed scheduled listings supplemented by exception reports as necessary. Supervisory managers tend to work with scheduled listings exclusively.

▪ No matter how large or small, any business deals with the areas of accounting, marketing, finance, and personnel.

▪ Modern offices might use word processing systems, electronic mail/message systems(EMMS) or E-mail, and teleconferencing systems in a service-oriented context.

▪ Portable personal computers that can link to communications systems make it possible to, in effect, take the office almost anywhere. Personal computers and communications links have also made it possible to perform many office functions at home, a form of work known as telecommuting.

▪ A management information system (MIS) is an information system designed to assist in the performance of management functions. It processes the transactions of an organization's day-to-day operations, and creates information in the form of reports, to support a manager's tasks of planning, organizing, directing, and controlling. Often a separate department exists within an organization for management information systems, headed by a vice-president for MIS.

▪ A decision support system (DSS) is an information system managers can use easily and provides highly refined information to help in making nonroutine decisions. It extends the concept of the MIS further, in that it is more user-friendly and flexible, can handle heterogeneous data, and performs more analysis on the data.

▪ Expert systems give technical advice in forms resembling the user's language. An expert system is made up of three components: a user interface, an inference engine, and a knowledge system. Part of the knowledge system consists of the rule set or knowledge base.

▪ An information resource management system (IRMS) coordinates the total acquisition, flow, storage, and distribution of information in an organization. An IRMS does everything that an MIS or DSS does, and adds on word processing and electronic mail/message systems.

▪ The person in charge of an organization's MIS, DSS, or IRMS, is caught in the dilemma facing businesses today: whether to encourage centralization or decentralization. Distributed data processing seems to hold the most promise for the powerful MIS, DSS, or IRMS of tomorrow.

wrap-up

The orders must go out

A company like Paul's House of Electronic Wonders thrives by serving its customers well. Once an order has been processed, people in the shipping department must see that the items are sent to customers as quickly as possible. If an item is out of stock, the purchasing department is notified. If some of the required items are in stock, but others are not, Paul's often sends a partial shipment.

Incoming goods go through the receiving part of the warehouse. The items are checked for damage and then stored. Highly valuable items and hazardous substances are stored in special areas to minimize the risk of theft or fire.

Penny Helmsley introduced Bonnie Meyer and Gene Tomaselli, the two trainees, to Herman Lemming, manager in charge of shipping and receiving. Herman explained to the trainees why it was important to properly enter the sales data. If the data were inaccurate, the customer would receive the wrong parts, or in some cases, nothing at all.

The computer-generated shipping forms showed the freight charges for the type of transportation the customer selected. Herman Lemming elaborated about these costs. "Usually items needed quickly were sent via an express courier service, while other items were shipped with a regular delivery truck. Sometimes a customer will request a particular shipper." He added, "selecting the proper shipping method could save us and our customers thousands of dollars a year."

By the time Bonnie and Gene returned to the marketing department after several days spent in shipping and receiving, they had become aware of the link between shipping and sales in a way that they would never forget. Expecting merely a loading dock and a few trucks, they had found them, as well as a specialized information system on shippers, sophisticated methods of handling shipping forms and labels on goods, and a concern that salespeople negotiate their sales and enter their orders in a realistic way that would cut costs for everyone.

key terms

These are the key terms in alphabetical order. The numbers in parentheses refer to the page on which each term is defined.

Decision support system (DSS) (86)
Demand report (76)
Electronic mail/message systems (EMMS) or E-mail (81)
Exception report (76)
Expert system (ES) (87)
Inference engine (88)
Information resource management system (IRMS) (90)
Knowledge base or rule set (88)
Knowledge system (88)
Management information system (MIS) (84)
Predictive report (76)
Scheduled listing (76)
Telecommuting (83)
Teleconferencing (81)
User interface (88)
Word processing system (81)

review questions

objective questions

True/false. *Put the letter T or F on the line next to the question.*

1. Expert systems are used to create scheduled listings. 1 _____

2. About 30 percent of a company's computer resources are devoted to accounting operations. 2 _____

3. The most important part of controlling is staffing the organization. 3 _____

4. Planning is a major function for supervisory managers. 4 _____

5. Electronic mail/message systems (EMMS) are used to create original documents. 5 _____

6. Teleconferencing systems allow people to hold meetings without being physically in the same location. 6 _____

7. Telecommuting and teleconferencing mean the same thing. 7 _____

8. Expert systems can only be used in a management information system (MIS) environment. 8 _____

9. Historically MIS grew out of managerial dissatisfaction with production-oriented data processing operations. 9 _____

10. IRMS offer less flexible operations to managers than MIS. 10 _____

Multiple choice. *Put the letter of the correct answer on the line next to the question.*

1. Another meaning for the term *rule set* is 1 _____
   (a) Inference engine.   (c) Expert system.
   (b) Knowledge base.   (d) User interface.

2. A method for communicating with people within an automated office is 2 _____
   (a) Telecommuting.
   (b) Electronic/mail message systems.
   (c) Word processing.
   (d) Teleconferencing.

3. The principal feature of a decision support system (DSS) is 3 _____
   (a) The ability to handle nonroutine types of decisions.
   (b) The capability to handle heterogeneous data.

(c) The capability of performing strong analytic modeling in a user-friendly environment.

(d) All three choices are correct.

4 _____ 4. The view that information is a valuable organizational asset caused the development of

(a) Decision support systems (DSS).

(b) Expert systems (ES).

(c) Management information systems (MIS).

(d) Information resource management systems (IRMS).

5 _____ 5. A(n) _____ is information system output least likely to be used by supervisory-level management for routine decision making.

(a) Scheduled listing.

(b) Exception report.

(c) Demand report.

(d) Predictive report.

Fill in the blank. _Write the correct word or words in the blank to complete the sentence._

1. A _____ organizes people and other resources to achieve an organizational goal.

2. Acquiring money and materials are featured in the _____ activity.

3. A(n) _____ coordinates the elements of an information system in order to optimize the flow and use of information in an organization.

4. The ability to quickly edit documents is a valuable feature of _____.

5. The _____ is software that performs logical operations in an expert system.

6. A(n) _____ system is used to monitor the amount of items a company has in stock.

7. The rise of the office in the home permits _____ between home and the office.

8. A DSS can process _____ data to assist in the handling of _____ decisions.

9. Strategic planning is an activity performed by _____ managers.

10. A(n) _____ report is generated when there is a deviation from normal limits.

short answer questions

When answering these questions, think of concrete examples to illustrate your points.

1. What are the features of an expert system?

2. How do expert systems relate to DSS?

3. What are the decision-making steps managers follow?

4. What are the office automation features of modern offices?

5. What types of reports are used by top managers?

6. What are the main features of a management information system (MIS)?

7. What is the difference between telecommuting and teleconferencing?

8. What are the main features of a decision support system (DSS)?

9. What are the main features of an information resource management system (IRMS)?

essay questions

1. What type of businesses have you worked at? How were information systems used in the office? In other parts of the organization?

2. What to does the phrase "the bills have to go out before the money comes in" mean in terms of an information system?

3. What are the differences between management information systems (MIS) and decision support systems (DSS)?

4. How do management information systems (MIS) differ from information resource management systems (IRMS)?

Answers to the objective questions

True/false: 1. F; 2. T; 3. F; 4. F; 5. F; 6. T; 7. F; 8. F; 9. T; 10. F

Multiple choice: 1. b; 2. b; 3. d; 4. d; 5. d

Fill in the blank: 1. manager; 2. organizing; 3. information resource management system (IRMS); 4. word processing; 5. inference engine; 6. inventory management; 7. telecommuting; 8. heterogeneous; nonroutine 9. upper-level; 10. exception

Why information systems were created: a bit of history

After studying this chapter you should understand the following:

- *The general historical trends in the development of information systems.*
- *How the four generations of computers differ.*
- *How user demand affected the development of information systems.*
- *How software has evolved to meet new demands.*
- *The challenges of future developments for information systems.*

chapter 4

Reminders

The old warehouse at Paul's House of Electronic Wonders (PHEW) still held a few boxes of computer parts. Herman Lemming looked over the room. As manager of shipping and receiving, he was charged with overseeing the move of the warehouse's contents to a new, larger facility. Bonnie Meyer, a sales trainee, was assisting him in monitoring the transfer of the goods. Philip Paul, the owner, strode toward Herman and Bonnie, his footsteps echoing in the nearly empty warehouse.

"The movers are almost done. Just a few small boxes to go," said Herman.

Because of today's much lighter and smaller hardware elements, this latest move was progressing more quickly than the previous one. With the growth in PHEW's electronics wholesaling business, additional warehouse space was needed once again.

"Remember how large computers were in the old days?" Herman asked Philip.

Philip Paul nodded. "Yeah, the first one I worked on had vacuum tubes and was a real power hog. Any one of the microcomputers around today could out perform that old beast. And programming it seemed to take forever!"

"When I joined this company transistor-based computers had pretty much replaced those vacuum-tube monsters." said Herman. "Still those machines were big compared to today. And, we still had to use punch cards. We used to ship truckloads of them. Now these new microcomputers can store data that used to take 500,000 of those old cards."

Bonnie asked Herman, "How much would half a million cards weigh?" She thought to herself how nice it was to have avoided the difficulties of using punch cards.

Herman thought for a while, then said, "Over a ton! Working punch cards was frustrating at times—you're lucky to only work at a display screen instead of dealing with those cards."

A forklift rumbled by carrying cartons holding printers. These were the latest laser printers available for small businesses and professional workstations. Philip Paul reflected on the printing power of each—power that would have cost tens of thousands of dollar was now available for just over one thousand dollars.

Herman walked over to the last few boxes on a shelf in the corner. He bent down and looked at the carton labels. He motioned Philip and Bonnie over to where he was standing. Cautiously Herman opened one of the dusty boxes. Philip and Bonnie peered over his shoulder. Squinting in the gloom they made out the shape of—vacuum tubes.

"Maybe we should have an antique sale." chuckled Philip Paul.

Birth of the modern computer

*The earliest
calculating
machines*

People have recorded data, processed them, and transmitted the results for thousands of years. Cave paintings communicated information to young hunters concerning the best way to stalk and kill animals. Early civilizations used clay tablets to record business transactions and keep government and community records. Calculating for such records can be tedious work. Simple devices allowed people to reduce the labor and increase the accuracy of recording and processing information.

The abacus

The first mechanical contrivance used for calculations was the ABACUS. Still in everyday use in parts of the world, such as Japan, China, and the Soviet Union, its origin dates back thousands of years. Shown in Figure 4-1, the abacus is based on a 10-digit number system. It offered a better way to perform the calculations that until its invention had been made by scratching symbols into clay tablets or on the bare ground, or by arranging pebbles in patterns. Extremely easy to manufacture, the abacus serves as an example of a product that has withstood the test of time. No device superior to the abacus was developed for thousands of years.

The Pascaline

In 1642, the French mathematician BLAISE PASCAL (1623–1662) invented the first mechanical calculator (Figure 4-2). Called the PASCALINE, the calculator could add and subtract. Pascal was the son of a tax collector, and the device he invented when he was 19 years old was meant to save the drudgery of manual tax calculations. But the Pascaline was not suc-

*Figure 4-1
The abacus.*

*Figure 4-2
Blaise Pascal and his calculator. The Pascaline
was read from left to
right and had two deci-
mal places to the right of
the decimal line (point).*

(a)

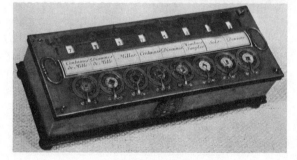

(b)

Figure 4-3
Jacquard's loom used
punch cards to set the
pattern for weaving.

cessful. The technology did not then exist to produce the needed parts in quantity and to a sufficient degree of exactness. Moreover, given the low wages paid clerks at the time, the drudgery of calculating by hand was cheaper.

Jacquard loom

Another invention that affected the creation of computers had nothing to do with mathematics. JOSEPH-MARIE JACQUARD (1752–1834) invented a weaving loom in 1801 that used a *punch card* reading system. The JAC-QUARD LOOM, illustrated in Figure 4-3, was controlled by wooden punch cards hooked with leather straps into a chain which carried the codes that ordered the machine to weave in a certain pattern. Rods attached to the different colored threads were able to pass through the cards where there were holes, and were blocked where there were not. Forms of this machine are still in use today. More importantly for the development of computers, the idea of controlling a machine by a variable program was born, and a now-venerable input-output medium, the punch card, was introduced.

The difference and analytic engines

The next major effort in developing machines to perform calculations was made by the English mathematics and engineering professor, CHARLES BABBAGE (1792–1871). Babbage (Figure 4-4) was concerned about the accuracy of mathematical tables for astronomy, military gunnery, and various business functions. The calculation tasks were divided among teams of workers with various skill levels. The most mathematically skilled would perform the initial calculations, and then solve the

Figure 4-4
Charles Babbage and
Lady Ada Lovelace.

equations at periodic intervals to serve as checkpoints for the other workers. Less skilled people would do simple additions and subtractions.

Babbage persuaded the British government to grant him money to develop a machine to calculate these tables. He called his machine the **DIFFERENCE ENGINE** (Figure 4-5). The difference engine's switches could be preset to generate tables of squares, cubes, and other functions following various algorithms (rules that break down calculations into simple, repetitive operations), and the machine would then show the

Figure 4-5
The difference engine
was used to calculate
numerical tables.

results. In theory, using the machine would be much faster and less error-prone than finding the answer by hand. After a number of years of unsuccessfully attempting to build a full-scale model of the difference engine, however, Babbage lost interest in the project. His major benefactor, the British government, was not amused.

But Babbage had bigger plans. He had an idea for a machine that could be applied to solving any mathematical problem; he called it the ANALYTIC ENGINE. The machine had two major parts: a "mill," which would perform various control and mathematical and logical comparisons, and a "store," which would hold the data until they were needed. The engine would be powered by the dominant energy source of his era, steam. Reputedly, it would be as large as a football field.

Babbage had many design problems with his project. Finally one of his mathematics students came to his rescue. LADY ADA AUGUSTA, THE COUNTESS OF LOVELACE (1816–1852), daughter of the British poet Lord Byron, translated an article concerning the analytic engine written by an Italian engineer. She added an extensive commentary concerning the input and output requirements and other features.

Lady Ada developed a series of instructions to tell the engine what steps to perform. She invented a programming technique called a *loop*, which directs a machine to perform a set of instructions repetitively. Lady Ada Lovelace became the world's first *programmer*. Her portrait is shown in Figure 4-4.

When funding for the analytic engine was cut off by a disgruntled British government, Babbage and Lady Ada attempted to raise funds by applying the machine to pick winning horses at the racetrack. This too was unsuccessful.

Though there was demand for the machine, the product failed. We know from Chapter 2 that the idea of having a control and calculation element (mill) and a primary storage element (store) conforms to the design of computers today, with their central processing unit and primary storage unit. So what went wrong with Babbage's idea? The degree of precision necessary to machine the internal parts required for the analytic engine was lacking. Thus the analytic engine was a product failure.

Would the machine have worked if the parts could have been produced? The answer is yes. A group of IBM engineers working with Babbage's plans developed a working model of his machine in the 1950s— 100 years later. More significantly, by the time of that experiment, IBM and other firms were already selling computers that incorporated Babbage's basic concepts. Lady Ada, who died of cancer at the age of 36, is memorialized by the programming language Ada, named for her by the U.S. Department of Defense.

Hollerith's tabulating machine
The idea of using punch cards to transmit coded data received further application in the work of HERMAN HOLLERITH (1860–1929), who is shown with his invention in Figure 4-6. The U.S. Bureau of the Census took almost 8 years to record and tabulate the data obtained from the 1880 census. The Census Bureau feared it would take $13\frac{1}{2}$ years to tabu-

Figure 4-6
Herman Hollerith and
his tabulating machine.

(a)

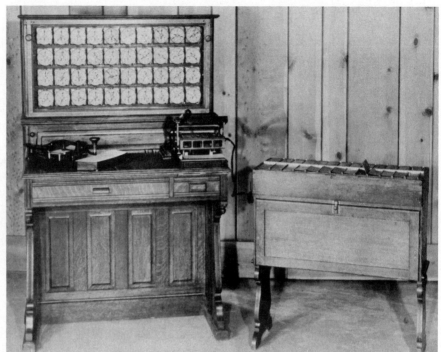

(b)

late the 1890 census, thus violating the constitutional requirement to hold a census every 10 years. A design contest was held and Herman Hollerith's design won. A statistician with the Bureau, he devised a paper punch card **TABULATING MACHINE** to speed up the process of summarizing the census records for the 1890 census. The tabulator, combined with card punching and sorting machines, reduced the time to process the data to $2\frac{1}{2}$ years, less than one-fifth of the time it would have taken under the old system.

Hollerith went on to found the Tabulating Machine Company to market these devices worldwide. He made a fortune in after-market sales producing and selling the punch cards used in the operation of the tabulating machines. These cards are still being produced, punched, bent, spindled, and mutilated throughout the world. His company was later merged into the Computing-Tabulating-Recording Company, which was eventually renamed International Business Machines Corporation (IBM).

Electromechanical accounting machines (EAMs)

Toward the electronic computer

The next major breakthrough in automating information processing was the **ELECTROMECHANICAL ACCOUNTING MACHINE (EAM)**. An electromechanical machine (Figure 4-7) uses electrical pulses to activate mechanical elements. These machines employed punch card technology to process data. Source document data were keypunched, verified, interpreted with human-readable type, sorted, extracted, merged, reproduced, and printed in a noisy factorylike setting. Feeding large piles of cards into machines was a physically demanding task. Today many of these accounting operations can be done by accessing a database and

Figure 4-7
Electromechanical ac-
counting machines.

invoking prewritten programs with a few simple strokes on a keyboard. The largest manufacturer of electromechanical machines was IBM.

The MARK I

The **MARK I**, or Automatic Sequence Controlled Calculator, developed from 1939 to 1944, was an electromechanical computer. A joint project by **HOWARD AIKEN** (Figure 4-8) of Harvard University and IBM Corporation, the MARK I could perform a multiplication operation in 3 seconds. An electromechanical computer represented an advance over an electromechanical accounting machine, because a computer controlled the processing steps without the frequent human intervention necessary with accounting machines. The MARK I was a massive machine, about the size of one wall of a house. After building the MARK I, Dr. Aiken

Figure 4-8
Dr. Howard Aiken (left),
Director of Harvard Uni-
versity Computer Li-
brary with the assistant
director, John Harr. The
MARK I or Automatic
Sequence Controlled
Calculator was invented
by Dr. Aiken. Input to
the MARK I was in the
form of paper tape. Out-
put consisted of punch
cards. He later developed
the Mark IV, shown
here.

discovered he had incorporated the key ideas of Babbage, with whose work Aiken had been unfamiliar. The MARK I was, in effect, a working model of the analytic engine.

The Atanasoff-Berry computer

Who invented the first electronic computer? Proper credit has been the subject of historical as well as legal disputes. An ELECTRONIC COMPUTER uses only electrical switches and circuitry to carry out processing or computing functions, instead of the slower mechanical relays of an electromechanical computer like the MARK I.

Based on a court decision, legal credit for the first electronic computer is given to a machine designed and built by JOHN V. ATANASOFF, a professor at Iowa State University, and his graduate assistant, CLIFFORD E. BERRY. The ATANASOFF-BERRY COMPUTER (ABC), developed from 1937 to 1942, preceded its nearest competition by several years. This computer (shown in Figure 4-9) was designed to solve special types of linear equations, and was not a true general-purpose machine.

The university, unfortunately, failed to patent the ABC, losing a potential $500 million in royalties. Ironically, when Dr. Atanasoff approached IBM for assistance in exploiting the project, he was turned down because IBM's president, THOMAS WATSON, SR., could see no commercial future for electronic computers. The ABC was known, however, to the inventors of the ENIAC, a machine that rapidly led to the first commercially available computers.

Figure 4-9
(a) The Atanasoff-Berry Computer and its inventors, (b) John V. Atanasoff and (c) Clifford E. Berry.

(b)

(c)

(a)

ENIAC

The ENIAC, short for ELECTRONIC NUMERICAL INTEGRATOR AND CALCULATOR, was built between 1943 and 1946. Created by JOHN W. MAUCHLY and J. PRESPER ECKERT of the University of Pennsylvania, it was used by the U.S. Army for calculating ballistics tables. Shown in Figure 4-10, it was considered to be the first general-purpose, fully electronic digital

Figure 4-10
(a) The ENIAC or Electronic Numerical Integrator and Calculator and its inventors, (b) Drs. John W. Mauchly and (c) J. Presper Eckert of the University of Pennsylvania.

(a)

b)

c)

Figure 4-11
John von Neumann proposed storing program instructions in the computer.

computer. The ENIAC used on-off digital pulses to solve a wide range of problems electronically. The ENIAC was a thousand times faster than the electromechanical MARK I. In bulk ENIAC was also enormous. It weighed 30 tons, was as big as a three-bedroom house, and employed over 18,000 vacuum tubes to store and process data. The lights in parts of Philadelphia dimmed when ENIAC was on the job. The machine was used until 1955. ENIAC read in and stored its data, but not its programs. Whenever a new program had to be run, operators had to reset switches and change around numerous wires on plugboards.

Following the completion and success of ENIAC, Eckert and Mauchly formed their own computer manufacturing company, called the Eckert and Mauchly Computer Corporation. Financial difficulties forced them to sell their firm to Remington-Rand, now a division of Unisys Corporation.

The stored program concept

The electronic machines discussed so far were cumbersome to program, with switches and plugboards that had to be changed by hand. Then a mathematician, JOHN VON NEUMANN (Figure 4-11), proposed a solution to this problem—the STORED PROGRAM CONCEPT. A stored program is one that is entered into and stored inside the computer the same way data are. Von Neumann suggested that instructions (given the technology of his era) could be read into a computer on paper tape and then stored in the banks of vacuum tubes along with the data the program was to manipulate. In this way, the program that a computer followed could be changed much more easily and quickly simply by inputting new instructions without the need to rewire the machine for modifications in a program.

The EDSAC, or ELECTRONIC DELAY STORAGE AUTOMATIC COMPUTER, created at Cambridge University in England, was the first stored program computer. EDSAC became operational in 1949. In effect, the EDSAC became the first working prototype of the computers we presently use. Now let's turn to these.

case in point

IBM's winning ingredient

It must be every inventor's dream to stumble on some device that creates a new field of endeavor and ensures success and fame. The International Business Machines Corporation, the world's largest maker of computers, fits this picture only to a degree. Herman Hollerith created the firm, first as the Tabulating Machine Company (in 1896), and eventually, after mergers, as the Computer-Tabulating-Recording Company (in 1911). The firm changed its name to IBM in 1924. The object of the firm was to sell Hollerith's punch card tabulating machines that had proven so successful with the 1890 census. For years "the IBM machine" was what people called devices that handled punch cards, though as the decades passed these machines diversified into many different devices made by various manufacturers. Electromechanical technology reached its high point with the MARK I computer, built in part by IBM.

However, when the inventor of the first electronic computer, John B. Atanasoff, suggested that IBM help market his ABC computer, the firm declined. The IBM president at that time, Thomas J. Watson, stated that he did not believe electronic computers had a future. With such a beginning, how did the computer giant get to be a giant?

IBM did enter the computer arena, following UNIVAC by 2 years, with the IBM 701, introduced in 1953. IBM started making the 650 in 1954, which was the most popular commercial computer for some years. Through the subsequent march of computer generations, IBM has sold more computers than all of the world's other computer makers combined. In 1987, the firm employed 390,000 people and had annual sales of over $54 billion (nearly six times the sales level of its nearest rival, Unisys Corporation).

At many points in its history, IBM has not had the latest, the fastest, or the most sophisticated computer to sell. Microcomputers had been selling like hotcakes for the better part of a decade before IBM decided to produce one. How, then, does this behemoth attract the lion's share of the computer market?

A large part of the answer is the people. Remember the five-element model of an information system—people, rules and procedures, data, software, and hardware? Along with its hardware (and later, software), IBM has always stressed the people element, encouraging loyalty among its employees, and offering the services of these employees to customers along with the hardware or software purchased.

IBM, of course, is not unique in stressing people: it would be hard to make your way through a recruiting brochure from almost any company without reading about the value of people to the organization. What many companies did not do, especially in the early years of computing, was offer support people who spoke the user's language. But when you bought an IBM computer, the services of a team of professionals—who would do their best to see that the machine did exactly what you wanted, and kept doing it—were thrown in.

Indeed, this "throwing in" was a point of contention in a lengthy suit brought by other computer manufacturers against IBM in the 1960s. The U.S. Justice Department ordered IBM to start charging for these people services. "Unbundling" then became the rule of the industry, and hardware, software, and people services began to be priced separately.

A reputation remains a reputation, however. Do a bit of field research by visiting installations with IBM computers, and ask why IBM was chosen over many other manufacturers of excellent machines. The odds are that you will hear the "people" argument, often referred to as "support." Good support inspires confidence, and though purchasers must pay for it, everyone wants it. Today, IBM is not unique in providing support services but there was a time when it almost was.

No matter what end of the computer industry is examined, people remain the most important of the five elements. Many factors make for successful computer hardware, but the world's largest computer manufacturer got that way by putting people first.

The evolution of commercial computers

Computers have been commercially available long enough that we divide them into "generations." Computer generations constitute different technological eras. The primary technological element is the central processing unit. Each generation of commercial computers differs considerably from other generations in terms of the technology used.

What is important is not only when a machine or component was invented, but how the new technology was commercially applied and popularized. Technology does not exist in a vacuum. There has to be a demand for it. For a technology-based product to become a success, consumers from either the public or private sectors must find some productive use for it.

Each computer generation has seen the adoption of new types of software. These software breakthroughs will be discussed within the generation they became commercially popular.

Dividing computer generations into these three categories—technology, demand, and software—is solely for convenience to help you learn. In reality, these three categories interact and affect each other in complex ways. As we shall see, demand may push the technology and software to new frontiers; or changes in technology may give rise to whole new areas of demand.

Technology

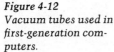

First-generation computers (1951–1958)

The major hardware characteristic of **FIRST-GENERATION COMPUTERS** was the use of **VACUUM TUBES** for internal computing operations. As shown in Figure 4-12, these devices were considerably faster than electromechanical devices for processing data. Calculations could be performed in **MILLISECONDS** (thousandths of a second). The main disadvantage of vacuum tubes was the amount of heat they generated. Special air-conditioning units were required to dissipate the heat. (Although heat problems became less severe in subsequent generations, mainframe computer rooms are still air-conditioned to this day.) Due both to the heat

Figure 4-12
Vacuum tubes used in first-generation computers.

level and the nature of the available materials, vacuum tubes had a short life and "blew out" frequently. Another disadvantage was the amount of space that circuits using vacuum tubes occupied. Compared to modern systems, first-generation computers were more prone to breakdowns.

Punch cards and punched *paper tape* were the main media for the input, output, and external storage of data and instructions, although on some machines *magnetic tape* was available. For internal storage, most first-generation computers used *magnetic drums*, large spinning cylinders with programs and data recorded on them.

Demand

The main demand for first-generation computers was to perform scientific applications, particularly military contract work. For business users, applications were primarily limited to batch processing of accounting and payroll operations, essentially an extension of the techniques used with the electromechanical accounting machines of an earlier era. Data for processing were entered sequentially, one record after another. Rules and procedures focused on standard operating conditions, and programs capable of handling exceptional situations were far more difficult to write.

The first commercially produced computer was the UNIVAC I, or UNIVERSAL AUTOMATIC COMPUTER, which became available in 1951. The U.S. Bureau of the Census purchased three of these machines to aid in tabulating the 1950 census. The UNIVAC I was designed by Eckert and Mauchly, the builders of the ENIAC, and completed while they were at Remington-Rand. The machines remained in use for over a decade at the Census Bureau.

The UNIVAC I gained a reputation as an electronic "brain" when, with only about 5 percent of the votes counted, it correctly predicted for CBS television that Dwight D. Eisenhower would win over Adlai E. Stevenson in the 1952 presidential election (Figure 4-13).

Not to be outdone by the competition, in 1953 IBM introduced its first commercial computer, the IBM 701. The primary market for this machine was large companies who already used IBM's electromechanical accounting machines and other punch card-dependent devices. A

Figure 4-13
The UNIVAC I or Universal Automatic Computer, the first successful commercial computer. Walter Cronkite (right), J. Presper Eckert, and an unidentified operator are shown here. In 1952, the UNIVAC I was the first computer to successfully tabulate early returns in a presidential election and predict the winner—Dwight D. Eisenhower.

Figure 4-14
The IBM 650 computer,
the most popular first-
generation computer.

year later, IBM introduced the IBM 650 (Figure 4-14), a machine that established the firm's dominance in the computer industry, which has continued (through many models) to the present day. IBM initially expected to sell 20 of its 650s; instead, it sold or leased over 1800. A major factor in IBM's success was that their computers were designed to be compatible with existing electromechanical accounting machines, using the same punch card codes, and to emulate and supplement the older generation of machines in solving business problems. As a result, users felt more comfortable with the IBM 650 machines than with computers made by rival companies. The 650 was viewed by purchasers as a less risky investment, one which complemented existing ways of doing business.

Software

Programs on some first-generation computers were entered by wiring plugboards, as with electromechanical accounting machines and the ENIAC. On others, programs were written in MACHINE LANGUAGE and read into the computer's memory as a stored program. The computer reads the machine language as a series of 1s and 0s—the numbers used in the *binary number system* that correspond to the actual circuitry of the machine. Number systems are discussed in greater detail in Chapter 5. Coding in machine language is a tedious process. To speed up the programming effort, symbolic languages called ASSEMBLY LANGUAGES were created, using symbols easier for people to work with and remember than strings of binary or octal code. A program written in the symbolic assembly language was then translated into the numeric machine codes. Figure 4-15 compares machine and assembly languages by showing the codes for an assignment function that adds the values in one field (B) to another (A). The general formula is A = A + B, which might be used to accumulate a running total for a customer's bill. Computer languages are examined in detail in Chapter 15.

Figure 4-15
Examples of machine
language code and as-
sembly language code to
add the value of B to A
(A = A + B).

Machine code:
111110100101001010010000000000001001000000001100
Assembly code:
AP   TOTALA,   VALUEB

*Second-generation
computers
(1958–1964)*

Technology

Two major hardware features of SECOND-GENERATION COMPUTERS were the use of transistors—replacing the fragile vacuum tubes of the previous generation—and the use of magnetic cores—replacing the first generation's magnetic drums for internal storage. The transistor was invented in 1948 at Bell Telephone Laboratories by WILLIAM SHOCKLEY, JOHN BARDEEN, and WALTER H. BRATTAIN. Shown in Figure 4-16, a TRANSISTOR is a solid-state semiconducting device. A SEMICONDUCTOR is a compound that has electrical properties between those of a conductor (like copper wire) and an insulator (like rubber). Transistors were much smaller, more reliable, less fragile, and cheaper than vacuum tubes, and produced far less heat.

Another feature of second-generation computers was the use of *magnetic core memory* for main memory rather than a magnetic drum. The "core", as it was called, consisted of tiny iron "doughnuts" wired together (Figure 4-17). The computer could store and access data and instructions by magnetizing and demagnetizing these tiny cores much more rapidly than reading and writing from a magnetic drum. With these improvements, second-generation computers could perform arithmetic and logical operations in MICROSECONDS (millionths of a second). Magnetic tape units were also more frequently used for peripheral operations such as input, output, and secondary storage, although punch card and paper tape systems were still used.

Second-generation computer manufacturers began to organize their computers into product lines or series. An example of a highly successful product line, the IBM 1400 series, is shown in Figure 4-18. A manufacturer's machines were compatible with one another but not with those made by rival companies; this encouraged the customer to stay with the same company when upgrading from one computer to another. Competitors of IBM in the second generation included Burroughs, Sperry-Univac, National Cash Register, Control Data, and Honeywell (collectively known as the BUNCH), as well as General Electric and RCA.

*Figure 4-16
The transistor, a breakthrough in solid-state technology. The developers of the transistor—William Shockley (center), John Bardeen (left), and Walter H. Brattain (right)—received the Nobel prize in physics for their work on semiconductors.*

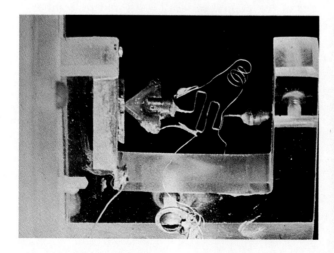

Figure 4-17
Magnetic core storage of
the type used in second-
generation computers.

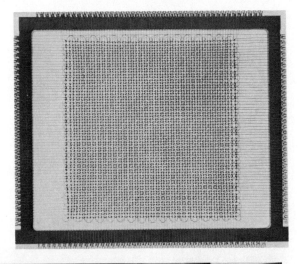

Figure 4-18
The IBM 1401, an exam-
ple of a second-genera-
tion computer system.

Demand

The major demand for second-generation computers was from government agencies and both large- and medium-sized businesses. Smaller businesses and individuals could not afford computers. The main business uses included accounting, payroll, marketing, and manufacturing applications, where data could be processed in batches. Universities used computers to process research projects as well as for their regular accounting operations. As with the previous generation, systems focused on standard operating procedures.

Software

The second generation saw the popularization of two programming languages, FORTRAN and COBOL. Examples of both of these languages are given in Figure 4-19. Even today these remain extremely popular languages.

The FORTRAN statement for adding the value of B to the total value A:

        A = A + B

The COBOL statement:

        004100   ADD B TO TOTAL.

or, another way:

        004100   COMPUTE TOTALA = TOTALA + VALUEB.

Figure 4-19
FORTRAN and COBOL, two second-generation languages. Dr. Grace Hopper worked on the development of the COBOL compiler. Compare the FORTRAN and COBOL statements with the examples shown in Figure 4-15. Note how much more readable the FORTRAN and COBOL statements are.

A mathematically oriented language, FORTRAN (short for FORmula TRANslator) was developed at IBM Corporation by JOHN BACKUS, and was introduced into the market in 1957. A standardized version was not available until the mid-1960s. A very powerful language for mathematical problems, it is useful in many scientific and engineering application areas. Business applications include market research and production control.

COBOL (short for COmmon Business Oriented Language) was released in 1959, largely through the efforts of GRACE HOPPER. For her distinguished efforts in developing programming languages, she was named "Man of the Year" in 1969 by the Data Processing Management Association.

Other languages were also developed during the second generation. In addition, simple operating systems were introduced. Programs written in languages such as FORTRAN and COBOL use a language translation program called a compiler to convert the program code into the computer's own machine language.

Technology

Third-generation computers (1964–1971)

The major technological breakthrough of THIRD-GENERATION COMPUTERS was the development of the integrated circuit. An INTEGRATED CIRCUIT combines transistors and related circuitry into one unit. Integrated circuits are etched onto small wafers of glass called SILICON CHIPS. Silicon chips have an advantage over previous types of circuitry with their ability to operate under greater temperature variations and vibration. A second-generation transistor would fail at about 120° F. In fact, it was the demand for transistors capable of withstanding high temperatures that led to the development of integrated circuits. Another advantage of integrated circuits is that the distance between the parts of a circuit is so small that electricity has a shorter distance to travel to carry out any given computer operation. And smaller, with computers, means faster.

Figure 4-20
An early integrated circuit.

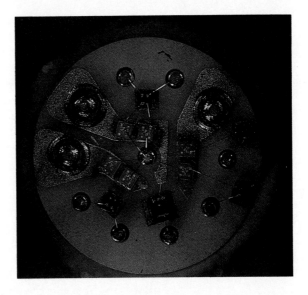

Integrated circuits have gone on to revolutionize not just computers but many other areas, from automobiles to zoology. An example of a third-generation integrated circuit is shown in Figure 4-20. As computers continued their steady march forward in speed, processing operations were measured in *microseconds* and eventually NANOSECONDS (billionths of a second).

The IBM 360 was the most significant computer of the third generation. Displayed in Figure 4-21, it was conceived as a general-purpose machine that would service a full circle of scientific and business users (the 360 model number represents the degrees in a circle). In previous generations computers usually specialized as "scientific" or "business" computers.

Figure 4-21
The IBM 360, the main-frame computer that signaled the start of the third generation.

Improvements in input, output, and external storage devices, and communications equipment, continued the trend toward faster processing. The most significant change was the increased popularity of the *magnetic disk*. Instead of using punch cards or magnetic tape systems, programmers increasingly stored software and data on magnetic disks. On a disk, as opposed to tape or cards, a record can be selected to be read without reading the preceding ones, which greatly increases data access speed for some applications.

Demand

In the United States, demand for third-generation computers was spurred by competition with the Soviet Union in the race to the moon and the development of more sophisticated missiles and warheads. To assure control of these sophisticated rockets and weapons, advances in computer circuitry and data communications were required.

To increase the reliability of electronic components, especially in outer space or under battle conditions, governments spent millions of dollars funding the development of integrated circuits. The development of advanced telecommunication systems allowed for data communications between computerized monitoring systems placed on board spacecraft and land-based data processing centers (Mission Control). There was no time to wait for data to be accumulated for a batch processing run. Instead responses had to be made to events in progress, in what is called *real-time processing*.

Software

Changes in software included the development of the first large-scale operating systems to manage all of a computer's hardware and software resources. System and application software, in addition, were developed to handle on-line processing of data.

The major language developed in this era was BASIC (Beginner's All-Purpose Symbolic Instruction Code). Developed by JOHN G. KEMENY and THOMAS KURTZ, two mathematics professors at Dartmouth College, BASIC was designed with the novice programmer in mind (Figure 4-22).

Figure 4-22
John G. Kemeny and Thomas Kurtz developed BASIC to teach novices programming.

Figure 4-23
*An advanced micropro-
cessor.*

*Fourth-generation
computers (1971–?)*

Technology

The technological change that distinguishes the FOURTH-GENERATION COMPUTERS from the third is the development of the microprocessor. A MICROPROCESSOR contains the control and arithmetic/logic units of the central processor etched on a single silicon chip (see Figure 4-23). Many microprocessors also have storage elements etched into the chip. Microprocessors are produced by LARGE-SCALE INTEGRATION (LSI) which is the process of placing thousands of integrated circuits on a chip. The first commercial microprocessor was produced by Texas Instruments Corporation in 1971. Since that time billions of microprocessors have found their way into everything from automobiles and computers to toasters and x-ray machines. The most notable product is the microcomputer or personal computer.

The first microcomputer was marketed in 1976. In 1977, Apple Computer Corporation, founded by STEPHEN WOZNIAK and STEVEN JOBS (Figure 4-24), released its first computer—the APPLE I. In less than a decade, Apple Computer Corporation rose into the Fortune 500. In the early 1980s Apple introduced the Macintosh, a microcomputer that had wide market acceptance. Many other companies joined the race to establish themselves in this new market, and a number of them failed. In 1981, IBM began selling its own microcomputer, called the Personal Computer or IBM-PC. The IBM-PC legitimized the role of the microcomputer in the workplace. Competing manufacturers were quick to offer machines, often called "clones", that could offer compatibility with the IBM-PCs. These clones could to varying degrees run the same application programs as the IBM-PC. With IBM's introduction of the Personal System/2 microcomputer the "clone" race has started all over again.

*Figure 4-24
(a) Stephen Wozniak and
(b) Steven Jobs, the
founders of Apple Com-
puter, with one of their
machines (c).*

(a)

(b)

(c)

Which companies and products now on the market will survive into the 1990s is subject to great speculation, as prices continue to fall for this sophisticated equipment.

Although microcomputers are the golden children of the fourth generation, great strides in the performance of other types of computers have also taken place. Processing speeds for the fastest computers can now be measured in nanoseconds and PICOSECONDS (trillionths of a second). Figure 4-25 shows representative fourth-generation computers.

Other parts of the information-processing industry have also undergone significant changes. Data input methods have become highly automated; for example, laser scanners can read product codes far faster than people can key in the prices using an old-fashioned cash register. In addition, the scanner transmits the transaction data to external storage units to aid in controlling inventory levels. External storage units are now capable of retaining far greater amounts of data in smaller physical units, speeding data-handling while lowering per-item cost. Magnetic disk systems have evolved into high-density hard disk models and inexpensive floppy disk systems. Fourth-generation output devices can create more personalized output than those of previous generations. Communications systems are using *fiber-optic cables* made of ultrathin glass filaments to transmit more data at faster rates of speed.

The major engineering trend in the fourth generation is toward further miniaturization of the components of computers. Currently it is possible to store over 4 million binary digits on a single silicon chip. There are experimental storage chips capable of storing over 16 million binary digits of data on one chip. These are examples of VERY-LARGE-SCALE INTEGRATION (VLSI), which is the process of placing a great number

(a)

(b)

(c)

Figure 4-25
Fourth-generation computers. (a) A mainframe system. (b) A minicomputer system. (c) A large microcomputer.

of integrated circuits on a chip. In addition to offering rapid processing speeds due to their small size, these circuits are also more reliable and use less power than their predecessors.

One area of great technological interest is the application of information-processing elements to the field of ROBOTICS, the study and application of robots. A ROBOT is a machine capable of coordinating its movements itself by reacting to changes in the system environment. The most common application of robots in the work world is carrying out routine assembly operations (Figure 4-26). Other robot-related applications will be discussed in future chapters.

Figure 4-26
Robots are everywhere.

Contributions to fourth-generation technology have come from many different countries. Increasingly firms in Western Europe and Japan have joined with North American companies to push the limits of technology. The production of computers and peripherals has become a global business. A single device might contain components designed, manufactured, or assembled in countries ranging from South Korea and Taiwan to Canada and Mexico.

Demand

Demand for greater levels of integration, with more and more circuitry packed into a chip, was pushed by the need to develop "smart" weaponry as well as for cheaper and more sophisticated consumer products. The result has been that for the first time, the average individual can afford a computer. Further demand rose for *distributed information systems*. A distributed information-processing system shares computing power among several different computers. For example, a company can link its computers into a communications network, and give different jobs to the different computers. Microcomputers or minicomputers can be linked into various network patterns with other micros, minis, or mainframe computers to share in information processing.

Since the late 1970s, there has been a tremendous rise in the popularity of microcomputers. Users are now able to purchase microcomputers and software at a reasonable price to help solve their computational and other information system problems at work, school, or home.

Software

Distributed data processing evolved further in the fourth generation with the development of system software capable of managing many users at once. *Database management systems (DBMS)* were developed first for large mainframe computers, and eventually for microcomputers. Database management software allows users with different application needs access to a shared database.

In addition, there has been a veritable explosion of prepackaged software programs, especially in the area of business applications. You can perform many information-processing operations without knowing how to write programs—all you need to know is how to start a program on your terminal or microcomputer with a few simple commands. Interpreting the results, however, does require you to be knowledgeable about the subject area. An example of a popular software package for business use is Lotus 1-2-3, a combination spreadsheet (visual calculator), file handler, and graphics package.

During the fourth generation, structured programming techniques have become more popular. Structured programming techniques substantially reduce the overall cost of writing, correcting, testing, and maintaining programs. The programmer is required to design solutions using special organizing rules. PASCAL is a programming language which requires the use of structured programming techniques. Developed by NIKLAUS WIRTH, Pascal is named after the inventor of the Pascaline calculator, discussed earlier in this chapter.

Mainframes aren't dinosaurs yet

When the *Wall Street Journal* and *Business Week* touted the fall of the mainframe empire . . . most of Silicon Valley should have cheered.

But personal computer industry leaders held back on the celebration because they knew something the reports had glossed over. The mainframe isn't dying, sales are just slower than before. . . .

But companies are still buying mainframes, says Dave Martin, president of National Advanced Systems of San Jose, a mainframe builder. . . . It's just they aren't buying them in every available size.

"People lump together small, medium, and large mainframes. Clearly, the action is moving into large mainframes and small personal computers. That says the middle ground—small and medium mainframes—have an extremely poor growth picture. . . ."

Mainframes are the biggest general-purpose commercial computers. The Computer and Business Equipment Manufacturers Association, a computer industry group in Washington, defines mainframes as all general-purpose computers costing more than $250,000. Most mainframes are housed in "glass houses," computer rooms with special power, raised floors, and air conditioning.

But where once virtually everything was done on the mainframe, now virtually anything can be done by a personal computer, which can perform calculations on information stored on mainframes and distribute the results through mainframe-controlled networks. In short, the mainframe has become a filing cabinet, traffic cop, and mailbox.

By the most predictable criterion—power—mainframes will present microcomputers with a moving target they aren't likely to catch, says Bill Husband, president of 20th Century Systems of Palantine, Ill., and senior consultant at Meridian Leasing of Deerfield, Ill.

To illustrate his point, Husband compares the basic mainframe of the decade, IBM's 3081KX computer, with one of the more powerful microcomputers of the day, IBM's PC-AT. The mainframe is capable of performing 15 million instructions per second (MIPS), the PC-AT can handle only 0.1 MIPS. Although the equivalent of the AT in the 1990s will run at 10 MIPS, he says, a mainframe will run at 1500 MIPS.

But the thesis that the mainframe is dead also involves another assumption: Mainframes and personal computers are interchangeable. And no leading analyst agrees with that.

Mainframes have never penetrated small and medium-sized businesses, and now that personal computers have taken hold, they never will. Mainframes dominated corporate America because they were once the only vehicle for automating operations. And it's hard to rip out that installed base now.

Mainframes will always have certain advantages, Husband says. Dale Kutnick, executive vice-president at Gartner Securities, notes that users of smaller computers—even of microcomputers—complain their machines can't manage multiple systems, measure performance of the computer, or administer the system so that different tasks can be performed in the proper order.

That puts mainframes in a bind. They have those required features but also have more overhead than personal computers. To users who do not particularly care about system performance measurement, system administration, security and disaster recovery, personal computers look like real bargains.

But there are functions that must be centralized, and those are the functions that mainframes will continue to perform: data base management, network management, and connectivity of disparate computer equipment. . . .

So, it's premature to say the reliance upon mainframes is over. As one waggish security analyst put it, "There will be a mainframe in the future. Just one. That's all we will really need. It may be the size of New Jersey, but we'll only need just one."

Source: Paul E. Schindler, Jr. "A Palace Coup? If You Think Personal Computers Will Usurp Mainframes, Think Again," *San Jose Mercury News,* 1 Feb. 1988, pp. 1E, 7E. Reprinted with permission from the San Jose Mercury News.

Another one of the most influential software designers of this era is BILL GATES, the owner of Microsoft Corporation. His firm produced the operating systems (PC-DOS and OS/2) that control processing within all of IBM's line of microcomputers.

Another fourth-generation development is programs permanently recorded on integrated circuits. Programs of this sort are called *firmware*, a blend of hardware and software. In a way, this harks back to ENIAC's plugboards, though on a microminiaturized level.

The fourth generation has also seen growing interest in ARTIFICIAL INTELLIGENCE (AI), which refers to efforts to capture the way humans think and learn in computer programs. Artificial intelligence has had an impact on areas as diverse as the study of human learning and memory, the development of expert systems, and the design of robots capable of complex tasks.

Toward future generations—fifth and beyond

Technology

Up to now, we have generally underestimated the impact of computers on our society. What might the future look like?

Some feel the technology of future generations will probably be based upon further improvements in the integration of circuitry. Reductions in the size of the circuits, and increases in density, have been predicted. Processing speeds will reach further into the picosecond range for faster computers. To maintain such processing speeds and density of circuits, the vital parts of the computer might be immersed in a solution of liquid helium or nitrogen. Recent developments in superconducting materials technology may lead to less stringent cooling requirements and allow greater applications with lower cooling costs.

Another breakthrough concerns the area of parallel processing computers. PARALLEL PROCESSING COMPUTERS can carry out many instructions at the same time. Today, even the fastest supercomputers have difficulty with such multiprocessing efforts. Typical applications include determining the stress on a rocket motor or an aircraft wing. Other suggested applications include balancing workstation production loads on automated assembly lines. Ironically, the reason present commercial computers do not process solutions in parallel steps goes back to the *stored program concept* John von Neumann suggested for solving the programming problems of the 1940s where instructions were executed one at a time. Figure 4-27 illustrates the difference between traditional processing and parallel processing and shows a parallel processing computer. True parallel processing computers that reach execution speeds up to 1000 times faster than traditional supercomputers (which have some parallel processing capabilities) have been tested. They accomplish this by linking together many (a thousand or more) microprocessors into a densely interconnected network.

Home and personal computer systems may continue to proliferate, providing more and easier-to-use computing power for your money. More sophisticated robots are already being created for use in the workplace. Researchers have begun experimentation on laser-optic computers, designs for biotechnological methods of storing information, and other ideas.

Education and training specialist

One career evolved fairly early in the history of commercial computers and has remained in demand ever since: teaching others how to use a particular computer system, programming language, or software package. While this function is sometimes carried out by the personnel involved in developing or installing a particular system—who then try to explain to users and others what the system does—often such training is given by a training and education specialist.

Two prerequisites are very important to obtain and keep such a job: (1) the ability to teach, and (2) familiarity with the topic being taught.

Teaching ability is usually found in people who are interested in the idea of showing others how to do something, who are talented in communicating with others, and who have had the opportunity to try it during their own schooling or career. Familiarity with the training topic is acquired by careful study of the particular subject to supplement a general familiarity with computer concepts.

Well-organized, large information centers maintain a department that does nothing but training. Specialized courses are aimed at each of the three different types of people involved with computers: users, technical staff, and managers. Smaller computer centers may hire outside training specialists or simply ask those involved with a project to explain it to others.

Training and education specialists are responsible for more than conducting courses. Some firms pride themselves on the in-house training opportunities they offer to help employees keep abreast of new technology and expand their skills. The training department is involved in selecting, designing, and coordinating the course offerings, and sometimes in establishing training schedules and goals for employees.

As for the courses themselves, there are many options. Courses can be taught by videotape and accompanying written materials supplied by a training firm or a hardware or software vendor. Courses can also be taught right on the employee's microcomputer or terminal. Regular classroom courses, however, remain a mainstay of the training process.

Training and education specialists are employed by organizations that use computers, firms that sell support services, hardware vendors, software vendors, and educational institutions. Training and education specialists can move to other careers within an organization. Since technical expertise is required to teach courses, it is possible to switch (or return) to programming or systems analysis. Administrative and managerial acumen are involved in designing courses and running the department, so successful training and education specialists could pursue careers in management.

Instruction-at-a-time
processor

1st instruction

2nd instruction

3rd instruction

⋮

nth instruction

$n + 1$st instruction

etc.

A parallel processor with n processors

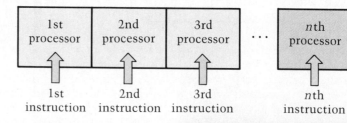

1st
instruction

2nd
instruction

3rd
instruction

nth
instruction

$n + 1$st
instruction

Figure 4-27
Comparing today's instruction-at-a-time computers (left) with a parallel processing computer (right). An actual parallel processing computer is also shown.

Demand

Demand for future generations of information systems is expected to come from the same institutions as before. Businesses will probably want faster computers to assist in reducing production and management costs. Information systems may also be used increasingly for earning money as well as saving money; predicting, for example, future investment or market penetration possibilities.

Governments will probably continue to sponsor research in new types of information systems in order to maintain competitive advantages for their strategic industries, and for the creation of more efficient weapons systems. Further use of robots is predicted, affecting the kinds and quality of work many of us may perform.

Possible solutions to global problems such as pollution may require advanced computing techniques (Figure 4-28).

Software

Here, the principal effort will be in the area of artificial intelligence—attempts to develop software that more closely resembles how humans think. Researchers are already considering how to move from machines that respond to on-off conditions for single tasks, to ones that can perform many tasks simultaneously, as humans do. The biological circuits in human brains process data more slowly than computers, but because we can deal with a number of data items simultaneously, we are able to think and reason. Computers, for all their speed, are incapable of thinking—so far.

A final note on trying to predict the future. Earlier in this chapter we mentioned that IBM Corporation predicted they would sell only 20 of

Figure 4-28
Fifth-generation com-
puters may aid in pre-
dicting the long-range ef-
fects of atmospheric pol-
lutants.

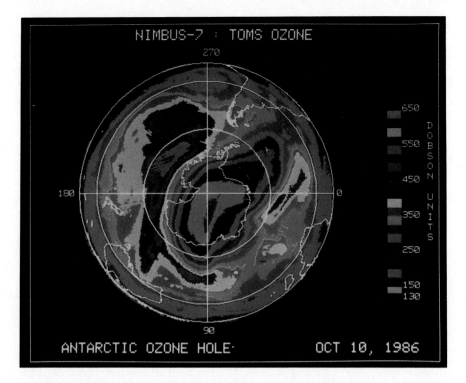

their first-generation IBM 650 series computers. They wound up building over 1800. With a breakeven point at about ten computers, imagine the return on investment. Given the transitions we have covered from movable beads and steam engines to pinhead-sized computers, think what possibilities, as yet unpredicted, await in the future.

summary

■   A successful information system product depends upon three factors: demand for the product, the technical ability to produce the product, and the software or instructions to make use of the product.

■   The first devices used for calculating include the abacus and Pascal's mechanical calculator, the Pascaline. Early in the nineteenth century Joseph-Marie Jacquard invented an automated loom that used a punch card reading system.

■   The nineteenth century also saw Charles Babbage's attempts to build first the difference engine, and then the analytic engine with the assistance of Lady Ada Lovelace, considered to be the first programmer. Although it was never a successful product, the analytic engine, as Babbage conceived it, contained all the basic elements of the modern computer.

■   Herman Hollerith developed a paper punch card tabulating machine to speed the processing of the U.S. Census of 1890.

■   Electromechanical accounting machines using punched card technology were developed to automate accounting procedures. Howard Aiken used this technology to build one of the first working computers, the MARK I.

■ The first electronic computer, the Atanasoff-Berry Computer, was completed in 1942. At the time, Thomas Watson, Sr., the head of IBM Corporation, felt electronic computers were not a marketable product. John Mauchly's and J. Eckert's giant ENIAC, successful in calculating ballistics tables, soon followed in 1946. The EDSAC and similar machines introduced John von Neumann's idea of stored programs to speed the processing of data.

■ The age of commercially available computers began in earnest with the UNIVAC I in 1951. Since then, computers have been divided into "generations" based on the changes in hardware.

■ First-generation computers (1951–1958) used vacuum tubes and magnetic drums to store data and instructions for processing inside the computer. Processing operation speeds were measured in milliseconds. The primary input, output, and external storage media were punch cards, paper tape, and (on some machines) magnetic tape. Accounting programs with a focus on standard operating procedures were emphasized. IBM established its leadership in the computer industry with the introduction of the 701 and 650 computer models. Data were organized into files which were dependent on specific application programs. Machine languages (using the binary number system), and assembly languages were used to write programs.

■ In the second generation (1958–1964), semiconducting transistors (developed by the team of Shockley, Bardeen, and Brattain) were used inside the computer for switching, and magnetic core elements for storage. Processing speeds increased into the microsecond range. Magnetic tape and punch card systems continued to dominate the input, output, and external storage elements of information-processing systems. Business applications expanded to include production and marketing. Data were still file oriented. Two higher-level languages were popularized: FORTRAN for engineering and scientific applications, developed by John Backus; and COBOL, designed by Grace Hopper, primarily for large businesses and government organizations.

■ Integrated circuits on silicon chips were incorporated into third-generation computers (1964–1971). The speed of processing rose into the nanosecond range. Magnetic disk systems served to handle data for external storage, although magnetic tape and punch cards were still used for input and output. Most business needs could be addressed in this generation. General-purpose computers, such as the IBM 360, were built to serve a wide variety of users. These computers were capable of real-time processing. Data communication systems were developed. BASIC, a programming language for novices, was created by Kemeny and Kurtz at Dartmouth College.

■ Large-scale integration (LSI) characterizes the fourth and present generation (1971–?), especially the development of the microprocessor or computer on a chip. Processing speed on the fastest systems reaches into the picosecond range. Magnetic disk systems have evolved into high-density hard disk models and inexpensive floppy disk systems. Microprocessors allow the creation of more sophisticated robots (through the study of robotics), personal computers, and fiber-optic cable-based communications systems.

■ Stephen Wozniak and Steven Jobs created the Apple I computer, helping to fuel the microcomputer age. Mature information systems are available for virtually any business-related problem. The IBM-PC firmly launched microcomputers into the workplace. Systems can handle both standard and exceptional operating conditions as well as distributed information processing. On-line databases handled by database management systems (DBMS) were initiated for large computer systems and are now available for personal computers. Niklaus Wirth devised Pascal, a structured programming language. Easy-to-use business-oriented software packages are available for personal computers.

■ Microsoft Corporation, founded by Bill Gates, developed the operating systems that control IBM and IBM-compatible microcomputers. The software packages can even be incorporated onto chips in the form of firmware. The quest to create computers that can "think" like humans has been pushed along by the development of artificial intelligence (AI) programming languages and very-large-scale-integrated (VLSI) circuits.

■ Recent developments in parallel processing computers and the introduction of superconducting materials will most likely lead to computing applications and speed far in excess of today's devices.

■ Future generations may see the continuation of present trends or some breakthrough that cannot be predicted. How the future will affect us remains, of course, unknown.

wrap-up

The march of the generations

It should be apparent that there have been many changes from the earliest computing devices to the rapid computers of the present. Even from the more recent time when we started counting computer generations (the arrival of the first commercially available computers) the nature of computers has transformed how society does business. A fourth-generation collection of circuits containing the equivalent power of thousands of the first generation's vacuum tubes, occupies no more space than would a fleck of dust on one of those vacuum tubes. Speed has changed as dramatically, and cost has plunged, making computing power available not only to government and big business but to anyone reading this book.

The table below summarizes the characteristics discussed for each of the four generations. These are divided into the five elements of an information system: people, rules and procedures, data, software, and hardware. In this case, however, we have put hardware first (before people), since hardware most clearly separates one generation from the next. The magnitude of the changes that have taken place in less than 4 decades is enormous.

System element	Generation			
	First (1951–1958)	Second (1958–1964)	Third (1964–1971)	Fourth (1971–?)
Hardware Computer	Vacuum tubes Magnetic drums	Transistors Magnetic core	Integrated circuits	Large-scale integrated circuits
Speed	Milliseconds	Microseconds	Nanoseconds	Nanoseconds and picoseconds
Input, secondary, storage, output, communications	Paper tape Punch cards Magnetic tape Standard output	Punch cards Magnetic tape Standard output	Punch cards On-line terminals Magnetic disk Standard output Telecommunications	On-line terminals Magnetic disk Floppy disk Robotics Standard and personalized output Fiber-optic cables
People (business users only)	Accounting	Accounting Production Marketing	Data communications General business	Information systems General business
Rules	Standard procedures emphasized	Standard procedures emphasized	Exception and standard procedures	Exception and standard procedures
Data	File oriented	File oriented	File oriented	Databases for large and personal computers
Software	Machine and assembly languages	FORTRAN COBOL	BASIC	Structured language: Pascal Easy-to-use business packages Artificial intelligence

name list

These people are listed in historical order with their principal contribution in parentheses. The numbers in parentheses refer to the page in which each person is first discussed.

Blaise Pascal (Pascaline) (102)
Joseph-Marie Jacquard (Punch card, Jacquard loom) (103)
Charles Babbage (Difference engine, Analytic engine) (103)
Lady Ada Augusta, the Countess of Lovelace (Analytic engine, Programmer) (105)
Herman Hollerith (Tabulating machine) (105)
Howard Aiken (MARK I) (107)
John V. Atanasoff and Clifford E. Berry (Atanasoff-Berry Computer or ABC) (108)
Thomas Watson, Sr. (IBM Corporation) (108)
John W. Mauchly and J. Presper Eckert (ENIAC or Electronic Numerical Integrator and Calculator) (108)
John von Neumann (Stored program concept) (109)
William Shockley, John Bardeen, and Walter H. Brattain (Transistor) (114)
John Backus (FORTRAN programming language) (116)
Grace Hopper (COBOL programming language) (116)
John G. Kemeny and Thomas Kurtz (BASIC programming language) (118)
Stephen Wozniak and Steven Jobs (Apple Computer) (119)
Niklaus Wirth (Pascal programming language) (122)
Bill Gates (PC-DOS and OS/2 operating systems) (124)

key terms

These are the key terms listed in alphabetical order. The numbers in parentheses refer to the page on which each term is defined.

Abacus (102)
Analytic engine (105)
Apple I (119)
Artificial intelligence (AI) (124)
Assembly language (113)
Atanasoff-Berry Computer (ABC) (108)
BASIC (118)
COBOL (116)
Difference engine (104)
EDSAC (Electronic Delay Storage Automatic Computer) (109)
Electromechanical accounting machine (EAM) (106)
Electronic computer (108)
ENIAC (Electronic Numerical Integrator and Calculator) (108)
First-generation computers (1951–1958) (111)
FORTRAN (116)
Fourth-generation computers (1971–?) (119)
IBM-PC (119)
IBM 360 (117)
Integrated circuit (116)
Jacquard loom (103)
Large-scale integration (LSI) (119)
Machine language (113)
MARK I (107)
Microprocessor (119)
Microsecond (114)
Millisecond (111)
Nanosecond (117)
Parallel processing computer (124)
Pascal (122)
Pascaline (102)
Picosecond (120)
Robot (121)
Robotics (121)
Second-generation computers (1958–1964) (114)
Semiconductor (114)
Silicon chip (116)
Stored program concept (109)
Tabulating machine (106)
Third-generation computers (1964–1971) (116)
Transistor (114)
UNIVAC I (Universal Automatic Computer) (112)
Vacuum tube (111)
Very-large-scale integration (VLSI) (120)

review questions

objective questions

True/false. *Put the letter T or F on the line next to the question.*

1 _____ 1. Pascal is an example of a second-generation programming language.

2 _____ 2. Vacuum tubes were used for processing in first-generation computers.

3 _____ 3. Grace Hopper was instrumental in developing the programming language BASIC.

4 _____ 4. The ENIAC could perform computations over 1000 times faster than the MARK I.

5 _____ 5. The analytic engine was a product failure because technology did not exist to machine the needed parts.

6 _____ 6. IBM delivered the world's first commercial computer.

7 _____ 7. Magnetic core memory is a feature of fourth-generation computers.

8 _____ 8. Demand for first-generation computers was generated by batch-oriented business applications.

9 _____ 9. The analytic engine was developed by the team of Charles Babbage and Lady Ada Lovelace.

10 _____ 10. Robotics is the study of creating hardware and software capable of thinking like humans.

Multiple choice. *Put the letter of the correct answer on the line next to the question.*

1 _____ 1. The programming language COBOL was developed by
   (a) John Backus.
   (b) Grace Hopper.
   (c) John G. Kemeny and Thomas Kurtz.
   (d) Niklaus Wirth.

2 _____ 2. The analytic engine was a product failure because of
   (a) The difficulty in machining the parts required to operate the machine.
   (b) The lack of demand by government and industry for the machine.
   (c) The inability of the designers to work out the logical processes to be used by the machine.
   (d) All of the above.

3 _____ 3. Which is the earliest form of calculating instrument?
   (a) MARK I.
   (b) Analytic engine.
   (c) Electromechanical accounting machine.
   (d) Pascaline.

4 _____ 4. Which person developed the punch card tabulating machine to help compile the results of the U.S. Census of 1890?
   (a) John von Neumann.
   (b) Herman Hollerith.
   (c) Howard Aiken.
   (d) Thomas Watson, Sr.

5 _____ 5. Transistors and magnetic core memory are distinguishing features of which generation of computers.
   (a) First.
   (b) Second.
   (c) Third.
   (d) Fourth.

Fill in the blank. *Write the correct word or words in the blank to complete the sentence.*

1. The team of _____ and _____ developed the Apple Computer.

2. The two major programming languages developed during the second generation were _____ for scientific applications and _____ for business applications.

3. On-line terminals and databases are primarily features of _____-generation computers.

4. The field of _____ refers to efforts to design programs that reflect the way people think and learn.

5. The "race to the moon" was an important stimulus for the development of _____-generation computers.

6. The _____ made it possible for computers to accept instructions as well as data into memory.

7. The interactive programming language, _____, was developed for novice users by the team of _____ and _____.

8. A fourth-generation language that stresses structured programming is _____.

9. To handle complex simultaneous processing needs _____ processing computers are under development.

10. The earliest form of calculating instrument was the _____.

short answer questions

When answering these questions, think of concrete examples to illustrate your points.

1. How does a parallel processing computer differ from earlier types of computers?

2. What are the major features of first-generation computers?

3. What are the major features of third-generation computers?

4. Match the software languages with the computer generation in which they first became popular.

5. How did the "race for the moon" affect the development of real-time processing?

6. Which computer generations favored the development of computers and software capable of easily handling exception procedures?

7. What is the study of robotics?

8. What was the principal means of secondary storage for each generation?

essay questions

1. Describe how demand for computers has affected the development of the four generations of computers.

2. Compare the features of the information system elements found in first- and fourth-generation computers.

3. What are the features expected to be found in fifth-generation computers? A trip to the library will help uncover some sources on this topic.

Answers to the objective questions
True/false: 1. F; 2. T; 3. F; 4. T; 5. T; 6. F; 7. F; 8. T; 9. T; 10. F
Multiple choice: 1. b; 2. a; 3. d; 4. b; 5. b
Fill in the blank: 1. Stephen Wozniak, Steven Jobs; 2. FORTRAN, COBOL; 3. fourth; 4. artificial intelligence; 5. third; 6. stored program concept; 7. BASIC, John G. Kemeny, Thomas Kurtz; 8. Pascal; 9. parallel; 10. abacus

part two

Hardware

Part One introduced information systems, briefly explaining what they are, the steps in their evolution, and the jobs they perform today. In Part Two, we focus on a key element of information systems—hardware.

Inside the computer: smaller and quicker

After studying this chapter you should understand the following:

- *What the parts of the computer are, and how they work together.*
- *How data are represented and stored inside the computer.*
- *The types of silicon chips the central processing unit uses for processing and storage.*
- *How microcomputers, minicomputers, mainframe computers, and supercomputers differ in terms of performance and price.*

chapter 5

The hardware surgeons

Nat Bergstein and David Cunningham drove into the parking lot at Global Electrical Equipment's appliance manufacturing facility in Oakriver.

"At least the smokestacks are still putting out smoke," David said.

"Manufacturing is controlled by the minicomputer," Nat said, "and it's all right. It's the mainframe that's down." Nat pulled the car right up to the visitor parking area. "Besides, they don't call it smoke here, they call it steam."

Nat and David gathered together their manuals and disk pack, left the car, and signed in at the front desk. A few minutes later they reached the computer center, where the atmosphere was one of crisis. Clayton Johns, the computer center manager, spotted them.

"Mr. Johns," Nat said, "let me introduce my colleague, David Cunningham." David and Clayton shook hands.

"Welcome, gentlemen," Clayton said. "The whole system's down, and everybody's on my back. If you can't get it running again by lunch, I might as well enlist in the French Foreign Legion!"

"I hear the food's good in the Legion," Nat said, leading the way to the computer console. "But we have to get your system up again. Otherwise I'll be in the Legion with you." Nat twirled the fastener on the lid of the disk pack he was carrying, and removed the pack. "Before we run the test program, tell me what's wrong," he said.

"The computer powers up all right," Clayton said, "but the operating system won't run. Instead it hangs up and displays the strangest system errors."

"And you think it's the hardware?" Nat asked.

"Definitely," Clayton said. "You see, the trouble began when the computer started terminating programs for illegal operations."

"Production programs?" David asked.

"Yes. Programs that have run fine for years."

"And now even the operating system itself won't run," Nat said. "Okay, this should tell us what's wrong." He took the disk pack and mounted it on a disk reader, returned to the console, entered a few commands, and got the machine to start running the test program. Several magnetic tape drives started twirling and the laser printer began spewing out pages.

"What is it testing now?" Clayton asked.

"Main memory," Nat said. "Let me just look at the printout." Nat and David crossed the room to the printer. "Good news. Memory's all right. All 32 million bytes of it. This program diagnoses faster than we can with our meters. The problem might not be hardware at all. It could be in the operating system. But we'll see. Right now the program is putting the arithmetic/logic unit through its paces. It checks every single circuit that does computations and logical operations."

The printer put out a one-page report. Clayton, Nat, and David bent over the machine to see it.

"The arithmetic/logic unit is working all right," Nat said. "Now it will move on to the control unit. We may as well get comfortable, this part of the program tries out everything in the house."

Clayton pulled up a chair at the console beside Nat. "The operating system won't even run," Clayton said, shaking his head and smiling. "Yet this diagnostic program of yours runs fine."

"It seeks alternatives," Nat said. "If it gets a parity error on data that passes through one register, it notes the fact and then tries again with another register. It's a thorough program for testing."

"Well if that program keeps me out of the Foreign Legion . . ." Clayton said.

"Relax," Nat said. "Your hardware surgeons are here."

The computer: what it is and how it works

Recall the definition from Chapter 2, that a COMPUTER is a very-high-speed electronic device that can accept data and instructions, use the instructions to perform logical and mathematical operations on the data, and report the results of its processing. There are two major types of computers: digital and analog. *Digital computers* count discrete (meaning "separate" or "unconnected") values. The digital computers most commonly used in business and industry are called *general-purpose digital computers. Analog computers* measure continuous values by using an analogy to the data (hence the name). For example, an equation might be expressed by using different voltage levels for its different values—much like a dimmer switch can control a light bulb. The inner workings of the digital computer will be examined here.

The hardware of a computerized information system is made up of four parts: (1) the computer, (2) input and output devices, (3) secondary storage devices, and (4) communications equipment. Figure 5-1 shows how the four components relate. This chapter deals only with the computer. Input and output devices, secondary storage devices, and communications equipment are covered in Chapters 6, 7, and 16 respectively.

The parts of the computer

The two parts of the computer are the central processing unit, or CPU, that contains the control and arithmetic/logic units, and the main storage unit. These two parts are shown in Figure 5-2.

■ The CENTRAL PROCESSING UNIT (CPU) carries out the instructions given it by software. It does this by processing the input data and producing the output information. Inside the CPU the CONTROL UNIT serves as the "brain" of the computer. It interprets program instructions and directs the other parts of the CPU; it also communicates with external input/output and secondary storage devices. The ARITHMETIC/LOGIC UNIT (ALU) performs calculations and logical operations with data, as directed by the control unit.

■ MAIN MEMORY or PRIMARY STORAGE stores data and instructions that have been input and are waiting to be processed, and stores the results of processing until they are released to output devices. Though main memory is closely associated with the central processing unit, main memory is *not* considered part of the CPU.

In the following sections we first examine the two parts of the CPU and then the functional subunits of main memory.

Control unit

The job of the CPU's control unit is to direct all hardware operations. The control unit interprets the instructions of the application or system program that is being run, one instruction at a time, and issues the necessary orders to the other parts of the system to carry out the instructions. The control unit also communicates with the input/output devices and secondary storage devices.

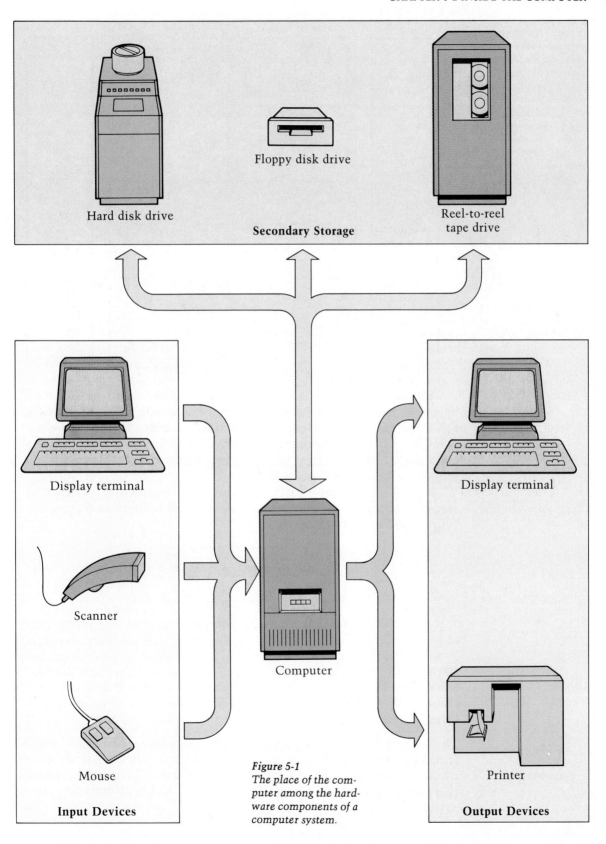

Floppy disk drive

Hard disk drive

Reel-to-reel
tape drive

Secondary Storage

Display terminal

Scanner

Mouse

Input Devices

Computer

Display terminal

Printer

Output Devices

Figure 5-1
The place of the com-
puter among the hard-
ware components of a
computer system.

Figure 5-2
The central processing unit and how it relates to main memory. The two functional units of the CPU are the control unit and the arithmetic/logic unit. The main memory of the computer is linked to both units. Arrows indicate the general flow of instructions, control, and data.

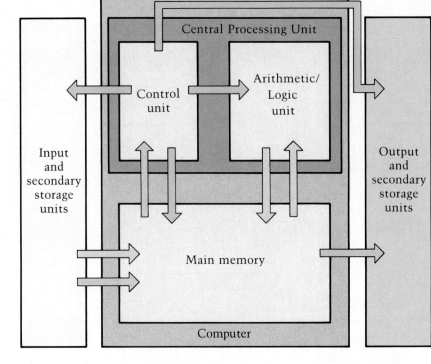

LEGEND

Control flow

Instruction flow

Data flow

The machine instructions supplied to the control unit consist of an operation code (op code) and one or more operands. The **OP CODE** tells the computer what operation to perform. An **OPERAND** tells the computer what the operation is to be carried out on. Usually the operand gives the address of data that are to be operated on. An **ADDRESS** is a unique location in main memory.

Here is an example of a machine-level instruction (written in assembly language) to subtract the value found in location B from the value found in location A:

Op code	Operand 1	Operand 2
SUB	A	B

A part of the control unit known as the **DECODER** reads the instruction code and matches it against a list of operations the computer can perform. When the decoder finds a match, the control unit sets the correct circuitry to carry out the operation. For instance, when the decoder encounters the command for subtraction, the control unit sends messages to the arithmetic/logic unit to set the electronic switches to perform subtraction.

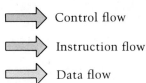

Arithmetic/logic unit

The arithmetic/logic unit (ALU) performs calculations and logical operations on data. The ALU circuitry works under the direction of the control unit. Given an instruction by the control unit—such as to compare two numbers to find out which is larger—the ALU performs the comparison.

There are two main components of the ALU: math gates and logic gates. A *gate* is an electronic switch with several entrances but only one exit. Data come in through the entrances and the answer comes out the exit. MATH GATES perform basic calculations, such as addition, subtraction, multiplication, and division. LOGIC GATES perform comparisons. Depending on the results of a comparison, the control unit tells the computer to do one of two things, as the program directs.

Main memory

Main memory—also called primary storage—holds data and instructions that have been input for processing, intermediate results, and the final results of processing until they are released to output devices. Main memory is divided into four functional areas (see Figure 5-3).

■ **INPUT STORAGE** holds data that have been read from an input device. Since input devices operate at slower speeds than the computer, part of the input storage area serves as a buffer. BUFFERS help free the computer to do other work while the slower input/output operations are completing. Input storage acts as a buffer, accumulating data until enough are present to justify processing them.

■ **PROGRAM STORAGE** holds instructions from both system and application programs, which enter the computer from an input device.

■ **WORKING STORAGE** holds the results of work in progress, such as intermediate answers to mathematical computations the computer is carrying out.

■ **OUTPUT STORAGE** holds information that has been processed and is ready to output. Like input storage, this area too can serve as a buffer.

Figure 5-3
Main memory and its four functional subcomponents.

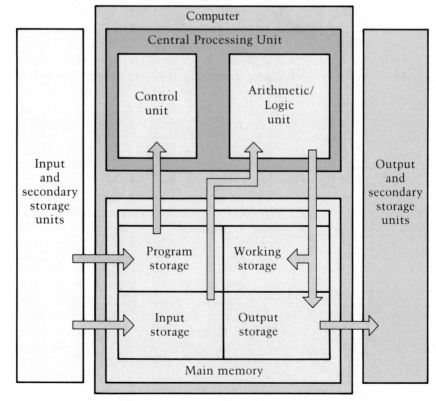

LEGEND

⟹ Instruction flow

⟹ Data flow

Output storage receives a quantity of output information from processing, and then retains the data so that they can be sent gradually out of the computer at a speed appropriate to the slower output devices.

As with a number of the computer concepts we will describe, these four types of storage are handled differently from one machine to the next. Even within a particular machine, as the computer processes its programs, it may increase or decrease the amount of main storage that it allocates for program storage, output storage, or whatever, depending on program needs. The point is that all four types of storage needs must be met by any computer.

Every location within main storage has a unique address. The address identifies one, and only one, specific point in the computer hardware. For an analogy we can think of addresses as referencing mailboxes that can only hold one letter (data item) at a time. If another letter (data item) is placed in the mailbox, it destroys whatever was there first. This process of writing new material into a storage location and erasing the old material in the process is called **DESTRUCTIVE WRITE**. Examining or copying data from a storage location, in contrast, does not destroy it. **NONDESTRUCTIVE READ** refers to the ability to look at or copy the data in a storage address without destroying it.

Registers

Among its various types of switches, the CPU relies extensively on registers. A **REGISTER** is a high-speed temporary storage unit for data or a program instruction. Registers are used in the control unit and the ALU. The circuitry of a register is designed such that data can be placed into a register, or removed from it, faster than from a location in main storage.

To illustrate some of the specialized functions registers perform, let's look at how the decoder uses them. The decoder matches instruction codes against a list of permissible codes, and when a match is found sets the correct circuitry to carry out the operation the code specifies. No fewer than four types of registers are used in the process. These are:

■ The *sequence control register*, which keeps track of the steps in the processing sequence.
■ The *instruction register*, which holds the operation code to be decoded and the operand.
■ The *address register*, which also holds the address specified in the instruction's operand.
■ The *instruction address register*, which holds the address of the next instruction to be fetched from main memory.

Well-designed registers permit the most efficient use of the most expensive parts of the CPU—the decoder and the math and logic gates. Registers reduce the distance signals must travel to and from these parts, and thus reduce idle time, much the way an airline reduces the amount of time an airplane is idle on the ground by collecting everything needed to service and fill the plane—fuel, luggage handlers, flight crews, passengers—near the plane at the right time.

career box

Hardware-oriented jobs

Hardware-oriented careers concentrate on the operation and maintenance of computer equipment. By equipment we mean the computer unit and peripheral devices for input, output, storage, and communication. As a rule, the lower-level jobs (such as that of computer operator) are the easiest to obtain in the information systems field, and the least challenging. You might wonder why, since computer hardware is such a technological marvel. *Designing* computer hardware is complex; *running* it is not. The higher-level positions (such as manager of computer operations) differ from the lower-level jobs by the addition of supervisory and planning responsibilities. The following list briefly describes various positions and their responsibilities in the hardware-oriented field.

■ *Manager of computer operations.* This person is in charge of keeping the computers and other hardware in an information-processing center running. Responsibilities include scheduling the activities of computer operators and maintenance personnel.

■ *Data communications/telecommunications manager.* This person is responsible for the design and continued operation of telecommunications and distributed processing networks.

■ *Data communications analyst.* A specialist within the telecommunications area, this individual designs telecommunications networks and software.

■ *Remote site administrator.* This person is responsible for managing a site in a distributed processing network. The individual in this job is often not an information systems professional, but a nontechnical worker who has taken on this function in addition to other duties.

■ *Computer operator.* This individual assists in running a computer, such as mounting and dismounting storage media. Under supervision, a computer operator may operate the main computer console. A *lead* computer operator typically manages the other operators during one shift, or directs the operations of equipment at a remote site.

■ *Production control supervisor.* Responsibilities of the production control supervisor are scheduling which job will run at a large computer center, balancing the full use of resources with the turnaround deadlines for the jobs.

■ *Magnetic media librarian.* The responsibility of this person is to control the storage and use of removable magnetic storage media.

■ *Minicomputer specialist.* This individual is an expert in a particular model of minicomputer. Responsibilities include installing and sometimes repairing the computer hardware and software, and programming and running the system.

■ *Microcomputer specialist.* This person is an expert in one or more particular models of microcomputers. Responsibilities include installing and sometimes repairing the computer hardware and software, and programming and running the system.

■ *Field service engineer.* An electronic technician trained by hardware manufacturers, this person services malfunctioning hardware and also pinpoints software problems.

■ *Data-entry operator.* The job of this person is to enter data into a computer system with one or more different types of data-entry devices.

■ *Word processing operator.* This job entails entering, editing, and outputting text on a word processing system.

Source: Based on information in Stephen R. Gray's, "1982 DP Salary Survey," *Datamation*, vol. 28, no. 11 (October 1982): 128. Excerpted from DATAMATION, © 1982 by Cahners Publishing Company.

The term **MACHINE CYCLE** refers to the interaction of the components of the computer for the time required to carry out one machine operation. It can be compared to a heartbeat. An electronic clock within the computer gives out pulses at regular intervals, which fix the machine cycle. Machine cycles are short: today's computers can squeeze hundreds of millions of machine cycles into a single second. A single program may require many millions of machine cycles to run.

The machine cycle has two substages, the instruction cycle and the execution cycle. During the **INSTRUCTION CYCLE**, the CPU fetches an instruction, figures out which operation to perform by decoding it, and then interprets the operand to find the data to perform the operation upon. During the **EXECUTION CYCLE**, the CPU performs the operation. Then the CPU moves on to the next cycle.

To illustrate how the components of the CPU interact with main memory, let's follow one machine cycle through the computer. Assume that a program and the data it will use are already in main memory, and that the operating system has instructed the CPU to start running the program. In this example the program will multiply two numbers (2 and 5), and then pass the result to storage.

In Figure 5-4 we can observe how the program instructions and its data are stored in main memory. The storage addresses are shown in parentheses. The intermediate and the results to be printed are shown in working and output storage respectively. Not all the storage areas are used.

During the *instruction cycle* the control unit fetches the first instruction from main memory. Within the control unit the decoder matches the instruction code against the machine's repertoire of possibilities (called the instruction set). Upon finding a match, the decoder sends messages to the arithmetic/logic unit to set the necessary gates to carry out the operation.

In our example (Figure 5-5) the sequence control register that keeps track of the addresses of the steps in the program is set at step 03. At this step the op code (MULT) and its operand (11)—the address for B—are fetched and placed into the instruction register. Then the op code is sent into the decoder and the operand is placed into the address register.

Figure 5-4
Storing in main memory. Program instructions and data are stored in main memory. The storage addresses are shown in parentheses. The intermediate stage is placed in working storage and the results to be printed are shown in output storage. Note: Not all the storage areas are used.

Program Storage									
(00)	(01)	(02)	(03)	(04)	(05)	(06)	(07)	(08)	(09)
Start program	Read data into addresses 10 and 11	Read contents of address 10 into ALU	Multiply contents in ALU by contents of address 11	Copy result from ALU into addresses 12 and 14	Read contents of address 12 into ALU	Square contents in ALU	Copy result from ALU into address 15	Print contents of addresses 14 and 15	Stop program

Input Storage		Working Storage		Output Storage					
(10)	(11)	(12)	(13)	(14)	(15)	(16)	(17)	(18)	(19)
2	5	10	Empty	10	100	Empty	Empty	Empty	Empty

Figure 5-5
How the decoder and registers work together. The sequence control register keeps track of the addresses of the steps in the program. At step 03 the op code (MULT) and its operand (11)—the address for 5—are fetched and placed into the instruction register. Then the op code is sent into the decoder and the operand is placed into the address register. Meanwhile, the instruction address register holds the address of the next instruction (04).

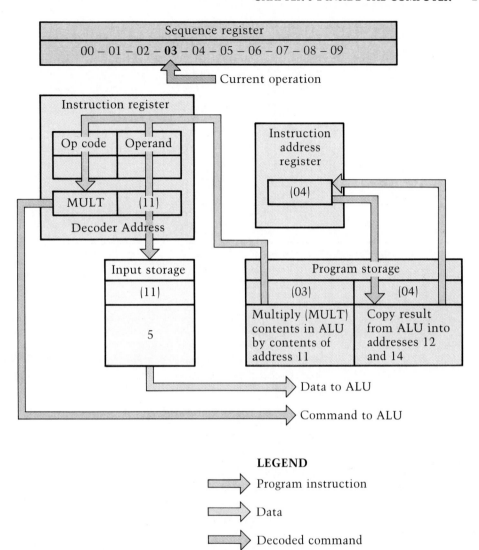

Meanwhile the instruction address register holds the address of the next instruction (04).

The ALU performs the operation. If the operation generates output (or intermediate results that will be used by another operation), the output or result is stored in main memory. In this example, during the *execution cycle* the values (2 and 5) are placed into the registers, fed into the math gate, and the result (10) is placed into a register (erasing the value 5) to be sent back to working and output storage (Figure 5-6). The machine cycle is complete—a tiny fraction of a second has gone by—and the machine begins the next cycle.

When the program directs the computer to produce output, it is transferred from main memory to the appropriate output unit, under the control of system software. When the program finishes running, the CPU is sure to find work with another application program, or with running instructions of the operating system itself.

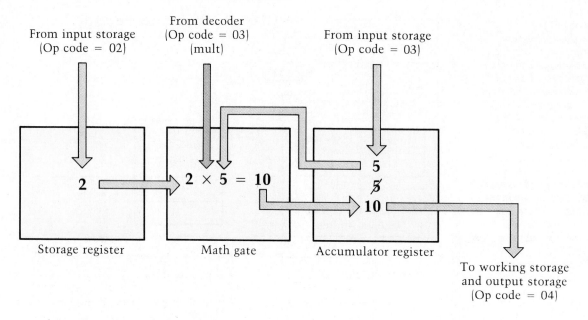

From input storage
(Op code = 02)

From decoder
(Op code = 03)
(mult)

From input storage
(Op code = 03)

2

2 × 5 = 10

5
5̶
10

Storage register

Math gate

Accumulator register

To working storage
and output storage
(Op code = 04)

LEGEND

Decoded command

Data

Figure 5-6
Using a math gate. The values (2 and 5) are placed into the registers, fed into the math gate, and the result (10) is placed into a register (erasing the value 5) to be sent back to working storage and output storage.

Data representation

Computers—fast as they are—need numbers, characters, and symbols presented to them in a very simple fashion. Digital computers respond only to yes or no, on or off signals. Therefore our rich and diverse number systems, alphabets, and symbolic codes must be translated into a two-state, on or off, pattern.

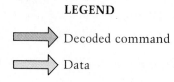

Bits, bytes, and characters

The **BINARY (BASE 2) NUMBER SYSTEM** is central to digital computers—they understand nothing but binary. It utilizes only the numerals 1, corresponding to the "on" state of an electronic component, and 0, corresponding to the "off" state. Binary is derived from the Latin word for "two." A single **BINARY DIGIT** (a 1 or 0) is known as a **BIT**, a word derived from "*binary digit.*"

A computer that could only use long strings of true binary numbers would be very limited. In theory, a binary number could have an infinite number of digits. Further, alphabetic characters and other symbols could not be represented. Communicating data would also be difficult. For these reasons, computers work with a larger unit than the bit, called a byte. A **BYTE** is a binary character (made up of adjacent bits) that the computer stores as a unit. Each binary character is made up of a unique pattern of bits. Although other sizes have been and are still used, on most modern computers, the usual number of bits per byte is 8. Another term you will sometimes encounter is a **NIBBLE** or **NYBBLE**. This is simply half a byte, which is usually 4 bits.

Binary-coded decimal (BCD) numbers
The decimal numbers 0 to 9 can be coded in sets called **BINARY-CODED DECIMAL (BCD)**. This is simply a code to represent characters including decimal numbers.

Let's see how we can convert the decimal number 79 into the form of a binary-coded decimal. Because the binary code in this case will be 4 bits wide, it can be labeled 4-bit BCD. We can convert the decimal number 79 ($7 \times 10^1 + 9 \times 10^0$) into two adjacent 4-bit BCD numbers— 0111 1001—by finding the binary equivalent for each decimal digit. (The arithmetic for this conversion for the decimal number 7 is $0 \times 2^3 + 1 \times 2^2 + 1 \times 2^1 + 1 \times 2^0 = 0 + 4 + 2 + 1 = 7$; and for the decimal number 9 is $1 \times 2^3 + 0 \times 2^2 + 0 \times 2^1 + 1 \times 2^0 = 8 + 0 + 0 + 1 = 9$.) This conversion process and other features of binary numbers and arithmetic are discussed in the appendix to this chapter, Number Systems.

EBCDIC and ASCII
Besides representing numbers, a byte can also represent letters, punctuation, and other symbols. This is done by following agreed-upon conventions used in designing hardware and software. The conventions say that certain patterns of bits in a byte will not be taken for binary numbers at all, but for a particular letter or symbol.

One such set of conventions, widely used, is known as EBCDIC. The acronym **EBCDIC** is short for **EXTENDED BINARY-CODED DECIMAL INTERCHANGE CODE**. Taking the 8 bits of a byte, EBCDIC assigns a bit pattern to each of the decimal numbers 0 through 9, lowercase and uppercase letters of the alphabet, and commonly used special symbols (such as plus signs and dollar signs). Some input/output devices need specialized control characters, and EBCDIC even has values that stand for these.

In all, 8 bits can represent 256 (2^8) characters, enough to account for our entire repertoire of numerals, letters, special characters, and control characters, with enough space left open for future use or customized meanings on particular systems. Figure 5-7 shows the EBCDIC system.

The other set of conventions also in wide use today is known as **ASCII**, short for **AMERICAN STANDARD CODE FOR INFORMATION INTERCHANGE**. Like EBCDIC, ASCII has a specific bit pattern assigned to every number, letter, symbol, and control code in common use. Unlike EBCDIC, which only uses 8 bits, ASCII has one version that uses 7 bits, and another—known as ASCII-8—that uses 8 bits. Figure 5-8 shows the ASCII-8 system.

Developed by IBM, EBCDIC is used on mainframes produced by IBM, as well as on mainframes produced by some other manufacturers. ASCII is commonly used by microcomputers and data-communication systems.

Char-acter	8-bit EBCDIC 8421 8421 (place values)	Char-acter	8-bit EBCDIC 8421 8421 (place values)
0	1111 0000	K	1101 0010
1	1111 0001	L	1101 0011
2	1111 0010	M	1101 0100
3	1111 0011	N	1101 0101
4	1111 0100	O	1101 0110
5	1111 0101	P	1101 0111
6	1111 0110	Q	1101 1000
7	1111 0111	R	1101 1001
8	1111 1000	S	1110 0010
9	1111 1001	T	1110 0011
A	1100 0001	U	1110 0100
B	1100 0010	V	1110 0101
C	1100 0011	W	1110 0110
D	1100 0100	X	1110 0111
E	1100 0101	Y	1110 1000
F	1100 0110	Z	1110 1001
G	1100 0111	+	0100 1110
H	1100 1000	$	0101 1011
I	1100 1001	.	0100 1011
J	1101 0001	<	0100 1100

Figure 5-7
How EBCDIC represents numbers, letters, and special symbols.

Char-acter	8-bit ASCII 8421 8421 (place values)	Char-acter	8-bit ASCII 8421 8421 (place values)
0	1011 0000	K	1100 1011
1	1011 0001	L	1100 1100
2	1011 0010	M	1100 1101
3	1011 0011	N	1100 1110
4	1011 0100	O	1100 1111
5	1011 0101	P	1101 0000
6	1011 0110	Q	1101 0001
7	1011 0111	R	1101 0010
8	1011 1000	S	1101 0011
9	1011 1001	T	1101 0100
A	1100 0001	U	1101 0101
B	1100 0010	V	1101 0110
C	1100 0011	W	1101 0111
D	1100 0100	X	1101 1000
E	1100 0101	Y	1101 1001
F	1100 0110	Z	1101 1010
G	1100 0111	+	1010 1011
H	1100 1000	$	1010 0100
I	1100 1001	.	1010 1110
J	1100 1010	<	1011 1100

Figure 5-8
How ASCII-8 represents numbers, letters, and special symbols.

Parity bits

When data are communicated between a computer and its peripherals, or from computer to computer over a communications link, they may sometimes be garbled. Often this garbling is caused by binary digits accidentally flipping from 1 to 0, or from 0 to 1, leaving the computer with a pattern it cannot understand. A PARITY BIT, or CHECK BIT, is used to detect the presence of such possible garbling. A parity bit is simply an additional bit appended to a byte. Thus an EBCDIC or 8-bit byte will have a ninth parity bit and a 7-bit ASCII byte will have an eighth parity bit.

Here is how the parity bit works. The ASCII-8 code for the letter G is 11000111. There are five 1s in the code. We can place another 1 in the parity bit, giving a total of six 1s. Six is an even number. We can follow the convention that all bytes in our computer system must contain an even number of 1s, counting the parity bit. Thus whenever the data value contains an odd number of 1s, as in the example, we simply set the parity bit to 1, to give an even total. If the data value already contains an even number of 1s, we set the parity bit to 0. This system is known as "even parity."

The opposite approach, "odd parity," requires that the total number of 1s in a byte plus its parity bit, be odd. For instance, the ASCII-8 code for a dollar sign is 10100110. There are four 1s in the code. If we need an odd number of 1s, we would set the parity bit to 1, giving a total of five 1s.

Figure 5-9
Using a parity or check
bit. The "even parity"
system is used here. The
letter G contains an er-
ror—a 1 instead of a 0—
and the total number of
1s in that byte, including
the parity bit, adds up to
7, an odd number.

Letter	Parity bit	ASCII-8 code
G	1	1 1 0 0 1 1 1 1
R	0	1 1 0 1 0 0 1 0
E	0	1 1 0 0 0 1 0 1
E	0	1 1 0 0 0 1 0 1
T	0	1 1 0 1 0 1 0 0
I	0	1 1 0 0 1 0 0 1
N	1	1 1 0 0 1 1 1 0
G	1	1 1 0 0 0 1 1 1
S	1	1 1 0 1 0 0 1 1

Figure 5-9 shows the parity bit settings for each of the characters that spell out "GREETINGS" using the even parity system. Parity bits can be used with EBCDIC, ASCII, or any other binary-based convention.

The parity bit does not change the data value contained in the byte itself. It is merely a protective measure to help spot many cases of garbled bytes. The parity setting is not under the user's control. If our computer uses even parity, every single byte of data will be checked at key points to assure that the number of 1s in the byte plus the byte's parity bit, is even. When an odd total turns up, something is amiss. In this situation the computer generally prints an error message stating there is a parity error, and outputs the suspect data (or instruction) byte as well. Other methods for verifying data integrity are discussed in Chapter 17.

Computer words

A **COMPUTER WORD** is made up of one or more consecutive bytes. The length of a computer word is a design feature of the particular computer, closely tied to the way that the CPU interprets and executes instructions (which themselves must be placed into bytes or words). Typical word sizes are 1 byte (8 bits), 2 bytes (16 bits), 4 bytes (32 bits), and 8 bytes (64 bits). Word sizes for microcomputers range from 8 bits in older machines to 32 bits in newer machines. Mainframe computers have word sizes ranging from 32 to 64 bits. Depending on how they treat words, computers may be classified as either fixed-length-word or variable-length-word machines.

Fixed-length systems
A computer with **FIXED-LENGTH WORDS** is designed to handle words that contain a specific number of bytes. By placing several bytes together in one word, and working with words as a unit instead of bytes, the size of the numbers that can be handled is increased, as is the speed of the computer. What makes it possible for the computer to work faster is that data and instructions can be obtained an entire word at a time and worked on a word at a time. Performing an operation on all of a word at once, so that calculations can be performed on all the digits of a number simultaneously, is known as **PARALLEL ARITHMETIC**. Parallel arithmetic is the opposite of **SERIAL ARITHMETIC** in which operations occur more slowly on a byte-by-byte basis.

Fixed-length-word computers are most often used for scientific and engineering applications, which require high processing speeds to perform complex calculations.

The drawback of the fixed-length system is that it tends to waste storage space. When data do not fill a word, the unused bytes of the word are left empty.

Variable-length systems

Computers with a **VARIABLE-LENGTH WORD** handle each byte or character individually. Many microcomputers and other smaller computers are of this type. Each byte having its own address minimizes wasted space in main storage, an advantage over fixed-length systems. The drawback is that performing operations on the data is slower because serial arithmetic must be employed.

Some larger computers, such as mainframes, are capable of performing either fixed- or variable-length-word operations. Thus when eliminating wasted storage space is the focus of an application, the variable-length system can be used; when calculation speed is the prime factor, the fixed-length approach can be taken.

Chips: the stuff computers are made of

Modern computers are packed with miniature electronic circuits etched onto small wafers of glass called **SILICON CHIPS** (see Chapter 2). The circuits are so tiny that many can be squeezed onto the small chip (see High RISC Chips). Figure 5-10 shows how chips are made.

Today's mainframe computers and minicomputers use semiconductor silicon chips throughout the central processing unit and the main memory unit. Chips are used in the control unit to monitor processing, decode instructions, and serve as registers. The arithmetic/logic unit uses chips to perform mathematical and logical operations. Main memory units have banks of chips capable of storing tens of millions of bytes.

Microprocessors

In microcomputers, the entire CPU is contained on a single silicon chip known as a **MICROPROCESSOR**. A microprocessor can contain the control unit, the arithmetic/logic unit, and some of the main memory. An example is shown in Figure 5-11.

Microprocessors are often categorized by word size, or the number of bits the processor can operate on. The earliest microprocessors could only handle 8-bit-sized words. Then 16-bit microprocessors were developed. Today, 32-bit microprocessors allow a substantial increase in processing speeds, since more data and instructions can be processed in a given time interval than with 8 or 16-bit systems. In addition, the larger word size makes it possible to build more main storage into the machine. The number of each memory location must be able to fit into a

High RISC chips

Silicon Valley has not seen such a bumper crop since it stopped growing peaches and prunes and began producing computer chips. Hardly a week has gone by this Spring without a ballyhooed announcement of a new semiconductor or a line of high-speed computers. At the center of the excitement is a new breed of microprocessors that promises to give computer manufacturers their biggest performance boost in a decade. Lightning fast, the chips make it possible to put the power of ten to 20 refrigerator-sized minicomputers into a . . . desktop-size machine.

Of all the announcements, none has generated as much anticipation as the one to be made this week by Motorola, the largest U.S. supplier of semiconductors (1987 sales: $6.7 billion). The electronics giant has etched 1.7 million transistors into a three-chip microprocessor called the 88000 that it hopes will become a standard component of the next generation of high-performance computers. Motorola may be right. Even before the new product was formally unveiled, more than 30 prospective customers, including Data General, Convergent, and Tektronix, had formed a users group to set guidelines for designing hardware and software to take advantage of the new chips. Says Motorola Vice President Murray Goldman: "This is the next major battleground in the computer world."

How do the new chips achieve their performance breakthroughs? In a word: RISC, for reduced instruction set computer. RISC is not a new technology, but a fresh approach to computing that challenges 25 years of semiconductor design. It focuses on a computer's most basic commands: the instructions that are embedded, or hard-wired, into the silicon circuitry of the machine's central processing unit. The first computers made do with a handful of primitive commands, such as LOAD, ADD, and STORE, which programmers combined to perform complex tasks. Lacking a command to multiply 6 times 5, for example, they had to instruct their computers to add five 6s together.

Over the years, the basic instruction sets grew in length, as miniaturization allowed computer designers to etch more circuits into silicon chips. The most advanced microprocessors began to resemble state-of-the-art calculators that could compute interest at the touch of a button. By the time Digital Equipment introduced its best-selling VAX 11/780 computer in 1977, the machine's instruction set had swelled to 304 commands.

But the increased complexity had its cost. Studies showed that 20 percent of the instruction were doing 80 percent of the work. The rest were like expensive extras on a limousine: rarely used luxuries that took up space and slowed performance. The advocates of RISC, declaring that it was time to go back to basics, stripped away the nonessentials and optimized the performance of the 50 or so most frequently used commands. . . .

At first, the industry was reluctant to switch to RISC. But the new crop of chips has made believers out of almost everybody. Sun, a company best known for its engineering computers, got into the chip business last summer when it began licensing a RISC processor to AT&T, Unisys, and Xerox. MIPS, which introduced its second generation of the chips last month, supplies microprocessors to Tandem, Prime, and Silicon Graphics. Hewlett-Packard has built an entire line of computers around RISC technology.

Most important, IBM is making a major commitment to RISC. IBM Vice-President Andrew Heller suggests that RISC technology could produce startling advances in electronic speech recognition, machine vision, and artificial intelligence—all of which require superfast microprocessors. Says Heller: "Computers that can listen and talk back, and recognize objects on sight, are not so farfetched. RISC will help make all that a reality, and it's going to happen this century."

Figure 5-10
How chips are made. (a) Computer chips are made from wafers of silicon. The process begins with an enlarged circuit design created with the help of computer-aided design methods. This design is scanned and stored in digitized form. (b) The silicon wafers are sliced from a pure silicon ingot. (c) The wafers are polished. (d) The circuit pattern from the original enlarged design is reduced to microscopic size and printed onto a photomask. Each of the little squares in the mask contains a copy of one layer of the design; each square represents a layer of a single chip. The mask is placed over a wafer, which is then exposed to ultraviolet light. The wafer has been previously treated with a light-sensitive "doping" compound. Where the mask blocks the ultraviolet light, the compound remains soft; the places exposed to light harden. The wafer is then placed in an acid bath and the soft, unexposed areas wash away.

(a)

(b)

(c)

(d)

(e) The fabrication process takes place in "clean rooms" 10,000 times cleaner than a hospital operating room.

(e)

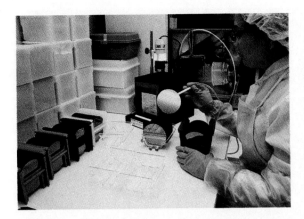

(f)

(g)

(h)

(i)

(f) Inspectors monitor the fabrication process. (g) The chips are soldered onto frames. (h) The chip and frame are placed in a protective jacket, which has connector pins to fit onto circuit boards. (i) Circuit boards containing chips are then assembled into a wide variety of products.

Figure 5-11
A computer on a chip. A microprocessor with all of the elements of a CPU.

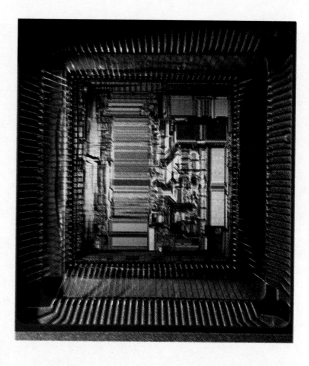

word; with larger words, more main storage can be used and referred to.

Even greater increases in processing speed can be obtained by combining microprocessors. In larger computers, the CPU may contain a number of microprocessors linked together.

Random-access memory (RAM) chips

It is in their role as main memory that silicon chips serve their most visible purpose: fast storage. Chips used for main memory have a variety of different names that reflect their various functions.

The mainstay of main memory is the highly price-competitive RANDOM-ACCESS MEMORY (RAM) chip. It is called "random access" because the address of any memory location can be reached ("accessed") without the necessity of checking or referring to any adjacent locations. RAM is the part of the computer's memory that stores and erases data and programs.

On some computers a special storage area of high-speed RAM chips sits between the rest of main memory and the CPU. Called *cache storage* (cache is a French word meaning a place for storing provisions, pronounced *cash*), this area holds data and instructions not yet ready to be transferred to the registers for processing. The aim is to save time fetching the instructions once the program needs them.

RAM chips are volatile; that is, they immediately lose their data when the power is turned off. To avoid costly losses of instructions or data, backup power supplies should be provided.

A memory chip can be thought of as a large grid with many rows and columns. At the intersection of a row and column, a bit can be stored. To find what is stored at any intersection, only the row and column numbers need to be known. With a RAM storage unit you can store data at storage locations, read them later, and then erase the data by writing over it.

Storage capacity on a chip is expressed in multiples of 2^{10} or 1024 bits, often called 1K (where K is approximately 1000). A common RAM storage chip of 256K bits has 256×2^{10}—or 262,144 bits. Many newer systems for home and personal applications use 256K RAM chips. If each byte in your computer is 8 bits in size, it takes eight of these 256K-bit chips to give you 256K *bytes* of primary storage. Currently, some RAM chips can hold just over 1 million bits, and 4-million-bit RAM chips are coming into production.

Read-only memory (ROM) chips

READ-ONLY MEMORY (ROM) chips are chips on which programs (or data) have been permanently encoded. A ROM can be read, but cannot be written onto or erased by the user. ROMs are used for a variety of purposes. They can be used to store programs. Many video games have a ROM chip contained in the cartridge that is slipped into the computer when you want to play that particular game. Within many microcomputers part of the system software is stored on ROM, as is the program that allows the computer to run application software written in the BASIC programming language. ROM is also used to store machine-level instructions for frequently used procedures, such as how to calculate square roots. ROM can be used to store entire applications programs. Some portable microcomputers, for example, come with word processing and spreadsheet programs built in on ROM. Software encoded or embedded into ROM chips is often called FIRMWARE because, strictly speaking, it is neither "hard" nor "soft."

Users of an information system may want to program and protect their own procedures on a read-only memory chip. PROGRAMMABLE READ-ONLY MEMORY (PROM) chips serve this purpose. Some PROMs are erasable under special circumstances so that they can be reprogrammed, and are called ERASABLE PROGRAMMABLE READ-ONLY MEMORY (EPROM) chips. The erasure process might involve exposing the EPROM to ultraviolet light or to an electrical charge—in which case the chip is known as *electrically erasable programmable read-only memory (EEPROM)*. PROMs and EPROMs give users greater flexibility in designing systems that meet their needs.

The CPU and computing power

The CPU in today's computers is an impressive device. This is true regardless of whether the CPU is a single-chip microprocessor in a microcomputer, or a multichip version in a minicomputer or a mainframe.

Figure 5-12 compares performance and price of the four main categories of computers—microcomputers, minicomputers, mainframes, and supercomputers. As you can see, the four categories overlap.

The race for faster supercomputers

. . . For most of the supercomputer era, the market for the most powerful machines has been dominated by one firm, Cray Research of Minneapolis. With 178 of its distinctive C-shaped models installed around the world, Cray accounts for 60 percent of all the supercomputers sold. The closest competitor, located directly across the Mississippi River in St. Paul, is the company from which Cray split off in 1972: Control Data Corp. CDC, which in 1983 created a supercomputer subsidiary called ETA Systems, is holding steady with a 12.7 percent market share. Coming up quickly is a trio of Japanese manufacturers—NEC, Hitachi, and Fujitsu—that entered the supercomputer race in 1983 and has since captured 23 percent of the world market.

But this tidy pie chart may soon be upset by the surprise entry of a new player that for the past two decades has been most conspicuous by its absence from the supercomputer market: IBM . . . announced that it had struck a deal with Steve Chen, one of the foremost supercomputer designers, who jolted the computer world . . . by suddenly leaving his post as a vice-president at Cray. With financial aid from IBM, Chen has set up his own company to develop a machine 100 times as fast as any currently on the market.

IBM has not only taken the plunge but has also put its prestige and enormous resources behind a radical kind of supercomputer that represents a dramatic break from the past . . . the computer Chen is building with IBM's backing will contain not 1, but 64 processors, all operating at the same time, in parallel, and thus significantly cutting down computing time. IBM's decision to support a major parallel-processing supercomputer project is a sign that technology is headed in that direction. Says H. T. Kung, computer scientist at Carnegie-Mellon University: "In one move, IBM legitimized two technologies: supercomputing and parallel processing." AT&T Bell Laboratories is expected to introduce a new parallel-processing computer.

Cray, IBM, and AT&T could be upstaged, however, by a determined gang of innovative computer designers who have already moved beyond 64 processing units to build machines that divide their work among hundreds, even thousands of processors. . . . [S]cientists at Sandia National Laboratories in Albuquerque announced that they have coaxed a 1024-processor computer into solving several problems more than 1000 times as fast as a single processor machine acting alone, an unprecedented speedup that suggests the performance of supercomputers may in the future be related almost directly to the number of processors they employ.

Much supercomputing research is funded by the U.S. government, whose appetite for high-speed, number-crunching power for both defense and intelligence uses seems boundless. . . .

The military-intelligence connection is nothing new for supercomputer manufacturers. One of the first Crays to come off the assembly line in 1976 was shipped to the Lawrence Livermore National Laboratory, where it made short work of the mind-boggling mathematical equations required to design hydrogen bombs. . . .

What is new is the rapidly growing appetite for supercomputer power in the private sector. In a classic case of a technology developed for a few specialized purposes finding application in all sorts of unexpected areas, supercomputing has spread from one industry to another like a benevolent virus. Semiconductor manufacturers use supercomputers to design ways to squeeze more transistors into a square-centimeter chip of silicon. Financial advisers use them to devise investment strategies of dizzying complexity. Biochemists need them to predict which molecules are worth testing as new medicines. Engineers rely on them to design new cars, jet engines, light bulbs, sailboats, refrigerators, and artificial limbs. . . .

Source: Adapted from Philip Elmer-DeWitt, reported by Thomas McCarroll/New York, J. Madeleine Nash/Minneapolis, and Charles Pelton/San Francisco, "Fast and Smart: Designers Race to Build the Supercomputers of the Future," *Time* 28 March 1988, 54–58. Copyright 1988 Time Inc. All rights reserved. Reprinted by permission from TIME.

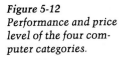

Figure 5-12
Performance and price
level of the four com-
puter categories.

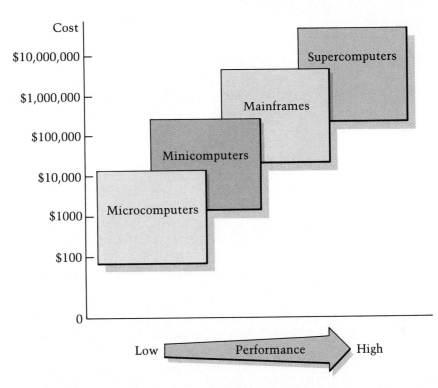

Figure 5-13
Comparing the different
types of computers.

Computer type	Characteristics					
	Size	*Memory*	*Speed*	*Peripherals*	*Cost*	*Environment*
Micro-computer	Desktop or smaller; some are portable	64K to 4M	Micro-seconds	Keyboard, printer, and disk drives	$500–$15,000	No special re-quirements
Mini-computer	About the size of a file cabi-net	500K to 16M	20–60 nano-seconds	Dozens of peripheral devices	$10,000–$250,000	Air condition-ing, security recom-mended
Mainframe	A large of-fice desk or file cabinet	8M to 512M	10–50 nano-seconds	Hundreds of devices	$100,000 to several million	Special cooling, fire protec-tion, security
Super-computer	Several large file cabinets	64M to 1024M	1–10 nano-seconds	Special high perfor-mance de-vices	$10 million plus	Special protec-tion required

The characteristics of each type of computer are summarized in Figure 5-13. Note that the general trend has been for computers in all four categories to offer better (lower) cost-to-performance ratios over the past years. A continuation of such trends will lead to even greater processing speeds, more internal storage, and lower prices in the future.

summary

▪ A computer is a very-high-speed electronic device that can accept data and instructions, use the instructions to perform logical and mathematical operations on the data, and report the results of its processing.

▪ The computer has two main components: the central processing unit (CPU) and main memory.

▪ Within the CPU are two functional units: the control unit and the arithmetic/logic unit (ALU).

▪ The control unit is the "brain" of the computer. It interprets program instructions, directs the other parts of the CPU, and communicates with external input/output devices and secondary storage devices. The machine instructions supplied to the CPU consist of an op code that tells the computer what operation to perform, and one or more operands that tell what the operations are to be performed on. The decoder interprets the op code. An address is a unique location in main memory.

▪ The arithmetic/logic unit (ALU) performs calculations and logical operations with the data, as directed by the control unit. Math and logic gates are the electronic switches in the ALU that perform these operations.

▪ Main memory (or primary storage) stores data and instructions that have been input and are waiting to be processed. It also stores the results of processing until they are released to output devices. Incoming data are placed in input storage, program instructions into program storage, intermediate results in working storage, and output in output storage. Buffers are used to compensate for speed differences between the computer and its peripheral devices. When data are stored in an address in main memory, they destroy any data that were there before (destructive write). Reading data from an address leaves them unaffected (nondestructive read).

▪ Registers are high-speed temporary storage units.

▪ The machine cycle has two phases—the instruction cycle and the execution cycle. During the instruction cycle, instructions are fetched, decoded, and the appropriate parts of the computer made ready. During the execution cycle, the computer performs the operation.

▪ With a computer, all numbers, letters, and symbolic codes must be translated to a two-state, on or off pattern using the binary (base 2) number system. Each binary number or digit inside a computer is known as a bit.

▪ A byte is a string of adjacent bits that the computer processes as a unit. The usual number of bits per byte is 8. A nibble (or nybble) is half a byte, usually 4 bits.

▪ Letters, decimal numbers, punctuation, and other symbols are represented by following conventions that designate certain binary-coded decimal patterns as their equivalents. EBCDIC (Extended Binary-Coded Decimal Interchange Code) is one convention. ASCII (American Standard Code for Information Interchange) is another.

▪ A parity or check bit is an extra bit added to an EBCDIC or ASCII byte to make it possible to detect communication errors.

▫   A computer word is made up of one or more consecutive bytes. Fixed-length-word machines handle words that contain a fixed number of bytes. Variable-length-word machines handle each byte individually. Some machines can use either system. Fixed-length-word machines can perform parallel arithmetic. Variable-length word machines use serial arithmetic.

▫   Today's mainframe computers and minicomputers use silicon chips throughout the computer. On microcomputers, the entire CPU is etched onto a single chip known as a microprocessor. Main memory is contained on random-access memory (RAM) chips. On some computers, a special storage area of high-speed RAM chips called cache storage sits between the rest of main memory and other parts of the CPU. Storage capacity is usually expressed in terms of K. 1K equals 1024 bytes.

▫   Read-only memory (ROM) can be read from but cannot be written onto. ROM is often used on microcomputers to store parts of the system software and machine-level instructions of frequently used procedures. ROM can also be used to store entire application programs. Software encoded on ROM is often called firmware. Variants on ROM are programmable read-only memory (PROM), and erasable programmable read-only memory (EPROM).

▫   The four categories of computers—microcomputers, minicomputers, mainframe computers, and supercomputers—differ in terms of a number of variables. Two of the most important are price and performance. Microcomputer systems can be purchased from under $500 up to $20,000; minicomputers from $10,000 to $250,000; mainframe computers from $100,000 to several million dollars; and supercomputers from $10 million and up. Performance parallels the increase in price, ranging from a machine cycle time measured in microseconds (millionths of a second) for microcomputers, through a declining range of times for the other three types of computer measured in nanoseconds (billionths of a second).

wrap-up

Modular replacement

"Well, that's it," Nat Bergstein said, looking at the last page of output from the diagnostic program.

"Have you found the problem?" asked Clayton Johns, Global Electrical Equipment's computer center manager.

"I believe so," Nat said. "It's in the control unit of the CPU."

"Does that program actually tell you what chip?" Clayton asked.

"No," David said. "It indicates functional components. The control unit of the CPU has a part known as the decoder. It figures out what the program instructions are and rigs up the circuits to carry them out. Some portion of the decoder hardware isn't working."

"Can you install a new one?" Clayton asked.

"Yes," Nat said. He picked up the phone and called his office.

"We'll be back on the air in 10 minutes," Nat said as he hung up the phone. "The new decoder is coming by taxi."

Nat leaned back in the console chair. "The funny thing is, the decoder was working right 99 percent of the time. A failure on the order of 1 percent—maybe a blown register or something—was enough to confound your operating system and as good as shut down the mainframe."

"Why would a register just burn out?" Clayton asked.

"Everyone assumes hardware is perfect," Nat said. "It *is* amazing in terms of its power and how tiny it is. But it isn't magic, and it still breaks."

"Or has flaws to begin with," David said.

A messenger placed a package with the decoder on the console. Nat unwrapped the circuit board with its chips already in place and walked to the CPU. He opened a panel, clicked off the power switch inside, and following a diagram in the book David held open, found the right board. Nat detached the old board, and set the new one in place.

"Okay Clayton," Nat said, closing the panel. "Fire 'er up!"

Clayton summoned a computer operator to sit at the console. "Bring up the real-time jobs first," Clayton said. "We can catch up on the batch runs later."

The operator nodded, and then made a number of entries at the console terminal. In a few moments the computer was up and running.

"So far so good," the operator said. "We've got forty users on line and the system hasn't croaked."

"Never underestimate the power of a CPU," Clayton said.

"That's for sure," Nat said. "Without it, where would we be?"

"In the Fren . . ." Clayton began.

"I know, I know," Nat said, packing up.

key terms

These are the key terms in alphabetical order. The numbers in parentheses refer to the page on which each term is defined.

Address (140)
Arithmetic/logic unit (ALU) (138)
ASCII (American Standard Code for
   Information Interchange) (147)
Binary-coded decimal (BCD) (147)
Binary (base 2) number system (146)
Bit (binary digit) (146)
Buffer (141)
Byte (147)
Central processing unit (CPU) (138)
Computer (138)
Computer word (149)
Control unit (138)
Decoder (140)
Destructive write (142)
EBCDIC (Extended Binary-Coded Decimal
   Interchange Code) (147)
Erasable programmable read-only memory
   (EPROM) (155)
Execution cycle (144)
Firmware (155)
Fixed-length word (149)
Input storage (141)
Instruction cycle (144)
K (155)
Logic gate (141)
Machine cycle (145)
Main memory or primary storage (138)
Math gate (141)
Microprocessor (150)
Nibble or nybble (147)
Nondestructive read (142)
Op code (operation code) (140)
Operand (140)
Output storage (141)
Parallel arithmetic (149)
Parity bit or check bit (148)
Programmable read-only memory (PROM)
   (155)
Program storage (141)
Random-access memory (RAM) (154)
Read-only memory (ROM) (155)
Register (142)
Serial arithmetic (149)
Silicon chips (150)
Variable-length word (149)
Working storage (141)

review questions

objective questions

True/false. *Put the letter T or F on the line next to the question.*

1. Assuming even parity, the parity bit for the 8-bit byte 11011010 is 1.   1 _____
2. The decoder is a key feature of the control unit of the CPU.   2 _____
3. Registers are high-speed temporary storage areas.   3 _____
4. Fixed-length-word computers are slower at mathematical computations than variable-length-word computers.   4 _____
5. Intermediate processing results are stored in the working storage area of main memory.   5 _____
6. The term computer means the same as CPU.   6 _____
7. Random-access chips are nonvolatile memory.   7 _____
8. Logical tests are performed in the control unit.   8 _____
9. Small minicomputers cost considerably more than large microcomputers.   9 _____
10. Modeling the stresses on the structure of a proposed aircraft would most likely be done on supercomputers.   10 _____

Multiple choice. *Put the letter of the correct answer on the line next to the question.*

1. The parts of the computer include the   1 _____
   (a) Input, arithmetic/logic, primary storage, and output units.
   (b) Control, arithmetic/logic, and output units.
   (c) Arithmetic/logic, control, and primary storage units.
   (d) Arithmetic/logic, control, and input units.
2. The number 676.4 is being moved from the accumulator register to primary storage for later use in the program. What part of main memory will it be stored in?   2 _____
   (a) Input storage.
   (b) Output storage.
   (c) Working storage.
   (d) Secondary storage.

review questions

3 _____
3. The op code
(a) Tells the decoder where to find whatever is to be operated on.
(b) Tells the decoder what instruction is to be carried out.
(c) Is located in working storage.
(d) Is an abbreviation for the term optional code.

4 _____
4. The operand
(a) Tells the decoder where to find whatever is to be operated on.
(b) Tells the decoder what instruction is to be carried out.
(c) Operates the logical gates.
(d) Is used to reset the sequence register back to the beginning of the program.

5 _____
5. Assuming even parity, which of these values has an error?
(a) 1 11011010
(b) 0 11010010
(c) 0 11001000
(d) 1 00000010

Fill in the blank. *Write the correct word or words in the blank to complete the sentence.*

1. The _____ unit is responsible for interpreting instructions.
2. The four parts of main memory are _____, _____, _____, and _____ storage.
3. A _____ chip cannot be altered by a programmer.
4. The _____ number system is the only kind understood by digital computers.
5. During the _____ cycle, the computer performs the specified operations.
6. The two parts of the CPU are the _____ and the _____ units.
7. Each location in memory has a unique _____.
8. A _____ serves as very fast temporary storage in the control and arithmetic/logic units.

9. The acronym EPROM stands for _____ _____ PROM.
10. The number of bits a computer can process at a single time is called a _____.

short answer questions

When answering these questions, think of concrete examples to illustrate your points.

1. What functions do the parts of the control unit perform?
2. Describe the differences between the instruction and execution cycle.
3. What is the function of a logic gate?
4. What are the differences between ROM and RAM chips?
5. Describe the functions minicomputers may perform in business environments.
6. What are the differences between ROMs, PROMs, and EPROMs?
7. What is cache storage?

essay questions

1. Compare and contrast the features of microcomputers, minicomputers, mainframes, and supercomputers.
2. Describe the two units of the CPU and how they interact with main memory.

Answers to the objective questions
True/false: 1. T; 2. T; 3. T; 4. F; 5. T; 6. F; 7. F; 8. F; 9. F; 10. T
Multiple choice: 1. c; 2. c; 3. b; 4. a; 5. c
Fill in the blank: 1. control; 2. program, input, working, output; 3. ROM; 4. binary; 5. execution; 6. control, arithmetic/logic; 7. address; 8. register; 9. erasable; 10. computer word

appendix: number systems

After studying this appendix you should understand the following:

- *How to write whole and fractional binary, hexadecimal, and octal numbers.*
- *How to convert between decimal, binary, hexadecimal, octal, and 4-bit binary-coded decimals (BCD).*
- *How to perform the fundamentals of binary arithmetic.*

Powers of 2: number systems and the computer

The number system we are all familiar with is the **DECIMAL (BASE 10) NUMBER SYSTEM**. The word *decimal* is derived from the Latin word for "ten" (*decem*). "Base" means the number of available numerals in the system. The decimal system has ten available numerals, consisting of 0 through 9. As you recognize that all the numbers we know can be made up of the numerals 0 through 9, then you have come partway to believing the same can be done using only the numerals 0 and 1.

As with all number systems, larger numbers can be represented by raising the base to different powers. Looking at powers of 10 shows how a number can be broken down into both real and fractional values. Under each power its decimal equivalent is written out.

$$10^3 \quad 10^2 \quad 10^1 \quad 10^0 \, \cdot \, 10^{-1} \quad 10^{-2} \quad 10^{-3}$$
$$1000 \quad 100 \quad 10 \quad 1 \, \cdot \, 0.1 \quad 0.01 \quad 0.001$$

Thus the decimal number 2409.325 is equal to $(2 \times 1000) + (4 \times 100) + (0 \times 10) + (9 \times 1) + (3 \times .1) + (2 \times .01) + (5 \times .001)$.

Figure 5-14 examines the decimal number 179 in detail. The value of each digit in the number is determined by its place value or position. In the top part of the figure we can look at the number 179 by its place values. The place values or powers of 10 can be multiplied by any number between 0 and 9, as shown in the bottom part of the figure. (In case you have forgotten: any number raised to the 0 power equals 1, thus 10^0 equals 1.)

Figure 5-14
Place values for the decimal number 179.

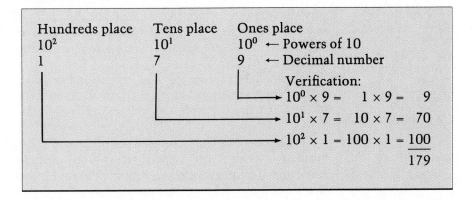

Figure 5-15
Comparing the first sixteen numbers in the decimal, binary, octal, and hexadecimal systems.

Decimal		Binary					Octal		Hexadecimal	
10^1	10^0	2^4	2^3	2^2	2^1	2^0	8^1	8^0	16^1	16^0
	0					0		0		0
	1					1		1		1
	2				1	0		2		2
	3				1	1		3		3
	4			1	0	0		4		4
	5			1	0	1		5		5
	6			1	1	0		6		6
	7			1	1	1		7		7
	8		1	0	0	0	1	0		8
	9		1	0	0	1	1	1		9
1	0		1	0	1	0	1	2		A
1	1		1	0	1	1	1	3		B
1	2		1	1	0	0	1	4		C
1	3		1	1	0	1	1	5		D
1	4		1	1	1	0	1	6		E
1	5		1	1	1	1	1	7		F
1	6	1	0	0	0	0	2	0	1	0

The binary number system

The *binary (base 2) number system* is central to digital computers. It utilizes only the numerals 1, corresponding to the "on" state of an electronic component, and 0, corresponding to the "off" state. A single *binary digit* (a 1 or 0) is known as a *bit*, a word derived from "*binary digit.*"

Here are some powers of 2 with the decimal equivalents displayed beneath each power.

$$2^5 \quad 2^4 \quad 2^3 \quad 2^2 \quad 2^1 \quad 2^0 \cdot 2^{-1} \quad 2^{-2} \quad 2^{-3}$$
$$32 \quad 16 \quad 8 \quad 4 \quad 2 \quad 1 \cdot 0.5 \quad 0.25 \quad 0.125$$

Thus the decimal equivalent for the binary number 110110.011 is $(1 \times 32) + (1 \times 16) + (0 \times 8) + (1 \times 4) + (1 \times 2) + (0 \times 1) + (0 \times 0.5) + (1 \times 0.25) + (1 \times 0.125)$ or 54.375.

Figure 5-15 compares the first sixteen numbers as represented in decimal, binary, octal, and hexadecimal. By the time we reach the decimal number 16, the equivalent binary number (10000) occupies 5 digits. You can see how bulky binary numbers become, and how octal and hexadecimal numbers reduce the space required for human-readable output of machine instructions or stored data. Hexadecimal compresses numbers the most (it is even tighter than the decimal system we are used to), but has a drawback—it includes letters as numbers. This reduces the readability, since we are not accustomed to reading letters mixed with our numbers.

Figure 5-16 represents the binary number 1001 in terms of its place values, showing why it is equal to the decimal number 9. Compare this result with the example using decimal number 179 shown in Figure 5-14.

Figure 5-17 relates the powers of 2 to the octal and hexadecimal number systems. Observe the patterns. For example, 2^{12}, 8^4, and 16^3 all equal the decimal value 4096. Since 8 and 16 are powers of 2, and require fewer symbols to represent a number than base 2, the octal and

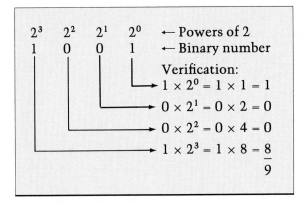

Figure 5-16
Place values for the binary number 9.

Binary	Octal	Hexadecimal
$2^0 = 1$	$8^0 = 1$	$16^0 = 1$
$2^1 = 2$		
$2^2 = 4$		
$2^3 = 8$	$8^1 = 8$	
$2^4 = 16$		$16^1 = 16$
$2^5 = 32$		
$2^6 = 64$	$8^2 = 64$	
$2^7 = 128$		
$2^8 = 256$		$16^2 = 256$
$2^9 = 512$	$8^3 = 512$	
$2^{10} = 1024$		
$2^{11} = 2048$		
$2^{12} = 4096$	$8^4 = 4096$	$16^3 = 4096$

Figure 5-17
Comparing place values of the powers of 2, 8 and 16. The equivalent decimal values are shown for each.

hexadecimal number systems are used to represent values stored inside a computer in less bulky form than binary.

It is possible to convert numbers from one number system to their equivalents in another. The binary equivalent for the decimal number 179 is shown in Figure 5-18. There are a number of ways to convert numbers from one base to another. In this figure we use a process that involves dividing the value written in one number system by the base of the second system—in this case 2. The remainder is placed in a column to the right of the original value. If there is no remainder, a 0 is placed in the column. Next the result of the division excluding the remainder is divided by the base 2. This process is continued until division is no longer possible. Reading the remainders from bottom to top gives us the original value written in base 2.

An alternative method is to refer to a table of values written in different number bases, as in Figure 5-17. Using a table is sometimes easier to follow. As shown in Figure 5-18, the largest value that is less than or equal to 179 is 2^7 or 128. This is the highest (leftmost) place, and we assign a 1 to it. Then we subtract 128 from 179 and get 51. Since the next place, 2^6 or 64, is greater than 51, the next place value is 0. We continue this process through the lower powers of 2 until there is no further remainder. To verify your answer, you can multiply the binary digit by the appropriate power of 2 and add up the results. You should end up with the same decimal number you started with.

To convert from binary to decimal is a simpler process. Just multiply each place value by the appropriate power of 2 (as you did to check your answer above). For example, the bottom of Figure 5-18 shows how binary 10111011010 converts into the decimal number 1498.

The octal number system

The **OCTAL (BASE 8) NUMBER SYSTEM** uses only the eight numerals 0 through 7. The term *octal* is derived from the Greek term for *eight* (*okto*). The octal number system is related to binary, as 8 is a power of 2 (2^3). Listed beneath each power of 8 is its decimal equivalent.

$$8^3 \quad 8^2 \quad 8^1 \quad 8^0 \quad . \quad 8^{-1} \quad 8^{-2} \quad 8^{-3}$$
$$512 \quad 64 \quad 8 \quad 1 \quad . \quad 0.125 \quad 0.016 \quad 0.002$$

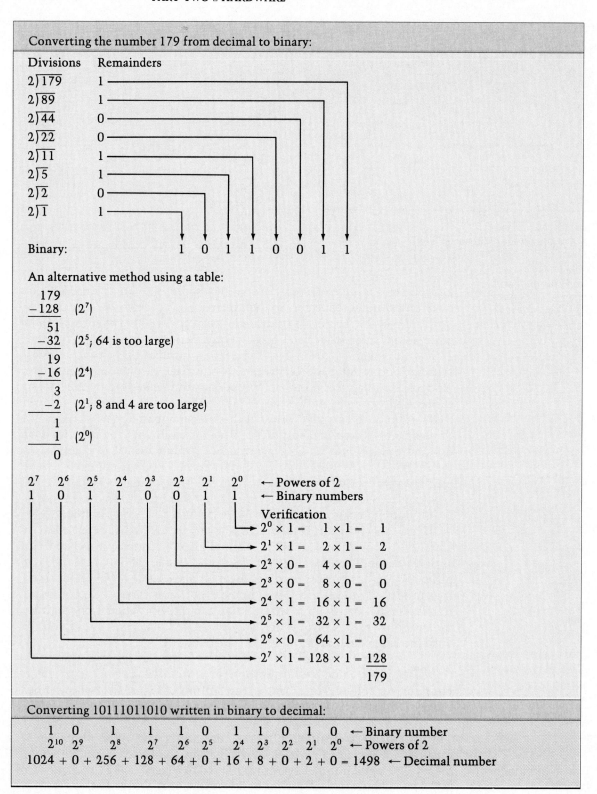

Converting the number 179 from decimal to binary:

Divisions	Remainders
2)179	1
2)89	1
2)44	0
2)22	0
2)11	1
2)5	1
2)2	0
2)1	1

Binary: 1   0   1   1   0   0   1   1

An alternative method using a table:

$$
\begin{array}{rl}
179 & \\
-128 & (2^7) \\
\hline
51 & \\
-32 & (2^5; \text{64 is too large}) \\
\hline
19 & \\
-16 & (2^4) \\
\hline
3 & \\
-2 & (2^1; \text{8 and 4 are too large}) \\
\hline
1 & \\
1 & (2^0) \\
\hline
0 & \\
\end{array}
$$

2^7	2^6	2^5	2^4	2^3	2^2	2^1	2^0	← Powers of 2
1	0	1	1	0	0	1	1	← Binary numbers

Verification

$2^0 \times 1 = \quad 1 \times 1 = \quad 1$
$2^1 \times 1 = \quad 2 \times 1 = \quad 2$
$2^2 \times 0 = \quad 4 \times 0 = \quad 0$
$2^3 \times 0 = \quad 8 \times 0 = \quad 0$
$2^4 \times 1 = \quad 16 \times 1 = \quad 16$
$2^5 \times 1 = \quad 32 \times 1 = \quad 32$
$2^6 \times 0 = \quad 64 \times 1 = \quad 0$
$2^7 \times 1 = 128 \times 1 = \underline{128}$
179

Converting 10111011010 written in binary to decimal:

1	0	1	1	1	0	1	1	0	1	0	← Binary number
2^{10}	2^9	2^8	2^7	2^6	2^5	2^4	2^3	2^2	2^1	2^0	← Powers of 2

$1024 + 0 + 256 + 128 + 64 + 0 + 16 + 8 + 0 + 2 + 0 = 1498$ ← Decimal number

Figure 5-18
Converting between binary and decimal.

Figure 5-19
Converting between octal and decimal.

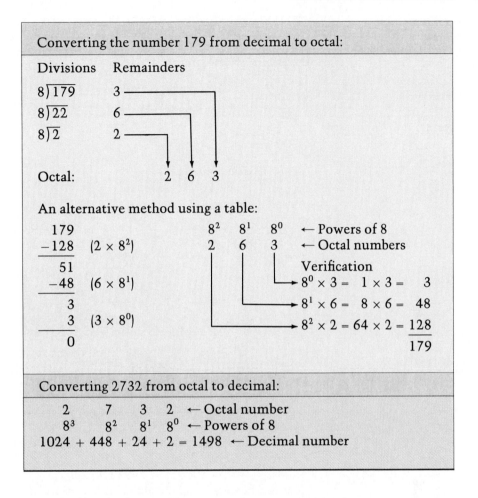

Converting the number 179 from decimal to octal:

Divisions   Remainders

$8\overline{)179}$ 3
$8\overline{)22}$ 6
$8\overline{)2}$ 2

Octal: 2   6   3

An alternative method using a table:

179   8^2 8^1 8^0 ← Powers of 8
−128 (2×8^2) 2   6   3   ← Octal numbers
 51   Verification
−48 (6×8^1) $8^0 \times 3 = 1 \times 3 = 3$
  3 $8^1 \times 6 = 8 \times 6 = 48$
  3   (3×8^0) $8^2 \times 2 = 64 \times 2 = 128$
  0   179

Converting 2732 from octal to decimal:

  2   7   3   2   ← Octal number
 8^3 8^2 8^1 8^0 ← Powers of 8
1024 + 448 + 24 + 2 = 1498   ← Decimal number

Thus the decimal equivalent of the octal number 4360.234 is (4×512) + (3×64) + (6×8) + (0×1) + $(2 \times .125)$ + $(3 \times .016)$ + $(4 \times .002)$ or 2288.306.

The procedures for conversion are essentially the same for octal as for the other number systems. As displayed in Figure 5-19, we can convert from decimal to octal as well as from octal to decimal.

The hexadecimal number system

The **HEXADECIMAL (BASE 16) NUMBER SYSTEM** requires sixteen numerals, 0 through 15. The term *hexadecimal* is derived by combining the Greek term for *six (hex)* with the Latin word for *ten (decem)*. Hexadecimal values are used to represent binary numbers in human-readable form (16 is equal to 2^4). Hexadecimal numbers reduce the space required for human-readable output of machine instructions or stored data.

The hexadecimal system challenges our creativity because our decimal system only ranges from 0 to 9 in a place column. The numbers 10 through 15 therefore need special symbols. For convenience, the alphabet letters A to F are used to represent these higher numerals. Listed beneath each power of 16 is its decimal equivalent.

16^3 16^2 16^1 16^0 · 16^{-1} 16^{-2} 16^{-3}
4096   256   16   1   ·   .0625   .0039   .0002

Figure 5-20
Converting between hex-adecimal and decimal.

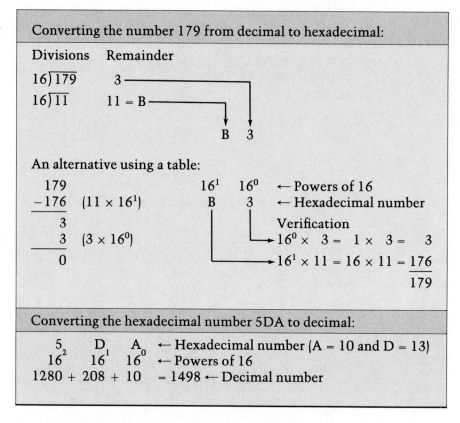

Converting the number 179 from decimal to hexadecimal:

Divisions   Remainder

$16\overline{)179}$ 3 ─────────────────┐

$16\overline{)11}$ 11 = B ───────┐   │

                                    B   3

An alternative using a table:

$$
\begin{array}{l}
179 \\
\underline{-176} \quad (11 \times 16^1) \\
\quad 3 \\
\underline{\quad 3} \quad (3 \times 16^0) \\
\quad 0
\end{array}
$$

16^1 16^0 ← Powers of 16

B   3   ← Hexadecimal number

Verification

$16^0 \times 3 = 1 \times 3 = 3$

$16^1 \times 11 = 16 \times 11 = \underline{176}$

179

Converting the hexadecimal number 5DA to decimal:

$$
\begin{array}{ccc}
5_2 & D_1 & A_0 \\
16^2 & 16^1 & 16^0 \\
1280 + & 208 + & 10
\end{array}
$$

← Hexadecimal number (A = 10 and D = 13)

← Powers of 16

= 1498 ← Decimal number

Thus the decimal equivalent for the hexadecimal number 3A7B.2C5 is $(3 \times 4096) + (10 \times 256) + (7 \times 16) + (11 \times 1) + (2 \times .0625) + (12 \times .0039) + (5 \times .0002)$ or 14971.1728.

A single hexadecimal number can represent four binary place values; therefore binary 1010 is A in hexadecimal. The decimal number equivalent is 10.

The conversion from decimal to base 16 is done in the same way as for binary (Figure 5-20, top). To convert from hexadecimal to decimal we simply multiply each place value by the appropriate power of 16 (Figure 5-20, bottom).

Binary-coded decimal (BCD) numbers

A bit is a single binary digit. A *byte* is a string of adjacent bits that the computer processes as a unit. The decimal numbers 0 to 9 can be coded in sets called *binary-coded decimal (BCD)*. Because the binary code in this case is 4 bits wide, it is labeled 4-bit BCD. We can convert the decimal number 179 into three adjacent 4-bit BCD numbers—0001 0111 1001—simply by finding the binary equivalent for each decimal digit. We can also easily move in the other direction, and convert from BCD into decimal. The four adjacent 4-bit BCD values 0001 0100 1001 1000 represent the decimal number 1498. BCD numbers are often used in processing business data—especially calculations involving money—because BCD can process fractional amounts like 0.1 where there is no exact binary equivalent. Processing is slower but avoids rounding errors which might create checks like $ 1.099999999999.

Binary arithmetic

In this section we will describe how to perform simple binary addition, multiplication, subtraction, and division.

Addition

The rules for binary arithmetic are the same as for any other number system, only the number of digits varies. The addition process works like this:

+	0	1
0	0	1
1	1	0 ← (Carry 1 to the next column)

or

$0 + 0 = 0$
$1 + 0 = 1$
$0 + 1 = 1$
$1 + 1 = 0 ←$ (Carry 1 to the next column)

Let's look at some examples.

```
          1        1111     111 ← (Carries)
  100     1001     10101    101
+  11    +  101   +11011    1011
 ----    ------   ------   +  110
  111     1110    110000    -----
                            10110
```

$(4+3=7)$, $(9+5=14)$, $(21+27=48)$, $(5+11+6=22)$ ← (Verification)

Notice how the carry operation works.

Multiplication

Multiplication is very simple using binary numbers. As shown in the multiplication table below only the result 1 occurs when 1 is multiplied by itself, otherwise the result is 0.

×	0	1
0	0	0
1	0	1

or

$0 × 0 = 0$
$1 × 0 = 0$
$0 × 1 = 0$
$1 × 1 = 1$

Unlike addition there is no carrying with binary multiplication (except for the partial products). The example below demonstrates binary multiplication.

```
  1111
    10
 ----
  0000 (Partial products)
 1111
 -----
 11110
```

Notice that multiplying by 0 gives a line of zeros. Multiplying by 1 simply repeats the line (with the digits moved left). Then the partial products are added together. Here are some more examples:

```
    101          110        10000          10101
 ×   10        × 11       ×    10        × 1011
  -------      -----      --------       -------
    000          110        00000          10101
    101          110        10000          10101      (Partial products)
  -------      -----      --------       00000
   1010        10010      100000          10101
                                        --------
                                        11100111
```

$(5 \times 2 = 10)$, $(6 \times 3 = 18)$, $(16 \times 2 = 32)$, $(21 \times 11 = 231)$ ← (Verification)

Since at each stage we are multiplying by either 0 or 1, the partial products are either all 0 or duplicates of the original number.

Subtraction

Subtraction is similar to decimal subtraction. The subtraction table shows the following:

−	0	1
0	0	1	← (Borrow 1 from the next column)
1	1	0	

or

$0 - 0 = 0$
$0 - 1 = 1$ ← (Borrow 1 from
$1 - 1 = 0$ the next column)
$1 - 0 = 1$

Here are some subtraction examples:

```
                 0                          0    ← (Change caused
    111         1011        1111         1101      by borrowing)
  −  11        − 110       −1010        −1011
  ------       -----       -----        -----
    100         101         101           10
```

$(7 - 3 = 4)$, $(11 - 6 = 5)$, $(15 - 10 = 5)$, $(13 - 11 = 2)$ ← (Verification)

Division

For division we perform standard operations as shown in the following examples:

```
        011                    111
   11) 1001            100) 11110
        00                    100
       ----                   ----
       100                    111
        11                    100
       ----                   ----
        11                    110
        11                    100
       ----                   ----
                               10  ← (Remainder)
```

$(9/3 = 3)$, $(30/4 = 7$ with 2 remainder$)$ ← (Verification)

Since each digit in the quotient can only be a 0 or a 1, binary division involves repeatedly subtracting the divisor until the final remainder is too small.

number systems exercises

1. Convert the following decimal numbers into binary, 4-bit BCD, octal, and hexadecimal.

   (a) 17   (c) 197
   (b) 56   (d) 1943

2. Convert the following 4-bit BCD numbers into decimal.

   (a) 1001 1000 0110
   (b) 1000 1001 0001
   (c) 0101 0100 0111
   (d) 0100 0001 0110 0110

3. Convert the following binary numbers into decimal, octal, and hexadecimal.

   (a) 1011   (c) 11011011
   (b) 1110110   (d) 11110101

4. Convert the following octal numbers into decimal, binary, and hexadecimal.

   (a) 51   (c) 714
   (b) 103   (d) 570

5. Convert the following hexadecimal numbers into decimal, binary, and octal.

   (a) F   (c) A5
   (b) 2B   (d) CBA

6. Perform addition upon these binary numbers.

   (a) 101 + 11
   (b) 1011 + 1010
   (c) 1010 + 1001 + 1000
   (d) 11011 + 1101 + 111 + 1000

7. Perform multiplication upon these binary numbers.

   (a) 11×11 (c) 1101×101
   (b) 10×101 (d) 10001×110

8. Perform subtraction upon these binary numbers.

   (a) 101 − 11   (c) 1001 − 1001
   (b) 1101 − 10   (d) 10011 − 1010

9. Perform division upon these binary numbers.

   (a) 100/10   (c) 10000/10
   (b) 1111/11   (d) 11110/110

These are the key terms in alphabetical order. The numbers in parentheses refer to the page on which each term is defined.

Decimal (base 10) number system (163)
Hexadecimal (base 16) number system (167)
Octal (base 8) number system (165)

Answers to number systems exercises

1. (a) 10001, 0001 0111, 21, 11; (b) 111000, 0101 0110, 70, 38; (c) 11000101, 0001 1001 0111, 305, C5; (d) 11110010111, 0001 1001 0100 0011, 3627, 797; 2. (a) 986; (b) 891; (c) 547; (d) 4166; 3. (a) 11, 13, B; (b) 118, 166, 76; (c) 219, 333, DB; (d) 245, 365, F5; 4. (a) 41, 101001, 29; (b) 67, 1000011, 43; (c) 460, 111001100, 1CC; (d) 376, 101111000, 178; 5. (a) 15, 1111, 17; (b) 43, 101011, 53; (c) 165, 10100101, 245; (d) 3258, 110010111010, 6272; 6. (a) 1000; (b) 10101; (c) 11011; (d) 110111; 7. (a) 1001; (b) 1010; (c) 100001; (d) 1100110; 8. (a) 10; (b) 1011; (c) 0; (d) 1001; 9. (a) 10; (b) 101; (c) 1000; (d) 101

Input and output devices: faster and friendlier

After studying this chapter you should understand the following:

- *Input and output concepts and trends.*
- *How terminals are used in information systems.*
- *The features of current display screens.*
- *Which types of input devices are used for source data automation.*
- *How impact and nonimpact printers differ, and various printing techniques.*
- *The role of voice, graphics, and microfilm for input and output.*

chapter 6

One Saturday's input and output

It was Saturday afternoon, and the Roberts family—Janis, George, and 9-year-old Meagan—drove off to run errands.

At a hardware store they picked up fertilizer, seeds, and a shovel. The clerk rang up the sale on a large register linked by cables to the store's computer. Janis paid with a credit card, which the clerk placed in a small machine next to the register. The machine read the magnetic strip on the back of the card and a few seconds later a message appeared on the register saying that the card was valid and that the credit limit had not been exceeded.

After stopping for sodas at a fast-food restaurant—where the cashier rang up the sale on a keyboard that had symbols for burgers, drinks, and fries—the Roberts family headed for the supermarket. While Meagan and George started pushing the cart down the aisle, Janis stopped at the deli department where she asked the clerk to slice some meats and cheeses. As each item was weighed, a printer hooked up to the scale printed a label complete with a bar-code pattern and a description of the purchase that Janis could read. The clerk attached the label to the package and handed it to her.

Janis caught up with her family at the dairy department, and they proceeded through the store to the checkout counter. The clerk passed the grocery items over a scanning device that read their bar-code labels. Janis paid for the purchase using her bank debit (ATM) card—much easier than writing a check.

Both Janis and George worked with computers at their jobs. George drove away from the supermarket thinking of the number of different computer input devices they'd seen on their shopping trip, and how clever such devices were becoming these days. Also, he realized that the family's cash supply was low.

He swung the car off in a new direction and headed for the bank. He inserted his debit card into the automated-teller machine and typed some codes. In return, the machine gave him his much-needed cash.

"Now it's time to head home before the ice cream melts," George said. He enjoyed gardening, and was looking forward to doing some this afternoon. After digging a little, he would press some seeds into the earth—which, he reflected, was not yet computerized.

Input and output devices: our contact with computers

In this chapter we will look at the machines that enable us to interact with the computer—the input devices that read our data, programs, and queries, and the output devices that provide us with the results of processing. Before we get to the actual devices, however, let's review general concepts and trends that apply to input/output ("input/output" or "I/O" means "input and output"). These concepts and trends apply regardless of the size of computer involved, whether micro, mini, mainframe, or supercomputer.

Input and output concepts

INPUT is the stage where data and instructions on how to process the data are brought into an information system. The most important requirement of the input stage is to capture accurate, timely, and useful data. The best processing and timely output cannot possibly overcome the effects of negligent input.

Data entry
DATA ENTRY refers to the process of getting the facts into a form that the computer can interpret. Data entry can be broken down into four steps:

1. Obtaining the source document with the data.
2. Preparing the source document for entry.
3. Entering the data from the document.
4. Verifying the data (checking that they were correctly entered).

A person can perform these steps one at a time. For example, you can obtain a sheet of data values (step 1), round off all the numbers to three decimal places (step 2), key in the numbers at a terminal (step 3), and check the numbers displayed on your terminal screen against the sheet of data values before transmitting the data (step 4).

Alternately, machines can do part of the job on their own. When the Roberts family went to the supermarket checkout, the bar-code reader did steps 3 and 4 by itself, with a little help from the computer to which it was hooked up.

Two major expenses incurred in running an information system are the labor and the material costs for the input process. To reduce these two expenses, there has been a push to design documents that can be read and checked by machine. Later in this chapter we will see plenty of devices that enter data on their own. Chapter 17 will discuss certain security problems involved with checking data by machines.

Types of output
Let's skip for a moment to the other end of the process. When a program has received its input and processed it into meaningful information,

output occurs. OUTPUT from an information system communicates the results of processing. There are three categories of output:

■ *Permanent, human-readable output.* The most common medium here is printed reports or forms. By "permanent" we do not mean that the output will outlast the Parthenon, simply that it will not disappear when you turn your display screen off.

■ *Temporary, human-readable output.* The most common medium here is the display screen.

■ *Permanent, machine-readable output.* This is output produced in a format that only machines can understand, and is meant to serve later as input to the same or another machine. The most common machine-readable media are magnetic disk and magnetic tape.

Our focus in this chapter will be on the first two kinds of output. The third, machine-readable output, will be covered in Chapter 7.

Medium and device
When looking at both output and input, we must distinguish between the medium and the device that works with it. Printed forms, visual displays, magnetic tape, magnetic disk, sound, and microfilm are various types of *media*. The corresponding *devices* are printers, display terminals, magnetic tape units, magnetic disk units, speech recognition and voice output devices, and microfilm units.

We use an *input device* to take the data contained on the medium and convey it to the computer's main storage. An *output device* can take information contained in main storage and convey it or record it on a medium. Some media (such as magnetic disk) are used for both input and output, and some devices (such as a magnetic disk unit) are used for accepting input and producing output.

Input, output, and the information system

The mix of input and output equipment an organization acquires must be considered and chosen in the context of the whole system. First to consider are the needs of the *people* using the system and how these needs translate into the *rules and procedures* by which they operate. If an organization needs *data* available quickly and accurately, it might consider using automated input methods. If time is not so important, data could be input from written forms by a person working at a terminal. A need for high-volume and attractive printed output calls for a sophisticated printer; a need for only a "quick and dirty" listing calls for a much simpler printer device. Within a single organization a variety of different input and output equipment may be required. Finally, appropriate *software* and *hardware* (computers and peripherals) must be obtained to permit the organization to use whatever input/output devices it selects.

Input and output trends

We have observed a number of trends in this book. In Chapter 4 we saw how computer hardware has become steadily smaller with each generation, and the computer steadily faster. Input/output also has its trends. One of these trends is toward source data automation. SOURCE DATA AUTOMATION refers to the use of machine-readable source documents

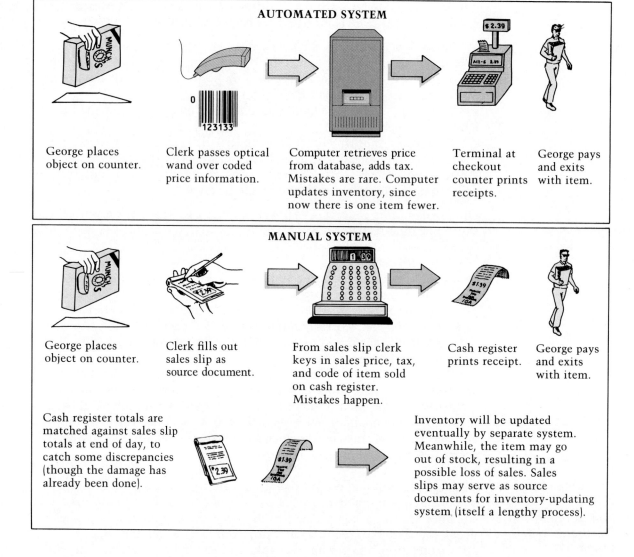

AUTOMATED SYSTEM

George places object on counter.

Clerk passes optical wand over coded price information.

Computer retrieves price from database, adds tax. Mistakes are rare. Computer updates inventory, since now there is one item fewer.

Terminal at checkout counter prints receipts.

George pays and exits with item.

MANUAL SYSTEM

George places object on counter.

Clerk fills out sales slip as source document.

From sales slip clerk keys in sales price, tax, and code of item sold on cash register. Mistakes happen.

Cash register prints receipt.

George pays and exits with item.

Cash register totals are matched against sales slip totals at end of day, to catch some discrepancies (though the damage has already been done).

Inventory will be updated eventually by separate system. Meanwhile, the item may go out of stock, resulting in a possible loss of sales. Sales slips may serve as source documents for inventory-updating system (itself a lengthy process).

Figure 6-1
Processing a store purchase on an automated and on a manual system.

for data entry which offers faster and more accurate input than manual data entry. Over the past decade, source data automation in real-time environments has developed at an explosive rate. It reduces the steps between acquiring data and entering them into the information system for processing. More timely data can enter the system, and more timely information can exit it. As for accuracy, although machines do make mistakes, enough checks are built into source-data-automation procedures to ensure that the process is less error-prone than manual data entry.

Another trend concerns output. Advances in output technology have increased the variety of output possibilities and made output easier to understand and use. Whether displayed on a screen, printed, or produced in some other medium, today's output can be presented various ways. Output which is "uncomputerlike" and geared to people's expec-

tations—a letter that looks like it rolled off a typewriter, for example—
is known as **USER-FRIENDLY OUTPUT**. Reports, for instance, can be produced on a printer that produces high, "letter-quality" output, or on a
printer geared to volume output that produces legible but lower-quality
output, or on a printer or plotter that creates professional-looking multicolor graphics.

Working with data to create information—known as input and output—has come a long way since the manual systems that were used
before computers arrived on the scene. At the start of the chapter, we
saw the Roberts family make a number of purchases. Figure 6-1 con-
trasts the way these purchases would have been handled with a manual
system with the faster, cheaper, and more thorough way a computerized
information system took care of them.

Terminals: the long arm of the computer

A **TERMINAL** is a computer input/output device that can send data to,
and receive information from, a computer through a telecommunications link.

Display terminals

DISPLAY TERMINALS consist of an input unit, a display screen, and a
screen control unit that links the two. Today the most common types of
terminals are the display terminal and a variant of the display terminal,
the point-of-activity terminal. There are several different types of input
units (Figure 6-2). These include the following:

■ **KEYBOARDS** are typewriterlike sets of keys used for entering numeric
and alphabetic data, and are the most common input unit on terminals.
■ **ELECTRONIC MICE** are palm-sized devices that can be moved across a
flat surface to move a pointer on a display screen. Some mice work by
detecting the motion of a ball mounted under the device. Others use
self-contained light beams to "read" points on a grid that represents the
display screen.
■ **GRAPHICS TABLETS** or **DIGITIZERS** are electrically wired surfaces upon
which a user can draw diagrams for entry as data.
■ **LIGHT PENS** are pencillike light-sensitive rods that can be pointed at a
display screen to perform functions indicated there or to draw diagrams.

Display terminals often use more than one of these input methods. A
user might enter data with a keyboard, and use an electronic mouse to
move a pointer quickly about the screen.

Terminal intelligence
A display terminal is classified as "intelligent" or "dumb" on the basis
of whether or not it can perform certain functions on its own. An **INTEL-
LIGENT TERMINAL**, or **SMART TERMINAL**, can do some processing on its

(a)

(b)

(c)

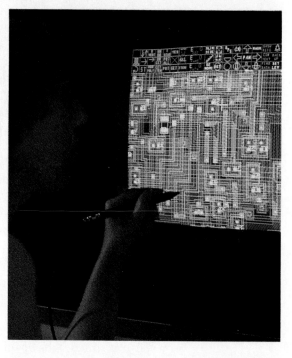
(d)

Figure 6-2
Four ways to enter data at a display terminal. Using a keyboard (a) and a mouse on a microcomputer (b). Using a digitizing tablet (c). Using a light pen (d).

own, such as perform preliminary editing and formatting of data being entered, without the help of the computer to which it is hooked up. Such terminals have a small microprocessor and a built-in memory, and can be programmed. The degree of "intelligence" varies, from a simple terminal with a few keys that can be programmed to do certain jobs, to a complex terminal with its own operating system and a great deal of internal storage.

There is a big difference between a microcomputer and a display terminal. Like any other computer, a microcomputer system consists of a central processing unit, has primary memory, one or more input devices, one or more output devices, and cables to hook all the parts together. A microcomputer sometimes functions as an intelligent terminal when it is linked in a network to a larger computer.

There is no ambiguity surrounding the definition of DUMB TERMI-NALS. These have no information-processing capabilities, but rather passively channel data to a computer. Any editing and formatting of data cannot be handled by the terminal, but must be performed by the computer receiving the data, although the editing operations appear on the display screen.

Screen technologies

Various technologies are currently used for display screens (Figure 6-3). Three common types are:

■ *Cathode-ray tubes (CRTs)*, which are like television picture tubes.
■ *Light-emitting diodes (LEDs)*, which produce green or red letters of the type found in many calculators and clocks.
■ *Liquid crystal displays (LCDs)*, which produce a dark gray display against a light background, also seen in calculators and watches.

Cathode-ray tubes are still the most common type of screen. They are used with both microcomputers and display terminals. CRT screens tend to be bulky. LED and LCD screens, in contrast, are very thin, making them ideal for lightweight portable microcomputers.

Display screens presently available have a wide range of color and graphics display capabilities. Two factors to consider are resolution and sharpness.

Resolution is determined by the number of pixels that can be displayed in a given area. A PIXEL (short for PICTURE ELEMENT) is the smallest element of a display screen assigned color and intensity. A monitor capable of displaying a matrix 640 by 480 pixels will have 307,200 picture elements. The highest resolution systems provide several million pixels.

Sharpness means how blurry or clear the pixel is. Monochrome screens provide sharper images because only one electron gun is used to project the image. Color monitors have three guns (one for each primary color) that do not line up perfectly—leading to a more blurry image. These color monitors range from only slightly better than a television set for a low-priced terminal, to extremely clear definition for sophisticated graphics terminals.

Figure 6-3
Display screens. (a) A cathode-ray tube (CRT). (b) A portable microcomputer with a liquid crystal display (LCD) screen.

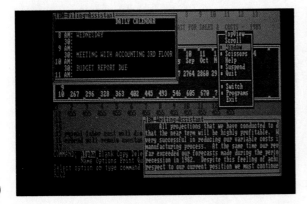

(a)

(b)

CRT screens fall into a number of general categories:

- *Monochrome screen monitors* display text and images in a single color such as green or yellow against a background color that is supposedly easy on the eyes (such as black or dark green).
- *CGA (color graphics adapter) monitors* use the same technology as most television sets and offer four colors (not including various hues) and the lowest resolution.
- *RGB (red-green-blue) monitors* are the original standard for IBM-PCs, offering sixteen colors and somewhat better resolution than CGAs, while using CGA technology.
- *EGA (enhanced graphics adapter) monitors* offer sixteen colors and better resolution than RGB monitors.
- *VGA (video graphics array) monitors* offer a choice of up to 256 colors and have still higher resolution.
- *CAD (computer-aided design) monitors* offer from 16 to 256 colors and the highest resolution.

The CURSOR is a movable, sometimes blinking symbol on a display screen that shows you where you are. Generally it indicates where the next character typed at the keyboard will be displayed.

A WINDOW is a part of the screen that displays instructions and data. Displays can be created that are much bigger than the screen volume (what the screen can hold); users can then examine these displays one screen (window) at a time. Electronic spreadsheets, discussed in Chapter 10, are often so large that they must be viewed a window at a time. Some programs split a screen up into parts, each of which can display a window, so that several windows can be seen at once (though each will be small) (see Figure 6-4). Windows can be overlapped, displaying just a portion of each, much as you might arrange papers on your desk. As you move from task to another you would expand the window of interest, allowing the previous window to recede into the background.

The process of SCROLLING is similar to using windows where the instructions and data shown on the screen are moved forward or backward or from right to left. If you are editing text with a word processing program, but want to view something edited earlier, activating the pro-

Figure 6-4
Windows allow you to see portions of several documents on the screen at the same time.

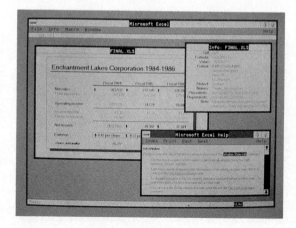

gram's scrolling feature can move the lines displayed backward until you reach the point you want. By scrolling forward—moving ahead—you can look in the opposite direction.

ICONS are pictorial representations of operations the computer can carry out. Displayed on a screen—usually at the margins—icons can be pointed to by the cursor. When a user selects an icon, the program then carries out the function shown. The icons in a word processing program for moving text from one place to another, for example, might be a scissors and a glue brush.

Display screens can do a lot of other things. They can be programmed to reverse the colors of the text and background for designated words or portions of the display, for emphasis; or they can flash part of the display on and off for the same purpose. In addition, many display terminals include a small, yet impressive, repertoire of sound output possibilities that can also be programmed as attention-getters.

Keyboards

Like display screens, today's keyboards come in different types. Typewriter-style keys are found on most high-quality display terminals where heavy usage is expected (Figure 6-5). These keys are sturdy individual boxes, like those found on electronic typewriters, and will take a lot of pounding.

Keyboards not only differ in type but in layout as well. In the past few years, IBM-style keyboards have changed from the PC-standard (Figure 6-5a) to the more current enhanced-AT (Figure 6-5b). All vary the location of their function keys, and the size and shape of calculator keypads and cursor control keys. Even the QWERTY key layout of typewriters (named to reflect the first six letters on the top row) has been rearranged. Let's take a brief look at the logic of this development.

Originally, the QWERTY design was developed by Christopher L. Sholes for use with the mechanical typewriters of the mid-1870s. Its purpose was to slow down the typist's fingers so that there were less jammed keys. The most common letters in the English language (notably A and S) were strategically placed under the slowest fingers humans have. More efficient designs that emerged later on, such as the one developed by August Dvorak in the 1930s, were ignored due to the overwhelming problems of retraining and redesign of equipment.

With the nonmechanical nature of modern keyboards, however, it became a simple matter to reprogram the input from the keyboard in any manner desired through switchable keyboards or simple software. Without buying anything new, businesses could share the same equipment among those typists trained on QWERTY layouts and those who were not. In the mid-1980s, the American National Standards Institute (ANSI) named the Dvorak keyboard as a second standard layout to QWERTY. It may well be that the Dvorak keyboard will become more popular and be used more widely in the 1990s (see Figures 6-5c and 6-5d for comparison).

Calculator-style keys are smaller and lack the same solid feeling (Figure 6-6a). These are found on simpler terminals, and are often used for entering numeric data rather than text. *Diaphragm-style "keys"* are

182

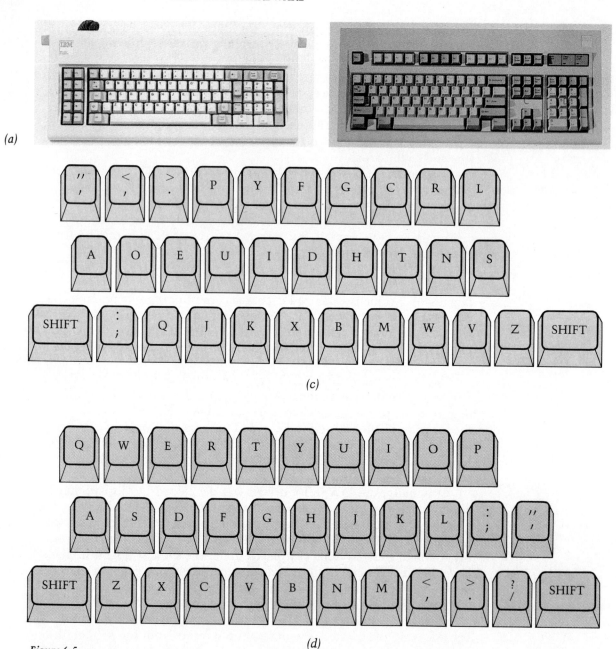

Figure 6-5
Typewriter-style keyboards. (a) A PC-style keyboard. (b) An enhanced AT-style keyboard. (c) A Dvorak keyboard (showing the locations of the alphabetic characters). (d) A QWERTY-style keyboard (showing the locations of the alphabetic characters).

areas on a flat plastic membrane that are treated electronically as keys, and do not stick up (Figure 6-6b). This type of keyboard is often used in environments where the keyboard may get wet or dirty, such as outdoors or in fast-food restaurants.

Of mice and pens

As we saw earlier, keyboards are not the only possible input device. An electronic mouse can be moved to shift the position of the cursor on the display screen quickly. The mouse's relative motion is converted into

(a)

(b)

Figure 6-6
Nontypewriter-style keyboards. (a) A calculator-style keyboard. (b) A diaphragm-style keyboard.

electronic signals, transmitted to the screen control unit, and then displayed on the screen.

Light pens can read a small portion of the display screen at a time. The data are conveyed to the computer, which can then identify the exact position on the screen being read. Pointing the light pen at an icon, for instance, can cause the program to carry out the function for which the icon stands. With a graphics package, pointing the light pen to a portion of an image can cause the computer to rotate the image so that a part of interest faces the viewer directly. On some systems diagrams can be drawn by moving the light pen across the screen.

Still other display screens have a grid of infrared beams that is broken when the screen is touched. The point in the grid where the break occurs indicates what the computer should do (see Figure 6-7).

Figure 6-7
Using a touch screen. The user can call up a function simply by touching the appropriate box and interrupting the light beams.

*Point-of-activity
terminals*

Years ago, data entry was routinely done at locations far removed from where the actual activity occurred. For example, data generated by credit card sales would be collected for entry and batch processing at a centralized computer center.

Today, input units are often located at the point where a specific activity occurs, to capture data at their source. We call these machines POINT-OF-ACTIVITY (POA) TERMINALS. Figure 6-8 shows sample applications.

The most common type of POA terminal is a POINT-OF-SALE (POS) TERMINAL that combines a cash register with a computer terminal linked to an information system. These units may receive their input via a keyboard or from a scanning device. (Scanning devices will be discussed later in the chapter.) POS terminals see frequent use in department stores, supermarkets, and fast-food restaurants.

Figure 6-8
Point-of-activity (POA) terminals. (a) Maintenance—a service engineer transfers data from computer. (b) Banking—tellers entering transaction data directly into the computer. (c) Warehousing—keeping track of inventory.

(a)

(b)

(c)

Point-of-activity terminals, in effect, go to the data in order to gather data in a timely and efficient manner and cut costs. The productivity of people using POA terminals can be boosted still further by source data automation.

Using the telephone as a terminal

In Chapter 2 we discussed how your computer can be directly hooked up to a telephone line through the use of a modem. For some applications, clients and users of information systems can communicate with a computer (through its attached modem) at the other end of a telephone line simply by using the tone-keying signals generated by pushing the buttons of a *push-button dialing telephone* (such as AT&T's Touch-Tone or GTE's Touch-Call telephones). One steadily growing business application is in the area of *telemarketing*. You may have received a telemarketing sales call where a prerecorded message urges you stay on the line and respond to a request for service by pressing certain buttons on the telephone. Similar systems allow users of advanced telephone systems to collect phone messages stored in an electronic mailbox.

Source data automation

With source data automation the input medium and the source document are one and the same. There is no need to convert source documents into machine-readable form, because they are already machine-readable. This reduces the amount of manual labor involved in entering data. With fewer steps there are fewer opportunities for error, and the data can be input more quickly.

In this section we will first look at the use of scanners for source data automation. Scanners read data directly from source documents and accumulate data far faster than the speediest typist could manage. In some instances, as we will see, data could not be gathered at all without scanners. In addition, we will show how human speech can be used for source data automation.

Optical scanners

OPTICAL SCANNERS use visible light to read characters, numbers, or patterns. The types we will discuss are optical mark readers, optical character readers, document readers, graphics and desktop scanners, and barcode readers.

An OPTICAL MARK READER (OMR) senses marks on special paper forms. The scanner converts the marks into binary code, and the results are transferred to tape or disk for further processing (see Figure 6-9). There is no need for a data-entry operator to key in data. You may have taken tests using optical scanning forms. Your answers were compared against an answer key form prepared by the instructor or testing service. Some systems require the use of special marking pencils. The U.S. Bureau of the Census, market research companies, and testing agencies make extensive use of optical mark readers.

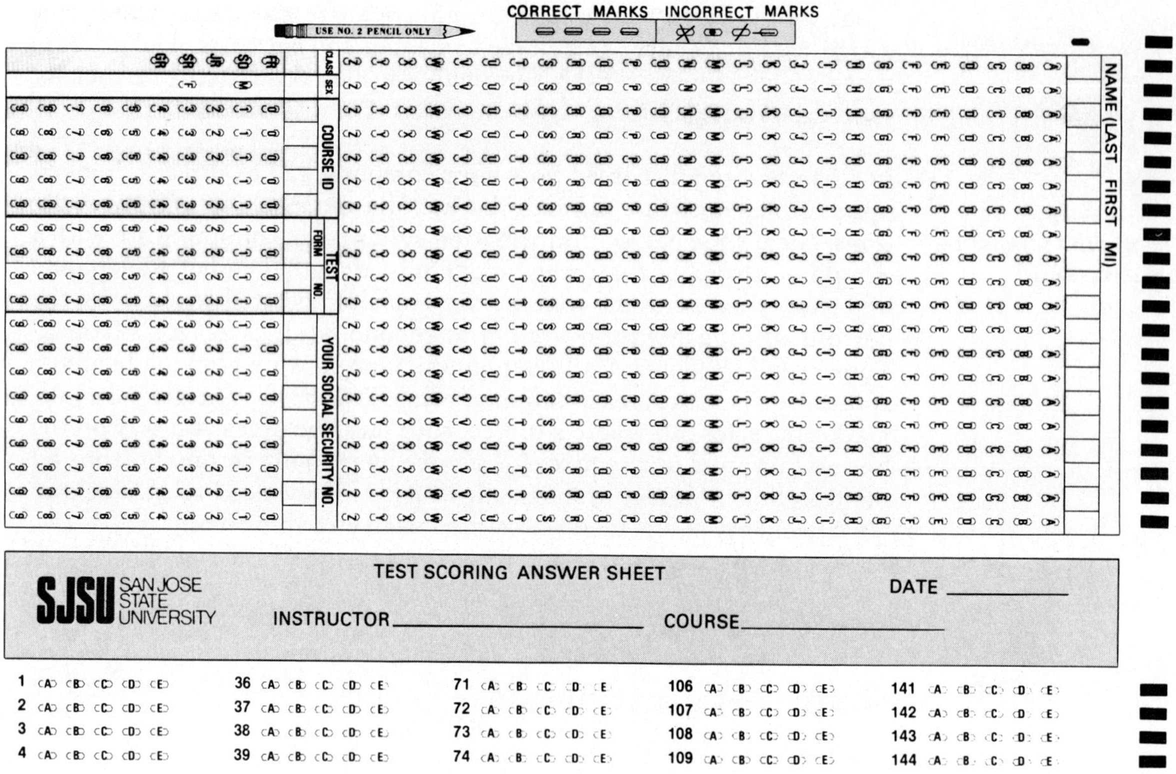

Figure 6-9
An optical mark reader senses special marks on forms like this test answer form.

Another type of scanner, the **OPTICAL CHARACTER READER (OCR)**, can detect printed letters and numbers as well as marks. Figure 6-10 shows an optical character reader and a form that it can read. Characters must be carefully printed to ensure accurate recording of the data. Some OCRs can recognize a variety of fonts (typefaces), while others can only recognize special fonts. OCRs are available to read paper rolls such as cash register tapes, documents smaller than page size, and full-page documents. Applications include mail-order catalog forms, accounting forms, tax forms, and billing by utilities.

DOCUMENT READERS are optical scanners that can read all forms of printed matter—text, diagrams, and pictures. The data captured can be immediately stored, displayed on a screen, or read aloud over a speech synthesizer. These machines assist in automating the input of typed documents in office automation systems. Disabled individuals—particularly the visually impaired—can obtain greater access to the information required to carry out their jobs or schoolwork. Scanners digitize text material by "reading" the pattern of each typed character into the computer, where it is identified and stored in a standard form that can be used for immediate processing, or saved on a disk file to be read later by a word processing program. In this way, text produced on a regular typewriter can actually be input into a computer without the need for retyping. Some scanners are able to identify handwriting patterns as well, pointing to the time when handwritten notes will serve as direct computer input.

Figure 6-10
(a) An optical character reader (OCR). (b) An insurance bill printed with an optical character font.

(a)

EVENTUAL COMPANY   **Premium Payment Coupon**

Policy	Insured	Date Due
CHAM 74 382 364	KEVIN J MORRIS	JAN 23 89
043		Monthly Premium
		$57·69

Please make check or other order for payment payable to
EVENTUAL. It will be accepted only subject to collection.

Mail with coupon with your remittance to:

EVENTUAL INSURANCE COMPANY
P.O. BOX 1677
CHICAGO, IL 60255

If you pay in person, please present your record book.

0 763873622 20000 29650 120 284000086   18

/06 73863 54000 1 298 510 78 500 114

(b)

Numbers printed
in an OCR typeface

GRAPHICS SCANNERS were created specifically to digitize art and other graphic patterns. Digitizing is a process that converts brightness patterns of the art into a corresponding numerical pattern. This pattern can then be stored on disk and later merged into desktop publishing documents. Digitizing uses a light-sensitive device to measure the reflection of light in each tiny portion, or *sampling cell*, of an image. It then creates a number quantifying its level of "brightness." In graphics scanners, up to 256 gray scale values are used to indicate anything from "totally black" (a value of 0) to "totally white" (a

Figure 6-11
Reading documents and graphics. (a) A movable scanner. (b) A desktop scanner.

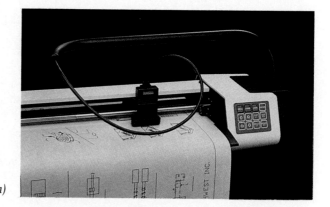

(a)

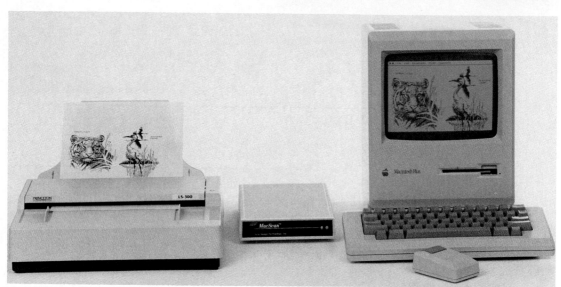

(b)

value somewhere between 0 and 255 depending on the number of gray tones). The overall resolution of the digitized image depends on the number of sampling cells and the number of different tones being scanned.

Inexpensive *movable scanners* use a light-sensitive input device that is attached to the printing head of a dot-matrix printer as in Figure 6-11a. In a clever role reversal, the printer is used for input instead of its normal output function. To scan a drawing, place it in your printer (as you would a blank piece of paper) and activate the program. The scanner moves across each line (with the printing head), measuring the light and dark patterns on the paper. The drawing moves up line by line until the entire image has been digitized into the computer. Movable scanners are slow, and the resolution they produce is not of the highest quality. Still, their low cost and simple operation provide an inexpensive add-on that greatly expands the graphics capabilities of information systems.

DESKTOP SCANNERS resemble small copying machines, and can produce much higher-quality images than the movable type. Because of their increased resolution, they are more useful with computer systems that employ lasers for final print (Figure 6-11b). The most sophisticated

Figure 6-12
A facsimile (FAX)
machine acts as a long-
distance copier.

optical input devices, called *flatbed scanners*, can scan an entire page at once, often achieving resolutions in excess of 2000 dpi (dots per inch). These machines find application in more graphics-oriented businesses such as advertising and engineering.

Scanners have also seen remarkable growth in business offices as FAX machines (Figure 6-12). **FAX**, short for **FACSIMILE TRANSMISSION MACHINES**, allow text or art to be electronically sent from one location to another. They are, in effect, long-distance photocopiers. One FAX machine scans the document page, converting its contents into electrical signals. These signals are sent over phone lines to another FAX machine that reconstructs the page and prints out a copy. Photographs, contracts, designs, and sketches are among the documents that are being "faxed" around the country.

A **BAR-CODE READER**, shown in Figure 6-13, is a scanner that reads data coded as lines (bars) of varying width. Initially introduced into high-volume supermarkets, their use has spread to smaller and more specialized stores. Almost all boxed, canned, or prepackaged goods bear a **UNIVERSAL PRODUCT CODE (UPC)** on the label. A low-intensity laser reads the coded data and sends it to the POS terminal, where the code is checked for accuracy. Then, the code is transmitted to the store's main computer, where the price and product data for each code are kept in the database. The main computer retransmits the product information to the checkout counter for preparing the sales slip. We will see in the example at the end of the chapter that products unique to a store can be tagged with UPC-like labels. Hand-held bar-code readers can also help stores keep track of shelf and stockroom inventory.

Bar-code technology has spread to virtually every industry. Applications include labeling shipping documents; marking airline travelers' luggage to sort them for loading onto the proper airplanes; tagging manufacturing assembly kits, subcomponents, or finished goods; and identifying library books.

Magnetic scanners

In a process known as **MAGNETIC-INK CHARACTER RECOGNITION (MICR)**, letters, numbers, and symbols written using an iron-oxide ink can be read magnetically (Figure 6-14). This type of input occupies an important niche in the business environment—the processing of checks through the banking system. The stylized numbers at the bottom of checks are magnetic ink characters.

MAGNETIC STRIP READERS are devices that read the data encoded on the backs of credit and bank debit cards (Figure 6-15). A range of retail outlets use this technology to check on the credit status of customers, or to electronically transfer funds from customers' bank accounts to the retailer's.

Three-dimensional scanners

A **THREE-DIMENSIONAL SCANNER** can look at objects in terms of their width, length, and depth. These scanners react to electromagnetic wavelengths and patterns ranging from x rays, through the visible light range, up to infrared and beyond. Applications include creating three-dimensional maps of underground geologic deposits, satellite mapping of large-scale climatic patterns (Figure 6-16), and the diagnosis of diseases.

The use of scanners in medicine has aided in the diagnosis of diseases that are difficult to spot visibly. Scanners have the enormous advantage of providing detailed data without physically intruding into the human body. The first machines in this field used a scanning technique known as *computerized axial tomography (CAT)* where x rays enter the body from three different directions, and are selectively absorbed as they pass through bones and tissues. The computer sorts out these absorption patterns using triangulation techniques to create a picture of a thin "slice" of the body.

A newer device uses the same general approach but detects the vibrations emitted by atomic nuclei rather than x rays. Scanners employ this technology, called *magnetic resonance imaging (MRI)*, to detect and analyze cancer growth rates (Figure 6-17).

Figure 6-13
Using bar-code readers.
(a) A low-intensity laser reads the bar-code patterns. The 12-digit bar code has 11 human-readable digits plus a check digit. (b) The checkout counter's microprocessor will display the item purchased on a small screen and print out a detailed receipt (c).

(a)

(b)

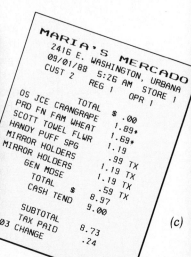

(c)

Figure 6-14
An MICR reader. MICR machines write, read, and sort checks throughout the banking system. The machine shown here can read both MICR and OCR codes and operate alone or in conjunction with a host computer. The check has four fields displaying data concerning the bank and federal reserve district, the payor's account number, the check number, and the amount of the check.

(a)

(b)

Identifies the bank
or savings and loan
the check is drawn on
(transit or FRABA field)

Account number
and transaction
code
(on us field)

Check
number

Amount of check
(amount field)

Figure 6-15
Magnetic strip readers are used to read the encoded data on the backs of credit and bank debit cards.

Figure 6-16
Three-dimensional scanners are used to gather data for many applications. This computer-enhanced image—which shows temperature levels within a hurricane—was derived from satellite data.

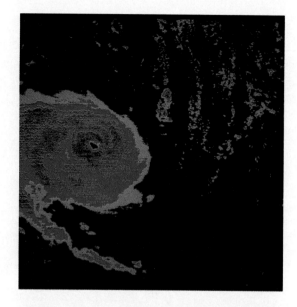

Figure 6-17
Computerized magnetic resonance imaging (MRI) scanners are used to view the inside of the body for diagnosis of disease.

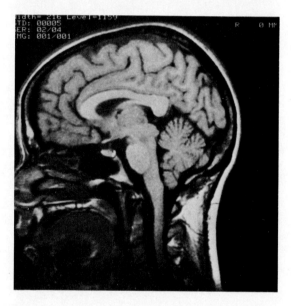

Speech recognition systems

Computers that listen when we talk, and that talk back, are not reserved for science fiction but have really arrived—though they do not yet have the versatility of the HAL-9000 machine shown in the movies *2001* and *2010*. Computers listening when we talk (Figure 6-18) is known as *speech recognition* (and also as "voice input" or "speech input"). A SPEECH RECOGNITION DEVICE can translate the human voice into signals for use as input media.

Voice-dependent speech recognition systems work with a particular speaker or speakers, who have to prepare the system for use by speaking into it so that it can record their voices to match input against. Once this is done, voice-dependent systems can have quite large vocabularies, up

Figure 6-18
Speech recognition sys-
tems—no-hands com-
puting.

to thousands of words and numbers. In effect, the input device takes dictation and feeds it to the computer.

Voice-independent systems are intended to work with any speaker. These systems require much more software for analysis of sounds and the vocabulary is usually far more limited than those of voice-dependent systems. Such systems tend to be used for production or warehouse activities where hands are not readily available for keyboard input. By following a small vocabulary, users can input commands to the computer to direct machinery, electric wheelchairs, robots, and elevators. Credit card approval systems also use speech recognition devices to accept and translate for the computer a credit card number, amount of purchase, and merchant's identification number, spoken through the telephone.

Speech recognition systems free the hands and have a futuristic quality about them. However, they are prone to errors (many detect possible error situations themselves and request further information), expensive, and the most limited type of input device in terms of the range of data they will accept. One area in which they already perform an invaluable service is in accepting data input from the blind and visually impaired, and from people whose physical handicaps prevent them from using a keyboard.

Toward friendlier output

The display terminals studied earlier in the chapter as input devices are also output devices. Information systems often rely on data output to terminal screens for quick answers to queries.

In many cases, however, people need to be able to retain output in order to use the information that it contains to make effective decisions. Printed computer output has always served this purpose.

Output destined for users or managers used to mean bulky printouts of oversized paper full of blurry, all-caps letters and equally blurry numbers. Many ended up in the trash bin, which, given the quality, did not seem inappropriate.

Today, the quality of print on the paper is better (it need not be all caps), paper comes in different sizes and colors, and color graphics can be mixed with text or produced separately. There is a wider variety of typestyles—called type fonts—on many modern printers. The general trend in output devices is to make output more attractive, less "computerlike" in appearance (or sound), and—as always—faster and cheaper whenever possible.

Impact printers

IMPACT PRINTERS have printing mechanisms that physically contact the paper. Impact printers can be categorized by print quality and printer speed. Print quality can be either *letter quality*, which means that the output looks good enough to have been typed, or *draft quality*, which means that the output looks as though it were produced by a computer printer.

Printer speeds vary as well, from comparatively slow **CHARACTER PRINTERS** which print only one character at a time, to more rapid **LINE PRINTERS** which print an entire line at once. Most character printers can print in either direction across the page (bi-directionally), which speeds their operation. Multiple copies of output can easily be created with impact printers, by printing on multi-ply paper.

Character printers

The most common type of character printers, **DOT-MATRIX PRINTERS**, have printing elements consisting of a series of tiny pins arranged in a cluster. To print a particular character—say the letter "G"—a hammer mechanism in the printer strikes that pattern of pins that will form the letter. The pins in turn strike a ribbon which prints the pattern of dots on the page. Figure 6-19 shows a dot-matrix printer and illustrates how it forms characters. Dot-matrix printers offer considerable flexibility. Pin patterns for letters can be altered to change their sizes and styles. These printers can produce graphs and other "artistic" output. (See Chapter 12: Desktop Publishing and Graphics.)

The quality of a dot-matrix printer depends on the density of the pins in the cluster. In general, the more pins, the higher the print quality and the more expensive the printer. Better dot-matrix printers have up to twenty-four pins capable of producing "near-letter-quality" or "nlq" output. Most dot-matrix printers have the option of striking the same location more than once to darken the character, or to slightly offset the pins to make the output look more complete, though this slows the printing process.

DAISY-WHEEL PRINTERS are character printers that produce typewritten letter-quality output. Figure 6-20 shows a daisy-wheel printer and its print element. The print element is called a daisy wheel because its

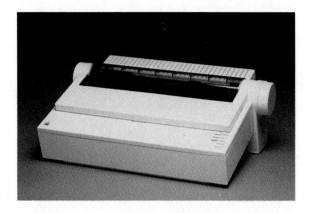

(a)

Figure 6-19
(a) A dot-matrix printer.
(b) A diagram of a dot-matrix printing mechanism. Characters are formed when selected pins are hammered against a ribbon. (c) Sample output.

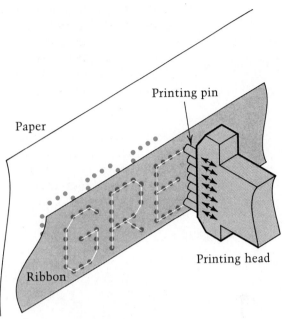

(b)

DRAFT 10 CPI	CORRESPONDENCE 10 CPI	LETTER QUALITY 10 CPI
DOUBLE STRIKE	DOUBLE STRIKE	DOUBLE STRIKE
EMPHASIZED	EMPHASIZED	EMPHASIZED
DOUBLE STRIKE & EMPH.	DOUBLE STRIKE & EMPH.	DOUBLE STRIKE & EMPH.
EXPANDED	EXPANDED	EXPANDED
DRAFT 12 CPI	CORRESPONDENCE 12 CPI	LETTER QUALITY 12 CPI
DOUBLE STRIKE	DOUBLE STRIKE	DOUBLE STRIKE
EMPHASIZED	EMPHASIZED	EMPHASIZED
DOUBLE-STRIKE & EMPHASIZED	DOUBLE-STRIKE & EMPHASIZED	DOUBLE-STRIKE & EMPHASIZED
EXPANDED	EXPANDED	EXPANDED
DRAFT 17.1 CPI	CORRESPONDENCE 17.1 CPI	LETTER QUALITY 17.1 CPI
DOUBLE STRIKE	DOUBLE STRIKE	DOUBLE STRIKE
EMPHASIZED	EMPHASIZED	EMPHASIZED
DOUBLE STRIKE & EMPHASIZED	DOUBLE STRIKE & EMPHASIZED	DOUBLE STRIKE & EMPH.
EXPANDED	EXPANDED	EXPANDED

(c)

spokes with the letters at the end resemble a daisy's petals. To print, a daisy wheel spins until the appropriate fully formed character is in position. A hammer then strikes the character against a ribbon, leaving an impression on the paper. It is easy to change the daisy wheel, thus changing the printer's typestyle. Daisy wheels are also widely used in electronic typewriters. Daisy-wheel printers are usually slower than dot-matrix printers.

(a)

(b)

Figure 6-20
(a) A daisy-wheel printer.
(b) A daisy-wheel print element.

Figure 6-21
Line printers like these use a row of dot-matrix pins to produce output across the page.

Line printers

The great advantage of line printers over character printers is that they produce a whole line of print at once. This makes them much faster than character printers. Some of the newer line printers use dot-matrix pins set along the width of the printer. Figure 6-21 shows an example of a line printer and its internal mechanism. Line printers can print up to about 3000 lines per minute. This is a maximum speed, attained for long print jobs. In practice, printers often work for short bursts of a few seconds, pause, and then go on to the next job.

Nonimpact printers

NONIMPACT PRINTERS are so called because their printing mechanism does not touch the paper. Nonimpact character printers include both inexpensive thermal printers and extremely versatile ink-jet printers which are illustrated in Figure 6-22.

Figure 6-22
Ink-jet printers provide
great versatility, includ-
ing the ability to create
color output.

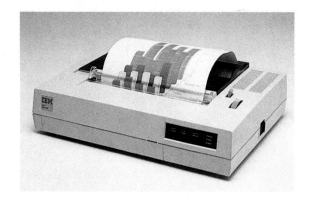

THERMAL PRINTERS are used to provide "quick and dirty" output. One type of thermal printer uses heated dot-matrix pins to "burn" the dots onto specially coated heat-sensitive paper. They are very popular among scientists and engineers for recording intermediate results where the quality of the output is not important.

INK-JET PRINTERS use electrically charged ink droplets to form "near-letter-quality" images on the paper. The droplets are sprayed between two electrically charged deflection plates. As the ink droplets pass between, they are deflected to form the appropriate characters. The font or typestyle of the ink-jet printer can be changed electronically, and some models can print simultaneously with different colored inks, and can produce graphical output. These printers are usually attached to personal computers in office settings.

HIGH-SPEED PAGE PRINTERS (Figure 6-23), primarily using laser-xerographic technology, produce an entire output page at one time. High-speed printers can produce over 45,000 lines of output per minute. They can print on both sides of a sheet, and can reduce a twelve-page report to a readable format on one double-sided 8½ by 11-inch sheet of paper. Moreover, since no impact is involved, these printers are quiet.

The LASER PRINTER or *engine* prints an entire page at once using a low-intensity laser to lay a dense matrix of dots (around 300 dpi). Characters can be printed with high resolution, giving the appearance of

Figure 6-23
Laser printers provide
high-quality printed out-
put at high speeds. (a) A
desktop laser printer. (b)
A high-capacity laser
printer can handle the
needs of many users in
an office network.

(a)

(b)

typed letters even at high operational speeds. Laser printers can also print graphics.

Laser printers range in price from around one thousand dollars to tens of thousands of dollars. At the lower price end they have become competitive with high-quality dot-matrix and daisy-wheel printers.

The ability of high-speed printers to create high-quality, user-friendly output, coupled with reductions in paper waste and labor costs, can justify a high cost when hundreds of thousands of sheets of paper are generated. With this type of printer, forms can be printed onto the paper along with the data that fill in the forms. The formats for forms can be stored on magnetic disk and called as needed by the processor directing the printer. In addition to forms, graphic output of many other types can be produced.

One disadvantage of nonimpact printers is they cannot print multi-ply forms, since the printing mechanism does not contact the top page at all. However, some of the faster nonimpact printers can produce multiple copies of the same report faster than the time it takes impact line printers to do a single run with multi-ply paper.

Such capable printing equipment has led to the rise of a business-support area known as reprographics. *Reprographics* refers to the computerized production of graphical and textual output in a variety of media. A reprographics center has a range of printing hardware available, and can print original output from the computer as well as duplicate existing output, produce slides and illustrations, or transmit output to intelligent copiers located elsewhere. Some facilities even have computerized typesetting capabilities—to produce books, manuals, and newspapers.

Graphical output devices

We have already mentioned two sources of graphical output: printers and display screens. The more sophisticated printers, particularly the high-speed page printers, are capable of producing high-quality illustrations and other graphical material. Many simpler printers also can produce graphics.

Display screens have varying degrees of graphics capability, ranging from those that can do charts and graphs for business presentations to those that can handle extremely complicated technical illustrations and high-quality computer art. Once created at a display terminal, a graphic design can be stored for future reference or output on a printer or plotter. Figure 6-24 shows some examples of computer-generated art.

PLOTTERS are devices that output computer graphics. They are available for all sizes of computer, including microcomputers. Figure 6-25 (page 202) shows the two main types of plotters, flatbed and drum. Flatbed plotters work with paper that lies flat in a frame. A pen directed by the device's control unit moves rapidly horizontally and vertically across the paper, drawing output from the computer. These devices come in a variety of sizes, work at an impressive speed, can use different colors, and create three-dimensional effects.

The drum plotter draws upon paper that is wound around a cylinder. The machine rotates the paper, and the pen moves back and forth, to

Figure 6-24
Computer-generated art.

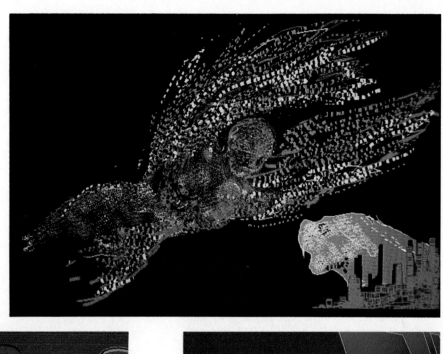

(a)

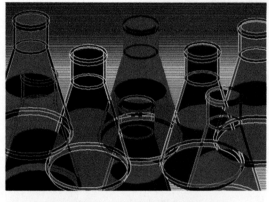

b)

(c)

d)

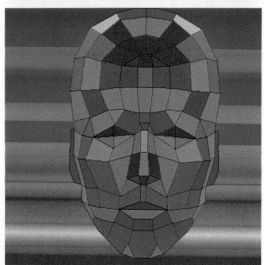

(e)

case in point

PC revolution enlists the handicapped

BOSTON—Before the personal computer came to be, handicapped persons were generally limited in their choice of computer careers.

The handicapped, most assumed, could work either as data-entry/data-retrieval specialists, or as programmers like those who trained them, said David Rose, executive director of the Center for Applied Special Technology (CAST), of Peabody, Mass., an organization that trains special-needs persons to use computers and other technology.

The PC revolution changed all that, Mr. Rose said. The user-friendliness of PCs, particularly Apple Computer Inc.'s Macintosh, gives the handicapped access to computer power they didn't have previously, he said.

"Now we know that the physically handicapped can go beyond being data-entry people to becoming computer managers and planners," Mr. Rose said.

"You used to have to justify this equipment at each level of management—now it's looked upon as equipment needed to get the job done," said Bert Cohen, a salesman at VTEK, a Santa Monica, Calif., manufacturer of equipment for the visually impaired.

To make PCs more accessible to special-needs users, many vendors have developed products designed to help handicapped persons as they assume greater responsibility in the workplace. Several of these developers gathered recently at a forum on technology and the handicapped at Northeastern University here.

One such developer is Personics Corp., of Concord, Mass., which demonstrated Head-Master, a headset that lets paralyzed persons operate a Mac. The device is equipped with transducers that transmit signals to a control unit placed on top of the Mac. The control unit uses the signals to sense the user's head movements, translating them into commands which emulate those of a mouse, thereby moving the cursor around the screen, explained Bonnie L. Weaver, marketing assistant at Personics.

In conjunction with Personics' Screen-Typer software, which displays a keyboard on the screen, users of HeadMaster can enter data by moving the cursor to the desired key, then puffing a breath into a mouth tube attached to the headset. Each puff enters a character on the screen.

"We had a 13-year-old kid who was paralyzed from a diving accident who made it through high school with HeadMaster—he lives with it," Ms. Weaver said.

An IBM PC-compatible version of Head-

---

reach the right positions in a diagram. Changes in pen and paper speeds can produce the desired curves and angles.

Not all plotters use pens; some use a dot-matrix printing technique like the dot-matrix printers described earlier.

Audio output devices

AUDIO OUTPUT DEVICES (Figure 6-26, page 202) allow the user to listen to the computer. Audio output devices exist that will speak any word, letter, or number given to them by the computer to output, just as a printer would print the same thing or a terminal would display it. The quality of the spoken speech remains somewhat artificial, but is improving.

Audio output devices often work in concert with the speech recognition systems discussed earlier in the chapter. Application areas for audio output include credit card verification systems, telephone directory assistance, on-board computers for military aircraft, and "talking

Master is in the works, she said. HeadMaster is priced at $995 for a headset, a control unit, and ScreenTyper software.

In addition to opening more sophisticated computer jobs, advancing PC technology is creating a significant number of less sophisticated jobs for the blind and visually impaired, said Brian Charlson, chief instructor at the Carroll Center for the Blind, Newton, Mass.

"In the past, there wasn't a computer available that would let a blind person do everything a receptionist has to do, such as answer phone calls, enter data on a computer and so on," he said. With more complex voice, print-enlargement and braille hardware and software available, he said, blind persons can handle jobs that sighted persons might consider "unsophisticated" but are quite challenging for the blind.

Mr. Charlson stressed that voice products have become an important feature for blind and visually impaired users. One such product was demonstrated by Kurzweil Computer Products Inc., of Cambridge, Mass. Its Personal Reader reads aloud printed material or on-screen text.

With the Personal Reader, a user scans printed text with a hand-held or desktop scanner, and hears the words "spoken" by a voice-synthesis unit. A cable attached to the voice unit enables the device to read information that appears on a PC display, explained Mary M. Harrington, senior marketing analyst with Kurzweil.

The system is priced between $8000 and $12,000 depending on configuration and will be available this summer.

Another company participating in the forum, Telesensory Systems Inc. (TSI), of Mountain View, Calif., offers a family of PC products for the visually impaired, including the VersaBraille II+, a personal computer that "displays" data in braille along a built-in twenty-character panel.

Introduced in 1982, the 12-pound system was "the first laptop computer," according to Gayle Yarnall, field marketing representative for TSI, who demonstrated the VersaBraille II+ at Northeastern. The company recently developed a software package for the VersaBraille II+ that allows users to access any program on a PC linked to the system. . . .

books" or other output for the visually impaired. Many automobiles and appliances have on-board computers that will tell the user when there is a problem. Some systems aid in musical composition and instrument-testing.

Microfilm output devices

Many documents and records need to be retained for a number of years because of various rules and procedures. Tax records, student data, and accounting records are examples. *Microfilm* is a reel of greatly reduced photographs of documents that saves space, and is therefore a popular medium for storing large quantities of documents. *Microfiche* places frames of microfilm on a flat card of film (up to about 1000 pages of a document per card), which can then be easily stored.

In the past, every page of a document to be recorded on microfilm had to be photographed by hand. Today, **COMPUTER-OUTPUT MICROFILM**

(a)

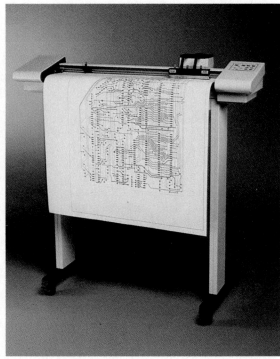

(b)

Figure 6-25
The two main types of
plotters. (a) The flatbed
plotter. (b) The drum
plotter.

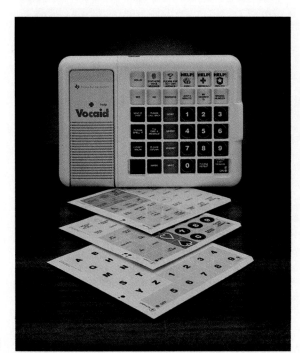

(a)

(b)

Figure 6-26
Audio output devices. (a) This device enables people
who otherwise can't speak to communicate short verbal
messages. (b) This device allows the visually impaired to
"see" what is on the screen by listening to a computer-
generated voice "read" the screen.

career box

Director of information systems

Why not aim for the top? As director of information systems, you would be in charge of the entire computer operation. In smaller companies, or in firms with a more traditional management structure, this position will be the highest one that relates to information systems. In larger organizations, or in firms with a more modern management structure, the director of information systems will report to the information resources manager or vice-president.

What would you manage? All five elements of an information system. Directors of information systems are sometimes in charge of hundreds or even thousands of people, including intermediary tiers of managers. In many organizations the director of information systems takes part in working out rules and procedures affecting information systems, together with other high-level managers. This includes identifying the need for new information systems to ensure that data flow smoothly into the computer center, and that timely and useful information flows out of it.

As far as hardware goes, the director of information systems is responsible for ac-

quiring it in the first place, seeing that it is used sensibly, and ensuring that it is up and running. A single computer, or dozens of them, may be involved. Software, too, is acquired or developed under the supervision of the director of information systems. Like all the elements in the picture, software must function well, or the director's job is on the line.

In smaller shops the director of information systems will be involved in day-to-day operations. In larger firms, he or she will be in charge of other executives who manage the major areas, such as database administration, telecommunications, and computer operations.

Directors of information systems are well paid and are in great demand. Prerequisites are proven technical competence and managerial ability. The best way to become a director of information systems is to work your way up through the information system ranks, demonstrating your technical proficiency and leadership skills. It's not unreasonable to expect to spend a decade or more in doing so. In a smaller shop this time might be shortened.

(COM) systems can produce up to 50,000 lines per minute of output on microfilm directly from computer-generated signals, using a high-speed camera. When a document needs to be retrieved for later use, a computer-assisted retrieval system can search for the correct microfilm reel (or microfiche card); the microfilm (or microfiche) can then be read using special readers, and photocopied onto paper if desired.

summary

■ Input brings data and instructions concerning how to process the data into an information system. Data entry refers to the process of getting facts into a form that the computer can understand. Output conveys the results of processing.

- As with all the other elements of an information system, the mix of input and output equipment an organization acquires must be considered in the context of the whole system.
- Trends in input and output include the use of source data automation and the production of user-friendly output.
- A terminal can send data to and receive data from a computer. Display terminals are the most common type of input device. They consist of an input unit, a display screen, and a screen control unit that links the two. Input units include keyboards, electronic mice, graphics tablets or digitizers, and light pens. An intelligent or smart terminal can do processing locally, whereas a dumb terminal cannot. A variety of screen technologies and features are employed by terminals, as well as different kinds of keyboards. Common features of display terminal technology include cursors, windows, scrolling, and the ability to use icons. High resolution monitors have more pixels (picture elements) per unit of area.
- Point-of-activity (POA) terminals are located at the point where a specific activity occurs to capture data at their source. The most common type of POA terminal is the point-of-sale (POS) terminal seen in stores.
- The buttons on push-button dialing telephones can be used to respond to computer-generated messages such as those used in telemarketing.
- With source data automation, the input medium and the source document are one and the same. The effect is to reduce the amount of manual labor involved in entering data. Source data automation uses optical scanners, magnetic scanners, three-dimensional scanners, and speech recognition systems. Optical scanning methods include optical mark readers (OMR), optical character readers (OCR), document readers, desktop scanners, and bar-code readers that read Universal Product Codes (UPC). Graphics scanners can be used to "read." Fax or facsimile transmission machines serve as long-distance copiers. Magnetic scanners include magnetic-ink character readers (MICR) and magnetic strip readers. In medicine, computerized axial tomography (CAT) and magnetic resonance imaging (MRI) assist in diagnosis and research.
- Output devices include display terminals, impact printers, nonimpact printers, graphical output devices, audio output devices, and microfilm output devices. Printers are the most frequently used device for permanent output. Impact printers can print a character at a time or a line at a time. Character impact printers are available that use dot-matrix or daisy-wheel printing mechanisms. Newer line printers use dot-matrix technology to print a line at a time.
- Nonimpact printers are the most sophisticated of all, particularly the high-speed page printers which employ laser technology. These laser printers are capable of producing graphical and textual output quietly at great speeds. Nonimpact character printers use thermal and ink-jet technologies. The availability of such capable printing equipment has led to the rise of a business-support area known as reprographics.
- Additional output devices include plotters, audio output devices, and computer-output microfilm (COM) systems that produce microfilm and microfiche output.

Cosentinos' vegetable haven

Japanese tourists taking photographs in an American food store! Seems unusual? Not in this case. Amid the click and whir of Nikons and Canons, we find ourselves not just in any grocery store, but one that can justify being a stop for tour buses. Welcome to Cosentinos' Vegetable Haven, in San Jose, California.

Founded in 1947 by four brothers as a fruit and vegetable stand, Cosentinos has since grown into a $20 million per year grocery business with a work force of 160 full- and part-time employees. Cosentinos is a two-store business and each store has less floor space than most chain supermarket stores. Computers barely existed when Cosentinos was founded; since then, Silicon Valley has grown up around the store, and Cosentinos' management did not fail to note the trend.

When bar codes and optical scanning devices were first introduced to retailing, many people predicted that this would lead to an even more sterile, artificial shopping experience for the consumer. This may often be the case, but it need not be. The strengths of Cosentinos are its vegetable and meat departments, where greengrocers and butchers have the same personal contact with customers that they have always had. For example, meat is not prepackaged; the butcher personally cuts and wraps it, based on your request. How can this be done in a highly automated store with laser readers at the checkout counters?

The butcher weighs the meat on an electronic scale, and keys in a short code number for the particular meat. The weight, product code, and price are electronically communicated to a bar-code-generating machine that prints a label for the meat. The label contains a machine-readable bar code as well as words and numbers that the customer can read. When the customer takes the meat package to the checkout counter at the front of the store, the laser scanner there will handle it exactly as it does all of the store's prepackaged items. The same procedure is followed in the bakery, produce, and deli departments.

The laser scanner system at the checkout counters was designed and installed by NCR Corporation. The prices for 22,000 items stocked in the store are stored on floppy disk. Laser scanners read the Universal Product Codes or the store-produced labels. The equipment cost about $75,000. Sal Cosentino, the manager, feels both the customers and employees have benefited from the use of scanners. "The scanners are more accurate, faster, and reduce the amount of theft," Sal says.

The store's computer communicates ordering information to the wholesalers' computers. The wholesalers retain extra copies of the price information in case the floppy disks develop problems. In addition, wholesalers provide the store with reports on how fast products are moving. Cosentinos' managers can change prices of items either at a terminal near the computer or by inserting a special key into a checkout register. The price changes are then communicated to the wholesaler, who prints new shelf labels and ships them to the store. As for the customer, he or she receives top-quality food, personalized service, and a receipt that describes each item and its price.

key terms

These are the key terms in alphabetical order. The numbers in parentheses refer to the page on which each term is defined.

Audio output device (200)
Bar-code reader (189)
Character printer (194)
Computer-output microfilm (COM) (201)
Cursor (180)
Daisy-wheel printer (194)
Data entry (174)
Desktop scanner (188)
Display terminal (177)
Document reader (186)
Dot-matrix printer (194)
Dumb terminal (179)
Electronic mouse (177)
Fax or facsimile transmission machine (189)
Graphics scanner (187)
Graphics tablet or digitizer (177)
High-speed page printer (197)
Icon (181)
Impact printer (194)
Ink-jet printer (197)
Input (174)
Intelligent terminal or smart terminal (177)
Keyboard (177)
Laser printer (197)
Light pen (177)
Line printer (194)
Magnetic-ink character recognition (MICR) (190)
Magnetic strip reader (190)
Nonimpact printer (196)
Optical character reader (OCR) (186)
Optical mark reader (OMR) (185)
Optical scanner (185)
Output (175)
Pixel (Picture Element) (179)
Plotter (198)
Point-of-activity (POA) terminal (184)
Point-of-sale (POS) terminal (184)
Scrolling (180)
Source data automation (175)
Speech recognition device (192)
Terminal (177)
Thermal printer (197)
Three-dimensional scanner (190)
Universal Product Code (UPC) (189)
User-friendly output (177)
Window (180)

review questions

objective questions

True/false. *Put the letter T or F on the line next to the question.*

1. Impact printers can produce multi-ply copies.   1 _____
2. Optical scanners are often used to detect brain tumors.   2 _____
3. Source data automation refers to machines automatically writing in optical character codes.   3 _____
4. Laser printers generally cost less than ink-jet printers.   4 _____
5. A daisy-wheel printer produces "dotlike" characters.   5 _____
6. A display terminal consists of an input unit, display screen, and a screen control unit.   6 _____
7. Bar-code readers are limited to retail operations.   7 _____
8. Obtaining, preparing, entering, and verifying data is known as the data-entry process.   8 _____
9. A magnetic disk is an example of a high-volume input/output device.   9 _____
10. A document reader is used to read the encoded characters on checks.   10 _____

Multiple choice. *Put the letter of the correct answer on the line next to the question.*

1. A common type of scanner used in the banking industry is the   1 _____
   (a) OCR.   (c) OMR.
   (b) CAT.   (d) MICR.
2. Which of the following is *not* an example of a nonimpact printer?   2 _____
   (a) Thermal printer.
   (b) Laser printer.
   (c) Dot-matrix printer.
   (d) Ink-jet printer.
3. Special symbols used on display terminals to illustrate particular functions are called   3 _____
   (a) Mice.   (c) Windows.
   (b) Icons.   (d) Cursors.

4. The most important factor in determining the variety of input and output devices used in an information system is the

    (a) Hardware available.

    (b) Rules and procedures concerning the proper mixture.

    (c) Information needs of the users.

    (d) Data capture needs of the organization.

5. Bar codes are commonly used in

    (a) Banks.

    (b) Medical laboratories.

    (c) Supermarkets.

    (d) College examinations.

Fill in the blank. *Write the correct word or words in the blank to complete the sentence.*

1. A terminal that only channels data to the CPU is known as a(n) _____.

2. A _____ printer uses metal pins that selectively strike a carbon ribbon against the paper.

3. Using _____ and the _____ features allow a person to view different parts of the data not yet on the display terminal screen.

4. The capture of data when and where a transaction occurs is a fundamental feature of _____.

5. A device designed to read the data encoded on the back of a bank debit card is called a _____.

6. Daisy wheels are _____-at-a-time _____ printers capable of "_____-quality" output.

7. The creation of high-quality, computer-generated output for printing, slide presentations, and other visual media is called _____.

8. Optical scanners that can read all forms of printed matter are called _____.

9. COM is an acronym for _____.

10. A _____ is an example of a high-speed page printer.

short answer questions

When answering these questions, think of concrete examples to illustrate your points.

1. What are the four parts of the data-entry process?

2. What are the three types of output? Do they overlap?

3. What is meant by the term source data automation?

4. What do the initials COM, OMR, OCR, UPC, and MICR stand for?

5. Describe the different types and uses of optical scanners.

6. Discuss some applications for magnetic and three-dimensional scanners.

7. What are different types of character printers?

8. What are the advantages of page printers?

9. What is meant by the term reprographics?

10. What types of businesses would use COM?

11. What types of businesses would use voice input and output?

essay questions

1. Discuss the effect of source data automation in business. Focus on an industry of your choice for this problem.

2. Compare and contrast impact printers with nonimpact printers.

3. Find ten ways in which source data automation affects your life today.

4. What is meant by the term user-friendly output? Discuss examples where such output may make your life easier.

Answers to the objective questions

True/false: **1.** T; **2.** F; **3.** F; **4.** F; **5.** F; **6.** T; **7.** F; **8.** T; **9.** T; **10.** F.

Multiple choice: **1.** d; **2.** c; **3.** b; **4.** c; **5.** c

Fill in the blank: **1.** dumb terminal; **2.** dot-matrix; **3.** windows, scrolling; **4.** source data automation; **5.** magnetic strip reader; **6.** character, impact, letter; **7.** reprographics; **8.** document readers; **9.** computer-output microfilm (COM); **10.** laser printer

Secondary storage: disks, tapes, and more

After studying this chapter you should understand the following:

- *The place of secondary storage in the storage hierarchy.*
- *How on-line and off-line storage differ.*
- *The main characteristics of magnetic disk storage and magnetic tape storage.*
- *How data are organized in sequential and direct-access storage.*
- *Typical uses for magnetic disk storage and magnetic tape storage.*
- *Which technologies offer mass storage capability.*
- *The characteristics of optical storage.*

chapter 7

A Monday kind of report

George Roberts wished he were at home gardening. Instead, he sat at his desk at Global Electrical Equipment. This Monday he had to prepare a difficult report. As quality-control supervisor, he had to evaluate how well his subordinates carried out their inspections of appliances manufactured at the Oakriver plant. Based mainly on his report, higher management would determine promotions and pay increases.

For an inspector, performing well meant rejecting bad appliances and approving good ones. Each type of appliance had an inspection quota that George's employees had to meet. For toasters, an inspector had to test at least 30 per hour, and had to correctly classify at least 29. Pushing that 29 figure nearer to 30 was what the best inspectors did. Periodic samples of inspected appliances were taken to estimate the number of correct inspections made by each inspector.

George got up and walked toward his assistant's office. The assistant would retrieve the data from Global's computer this morning while George worked on other administrative tasks. Then in the afternoon, George—using the data—could write the report. George recalled an article in a recent company newsletter that told about the billions of items of data stored at Global's computer center. Most of the data were kept on magnetic disk packs. A photograph in the article had shown a wall entirely occupied by a long row of disk storage units that read the data from the packs and also wrote new data onto them.

George's assistant would be able to obtain the right data from his office terminal, and rapidly enough so that George could write his report today. Unauthorized people could not view the data, just as George and his assistant could not access data maintained by other departments. The operating system kept it all straight. Data that the computer didn't need to work with at any given time were not stored in it at that time. Instead, they were stored until needed on the disks or tapes. The most-used disks and tapes were right in the computer room in close proximity to the computer, and the others were stored in the data library. The data library was nicknamed the "vault" because of the various security measures used to protect these valuable resources. George entered the office his assistant shared with several other people.

"Ward," George said, "I have to prepare my favorite report again. So I need performance data on all quality-control inspectors this morning."

"Which report?" Ward asked.

"You know." George moved his finger across his neck in a cutting motion, accompanied by an appropriate noise.

"Oh." Ward frowned. "Sure thing. I'm certainly glad I'm not one of the people on that report!"

The role of secondary storage

SECONDARY STORAGE, also known as EXTERNAL STORAGE, supplements main memory by holding data and instructions in machine-readable form outside of the computer.

The storage hierarchy

We can think of computer storage as being arranged in a storage hierarchy, as shown in Figure 7-1. A STORAGE HIERARCHY concerns the speed and cost of different types of data storage—with storage at the top being the costliest and fastest. As we move down the hierarchy, speed slows, and costs drop.

The top level of the hierarchy in the figure is occupied by the main memory of the computer. The next level of the hierarchy is occupied by secondary storage. Within secondary storage, there is a subhierarchy, ranging from the high-speed and more expensive hard disks down to the slowest and cheapest tape cassettes.

Just as speed and price decrease as we go down the hierarchy, so capacity increases. Main memory can hold from thousands (*kilobytes*) up to millions (*megabytes*) of bytes. Within secondary storage, large hard disk systems have capacities measured in GIGABYTES or Gs (billions of bytes). Even this number is not big enough for some organizations. With their many large-scale secondary storage devices, they must measure storage needs in terms of TERABYTES or Ts (trillions of bytes).

For an analogy, consider your brain's short-term memory as equivalent to the computer's primary storage, and your class notes as equivalent to secondary storage. When you study for an exam you will refer to those class notes to "refresh" your brain's memory.

Information systems and secondary storage

As with other hardware, the role secondary storage plays in an information system depends on the needs of management and other users. *People* have to evaluate which storage media will give them a cost-effective mixture. Still other people will need to administer access to the data held on the media (see the Career box: Media Librarian).

The characteristics of the *data* to be processed also strongly determine storage requirements. As you will recall from Chapter 2, the smallest usable unit of data is the field. Records are a collection of related fields; files a collection of related records; and a database a collection of interrelated files. The storage requirements of an information system with a vast, complex on-line database are clearly different from those of a system with a few files that need to be updated once a month. The addition of text and video data to transaction data increases the storage needs of the information system.

To enforce management decisions, *rules and procedures* for storing and securing data on various media must be developed and implemented. Secondary storage devices are controlled by system *software*. The software in turn determines how the *hardware* (the computer and its secondary storage devices) interact.

Figure 7-1
The storage hierarchy.

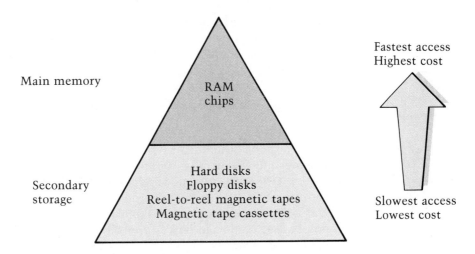

Main memory — RAM chips

Secondary storage — Hard disks / Floppy disks / Reel-to-reel magnetic tapes / Magnetic tape cassettes

Fastest access
Highest cost

Slowest access
Lowest cost

Selecting the secondary storage mix

We already mentioned that cost and speed were key differentiations of the media. In choosing the right secondary storage mix for an organization another important consideration is security.

Storing data in any form incurs *costs*. One goal in determining the best storage mix for an information system is to minimize the total cost of data storage. Costs go beyond the purchase price of the particular device used, such as a magnetic tape unit. Specifically, costs comprise:

■ *Storage cost.* This includes the cost of purchasing the secondary storage device and the media it uses, the cost of making extra copies of the stored material, the security costs necessary to protect the material, and the warehousing costs of keeping the media and extra copies when not in use.

■ *Access cost.* The price of reading data from a secondary storage device, or of writing data to a secondary storage device is the access cost. The faster the device, the lower the access cost for retrieving a given data item.

■ *Handling cost.* This refers to the labor and other expenses necessary to place the secondary storage medium on the secondary storage device, and to remove the medium from the device.

After cost, the second factor to consider in choosing a storage mix for an information system is *speed*. ACCESS TIME is the amount of time necessary to find and retrieve a data item from secondary storage and place it into main memory. Note that access time is not the same as RESPONSE TIME, which is the amount of time between making an inquiry or request and the start of the response. For example, if George Roberts types in a request at his terminal, the total time that elapses until the terminal starts displaying his answer is the response time. Buried within this time is the access time needed for the computer to read the data item George asked about.

After cost and speed, the third factor in choosing a secondary storage mix is *security*. Programs and data must be kept safe and secure; they must be protected against accidental or deliberate destruction or alteration. Generally speaking, security measures increase costs and slow down speed, but are justified in the long run by the money and time saved by not allowing leaks of vital information or having to generate original data. Chapter 17 will discuss data security in greater detail.

On-line and off-line storage

Secondary storage can be either on-line or off-line. The computer has direct control over ON-LINE STORAGE and can access data and software stored there without human intervention. On-line storage systems generally use magnetic disk as the storage medium, but can also use magnetic tape and other media. On-line storage is required for real-time processing, and is generally used for time-sharing as well.

OFF-LINE STORAGE is not under the direct control of the computer. As soon as an on-line device is turned off, it becomes off-line. In the same way, when a reel of magnetic tape or a removable disk is taken out of the device that reads and writes upon it, the tape or disk is off-line. Some off-line storage is archival in nature, retaining information in a machine-readable form in case an organization needs it again at some future time.

Sequential and direct access

Data held in secondary storage can be accessed by two methods: sequential or direct. SEQUENTIAL ACCESS refers to the necessity of reading every record leading up to a sought-after record. The most common medium for sequential access is magnetic tape. If we have a file containing 40,000 records, and we want to read record number 40,000, we have to first read the other 39,999 records to get to the last one.

DIRECT ACCESS refers to the ability to retrieve or write a given record without first having to process all of the records leading up to it. Direct access offers a fast way to retrieve or write data. The most common type of direct-access medium is magnetic disk.

Media that permit direct access to data also permit sequential access. Direct access, for instance, is used to recall a word processing document stored on disk. As you scan through the text, later pages of the document will be read sequentially. We will examine concepts concerning both sequential and direct-access file designs in Chapter 11.

Magnetic disk storage

Magnetic disks provide very fast, high-capacity secondary storage. They are the medium of choice for applications that need ready availability of large amounts of data. For example, law-enforcement agencies store data about stolen vehicles on magnetic disk systems because disk storage has enough capacity to hold all the relevant data about license plate numbers and vehicle type, and can deliver the data fast enough for officers to act upon them. Other applications include storing credit and check verification data, maintaining current levels of inventory in a warehouse, storing financial quotations, and recording patients' laboratory test results at hospitals.

Magnetic disk storage is also used for many routine day-to-day business processing tasks. Databases are usually stored on disk, as are operating systems and other frequently used programs. In an information system that includes both magnetic disk and magnetic tape for secondary storage, disk is typically used for programs with a higher priority or of greater importance, as well as for programs that work with a large quantity of data.

New data can be entered onto disk from source documents through a device that operates off-line from the computer. Such key-to-disk or key-to-diskette systems (Figure 7-2) consist of a keyboard, display screen, and a unit to enter the data onto the disk. These devices allow for a certain amount of editing and checking of the data. Once the data are entered, the disk or diskette containing the data can then be removed. Later the data can be read for input to a computer program.

Types of magnetic disks

All types of magnetic disks share a vital trait, the ability to store data so that programs can have *direct access* to the data. Magnetic disks are slower in their operation than main memory, but can hold considerably more data. Main memory can contain from tens of thousands to millions of bytes, whereas magnetic disks can hold from hundreds of thousands to billions of bytes.

MAGNETIC DISKS are circular, like phonograph records, and are coated with a magnetic surface. In the surface, particles can be aligned into bit patterns to record data. MAGNETIC DISK UNITS read data from, and write data upon, magnetic disks. Such units contain the read/write mechanism, the drive motors, and support circuitry. A magnetic disk unit is often called a DASD—short for DIRECT-ACCESS STORAGE DEVICE. Magnetic disks are divided into two categories: hard disks and floppy disks.

Figure 7-2
Entering data on a key-to-disk system.

Hard disks

HARD DISKS are made of metal and, as their name indicates, are rigid. They have a greater storage capacity than floppy disks. Hard disk systems are available for any size computer. Figure 7-3 shows a common type of hard disk system used for microcomputers. Figure 7-4 shows a large system commonly used with mainframe computers.

One or two hard disks can be placed into a sealed DISK CARTRIDGE (Figure 7-5). A number of disk platters can also be stacked vertically into a DISK PACK (Figure 7-6). Disk cartridges and disk packs can be permanently installed in the DASD or be removable. In addition, large units exist that combine multiple-disk units to hold billions of bytes.

Access arms within a DASD hold the read/write mechanism. When the disk reaches an operating speed of about 3000 to 4500 revolutions per minute, the access arm can move the read/write head over the disk. Figure 7-7 shows a stack of read/write heads. The arm holds two read/write heads, one for each side of the disk. The head does not touch the surface of the disk at all, rather its aerodynamic qualities allow it to float just above the surface.

Figure 7-3
A "Winchester" hard disk system used for microcomputers. Systems like this can store over 40 million bytes.

Figure 7-4
A large multiple-disk storage system.

Figure 7-5
Removable disk car-
tridges.

Figure 7-6
Mounting a removable
disk pack.

Figure 7-7
The read/write mecha-
nism of a disk head. It
floats over the disk sur-
face.

Floppy disks

The other category of disk, FLOPPY DISKS or DISKETTES, are made from flexible plastic. They remind most people of small phonograph records. Shown in Figure 7-8, floppy disks for microcomputers come in two main diameters: $5^1/_4$ inches and $3^1/_2$ inches. Floppy disks in the $5^1/_4$-inch size remain permanently in a special square envelope made of light plastic or cardboard. The envelope protects the disk, and has small openings to allow the read/write mechanism access to the disk surface. Floppy disks in the $3^1/_2$-inch size are encased in rigid plastic and have a protective metal flap over the openings for the read/write mechanism.

Data and programs stored on a floppy disk can be protected from accidental erasure or "write-protected". For the $5^1/_4$-inch disk an adhesive tab must be placed over the write-protect notch (located to the left of the label). A plastic locking tab located on its underside serves the same purpose for $3^1/_2$-inch disks.

A floppy disk is placed by hand into a floppy disk drive (Figure 7-9). Floppy disk drives are available for any size of computer, though they

Figure 7-8
Examples of floppy disks. There are two major sizes—5¼-inch (a) and 3½-inch (b). The 3½-inch size (bottom) has a protective shield over the actual disk.

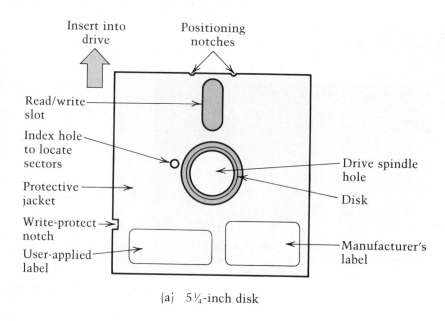

Insert into drive

Positioning notches

Read/write slot

Index hole to locate sectors

Protective jacket

Write-protect notch

User-applied label

Drive spindle hole

Disk

Manufacturer's label

(a)   5¼-inch disk

Figure 7-9
A disk drive for a 3½-inch floppy disk. When the disk is inserted into the drive the protective shield moves aside.

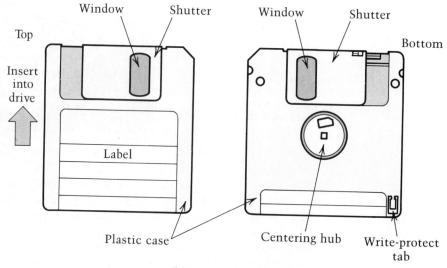

Top

Window   Shutter

Insert into drive

Label

Window   Shutter

Bottom

Plastic case

Centering hub

Write-protect tab

(b)   3½-inch disk

are most commonly associated with microcomputers. In contrast to hard disk systems, the read/write mechanism physically touches the floppy disk surface. Typical floppy disks store only a fraction of the amount (a twentieth or less) that a comparable hard disk can hold. Floppy disk capacities range from about 360,000 bytes (360 kilobytes) to over 1.4 million bytes (1.4 megabytes).

Figure 7-10
A Bernoulli box.

Bernoulli boxes

A **BERNOULLI BOX** is a removable disk cartridge usually used with micro-computers (see Figure 7-10). The disk material is made of the same magnetic-oxide coated flexible plastic used for floppy disks. The disk drive mechanism rapidly rotates the disk creating the Bernoulli effect that lifts the read/write head away from the surface just as rapidly moving air "lifts" an airplane's wing. Bernoulli boxes have about the same capacity as a hard disk of similar size. Because they are removable, users can take their data and application programs with them—a feature that enhances both security and convenience.

*Retrieving data
from magnetic disk*

We have already seen how access arms and read/write heads handle reading and writing data from disk. Since some programs require data records to be read and written many thousands of times, speed is an important consideration. Speed in this case means *access time*, the amount of time necessary to retrieve a data item from secondary storage and place it into main memory, or, conversely, the amount of time necessary to locate an appropriate secondary storage location and transfer data from main memory to the location.

Access time is made up of three stages: (1) seek time, (2) search time, and (3) data-transfer time. **SEEK TIME** is the time required to position the read/write head over the right part of the disk. **SEARCH TIME** is the rotational time it takes for the data to spin under the head (or, when writing, for the appropriate locations to spin under the head to receive the data). Once the data (or write location) has been found, the data must be transferred to the computer (for a read), or to the disk (for a write). The time for this transfer is the **DATA-TRANSFER TIME**.

Hard disk systems take from about 10 to 100 milliseconds (thousandths of a second) for the seek and search time together, and have a data-transfer rate from 250,000 to over 4 million bytes per second. To reduce seek and search times on hard disks, some DASDs have multiple read/write heads for each surface. Others totally eliminate seek time by substituting fixed heads over every track. These types of systems are faster, but more expensive.

Floppy disks take from 75 to 600 milliseconds for the seek and search time together, and have a data-transfer rate of about 30,000 to over 60,000 bytes per second. These rates may seem fast, but most computers operate in the millionth to billionth of a second range. In other words, a computer with a 60-nanosecond (billionths of a second) instruction execution time can perform a million operations during the time that a hard disk with a seek and search time of 60 milliseconds (thousandths of a second) finds one data item.

With either hard or floppy disks, special disk management software, and circuitry built into the DASD, directs the storage and retrieval of data and instructions. These disk control packages can even place frequently used materials in parts of the disk that can be gotten at more quickly and rarely used material in slower-to-reach areas, thus minimizing arm travel.

Formatting hard and floppy disks

The number of bytes that can be stored on a disk depends on its format. FORMATTING refers to the way a particular computer and its operating system's disk management software order the disk drive to position magnetic markings on the surface of the disk in preparation for the bytes of data and programs to be stored. Normally a disk is formatted just once.

Let's see how data and programs are organized on a hard disk. Each side of a hard disk in a disk pack or stack of disks is called a surface. Permanently installed disks and many removable disk packs make use of all the surfaces. Other removable disk packs use all but the top surface of the top disk, and the bottom surface of the bottom disk, which are the surfaces most likely to be contaminated.

Let's view the disk surface from above. If we could see the magnetized bits, they would appear to be arranged along concentric rings. Each ring is known as a TRACK. The number of tracks a disk can hold varies from about 300 to 1000. Traveling along a single track, we can store around 10,000 bits per inch. Figure 7-11 is a schematic drawing of a disk pack showing the relationship of disks, surfaces, tracks, and the access mechanism.

CYLINDERS are a conceptual "slice" of a disk pack made up of vertical stacks of tracks. The first cylinder on a disk is made up of all the first tracks; the second of all the second tracks; and so on. Thus if each disk has 600 tracks, the disk pack has 600 cylinders. Some systems place the data for a file onto one cylinder at a time, while other systems fill the disk on a track-by-track basis. Working with one cylinder at a time shortens seek time, since for most operations the read/write heads will already be over the right cylinder.

SECTORS are pie-shaped sections radiating out from the center of the disk. Usually each of the tracks within a sector holds the same number of bytes. This means that the larger-diameter outer tracks are written less densely than the shorter-diameter inner tracks.

Figure 7-11
The relationship of disks, surfaces, tracks, and the access mechanism in a disk pack.

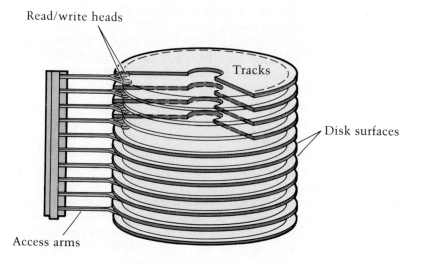

Read/write heads

Tracks

Disk surfaces

Access arms

Figure 7-12
Tracks and sectors on a floppy disk. Usually the disk surface is divided into eight to twenty sectors. This disk has nine sectors.

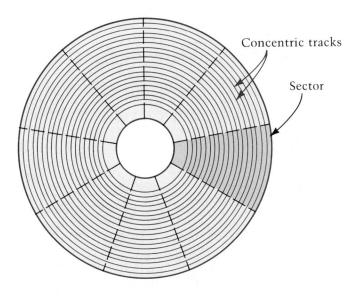

Concentric tracks

Sector

Floppy disks have less dense formats than hard disks. Like hard disks, floppies have tracks. The tracks for floppy disks are not as densely packed as for hard disks. Floppy disks contain between 40 and 100 tracks, storing about 6400 to 12,800 bits per inch. Some floppy disks only use a single surface; we call these single-sided disks. Other floppy disks—double-sided disks—use both surfaces.

Floppy disks generally use sectors for organizing data on the disk surface (Figure 7-12). Disks with the sectors predefined on them are called hard-sectored; disks without predefined sectors are called soft-sectored. Most floppy disk drives sold today use soft-sectored disks. A floppy disk formatted on one microcomputer can be transferred to another manufacturer's computer if their data formatting procedures and disk circuitry are compatible.

Advantages and drawbacks of magnetic disk storage

The main advantage of using magnetic disks for secondary storage is that they can maintain a lot of data on-line. The time delays due to frequent mounting and removing of media common with tape are reduced with disks. Another key advantage is that disks permit fast, efficient direct access.

There are drawbacks as well. Disks are sensitive to environmental hazards. Tiny particles of dirt, bacteria, or hair can cause major complications if they come in contact with the surface of a disk (Figure 7-13) (although most hard disk systems are sealed against these environmental hazards). Too much handling of a disk can distort it, causing the read/write head to crash on the surface and damage data and possibly the DASD as well. Electromagnetic radiation can also damage data, but special shielding can reduce this risk. Creating backup copies of disk files is a must. They should be stored far enough from the computer that originals and backups could not possibly be destroyed by the same disaster.

Figure 7-13
The read/write mecha-
nism of a disk drive is
very sensitive to environ-
mental damage. Even
dust or smoke particles
can cause a crash.

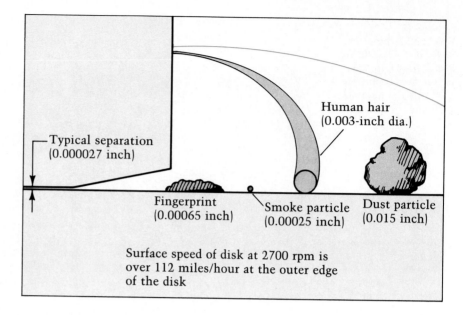

Typical separation
(0.000027 inch)

Human hair
(0.003-inch dia.)

Fingerprint
(0.00065 inch)

Smoke particle
(0.00025 inch)

Dust particle
(0.015 inch)

Surface speed of disk at 2700 rpm is
over 112 miles/hour at the outer edge
of the disk

Vulnerability to unauthorized access is another drawback. A disk can hold data from a variety of sources. A small number of disks—even only one—may contain all of an organization's data. If these disks are on-line, there is a possibility that someone could deliberately or accidentally read, change, or destroy data without anyone being aware of it. Software packages are available to help reduce these risks. A simple solution is to use removable disk packs—when data are not required, the pack can be taken out of the disk unit and stored in a safe area.

Magnetic tape storage

MAGNETIC TAPES provide rapid, high-capacity secondary storage. In both of these areas, however, magnetic tape cannot compete with magnetic disk, which is much faster and holds much more. But tape is substantially cheaper. Magnetic tape can provide only *sequential access* to data records. We will examine concepts concerning sequential access in Chapter 11.

As with disk files, tape files may be created as program output, and used as input to another program or to the same program at a later time. In addition, off-line key-to-tape devices can be used to enter data.

Magnetic tape is generally the medium of choice for off-line and archival storage of data. Tapes are frequently used to make backup copies of files stored on disk. Reels of tape are inexpensive, compact, and easy to move and store. Batch processing programs often use magnetic tape for data input and output.

An important specialist in today's large and diversified computer centers is the media librarian. The media librarian is responsible for controlling the storage and use of removable magnetic storage media—magnetic disks and magnetic tapes.

In early computer centers, the computer operators themselves took care of cataloging the tapes on an impromptu basis. Imagine a conventional library with no catalog for the books and with no particular organization on the shelves—or with a catalog and organization begun by one person in a certain way, taken up again in an altogether different way by another, and forgotten by a third. Before the creation of the job of media librarian, this type of library existed in many otherwise sophisticated computer centers. The result was lost time hunting for the tape or disk sought and needless duplication of materials.

The media librarian pays attention to details, yet cannot be overwhelmed by rush requests or by the sheer volume of materials handled (it is not uncommon for thousands of labeled and numbered tapes to hang on the storage racks). The librarian will be responsible for either devising a classification system for labeling and storing the media, or for following the system already in effect. Disks and tapes are usually checked in and out of the library with an accompanying form filled out by the responsible party. The aim is to keep unauthorized material out of the hands of people who have no legitimate need for it or permission to use it. The skills of classification, efficient storage logistics, and smooth check-in/check-out control, are those of a librarian. Accordingly, media librarians often have degrees in library science, like their counterparts in book libraries.

Some familiarity with computers will be acquired when pursuing a library science degree, since the field is highly automated. It is not necessary to have additional computer experience to become a media librarian. Library or other detail-oriented administrative experience would be a plus.

People and managerial skills are important. The media librarian interacts with people, some of whom must be diplomatically told no to their request. The librarian may help plan the efficient use of media, together with the director of information systems or the database administrator. The media librarian may also work with the information system security specialist and manager of computer operations to ensure that check-in/check-out procedures effectively hinder improper use of data, yet do not unduly impede the organization's work.

Types of magnetic tape

Magnetic tape is thin plastic, coated with a magnetic surface. Particles in the surface can be aligned into bit patterns to record data. Magnetic tape comes in either reel-to-reel or cassette form. Both types are shown in Figure 7-14, together with the MAGNETIC TAPE UNITS that read from and write to them. A newer magnetic tape technology is also available: videotape. Magnetic tape units are sometimes referred to as TAPE DRIVES. Write-protect measures are available for each type of device.

Reel-to-reel tape systems

REEL-TO-REEL MAGNETIC TAPE records data one byte at a time, spreading the bits that make up the byte across the width of the tape. Figure 7-15 shows an example of how the message "GREETINGS" is represented in a code called EBCDIC on a tape containing nine tracks. For tape, a track runs along the length of the tape, and records a certain bit of each byte (the first track records the first bit of all the bytes, the second track records the second bit, and so on). Each of the 8-bit EBCDIC bytes has a ninth bit for parity (a way of checking the validity of the coded data), which is why the tape has nine rather than eight tracks. (We discussed parity bits and the EBCDIC coding system in Chapter 5.) To prevent accidental erasure of data a "write-enable" ring must be attached to the tape reel in order to write data onto the tape—no ring, no write!

Figure 7-14
Magnetic tapes and the tape drives that read them. (a) Reel-to-reel tape. (b) A reel-to-reel tape drive. (c) A cassette tape and drive.

(a)

(b)

(c)

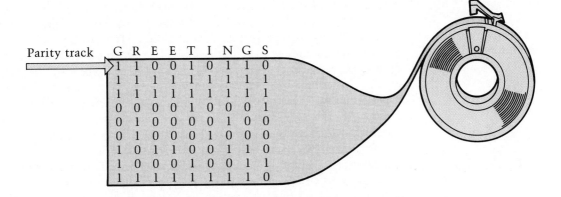

Parity track

G	R	E	E	T	I	N	G	S
1	1	0	0	1	0	1	1	0
1	1	1	1	1	1	1	1	1
1	1	1	1	1	1	1	1	1
0	0	0	0	1	0	0	0	1
0	1	0	0	0	0	1	0	0
0	1	0	0	0	1	0	0	0
1	0	1	1	0	0	1	1	0
1	0	0	0	1	0	0	1	1
1	1	1	1	1	1	1	1	0

Figure 7-15
Using magnetic tape. How the message "GREETINGS" is represented in code called EBCDIC on a tape containing nine tracks.

Magnetic tape cassettes

MAGNETIC TAPE CASSETTES look like audiocassettes and are used primarily with microcomputers. Cassettes handle data differently: the bits for a character follow one another in a single track. When all of the bits for one character are finished, then the bits for the next character begin. Many large microcomputers can hold tape cassettes for backing up their hard drives.

Videotape systems

Again relying upon technology first put to commercial use in the entertainment industry, **VIDEOTAPE SYSTEMS** can store vast amounts of data, providing sequential (not direct) access to data. Instead of recording a picture for later playback, a video cassette recorder can register bit patterns and, when needed, read these values back. In fact, the same types of video recording tape used in the home to record television shows can be used. One version holds 5 gigabits of data on a single VHS tape. Some videotape systems can be programmed to perform automatic backup operations, just as you would program them to tape a favorite television show.

Such high-data capacities are made possible by positioning a rapidly rotating read/write head at a slight angle (6 degrees for VHS-style systems) across the tape's path (Figure 7-16). The tape moves at standard recording speeds, permitting the creation of tracks about 4 inches long that can hold 16 kilobytes of data per track.

Figure 7-16
Using videotape technology, up to 16 kilobytes of data can be written onto each diagonal 4-inch track.

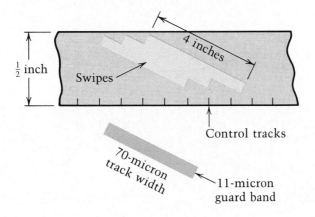

Once a magnetic tape is mounted in a magnetic tape unit, the unit will read or write upon the tape as directed by the computer. Reading or writing is done as the tape passes by a fixed read/write head. Reel-to-reel tapes move at speeds up to 200 inches per second, and hold data at a density ranging from 800 to 18,000 bytes per inch. Reel-to-reel tapes are usually 2400 feet long, and wound on a reel 10½ inches in diameter. The data-transfer rate for these tapes can approach 2 million bytes per second. In practice, however, transfer rates are usually much lower because of the frequent stops and starts the tape drive makes.

To allow for these starts and stops, magnetic tapes must contain either interrecord gaps or interblock gaps. These gaps are simply a sufficient amount of space between data records to allow the tape to reach operational speed before reading or writing data, and to allow the tape to slow down after reading or writing is finished. INTERRECORD GAPS are placed between each record (Figure 7-17a). This can take up a prohibitive amount of space—as much as 90 percent of a tape, for instance, might consist of interrecord gaps rather than data.

To economize on space, records may be written adjacent to each other in blocks. The number of records in a block is called the BLOCKING FACTOR. An INTERBLOCK GAP then provides the start-up/slow-down time

Figure 7-17
How records are arranged on magnetic tape. (a) Interrecord gaps permit reading and writing single records at a time. (b) With interblock gaps groups of records can be stored more efficiently. The number of records in a block is called the blocking factor.

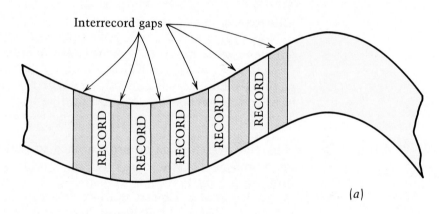

Interrecord gaps

(a)

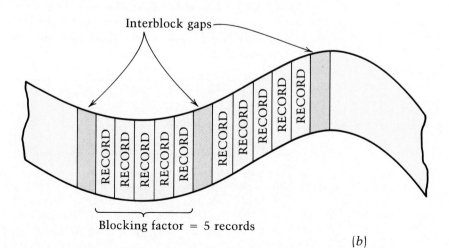

Interblock gaps

Blocking factor = 5 records

(b)

the tape drive needs, and interrecord gaps are eliminated (Figure 7-17b). A single read then transfers a block, consisting of a number of records, to the computer, where the block is placed in a buffer. A BUFFER is a temporary storage area used to accumulate data from the relatively slow input device until enough data are present to justify processing by the more rapid computer.

In the case of writing data, a buffer receives a burst of output data from the computer when it is ready, and parcels the data out at the appropriate speed to the slower output device. Besides helping out with this speed disparity between the computer and the input/output devices, buffers are handy for receiving blocks. If blocks rather than records are being read or written, then the block size must be kept small enough to fit into the buffer. Buffers are located in the computer and in the tape units.

Gaps notwithstanding, an enormous amount of data can be stored on a single magnetic tape. Assuming a 2400-foot tape, and allowing for interblock gaps, approximately 140 million bytes—the equivalent of 50 copies of this book—can easily be stored on the tape. To store the same amount of data on punch cards would require more than 1.7 million 80-column cards. The tape would weigh 3 pounds; the cards over a ton!

Advantages and drawbacks of magnetic tape storage

The main advantages of using magnetic tape for secondary storage are that tape is inexpensive, compact, and provides fairly fast retrieval of data. Tapes cost about $20 each, and the price per byte stored on a tape is negligible. The cost of storing an individual tape in a tape library is fairly low as well. Often copies of important records are stored in underground fireproof vaults far from the computer center where the tape was originally made. Corporations maintain vital proprietary information, stockholder data, and customer and personnel records in such vaults, as insurance against a disaster at the main computer center.

The major drawback of tape is that data can only be retrieved and written sequentially, as discussed earlier in the chapter. Of course many business operations, such as payroll, lend themselves to processing in sequential fashion. In addition, there are environmental hazards, as with disks. Environmental dangers include exposure of a tape to a magnetic field, dust from a tape drive or elsewhere sticking to a tape, and extreme temperatures. Any of these can distort or destroy data.

Mass storage

Imagine storing all of the accounts of millions of insurance customers, or the ticket information for people who fly on commercial airlines, or—bigger yet—the files for the U.S. Social Security Administration. Files of this size would overwhelm the resources of single magnetic disk or tape systems. MASS STORAGE DEVICES hold the data contained within very large files and databases. There are several different types of mass

Figure 7-18
A mass storage system using magnetic strip cartridges.

storage devices of interest to us: magnetic strip cartridge systems, multiple-disk systems, optical disk devices, and videotape units. In this section we will examine the magnetic media.

Magnetic strip cartridge systems

The **MAGNETIC STRIP CARTRIDGE SYSTEM**, or **DATA CELL**, is one of the most common types of mass storage (Figure 7-18). This device stores data on short strips of magnetic tape. The strips are wound up and placed in cartridges that serve as containers, and the cartridges are stored in individual cells of a giant honeycomblike structure.

To retrieve or write data, a mechanism scoots to the storage location of the appropriate cartridge, pulls the cartridge from the honeycomb, removes the tape from the cartridge, and reads the data from it or writes the data upon it. Some systems first transfer the contents of the strip to disk storage and then read from the disk; or write data to the disk and then transfer the contents to the strip.

Slower than disk systems, these devices offer a compromise between off-line and on-line storage. That is, all of the data are in fact on-line—they do not have to be fetched by a person from a library somewhere, but only by a mechanism from within the system itself. It does, however, take a little time to actually get at any of the on-line data. Seconds can easily be tallied while waiting. Like disks, the devices offer direct access to data. Enormous quantities of data can be held (some systems can hold over 500 gigabytes of data).

Multiple-disk-drive systems

Another type of mass storage teams up magnetic disk units into **MULTIPLE-DISK-DRIVE SYSTEMS** that can coordinate dozens of DASDs and occupy several large rooms. One system, the IBM 3380, can manage thirty-two disk drive units holding over 240 gigabytes of data. These systems are frequently used for large-scale real-time applications that handle vast amounts of data, such as travel reservation systems and credit card validation systems.

Optical storage systems

*Optical disk
systems*

An **OPTICAL DISK SYSTEM** (Figure 7-19), also known as a laser disk system, can store and retrieve billions of bytes of data. Certain optical disk systems are available for microcomputers. The same technology has made possible the *CD-ROMs* (Compact Digital–Read-Only Machines) that revolutionized sound recording and home audio systems. Optical disks offer **WORM (WRITE-ONCE READ-MANY)** technology. With WORM technology, data can be entered permanently once and then accessed as often as needed. Such technology is ideal for archival transaction, text, voice or image data.

An optical disk system works by using the intense light of a laser to melt tiny bubbles into the surface of a disk. These bubbles change the optical qualities of the surface. A lower-power laser can then read the pattern and transfer the bits to the computer. Optical disk systems operate on the same principles as video disks used to record and show movies in the home.

Compared to a magnetic hard disk, an optical disk of the same diameter has a much greater capacity, about twenty times as much. Optical disks provide direct access to data.

To date, optical disk systems have two drawbacks: access speed and the inability to erase data. Current access times are slower than for hard disk systems. Efforts are underway to speed up access times.

A more critical drawback of optical disk systems is that the little bubbles that record that data are permanent. This means that the data on optical disks cannot be erased; therefore, the disks, which are expensive, cannot be reused. Attempts are being made to produce erasable disks by using either a combination of magnets and lasers or by developing surfaces that can be optically altered back to their original state.

The main application of optical disks is to provide archival storage of documents that are needed for reference but that will not require any

Figure 7-19
*Optical storage systems
use laser technology for
storing archival data.
Such systems can hold
billions of bytes of data.
One optical disk can
hold as much informa-
tion as an encyclopedia.*

case in point

Hospital cures paper plague

NEW YORK—A community hospital here is installing an optical disk-based storage and retrieval system that provides instantaneous access to patient admission, billing information and medical records from networked workstations.

Maimonides Medical Center, a 700-bed, non-profit hospital serving the Borough Park section of Brooklyn, is counting on the storage and retrieval system to make its operations more efficient by reducing reliance on paper. Microfilm was initially used to relieve the hospital's paper glut, but it has proven too tedious and inefficient to work with, hospital officials said.

"We're just inundated with paper," noted Bill Dipple, Maimonides' assistant director of finance, pointing to New York state laws that mandate the retention of patient financial records for six years and health records indefinitely. "We just plain ran out of space to put it all."

Cost comparison
Without the optical-based storage and retrieval system, the hospital would have had to rent warehouse space—costing at least $18 per square foot—to store the mountains of paper it generates, Dipple maintained. "We're investing $400,000 in this system," he said. "That's not expensive if you measure it against the cost of warehouse space over time."

Maimonides contracted with Advanced Graphic Applications, Inc. (AGA), a New York-based systems integration firm, to build the system. AGA has developed software that manages the flow of information throughout an organization—be it data, image or voice—using write-once read-many optical devices as the primary storage medium.

AGA installed an Ungermann-Bass, Inc. token-ring network at the hospital to provide shared access to admission records from IBM Personal Computer AT or Personal System/2-

class machines over twisted-pair wiring. The network will eventually be used to facilitate voice messaging of test results from the radiology laboratory to attending physicians, Dipple said. . . .

The hospital intends to link its radiology and cardiology departments, located within a two-block campus, to the network using modems and existing twisted-pair telephone wiring. "We need to see where a patient has been during his stay in the hospital. This eliminates all the hunting" for records.

Upon admission, all of a patient's vital information, including medical history and insurance, is entered into a Burroughs Corp. Model 3955 mainframe. Each evening, after midnight, the information from the mainframe is downloaded onto tape in batch mode and into the network's file server via a tape-to-tape transfer.

Patient information written on paper can also be entered into the optical disk-based storage and retrieval system from various locations throughout the network using scanners attached to workstations. . . .

Optical prescription
Ultimately, the hospital hopes to create an interface that would enable data to be automatically transferred from its mainframe to the optical system. In addition, it is considering using optical storage as a primary medium for image as well as for data processing, noted Akiba Keehn, Maimonides' MIS director. . . .

The new system is already proving its worth to the hospital's administration, Maimonides' Dipple declared.

"When an outside organization such as Medicaid or Medicare seeks information, it used to take a week to 10 days. It now takes half a day," Dipple said.

"At first, I was skeptical of optical systems, particularly the networking part," Dipple recalled. "But this system is so soft, it takes about 20 minutes to train someone to learn how to use it."

Source: Alan Alper, *Computerworld,* vol. XXII, no. 20, May 16, 1988, 55, 58. Copyright 1988 by CW Publishing Inc., Framingham, MA 01701. Reprinted from Computerworld.

changes. Such documents might include accounting, banking, insurance, and payroll records. The fact that the documents cannot be changed is a useful feature for auditors.

The **OPTICAL CARD SYSTEMS**, now being introduced, use lasers to write data onto and read data from a card about the size of modern credit cards. An application suggested for such cards is encoding a person's financial and medical data upon a single card. The card could be used to record electronic transactions, eventually replacing credit cards, ATM debit cards, and in many situations, checks and cash. These cards should be able to store several million bytes of data. Widespread use of optical cards could raise privacy and security questions in terms of who has the right to view, alter, or correct errors in such sensitive data.

Optical card systems

Other types of secondary storage

Although we have covered quite a few different types of secondary storage systems, we have not yet exhausted the possibilities. In this final section we will look at three more: charge-coupled devices, bubble memory, and ferro-electric RAM.

CHARGE-COUPLED DEVICES (Figure 7-20) are a form of semiconductor storage. A very fast storage medium, these devices use tiny storage cells to hold charges that represent desired bit patterns. The data bits are transferred to and from the device in small "pipelines" when required. Direct access is not possible, only sequential access to one *bit* at a time. Unfortunately, when the power is turned off, charge-coupled devices lose the data being stored there.

Another rapid type of storage, although not quite as fast as charge-coupled devices, is bubble memory. **BUBBLE MEMORY** uses tiny, movable bubbles implanted in a thin film on a garnet wafer to store data. The bubble pattern is read sequentially. What long-term role charge-coupled devices and bubble memories will play in the area of secondary storage remains to be seen. Bubble memory chips are already used for main

Figure 7-20
A charge-coupled device, slightly longer than ¼ inch.

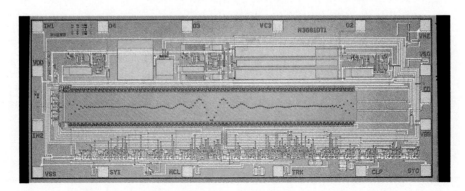

Are disks to be just a memory?

This article, reprinted in part from the British weekly, *The Economist*, points to a new technology that could change how data are kept in secondary storage. (Note the British spelling "disc" rather than the American "disk.")

Floppy discs are to computers what brittle old 78s were to gramophones: a joy for a while, but not long for this world. Such a thought frightens the makers of computer discs and disc drives. Their comfortable seat in the $20 billion-a-year electronic memory business could be snatched from under them. Within the next ten years the mechanical disc-drives found on nearly all computers could be replaced by data-storing micro-chips.

Instead of merely using microchips to process information, why not let them serve as a "solid-state disc" to store it too? Memory chips are tiny and have no moving parts. Because mechanical delays do not slow them down, they are usually five (and can be 50) times as fast as rotating memories. Future personal computers could have removable cartridges, like thick credit cards, each holding as much information as several of today's hard discs.

Until recently, solid-state memories had just a few specialized uses. They are now finding their way into a broader variety of machines, including some consumer products such as hand-held computers. Several big computer companies are designing new products around the capabilities of memory chips. IBM, for one, thinks that much of the future belongs to solid-state memory. But how will the revolution start?

The most popular memory chips today are "dynamic random access memories" (DRAMs). . . . But today's DRAMs are used mostly as temporary memories to hold programs and data that have been fed in from a disc. Such memory vanishes when a computer is switched off. It has to be loaded back into the computer from its permanent home on a disc each time the computer is used.

Forgetful DRAMs cannot replace discs.

Picture a DRAM as an array of tiny storage batteries or "capacitors." Data are stored by charging some of these capacitors; the charged and uncharged states correspond to the 1s and 0s of binary code. This way of keeping information is unstable because the charges leak away spontaneously. DRAMs are therefore "volatile" and must be fitted with external power sources that refresh the charges thousands of times each second.

The ceramic solution

A new sort of chip may help solve some of these problems. Two small companies, Ramtron in Colorado Springs, Colorado, and Krysalis in Albuquerque, New Mexico, have come up with "ferro-electric random access memories" which are naturally nonvolatile and lend themselves to compact designs. They take advantage of the curious properties of a ceramic material, lead zirconate titanate (PZT).

To understand how ferro-electric RAMs work, imagine that the capacitors on a DRAM have been replaced or supplemented by tiny bar magnets. Binary data can be written on this magnetic array by swiveling the magnets so that either their "north" or "south" poles are upright; the orientations correspond to the charged and uncharged states of capacitors on a DRAM.

Ferro-electric RAMs get close to this sort of arrangement by laying a thin film of PZT over a silicon chip. Crystalline elements in the PZT have opposite charges at each end that can be reversed by an electric field. Because the orientations—north or south—of these tiny "bar magnets" are fixed and intrinsic, they do not weaken or vary over time. Binary data encoded in the electrical orientations of a PZT layer will last.

. . . Permanent memory is not their only advantage over DRAMs. Ferro-electric components produce signals that are ten times as strong as those of DRAM capacitors, so it is easier to make them smaller without garbling stored data. . . .

Source: Reprinted in part from "Computer Discs Spin Off into History," *The Economist,* May 14 1988, 87. Reprinted with permission.

memory in some devices, especially those requiring ruggedness and nonvolatility, like portable computers.

The latest contender for providing cheap secondary storage is the ferro-electric RAM chip. FERRO-ELECTRIC RAM possesses nonvolatile memory made possible by the use of a special ceramic film over a silicon base. The crystals in the ceramic act as tiny bar magnets. The market potential for this technology could be enormous (see the box: Are disks to be just a memory?).

File design: applying secondary storage media

With an understanding of the physical characteristics of secondary storage media, especially magnetic tape and disk, we can examine the methods used to store, retrieve, and manage data. *File design* refers to the technique used by a file to store and retrieve data from secondary storage.

In Chapter 11, in Part Three on Productivity Software, we will look at the way records are organized into a file, which has a fundamental effect on the way programs process data from the file. We will also learn the details of how files and databases are constructed and used.

summary

■ A computer lacks the main memory capacity to store all of the data and programs at once that an information system needs. Secondary storage fills the need for additional memory, holding data and instructions in machine-readable form outside of the computer but under the computer's control.

■ Within an information system, storage can be thought of in terms of a storage hierarchy. Main memory, at the top of the hierarchy, is the fastest, most expensive, and most limited in capacity. Secondary (or external) storage, at the bottom of the hierarchy, has great capacity and is slower and less expensive. Of the technologies commonly used for secondary storage, hard disk systems are the fastest, have the greatest capacity, and are the most expensive. Capacity can be measured in terms of kilobytes, megabytes, gigabytes (Gs), and terabytes (Ts).

■ Considerations that go into selecting a storage mix are cost, speed, and security. Speed is generally measured in terms of access time—the time needed to transfer data from storage to main memory. Users, however, are usually most interested in response time—the time between making an inquiry and receiving a response.

■ Secondary storage can be either on-line (under computer control) or off-line (not under computer control).

■ Magnetic disks provide very fast, high-capacity secondary storage, and offer direct access to data. Magnetic disk units (often called DASDs for direct-access storage device) read from and write on magnetic disks.

Disks come in two types—hard (rigid) metal or flexible (floppy) plastic. Hard disks may be permanently installed in the DASD or placed in removable disk packs or small disk cartridges such as Bernoulli boxes.

■   Access time is made up of three stages: seek time, search time, and data-transfer time.

■   Data on disks are arranged in concentric rings, called tracks, on the surface of the disk. With multiple-surfaced disk packs, the set of concentric tracks above and below each other make up a cylinder. Disks can also be broken into pie-shaped segments called sectors. The process of formatting determines the exact location of tracks, cylinders, and sectors on the disk surface.

■   Magnetic disks are sensitive to environmental hazards and vulnerable to unauthorized access.

■   Magnetic tapes provide secondary storage that is neither as fast nor as high-capacity as disk, but is cheaper. With magnetic tape, only sequential access to data is possible. Magnetic tape units or drives read reel-to-reel tapes; cassette readers read cassette tape. More recently, videotape technology has come to offer a means to cheaply store data. Like disks, tapes are sensitive to environmental dangers.

■   To allow the drive mechanism room to start and stop, interrecord gaps are placed between data records. Groups of records can be compressed into and separated by an interblock gap. When data are grouped into blocks they are transferred a block at a time from tape to a buffer in the computer. The number of records in a block is called the blocking factor.

■   Mass storage refers to devices and media that can store very large quantities of data on-line. Mass storage systems include magnetic strip cartridge systems, multiple-disk systems, optical disk devices, write-once read-many (WORM) systems, and optical card units.

■   Looking to the future, charge-coupled devices, bubble memory, and ferro-electric RAM are among the technologies that might transform the future of secondary storage.

Wrap-up

Secondary storage at Global Electrical Equipment

At Global Electrical Equipment, as we saw at the beginning of the chapter, George Roberts sought data on how well his employees were doing. Using this data he would prepare a report the same day for his own manager, who would use it to determine salary increases and promotions. The data George needed were contained on secondary storage. Let's look more closely at what that means.

The data on inspector performance were maintained on-line on a multiple-disk-drive system. The purpose of keeping it on-line was to allow ready access for just such uses as George had in mind, and to permit frequent updating of data and the addition of new data. Keeping the data on disk made possible direct access to sought-after items by query programs such as the one George's assistant would use from his terminal.

Besides the on-line data, a second copy existed off-line on magnetic tape. This was strictly a backup copy, for use only if something happened to the originals.

Ward sat at his terminal and requested the data George needed. The computer system permitted both Ward and George to view these particular data. They could not, however, look at data kept by the marketing, engineering, or accounting departments.

Just before lunch, Ward handed George a one-page report containing the needed information.

"Thanks Ward," George said, taking the page. "And now . . ." George began.

Ward finished it for him, making a slicing motion with his finger at his neck.

George placed the report on his desk and skimmed the figures. For each inspector, he could see the average number of inspections per hour and the average number of incorrect choices per hour. These inspection averages were obtained by resampling some of the appliances each inspector accepted or rejected. Much of it was as he had guessed—but there were a few surprises.

For example, Irma Halpern turned out to be even better than he'd thought. She had inspected an average of thirty-eight machines an hour—eight more than the standard—yet she averaged only one incorrect choice per hour. George was always glad to go to bat for his people and get them promotions, when they were merited. For Irma, it certainly was. George scanned the figures for the other inspectors. This was the kind of information he could get enthusiastic about. His manager would sense that and probably grant most of George's requests for his employees.

Soon George would have his report finished, could feel proud of himself, and would go home early and get in a bit of gardening before dinner. He deserved it, he decided. Looking up briefly from his work, however, he noticed that heavy rain had begun.

234

key terms

These are the key terms in alphabetical order. The numbers in parentheses refer to the page on which each term is defined.

Access time (211)
Bernoulli box (217)
Blocking factor (224)
Bubble memory (229)
Buffer (225)
Charge-coupled device (229)
Cylinder (218)
DASD (direct-access storage device) (213)
Data-transfer time (217)
Direct access (212)
Disk cartridge (214)
Disk pack (214)
Ferro-electric RAM (231)
Floppy disk or diskette (215)
Formatting (218)
Gigabyte or G (210)
Hard disk (214)
Interblock gap (224)
Interrecord gap (224)
Magnetic disk (213)
Magnetic disk unit (213)
Magnetic strip cartridge system (or data cell) (226)
Magnetic tape (220)
Magnetic tape cassette (223)
Magnetic tape unit (or tape drive) (222)
Mass storage device (225)
Multiple-disk-drive system (226)
Off-line storage (212)
On-line storage (212)
Optical card systems (229)
Optical disk systems (227)
Reel-to-reel magnetic tape (222)
Response time (211)
Search time (217)
Secondary storage (or external storage) (210)
Sector (218)
Seek time (217)
Sequential access (212)
Storage hierarchy (210)
Terabyte or T (210)
Track (218)
Videotape systems (223)
WORM (Write-Once Read-Many) device (227)

review questions

objective questions

True/false. *Put the letter T or F on the line next to the question.*

1. Primary storage is generally more expensive than secondary storage. 1 ____
2. Optical disk systems offer less storage than comparably sized magnetic disk systems. 2 ____
3. Magnetic tapes are used for direct access systems. 3 ____
4. Because of the reliability of today's storage devices there is no need to backup your files. 4 ____
5. The most expensive type of secondary storage is magnetic tape. 5 ____
6. On-line storage is more vulnerable to security breaches than off-line storage. 6 ____
7. Floppy disks can hold about twenty times more data than comparably sized hard disks. 7 ____
8. The total cost for secondary storage is only the cost of accessing the data. 8 ____
9. Data coded on tape can only be placed at a right angle to the tape's length. 9 ____
10. WORM technology does not permit users to easily alter stored data. 10 ____

Multiple choice. *Put the letter of the correct answer on the line next to the question.*

1. Archival data stored on optical laser disks can include: 1 ____
   (a) Text and transaction data.
   (b) Text, transaction, voice/image data.
   (c) Transaction data.
   (d) Transaction and image data.
2. A disk pack with 1 gigabyte of storage can hold approximately how many bytes? 2 ____
   (a) 1,000.
   (b) 1,000,000.
   (c) 1,000,000,000.
   (d) 1,000,000,000,000.
3. In order to speed read/write operations, records on magnetic tape are often grouped into what? 3 ____
   (a) Sectors.　(c) Tracks.
   (b) Blocks.　(d) Files.

4. The secondary storage mixture selected for an information system depends upon:

(a) The cost of the total secondary storage mix.

(b) The security level desired for the data.

(c) The response time required by the users of the information system.

(d) All of the above factors must be considered in selecting the secondary storage mixture.

5. Fly-By-Night Airlines uses its information system to service the reservation requests of passengers as well as for traditional business operations such as payroll. What type of secondary storage mixture would be best for the airline?

(a) Direct-access storage systems.

(b) Sequential access storage systems.

(c) Mass storage systems.

(d) A combination of all of the above types.

Fill in the blank. *Write the correct word or words in the blank to complete the sentence.*

1. Microcomputers most commonly use magnetic _____ secondary storage.

2. The acronym DASD means _____.

3. A _____ uses a laser to write data for direct access retrieval.

4. The _____ time refers to the interval required to retrieve data from secondary storage and place it into main memory.

5. The _____ allows us to visualize differences in storage in terms of cost and speed.

6. The _____ time is the amount of the time between the start of an inquiry and the receipt of a response.

7. The process of preparing a disk or diskette for data storage is known as _____.

8. Data on disks are often written onto tracks contained within pie-shaped areas called _____.

9. With _____ access, to read the last record in a file of 550 records requires reading all 549 preceding records.

10. The acronym WORM means "write _____ read _____."

short answer questions

When answering these questions, think of concrete examples to illustrate your points.

1. What are the differences between primary and secondary storage?

2. What are the differences between off-line and on-line storage?

3. What is the difference between an interrecord gap and an interblock gap? Why are these gaps used?

4. What are the differences between hard and floppy disks?

5. What are some examples of mass storage devices?

6. What is WORM technology?

essay questions

1. What are the advantages and disadvantages of magnetic disk storage?

2. What are the advantages and disadvantages of magnetic tape storage?

3. Recalling the chapter opening and the wrap-up example, defend the position of not allowing George Roberts the right to alter the original data in the database.

4. Referring to the previous question, should George be able to alter these figures? If so, why? Should the reasons for the alterations be recorded? Why?

Answers to the objective questions

True/false: 1. T; 2. F; 3. F; 4. F; 5. F; 6. T; 7. F; 8. F; 9. F; 10. T
Multiple choice: 1. b; 2. c; 3. b; 4. d; 5. d
Fill in the blank: 1. disk; 2. direct-access storage device; 3. optical disk; 4. access; 5. storage hierarchy; 6. response; 7. formatting; 8. sectors; 9. sequential; 10. once, many

part three

Productivity software

Parts One and Two of this book introduced information systems, their evolution, current uses, and hardware. In Part Three, we look at the productivity software that enables users to apply their microcomputers directly to their business needs:

Software packages: programs off the shelf

After studying this chapter you should understand the following:

- *The chief advantages and disadvantages of using prewritten software.*
- *The general types of prewritten software that have found wide application in both business and the home.*
- *Some important business application areas—accounting, management, and marketing—for which specialized packaged software is available.*
- *The types of home-use software available for fun, education, and convenience.*
- *Where to obtain canned software.*
- *How to evaluate prewritten software.*

chapter 8

A canned festival of lights

The Oakriver University Information Processing Center was ablink with dazzling color graphics. People moved from one display to another as at a carnival, pausing here and there, and then walking on as the spirit moved them. Alice Smith—the systems analyst who arranged the hands-on demonstration—circulated among them. The aim today was to let everyone know what prewritten software was available. The idea seemed to be working.

"This is the most interesting meeting the Computer User's Committee has ever had," Miguel Abreu, the committee chair, said to Alice. "Did it take long to set all this up?"

"No, we really just had to move a few more microcomputers in. The software is all canned."

"Then I guess it's true," Miguel continued. "You can just take programs off the shelf, plug them in, and they work."

"If they're good, yes," Alice said. "But you have to do careful evaluating too. Some packages are just fluff. As with buying anything, when you take the wrapping off and try it out you may be disappointed."

Elizabeth Slater, from the School of Business, looked up as Alice passed. Elizabeth was seated watching a tutorial program extol the virtues of a new electronic spreadsheet. "Do you have written descriptions of all of these programs?" she asked.

"Of course," Alice said, "on the tables in the middle of the room."

"Alice!" Jasper Thomas called from across the room. "I never saw graphics of this quality!" He gazed at a screen where shapes that looked like peach-colored giant ants were moving. "The Physics Department will probably want to buy this package."

"What would you run the program on?" Alice asked.

"Well, I suppose on microcomputers," Jasper said. "We have quite a few of them."

"Unfortunately, this particular package only runs on minicomputers, and requires very expensive special-purpose display terminals."

"Come on, Jasper, what does Physics need with that, anyway?" Daniel Powers said from the next terminal. "You scientists are happy with a blackboard and a piece of chalk. We engineers, however, use computer-aided design right and left." He motioned to his screen, which showed a cross section of a roadway with the different layers represented in varying colors and textures.

Miguel Abreu tapped Alice on the shoulder and pointed to the back of the room. "Is that a canned program too?" he asked.

Alice turned and saw one of the computer operators working with a fast-paced video game. Alice laughed. "Actually I think she wrote it herself," Alice said. "I don't think the University will fund the purchase of those!"

"That's good, because I can see we're going to run out of money fast," Miguel said. "All these respectable middle-aged people want to buy everything in sight, like kids in a toy store."

"They haven't seen the price tags yet," Alice said. "That may bring a few of them in line."

Prewritten programs ready to run

*Speeding up
the program
development cycle*

Anyone with the proper skills can create programs; however, most users should first seek out prewritten software. **PREWRITTEN SOFTWARE** refers to programs that were written and tested by someone else and that are ready to run. The terms *prewritten software*, **CANNED PROGRAMS**, **PACKAGED SOFTWARE**, and **OFF-THE-SHELF PROGRAMS** are used interchangeably. These programs may have been created by someone else within the same organization, obtained free or on an exchange basis from a computer users' group, or purchased (or leased) from an outside supplier. Most often, prewritten software is purchased. A number of companies exist that write software for sale. Major hardware manufacturers also write and sell software. For-purchase software packages are the ones that have had a major impact on the world of business management over the last decade, and will be the main focus of this chapter.

Although much of the chapter deals with software for microcomputers, vast amounts of prewritten software are also available for minicomputers, mainframes, and supercomputers.

*The advantages and
disadvantages of
prewritten software*

An advantage of using prewritten software—assuming it meets the needs of your specific problem—is its immediate availability for use. Ideally you can simply purchase the program, read the introductory instructions, work with a tutorial program that accompanies it, and begin to solve your problem. In contrast, developing software at your computer center can take months or even years.

A second advantage is that good off-the-shelf programs have most of their major problems already ironed out. They have been tested and corrected as time (and resources) allow.

They also reflect an attempt at standardization. Since many people are expected to use the software, the developer has sought to provide capabilities common to many needs. In addition, if high-quality user documentation is available, you can learn how to use the package quickly.

Off-the-shelf programs also reflect a level of sophistication not easily attainable by single users. In many cases, they were developed by an expert team of analysts and programmers, and, when done well, reflect the most recent techniques in memory conservation, speed, and power.

A final advantage is the lower cost of purchasing a program compared with the cost of developing it yourself. The development costs are passed on to the many purchasers of the product instead of being borne by you or your department alone.

There are also some disadvantages to using prewritten software. One is uncertainty as to whether the software will perform as promised. In some cases the virtues of a particular canned program are oversold. Another is that you may pay for more than you need. To make their software more marketable, suppliers often pack features into programs that you might not need but nonetheless must pay for. For example, many spreadsheet programs provide mathematical functions that you may never use. In comparison with the cost of custom programs, however, the cost of these extra features may be insignificant.

The standard approach of prewritten software is another drawback at times. Perhaps you need a particular design of the screen, or layout of report, not offered by the program. Should you want to change a canned program, you will discover a third drawback. To avoid "piracy" of their products, most sellers of software protect the programs so that users cannot have access to the actual code for the program. This is certainly a reasonable precaution for the vendors. Without it they stand to lose money to people who make illegal copies or modifications of their property. As a result, however, modifications in the software may be impossible, or illegal, or, in any case, quite tricky to make. Certain programs circumvent this problem, in part, by allowing you to write your own special functions in a separate subprogram which can then be called by the package.

If you're a programmer or a company with a programming staff, a final disadvantage of buying rather than writing software is the loss of potential income from selling the program yourself. Many business-oriented software packages were originally developed internally by a company to help solve a problem, and then sold to other companies with similar problems. The rights to a program can be assigned to a software supplier or marketed directly by the company itself. Large computer firms such as National Cash Register Corporation, Hewlett-Packard, and IBM, have followed the self-marketing approach.

Canned software and your information system

Like software produced in-house or custom-built, prewritten software has an effect on the other elements of the information system. The *people* in the system must be trained in the proper use and maintenance of these packages. Users need to know what the software package can do for them. They need to be trained individually or in groups on how to make best use of the software. Information system staff must be able to answer questions from users, as well as ensure that the prewritten package can make use of the other elements of the information system—that the package can, for instance, use existing data and run on existing hardware.

Rules and procedures need to take into account the tremendous rise in the variety of canned software available. For instance, if departments and individual users throughout a large organization are buying their own canned software right and left and tapping into the company's database, the security procedures that protect the data as well as prevent unauthorized access may have to be rethought.

Besides being accessible to those who need it, and inaccessible to those who don't, *data* must be in a form the prewritten software can use. Usually database management software—itself prewritten—can aid in linking a canned program to the data. Other *software* may need to be linked up with the canned programs to provide special operations. Proper *hardware*—such as color terminals for graphics packages—allows the user to exploit the software to its fullest. Mainframes generally allow you to run bigger and faster packages, whereas microcomputers give you greater control over what you do with the package.

Let's expand upon the software aspect of our information system and its relationship to canned programs. What makes canned software easy to use is the way it is designed for the nonprogrammer. Canned programs may be coded in assembly language or in a mid- or high-level language such as BASIC, C, FORTRAN, or Pascal (the topic of Chapter 15). In addition, system programs (also covered in Chapter 15) are used by the canned software. The beauty of a canned program is that in order to make use of its power, you do not need to know how to write in a programming language, nor very much about how the canned program and system programs interact.

Much of the most popular canned software presents a series of choices concerning use of the program that are known as a MENU. This is analogous to a restaurant's menu. You see what alternatives are available and select one that is appropriate. Depending on the software, the menu can be flexible (allows user-specified substitutions) or inflexible (no substitutions, please).

If you don't understand what an item is on a restaurant menu, you ask for help or clarification from the person taking your order. Similarly, canned software often allows you to ask for help. How helpful the response to your query is determines whether you will patronize the restaurant—or use the software—again (provided you have a choice).

Prewritten software is generally designed to execute in a modular fashion. The first module allows the user to enter the program. At this point the user can select from the menu what he or she wants to do. The menu of a word-processing program, for example, would include such choices as creating a new document, recalling an old document for modifications, destroying an old document, or printing a document. Once you make a choice, the program then generally switches to a submenu for that choice. If you selected printing the document, the submenu choices might include printing all or part of the document, using special typestyle and page format options, and printing onto paper or writing onto a magnetic medium such as a diskette. Help modules aid in learning how to use the program. The final module allows you to exit the package easily.

Wrapping the package
Packaged software is often supplied to the purchaser on a magnetic input/output medium. For a microcomputer this usually means one or more floppy disks that contain the canned program (Figure 8-1). For larger computers the program is often supplied on one or more reels of magnetic tape; the computer then reads the program from the tape and stores it on disk for more rapid future reference. For information systems that use removable disk packs rather than nonremovable disks, the canned software can also be supplied on such a disk pack.

Another alternative increasingly being used for a number of microcomputer systems is supplying the program right on a memory chip, generally a read-only memory chip (ROM), from which programs can be read into the computer system for use, but upon which no changes can

Figure 8-1
Microcomputer software
packaging. The package
for Lotus 1-2-3, an inte-
grated program that
includes spreadsheet, da-
tabase, and graphics ca-
pabilities, contains the
software itself on a set of
floppy disks, a manual,
and a keyboard template.
Most major micro-
computer packages in-
clude similar elements.

be made. Software supplied this way is convenient and fast. It also provides better protection against piracy for the software developer.

Even the simplest canned program comes with documentation of some sort. Many packages are accompanied by tutorial programs. Very expensive mainframe packages may even be installed by personnel from the software company, who also iron out bugs and train users in getting the most out of the software.

Multipurpose packaged software

Horizontal and
vertical software

Prewritten software can be general in nature, useful to many different businesses, or more specific, serving the needs of one particular industry. HORIZONTAL SOFTWARE is the term given to those packages that provide general capabilities to many businesses. VERTICAL SOFTWARE are those programs that are most appropriate to one specific type of business. Word processing is horizontal since most businesses benefit from its use. Insurance premium programs, however, are vertical since they are useful only to insurance companies. Recently, the term *vertizontal software* has entered our vocabulary. It characterizes software that is more general than vertical, but not as much as horizontal. Amortization programs would fit this new category, serving a number of businesses involved with loans and interest rates (banks, real estate, and mortgage companies), but not as many as a more horizontal program, such as an accounting program, might serve.

In this section we will look briefly at the most extensively used types of horizontal packaged software: word processing software, electronic spreadsheets, database management systems, electronic mail/message systems, graphics packages, desktop publishing programs, and combined packages. These are the software products that have set the pace for the software industry recently, particularly that portion of it devoted to microcomputers. The more important horizontal packaged software will be examined more closely in the chapters that follow.

Word processing software

WORD PROCESSING SOFTWARE is used to enter, modify, arrange, and print text material. The text material may include almost anything—accounting reports, business letters, lines of computer code, term papers, legal documents, recipes, novels, or personal letters. Word processing can be done on any size computer, although it is most often performed with microcomputers. Word processing software is available for use on a general-purpose computer. For applications that do extensive word processing and nothing else, dedicated word processors are available—minicomputers or microcomputers especially designed for, and limited to, word processing.

Popular among secretaries, managers, and writers, word processing software enables users to make changes as often as necessary in a document without having to type the document over. Once you have entered the text, you can easily change it, and check it over again on the display screen, before printing it. To make changes in a document that has already been printed, you need only type the changes and print it out again. Figure 8-2 shows an example of text entry and correction using word processing software.

Originally, word processing could be done only in English, in part because the input process could move only from left to right across the page or screen (unsuitable for many Middle-eastern languages such as Arabic, which moves from right to left). Software now exists to do word processing in virtually any language (Figure 8-3). We examine word processing in detail in Chapter 9.

Electronic spreadsheets

An **ELECTRONIC SPREADSHEET** is a type of software that offers a financial worksheet on a display screen and an easy way to change figures around within the worksheet. The term *spreadsheet* comes from the name given the paper printed with rows and columns used as worksheets by accountants. Electronic spreadsheets are used principally on microcomputers. Their strength and popularity rests on their ability to do projections: you can alter values or formulas on the spreadsheet and let the program update all of the related values based on your change. This is very handy for doing financial plans and budgets.

A typical spreadsheet can be thought of as a large grid with several thousand cells arranged in rows and columns. We can use a simple example to show how spreadsheets work. A sales manager wants to examine her company's operating income by month for the year 1989. Figure 8-4 shows the spreadsheet displayed on her screen. She has entered a formula in cell G17 to subtract the contents of cell G15 from the contents of cell G14. The result, 30, the projected operating income for April, appears.

She can then alter the spreadsheet and observe how the altered data

Subversive word processors

A few of us who love writing on computers suspect that, in some dark way, machines have ruined our style. It's probably true. Most current word-processing programs simply outdistance our writing skills, and their promised ease turns out to be a deception. When programs are loaded with user-friendly, obsessively distracting features, an already difficult job can get out of control.

All writers face the same basic challenges of creating ideas, organizing information, and revising for a better effect. A computer could help them, but it really doesn't know how.

Simply trying to get started is a hard job for anyone, and any word processor that softened this block would be a help. It should encourage moving forward at top speed and saving corrections until later.

I like to think of this as separating creativity from analysis. Peter Elbow, a widely published teacher of writing, calls it "freewriting" and has shown that writers develop ideas more easily when they keep thinking of the subject and ignore trivial mistakes. Sophisticated word processing programs don't understand this—they encourage instant revision.

Simple programs like Bank Street Writer, on the other hand, make shifts to the revising mode so awkward that users forge ahead out of necessity, abandoning all hopes of a perfect first draft. The rigidity irritates some, but many writers find their ideas flow more smoothly and their sentences sound less stilted. Because it will just boot up and go with no housekeeping, Bank Street Writer is comfortable, an Underwood among Selectrics.

Average writers fall back on pet rituals to plan their attack. They plot connections with elaborate maps, trees, and other designs, or they catalog relationships by outlining, listing, and serious notetaking.

Can a computer handle this planning more effectively? Well, at least it can make it neater. An outlining program like Thinktank emulates most of these creative strategies and has real potential for the writer.

I use it every day, but I'm still not good enough for it. I have this habit of tinkering with structures and conceptual arrangements, never seeming to know when to get busy and write. And who would? Computer outlining is so much fun that it's seductive.

So there goes style again. When an outline gets too good, it gets tight in the seams, leaving no room for the spontaneous thoughts and loose rhythms that separate quick writing from the dead. We learned that by doing outlines in high school.

Then there is revising. If you still believe that computers make writing easier, you're probably thinking about the power of insert and delete. Besides, moving blocks of copy is almost as much fun as outlining.

But too many writers squander this power on surface corrections and minor rearrangements. We move one awkward paragraph ahead of another and call it an improvement.

Not that we're lazy. We might not have seen the real problem. When that happens, a computer can get downright subversive and respond in a literal-minded way, as if all our commands were purposeful and exact. When we get really involved, we begin to think that they are.

I recently asked my students to rewrite some essays that they had turned in, and I watched while they processed their texts into flabby, textureless mush. They just Cuisinarted everything because it was easy.

Source: John Strommer, *Popular Computing*, May 1985. Reprinted with permission, from the May 1985 issue of Popular Computing magazine. © McGraw-Hill, Inc., New York. All rights reserved.

Marked text
to be moved

After the text is entered,
the block to be moved
is highlighted and the
cursor moved to the new
location.

Cursor

If you are working on a typewriter and decide after you have typed something that you don't like the word order you have chosen you usually have to start over on a new sheet of paper. With a word processing program, you can make the change electronically.

Corrected text after the
block has been moved and
the paragraph reformatted.

If you are working on a typewriter and decide that you don't like the word order you have chosen after you have typed something, you usually have to start over on a new sheet of paper.
With a word processing program, you can make the change electronically.

Figure 8-2
Entering and correcting
text using word process-
ing software.

Figure 8-3
A multilingual keyboard
for multilingual word
processing.

affect related cells. Such a tool allows users to ask "What if?" questions and to see the results with far less effort (and far more accuracy) than older paper-and-pencil and calculator methods. As with any projection, however, the results will only be as good as the data entered and formulas applied. Setting up spreadsheets inaccurately has cost some compa-

Database managers

nies considerable sums of money (see Case in Point box). Chapter 10 presents a detailed look at popular spreadsheet programs.

A database is made up of a set of interrelated files. **DATABASE MANAGEMENT SYSTEMS (DBMS)** are programs that enable users to create, access, and modify databases. They are used extensively on computers of all sizes. A database management system contains three different types of software:

1. *Data definition software.* This provides users with a means of describing the characteristics of the data and the interrelationships among different data elements.

2. *Data manipulation software.* This allows users to enter, alter, and delete data from the database.

3. *Data inquiry software.* This enables users to extract data from the database in response to questions.

Oakriver University maintains a central database on faculty members. For a given faculty member the database contains the department,

Figure 8-4
Using an electronic spreadsheet. Susan Paul enters a formula in cell G17 that gives the company's projected operating income for April.

Formula in cell G17

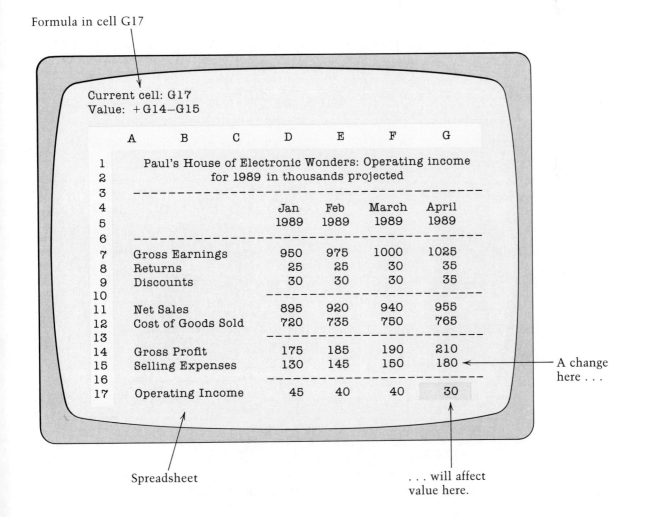

	A	B	C	D	E	F	G
		Current cell: G17					
		Value: +G14—G15					
1	Paul's House of Electronic Wonders: Operating income						
2	for 1989 in thousands projected						
3	---						
4				Jan	Feb	March	April
5				1989	1989	1989	1989
6	---						
7	Gross Earnings			950	975	1000	1025
8	Returns			25	25	30	35
9	Discounts			30	30	30	35
10				------	------	------	------
11	Net Sales			895	920	940	955
12	Cost of Goods Sold			720	735	750	765
13				------	------	------	------
14	Gross Profit			175	185	190	210
15	Selling Expenses			130	145	150	180
16				------	------	------	------
17	Operating Income			45	40	40	30

A change here . . .

Spreadsheet

. . . will affect value here.

home address and telephone, degrees earned, courses taught, and publications. Figure 8-5 shows how an authorized user might use the data inquiry software to gain information about a particular instructor. We will learn more about databases in Chapter 11.

An ELECTRONIC MAIL/MESSAGE SYSTEM or EMMS, allows people to send memos, messages, facsimiles (copies) of illustrations and photographs, and other materials electronically. The information or materials can be sent within an office, between branch locations, or across the world through satellite-based communications (see Chapter 17).

As we saw in Chapter 3, such systems are part of the information-age office. The flow of messages and paperwork can be speeded up using an EMMS. When messages are sent from one terminal to another, a paper copy may not be needed at all; indeed, some companies claim to run a virtually "paperless" office.

An EMMS works as follows. When you want to send a memo or message, you enter it into the system. Most likely you would do this with a word processing system to speed the creation of the message. You indicate one or more recipients of the information, and specify other

Electronic mail/
message systems

Figure 8-5
Using a database management package. Here an administrator at Oakriver University uses data inquiry software— part of the DBMS—to gain information about a particular instructor from Oakriver's faculty database.

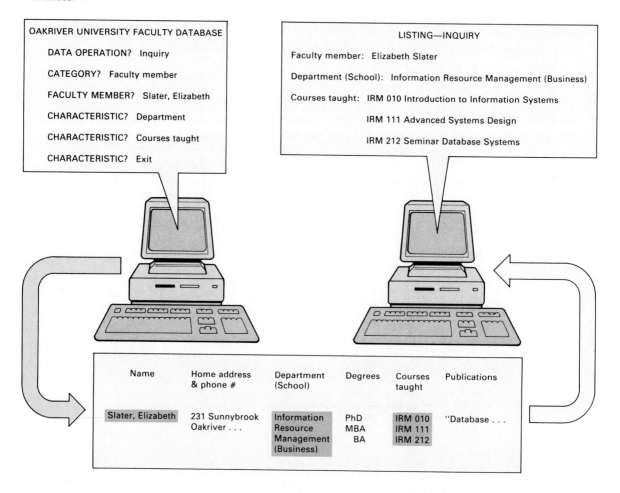

case in point

A case for horizontal "mainstream" software

. . . Self-employed professionals are the lone rangers of personal computing, often running the business side of their practices single-handedly or with a one-person support staff. When they set up their offices, sometimes at home, they don't have access to a corporate-type internal consultant for advice. They rely heavily on the software publisher for support, and, if the program takes too much time to master, most solo professionals won't bother. Time is literally money for almost all professionals, who, by definition, sell their expertise by the hour and don't get paid during the days and weeks they might spend wrestling with a new program. . . . The particular program or combination of software packages a professional chooses often determines whether the personal computer is viewed as a frustrating toy or a complete support staff on a hard disk.

When he consults to such professionals on their choice of software, Stanley Yocum, president of Seamark Consulting Group, Inc., of Long Beach, Calif., tries to steer his clients away from vertical market packages in favor of tried and tested popular off-the-shelf packages. "Chances are better than 80 percent that they will find mainstream software that will *do* 80 percent of what they need to run their office," Yocum asserts. "In the long run," he adds, "it will be cheaper for them to accommodate their practices to the 20 percent the software might not do exactly the way they want, rather than spending thousands of dollars on a sophisticated customized time and billing package or trusting their record keeping to a vertical market package that comes with documentation which won't make sense until after they've mastered the program. . . ."

Small vertical market publishers generally don't provide the high-quality documentation and hand-holding support that characterizes the best off-the-shelf packages. "Nor are you likely to find a book to help you understand the program better or a local consultant who knows anything about it," Yocum argues. . . .

[In addition, professionals'. . .] requirements are "rarely more than 20 percent different from what most other professionals need in order to run their offices," Yocum counters. They can really get most of what they need from good off-the-shelf word processors, spreadsheets, and databases. . . .

As off-the-shelf software keeps getting better, more professionals are likely to discover there is not much justification for profession-specific programs to support the business side of their practices. Some combination of a word processor, spreadsheet, and data base manager, with perhaps a tax program to round things out, can often provide more computing power and flexibility than the costlier, and sometimes riskier, vertical market applications.

details concerning the communication, such as whether or not a message is confidential and whether or not a response is required.

The message is then routed by the EMMS to the terminal(s) of the recipient(s) indicated. To read a confidential message, the user would have to first enter a password. Anyone who did not know the password would not be able to just sit down at a terminal and view the message. If the "message" sent is in the form of a photograph or facsimile, then it would be transmitted to equipment capable of reproducing it rather than a standard terminal.

Individual microcomputer users can also communicate with one another through messages without buying an EMMS. For a subscription and/or a service charge, microcomputer users can transmit messages over telephone lines to an information service such as The Source or CompuServe. The computers run by the service will "post" the message on an electronic bulletin board. An **ELECTRONIC BULLETIN BOARD** is a computer-maintained list of messages that can be posted and read by different computers, often concerning a topic of common interest. Curious "readers" can look at the messages the bulletin board contains, and read and respond to those they wish. Typical topics are science fiction novels, good restaurants in the area, and microcomputers.

Graphics packages

Although printed text is the dominant medium for computer output, it is by no means the only one. **GRAPHICS PACKAGES** allow the construction and output of pictorial information. The information can be displayed on a screen, plotted on a hard-copy pictorial output device known as a plotter, produced by a printer, or converted to transparencies for projection. Graphics packages are available for all sizes of computers—mainframes, minicomputers, and microcomputers. We will see more on graphics in Chapter 12.

Figure 8-6
A picture is worth a thousand words—some examples of the graphs and diagrams graphics packages can produce.

Businesses use graphics packages to develop charts that summarize situations at a glance (as in Figure 8-6). The old saw that "a picture is worth a thousand words" still rings true, and a continual concern in designing output in any medium for management is presenting it in brief, summary fashion. Graphical output is well suited to this. A typical use is to show summarized statistics to management. Corporate

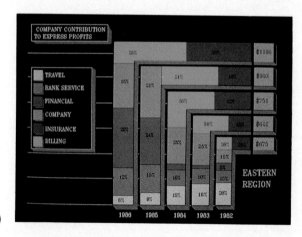

(a)

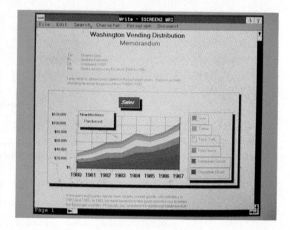

(b)

Figure 8-7
Computer-aided design.

income might be displayed in a multicolored "pie chart," showing which slices of the pie came from which sources. Sales projections could be shown with a bar-chart display.

Nonbusiness applications of graphics include producing weather reports, contour maps, and computer art. **COMPUTER-AIDED DESIGN (CAD)** systems use computers to facilitate design of a product (Figure 8-7). The designer works at a terminal, drawing graphical designs either with a special pad that transfers the data to the computer, or directly on the display screen using a light-sensitive rod known as a light pen. The engineer can manipulate and alter the design at the terminal. The type of display screen and printer or plotter used for a CAD system must be of a higher quality than that necessary for creating graphics for management use.

It is difficult to write programs yourself that produce high-quality graphics. In fact, graphics was one of the first areas historically to employ canned programs. Before the advent of display screen output or of printers that could draw, graphic output was by plotter only. Packaged subroutines were supplied with the plotter; users could call the subroutines, giving quite specific data such as where the pen should be placed on the page in terms of x-y coordinates, and the subroutine would handle the still thornier instructions for getting the pen there.

Modern graphics software meets most users at a much higher level. User-friendly graphics packages like the one illustrated in Figure 8-8 guide users quickly and painlessly to elegant output that can easily outdo those thousand words. The user selects the desired output from a menu. Then one or more screens appear asking the user to specify details about the selected graphical form, such as color and texture, and to give the data values to be displayed along with appropriate labels. The actual graphics display is then produced on the specified device.

Integrated packages

A number of **INTEGRATED SOFTWARE PACKAGES** contain the features of several of the software packages discussed above. For example, programs like Lotus's 1-2-3, Microsoft's Multiplan, and Borland's Quattro combine three elements: electronic spreadsheets, database (file) management, and graphics (Figure 8-9). Another Lotus product, Symphony,

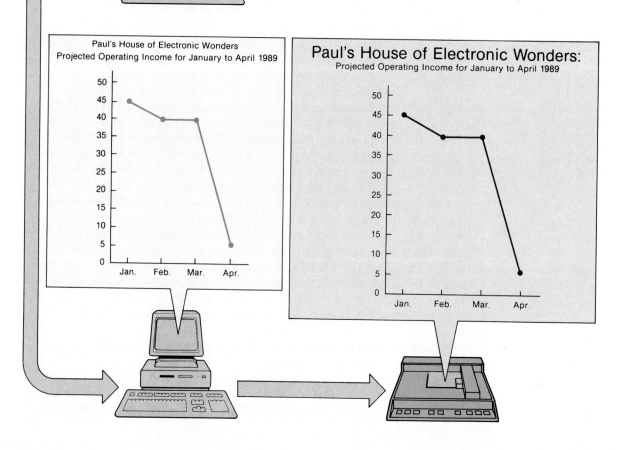

GRAPHICS MENU

BAR CHARTS
PIE CHARTS
LINEAR GRAPHS
STACKED GRAPHS
TWO-DIMENSIONAL GRAPHS (XY)
HELP
QUIT

TO MAKE A SELECTION TYPE THE FIRST LETTER: L

LINEAR GRAPHS
TITLE: Paul's House of Electronic Wonders:
SUBTITLE: Projected Operating Income for January to April 1989

MENU

SYMBOL ONLY
LINE ONLY
BOTH LINE AND SYMBOL
VALUE LABEL ONLY
EXIT LINE GRAPH

TO MAKE A SELECTION TYPE THE FIRST LETTER: B

COLOR SELECTION

MONOCOLOR (BLACK)
BLUE
GREEN
RED
YELLOW

TO MAKE A SELECTION TYPE THE FIRST LETTER: G

DATA

LABEL	VALUE
Jan.	45
Feb.	40
Mar.	40
Apr.	6

Paul's House of Electronic Wonders
Projected Operating Income for January to April 1989

Paul's House of Electronic Wonders:
Projected Operating Income for January to April 1989

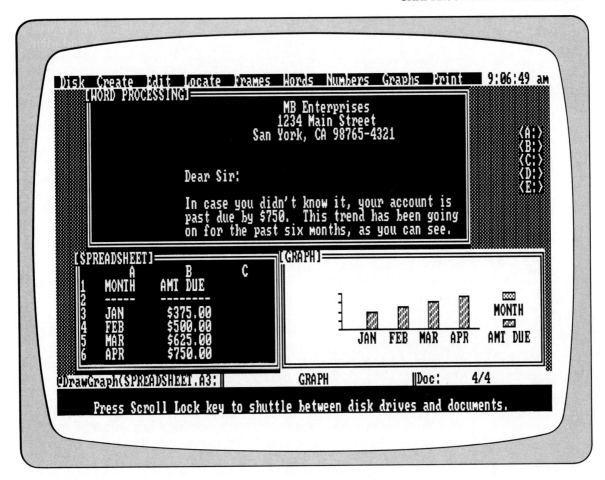

Figure 8-9
A screen from an integrated software package. The overlapping windows show its word processing, spreadsheet, and graphics capabilities.

Figure 8-8 (opposite)
Using a graphics package to produce a graph.

adds word processing capabilities. Ashton-Tate's Framework, and Software Publishing's PFS: First Choice, also combine database, spreadsheet, word processing, and telecommunications capabilities. These multiple-use packages allow a user to move from one feature to another with great ease, say from word processing to database management. A user might create a spreadsheet using data from the company's database, and then switch to the word processing function and incorporate the spreadsheet into a memorandum.

Combined packages offer a lot of software for users who require a variety of prepackaged functions. Their price tag is higher, however, and they usually require more memory than single-use packages. Still, it may be argued that the cost is actually cheaper, since you are getting four packages in one. It comes down to a matter of preference. Some users appreciate the consistency of menus and commands found in integrated packages. They like the ease of moving from one application to another without changing software, and the ability to easily incorporate data from one application into another. Others feel that in trying to be a "jack of all trades," integrated packages are not as powerful in each area as separate programs. They further argue that since data can be transferred among separate packages with the proper programs, they are bet-

Figure 8-10
Desktop publishing can produce professional-looking output combining text and images in a pleasing layout.

ter off using separate, more powerful, software. In general, users who do not really need all of the functions are probably better served by purchasing only those single programs that they do need.

Desktop publishing

A relative newcomer to the world of prewritten packages, DESKTOP PUBLISHING PROGRAMS enable users to combine text and graphic material in the same document and then manipulate them into a pleasing layout (see Figure 8-10). Users can control the size and style of type, the number and widths of columns, and the placement of all items on the page. With the proper equipment, such as high-resolution monitors and laser printers, desktop publishing programs can be used to produce newsletters, books, brochures, and letters that come close to the quality of typeset material.

Business managers are well acquainted with the importance of a good presentation. Over the next few years, as equipment capability increases and prices drop, we will see a significant increase in the use of desktop publishing in both large and small businesses. Chapter 12 examines the development and application of desktop publishing programs in today's business world.

Packages for general business

The multipurpose canned software just described is useful in many different home and office settings. We will now shift our focus to packaged horizontal software intended specifically for business functions. These packages come in all sizes, to meet needs ranging from the one-person business or small office with a microcomputer, to major corporations with their powerful mainframes. Even large organizations with extensive in-house staffs of programmers and systems analysts still evaluate and, when appropriate, purchase packaged software for specific needs; their information systems thus consist of a blend of custom-designed in-house software and packages obtained without the birth pains of development.

Accounting

There are well over 1000 ACCOUNTING PACKAGES available to computer users today. They range from simple bookkeeping and check-register programs for users of home computers, to complex packages costing $100,000 or more for use by corporations.

Some of the advantages of using canned accounting packages can be seen by looking at a small business the size of Freddy Johnson's Travel Agency, with its 71 employees. The growing success of the company, a sharp drop in hardware prices, plus the need to remain competitive, make it possible for the travel agency to install a computer system to handle accounting and other functions (Figure 8-11).

Instead of programming in-house (which is timely and costly), the agency can purchase canned packages to handle basic accounting needs: a payroll system to write the 71 paychecks and maintain records of employee taxes withheld and other deductions; an accounts payable system to control company bills; and an accounts receivable system to generate customer bills and track those still outstanding. A general ledger program can replace the agency's main bookkeeping records, producing

Figure 8-11
Monogram's Dollars & Sense is a popular home accounting package for microcomputers. This screen displays a partial list of accounts that have been set up by the user.

```
Edit Accounts/Budgets                    Net Annual Budget Balance:        0.00

NUM     ACCOUNT NAME       TYPE      START BALANCE   MONTHLY BDGT   VARIABLE BUDGET

100  Personal Checking   Check         1,250.00          0.00
101  Brokerage           Asset         9,200.00          0.00
200  Cash                Asset            50.00          0.00
201  Credit Union        Asset         4,400.00        124.33      [ Variable ]
202  Stocks & Bonds      Asset        87,135.00        600.00
203  Stock Savings Plan  Asset        24,115.93        400.00
204  Home                Asset       204,900.00          0.00
300  Mortgage            Liability   141,106.00         80.00
301  Auto Loan           Liability     4,750.00        200.00
302  Visa                Liability       250.00          0.00
303  American Express    Liability       419.12          0.00
400  Gross Income        Income           0.00       5,300.00
401  Interest Income     Income           0.00          12.00
402  Dividends           Income           0.00         700.00
403  Check Interest      Income           0.00           6.00
404  Cap Gains - Long    Income           0.00           0.00
405  Cap Gains - Short   Income           0.00           0.00
406  Unrealized Gains    Income           0.00           0.00

(Esc to Main Menu)
F1Help 2New 3Opts 4Backup 5Delete/Undo 6Chk Info              10Save
```

computerized balance sheets and income statements. Another common computerized accounting function—inventory—is not required at Freddy Johnson's, since services rather than physical products are sold. Similarly, tax preparation programs would not be required.

When a company switches from a manual to a computer-based information system, it does so first with accounting. Prewritten software—carefully evaluated before purchase to make sure it will meet company needs—can deliver the sought-after results in a hurry: more efficient and timely issuance of bills and checks, more up-to-date maintenance of accounting records, lower costs for carrying out the accounting process, and improved cash flow due to measures such as careful tracking of money owed. In addition, the ease of computerized systems enables managers to generate "statements of financial condition" at any time they wish, not just at the end of accounting periods.

Management

As with accounting packages, users can choose from a wide range of MANAGEMENT-ORIENTED SOFTWARE. Application packages exist in the areas of personnel management, operations management, forecasting, facilities maintenance, and resource management.

In the area of personnel management, for example, prewritten software exists to help managers set up work schedules, create confidential databases for personnel records, and manage the various employee benefit plans. In the area of operations management, production control programs assist in scheduling production, in monitoring output, and in quality control. In forecasting, the most popular purchased tool is the electronic spreadsheet (discussed earlier in this chapter and in Chapter 10); other packages exist which—based on the input you supply—will project possible future consequences of present actions. Facilities maintenance packages control the air-conditioning, heating, lighting, and security systems in offices, warehouses, and factories. Resource management packages assist in determining the optimal levels of production given an organization's financial, material, and labor resources.

Finance

FINANCE PACKAGES address such concerns as forecasting the company's budget for the next fiscal year, determining the credit-worthiness of clients, or modeling the outcomes of various investment decisions. Often these financial models are included as part of electronic spreadsheet packages. Nonetheless, special prewritten software is available. A package might, for instance, help Oakriver University decide whether or not to put up a new building for the Foreign Languages Department. A prepackaged capital expenditure analysis program could aid administrators in seeing if the investment made sense in the long run, or whether the university might save money and yet meet expansion needs by postponing construction and giving the department two floors of space in another building slated for demolition in 10 years.

A user-friendly series of prompts would elicit the data from a responsible person within the university with access to the relevant financial information and other figures needed for modeling. The program would then project the costs and benefits of different options. The program's output might show that erecting the building now, rather than waiting 10 years, was the better option, based on the assumption that construction costs will continue to escalate. The money saved by not building now, invested in low-risk, managed-growth securities would not grow enough in 10 years to match the differential in construction costs.

Naturally, the principle that the output of a program can be no better than its input, applies. Like management packages, finance packages are meant to be used by those who are experts in their areas of inquiry. The output of such packages is not extensive information, but vital information. Standard accounting packages, on the other hand, are heavy on output, and do not demand the same skill level of intelligent use since they deal with more routine operations.

Engineering

Another area where packaged software is available to help skilled people make important decisions is in engineering. Engineers can produce three-dimensional graphical designs at a terminal, alter them to their specifications, rotate the designs to examine different views, and create a hard copy of the design as well as of the specifications that produced it. This is possible using *computer-aided design* (discussed earlier in the "Graphics Packages" section). Engineers and their support personnel also can purchase canned software to aid in testing products at various stages of design and production and to carry out quality-assurance procedures.

Manufacturing

There are two major applications for prewritten software in the manufacturing process: computer-aided manufacturing and materials management. COMPUTER-AIDED MANUFACTURING (CAM) uses a computer to direct the production and assembly process. CAM systems usually direct machine tools and robots, and come in a wide variety of types. With recent packages, the user can select the correct sequence of operations from a menu and give specifications—cutting depth, for instance—for the operation.

Materials management is concerned with the control of manufacturing inventories. Raw materials on hand can be tallied, reorder points determined, and purchases made in a timely fashion that will neither keep the manufacturing process waiting for lack of materials, nor stockpile excessive quantities of those materials (Figure 8-12). Inventories of the finished product can also be controlled.

Marketing

In marketing an important goal is to know your customer. Sales-call packages help coach salespeople on how to make the right approach. A popular package for salespeople allows the user to develop a "psychological profile" of a potential customer. From this profile, the package then generates a suggested sales approach in terms of how to pitch the sales presentation. For example, if the psychological profile shows the client is put off by pushy methods, the salesperson will be advised to use a "soft-sell" approach.

Those involved in marketing have access to a variety of other software tools as well. Specific packages exist for sales analysis and market research; generalized packages such as database systems can be helpful

Figure 8-12
Software for materials resource management helps managers plan their resource needs for efficient production.

for marketing applications. Sales-order software helps speed up the order-processing effort by allowing the salesperson to transmit orders to the information system.

Packages for fun, education, and convenience

In addition to multipurpose packaged software and packages for generalized business use, there are plenty of prewritten programs strictly for having fun, for education, and for obtaining services in the convenience of your own home.

Computer games

The stock exchange has closed for the day, so it's time to put that spreadsheet away and have some fun. Computer games, a microcomputer phenomenon, are played by watching the action or questions on the display screen and responding using the keyboard, joysticks, or a mouse. Joysticks are movable levers like an airplane's control stick, used to control cursor movement or some other facet of a computer game. A "mouse" allows similar control through hand movements on a desk. Today, computer games range from those that provide challenge to nothing more than one's reaction time, as in firing missiles at the enemy, to those requiring great patience and mental skill, as in unraveling computerized mystery or adventure stories. There are games that appeal to virtually every age group and interest, providing tests, simulations, art, music, advice, and even magic. Games like Microsoft's Flight Simulator and Chuck Yeager's Advanced Flight Trainer can actually teach you instrument navigation and flying techniques. AdLib's Personal Music System lets you compose and play music. Psion, a chess program, plays an excellent game of chess with actual chess pieces appearing on the screen. Show-Biz Services' Computerized Magician Series enables you to perform magic with cards, numbers, and ESP, using your computer as an assistant. Figure 8-13 shows some typical microcomputer games.

While most games are designed for home use, a few have secretly

The office of the present and future—the information-age office—bristles with computerized equipment: word processing systems, electronic mail/message systems, intelligent copiers, facilities for teleconferencing, and more. The core of this or any office remains people, and the office administrator who is effective in managing people and in coordinating high-tech equipment is a new breed.

Computers are having ever more impact in office automation. The technologically proficient office administrator can therefore be expected to have rich and varied career opportunities.

Office administrators exist at different levels. The individual on top, the administrative office manager, is responsible for seeing that offices meet the needs of the organization. This means planning and controlling the people, financial resources, materials, and relevant automated systems. The systems include word processing facilities, records management, telecommunications, and teleconferencing. Sometimes the administrative office manager is charged with acquiring and disseminating information in the broadest sense, including not only the systems just mentioned but the traditional computer functions of systems analysis, programming, and computer operations.

At the next lower level, the middle-level office administrator assists top management in planning policy, and plays a more active role in carrying it out. The supervisory-level office administrator, the lowest in the hierarchy, carries out plans that middle management develops, and typically supervises a particular area, such as word processing, control of interoffice communications, or purchase of materials. More managers are required at the supervisory level than at the middle level, and the fewest openings exist at the top.

How do you become an office administrator? As a fairly new career, in an area undergoing fast-paced change, there is no sure route. The ability to interact with people effectively is one prerequisite. A business administration background wouldn't hurt. Above all, though, today's office administrator must demonstrate technical comprehension of automated equipment. Knowledge of information systems figures heavily, and hands-on experience in word processing, telecommunications, or other relevant areas, can separate you from the pack in today's job market.

(a)

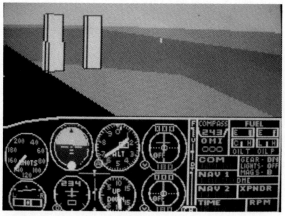

(b)

Figure 8-13
Screens from typical
computer games.

migrated into the business office, appearing during lunch hours or other breaks. In a playful mood, programs like Gato and Yacht offer a "no sound" option and a hidden "boss switch" to hide the game in case your boss walks in unexpectedly. By pressing one or two keys, the game screen is immediately replaced by a businesslike spreadsheet (Figure 8-14). When the boss leaves, another keypress brings the game back!

Computer-assisted instruction

In COMPUTER-ASSISTED INSTRUCTION (CAI), a computer is used to teach material to a student or other user, generally on an interactive basis such that the computer corrects incorrect answers immediately after the student gives them. These programs are available for mainframes, minicomputers, and microcomputers, but our focus here will be on microcomputers. CAI packages (see Figure 8-15) run the educational gamut, from flash-card programs for prekindergartners to continuing-education instruction for postgraduate professionals. Packages exist to teach computer languages and speed-reading, prepare students for examinations, and drill students in Morse code.

Figure 8-14
(a) Yacht's "normal"
game screen. (b) After
pressing the "boss
switch," a fake spread-
sheet appears in its
place.

CAI is also used in the business world to aid in personnel training. A worker might be trained to use a new machine or a new process on an old machine with the help of instructional programming. The flight simulators used to train pilots are a particularly sophisticated example

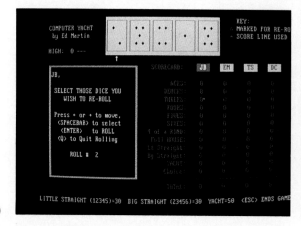

(a)

(b)

(a)

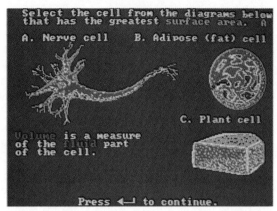

(b)

Figure 8-15
Computer-assisted in-
struction (CAI) allows
students to learn at their
own pace.

of computerized instruction. On a more routine level, the tutorial pro-grams accompanying many popular software packages are also examples of CAI.

The trick to a good CAI package is to have features that allow a user to move at his or her own pace. Most CAI packages adopt a format of short questions to which only one answer is possible; this is amenable to drilling simple mathematical operations, checking a spelling answer, or answering a series of true/false or multiple-choice questions. Unfortu-nately CAI packages do not do the complete job. Knowing that an answer is wrong is not enough; the person needs to know why. For this a teacher is usually required, as in the past.

Home managers

Tired of the tedium of manually balancing your checkbook? Of finding the perfect recipe for that perfect dinner party? Of filing the addresses of relatives and friends? Well, HOME-MANAGEMENT SOFTWARE—which per-forms convenience-oriented services as well as some accounting for microcomputer users—is just for you. Or maybe not.

Many home-management packages are available. Figure 8-16 illus-trates one product at work. Whether many of these packages are in fact economically worthwhile is something only you can decide. If you write only twenty checks a month and feel comfortable with rudimentary arithmetic, you may find it cheaper, and perhaps faster, to balance your

Figure 8-16
Andrew Tobias's Manag-
ing Your Money is a pop-
ular package for moni-
toring and controlling
home finances.

checkbook with paper and pencil and a small calculator than with a computer.

In addition to packages you can use at home, there are a variety of information-processing services that you can plug your home computer into—for a fee—using telephone lines. These include home banking services to handle such matters as paying bills; at-home ordering service for appliances and consumer goods; services that provide stock market and other financial reports; database-search services; and more. Indeed, today the computer has come home—a number of services will sell you processing time on their powerful minicomputers or mainframes, which you can utilize through your own microcomputer over phone lines. Computer services available by teleprocessing are discussed in Chapter 17.

Selecting packaged software

As with selecting a programming language, choosing prewritten software can be quite a challenge. The first step is to identify what your needs are; that is, what problem you wish to solve. You can turn to various sources that regularly evaluate software, such as trade journal reviewers and independent software-testing houses. In addition, it helps to know what questions you need to find answers for. The following questions are useful for microcomputer and mainframe systems.

■ *What does the program do?* This question refers to the tasks the program performs. You must determine what your present and future needs are, and then find the package to satisfy them. For example, one accounting program might handle 200 entries for accounts payable, while another package might handle up to 500.

■ *What machines will it work on?* Not every software package will work on all models of the type of computer it is geared to. Some microcomputer packages can be transferred from one microcomputer to another, while others are unique to one system.

■ *Will you need to modify your hardware?* A new software package may require more main memory than you currently have, or a disk drive system with a larger capacity. Other software may demand output hardware capable of producing high-quality graphics. Always test software on a system similar to the one you will use it on before you buy it.

■ *What do you do if the software doesn't work?* Find out what kind of warranty (if any) accompanies the software. Faults may show up in the actual software, in your equipment, in your installation and use of the software, or because you bought the wrong kind of software to begin with. When the software is defective, your legal recourse varies from state to state. Some suppliers provide support in diagnosing and correcting problems. In the case of major packages for mainframes, this support can be quite extensive. You should also try to evaluate the financial viability of the software vendor prior to purchase—less stable companies come and go frequently in this market.

■ *Are there classes or books available to explain how to work with the software?* Many classes and books are available for the most popular software systems. For microcomputer software, classes may be offered through university extension programs, the store where you purchased the software (sometimes for free), and through private classes or tutors.

■ *Does the software come with an accompanying training or tutorial program?* A good tutorial will let you progress at your own pace and allow you to skip over material you already know. It should be written in a user-friendly style.

■ *How good does the user documentation look?* Ask the sales-person to show you a copy of the documentation supplied with the program. Not only should the documentation be complete, but it should be written in a style you can understand.

■ *How much does the software cost?* You should consider not only the initial cost of the software, but also any possible associated costs, such as the cost of buying additional hardware, training people to use the software, changing the data into a usable form, and updating the system as your needs change. For example, a good accounts receivable program should accommodate more customers as a business grows.

■ *How much will it cost to upgrade the software?* As your needs change, you should be able to continue using the software. Perhaps there are options or additional parts of the package that can be added to expand your system. In any case, if you upgrade your hardware, you want the existing software to be able to run on it.

■ *Can you make copies of the software for your own protection? If not, are you given a backup copy?* If copies can be made, you will need to do so, and to keep them in a different location than the original, so that you can still use the program if the original is damaged. Some software packages are protected against copying to protect the copyright of the vendor and prevent unauthorized copies. For these systems the vendor usually supplies a backup copy with the original. If you can't make your own backup copy and the vendor doesn't supply one, you could find yourself, at least temporarily, without working software.

Sources of prewritten software

Prewritten software is only helpful, of course, if you know that it exists and know where to obtain it. Most of us find out about prewritten software much the same way we learn about good movies and books. Friends recommend them; we read reviews; we see advertisements. Smart business users read computer and business publications from time to time to see what is current. Often, colleagues can be asked if they have experience with a particular package, or salespeople and vendors will advertise their latest offerings if you're on their mailing list.

Prewritten software can be obtained from many sources. It can be ordered directly from the manufacturer or distributor, or purchased in a computer or software store, usually at full retail price. Many users find that buying from a store provides them with the opportunity to see the software demonstrated before purchase and to obtain it immediately. Many stores offer assistance in selection and use, and provide customer support after purchase. Local stores can also be convenient in the event of exchange or malfunction.

Software is available through mail-order companies, which usually offer substantial discounts. Of course, the ability to try out software and the ease of exchange is diminished. In addition, immediate purchase is not possible since packages must be shipped.

Software can also be obtained through book and magazine publishers who may offer software in printed form for typing into your computer, or disk versions for immediate use.

There is also **PUBLIC-DOMAIN SOFTWARE**. These prewritten programs are offered free of charge (or for a minimal copying fee) and may be copied and distributed freely. In many cases, these programs can be obtained through friends, computer user groups, or electronic bulletin boards. While many of these programs are trivial, some are excellent, even surpassing their commercial counterparts. "Why would anyone want to offer software for free?" you might well ask. We can envision a few possible motivations: Perhaps the software is too specific for commercial success, or is offered only after the author has given up trying to market it. The author might simply be a computer enthusiast who wants to encourage others to use computers. More likely, the author is not well known and is using this program as a calling card or "loss leader" to gain a reputation, hoping that future programs will then be recognized and achieve commercial success. Whatever the reason, public-domain software can be an excellent source of interesting programs for business and home.

Lastly, **PUBLICLY SUPPORTED SOFTWARE**, or **SHAREWARE**, offers another interesting avenue for program acquisition. Although these programs can also be freely copied and distributed, they are not public-domain programs—the author retains copyright and there is a user's fee attached. Shareware attempts to respond to the need for users to try out software before purchase; it says much about the author's inherent trust of the marketplace. Imagine for a moment: You dine at a restaurant, but receive no bill when you leave. Instead, you tell the cashier what you ate and then pay some reasonable price for it. This is, in essence, how shareware works. You can copy a shareware program, take it home or to your business, and use it for some reasonable length of time. Only after you decide that it is useful and that you plan to continue with it, do you send some fee (ranging from $5 to $100) to the author. If you decide not to use it, you pay nothing. Often this registration fee also entitles you to full documentation of the program, perhaps a new version, or even some reimbursement if you encourage other users to purchase it. How much fairer can it be? You use it as much as you wish, decide on its practicality, and only then pay a very reasonable fee for registration and support. For example, ButtonWare shareware products in word processing, spreadsheets, database, and communications have successfully matched the power of programs costing $400 or more, for less than one-fourth the price. Shareware is an interesting approach: It eliminates the "buy-before-you-try" problem, ensuring that the program meets or exceeds your individual needs prior to purchase. It also relies on the inherent honesty of human nature for its commercial success, and provides a reasonable product at a reasonable cost.

The need for installation

Many canned programs have specific hardware requirements that vary from the "normal" computer configuration. Some may require additional memory. Others may need a color or graphics screen. Certain multidisk programs run better if used on a hard disk. Since program designers can't predict exactly what type of equipment you have, or how you will wish to use the program, they often include an **INSTALLATION PROGRAM**—a set of options that allows you to match the program to your specific hardware. More likely than not, software must first be installed on your particular computer before it can be used. Installation configures the program for your specific needs. It usually includes defining the default locations of the program and data (using a disk identifier such as A:, B:, or C:), and selecting the type of monitor and printer to be used. The **DEFAULT SETTINGS** are those that are used unless you change them later on. In addition, programs will allow you to adjust other parts of their operation (color, speed, capabilities) to suit your own tastes.

Self-booting programs

Software can also be adjusted to self-boot, or start itself, without the need for the user to type any commands. Many users prefer to have each disk go directly into its program when the computer switch is turned on. These so-called turn-key setups make program start-up automatic. Other users prefer to type commands or respond to menus to start each program. The choice is yours.

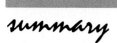

- Prewritten software refers to programs that were written and tested by someone else and are ready to run. The terms *prewritten software*, *canned programs*, *packaged software*, and *off-the-shelf programs*, are used interchangeably. Most often, prewritten software is purchased. The main advantage of using prewritten software rather than writing it yourself is that it is ready for immediate use. The main disadvantage is that you may pay for more program capabilities than you really require or, at the other extreme, may not get a program that exactly fits your needs.

- Software exists in two basic forms. Horizontal software is general in nature and can be applied to many different businesses. Vertical software tends to be more specific and serves the needs of a particular industry.

■ Many software packages provide menus, allowing you to select the desired functions from a list of possible options.

■ Increasingly, canned software is being written onto read-only memory (ROM) chips—a convenient feature for the user and an excellent protection against piracy for the software developers.

■ Electronic bulletin boards allow interested users an opportunity to communicate messages and other correspondence to users who share similar interests.

■ Multipurpose packaged software is used in business, at home, and in the schools. The main products are word processing software, electronic spreadsheets, database management systems (DBMS), electronic mail/message systems (EMMS) (including electronic bulletin boards), graphics packages (including computer-aided design systems), desktop publishing programs, and integrated packages. These are the canned programs that have set the pace for the software industry recently.

■ Packages for general business include accounting, management, finance, engineering, manufacturing, and marketing. Even large organizations with extensive in-house staffs of programmers and systems analysts still use packaged software for specific needs.

■ Computer-aided design software allows engineers and designers an opportunity to speed up the time required to create and modify product plans. They can use light pens to write product modifications "onto" the display terminal screen.

■ Management-oriented prewritten software packages allow opportunities to increase the productivity of information system users in the workplace. Computer-aided manufacturing (CAM) permits the use of more efficient machinery in the production of goods. Materials management uses software to help determine the material requirements during the entire production process. Sales-call packages assist users in interpreting the needs of the purchaser.

■ Other popular types of packaged software include computer games, computer-assisted instruction, and home management software.

■ When choosing prewritten software, you must first identify your needs. Then, a few questions can determine if the software meets those needs with regard to equipment required, accompanying tutorial or training programs, and cost. Carefully selected prewritten software can do what it is supposed to—save users the time, expense, and difficulty of writing the software themselves.

■ Prewritten software can be obtained from many sources, including direct purchase from manufacturers, distributors, publishers, computer stores, software stores, and mail order. Stores tend to offer the most user support; mail order usually offers the cheapest prices. Public-domain software is freely available from colleagues, electronic bulletin boards, and user groups. Publicly supported, or shareware, programs can be copied freely, used for a trial period, and then registered for a small fee.

■ Prewritten software is usually accompanied by an installation program that allows it to be matched to specific computer hardware.

wrap-up

The need to evaluate prewritten software

Alice Smith gathered the participants around her for an impromptu meeting before they left. "I'm glad to see everyone has taken literature on the software they're interested in," Alice said.

"And we thank you, Alice, for letting us try it out," said Miguel Abreu, the committee chair.

"The programs will be here for you to use the rest of the week," Alice said. "I would also urge you to read this carefully." She passed out a document produced by the Information Processing Center.

"This memo shows some factors you should consider when comparing programs. Things like what machines it runs on, how much it costs, and whether it really does what you want it to."

"How will the selection procedure work?" Jasper Thomas asked.

Miguel answered, "As representatives of your respective schools, you have decided, with your colleagues, what you need. But two more groups have a say as well. The first group is the committee as a whole. That's because we have to balance our budget and make sure we're not creating a hodgepodge of duplicate services and programs. The second group is the Information Processing Center."

"You see," Alice said, "it's our obligation at the Center to see that the software you choose is well programmed and decently documented. Also, we like some evidence of vendor support."

"Why are these considerations so important, Alice?" Jasper asked. "You people can always fix up a program if it doesn't run properly, can't you?"

"Most times, Jasper, we can," Alice said. "But we are up to our ears in programming your in-house software. With a solid programming backlog of several months, we want to make sure that any 'packaged' purchases really are packaged. After all, that's why you're buying them—to eliminate the need for you or me to program them."

Only slightly sobered by Miguel's and Alice's concluding admonitions, the committee members filed past the sparkling animated displays, clutching their piles of brochures. Jasper couldn't resist making one last attempt to "land" at LaGuardia Airport in New York before he left. Now how was he going to justify that Flight Simulator in his budget?

key terms

These are the key terms in alphabetical order. The numbers in parentheses refer to the page on which each term is defined.

Accounting package (255)
Canned program (240)
Computer-aided design (CAD) (251)
Computer-aided manufacturing (CAM) (257)
Computer-assisted instruction (CAI) (260)
Database management systems (DBMS) (247)
Default setting (265)
Desktop publishing program (254)
Electronic bulletin board (250)
Electronic mail/message system (EMMS) (248)
Electronic spreadsheet (244)
Finance package (256)
Graphics package (250)
Home-management software (261)
Horizontal software (243)
Installation program (265)
Integrated software package (251)
Management-oriented software (256)
Menu (242)
Off-the-shelf program (240)
Packaged software (240)
Prewritten software (240)
Public-domain software (264)
Publicly supported software (264)
Shareware (264)
Vertical software (243)
Word processing software (244)

review questions

objective questions

True/false. *Put the letter T or F on the line next to the question.*

1. A user of a software package needs to know how to write programs in the language in which the package was written. 1 _____

2. Spreadsheet packages are simulated electronic financial worksheets. 2 _____

3. Software packages are only available for micro- and minicomputers 3 _____

4. Computer-aided design (CAD) does not require graphics hardware support. 4 _____

5. An otherwise good package might not be used if the user documentation is poor. 5 _____

6. The availability of upgrades is not an important factor in selecting software. 6 _____

7. The term EMMS means the same thing as electronic bulletin board. 7 _____

8. A major advantage of off-the-shelf software is its almost immediate availability. 8 _____

9. Prewritten software always performs as promised. 9 _____

10. A "boss switch" allows business users to prepare reports for superiors easily. 10 _____

Multiple choice. *Put the letter of the correct answer on the line next to the question.*

1. Which of the following is *not* usually a factor in selecting a software package? 1 _____
   (a) Price.
   (b) Existing features.
   (c) Documentation.
   (d) Ease of rewriting the program code.

2. Spreadsheet packages allow users to 2 _____
   (a) Manipulate data in subparts of the grid.
   (b) Manipulate data in columns.
   (c) Manipulate data in rows.
   (d) All of the above answers are correct.

3. The most important advantage of word processing is 3 _____

(a) The decrease in time needed to "type" original documents.
(b) The availability of spelling-checker packages.
(c) The decrease in time required to edit text.
(d) The capacity to integrate text and other types of data processing.

4. The computerized production of graphical and textual output in a variety of media is called
(a) Computer-aided design.
(b) Integrated software.
(c) Computer-aided manufacturing.
(d) Electronic mail/message systems.

5. Integrated software packages usually do not include
(a) Electronic bulletin boards.
(b) Spreadsheets.
(c) File (database) management.
(d) Graphics.

Fill in the blank. *Write the correct word or words in the blank to complete the sentence.*

1. Buyers of prewritten software generally pay _____ than purchasers of custom software.
2. Prewritten software often presents you with a _____ listing a series of choices available to you.
3. Packaged software is generally designed to execute in a _____ fashion.
4. Publicly supported software is also known as _____.
5. _____ software is useful to one specific industry.
6. Computers designed exclusively for word processing are called _____.
7. Software _____ is a major problem for creators and marketers of prewritten software.

8. The availability of yearly _____ is a crucial feature in selecting a tax preparation package.

short answer questions

When answering these questions, think of concrete examples to illustrate your points.

1. What are two advantages of purchasing prewritten software?
2. What are two disadvantages of purchasing prewritten software?
3. What are the main features of a database management system?
4. What is the key feature of a word processing package?
5. How does an electronic bulletin board differ from an electronic mail/message system?
6. Describe some of the features found in integrated software packages.
7. What is the difference between public-domain and publicly supported software?
8. What are the uses for electronic mail/message systems?

essay questions

1. What are the advantages and disadvantages of prewritten software?
2. What packaged software might you require for your occupation or your educational training?
3. How does canned software fit into an information system?

Answers to the objective questions
True/false: 1. F; 2. T; 3. F; 4. F; 5. T; 6. F; 7. F; 8. T; 9. F; 10. F
Multiple choice: 1. d; 2. d; 3. c; 4. a; 5. a
Fill in the blank: 1. less; 2. menu; 3. modular; 4. shareware; 5. vertical; 6. dedicated word processors; 7. piracy; 8. updates

Word processing: manipulating text and ideas

After studying this chapter you should understand the following:

- *The importance and capabilities of word processors.*
- *Typical word processing business applications.*
- *How to interpret word processing screens.*
- *The differences between a word processor and a typewriter.*
- *The basic and advanced word processing functions.*
- *Supplemental programs that can be used with word processing.*

chapter 9

Report deadlines

Ann sat nervously in front of the microcomputer screen. She stretched her fingers over the keyboard while Janis Roberts, manager of Freddy Johnson's Travel Agency, looked on. Ann had skipped lunch to finish this work, stopping only when the stiffness in her neck and fingers forced her to take a break. This was Ann's first big assignment since completing the word processing course at Oakriver University. She could have used more practice with the word processor—especially using this keyboard, which differed from the one she used at school. Her fingers kept pressing the wrong key for SHIFT, forcing her to backspace and retype more often than usual. If only she was better acquainted with the keyboard layout, she'd be fine. But there was no time for that now. Janis didn't say a word, but Ann knew from her expression that time was short, and excuses wouldn't help. The job simply had to be completed.

Ann had arrived at work that morning to learn that an important meeting had been moved up, well ahead of schedule. With only hours left before the meeting, Ann had been asked to put her word processing training to the test—a typewriter was clearly too slow for all the work that had to be done. After 4 hours of straight typing, she was tired, but could not let Janis down.

After her brief rest, Ann searched through the filenames on disk and retrieved the first ten pages of the proposal she had saved a few minutes ago. Even though she was under intense pressure, her training had taught her to constantly make backup copies of her work for safekeeping. She couldn't afford to lose any part of this report if something unforeseen happened to the computer.

"There's still so much to do," she thought. "Even if I can read Freddy's handwritten notes, the current margins and spacing are all wrong, the paragraphs must be changed around, the itinerary is incomplete, and typing errors must be corrected." Not being the best speller, she also dreaded the editing that would follow after the entire report had been typed. But there was no turning back. The meeting could not be postponed, and the report must be ready. Ann began to type.

Applications and evolution

The development of the modern word processor

Although Ann's use of word processing would seem almost magical to an onlooker, Ann was simply making use of a modern tool to carry out tasks that had been done by others long before she, or the computer, was born. WORD PROCESSING, after all, is the creation, adjustment, and printing of text material—a process that began with the use of paper and the quill pen centuries ago. Since then, many tools have improved the appearance of the printed word while decreasing the time and effort needed to produce it.

Movable type, invented by Gutenberg in the 1400s, led to the widespread use of books and newspapers, but it wasn't until the invention of a mechanical typewriter in the 1800s, that personal communication began to develop in earnest. The manual typewriter remained virtually unchanged until the 1940s when IBM's electric typewriter enabled typists to produce consistently dark type faster and easier. IBM improved its design in the 1960s with its Selectric typewriter, which replaced the hammerlike typing of earlier models with a rotating element resembling a golf ball. This removable typing element was faster, quieter, and allowed typists to easily change the typestyle of their work.

In 1968, IBM coined the phrase "word processing" to refer to automated typing machines that could retype documents without additional human effort. Such machines included the Magnetic Tape Selectric Typewriter (MT/ST) and the Magnetic Card Selectric Typewriter (MC/ST). Both used magnetic media to record typists' keystrokes for future use. The 1970s saw a major change away from paper-intensive machines

Figure 9-1
The first practical typewriter was designed in 1867 by Sholes, Soulé, and Glidden.

Figure 9-2
The IBM Selectric eliminated the moving carriage and used a typing element instead of individual letters.

Figure 9-3
A modern typewriter
uses a daisy-wheel typing
element, and a one-line
screen to preview typing.

Figure 9-4
Word processing is now
done on a CRT-based
microcomputer.

with the introduction of CRT-BASED WORD PROCESSORS. These machines were computers that displayed typed material on screens (CRTs), allowing extensive changes to be made to the text before it was printed out on paper. CRT-based word processors also stored documents on magnetic disk and used separate printers to produce *hard copy*, or printed text. Dot-matrix printers produced legible draft text quickly, while daisy-wheel printers were used to generate letter-quality text the equal of the best typewriters. The modern word processor had been born!

Today, businesses can choose among several word processing tools. The electronic typewriter provides many automatic features (such as centering, spelling check, and automatic erase) but still types text directly on paper as any typewriter would. DEDICATED WORD PROCESSORS are powerful stand-alone computers equipped with special keyboards and built-in programs that offer many sophisticated capabilities to the professional writer. Minicomputer- and mainframe-based word processors are also available but not widely used. Microcomputer-based word processors are most common, using a personal computer and specialized applications software for word processing. The advantage to such machines is that they are available for other business functions when they are not being used for word processing. Most of these modern word processing alternatives share similar basic capabilities, but this chapter will stress the general-purpose microcomputer-based word processor in most examples.

Common
capabilities

Microcomputer-based word processors make use of the same hardware found in typical microcomputer systems (a CPU, screen, keyboard, disk drive(s), and printer), but require special software to enable the computer to do all the required word processing functions. Although the choice of word processing software affects the speed, capacity, and advanced functions available to the user, most modern word processing software packages offer the same basic capabilities. These functions allow users to create text material, edit it, print it, and save it for later use. Let's examine the most common ones.

TEXT ENTRY does not differ greatly from typing. In most instances, the familiar typewriter QWERTY layout is used, with SHIFT, TAB, SPACE, and BACKSPACE keys used normally. A TYPE-AHEAD BUFFER collects each keystroke and feeds it to the computer when the program is ready for it. In this way, the user can type as fast as possible, without losing keystrokes when the program is adjusting the screen (as in word wrap below).

WORD WRAP is a process that automatically continues words that do not fit on one line onto the next line. It eliminates the need for the typist to press the RETURN key each time he or she reaches the right margin. Instead, the typist simply continues to enter text. Words that do not fit within the right margin will be moved automatically by the computer down to the next line, starting at the left margin. The only time a typist must press the RETURN (or ENTER) key is at the end of a paragraph or to skip a line. Some word processors offer a hyphenation feature that automatically splits words with more than one syllable if they will not fit on the current typing line.

INSERTION allows new text material to be added to a document without destroying old text. It provides a major advantage over typewriting. In most cases, word processors are set to operate in a TYPEOVER mode, which allows new text to be typed directly over old text, replacing it letter for letter. However, unlike "regular" typing, when INSERT is activated (usually by pressing the INSERT key), new text can be added into the document wherever the user wishes. The program will simply push the old text over to make room for the new text.

DELETION is the process by which text is removed from a document. It offers a similar advantage over typing, but in reverse. In this case, text can be easily removed from any part of the document with the remaining words automatically closing in the gaps.

Page formatting enables users to alter left and right margins, change tabs, adjust line spacing, change page lengths, set top and bottom margins, and center text. However, unlike typewriters, these alterations can change text that has already been typed, as well as material not yet entered.

REFORMATTING of paragraphs occurs when insertions, deletions, or changes in margins and tabs alter the layout of the text. Depending on the software, text can be reformatted automatically to fall neatly within margins again, or the user may have to press keys to begin this action.

JUSTIFICATION means the aligning of words along a margin. Regular typewriting justifies the left margin while leaving the right margin "ragged." With a word processor, users have a choice of left, right, or full justification (where words are aligned on both margins). The computer achieves this by placing additional spaces within words as needed (see Figure 9-5).

Centering is easy with a word processor. Typing requires users to find the center and then backspace one count for every two letters; word processing centers automatically when the user presses one or two appropriate keys.

Cursor control allows users to move and edit anywhere within their document. A handy placemarker, the *cursor*, appears on the screen to show users their exact typing position. While its shape may vary from an underline in one program to a box in another, the cursor is always included as a visual reference on the screen.

Figure 9-5
WordStar text achieves
full justification by plac-
ing extra spaces between
words. (a) Full justifica-
tion of right and left
margins. (b) Regular typ-
ing with "ragged" right
margin.

```
This  is  text  that  has  been  set  for  full
justification at both right and left margins.
Note the extra spaces in between some of the words
so that the last word of each line, except for the
last  line  of  the  paragraph,  ends  at  the  right
margin.
```

(*a*)

```
This text is left justified just as in regular
typing.  There is normal spacing between words,
which do not necessarily end exactly at the right
margin forming a ragged line on the right.
```

(*b*)

Character formatting controls the way letters will appear when printed. Users can select typestyle, size, boldface, or underlining as they choose. Many word processing programs use special symbols or colors to indicate these settings; other newer programs offer WYSIWYG ("what you see is what you get") capabilities that enable the screen to display text as it will appear when printed (Figure 9-6).

Move and *Copy* commands enable users to "cut and paste" words or paragraphs. In earlier times editors used scissors and rubber cement to physically cut out typewritten copy and paste it where it belonged. Word processing allows this to be done directly on the screen, and even from one document to another.

SEARCH and **SEARCH AND REPLACE** allow users to scan through an entire document to locate specific words or phrases. Once found, the program can be set to automatically replace the phrase with another. For example, the word *silly* could be changed to *ridiculous* everywhere it occurred in a document with a few simple keystrokes. Try doing that on a typewriter!

SAVE and **RETRIEVE** capabilities enable users to store copies of their documents on magnetic disk and recall them later for review, editing, and printing. Writers can save portions of their work, retrieve them

Figure 9-6
The Apple Macintosh
offers a true WYSIWYG
screen.

Comparing major word processors

Most word processors offer similar capabilities even though they may use different keys to accomplish each task. The following list compares a number of the functions in four popular microcomputer word processing programs. Most of these programs can be customized to use different keys, or be programmed to allow the use of a mouse to simplify many of the on-screen editing operations.

Function	WordStar 4.0	WordPerfect	Multimate	Word
START-UP	ws <ENT>	wp <ENT>	wp <ENT>	word <ENT>
Boldface	<F4>	<F6>	<ALT-Z>	<ESC>FC<SP><ENT>
Center	<SHFT*-F2>	<SHFT-F6>	<F3>	<ALT-C>
Create	open* <D>	turn on	open <2>	turn on
Delete:				
Word	<F6>	<CTRL-BACK>	<DEL>	<F8> <DEL>
Line	<F5>	<CTRL-END>		<SHFT><F9> <DEL>
Block	<SHFT-F5>	<DEL> <Y>		<F6>move<DEL>
Goto Page	<CTRL-Q> I	<CTRL-HOME>	<F1>	<ESC> J # or ALT-F5
Help	<F1>	<F3>	<SHFT-F1>	<ESC> H or ALT-H
Line Space	<CTRL-O> S	<SHFT-F8>	<F9>	<ALT-P> single <ALT-O> double
Mark Block:				
Start	<SHFT-F9>	<ALT-F4>	see MOVE	<F6>
End	<SHFT-F10>	then move	command	then move
Move Block	<SHFT-F7>	<CTRL-F4>	<F7>	Mark text <DEL> Move <INS>
Page Break	type .pa	<CTRL-ENTER>	<F2>	<CTRL-SHFT-ENT>
Print	open <P>	<SHFT-F7>	<F10> 3	<ESC> P
Retrieve	open <D>	<SHFT-F10>	open <1>	<ESC> T L
Ruler Line	onscreen	<CTRL-F3>	onscreen	<ESC> W O 5 TABs Y <ENTER>
Save/Continue	<F9>	<F10>	<SHFT-F10>	<ESC> T S
Save/Exit	<F10>	<F7>	<F10>	<ESC>QY
Search	<CTRL-Q><F>	<F2>	<F6>	<ESC> S
w/Replace	<CTRL-Q><A>	<ALT-F2>	<F7>	<ESC> R
Spell Check	<F4> or <F3>	<CTRL-F2>	<CTRL-F10>	<ESC> L S
Thesaurus	Load WF first <ALT-1>	<ALT-F1>	—	<CTRL-F6>
Underline	<F3>	<F8>	<SHFT->	<ALT-U> on <ALT-SPACE> off

*Note: "open" means "at the opening menu"; <SHFT> = SHIFT key

Additional features offered in these word processing programs are listed below.

Function	WordStar 4.0	WordPerfect	Multimate	Word
Copying from outside documents	yes	yes	yes	yes
Footnotes	no	yes	no	yes
Indexing	yes	yes	no	yes
Mail merge	yes	yes	yes	yes
Math functions	yes	yes	yes	yes
Two documents in memory	no	yes	no	yes

when needed, and save them again in edited form. Secretaries can save form letters on disk to be recalled and filled in whenever necessary. Often, businesses have been able to reduce paper storage by keeping "electronic" copies of documents on disk, instead of paper copies in filing cabinets.

PRINTING is the creation of hard copy—the final step in most word processing procedures. Since most businesses still rely on paper for such items as letters, invoices, checks, and reports, the capability to print is an important part of a word processor. Word processors have greatly reduced paper waste by enabling editing and typographical errors to be corrected on the computer screen first, printing to paper only when the user is satisfied with the document.

Applying word processing to business

Business managers will not spend money for new equipment unless they are convinced of its worth. The purchase of millions of word processing programs by businesses is a good indication of their importance to management. But just how do word processors help businesses become more efficient? Let's look at a few illustrations.

Text rearrangement and error correction

Remember the last time you typed a term paper or report? How many times did you stop to correct an error, or throw out a page that required major readjustments? You're not alone. All typists, even the best ones, make mistakes. All writers, *especially* the best ones, review and rewrite their work. There is always a need to insert, remove, and correct the content and arrangement of words and paragraphs. However, when documents are typed directly on paper, they are *inflexible* products that require much time and effort, not to mention correction fluid, for these changes. Although the use of a word processor will not reduce the need for careful editing and review, it does change the nature of documents by making them totally *flexible*. Major changes to characters, words, paragraphs, and even margins, can be made with ease. Unlike words on paper, everything on the computer screen is adjustable before a final perfect copy is printed. Not only does this significantly reduce the time it would normally take for a finished product, but personal productivity increases as well. Typists type faster, knowing they can easily correct errors; writers are freer to experiment with words and presentation, knowing it takes little effort to move things around for best effect.

The capability to rearrange text is an advantage applicable to every business communication situation. Publishers of newspapers, magazines, and books have used word processing extensively in the past few years to provide a faster and more accurate method of moving from writing, through editing, to final production, using documents transmitted by phone or disk from one word processor to another. This textbook was produced using such a method.

Paragraph assembly

BOILER PLATING, or paragraph assembly, is a word processing technique that enables users to combine previously typed material into a new document. It has had significant application in businesses that routinely use similar paragraphs in many of their communications. For instance, although lawyers must create specifically worded contracts for many clients, the general paragraphs used in each may be remarkably similar. Rather than type each contract from "scratch," lawyers can use a word processor to store all the common paragraphs they use. When a new contract is being drawn up, they simply "assemble" selected paragraphs and add specific data such as names and dates, to quickly create a new contract, perfectly typed. In many states, lawyers can buy programs that already contain all appropriate paragraphs for documents such as wills and real estate contracts.

Mail merge

MAIL MERGE is closely related to paragraph assembly. The user can prepare blank form letters and merge them with specific data contained in a

Figure 9-7
Mail merge. Form letters (a) reserve space for data that will be added automatically from a file (b) when the program is run to produce customized, printed letters (c).

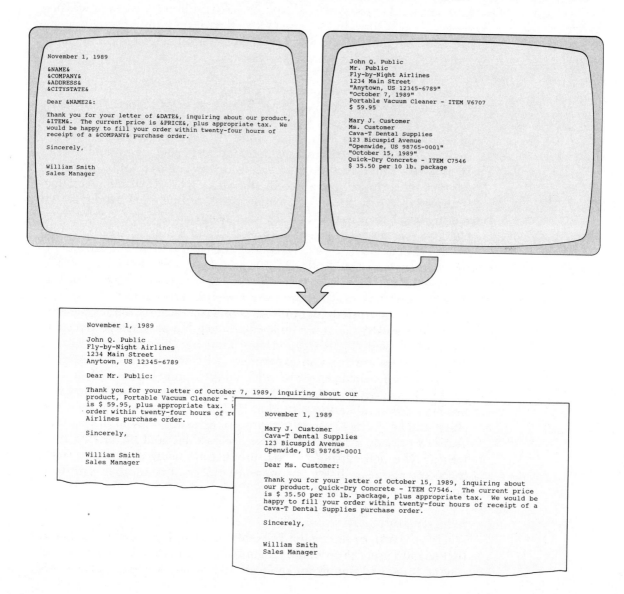

Figure 9-8
Typeset material (a) is easier to read, looks better, and takes up less space than regular typewritten material (b).

This text example is shown typeset (a) and typed (b). Notice that the typeset text looks more professional. It is easier to read and takes up less space than the typewritten one. If you had to read a long book (like this textbook), would you rather have it typeset or typewritten?

(*a*) Typeset text

```
This text example is shown typeset (a)
and typed (b).  Notice that the typeset
text looks more professional.  It is
easier to read and takes up less space
than the typewritten one.  If you had
to read a long book (like this
textbook), would you rather have it
typeset or typewritten?
```

(*b*) Typewritten text

computerized filing system to produce personalized letters. For example, the accounting department secretary creates a form letter requesting overdue payments, leaving spaces (and special codes) for the recipient's name, address, amount involved, and date due (see Figure 9-7). In the past, this letter would have to be retyped over and over again, once for each client. The time required, and the potential for error, was great. By using the word processing feature of mail merge however, the computer is instructed to locate its records for clients with overdue accounts, and merge each set of data with the form letter to produce a perfectly typed letter for each client. While the computer diligently works at this task, the secretary is free to devote attention to other matters.

Typesetting

Typeset material is easier to read, more compact, and more attractive than regular typewritten material (see Figure 9-8). Many businesses use typesetting for sales brochures and annual reports, finding it cost-effective when large quantities are printed. However, the use of a word processor allows documents to be transferred to typesetting machines with relative ease, reducing the effort and cost required to produce professional-quality copy. In the mid-1980s, the introduction of specialized *desktop publishing* programs, combined with the use of laser printers, revolutionized the way word processors could be used to manipulate text and graphics to produce camera-ready material for publication (see Figure 9-9 and Chapter 12).

Figure 9-9
Desktop publishing allows users to create professional-looking camera-ready copy on their microcomputers.

The word processor at work

To get a better understanding of how word processors operate, we will consider a typical word processing program as it would appear to the user. Although there are many different word processing programs, their functions and screens are remarkably similar. Once you become familiar with one, you can learn others with relative ease.

Interpreting the screen display

Word processing programs make extensive use of the computer screen to display typed material and convey useful data to the user. For our purposes, we can think of a word processing document as if it were typed on one continuous roll of paper—much like an ancient scroll. The computer screen is like a window that we slide up or down this long scroll to see any desired portion (see Figure 9-10). Not surprisingly, this technique is called SCROLLING. As we scroll down, for example, new text lines appear at the bottom of the screen while old lines disappear at the top. This can be frightening to new users who think they've just lost all their earlier work. Nothing is lost, though. The entire document is still in the computer's memory. As with any window, we can only see as much of the document as will fit on the screen (window) at any one time.

Since it is difficult to judge our location as we move around this scroll, the screen also constantly displays data that identify where we are and what we are doing. Figure 9-11 shows four word processing screens popular in businesses in the 1980s: WordStar, WordPerfect, Multimate, and Word. Their screen layouts differ, but they usually display 80 typ-

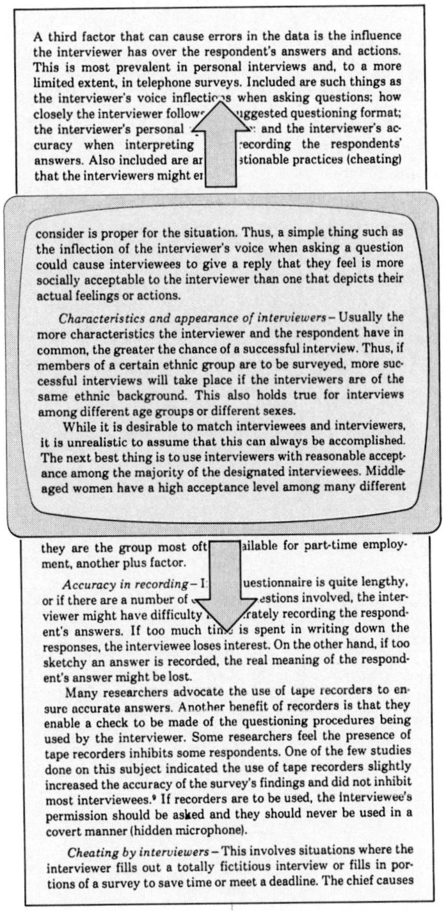

Figure 9-10
The computer screen acts like a window, displaying portions of the entire document as we scroll up and down.

> A third factor that can cause errors in the data is the influence the interviewer has over the respondent's answers and actions. This is most prevalent in personal interviews and, to a more limited extent, in telephone surveys. Included are such things as the interviewer's voice inflections when asking questions; how closely the interviewer follows the suggested questioning format; the interviewer's personal ... ; and the interviewer's accuracy when interpreting ... recording the respondents' answers. Also included are an ... stionable practices (cheating) that the interviewers might en ...
>
> consider is proper for the situation. Thus, a simple thing such as the inflection of the interviewer's voice when asking a question could cause interviewees to give a reply that they feel is more socially acceptable to the interviewer than one that depicts their actual feelings or actions.
>
> *Characteristics and appearance of interviewers* – Usually the more characteristics the interviewer and the respondent have in common, the greater the chance of a successful interview. Thus, if members of a certain ethnic group are to be surveyed, more successful interviews will take place if the interviewers are of the same ethnic background. This also holds true for interviews among different age groups or different sexes.
>
> While it is desirable to match interviewees and interviewers, it is unrealistic to assume that this can always be accomplished. The next best thing is to use interviewers with reasonable acceptance among the majority of the designated interviewees. Middle-aged women have a high acceptance level among many different
>
> they are the group most oft ... ailable for part-time employment, another plus factor.
>
> *Accuracy in recording* – I ... uestionnaire is quite lengthy, or if there are a number of ... estions involved, the interviewer might have difficulty ... rately recording the respondent's answers. If too much time is spent in writing down the responses, the interviewee loses interest. On the other hand, if too sketchy an answer is recorded, the real meaning of the respondent's answer might be lost.
>
> Many researchers advocate the use of tape recorders to ensure accurate answers. Another benefit of recorders is that they enable a check to be made of the questioning procedures being used by the interviewer. Some researchers feel the presence of tape recorders inhibits some respondents. One of the few studies done on this subject indicated the use of tape recorders slightly increased the accuracy of the survey's findings and did not inhibit most interviewees.[9] If recorders are to be used, the interviewee's permission should be asked and they should never be used in a covert manner (hidden microphone).
>
> *Cheating by interviewers* – This involves situations where the interviewer fills out a totally fictitious interview or fills in portions of a survey to save time or meet a deadline. The chief causes

ing columns across, and at least 20 single-spaced lines down. Let's examine their typical contents:

- A status line.
- A ruler line.
- Text entry area.
- Character indicators.

A **STATUS LINE** is a line of text that remains either at the top or bottom of the screen (depending on the program) at all times to present data about current conditions in the document and program. These data include such items as the document name, position identifiers, typing parameters, and message centers.

A *document name* identifies the document file currently being edited. Most status lines show both the disk location and name, as in B:SAMPLE (Figure 9-11a), which indicates that a document called SAMPLE will be stored on the B disk. Typically, document names do not exceed eight letters in length and may be followed by a three-letter extension, as in INVOICES.JAN. Word processing programs that allow more than one document to be edited at a time may use the name or simply a designating number, as in DOC 1 seen in Figure 9-11b.

Figure 9-11
Workscreens. (a) Word-
Star's characteristic
menus can be hidden to
allow more work space
on the screen. (b) Word-
Perfect presents a bare
workscreen with a mini-
mum of information. (c)
Multimate's workscreen.
(d) Microsoft Word's
workscreen.

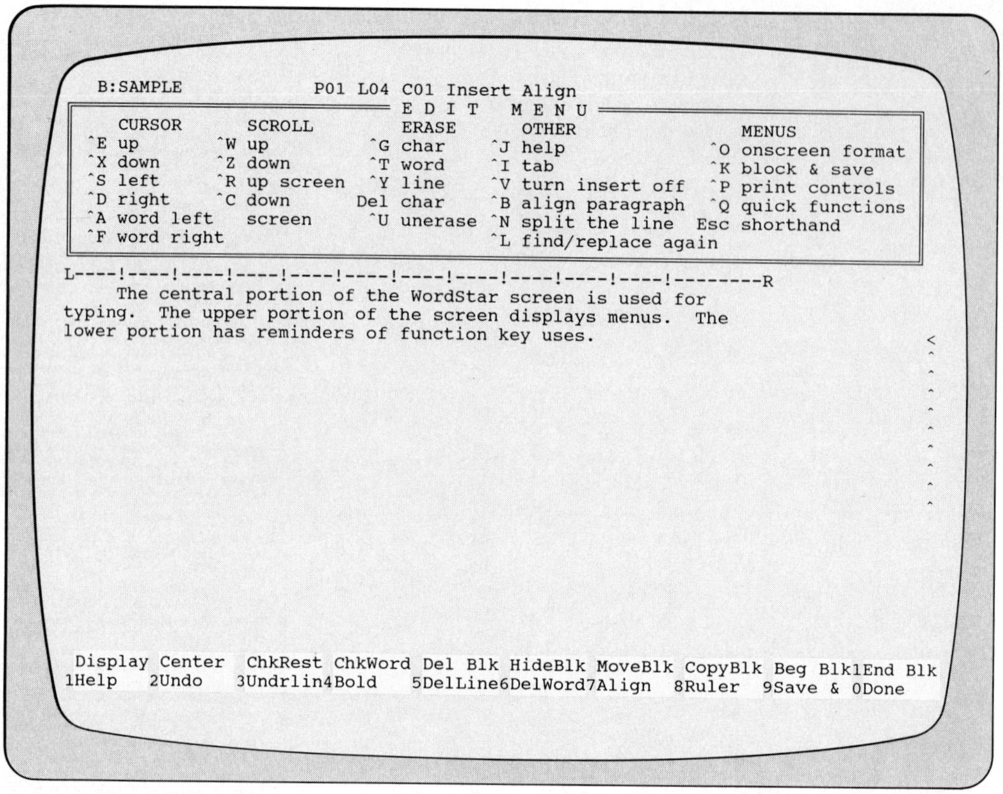

```
   B:SAMPLE              P01 L04 C01 Insert Align
                      ══ E D I T   M E N U ══════════════
     CURSOR      SCROLL         ERASE       OTHER              MENUS
 ^E up        ^W up          ^G char    ^J help          ^O onscreen format
 ^X down      ^Z down        ^T word    ^I tab           ^K block & save
 ^S left      ^R up screen   ^Y line    ^V turn insert off ^P print controls
 ^D right     ^C down        Del char   ^B align paragraph ^Q quick functions
 ^A word left    screen      ^U unerase ^N split the line Esc shorthand
 ^F word right                          ^L find/replace again
L----!----!----!----!----!----!----!----!----!----!----!-------R
        The central portion of the WordStar screen is used for
typing.  The upper portion of the screen displays menus.  The
lower portion has reminders of function key uses.
                                                                <
                                                                ^
                                                                ^
                                                                ^
                                                                ^
                                                                ^
                                                                ^
                                                                ^


    Display Center  ChkRest ChkWord Del Blk HideBlk MoveBlk CopyBlk Beg Blk1End Blk
    1Help   2Undo   3Undrlin4Bold   5DelLine6DelWord7Align  8Ruler  9Save & 0Done
```

(a)

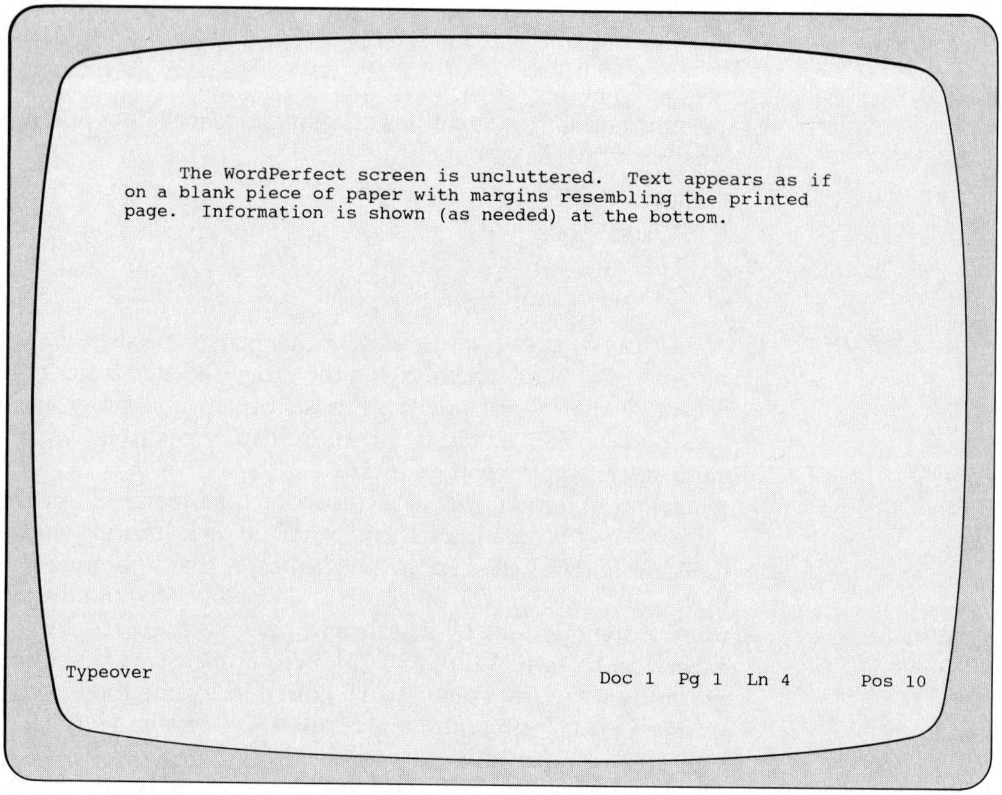

```
        The WordPerfect screen is uncluttered.  Text appears as if
on a blank piece of paper with margins resembling the printed
page.  Information is shown (as needed) at the bottom.








Typeover                              Doc 1  Pg 1  Ln 4      Pos 10
```

(b)

```
DOCUMENT: sample                    ‖PAGE:   1‖LINE:   4‖COL:   1‖
|1..»....»....».................................»...................«
       »A Multimate screen closely resembles the WANG word processor
with information contained at the top.  The remainder of the
page is available for typing.«
```

```
                                                      S:↑ N:↓
```

(c)

```
‖
║ Microsoft's Word for the IBM contains a boxed-in area on the
║ screen for text, and a list of available commands at the
║ bottom.  These menus can be activated by pressing the ESCAPE
║ key or using a mouse.
  ◊
```

```
COMMAND: Alpha Copy Delete Format Gallery Help Insert Jump Library
         Options Print Quit Replace Search Transfer Undo Window
Edit document or press Esc to use menu
Page 1   {}                              Microsoft Word:
```

(d)

POSITION IDENTIFIERS are numbers to help users keep track of their typing position on the screen. They usually indicate the current page, line, and column number on the status line for easy reference. These numbers change as the user moves through the document.

Some status lines also display *typing parameters*—the settings chosen by the typist for layout and spacing, such as automatic insert, right-margin justification, and double-spacing. Others may show when the SHIFT, CAPS LOCK, or NUM LOCK keys have been pressed on the keyboard.

There are times when the computer must communicate with the user to request input, indicate some action, or simply guide the user through a procedure with many steps. This can be done with a screen area reserved as a *message center.* In many instances, a portion of the status line is reserved to display these messages when required. Many word processing programs also use **PULL-DOWN MENUS** that appear on the screen only when needed so as not to block the text material more than necessary (see Figure 9-12). These techniques allow much more information to be conveyed to the user without complicating the word processing workscreen. Detailed reference material in the form of *help screens* can be called up onto the screen, read, and removed, without affecting the document being written. **WINDOWS**, smaller subdivisions of the screen, enables users to work on more than one document at the same time. Text from one report can be copied or moved into another easily (see Figure 9-13a).

A **RULER LINE** defines the horizontal typing area in a word processor and provides visual references to margins, typing columns, and tab settings. It can appear directly below or above the status line depending on

Figure 9-12
Pull-down menus.

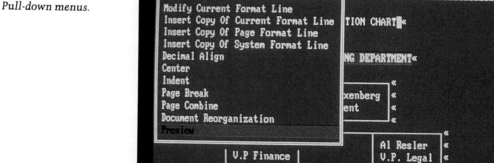

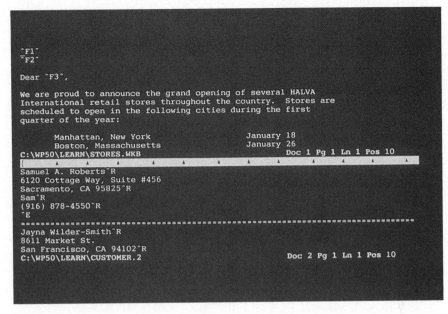

Figure 9-13
(a) WordPerfect's split screen can easily display portions of two documents at the same time. (Note the ruler line.) (b) A few typical ruler lines.

(a)

Multimate's ruler line

Word's ruler line

WordPerfect's ruler line

Wordstar's ruler line

(b)

the word processing screen layout. In many programs, it can be made either visible or invisible by the user. Although some typists prefer it, there is less need for this line in newer word processing programs that use WYSIWYG ("what you see is what you get") screens since they display the page exactly as it will appear when printed. Figure 9-13b displays some typical ruler lines from word processing screens.

The **TEXT ENTRY AREA** of the word processing screen holds the text material that will later appear on paper. It is usually the largest area on the screen, and unless it is reduced in size by windows or menus, it occupies most of the remaining screen space. Text entered by the typist, or loaded into the program from disk, appears here, as it would on a piece of typing paper.

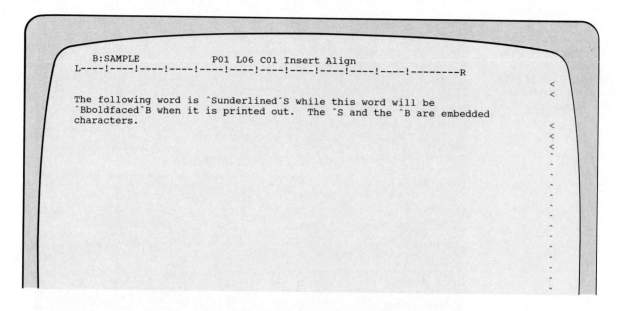

```
    B:SAMPLE              P01 L06 C01 Insert Align
L----!----!----!----!----!----!----!----!----!----!----!--------R

The following word is ^Sunderlined^S while this word will be
^Bboldfaced^B when it is printed out.  The ^S and the ^B are embedded
characters.
```

Figure 9-14
WordStar's "control characters" are embedded symbols that show the beginning and end of alterations to text.

Character indicators are used in the text entry area to provide visual clues about the way words and letters will appear when printed on paper. Most word processing programs can underline and boldface. However, more sophisticated programs offer adjustments to width, height, and typestyle, as well as superscripts or subscripts. Programs using WYSIWYG screens display these changes exactly as they will appear on paper. Other programs use different methods to indicate these character adjustments. Before the widespread use of color screens, software developers had to be creative in designing methods of identifying these changes. Early techniques, still useful with monochrome screens today, identified altered characters by using one or more of these visual clues:

■ **EMBEDDED SYMBOLS** are special characters placed before and after the text that is being altered. First-time users might be confused by these extra symbols on the screen, but after some practice, will have no difficulty interpreting these codes. For example, WordStar is well known for its use of "control characters" for underlining and boldface (see Figure 9-14).

■ **HIGHLIGHTING** is the use of increased character brightness on the screen to indicate the text to be altered. Multimate employs highlighting to show text that is being inserted or deleted.

■ **INVERSE VIDEO**, the reversal of foreground and background colors, can also indicate changed text. For instance, if a screen normally displays green characters on a black background, inverse video would show black characters on green. WordPerfect uses inverse video to indicate blocks of text (see Figure 9-15).

The addition of color screens greatly expanded the ability of word processing programs to indicate character changes. Colors can show any single text alteration. They can also display combinations of effects,

Figure 9-15
Inverse video is an effec-
tive method to indicate
changes to text on the
workscreen or call the
user's attention to menu
selections.

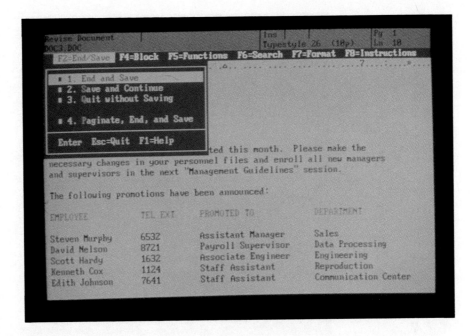

such as a word that is both underlined *and* italicized. In many instances, word processing color schemes can be customized by users to suit their own tastes, or to provide standardization for those who operate more than one word processor. Colors can also be used as visual clues to identify different versions of the same word processor set up for various applications.

Since both monochrome and color screens are used extensively in business, word processing programs must work effectively with both types of monitors. Each word processor solves the problem differently, using a combination of techniques to display text characteristics. The word processing "classics"—WordStar, Multimate, and WordPerfect—all use color effectively to identify changes in text. WordStar 4.0 uses embedded characters to maintain compatibility with its earlier (and extremely popular) version, WordStar 3.3, but it also improves readability through the combined use of color, highlighting, and inverse video—all on the same screen (Figure 9-16).

Using the keyboard

Most word processing programs have been designed to use the standard IBM-PC keyboard introduced in the early 1980s. Yet, newer keyboard layouts (as we've seen in Chapter 6) offer different styles to the business user (see Figure 9-17). Users are no longer limited to one particular keyboard, but can choose among several alternatives. Even the traditional QWERTY arrangement of keys, once the standard for all keyboards, has been joined by a new standard DVORAK arrangement as discussed in Chapter 6.

There are too many variations of key use and keyboard location for us to examine each in detail, but there are enough common keys to make a quick tour of a typical keyboard useful.

Figure 9-16
Some word processors can use embedded characters, color, highlighting, and inverse video to display character changes.

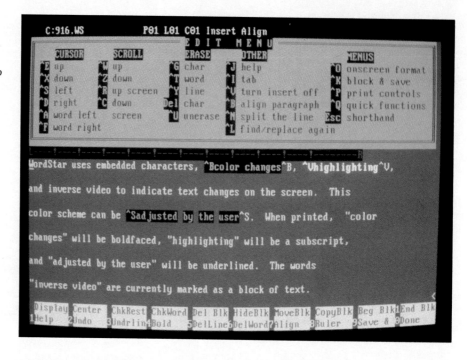

Figure 9-17
The Apple extended keyboard is much like the newer IBM standard: function keys along the top and separate cursor control and numeric keys.

Typewriter keys

The central portion of the keyboard contains the alphabetic, numeric, and punctuation keys found on every typewriter. Included in this group are the SHIFT, CAPS LOCK, SPACE BAR, TAB, and BACKSPACE command keys. These keys perform the same function in word processing as they do in "normal" typing. Additional numeric keys (the 0 and 1), square brackets, and a few mathematical symbol keys are usually added as well.

Cursor control keys

Word processing programs also make use of keys that control the movement of the screen cursor. Some keyboards offer only two keys to control vertical and horizontal movements, most keyboards provide four separate keys to move the cursor LEFT, RIGHT, UP, and DOWN. In addition, positioning keys such as HOME, END, PAGE UP, and PAGE DOWN, enable word processor users to move the cursor around the document quickly and efficiently. These keys are often found in a separate keypad area, serving double duty as both cursor control and numeric (calculator-style) entry. However, many users prefer newer keyboard designs that provide separate, single-function keys for cursor control and others for numeric entry.

"Shiftlike" keys

The familiar SHIFT key performs a very valuable service for the typist—it doubles the usefulness of each key. Letters can be typed in upper- or lower-case; numbers or symbols can be entered from the same numeric keys. This idea has been extended on computer keyboards with the inclusion of two "shiftlike" keys called ALTERNATE (ALT) and CONTROL (CTRL). When used in the same manner as the SHIFT key, they allow each key to serve two additional purposes. Most word processors use these shiftlike keys in conjunction with others on the keyboard to activate and control many of their powerful functions. For example, pressing <CTRL> and <PgDn> in WordPerfect will delete all words to the end of the current page. Using <CTRL> and <O> in WordStar will activate on-screen menu functions.

"Soft" function keys

Since the first introduction of microcomputer-based word processors, additional keys have been added to the keyboard to further expand its usefulness. IBM keyboard layouts place ten function keys (labeled F1 through F10) in two vertical rows on the left side of the keyboard. More recent keyboards place twelve or more keys horizontally across the top. Unlike alphabetical or numeric keys whose uses remain constant for most computer applications, the specific use of each function key is redefined by each program the computer uses. In this sense they provide "soft" functions—functions that can be "molded" like clay to fit the specific needs of each program.

This flexibility has been exploited to its fullest by today's word processing programs that combine the ten function keys with SHIFT, ALT, and CTRL to provide forty distinct functions. Here's how we get forty functions: we get ten different functions when we press the function keys alone; ten more when we press them while holding the SHIFT key; ten more with ALT; and the last ten when we use them with CTRL. To reduce confusion, most programs provide a printed cardboard or plastic *template* that fits around the function keys on the keyboard for easy reference by the user (see Figure 9-18). Some programs provide a list of function keys directly on the screen itself or in help screens to be called upon when needed.

Figure 9-18
A keyboard template for use with WordPerfect. The color codes indicate when to press SHIFT, ALT, or CTRL.

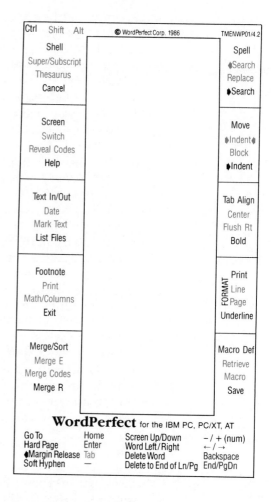

Three special keys

There are three additional keys that have no counterpart on the regular typewriter keyboard but are of "key" importance to word processing: the ESCAPE key, the INSERT key, and the DELETE key.

The ESCAPE (ESC) key allows a user to cancel a command; in effect, one can "escape" from a particular procedure and return to the work-screen without disturbing the text material. One word processing program, Perfect Writer, used the ESCAPE key to activate an extensive set of menus that led the user through most necessary procedures without the need for FUNCTION keys. A second press of the key would return the user to the screen to continue typing.

The INSERT (INS) key is a "toggle" switch that enables or disables the capability of the program to add new text to the screen. As we discussed earlier, word processing programs can either be in an *insert* or *typeover* mode. By pressing the INSERT key, the user can switch (or *toggle*) back and forth between these two modes.

The DELETE (DEL) key works much like the backspace key—it removes one character from the screen at a time. The DELETE key's operation, however, varies slightly from program to program. In many word processors, it deletes characters at or to the right of the cursor; in others, it deletes to the left. It can often be used in combination with the CONTROL, ALTERNATE, or FUNCTION keys to remove large portions of text material (called TEXT BLOCKS) extremely efficiently.

The UNDO procedure

The inclusion of such a powerful function as "block delete," which may inadvertently destroy large portions of a document, prompted software designers to include an UNDO procedure into later versions of their word processors. In most cases, users can "undo" or cancel the most recent delete command, and retrieve valuable material that would otherwise have been lost. Even so, most experienced word processing users are careful to keep copies of their documents on another disk in the event of such a catastrophe as deleting major portions of a document that may be too large to "undo."

The ENTER key

Even though they are located in the same position on the keyboard, the computer's ENTER key and the typewriter's RETURN key do not perform exactly the same function. A typewriter's RETURN key must be pressed at the end of each physical line to return the typewriter's carriage to the left margin and move to a new line. In word processing, the ENTER key is only pressed at the end of a paragraph or when a line is to be skipped. It is not used at the end of each typewritten line. As we discussed earlier, the computer's word wrap automatically returns the cursor to the next line when there is no space left on the current line. The proper use of the ENTER key is one of the hardest lessons for typists to learn when using a word processor. They must, in fact, "unlearn" their RETURN key habits.

The use of the ENTER key is perhaps the least understood of all the word processing functions. Here's what happens: whenever the ENTER key is pressed, it places a special (and usually invisible) marker, called a *hard return*, into the text. When placed incorrectly, as at the end of every typewritten line, these markers prevent proper adjustments of text after insertions, deletions, or margin changes are made later on. In effect, they defeat one of the major reasons for using the word processor—the ability to easily modify written material.

Basic entry techniques

All in all, using a word processor is not that different from using a typewriter. There are a few more keys to learn and techniques to master, but most of these involve the greater editing capabilities of the word processor. The basic entry techniques of character typing, shift, tab, and backspace, are virtually identical to those on a typewriter. So much so that even a novice can feel comfortable typing on a word processor after a short amount of practice (especially with the ENTER key).

Perhaps the hardest skill to master when first learning a word processor is how to start the program itself. We will briefly examine the start-up procedure as it compares to an electric typewriter. There are three beginning steps involved in "normal" typing. First, we prepare the typewriter by turning on its power. Next, we must insert blank paper into the carriage and adjust it so that it is neatly aligned. Finally, we move to our starting position for typing.

Word processors are not that different. First, we start the computer and load our word processing program into the computer's memory. Next, we open a new file for use—the equivalent of setting up the paper. Finally, we position the cursor to begin typing.

A few examples may help illustrate this procedure as well as the similarities among word processors themselves. Examine these routines for starting WordStar, Word, and WordPerfect on an IBM personal computer. We will assume that the computer has two disk drives, and that we wish to create a document called "TEST."

Starting the computer

First we must get the computer ready. There are many ways to start a computer depending on the particular model and the software being used. Let's say that we are using an IBM or compatible, and that our program has already been installed for use in the computer. We place a start-up DOS disk in drive A, turn on the power, and type in the date and time (some computers have a battery-powered clock that eliminates the need to type this information). An A> (A prompt) appears on the screen showing that the computer is ready for the next command. We now replace the start-up disk with our word processing program disk in drive A, and put a data disk in drive B as in Figure 9-19.

To start WordStar we type WS and press <ENTER>. A copyright notice appears briefly, followed by the OPENING MENU (see Figure 9-20). We press <D> to open a document. The screen requests a filename, so we type TEST (a name invented for this example) and press <ENTER>. The screen now asks if we wish to create a new file; we press <Y> for "yes." A blank workscreen appears and we can begin typing.

WordPerfect and Word are even easier to start. We type WP (for

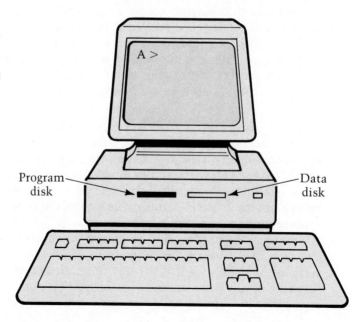

Figure 9-19
The IBM is ready to start the word processing program. The program disk is in drive A, data disk in drive B, and an A> appears on the screen.

A >

Program disk

Data disk

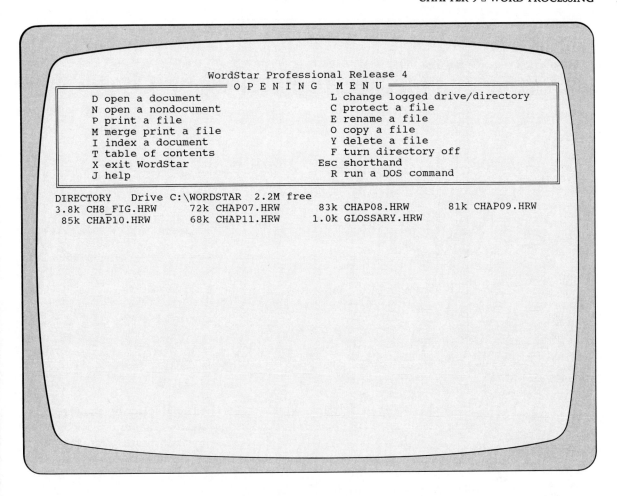

```
                    WordStar Professional Release 4
                 ═══════ O P E N I N G   M E N U ═══════
    ┌──────────────────────────────────────────────────────────────────┐
    │   D open a document          L change logged drive/directory      │
    │   N open a nondocument        C protect a file                     │
    │   P print a file              E rename a file                      │
    │   M merge print a file        O copy a file                        │
    │   I index a document          Y delete a file                      │
    │   T table of contents         F turn directory off                 │
    │   X exit WordStar           Esc shorthand                          │
    │   J help                      R run a DOS command                  │
    └──────────────────────────────────────────────────────────────────┘

  DIRECTORY    Drive C:\WORDSTAR  2.2M free
  3.8k CH8_FIG.HRW      72k CHAP07.HRW    83k CHAP08.HRW     81k CHAP09.HRW
   85k CHAP10.HRW       68k CHAP11.HRW    1.0k GLOSSARY.HRW
```

Figure 9-20
WordStar's Opening Menu. Note the <D> at the upper left for "Open a Document."

WordPerfect) or WORD (for Word) and press <ENTER>. A copyright notice appears briefly, followed by a blank workscreen. We can begin typing immediately and name the document later.

These procedures quickly become second nature to the user and take less time than placing paper into a typewriter. In fact, the word processor will constantly supply us with "new paper" as we type (as long as we have room on our disk).

This process can be simplified even further if the computer has a hard disk drive. We can copy the start-up and word processing programs onto the hard disk, eliminating the need to use floppy diskettes at all except for backup files. By adding an automatic start-up program, an *autoexec* file, we can program the word processor to start automatically when the computer is turned on. Some users purchase menu programs, such as Microsoft's Windows, that let them select any program by pointing to it with a mouse, rather than typing any commands at all. The start-up choice is one of personal preference and computer capability.

Once on the workscreen, however, the word processing program accepts text as easily as a typewriter. As each letter is pressed on the keyboard, it appears on the screen at the position shown by the cursor. The cursor then moves to position the next letter. Mistakes can be corrected

Figure 9-21
As new words are en-
tered, they are "wrap-
ped" past the right mar-
gin and onto the next
line automatically.

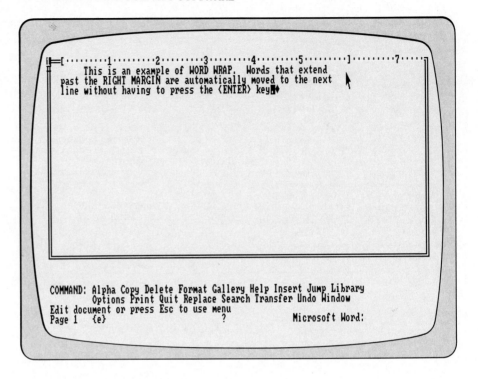

by backspacing or deleting, which erases the typed letter on the screen. There is no need for correction fluid or "white-out" paper.

As each word is typed, the program's built-in word wrap feature checks the remaining space on the line. If there is not enough space left for the word, it is automatically moved to the next line while the typist continues uninterrupted (see Figure 9- 21).

Saving and
retrieving
documents

If we only used documents once, or typed them perfectly the first time, typewriters would be more than sufficient for our needs. However, that is rarely the case. Mistakes require correction. Editing may involve considerable rearrangement of text. Perhaps the document cannot be finished in one session. Often, we may wish to reuse the document in the future, or transfer it for use with some other application program (such as desktop publishing). For these and other reasons, every word processor has the capability to save documents onto disk and retrieve them from the disk when they are needed for additional work.

In general, there are three techniques available to word processing users who wish to save documents:

- Save and continue.
- Save and quit.
- Save and exit.

Save and continue copies the entire document to disk and then returns the cursor to the exact screen position it left when the save command was issued. This ability to continue where one left off encourages users to create backup copies of their work easily and often. Most experienced users recommend that backups be made after every 10 minutes of work. This ensures that a replacement copy is readily available on disk should something happen to the document currently on the screen. At worst, the recovered document will only be missing the last few changes that were made. Experience is a harsh teacher. The time you forget to backup your work will be the one time you most desperately need that other copy!

Save and quit copies the document to disk and then erases it from the screen. This technique is useful when you've finished working with the document but wish to continue using the word processing program to do other tasks.

Save and exit copies the document to disk and then leaves the word processing program entirely, returning to the computer's operating system. This is useful when we have no further need of the word processor for the present.

Of course, we also have the option to *abandon* the document entirely; that is, not save the document, or at least not save the latest changes to it. This does not erase disk copies of the document saved previously, but simply allows us to not record the most current changes entered since last we saved it.

Once documents are saved to disk, users can copy, rename, or erase them either with word processing commands, through disk operating system commands, or menu programs. More importantly, documents can also be retrieved—copied back into the computer's memory—for additional word processing editing and use.

With save and retrieve capability, users can prepare drafts, save them to disk, and then retrieve them at will to edit and update their contents. Many word processors also enable users to save or retrieve portions of documents without accessing an entire file. Some permit portions of one document to be read into another. Other programs can keep two documents in memory at the same time, letting the user switch between them to retrieve and combine portions as needed (as we've seen in Figure 9-13). Users can save appropriate paragraphs in separate files, retrieving and combining them into a new, specialized letter or report.

Editing and rearranging

For all their advantages in text entry, word processors have their greatest use after text has been entered. Typing is relatively easy. Editing is much more difficult. It is the correction of typographical errors and the additions, deletions, and alterations of words that take up so much time and effort. This is where word processors stand out.

EDITING is the manipulation of text into a more useful and understandable form. In addition to correcting errors in spelling, grammar, and punctuation, careful editing can make writing more concise and meaningful. This is essential to business communications where brevity and clarity are highly regarded. Although certain editing functions can be automated with a word processor (as we will see shortly), the ability to write and edit clearly remains a skill that is undeniably human. Here is a perfect blending of human with machine. The word processor provides the flexibility to make major changes easily, freeing the user to concentrate on style and creativity when shaping the final product.

Through the use of word processing commands, writers have absolute freedom to copy, move, replace or add text to suit their purposes.

Did you ever pause at a typewriter, unable to continue until you found the "perfect" word to express your thoughts? Typewriters force you to do this by creating text that is permanent. Editing is restricted to minor typeovers. Word processing has no such restriction. When you're at a loss for words, simply leave a placemarker in the text and continue typing. You can fill in the missing words later; the computer will rearrange the text to match.

In fact, any change can be made to text on the workscreen. We can add or delete letters, underlining, capitals, commas, quotations, or periods. We can change spacing, adjust margins, alter tabs, center, uncenter, indent, or remove indentations. *Nothing* is permanent. Typists find this ability to change actually increases their typing speed. They type faster knowing that errors can be fixed easily and quickly.

Another important editing feature of the word processor is the BLOCK command, which enables users to identify words, sentences, paragraphs, or larger sections of text. Once identified, these "blocks" of text can be moved, copied, or even deleted. Some programs allow blocks to be capitalized, underlined, and centered as well. Sentences can be moved from the middle of a report to its beginning. Entire paragraphs can be rearranged to improve readability. Large-scale changes to text can be accomplished with a few keystrokes. As we saw earlier, block commands can also be used to transfer text from one document to another, or even build a new document by combining material from other files. Here is how a block of text can be moved in WordPerfect. Although specific keys differ, the technique is remarkably similar in most word processors:

Block moves in WordPerfect (see Figure 9-22)
1.   Move the cursor to the start of the block to be moved. Mark this spot by pressing <ALT><F4>. The words "BLOCK ON" appear at the lower left of the screen.
2.   Move the cursor to the end of the block. As you move, the block appears in inverse video. Press <CTRL><F4> and then <1> to cut the block from the text. It disappears!
3.   Move the cursor to the new position for the block. Press <CTRL><F4> and then <5>. The block reappears in its new position.

It is clear that users who master block commands will significantly improve their efficiency when using any word processor.

The final goal: hard copy

Although businesses are becoming more automated with each passing day, they still rely on printed material for much of their communication. Certainly the use of electronic mail/message systems is growing, but the day of the "paperless" office is not as close as some experts would lead us to believe. Letters and bills must still be printed and sent to clients by mail. Contracts and checks must still be signed in ink. Filing cabinets will still be filled with the paperwork of business transactions for years to come.

What good, then, are a word processor's wonderful capabilities to

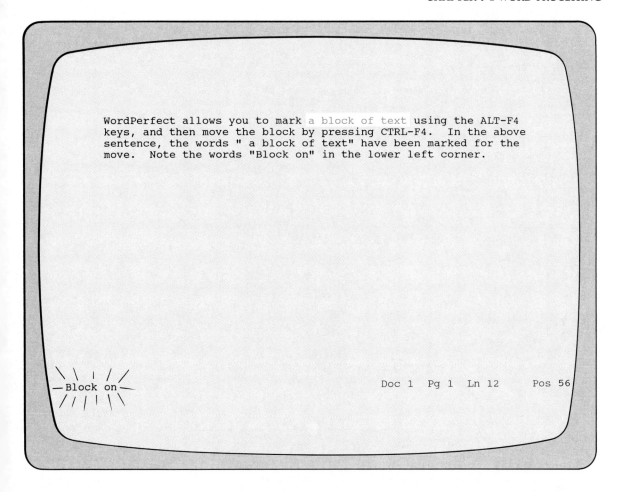

WordPerfect allows you to mark a block of text using the ALT-F4
keys, and then move the block by pressing CTRL-F4. In the above
sentence, the words " a block of text" have been marked for the
move. Note the words "Block on" in the lower left corner.

—Block on—

Doc 1   Pg 1   Ln 12   Pos 56

Figure 9-22
WordPerfect has a block
of text marked and ready
to be moved.

manipulate, store, and retrieve text unless it can be used to produce
printed output as well? This is still the ultimate goal of every word processing system: the production of hard copy; the creation of a neatly
printed document on paper.

Not surprisingly, it is no great feat to produce a printed copy of a
word processing document. Word processors come complete with standard *default* settings for printers that specify margins, page length, and
spacing. Once we have edited the screen version to our satisfaction, we
can print out one or more copies for final review and use. If we do not
like the appearance of the copy, we can override the default settings to
adjust margins, spacing, or in some cases, even print size, to suit our
needs. Then we can simply print it again. In addition, word processors
offer features that are not easily done by hand:

▪ *Headers* are additional lines that can be placed at the top of each
printed page to identify subject matter, chapters, sections, or pages (see
Figure 9-23). They need only be typed once and the word processor will
dutifully repeat them, unless a different header is specified in the text.
Some word processors allow users to specify different headers for use
with odd or even page numbers, as you might find in long reports or
books.

Figure 9-23
A typical header need only be typed once in a document. It is then repeated on each printed page.

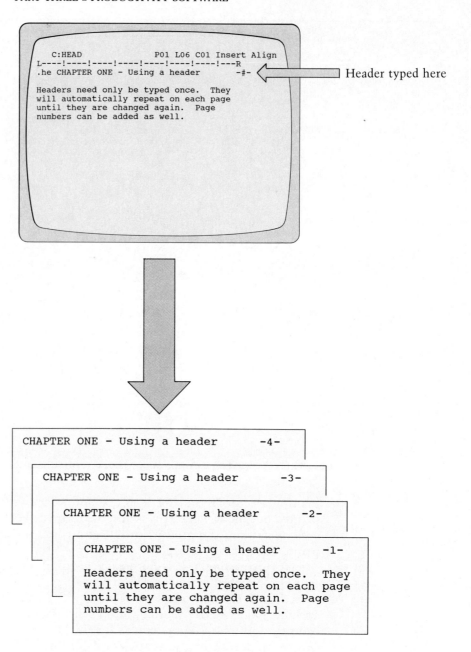

Header typed here

■ *Footers* are identical to headers except that they are used at the bottom of each page. Footers usually show page numbers, which can be automatically centered or placed left and right as desired. The user has total control over whether to include headers, footers, both, or neither, in each document.

■ *Page layout* can be done automatically. Once it is given instructions regarding size of margins and page length, the word processor will automatically format each page with the proper amount of lines to fit. Change the margins and all lines will be readjusted. Of course, you can "force" *page breaks* wherever you want them, but imagine how easy it is

career box
Technical writer

Did you ever try to put together a computer, or learn a new piece of software, by following the instructions that came with your purchase? Many times, the lack of clear, concise directions made it almost impossible to succeed unless you were a technical genius.

In the age of sophisticated computer hardware and software, the need for skilled technical writers has significantly increased. It is not enough to include a short explanation of the new product. Instead, users want to learn its operation quickly and easily using a manual they can understand. They need to know how to start up, how to use the basic parts of the product, and, later on, how to apply its advanced features. In many instances, the manual itself becomes the most important marketing feature of the product.

According to Career Associates, a career in technical writing does not require a scientific or engineering background, but rather ". . . an excellent command of the English language and the ability to write logically, clearly, and accurately. Your research and reporting skills must also be sharp, because you must gather all the facts and concepts for your writing from the engineers, systems analysts, and programmers who develop and design the technology."[1] After you've gathered the information, and, perhaps, gained experience in the use of the product, your job is to present it in an accurate and understandable manner. While typing skill is important, the ability to separate a complex procedure into small, logical steps (much like a programmer does) is essential. The ability to write clearly and concisely is also important.

Most technical writers use a word processor to type and edit their work on computers, and they also have some experience in layout and design. The potential technical writer might do well to gain some experience with word processing and even desktop publishing. He or she must be able to work with a production staff responsible for the manual(s) and understand the use of descriptive graphics when needed for illustration. The job market looks better than average for technical writers, especially in the areas of microcomputers and related software. While very few companies maintain a staff of full-time writers, there is a substantial market for freelance technical writers to prepare and edit brochures, training manuals, and reference manuals to accompany hardware and software products.

Typical entry-level salaries range from $18,000 to $20,000, but can be higher based on writing experience and knowledge of the technical vocabulary. Experienced writers can earn between $35,000 to $60,000 annually. Of course, technical writers can branch out on their own and write instruction books for general sale as well. Walk into any bookstore and notice how many "How to . . ." books on machines, computers, software, or engine repair there are. Where do you think they came from?

[1]"Technical Writing," in *Career Choices for Students of Communications and Journalism* by Career Associates. New York: Walker Publishing Company, 1985, p. 122. Reprinted with permission.

to remove (or add) a few paragraphs and then let the word processor reformat your entire report automatically.

■ *Page numbering* can be turned on or off as desired. When this feature is on, the computer will number every page and print them appropriately in headers or footers.

■ *Typestyles* depend on the printer being used. Some printers make it possible for different typestyles to be used within the same document. On dot-matrix or laser printers, character typestyles (or font) can be intermingled easily. In many programs, size can be adjusted as well, switching among such choices as *pica* (10 characters per inch), *elite* (12 characters per inch), *compressed* (16 to 18 characters per inch), or *expanded* (5 characters per inch). Daisy-wheel printers are more restrictive, using only one typestyle at a time. Although underlining and boldface will work automatically, users must manually replace type wheels on the printer to achieve any other changes in printed style. It is important for word processing programs to be installed with the correct codes so they can take full advantage of your printer's capabilities. Often, word processors come with a large selection of *printer driver* programs to match them to your particular needs.

Advanced functions

Most word processors offer similar basic functions. However, as available computer memory increased, more sophisticated programs began to offer features far beyond the original "basic" word processing package. Many of these features have become standard on today's programs and are expected by potential purchasers. Some of the most useful of these advanced functions are described next.

Spelling checker

A **SPELLING CHECKER** is a program that locates potential misspellings in text material. It provides welcome assistance to the poor speller or inaccurate typist. Spell-check programs can be part of a word processing package or purchased separately. They generally contain a large list or *dictionary* of words, perhaps 100,000 or more, kept separately on diskette. When activated, the spell-check program matches each word in the word processing document with words in its dictionary. Those words that do not match are brought to the user's attention. This procedure can quickly and effectively discover misspellings and typing errors, such as extra or missing letters and spaces, but it is not perfect. It will not locate incorrect usage or typographical errors that form other words in the dictionary. For example, "I wouldn't dot hat," will not be marked for correction even though it should read "I wouldn't *do that*." The words *dot* and *hat* are spelled correctly. Similarly, "I herd that," will not be found since *herd* is another legitimate word.

Recent spell-check programs allow users to check individual words even as they type. If the word cannot be found in the dictionary, the program will offer a list of alternate words right on the screen. Users can then select the proper one to replace the misspelled word in the text, ignore the suggestions, or correct the error themselves. Figure 9-24 shows a WordPerfect spell check in progress.

Figure 9-24
Typical of modern word processors, Word-Perfect's on-line spell-check program finds errors and suggests solutions.

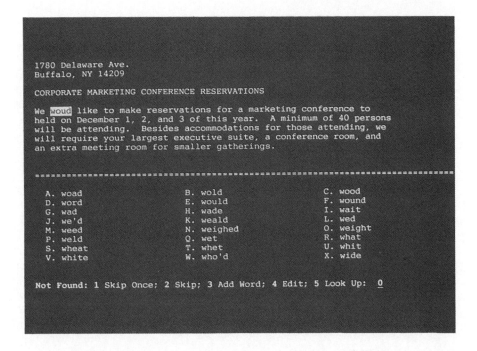

```
1780 Delaware Ave.
Buffalo, NY 14209

CORPORATE MARKETING CONFERENCE RESERVATIONS

We woud like to make reservations for a marketing conference to
held on December 1, 2, and 3 of this year.  A minimum of 40 persons
will be attending.  Besides accommodations for those attending, we
will require your largest executive suite, a conference room, and
an extra meeting room for smaller gatherings.

■■■■■■■■■■■■■■■■■■■■■■■■■■■■■■■■■■■■■■■■■■■■■■■■■■■■■■■■■■■■■■■■■■■■■■■■

     A. woad              B. wold              C. wood
     D. word              E. would             F. wound
     G. wad               H. wade              I. wait
     J. we'd              K. weald             L. wed
     M. weed              N. weighed           O. weight
     P. weld              Q. wet               R. what
     S. wheat             T. whet              U. whit
     V. white             W. who'd             X. wide


Not Found: 1 Skip Once; 2 Skip; 3 Add Word; 4 Edit; 5 Look Up:  0
```

In addition, most spell checkers enable the user to create his or her own dictionaries to enlarge the vocabulary of the program. Proper names or technical terms used often can be added to the list that will be automatically checked. As an extra bonus, many spell-check programs will display a total *word count* when an entire document is finished. Writers who prepare manuscripts based on word counts can quickly and easily gauge how much text must be added or deleted to meet the document's size requirements.

Electronic thesaurus

An **ELECTRONIC THESAURUS** is a program that aids writers who are looking for "just the right word" to express a particular thought. It is the computer's equivalent to the printed thesaurus often found on writers' bookshelves, containing collections of *synonyms* (words with similar meaning) for many English words. Much like a spelling checker, an electronic thesaurus contains an extensive dictionary on diskette. When activated directly from the workscreen, it lists every synonym in its file for the word in question. The user can then select the desired alternative from the list (or choose to ignore them all). For instance, WordPerfect's thesaurus lists the following synonyms for the word *word*: expression, statement, utterance, locution, term, charge, command, dictate, mandate, order, gossip, hearsay, rumor, scuttlebutt, communication, directive, information, message, report, assurance, guarantee, pledge, and promise. We need only indicate one of these choices and it would immediately replace the term *word* on the screen. We could then move to another word and repeat the process.

case in point

Can computers make you a better writer?

Please pause with me now to consider CAW. You're confused? Oh, well, CAW is what the literate and some software developers call computer-aided writing. Yes, it's a valid concept. No, it's not all the rage.

I first experienced CAW with awe, back in the CP/M days, as I sat glued to the screen— for all of the 10 minutes or so it took to operate on a moderately large file—watching programs like Punctuation & Style and Grammatik claw through my WordStar efforts. It seemed so . . . futuristic: a computer program "reading" my stuff, telling me my sentences were long and complicated, that I used clichés, was occasionally offensive to feminists, and often forgot to pair up parentheses.

Today, I almost never forget to pair up parentheses. But despite all that help, early on, I still (obviously) am partial to long and complicated sentences, still make liberal use of my favorite clichés, and am still occasionally offensive to feminists. As you can see, this represents the Zen approach to CAW; nothing need change except your awareness of what you're doing.

At least you will become aware sooner, these days. The latest style checker can operate with great dispatch, generates a "readability index," and then tells you what it is about your miserable excuse for a writing style that impairs it.

The implications are clear: If a particular message demands a reading competence much over the sixth grade level, a substantial portion of "literate" America will not totally absorb it.

Thus the flaw in CAW: As applied in the programs thus far available to personal computer users, CAW is really intended to be CAWC (computer-aided written communication). Not to demean the considerable skills involved in writing clearly and consistently at the sixth-grade level, this kind of discipline has no chance of producing a finished Faulkner or Fitzgerald every 2.3 generations. CAWC/CAW as it currently exists for basic purposes is far too rule-bound to serve higher forms of communication. Where is the program, for instance, that evaluates the stylish implementation of verbless sentences? Like this one. Or imperatives? Read Hemmingway. Or contemporary usage? No way.

More to the point, perhaps, is the fact that it *is* possible to write horribly at the sixth- or seventh-grade level. In any case, I can accept CAWC for what it currently is: a selectively useful software tool that is subject to interpretation.

But what about CAW? Is there really anything around that improves the art of writing as opposed to communication? A while ago a friend of mine, who is a lawyer, was writing an instructional book on income taxes in the form of hypothetical case studies. He decided to create fictional character names for his situations that would also be puns, thus lending some relief to the driest of topics. We were commuting together in his car so he recruited my help. I'm telling you we slaved over it. We could have used a computer program to generate the double meanings. So, for example, if you entered "average housewife," it would return *Rona DeMille*. To your "female Karate instructor" query, it would immediately respond: *Marcia Lartz*. Now that would be an implementation of CAW worth crowing about.

———

Authors' note: This article scored 9.64 and 12.4 on two different computerized readability scales. The style checker found long, incomplete sentences, clichés, weak and/or wordy comments, and disliked the word "but." Suggestions included "use an active voice, shorter sentences, and more common words." The spell-checker even suggested that "Faulkner" might be "falconer." An interesting follow-up: When we ran the style checker's comments back through itself, it found its own comment of "use more common words" to be too ambiguous!

Source: "Let's Hear It for CAW" (from an article in *Personal Computing*, August 1987 by Robin Nelson, now editor of *Computer and Communication Decisions*.) Copyright, Personal Computing. Reprinted and excerpted with permission.

Both spelling checkers and thesauruses make use of separate disks that contain their reference lists. This requires the user to switch disks when these programs are activated, and then switch back to the main program disk when finished. To alleviate this problem, many users copy all their word processing disks onto a hard disk. Then, each feature can be called upon instantly without switching disks. In addition, hard disks are much faster than floppies.

Footnotes

Additional notations placed at the bottom of pages (or at the end of a report) to provide references or explanations are called *footnotes*. Some word processors, notably WordPerfect, WordStar 5.0, and Word, provide automatic footnote capabilities. The user simply indicates where the footnote is desired and its content. The program automatically positions and formats the footnote to fit, with no further work on the part of the user. If you use footnotes, you'll greatly appreciate the time, effort, and headaches saved by this feature.

Indexing

INDEXING provides readers with easy reference to words and ideas contained within a book or report. It is a painstaking process to create a good index. First, you must identify all the important words to be indexed and alphabetize them. Then you locate every occurrence of these words throughout the document. Finally, you must type the alphabetical list with all appropriate page numbers for reference. Imagine the opportunities for error! Electronic indexing automates this entire process. Many programs offer *full indexing*, which alphabetizes and references every word in the document, or *selective indexing*, which allows the user to mark words for indexing. In both cases, the word processor then creates the index—a separate document alphabetically listing every word and all its appropriate page references.

Supplementing the word processor

As word processors increased in power and sophistication, software companies developed adjunct programs that could be applied directly to the documents created by the word processor. Many of these programs were intended to help writers improve the clarity and style of their letters and reports. For many writers, using these adjunct programs is like having an experienced editor carefully review their work and offer suggestions for improvement. In fact, these programs are small *expert systems* that have been programmed to look for common writing errors and suggest corrections. Although there are many currently available, they can be classified into two main groups: grammar checkers and style checkers.

Grammar checkers

GRAMMAR CHECKERS are programs that look for errors in basic punctuation and syntax. They are designed to work with files from many different word processors. They can detect missing capitalization, run-on sentences, incomplete sentences, repeated words, incorrect spacing, and poor use of periods, semicolons and the like. When they discover each error, they will "flag" it for review. Some will even suggest the correct form, but it is still up to the user to decide whether or not a correction will be made.

Typically, a user will save a complete or partial document on disk, exit the word processing program, and then start the grammar-check program. This program, like the word processing program, might be on a separate disk, or stored on a hard disk for easy accessibility.

The program then asks for the name of the file to "check" and begins its work. Depending on the length of the file, and the sophistication of the grammar checker, it could take 5 minutes or more to complete a thorough analysis.

Style checkers

STYLE CHECKERS are adjunct programs like grammar checkers, and come in many varieties. Some will identify individual clichés, pedantic phrases, and poor word usage and then suggest alternative structures. Others will measure general traits about your writing to include sexist language, readability, and sentence length, and give you a score for each based on accepted language scales (Figure 9-25a). Writers can then return to their document and edit as necessary, reevaluating their style as often as desired. Style checkers operate in a similar manner to grammar checkers, and can print comments directly in a file for later review. Some even prepare alphabetized lists of all the words you've used, their frequency in the document, and whether they are used in common English.

File conversion utilities

At times, we may wish to switch from one word processor to another. Perhaps we've purchased new software and want to edit some of our old files. Maybe we are using a word processor at home that is different than the one at work. While some word processors create standard ASCII files that can be shared by other programs, most store their files in a form that is unreadable by other word processors. Enter the file conversion program! This utility allows users to convert their files to match the format required on other word processors. Thus, WordStar files can be translated to Word or Multimate files, and vice versa. While some file conversion programs are included with word processing programs, others must be purchased separately. There may also be symbols in one word processor that cannot convert to the other. Even so, before you retype any document for use in a different word processor, check the availability of a file conversion program. It is much faster and easier than retyping.

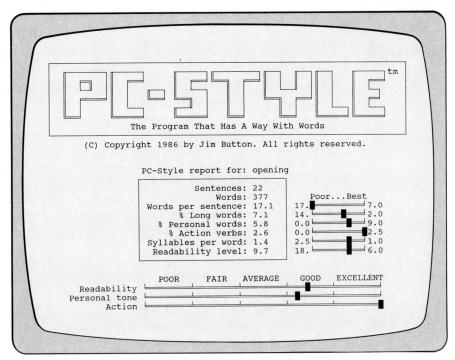

Figure 9-25
(a) PCStyle has completed its rating of this document in a few moments. (b) RIGHTWriter embeds comments directly into a document.

PC-STYLE™

The Program That Has A Way With Words

(C) Copyright 1986 by Jim Button. All rights reserved.

PC-Style report for: opening

Sentences:	22
Words:	377
Words per sentence:	17.1
% Long words:	7.1
% Personal words:	5.8
% Action verbs:	2.6
Syllables per word:	1.4
Readability level:	9.7

Poor...Best
17. ————— 7.0
14. ————— 2.0
0.0 ————— 9.0
0.0 ————— 2.5
2.5 ————— 1.0
18. ————— 6.0

POOR   FAIR   AVERAGE   GOOD   EXCELLENT
Readability
Personal tone
Action

(a)

"There's still so much to do," she thought. "Even if I can
read Freddy's handwritten notes, the current margins and spacing
are all wrong, the paragraphs must be changed around, the
        <<* 21. PASSIVE VOICE: be changed *>>ˆ
itinerary is incomplete, and typing errors must be corrected."
            <<* 21. PASSIVE VOICE: be corrected. *>>ˆ
                <<* 17. LONG SENTENCE: 32 WORDS *>>ˆ
                    <<* 31. COMPLEX SENTENCE *>>ˆ
Not being the best speller, she also dreaded the editing which
would follow after the rest of the report had been typed. But
            <<* 21. PASSIVE VOICE: been typed. *>>ˆ
                <<* 23. SENTENCE BEGINS WITH BUT *>>ˆ
there was no turning back. The meeting could not be postponed,
and the report must be ready. Ann began to type.
                    <<** SUMMARY **>>

    READABILITY INDEX: 8.12
Readers need an   8th grade level of education to understand.

    STRENGTH INDEX: 0.22
The writing can be made more direct by using:
            - the active voice
            - shorter sentences
            - more common words

    DESCRIPTIVE INDEX: 0.64
The use of adjectives and adverbs is within the normal range.

(b)

summary

■ Word processing is the creation, editing, and printing of text material—a process that has evolved since the use of paper and pen. It has developed through such inventions as movable type, the typewriter, and the CRT-based word processor.

■ Modern word processing options include electronic typewriters, dedicated word processors, mainframe- and minicomputer-based word processors, and the popular microcomputer-based word processor.

■ Microcomputer word processors require special software to control the word processing functions that include: text entry, word wrap, insertion, typeover, deletion, formatting, justification, centering, cursor control, move, copy, search, search and replace, save, retrieve, and printing. In some programs, an "undo" procedure allows users to erase their most recent command.

■ Word processors help business users become more efficient by substantially improving the flexibility of documents through text rearrangement, error correction, paragraph assembly, boiler plating, mail merge, and typesetting capabilities.

■ Most word processing takes place on a workscreen that allows users to scroll up or down a document to type or edit. This screen usually includes a status line with position identifiers, a ruler line, and character indicators such as embedded symbols, highlighting, inverse video, or color. Screens can also employ pull-down menus or windows to allow additional text material on the screen at the same time.

■ Keyboards used with word processors include alphabetic and numeric typewriter keys, cursor control keys, function keys, and the special keys of escape, alternate, and control. A type-ahead buffer may be used to allow the typist to continue working while the computer adjusts the screen.

■ The word processor's ENTER key differs in use from the typewriter's RETURN key. It is not pressed after every line. Instead, word wrap automatically moves words that do not fit onto the next line. Changes in line size can automatically be reformatted to fit within margins. Full justification can be used to align text neatly along both margins.

■ Documents can be saved onto disk and retrieved later for additional work. It is a good idea to create backup copies for safekeeping.

■ Editing is the manipulation of text into a more useful and understandable form. An important editing feature is the text block command, which enables users to make large-scale changes to text.

■ The final goal in word processing is the creation of a printed page, or hard copy. Word processors allow alterations to headers, footers, page layout, typestyle, and page numbering as desired.

■ Advanced word processing functions can include spell checkers, electronic thesauruses, footnotes, and indexing.

■ Word processors can be supplemented with adjunct programs that check the grammar and style of the document.

Wrap-up

Deadlines met

Let's rejoin Ann at her desk. Janis has been busy deciphering Freddy's handwriting and dictating to Ann. Ann didn't stop to fix mistakes, but just typed into the word processor as quickly as possible.

When she finished the rough draft, Ann printed out the itinerary portion and brought it to Janis for review. She made sure to print it triple-spaced, leaving more than enough room for written additions. While Janis filled in the missing data, Ann went back to the computer and started the built-in spelling checker. As each error appeared on the screen, she corrected it herself or selected one of the computer's correct spelling choices. Janis returned with the completed itinerary that Ann used to fill in the missing sections of the document.

Now it was time for "clean up." Ann ran her grammar- and style-check program. It found a few run-on sentences, some missing punctuation, and a repeated word. Ann corrected these flaws quickly. Then, she printed a double-spaced draft of the entire document on her dot-matrix printer and made copies on the photocopier. Freddy, Janis, and Ann got together to review them for style and content. Freddy felt that the word *fantastic* was overused and would have negative results at the meeting. Janis didn't like the order of paragraphs on page 20. Ann spotted an error, "We hope you enjoy your *tip*," that the speller could not pick up. Ann made notes of the changes.

Retrieving the document once more, Ann located each appropriate page and altered the document to match her notes. She moved the paragraphs around, deleted a few sentences, and used the on-line thesaurus to replace *fantastic* with *fabulous, fanciful, marvelous,* and just plain *great.* She almost forgot to change *tip* to *trip.*

Now, after a quick command to widen the left margin to allow space for a binder, Ann was ready to print. She saved the document on disk, and took it into Janis's office where the laser printer was located. A few commands later and the report was being printed, letter-perfect, at twelve pages a minute. Within 3 minutes, it was done. Janis gave it one last look for good measure.

Ann ran to the photocopier, made ten copies, and inserted them into presentation binders. Five minutes after the meeting started, Ann walked in with a stack of impressive reports—one for each participant. Then she calmly walked out and collapsed at her desk!

key terms

These are the key terms arranged in alphabetical order. The numbers in parentheses refer to the page on which each term is defined.

Boiler plating (277)
CRT-based word processor (273)
Dedicated word processor (273)
Deletion (274)
Editing (295)
Electronic thesaurus (301)
Embedded symbols (286)
Grammar checker (304)
Highlighting (286)
Indexing (303)
Insert/Insertion (274)
Inverse video (286)
Justification (274)
Mail merge (278)
Position identifiers (284)
Print (277)
Pull-down menu (284)
Reformatting (274)
Retrieve (275)
Ruler line (284)
Save (275)
Scrolling (280)
Search (275)
Search and Replace (275)
Spelling checker (300)
Status line (281)
Style checker (304)
Text block (291)
Text entry (273)
Text entry area (285)
Type-ahead buffer (273)
Typeover (274)
Windows (284)
Word processing (272)
Word wrap (274)

review questions

objective questions

True/false. *Put the letter T or F on the line next to the question.*

1. The electric typewriter was actually the first CRT-based word processor. 1 _____

2. Hard copy is text that appears on a monochrome screen. 2 _____

3. Microcomputer-based word processors use the same hardware found in typical microcomputer systems. 3 _____

4. Word wrap reduces the need for typists to use the ENTER key. 4 _____

5. If a screen is not set in the INSERT mode then it is in the TYPEOVER mode. 5 _____

6. Normal typing will result in full justification of the right and left margins. 6 _____

7. Save and retrieve commands are closely associated with cut and paste routines. 7 _____

8. Boiler plating is another term for paragraph assembly. 8 _____

9. A visual indication of left and right margins can be found on the workscreen's status line. 9 _____

10. Soft function keys are made of special plastic that feels soft to the touch. 10 _____

Multiple choice. *Put the letter of the correct answer on the line next to the question.*

1. Which of the following keys is considered to be a "toggle" switch? 1 _____
   (a) INSERT.   (c) ENTER.
   (b) ESCAPE.   (d) UNDO.

2. Which of the following procedures is not an option with the SAVE command? 2 _____
   (a) Continue.   (c) Exit.
   (b) Quit.   (d) Start over.

3. All of the following items are presented on a typical workscreen status line *except* 3 _____
   (a) Page.   (c) Margin.
   (b) Line.   (d) Column.

4. Increased character brightness on a computer screen is accomplished through a feature known as 4 _____

(a) Highlighting.   (c) Color.
(b) Inverse video.   (d) Embedded symbols.
5. The final goal of any word processor is
   (a) Saving the document on disk.
   (b) Preparing backup copies.
   (c) Creating hard copy.
   (d) Adjusting tabs and margins.

Fill in the blank. *Write the correct word or words in the blank to complete the sentence.*

1. In the technique called _____, the word processor's "window" is moved to display new text on the screen.
2. Screens that display text exactly as it will appear when printed are exhibiting a feature called _____.
3. The _____ key works much like the backspace key.
4. The feature _____ automatically moves text to another line if it doesn't fit within the right margin.
5. The placeholder on a computer screen is called the _____.
6. The identification of large areas of text for deletion, movement, or copying, can be done through a _____ command.
7. Additional lines that can be added automatically to the top of each page are called _____.
8. Spelling checkers use separate lists of words called _____ that are kept on diskette.
9. Two keys that have a similar purpose to the SHIFT key are the _____ and _____.
10. A cardboard list, called a _____, can be placed around the function keys to display their use in each program.

short answer questions

When answering these questions, think of concrete examples to illustrate your points.

1. What is a word processor?

2. How do WYSIWYG screens differ from other screens?
3. Why is the UNDO command useful in a word processor?
4. What is the major difference between a typewriter's RETURN key and a word processor's ENTER key?
5. What types of errors will *not* be found by a spelling checker?
6. What is backup and why is it important?
7. Name three business operations that can be improved using a word processor.
8. What is the difference between the commands SEARCH and SEARCH AND REPLACE?
9. Explain the use of the CTRL key in word processing.
10. What is mail merge?

essay questions

1. It is has been said that word processors are more "flexible" than typewriters. Explain this concept and give examples.
2. If you learn to use one word processor well, you should have no trouble learning another. Indicate whether or not you agree with this statement and provide examples to support your conclusion.
3. Describe how spelling checkers and electronic thesauruses can be used to improve writing skills.
4. If you were asked to participate in the selection of a word processing program, which features would you rate of most importance to your decision? Why?

Answers to the objective questions

True/false: 1. F; 2. F; 3. T; 4. T; 5. T; 6. F; 7. F; 8. T; 9. F; 10. F
Multiple choice: 1. a; 2. d; 3. c; 4. a; 5. c
Fill in the blank: 1. scrolling; 2. WYSIWYG; 3. delete; 4. word wrap; 5. cursor; 6. block; 7. headers; 8. dictionaries; 9. ALT and CTRL; 10. template

Electronic spreadsheets: thinking in rows and columns

After studying this chapter you should understand the following:

- *The importance and capabilities of spreadsheets.*
- *How to interpret spreadsheet screens.*
- *How to enter and manipulate data in the spreadsheet.*
- *The basic functions available with electronic spreadsheets.*
- *Supplemental programs that can be used with spreadsheets.*

chapter 10

The accountant at tax time

For the past 2 years, Jill had been an adjunct professor at Oakriver University and a practicing CPA (certified public accountant). She firmly believed that teachers who could draw upon *current* business experiences provided more meaningful instruction for students. Her class ratings and attendance, along with the growing success of her practice, proved that her approach was valid.

However, success did not come easy. As her accounting practice grew, so did the time required to maintain it. Lately, there was not much time, or energy, left for teaching. Her social life was nonexistent. Jill discovered, as most accountants do, that this condition always grew worse during "tax season." For Jill, it was doubly compounded as more and more clients sought her tax preparation help. Although she welcomed her growing success, Jill dreaded the thought of giving up teaching or sacrificing her personal life. Clearly, a solution was needed. As if by magic, it arrived in the next day's mail!

A brochure announced that Oakriver University was offering a course in microcomputer spreadsheet use especially designed for practicing CPAs. Jill eagerly enrolled in the course.

Over the next few weeks, Jill learned how to apply computers and spreadsheets to general ledger, accounts receivable, accounts payable, inventory, and payroll. She spoke with other accountants who had been using ready-made tax preparation software. She saw printers that could generate completed tax returns in a matter of seconds. It was all too clear that she had been living in the "Stone Age" of accounting. Now that she had some computer spreadsheet experience, she decided to quickly change that.

Pooling most of her consulting fees, and armed with helpful suggestions from colleagues and instructors, Jill purchased a microcomputer with a printer and color screen. She also bought a spreadsheet program, blank diskettes, and a tax spreadsheet template for the current year to automate much of her tax work. A few days of practice and Jill was ready for the new tax season. She also dusted off her social calendar!

Applications and evolution

The incredible roll of paper

Though microcomputer spreadsheets appeared only a short time ago, their manual counterparts have been around for ages. A SPREADSHEET, or worksheet, after all, is nothing more than a table—a set of boxes neatly arranged in columns and rows. Accountants have used "columnar paper" worksheets as an effective way of presenting large volumes of financial data, usually numbers, in a concise manner. As Figure 10-1 shows, the vertical COLUMNS on the spreadsheet intersect with horizontal ROWS to form individual boxes or CELLS. It is these cells that are used to hold various data—numbers, words, or the results of calculations.

Paper spreadsheets rarely exceed 14 columns and 40 rows (Figure 10-2). However, computer spreadsheets are much more extensive, in

Figure 10-1
Cells are formed by columns and rows.

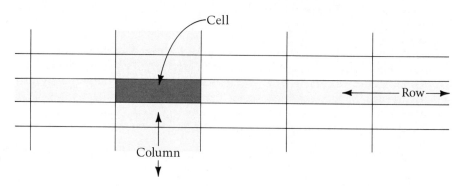

Figure 10-2
A typical sheet of columnar paper.

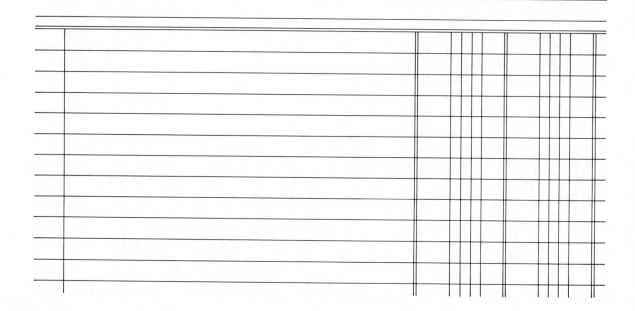

Figure 10-3
The original electronic
spreadsheet: VisiCalc.

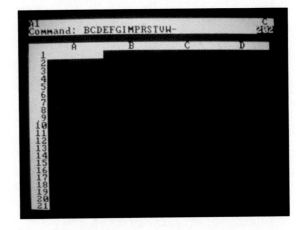

some cases providing space for up to 16,000 columns and rows. To hold the same data as these computer versions, you would need a piece of paper over 200 feet long and 1200 feet wide! Imagine the folder you would need to carry it.

The development of the modern spreadsheet

Paper spreadsheets have been used for many years, but the ELECTRONIC SPREADSHEET is a modern concept. It owes its existence to a former Harvard MBA student, Dan Bricklin, who was fed up with the constant changes and recalculations required by his accounting assignments. He wanted to replace his paper spreadsheet and hand calculator with a microcomputer program that would let him manipulate columnar data much like a word processor allows us to manipulate text. His dream was realized in 1978, when he and his friend, Bob Frankston, created Visi-Calc (short for *visi*ble *calc*ulator), shown in Figure 10-3.

Although small by today's standards, VisiCalc was the best-selling software program of its time, handling spreadsheets up to 64 columns by 256 rows. It also offered built-in statistical functions, logical "if" statements, simple formatting, editing, and, most important, the capability to create mathematical relationships among cells. Apple II microcomputer sales soared as businesspeople quickly realized the potential of this new software/computer combination.

The success of VisiCalc prompted other software companies to jump on the electronic bandwagon. "Visi-clones" flooded the marketplace. Most were remarkably similar, borrowing (some experts say "stealing") VisiCalc's approach to its menu system, screen display, and general spreadsheet operations. Programs like SuperCalc, Multiplan, PC-Calc, PFS:Plan, Perfect Calc, and Lotus 1-2-3 became the successful offspring of VisiCalc, which retired to its place in history as the "parent" of modern spreadsheets.

Of these second-generation spreadsheets, Lotus Corporation's 1-2-3 (see Figure 10-4) became a business favorite almost overnight. While not necessarily the best spreadsheet, its increased power, ease of use, and extreme flexibility appealed to many users. In addition, Lotus 1-2-3 offered three (thus its name) components integrated into one package: spreadsheet, graphics, and elementary database (file management) capa-

Figure 10-4
The Lotus 1-2-3 package.

bilities. Far beyond the original VisiCalc, the first version of Lotus 1-2-3 offered 256 columns by 2000 rows, helpful menu command lines, statistical formulas, advanced keystroke programming commands, formatting capabilities, and on-line help screens. Now past its third revision in size and capabilities, Lotus 1-2-3 still retains its substantial business following.

However, Lotus is not alone in the highly competitive and profitable spreadsheet market. History repeated itself in the mid-1980s when "Lotus-clones" appeared. By 1988, Mosaic's Twin, Paperback Software International's VP-Planner, and Goldstein Software's Joe Spreadsheet, were offered at one-third to one-tenth Lotus's price! They generally ran slower than Lotus 1-2-3 and did not match all the capabilities of 1-2-3's more recent release. Yet, being newer, some offered additional commands not found in the Lotus 1-2-3 program. Even though their screens, speed, and capabilities varied somewhat, each was so close to Lotus 1-2-3's "look and feel" that most commands and data files were totally compatible.

At the same time, Microsoft's Excel spreadsheet, already a best-seller for the Apple MacIntosh, was offered for IBM-compatible computers. Borland's Quattro offered speed and extended capabilities and Garrison Corporation's BoeingCalc extended spreadsheets into three dimensions offering 16,000 rows, columns, and pages! Each of these programs offered newer approaches to menus, screens, and capabilities, yet allowed users to access commands through Lotus-like "standard" keystrokes if desired.

As always, competition had fueled the swift growth of spreadsheet size and capability. In one decade, electronic spreadsheets progressed from college "homework-helpers" to essential parts of most microcomputerized businesses throughout the world. It is likely that they will continue to grow well into the 1990s.

The standard capabilities

Although they resemble paper spreadsheets in their use of columns and rows for data entry, all electronic spreadsheets provide a basic set of capabilities that greatly expand the size and versatility of their paper counterparts. For example, they allow users to create *formulas* that mathematically link one cell to another. Formulas are a significant improvement over paper techniques, for they will automatically display new results whenever values in related cells are modified. If a formula is used to calculate a column's total, then a new total will appear each time any number is changed in that column, as in Figure 10-5. Our time and effort are not wasted in recalculation.

Most of the capabilities of electronic spreadsheets contribute directly to their flexibility, the ease with which they can be modified to meet particular needs—a key aspect of spreadsheet use. Even the least expensive electronic spreadsheet allows us to modify any spreadsheet setting as often as we like. We can edit cell contents, make columns wider or narrower, or change how we display (called *format*) the con-

Figure 10-5
When values are
changed, formulas auto-
matically calculate new
results. (a) Before.
(b) After.

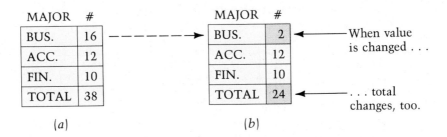

(a)   (b)

Figure 10-6
Examples of formatting.

When formatted as:	The number 1234.567 will look like:
General format	1234.567
NO DECIMALS	
Fixed	1235
Comma	1,235
Currency	$1,235
Percent	123457%
TWO DECIMALS	
Fixed	1234.57
Comma	1,234.57
Currency	$1,234.57
Percent	123456.70%
Hidden	
Scientific	1.23E+03

tents of any cell. As seen in Figure 10-6, we can show values with or without decimals, commas, or dollar signs. We can create our own mathematical formulas, or choose from many powerful built-in functions. If you've ever totalled a list of numbers, or had to calculate means and standard deviations with a hand calculator, you can appreciate the time saved with this capability alone. A one-word command will do the job, and will instantly change the result whenever the list is modified. We can also add or delete rows or columns and copy cells from one location to another. We can add new data and erase old. Of course, we can also save spreadsheets (or any part of them) to disk for later use. We can load them back into the computer's memory, modify them if needed, and print them out at will.

We can also create (or purchase) reusable templates (see Figure 10-7). **TEMPLATES** are simply spreadsheets that contain everything but our specific data. Their design, column widths, headings, formulas, and cell formatting are complete. We need only load them into memory and fill them in. For example, we can use last year's payroll spreadsheet by simply erasing some of the old data and modifying other parts (social security percentage or tax tables) to bring it up to date. The time savings alone would more than cover the initial cost of the program.

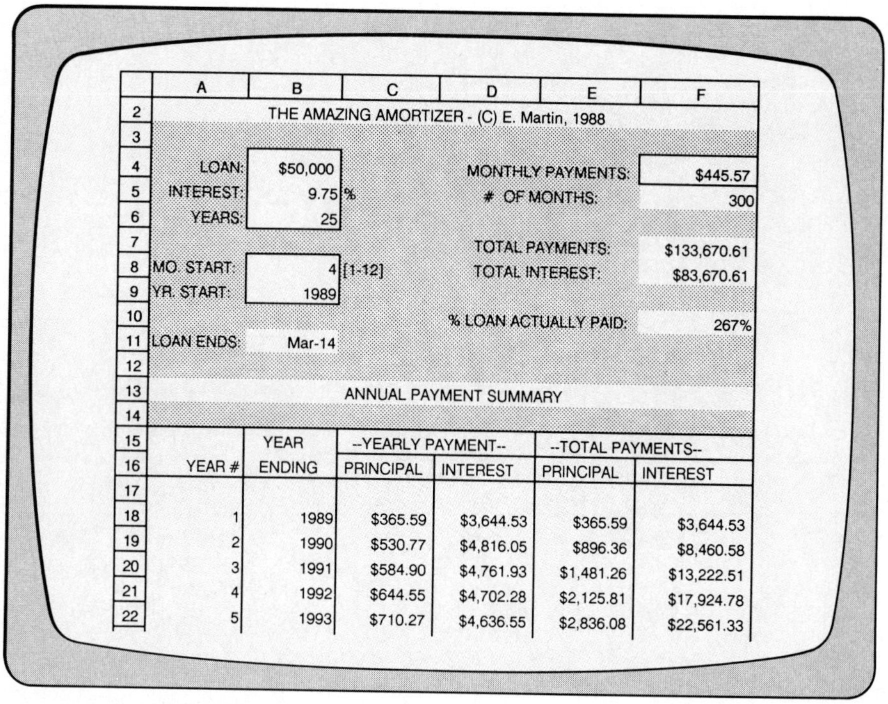

Figure 10-7
An amortization tem-
plate. Entering data in a
few cells automatically
changes the rest of the
spreadsheet.

	A	B	C	D	E	F
2			THE AMAZING AMORTIZER - (C) E. Martin, 1988			
3						
4	LOAN:	$50,000		MONTHLY PAYMENTS:		$445.57
5	INTEREST:	9.75 %		# OF MONTHS:		300
6	YEARS:	25				
7				TOTAL PAYMENTS:		$133,670.61
8	MO. START:	4 [1-12]		TOTAL INTEREST:		$83,670.61
9	YR. START:	1989				
10				% LOAN ACTUALLY PAID:		267%
11	LOAN ENDS:	Mar-14				
12						
13			ANNUAL PAYMENT SUMMARY			
14						
15		YEAR	--YEARLY PAYMENT--		--TOTAL PAYMENTS--	
16	YEAR #	ENDING	PRINCIPAL	INTEREST	PRINCIPAL	INTEREST
17						
18	1	1989	$365.59	$3,644.53	$365.59	$3,644.53
19	2	1990	$530.77	$4,816.05	$896.36	$8,460.58
20	3	1991	$584.90	$4,761.93	$1,481.26	$13,222.51
21	4	1992	$644.55	$4,702.28	$2,125.81	$17,924.78
22	5	1993	$710.27	$4,636.55	$2,836.08	$22,561.33

Applying
spreadsheets
to business:
"What if? . . ."

It is clear that electronic spreadsheets provide significant benefits at the operational level of business. With no great leap of imagination, we can see the immediate possibilities in payroll, accounts payable, accounts receivable, inventory management, financial analysis, sales order tracking, personnel—the list is virtually endless.

However, the characteristics of electronic spreadsheets also make them appealing to managers at all levels of business. Their ability to interrelate cells, calculate quickly, and be easily modified, make them important *modeling,* or predictive, tools for decision makers. With electronic spreadsheets, managers can play the "What if?" game. That is, they can vary numbers and formulas, and examine the financial consequences of potential actions. As long as appropriate data are contained in a spreadsheet (or can be moved into one), managers can manipulate assumptions, develop projections, and investigate trends. The speed and flexibility of the electronic spreadsheet allows them to quickly review and compare alternatives—a process rarely done with paper spreadsheets. In short, they can "financially experiment" with many new approaches, improving the rationality of their decisions. A manager preparing for upcoming negotiations might ask, "What if we gave 5 percent raises to workers who have been with the company more than 10 years?" "What if the raise is 4 percent?" "What if we include all workers at 3 percent?" "How about a raise directly related to years of service but not to exceed 7 percent?" Each alternative could quickly be examined, printed out for review, and evaluated.

A loan officer might investigate "How great a loan can be carried if applicants can afford $1000 a month at 10 percent for 20 years?" "What

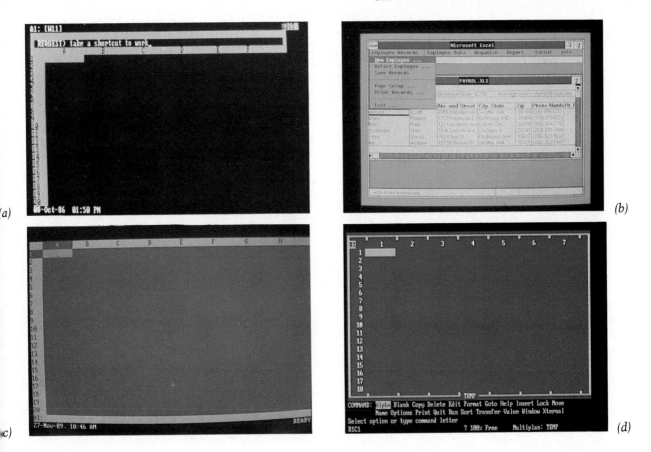

(a)

(b)

(c)

(d)

Figure 10-8
Spreadsheet screens are quite similar: (a) Lotus 1-2-3. (b) Excel. (c) Quattro. (d) Multiplan.

if they can afford $1100?" "What if the interest rate is reduced to 9 percent or the years extended to 25?"

The importance of these functions to business cannot be overstated. Talk to anyone who has recently been interviewed for a business position. In most cases, they will have been asked, "How well do you know microcomputer spreadsheets?" For the rest of this chapter, when we use the word *spreadsheet*, we are referring to the electronic microcomputer spreadsheet.

The spreadsheet at work

Finding your way around the screen

Most spreadsheet use takes place directly on the microcomputer's screen with the results saved on disk or printed. Since most spreadsheets were based on the original VisiCalc program, their screen layouts and general operation are quite similar. After all, how many different ways can you present columnar data and the necessary commands that go with them? These similarities are shown in Figure 10-8, which compares

Spreadsheet errors can cost millions

If you're like most managers, the decisions you make based on personal computer spread sheets are already big and getting bigger. The scope of those decisions is getting wider. And, the likelihood for serious problems is growing.

A Dallas-based oil and gas company recently fired several executives for oversights costing millions of dollars in an acquisition deal. The errors were traced to faulty financial analysis in a spreadsheet model.

How can we avoid disasters such as the one in Dallas? What are the problems we should look out for? How can we improve spread sheets so that they will improve high-quality decision making?

The old computing dictum, "garbage in, garbage out," used to imply a clear answer to the question of spread sheets' reliability: They were just as good or bad as you made them. But the acclaim given personal computers and the wholesale adoption of spread sheets as planning tools seems to have turned the old adage on its ear. "Garbage in, garbage out" has become "garbage in, gospel out."

Managers and executives responsible for decisions based on personal computer spread sheets should look behind those reassuring printouts to the logic and makeup of the spread-sheet models themselves.

The following problems are accompanied by real examples taken from businesses I have analyzed or worked with:

1. A model is logically inconsistent; rules applied to one part of the spread sheet should be applied to another part, but are not. In forecasting revenues, a California manufac- turer applied price discounts to one part of a product line, but overlooked them when fore- casting sales of complementary products. Ac- tual sales for the complementary lines turned out to be higher than forecast, and bottle- necks resulted when production could not keep up with delivery.

2. A model, though logically consistent, is conceptually flawed. Here, bad formulas are faithfully reproduced throughout a spread- sheet model. A finance officer with a large savings and loan association submitted five- year forecasts for divisional profits. How- ever, a mistake in a formula for compound growth resulted in the figures becoming pro- gressively overstated for years two through five of the forecast.

3. Data format is inconsistent or garbled. Typically, these problems occur when dif- ferent types of data are used side by side in the same or parallel model. For example, a national retailer, accounting for manpower needs, discovered field reports stated in per- sons, man-hours, man-days and man-months. Consolidation proved impossible until an ex- haustive rewrite of field reports was com- pleted.

4. The wrong tool is used for the task. This problem is common and growing. An interna- tional distributor of industrial goods based its plans for sales to a South American country on an analysis of that country's manufactur- ing capacity. But, the distributor's products were only used in secondary manufacturing, a small part of the country's total output. The distinction was not made in the spread sheet so that sales were far below forecasts; produc-

tion and inventory costs ended up consuming thousands of extra dollars.

In all of these examples, gross inconsistencies or major problems will quickly stand out. Many times, though, subtle problems will not be readily detected.

Worse, problem detection becomes more and more difficult as data users are removed from the data's source. This frequently occurs when one department uses data generated by another department's spread sheets. Even if detected, problems may be nearly impossible to trace, not to mention correct.

Managers are not without tools to address this mushrooming problem. A carefully followed set of "spread-sheet audit" procedures combined with software for isolating mistakes can all but eliminate most common spread-sheet problems.

The steps to be followed are straightforward:

1. Insist on an audit of all spread sheets used for important decision making. Recently available software, such as—DocuCalc for Apple computers or the Spreadsheet Auditor for IBM PCs, gives two-dimensional printouts with detailed listings of the spreadsheet formulas—thus making verfication of the model's underpinnings routine.

2. Create and enforce an audit trail. As data, printouts or diskettes move beyond their source, this becomes indispensable. In addition to the printout of the formulas mentioned above, an audit trail should include the name of the model's author, the date it was created, a unique name or number, what type of input and output are expected, and a brief narrative describing the purpose and operation of the model.

3. Establish responsibility for the model. Do not let it wander. Changes to the model should be made by authorized personnel only. More importantly, managers using other departments' spread sheets should be responsible for them as if they were their own. Enforcement of this rule will bolster enforcement of rule No. 2 above. A manager responsible for a spread sheet's output will insist on an audit trail and will not just blindly "plug in his own numbers."

4. Require a re-audit each time the model is modified. Document these changes in the audit trail. Spread sheets seem to take on a life of their own, growing in size and complexity as more and more variables are factored into the model. Even minor changes can have unintended effects on otherwise sound spread sheets.

In addition to these specific rules, a final suggestion may be useful: Raise the visibility of the issue. Find out who is using spread sheets for what sort of decision making. If the decisions are important, ensure that procedures similar to these are implemented and followed.

Figure 10-9
A spreadsheet screen is
really a window.

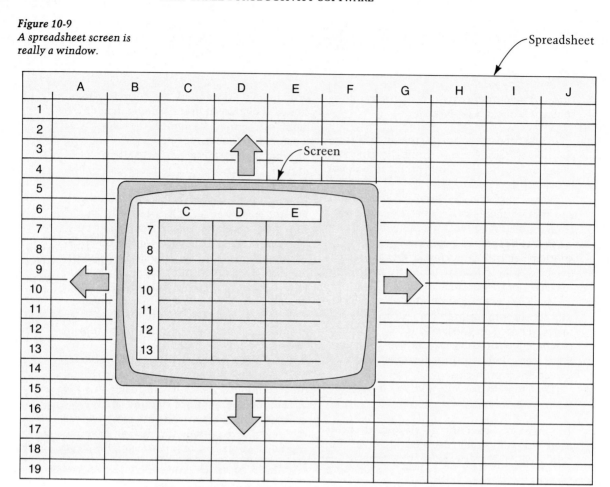

the original VisiCalc screen (in Figure 10-3) to some of the more popular
current programs.

Some programs display messages for users in the top three lines of
the screen. Others may use the bottom, side, or some combination of the
three. Yet, all provide the same basic utilities and present their spreadsheets in a similar fashion.

When viewing a spreadsheet screen, imagine that you are looking
through a window that can only show you a portion of a much larger
sheet (as in Figure 10-9). We can move this window to display various
areas of the spreadsheet, but unless our spreadsheet is small, it is rare
that all of it can fit on the screen at once. Computer screens can usually
display about eight columns (more if column widths are narrow) and
twenty rows. The use of higher resolution screens and software can significantly expand these limits. In general, users learn how to design
their spreadsheets to make the best use of their specific screens.

Figure 10-10 displays a typical upper left corner of a spreadsheet. As
in most spreadsheets, vertical columns are identified with letters and
horizontal rows with numbers for easy cell reference. In our example,
we can see columns A–H and rows 1–5. Columns beyond the first
twenty-six use two letters for identification as in AA1. The CONTENTS

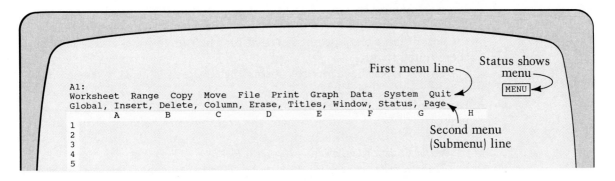

```
A1:                                         First menu line     Status shows
Worksheet  Range  Copy  Move  File  Print  Graph  Data  System  Quit        menu
Global,  Insert,  Delete,  Column,  Erase,  Titles,  Window,  Status,  Page   MENU
          A          B          C          D          E          F          G          H
1                                                                   Second menu
2                                                                   (Submenu) line
3
4
5
```

Figure 10-10
Command menus activated in a line.

LINE, at the top (or in some programs, bottom) of the screen, always identifies the current or active cell and displays its contents. The ACTIVE CELL is the cell into which we are able to enter data. The address A1 indicates that this cell is the intersection of column A and row 1. Some spreadsheets, such as Multiplan, identify columns and rows with numbers only. In this case, the cell in the upper left corner would have an address of R1C1 (for row 1, column 1). It's simply a matter of user preference. Newer programs such as Microsoft's Excel offer both addressing methods, allowing users to select the address format they prefer.

Programs often use the upper right corner of the screen to display the current status of the program. In most instances, the word "READY" appears, but in some cases, it will flash "WAIT" or some other comment for user notice.

Between the contents line and the spreadsheet itself are two additional blank lines. These are used for data entry and display of the various *command menus* that appear during use of the spreadsheet. Figure 10-10 indicates a command menu.

The highlighted area on the spreadsheet itself visually displays the active cell's location. It will move as we move the cursor around the spreadsheet.

Finally, the bottom of the screen may be used by some programs to display the date and time (if desired), or in other programs, the spreadsheet's filename. This line may also contain messages concerning spreadsheet operations or keyboard settings.

Remember that though screens may vary from one program to another, they display essentially the same information. Once you've learned one, it is a simple adjustment to use another.

Using the keyboard

Most spreadsheets were designed for use with the additional keys on the standard IBM-style keyboard. Pressing UP, DOWN, LEFT, or RIGHT arrow keys moves the highlighting cursor one cell in the desired direction. Although this is all we really need to get around the spreadsheet, we can achieve larger "jumps" with other keys. PgDn (Page Down) shifts our view one full screen down; PgUp (Page Up) moves one full screen up. Large horizontal movements can be achieved by pressing the TAB key to jump a screen to the right, or SHIFT-TAB for a full screen jump to the left. In most programs, a special "GO TO" key (F5 in Lotus 1-2-3) is also available. As in *Star Trek*'s transporter beam, the user types the coordinates of a specific destination (the cell address) and is moved there immediately.

Other keys have more normal functions. The alphabetic and numeric keys, SHIFT, BACKSPACE, CAPS LOCK, and SPACE BAR work as they normally would on a typewriter. Mathematical formulas make use of *, /, +, and −, as well as parentheses ( ), relational operators >, <, =, <>, the decimal point ., and the @ symbol. These will be discussed later when we examine formulas.

Only a few keys function in a special way when used with the spreadsheet. The ENTER key does not return the cursor to the left margin, nor does it move a line down. It simply enters data into the active cell. The ESC (Escape) key is used by most spreadsheets to erase the previous entry. It allows users to take one step back. Users can press ESC as many times as needed to exit from a command routine or cancel an entry before it is entered.

For almost every spreadsheet program, the most useful key by far is the "slash," or division, key. Pressing /, starts the hidden command menus and opens up all the powerful routines available in the spreadsheet. Once initiated, these menus lead the user through a series of keystrokes or cursor movements to accomplish almost any purpose from adjusting column widths to saving or printing portions of the spreadsheet. Figure 10-11 shows successive menus that would appear in Joe Spreadsheet to erase the current spreadsheet. Of course, experienced users need not bother reading the menus, but can simply press the first letter of each command to achieve the same results. Thus, the four menus representing / WORKSHEET ERASE YES, could be accomplished by typing /WEY directly.

Some spreadsheets, such as Excel and Lotus 1-2-3, can be controlled by using an electronic mouse in addition to the keyboard. Many users find it easier and faster to "point and click" the mouse instead of using arrow keys and typing commands as seen in Figure 10-12. However, mouse use can also increase the possibility of error, since it is easy to move to the wrong cell or menu with a slight flick of the wrist.

Labels, values, and formulas

Consider a paper spreadsheet for a moment. There are really only three types of entries that can be put into any box on the paper: words or symbols, numbers, or the result of some calculation (which is also a number). Electronic spreadsheets offer similar options. We can enter data into cells in the form of labels, values, or formulas.

■ LABELS are any combination of typewritten characters used to display nonnumeric data. They can be actual words or simply a set or string of symbols such as a row of dashes or asterisks. Labels can be used for column or row headings or for entries that contain alphabetic or other characters. For example, a name, address, or birthdate, would be typed as a label. In general, any entry that begins with a letter (A to Z or a to z), or a quotation mark, is recognized as a label.

■ VALUES, on the other hand, are strictly numeric entries, upon which we can perform some mathematical calculation. For instance, age, sal-

Figure 10-11
Erasing a spreadsheet in Joe Spreadsheet. (a) / (b) WORKSHEET. (c) ERASE. (d) YES. (e) Result . . . a new sheet.

323

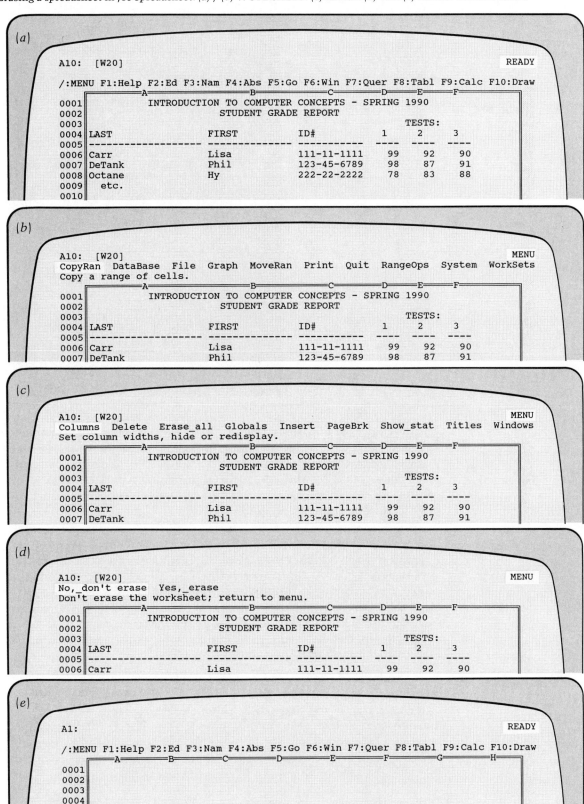

Figure 10-12
A mouse can be used to control many spread-sheet operations.

ary, unit price, or hours worked are all values. They use the numerals 0 to 9, and can include a decimal point, or begin with a plus or minus sign if needed. Any entry that begins with one of these symbols will be recognized as a value by the spreadsheet program. Although values are entered *without* commas, they can be formatted in various ways to display decimals, commas, and dollar signs.

■   **FORMULAS** are used to relate values in one or more cells. They result in new values being calculated and displayed in the cell. If, for example, we wish to subtract the value in cell B1 from 100 and have the results appear in cell C1, we could type 100 − B1 into cell C1. If the value in cell B1 is 25, then a 75 immediately appears in cell C1. Once we have created a formula, any change we make in referenced cells will affect the calculated result. If we change cell B1's contents to 40, then cell C1 will automatically calculate 100 − 40 and show 60 as the result. Compare Figures 10-13a and 10-13b.

Spreadsheet formulas use standard symbols for math operations, as displayed in Figure 10-14. They also follow the universally accepted order of parentheses first, then exponentiation, multiplication, and division, and finally addition and subtraction. The first letters of the sentence, "Please Excuse My Dear Aunt Sally," is a useful mnemonic device to remember this important order of operations, which can affect the outcome of your formulas. Examine the next three formulas. They

Figure 10-13
Changes in referenced cells will affect the calculated result. When cell B1 is changed from (a) 25 to (b) 40, the result of the formula in cell C1 changes from 75 to 60.

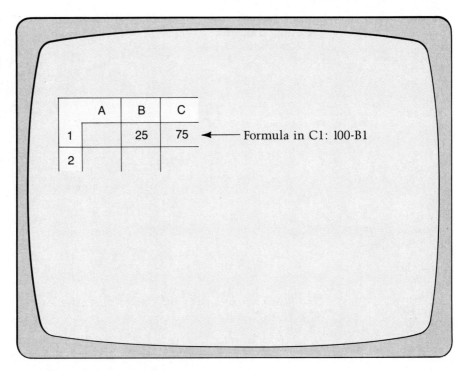

Formula in C1: 100-B1

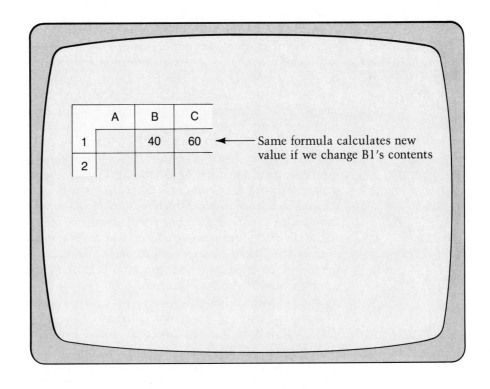

Same formula calculates new value if we change B1's contents

Figure 10-14
Mathematical and relational operators.

Mathematical operators		
Symbol	*Meaning*	*Example*
( )	Parentheses	(6+4)
^	Exponentiation	7^2
*	Multiplication	5*2
/	Division	9/5
+	Addition	7+8
−	Subtraction	9−3
Relational operators		
Symbol	*Meaning*	*Example*
=	Equals	5=5
>	Greater than	9>6
<	Less than	7<10

are identical except for the use of parentheses, which drastically alters their results:

$$20 - 2/3 - 1 \wedge 2 = 18.333$$
$$(20 - 2)/(3 - 1) \wedge 2 = 4.5$$
$$((20 - 2)/3 - 1) \wedge 2 = 25$$

Common errors in using formulas

A word about handling "false starts." Although electronic spreadsheets are powerful, they are not foolproof. At times, formulas might start with a cell reference, or labels might start with a number (as in a telephone listing). Users must be careful to distinguish among values, labels, and formulas, especially when the first character might mislead the program into displaying the wrong type of entry. If we type A1-B1, it will be misinterpreted as a *label* since it starts with a letter! No answer will appear. If we start the formula with the plus sign, as in +A1-B1, we tell the program to treat the result as a value (as it should be).

If we type April 25, 1988 as **4-25-88**, the result appears as **-109**! The program interpreted our entry as a *value* (4 minus 25 minus 88) since we began it with a number. Worse yet, **4/25/88** would yield .001818, or 4 divided by 25 divided by 88! For the same reason, phone numbers and social security numbers (which contain dashes) must be treated as labels, not values. Otherwise, we will see such results as **-3244** when we really mean **111-22-3333** or **-1455** instead of **312-555-1212**. While there are a number of ways to handle these problems, a simple rule will help in most cases: When in doubt, start labels with a quotation mark; start values with a plus sign. As you develop expertise with a particular spreadsheet, you will also learn how to use other symbols to differentiate and control each type of entry.

Be careful about formula use as well. Careless planning may result in CIRCULAR REFERENCES in which formulas end up referring to themselves! For example, typing +A1+A2+A3 in cell A3 results in a circular refer-

Figure 10-15
A circular reference.

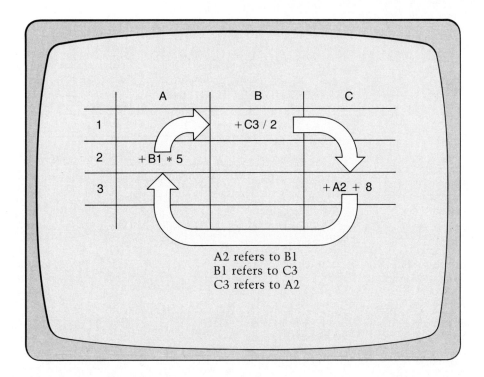

A2 refers to B1
B1 refers to C3
C3 refers to A2

ence since the formula in cell A3 includes A3 itself. While this one is obvious, many are not. How about the classic circular reference shown in Figure 10-15? Even though the cell is not mentioned in its own formula, one can see that the calculation of each formula ultimately leads back to the first cell!

Using built-in functions

BUILT-IN FUNCTIONS are available in all electronic spreadsheets to automate many standard procedures. You can certainly write your own formulas, but it is much easier and quicker to use these functions to perform advanced calculations for you. Built-in functions usually fall into one of seven categories: mathematical, statistical, financial, logical, string, date or time, and special. To use them, you simply type the name of the function, followed by one or more arguments enclosed within parentheses. The **ARGUMENT** identifies data on which the function will work. It can be a single value, a cell address, or a range of cells depending on the particular function in use (as seen in Figure 10-16a). In some spreadsheets (notably Lotus 1-2-3 and compatibles), an @ symbol must be used as the first character of each function's name. Putting this together, we could total all the numbers in cells A1 through A10 by entering @SUM(A1..A10). The "@SUM" is the function name for total, and the argument "(A1..A10)" indicates the **RANGE** of cells we wish to total. In most cases, range is expressed by listing the upper left corner cell first, followed by the lower right corner cell. Figure 10-16b lists examples of Lotus 1-2-3's extensive built-in functions.

Examine Figure 10-17a, which displays part of a simple payroll

Figure 10-16
(a) Argument formats. (b)
Built-in functions.

(a)

Single value: @SQRT(24)	Calculates the square root of the single value 24.
Cell address: @INT(C12)	Calculates the integer of the value in cell C12.
Cell range: @AVG(B1..B22)	Averages the values in the range of cells B1 to B22.

(b)

Illustrative list of Lotus 1-2-3 functions

Mathematical		Statistical	
@ABS	Absolute value	@AVG	Averages values in list
@COS	Cosine	@COUNT	Counts entries in list
@INT	Integer	@MAX	Maximum value in list
@LOG	Common logarithm	@MIN	Minimum value in list
@ROUND	Rounds off numbers	@STD	Standard deviation of list
@SIN	Sine	@SUM	Adds all values in list
@SQRT	Square root	@VAR	Population variance
@TAN	Tangent		

Logical		Special	
@IF	If-then statement	@@	Secondary lookup
@ISNUMBER	Tests for numeric	@CELL	Cell attributes
@ISSTRING	Tests for string	@CHOOSE	Selects from list
		@HLOOKUP	Horizontal table
		@VLOOKUP	Vertical table

Financial		String	
@CTERM	Compounding periods	@CHAR	ASCII character
@DDB	Double-decline depreciation	@EXACT	String comparison
@FV	Future value	@FIND	Substring search
@IRR	Internal rate of return	@LENGTH	Length of string
@NPV	Net present value	@MID	Substring extraction
@PMT	Loan payment	@LOWER	Convert to lowercase
@SLN	Straight-line depreciation	@PROPER	First letter capitals
		@REPEAT	Duplicates symbols
Date and Time		@TRIM	Removes excess space
@DATE	Serial date		
@NOW	Current date and time		

spreadsheet. Row 1 and column A both use labels for headings, but column A also uses labels for employee names. We have formatted the values in column B as integers; values in columns C and D have been set to display two decimals and include commas where needed. Note that row 2 values are formatted with dollar signs as well. All entries in columns A, B, and C, rows 1 to 5 have been typed in with formatting added afterwards with some simple commands.

Formulas were entered in column D cells to automatically multiply hours times pay, such as +B2*C2 in cell D2. The results of these multiplications (not the formulas themselves) appear in cells D2 through D5. In row 6, the built-in SUM function totals the four cells in each column. Similarly, row 7 uses the built-in AVG function to average.

Using even such a simple spreadsheet, a manager could quickly examine individual worker data or note that the average employee

Figure 10-17
Sample payroll spread-
sheets. (a) Payroll. (b)
With changes added.

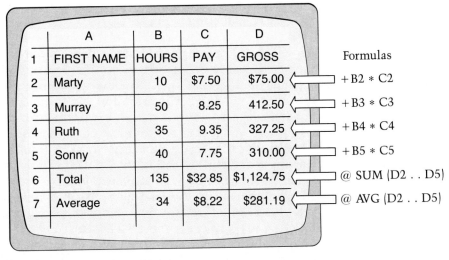

Formulas

	A	B	C	D	Formulas
1	FIRST NAME	HOURS	PAY	GROSS	
2	Marty	10	$7.50	$75.00	+B2 * C2
3	Murray	50	8.25	412.50	+B3 * C3
4	Ruth	35	9.35	327.25	+B4 * C4
5	Sonny	40	7.75	310.00	+B5 * C5
6	Total	135	$32.85	$1,124.75	@ SUM (D2 . . D5)
7	Average	34	$8.22	$281.19	@ AVG (D2 . . D5)

(a)

	A	B	C	D
1	FIRST NAME	HOURS	PAY	GROSS
2	Marty	15	$7.50	$112.50
3	Murray	50	8.25	412.50
4	Ruth	35	9.50	332.50
5	Sonny	40	7.75	310.00
6	Total	140	$33.00	$1,167.50
7	Average	35	$8.25	$291.88

Formulas have
automatically
changed the
GROSS in cells
D2 and D4, and
the appropriate
TOTALS and
AVERAGES
throughout the
spreadsheet.

(b)

worked approximately 34 hours for a gross pay of $281.19. It is also clear that the total payroll for the period is $1124.75. Now the interesting part. If we change an hour or pay entry (in columns B or C), the formulas we have created will automatically adjust results to reflect our changes. For example, in Figure 10-17b, we've changed Marty's hours and given Ruth a raise. Examine the GROSS, TOTAL, and AVERAGE to see the changes automatically performed by the spreadsheet.

With such capability, a manager could easily go beyond simple recordkeeping to investigate how proposed individual salary increases would affect total payroll, how many "person-hours" a particular project required, or the implications of an "across-the-board" percent increase or reduction of hourly wages.

As with word processing files, spreadsheets can be *saved* to a disk, and then *retrieved* later for further editing or use. This capability greatly expands the usefulness of electronic spreadsheets to business and saves countless hours in their creation and application. We might wish to save our spreadsheet for use with the next payroll, for instance. Or we might want to expand it into a much more comprehensive sheet in the future.

We can easily save a spreadsheet at any point in its development by starting the menu, selecting the SAVE routine, and naming a file. In Quattro, for example, the sequence of keys pressed is: / (to start the command menus), F (for File), S (for Save). A menu screen similar to Figure 10-18 would appear. We would then type the filename (perhaps PAYROLL1) and press the ENTER key. Everything about the file is saved: column widths, formulas, labels, even the current position of the cursor. We can save backup copies by using a different filename, or making changes to our original design and saving each as a separate new spreadsheet, slightly different from the first.

Retrieval is just as simple. To bring back a previously saved spreadsheet or a blank template, activate the menu, select the RETRIEVE routine, and type a filename. Most programs display a list of files as well. This allows us to select one for retrieval by moving the cursor to it rather than typing its name. Using Excel as an example, the sequence <ALT-F> O (to open a file) brings up the screen displayed in Figure 10-19. We could also get this screen by using a mouse to point to the word "FILE" in the menu line, and then move down to the word "OPEN" that will appear beneath it. In our example, there are three spreadsheet files available for retrieval, and the cursor has been moved to select the "BUDGET" file. Pressing <ENTER> at this point (or pointing to the word OK) would bring the file named BUDGET onto the screen.

Figure 10-18
Quattro's pop-up win-
dow menus on the right
side of the screen offer a
list from which users can
select the operation they
wish.

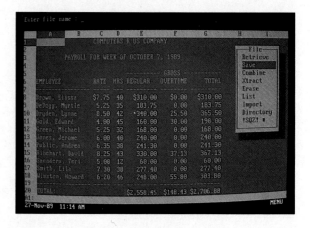

Figure 10-19
Excel's menus simplify
command use.

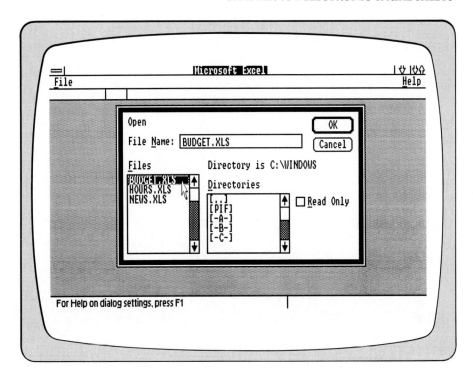

Editing and rearranging

Unlike their paper ancestors, which can be altered only with great difficulty, computerized spreadsheets are extremely flexible. Where paper spreadsheets are chiseled in stone, electronic ones are set in soft clay. They can be stretched, compacted, molded, and remolded as needs and whims dictate. The freedom they provide us as managers and decision makers cannot be overstated. It is especially helpful during initial development stages when we can experiment with different arrangements for best effect. Working with a new spreadsheet is like playing with children's blocks. We can add, take away, and move them around until we are satisfied with how it looks. There are five major capabilities that help us do this: insert, delete, move, copy, and edit.

Insert and delete

The ability to create new rows and columns, or remove others entirely, allows us to manipulate the very structure of the spreadsheet. This is essential when we seek to maximize the effective presentation of data. Adding rows or columns, unthinkable with paper, is no major obstacle on a screen. Suppose we wish to add a LAST NAME column to our payroll spreadsheet? Just move the cursor to the desired position (column B in Figure 10-17) and insert a new column by pressing /WIC (for Worksheet Insert Column) and ENTER. Columns to its right automatically shift over to make room. Every formula on the spreadsheet automatically adjusts to compensate. Now, change column width and formats if needed or simply type in appropriate headings and data. Figure 10-20

Figure 10-20
The payroll spreadsheet
after a column has been
added.

	A	B	C	D	E
1	FIRST NAME	LAST NAME	HOURS	PAY	GROSS
2	Marty	Graw	15	$7.50	$112.50
3	Murray	Hill	50	8.25	412.50
4	Ruth	Less	35	9.50	332.50
5	Sonny	Days	40	7.75	310.00
6	Total		140	$33.00	$1,167.50
7	Average		35	$8.25	$291.88

shows the result. We could also insert *rows* for new employees (/WIR) or delete columns and rows just as easily.

Move
The *move* function enables us to rearrange columns, rows, or individual cells. For example, we might wish to move the LAST NAME column to the left, or rearrange the sequence of employees, both of which have been done in Figure 10-21.

Copy
The ability to duplicate labels, values, formulas, and even formatting elsewhere in the spreadsheet is provided by *copy*. The convenience it offers is a time-saver in spreadsheet development. If we had 1001 employees, we would type the proper formulas and formatting for the *first one only*, and then use the copy command to duplicate them for the other thousand. We can copy one cell or any range (group) of cells. The range concept is an important one; every spreadsheet uses it. It is simply a rectangular area on the spreadsheet that can be as small as one cell, or as large as the entire sheet. Figure 10-22 displays typical ranges: a cell, a column, a row, or a block of cells. Formatting, copying, moving, erasing, and printing all depend on the user indicating ranges to the program.

Edit
Though we can always retype any cell's contents, there are times when only a slight adjustment to a formula or label is required, such as to correct typing errors, expand an earlier design, or update new conditions (a change in name or deduction). The *edit* function is like a tiny word pro-

Figure 10-21
Spreadsheet with LAST NAME column moved and names sorted alphabetically.

	A	B	C	D	E
1	LAST NAME	FIRST NAME	HOURS	PAY	GROSS
2	Days	Sonny	40	$7.75	$310.00
3	Graw	Marty	15	7.50	112.50
4	Hill	Murray	50	8.25	412.50
5	Less	Ruth	35	9.50	332.50
6	Total		140	$33.00	$1,167.50
7	Average		35	$8.25	$291.88

Figure 10-22
Typical ranges: Cell (A1.A1), column (B1.B6), block (C1.E4), and row (A8.C8).

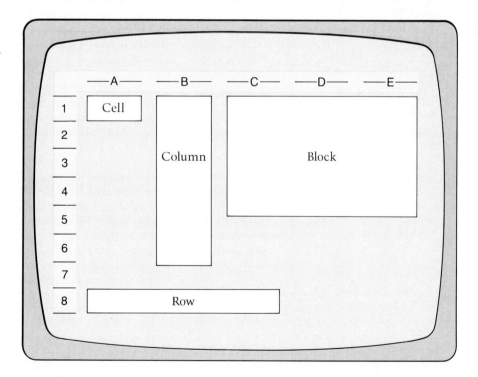

cessor that enables us to recall a cell's contents, and adjust it without having to retype it. Certainly not as useful as the extremely powerful reshaping tools mentioned above, it has its place in fine-tuning the appearance of the spreadsheet.

Spreadsheet traps

Electronic spreadsheets enhance the ability to present and analyze columnar data, but they also increase the risk of miscalculation and misinterpretation. No matter what form of data reporting you choose, it is still your responsibility to verify the accuracy of the reported results. Here are a few insights into overcoming some of the hidden traps awaiting unsuspecting newcomers to spreadsheet use.

Design. Readability is an important concern in preparing spreadsheets. Plan your layout before you begin, taking into account the final printing size, the interrelationship of columns and rows, underlining, headings, and white space. Trying to cram too much material onto one sheet may confuse you and others. It is a general rule that macros are placed in the upper left corner with proper identification for easy reference. Newer three-dimensional worksheets can contain macros on a separate sheet.

Annotation. Place notes at the bottom of the spreadsheet to highlight assumptions and formulas that may not be self-evident. For example, you might wish to note that a particular column was calculated with a specific formula, or the reasoning behind an IF statement you developed. You can always leave the notes off the final printing, but retain them for your own reference on disk.

Constants. Try not to build constants—actual numbers that do not change—into cell formulas; rather list them in their own cell and have other formulas refer to them. This method allows you to see the constant as well as modify it easily. In payroll, for instance, list the social security annual percentage in a separate cell, say F5, at the top of the social security deduction column (column F); then build a formula in each employee row to multiply the salary by cell F5 to calculate the proper deduction. This way, not only do you know the deduction, but cell F5 can be changed next year to reflect the new rate.

Ranges. Ranges for built-in functions must be used with care. First of all, they must be correct. If we wish to add cells A10 through A15, we must make certain that we didn't type (A11.A15). Experience also tells us that ranges must be flexible enough to "grow" as new rows or columns are added. For example, if we wish to add cells A10 through A15, we might have the formula include the cells directly above and below the range as in @SUM(A9..A16). If we add a new row above or below the old, the range will automatically change to include it. Inexperienced users often find that they have added new rows OUTSIDE the range that are therefore not included.

Verify all results. The computer is not responsible for the information—you are. Your reputation for accuracy and reliability is on the line each time you submit a spreadsheet to a superior. Therefore, take a few minutes to check the results of all major formulas. Do they seem reasonable? Have they included all required cells? A simple technique is to add values across first, then total down. Compare this result to adding down each column first, and then totaling across. They should be the same.

Also, make sure reported values make sense. For instance, it might not make sense to add up employees' commission percentages—an average may be more meaningful.

Formulas. Formulas should not be replaced with values. Just because 25 percent of 200 is 50, do not type 50 in the cell that should hold a formula. Although the answer will be correct for now, when you change the percent, or value, later, the reported answer will no longer be right.

Formats. Formats are useful but can lead to misunderstood results. For example, displaying all values as integers does not mean they *are* integers—in fact, the spreadsheet still retains them with decimals and all. Thus, if we multiply .8 by 4, we get 3.2. But if we format these cells to use integers, the spreadsheet will display the erroneous fact that 1 times 4 is 3! Be careful when formatting dollars and cents. It is more accurate to use the @INT or @ROUND functions to ensure that the numbers you see are the actual values in each cell.

Figure 10-23
Printouts can be rotated to fit lengthwise on continuous paper.

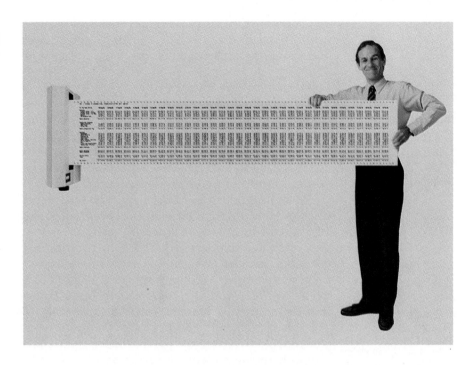

Producing hard copy

The computer allows us to easily update data or quickly investigate "What if?" scenarios on the screen, but we must ultimately be able to print copies of our work on paper. Businesses are changing; however, they still require paper, or hard copy, for presentations, reports, and other communications. We do not mail annual reports to stockholders on disk; nor do we carry computers on public transportation to review financial spreadsheets on the way to work (not yet, anyway). Therefore, one outcome of electronic manipulations is the creation of a paper spreadsheet.

The flexibility of electronic spreadsheets is useful here, too. We can print *hard copies* of each spreadsheet "What if?" scenario for comparison. We can print entire spreadsheets, or any portion of them. With certain printers (dot-matrix, ink-jet, or laser), we can change type size to expanded, compressed, boldface, draft, or near letter-quality. Some programs, like Microsoft's Excel, enable us to mix typestyles on the same spreadsheet for emphasis.

Of course, our spreadsheets may be larger than the paper on which we plan to print them. When this occurs, we have a number of options. We can adjust margins and type size to pack more data onto the sheet. We can use borders to reprint column or row headings on every page for readability. We can design layouts or add page breaks to match paper sizes, or let the program automatically print whatever will fit on each page. We can use each page separately, or cut and paste the parts together to recreate the entire sheet.

Some programs will rotate the entire spreadsheet so that it prints *down* the page instead of across it. Wide sheets can then be printed on continuous paper (as seen in Figure 10-23) without the need to cut and paste them together later.

The worth of electronic spreadsheets is pure gold to many businesses. And like gold, their ability to be reshaped easily allows us to design and transform them as often as our needs change.

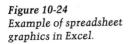

Advanced functions

Most modern spreadsheets offer capabilities far beyond the basic ones we've examined. Many integrate *graphics packages* into their design to aid users in the creation of elementary bar, line, or pie graph displays of columnar data (more on this in Chapter 12). While not the best graphics available for computers, these packages greatly reduce the time and effort needed to prepare reasonable presentation graphics for trend analysis and visual data comparisons, as seen in Figure 10-24.

Most programs can visually split the screen into *windows* that allow users to view different parts of the spreadsheet at the same time (Figure 10-25), or allow users to "lock in" column or row headings to provide easy reference no matter where the cursor may be moved.

Programs can also extract parts of one spreadsheet and combine them with another, allowing data created for one use to be moved elsewhere. More advanced programs can bring two or more spreadsheets into the computer's memory at the same time. This multiple spreadsheet capability, and the use of overlapping windows, enables visual comparisons of different spreadsheets, data transfer from one to the other, or in some cases, the creation of links among cells in *different* files. For example, an annual summary might automatically load totals from four quarterly reports.

Other recent advances increase the security aspects of spreadsheet use. Passwords can be added to files to reduce the risk of tampering or

Figure 10-24
Example of spreadsheet graphics in Excel.

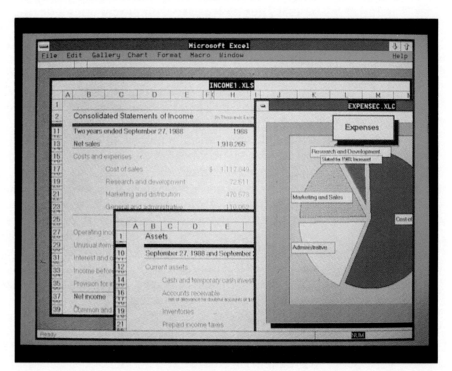

Figure 10-25
A split screen in
Quattro.

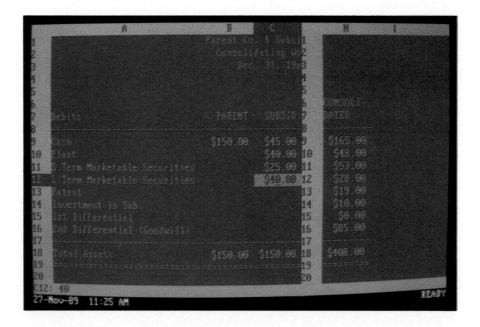

unauthorized access. Some spreadsheets also allow users to create hidden cells, or even to hide columns, which completely disappear from the screen. Although the cells can be used in other calculations, they cannot be printed or viewed when in this hidden state. Sensitive data can be protected but still accessed.

Introducing macros

Perhaps the most advanced capability of spreadsheets is the ability to create MACROS—lists of instructions to the computer. Anything you can do by pressing keys or moving a cursor, you can do automatically with a macro. But you can do it much faster, and with only one keystroke! Macros are very useful for procedures we may repeat often, or for complicated routines that we need from time to time. In Lotus 1-2-3, for example, we could create a macro named "E" containing the keystrokes we normally use to save a file and erase the spreadsheet, namely /FS<ENTER>R/WEY. Then, whenever we press <ALT><E>, the file will be saved and the screen erased. We can also create MENU MACROS, which appear like regular menus on the screen to provide additional capabilities. Figure 10-26 lists a print macro and shows a menu macro in operation.

Beyond the spreadsheet

Database techniques

In addition to spreadsheets and graphics, many programs also offer elementary database (file management) capabilities. Although these cannot compete with more powerful database management programs, they

Figure 10-26
(a) A print macro.
(b) A menu macro in operation.

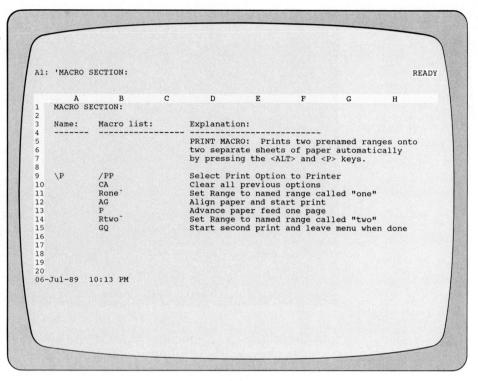

```
A1:   'MACRO SECTION:                                                          READY


         A        B          C         D          E          F         G          H
1    MACRO SECTION:
2
3    Name:     Macro list:           Explanation:
4    -------   -----------------     --------------------------
5                                    PRINT MACRO:  Prints two prenamed ranges onto
6                                    two separate sheets of paper automatically
7                                    by pressing the <ALT> and <P> keys.
8
9    \P        /PP                   Select Print Option to Printer
10             CA                    Clear all previous options
11             Rone~                 Set Range to named range called "one"
12             AG                    Align paper and start print
13             P                     Advance paper feed one page
14             Rtwo~                 Set Range to named range called "two"
15             GQ                    Start second print and leave menu when done
16
17
18
19
20
06-Jul-89   10:13 PM
```

(a)

```
A12: [W20] '/XMA13~                                                            MENU
FALL  SPRING  PRINT  X-PRINT  QUIT
Print Entire Report
         A                 B                  C              D
1    ADVANCED LOTUS WORKSHEET - AUTOMACROS AND MENUES - E.MARTIN  1989
2
3    MACRO SECTION:
4
5    MACRO NAME:            MACRO LIST:                    EXPLANATION:
6
7    \0                     {PGDN}{GOTO}H21~@TODAY~        Auto macro puts today's
8                           {GOTO}A21~@TODAY~{GOTO}B25     date in proper cells
9
10   MENU MACRO:
11
12   /XMA13~
13   FALL                   SPRING             PRINT          X-PRINT
14   Move to Fall Report Move to Spring Report Print Entire Report Security
15   {GOTO}A21~             {GOTO}H21~         /PPCARFL~AG    {GOTO}D25~
16   {GOTO}B25~             {GOTO}I25~         PRSP~GQ        /PPCARFL~A
17                                                           {GOTO}D25~
18
19   WORKSHEET BEGINS HERE:
20
06-Jul-89  10:24 PM                          CMD
```

(b)

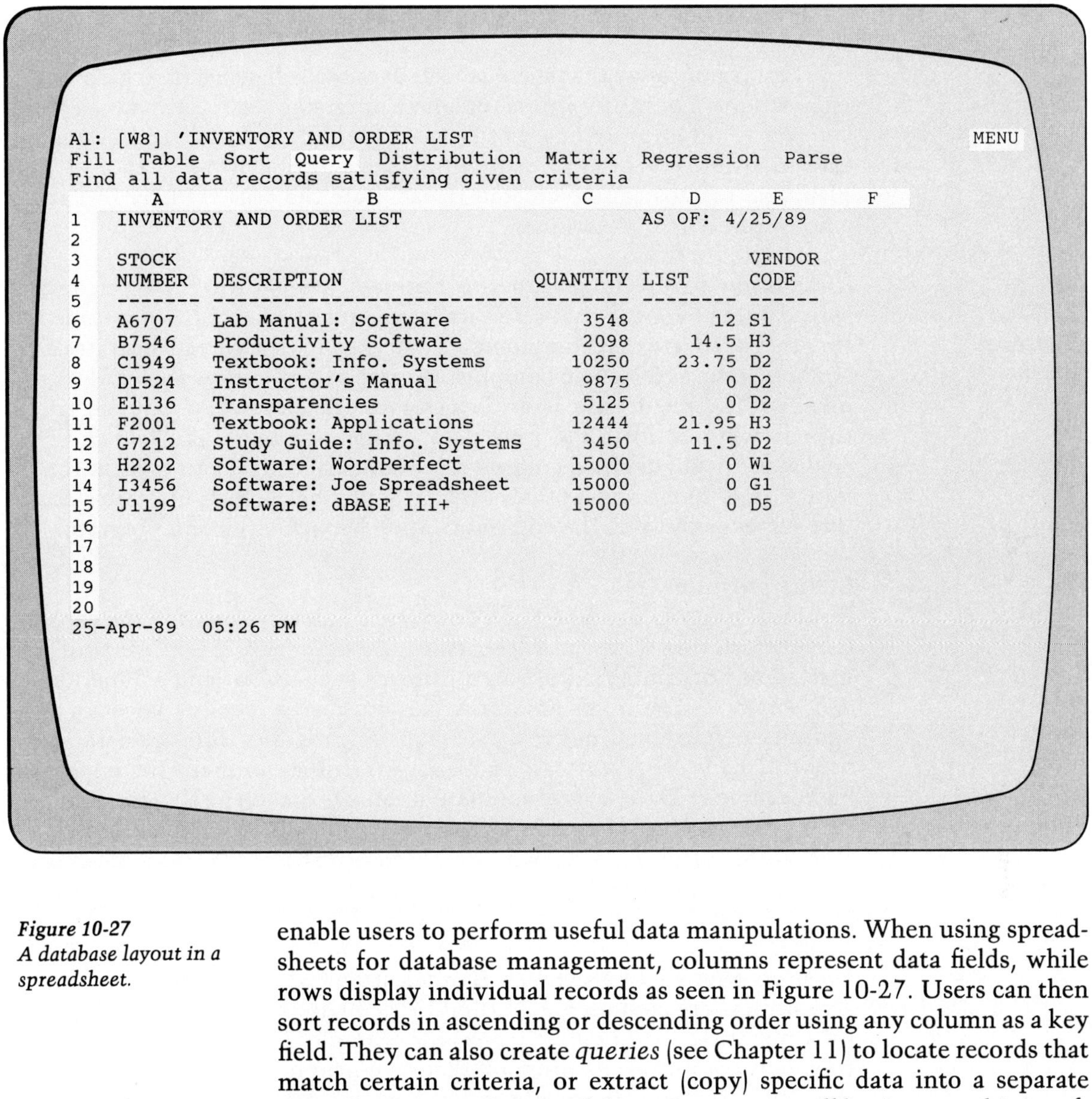

```
A1: [W8] 'INVENTORY AND ORDER LIST                                      MENU
Fill  Table  Sort  Query  Distribution  Matrix  Regression  Parse
Find all data records satisfying given criteria
          A              B                C        D       E        F
1    INVENTORY AND ORDER LIST                    AS OF: 4/25/89
2
3    STOCK                                                VENDOR
4    NUMBER  DESCRIPTION                QUANTITY LIST     CODE
5    ------  -------------------------  -------- -------- ------
6    A6707   Lab Manual: Software           3548       12 S1
7    B7546   Productivity Software          2098     14.5 H3
8    C1949   Textbook: Info. Systems       10250    23.75 D2
9    D1524   Instructor's Manual            9875        0 D2
10   E1136   Transparencies                 5125        0 D2
11   F2001   Textbook: Applications        12444    21.95 H3
12   G7212   Study Guide: Info. Systems     3450     11.5 D2
13   H2202   Software: WordPerfect         15000        0 W1
14   I3456   Software: Joe Spreadsheet     15000        0 G1
15   J1199   Software: dBASE III+          15000        0 D5
16
17
18
19
20
25-Apr-89   05:26 PM
```

Figure 10-27
A database layout in a spreadsheet.

enable users to perform useful data manipulations. When using spreadsheets for database management, columns represent data fields, while rows display individual records as seen in Figure 10-27. Users can then sort records in ascending or descending order using any column as a key field. They can also create *queries* (see Chapter 11) to locate records that match certain criteria, or extract (copy) specific data into a separate reporting area on the spreadsheet. For many small businesses, this is sufficient for database operations.

Integrated packages

As we have seen in Chapter 8, a number of software companies offer spreadsheet programs as part of a larger package that integrates, or combines, a number of business-related packages together into one program. Technically speaking, most modern spreadsheets are actually integrated packages for they combine spreadsheet capabilities with database and graphics. However, truly integrated software usually includes word processing, may also include communications capabilities as well, and allow sharing of data among all applications. Software Publishing's PFS:First Choice, Ashton-Tate's Framework, Lotus's Symphony, and

Software Group's Enable are current examples of more fully integrated software.

That is not to say that spreadsheets cannot exchange data with other applications. The more popular business programs can reformat data for transfer to other programs. Lotus 1-2-3 files, for instance, can be read into MicroPro's WordStar or Ashton-Tate's dBASE III+. With a little planning, macros can be created to facilitate the easy transfer of data among different applications.

Spreadsheet adjuncts

In addition to the huge appetite business has shown for electronic spreadsheets over the past 10 years, a secondary market has developed for other software that complements and expands the spreadsheet itself. Software such as SQZ! can compress the size of saved spreadsheet files as much as 90 percent, increasing disk storage capacity, while reducing the time it takes to load and save data. Other programs like NOTE-IT! enable us to add detailed comments to spreadsheet cells to explain formulas or assumptions. Lotus's HAL provides an English-like interface that further simplifies the communication between user and program.

Utility programs

Print utility programs like Funk Software's Sideways provide the capability of printing wide spreadsheets (or any other ASCII text) vertically instead of horizontally. *Keyboard utilities* such as Borland's Superkey and Software Research's Smartkey allow users to redefine keystrokes and create additional macros. *File transfer programs* convert data for use with many other software packages, even other normally incompatible equipment. DataViz's MacLink Plus allows data to be shared among such programs as Lotus 1-2-3, Symphony, dBASE, Multimate, Word-Star, Word, Excel, and Jazz, whether they are on the Apple MacIntosh or an IBM-PC compatible!

Compilers

For users who wish to share their applications with other offices, there are spreadsheet compilers. @LIBERTY is a compiler that can create a fully operational worksheet using, for example, Lotus 1-2-3, and then copy it as a self-running program that no longer needs Lotus. The functions and macros work exactly as designed, but formulas cannot be seen or changed, and labels cannot be erased. Instead of buying many copies of an expensive spreadsheet, companies can buy one spreadsheet program, and then distribute working copies of created worksheets to their staff.

Adjunct software also helps compensate for the technological "gaps" that appear after software has been in use for a time. These gaps appear for many reasons. Perhaps the original spreadsheet developer overlooked a specific utility, or underestimated its worth to the potential user. Sometimes users, after becoming acquainted with a program, suggest new additions to enhance a spreadsheet's power or ease of use. Or, the computer hardware might now offer capabilities that were not available when the spreadsheet was last revised. Perhaps the potential market for the utility is too narrow for a general spreadsheet to bother with it. Whatever the reason, adjunct software seems to flourish during the period when spreadsheet software companies are planning their next revisions. After all, when the new spreadsheet revision appears, some of the more powerful and convenient adjunct capabilities will be incorporated directly into it, eliminating the need for users to purchase the adjunct programs.

Yet, there will always be a market for adjunct software. Many users will not upgrade to a new version, being content with the older copy of the spreadsheet program. For those who do upgrade, the newer versions will lack other capabilities not yet possible or even conceived. These will ultimately be met by newer adjunct software. And so the cycle continues.

The era of the workpad and cube

Spreadsheet programs have grown considerably in size and power while retaining the two-dimensional approach characteristic of paper. During the mid-1980s, the one-sheet format was expanded with three major improvements: (1) extract and combine utilities that allowed data to be moved from one spreadsheet to another; (2) window techniques that enabled users to display more than one spreadsheet at a time; and (3) inter-worksheet formulas that could interrelate cells on different worksheets. The trend to look beyond the normal column/row spreadsheet was clear. Finally, in 1987, BoeingCalc replaced the work*sheet* with its WORKPAD—a subtle yet important distinction. Instead of individual two-dimensional spreadsheet files being interconnected through macros or formulas, users now had the capability to create one file in *three* dimensions—each cell defined by a column, row, and *page*. As seen in Figure 10-28, BoeingCalc defined the upper left cell on its first page as 1A1; the upper left corner cell of the next page was 2A1, and so on. The cell in the fourth column, third row, on page 6 would be 6D3. In fact, BoeingCalc is capable of creating a workpad file containing 16,000 pages, rows, and columns—a staggering 4 trillion cells—restricted only by the size of computer memory and secondary storage.

In 1988, Lotus Corporation introduced Lotus 1-2-3 Release 3, incorporating three-dimensional spreadsheets called CUBES. Similar to a workpad, each sheet of Lotus's stack is labeled page first, but with a letter, as in A:A1. The address 6D3 in BoeingCalc would appear as F:D3. The possibilities for these three-dimensional solid spreadsheet files are interesting. The top page might be used for an annual summary, followed by twelve monthly reports, using formulas and ranges that operate across the length, width, and depth of the sheet.

Figure 10-28
BoeingCalc's Workpad,
the state of the art in
three-dimensional
spreadsheets.

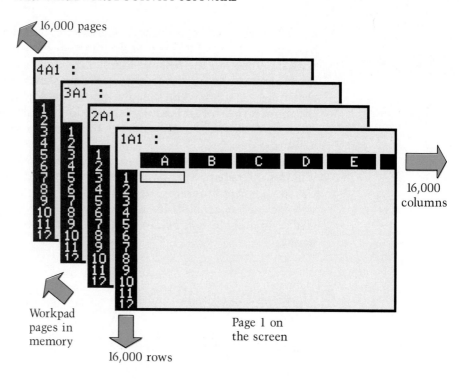

16,000 pages

16,000 columns

Workpad pages in memory

16,000 rows

Page 1 on the screen

It is clear that spreadsheets will continue to be important software packages to the business user. But it is also clear that users will have to expand their thinking from columns and rows to include three-dimensional pages as well. VP-Planner Plus already has capabilities beyond three dimensions. Don't be surprised if there are software developers out there right now wondering what five- and six-dimensional spreadsheets might be, and how to fit them onto a computer screen!

summary

▪ An electronic spreadsheet, or worksheet, is the computer equivalent of accounting columnar paper. It is arranged in vertical columns and horizontal rows that intersect to form cells.

▪ The first modern electronic spreadsheet, VisiCalc, appeared in 1978. Most spreadsheets use similar grids and menus but Lotus 1-2-3 has become a business standard.

▪ The major advantage of electronic spreadsheets is their flexibility—the ease with which they can be modified. This allows them to act as modeling tools for "What if?" investigations.

▪ Most spreadsheet screens use letters to identify columns and numbers for rows, forming such cell addresses as A1 or Z20. Others use numbers for both, as in R5C3.

▪ A screen cursor highlights the active cell that will hold our current typing.

■   The menu command line is activated in most programs by pressing the / key. In some, the line is always there for access through mouse movements.

■   Entries can contain labels for alphabetic or other nonnumeric data; values for numbers; or formulas used to interrelate cells.

■   Built-in functions can be used to simplify many standard mathematical calculations. They are composed of a name, followed by an argument enclosed in parentheses that identifies the data range on which the function will work.

■   Spreadsheets can be saved to disk and retrieved when needed for editing or printing.

■   Advanced spreadsheet capabilities include graphics, windows, extract, combine, multiple spreadsheets, passwords, hidden cell, database management, and macro commands.

■   Macros can be created to automate keystrokes and create helpful user menus.

■   Additional adjunct software can extend the usefulness of spreadsheets with notes, disk storage, print and keyboard utilities, file transfer programs, and compilers.

■   Workpads and cubes refer to spreadsheets that have been extended into three dimensions to include columns, rows, and pages.

career box

The "electronic" accountant

Electronic spreadsheets and computers have certainly changed the way most accountants work. They have had, perhaps, a more significant effect on the self-employed Certified Public Accountant (CPA), by automating much of the time-consuming calculations and reports that need to be generated in such enterprises. For instance, one self-employed CPA in Brooklyn, New York, told us that he has automated more than 80 percent of his work in the past 2 years alone by using a microcomputer, an electronic spreadsheet, and a word processor. If you are considering an accounting career in private practice, or even in a business's accounting office, you may learn much from his insights into the computerization of his practice, which specializes in small businesses (under 12 employees) and individuals.

After 10 hours of training in spreadsheets at a local community college, and practicing for another 30 hours on his own, he gained enough experience to create his own spreadsheets for such uses as cash disbursements/cash receipts journals, bank reconciliations, payroll books, and quarterly/annual reports. He has also created macro programs to streamline some of these procedures. In the past year, he has almost doubled his client list while cutting down on the amount of time he actually spends preparing the material.

During "tax season," he uses Tax Time (a prepackaged Lotus 1-2-3 template) to automate the calculations and form completion that previously consumed much of his time and attention. The normal tedious (and error-prone) task of filling out tax forms, and examining the consequences of various deductions that optimize the legal minimum tax, have become quick and accurate.

The ability to work at home and control his own time is what attracted him to self-employment in the first place. As a result of using electronic spreadsheets, he now enjoys more freedom in time, while reducing the need for personnel. He has cut his dependence on (and cost for) outside secretarial work. He can now prepare most forms, letters, and reports quickly and efficiently by transferring spreadsheet results directly into word processing documents. He has more time to pick and choose his clients, and more time to set aside for his family. He can be at home when his children are ill, or even attend special school functions that he missed when he worked in a 9-to-5 environment (or when his work schedule overwhelmed him prior to his computerization).

However, he cautions against computers and spreadsheets as a replacement for accounting expertise. First of all, you must be properly trained, experienced, and certified before you can start your own accounting practice. It is still the human who advises clients, oversees their paperwork, and helps them keep track of financial matters. You must know accounting by hand before you can successfully use a computer in your work.

In addition, there are some things that just work better manually. Large spreadsheets (the kind that take up four or five computer screens) still seem to be easier by hand. There's something about being able to glance quickly around the entire sheet that is preferable to some practitioners. On the other hand, some tasks are just too small to bother using the computer. Electronic spreadsheets can be a useful tool to the self-employed practicing accountant, if they are used wisely and appropriately. The time and clerical work they save can be used to further expand your business, or give you time off to enjoy the money you have earned.

wrap-up

April 15th—11:59 p.m.

In the past, around this time of year, Jill would be at her desk in her home office, calculator close at hand, putting the final touches on some late 1040 tax forms. Her clients could then sign the returns and deposit their envelopes in the central post office mailbox before the midnight deadline.

Tonight though, as she walked into her office, Jill glanced around the room in amazement. It was quite a contrast to years past. She remembered, as if it were yesterday, how she would normally be surrounded by stacks of blank forms, federal and state tax schedules, client data sheets, hastily scribbled phone messages, rolls of calculator paper, and bottles of correction fluid. At times there might even be a last-minute client sitting in the rocking chair across the room, reviewing forms that she passed over her head as she worked. She disliked the intricate tax forms, even though they provided a welcome addition to her accounting practice. Like a row of upright dominoes, every change in them started a chain reaction of alterations in accompanying schedules and forms: new numbers to add; new percentages to calculate; new forms to fill out; new clients to strangle.

But not this year! Tonight, the office was dark; the desktop was clear. The calculator was gathering dust in the back of her closet.

Thanks to her new computer, electronic spreadsheet software, and commercial tax template, Jill had finished most of her work a week ago. Of course there were some automatic extensions filed for clients and some last minute changes, but all went smoothly and quickly. So what if one client just discovered $253 in extra income, or another forgot $450 in tips? Jill simply had to retrieve their files and retype the appropriate cells. Then she would sit back and watch the spreadsheet template automatically recalculate related cells in every form. Let the computer worry about which dominoes fell and which didn't. All Jill had to do was have the program reprint the amended forms when she was done entering the new data. This was easy, too, using the menu macro supplied with the template. Less than 10 minutes from start to finish. She wasn't even upset when the client whose forms she had just printed out called her back to add another forgotten medical expense.

So tonight, a date well known to most taxpayers, Jill had stopped in her office, but not to do any tax work. Instead, she stayed only as long as it took to put on her answering machine. On this important date in the Internal Revenue Service's calendar, Jill was doing something important for herself—going out to a movie!

key terms

These are the key terms arranged in alphabetical order. The numbers in parentheses refer to the page on which each term is defined.

Active cell (321)
Argument (327)
Built-in function (327)
Cell (312)
Circular reference (326)
Column (312)
Contents line (320)
Cube (341)
Electronic spreadsheet (313)
Formula (324)
Label (322)
Macro (337)
Menu macro (337)
Range (327)
Row (312)
Spreadsheet (312)
Template (315)
Value (322)
Workpad (341)

review questions

objective questions

True/false. *Put the letter T or F on the line next to the question.*

1. Accountants were using electronic spreadsheets before the 1900s.   1 _____
2. The intersection of columns and rows are called cells.   2 _____
3. HarvardCalc was the first modern electronic spreadsheet that became the model for all others.   3 _____
4. All formulas must begin with an "@" sign.   4 _____
5. Although spreadsheets perform clerical tasks well, they are not useful to upper- or middle-level managers.   5 _____
6. Spreadsheet rows run horizontally across the screen.   6 _____
7. The address B1 in Lotus 1-2-3 is equivalent to R2C1 in Multiplan.   7 _____
8. Spreadsheet labels should be used to display telephone numbers.   8 _____
9. Spreadsheet programs interpret entries that start with quotation marks as formulas.   9 _____
10. The set of symbols between the parentheses in @SUM(A1..A10) is considered an argument.   10 _____

Multiple choice. *Put the letter of the correct answer on the line next to the question.*

1. Which one of the following is a formula?   1 _____
    (a) '7/8/81   (c) +A1
    (b) '718-555-1212   (d) Smith
2. Which of these is *not* a category of built-in functions?   2 _____
    (a) Rational   (c) Date
    (b) Financial   (d) Logical
3. Which of these statements best describes formulas that make use of circular references?   3 _____
    (a) They are useful in graphic applications.
    (b) They should be avoided.
    (c) They cannot be typed into a spreadsheet.
    (d) They are only available in advanced versions.

4. The opposite of the SAVE command is which command?
   - (a) SPEND
   - (b) RETRIEVE
   - (c) PRINT
   - (d) UNDO

5. Duplicating formulas in other cells can be accomplished with which of these commands?
   - (a) INSERT
   - (b) DUPE
   - (c) COPY
   - (d) EDIT

Fill in the blank. *Write the correct word or words in the blank to complete the sentence.*

1. Printed spreadsheets are referred to as _____.

2. Programs that combine spreadsheet capabilities with graphics and database are called _____.

3. _____ allow users to view different parts of the screen at the same time.

4. Removing and saving portions of a spreadsheet can be accomplished with the _____ command.

5. _____ are useful techniques for automating keystroke sequences that we use often.

6. _____ software can improve the utilities offered by a spreadsheet.

7. The concept of a workpad adds the dimension of _____ to the rows and columns of spreadsheets.

8. Spreadsheets that contain formulas but no data are called _____.

9. When managers use spreadsheets to examine "What if?" questions, they are using the spreadsheet as a _____ tool.

10. The cell into which our current typing will be placed is called the _____.

short answer questions

When answering these questions, think of concrete examples to illustrate your points.

1. What is a spreadsheet?
2. How do electronic spreadsheets differ from paper ones?
3. What three major types of entries can be used in an electronic spreadsheet? Give examples of each.
4. What information items are displayed on a typical spreadsheet screen?
5. Describe the two general systems for locating cells.
6. What is the difference between extract and save?
7. Explain the use of the cursor keys in a spreadsheet.
8. What is an active cell?
9. How do windows improve the capabilities of a spreadsheet?
10. What are the advantages of using built-in functions?

essay questions

1. We have seen that managers can use spreadsheets for "What if?" analyses. Explain this concept and its importance to decision-making.
2. If you were asked to select a spreadsheet for company adoption, what factors would influence your decision? Explain your reasons.
3. Adjunct programs are necessary for effective spreadsheet use. Indicate whether or not you agree with this statement and support your position with examples.
4. Does it matter which spreadsheet program you learn? If so, identify which one you would choose and explain why. If not, explain why no specific program should be preferred.

Answers to the objective questions
True/false: 1. F; 2. T; 3. F; 4. F; 5. F; 6. T; 7. F; 8. T; 9. F; 10. T
Multiple choice: 1. b; 2. a; 3. b; 4. b; 5. c
Fill in the blank: 1. hard copy; 2. integrated programs; 3. windows; 4. extract; 5. macros; 6. adjunct; 7. page; 8. templates; 9. modeling; 10. active cell.

Database management: harnessing the power of files

After studying this chapter you should understand the following:

- *How fields, records, files, and databases are related in the data hierarchy.*
- *The main characteristics of the three types of file design.*
- *How hierarchical, network, and relational databases differ.*
- *What advantages databases offer over files.*
- *The key steps in creating, using, and maintaining a database.*

chapter 11

Who gets the promotion?

Lesley Stevens glanced at the computer in her office at Paul's House of Electronic Wonders. She noted how its screen reflected in the shiny new sales manager nameplate on her desk. She was justifiably proud. When Susan Paul had moved Penny Helmsley up to the vice-president's office, Lesley replaced her in sales. Business had increased dramatically and Philip Paul, the firm's owner, now wanted to open a retail outlet. It was her job to recommend its new manager.

"Promote from within," Philip had said at their morning meeting. "Let's reward loyalty and hard work." Lesley herself had come up through the ranks and welcomed this approach. Weeks ago, in fact, she had anticipated the new expansion and had already identified three warehouse managers and two salespeople for the job. But, she had to be sure that her final choice was good for the company, and rewarded past performance as well as future potential. Clearly some objective help was needed for this decision.

Lesley turned to the keyboard. She typed her password and a few commands to copy file portions from the mainframe onto her computer's hard disk. While she disliked typing, she recognized the necessity of maintaining confidentiality of employee data—always an important concern.

Lesley now reached for the electronic mouse on her desk. She moved her hand to guide the cursor past familiar picture icons on the screen and then "clicked" the mouse but-ton to make her selection. Typing was never one of her strong points and she congratulated herself for purchasing a window program, which greatly simplified her access to the computer. Pressing the button had started her database management program, customized for "mouse-use" by Ed Wieland, one of the systems analysts. She selected the "Personnel Query" menu.

Under her direction, the computer searched related files, extracted records, sorted data, and printed reports. Lesley produced seniority and experience lists, attendance records, past performance ratings, and department growth charts. At her request, the reports were limited to the five candidates for the position, ignoring other employees so that comparisons could more easily be made. Lesley also reviewed buyer and supervisor complaints filed for each candidate.

She now had enough material for review. As always, she marveled at the ease with which it had been obtained. Without a computer, it would have taken hours (if not days) to gather these data into such useful forms, yet only 20 minutes had passed since she first began! Lesley ended the program and turned to the paperwork. Searching the computerized database was easy; the difficult task was still ahead—integrating this new information with her own evaluation of personalities and capabilities to make the final selection. She was determined to have her recommendation on Philip's desk before close of business.

File evolution

Information systems are used to process data into forms useful for making sound decisions. As we've seen, data are valuable resources, and the ability to retrieve and organize data in a timely fashion can greatly improve managerial decisions. For years, organizing and handling computer data has been a focus of systems analysts and programmers. With microcomputer advances, this has become an important skill for managers as well. We will review the data hierarchy, look at various file designs, and see how database management systems are used to create, use, and maintain databases.

The data hierarchy

As we learned in Chapter 2, data in information systems fall within a DATA HIERARCHY, or scale, comprising four categories: the field, record, file, and database (see Figure 11-1a). Some people include CHARACTERS in this list; we do not. A character is simply an individual letter, number, or symbol. Although it is the basic building block of all data, it has no meaning in an information system *until* it has been defined in a data field.

Moving from the lowest level of the data hierarchy to the highest, let us briefly review the four categories:

▪ A FIELD is the smallest component of the hierarchy that conveys a specific meaning or purpose. It uses one or more characters to represent a single data item. As seen in Figure 11-1a, a NUMERIC FIELD contains only numbers, such as the employee identification number. An ALPHABETIC FIELD (or CHARACTER FIELD), such as the job title field, contains only alphabetic characters. An ALPHANUMERIC FIELD contains any combination of numbers, alphabetic characters, and symbols. Social security numbers is such a field, using both numbers and dashes as special characters.

▪ A RECORD is a set of one or more fields concerning one individual or case. In Figure 11-1a, the record contains the employee identification number, name, job title, social security number, and salary fields for a specific employee. Each employee has his or her own record.

▪ A FILE is a set of one or more related records, grouped together by purpose. For example, we may have a payroll file containing individual employee pay records, or an accounts receivable file with invoice records. The file in Figure 11-1a consists of one record for each of the company's employees.

▪ A DATABASE, the highest step in the hierarchy, is a set of related files. The payroll file and job classification file are combined into a database in Figure 11-1a. One database may contain all the data necessary to run the business.

Figure 11-1b presents this concept in a more graphic form. If we imagine one gigantic filing cabinet holding all the data needed for our

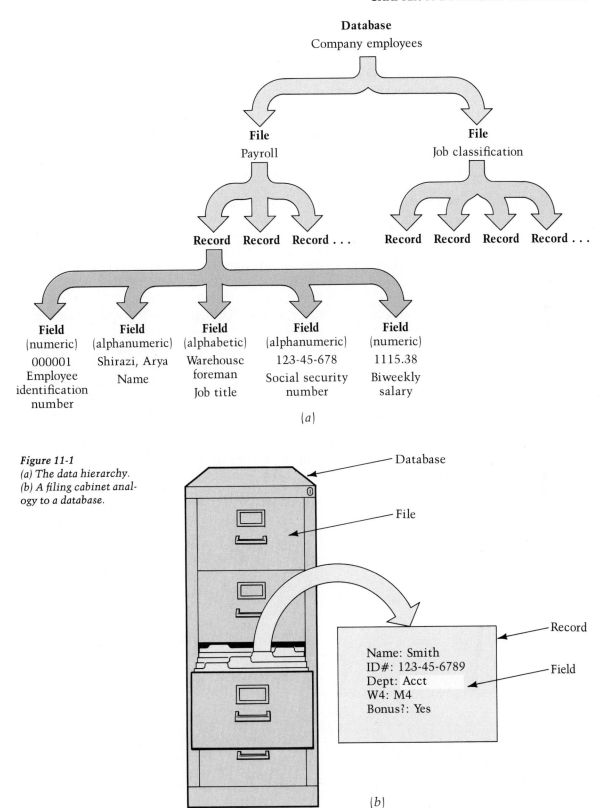

Database
Company employees

File
Payroll

File
Job classification

Record   Record   Record . . .

Record   Record   Record   Record . . .

Field
(numeric)
000001
Employee
identification
number

Field
(alphanumeric)
Shirazi, Arya
Name

Field
(alphabetic)
Warehouse
foreman
Job title

Field
(alphanumeric)
123-45-678
Social security
number

Field
(numeric)
1115.38
Biweekly
salary

(a)

Figure 11-1
(a) The data hierarchy.
(b) A filing cabinet analogy to a database.

Database

File

Record

Name: Smith
ID#: 123-45-6789
Dept: Acct
W4: M4
Bonus?: Yes

Field

(b)

business, then the database is the entire cabinet; each of its drawers is a file holding a smaller subset of data; each file drawer contains individual records; each record is made up of specific pieces of data grouped into fields, which are in turn made up of one or more characters.

Historically, files came before databases. Although databases represent an evolutionary step above files, they are, in fact, constructed *from* files. In the next section we will examine different FILE DESIGNS—techniques used to store and retrieve data. There are three main types of file designs: (1) sequential, (2) indexed sequential, and (3) direct access.

Sequential files

SEQUENTIAL FILES arrange records in a predetermined order. The payroll records in Figure 11-2 are arranged in an ascending sequence by employee identification number. The field used to order the file is known as a KEY. It can be unique, identifying a single record, or nonunique, referring to a group of records. Sometimes one key is not sufficient to uniquely identify a particular record. For example, "employee last name" might not differentiate employees adequately. We might then add an additional key, perhaps "first name." When more than one key is used, the most important key is known as the *primary key*, and the supplemental key is called the *secondary key*. Typically, computer records use single unique keys (such as a social security number or an invoice number) for each record. However, when we wish to locate a group of records, nonunique keys can be used. For instance, we might group certain employees' records together by using their job title as a nonunique key field.

Regardless of the key chosen, a sequential file is generally arranged in ascending or descending order according to one or more keys contained in the record. As we have seen earlier, sequential files provide

Figure 11-2
Sequential file organization. Records follow one another in record key sequence.

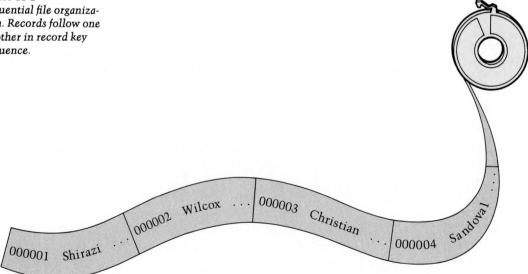

only SEQUENTIAL ACCESS to records. That is, records must be read in the order in which they appear in the file.

Most modern business programs that use sequential files follow a model for updating that employs three separate files: First, the program reads the "old" master file in need of updating, and a transaction file containing the updates. The program then writes an updated "new" master file that incorporates the changes from the transaction file and the old master file. In Figure 11-3 the program reads the first record in the transaction file (record key 000004) and then reads one record at a time from the old master file looking for its matching key. Each record that doesn't match is simply copied to the new master file. The program in this example will copy records 000001, 000002, and 000003 unchanged to the new file.

When a match is found, the program follows the directions of the transaction. Record 000004 matches the transaction record key. The action code in the transaction record specifies a delete; perhaps the employee quit or was fired. Accordingly, the program deletes the record by *not* writing it onto the new master file.

Having finished the first transaction, the program reads the next transaction record, 000006. Appropriately, it reads master record 000005 and copies it unchanged to the new file. It then reads master record 000006—a match! The transaction is an update, changing the employee's title and salary; obviously the employee was promoted with a raise. The program writes the updated version of record 000006 onto the new master file.

Next, transaction record 000008 is read. Old master file record 000007 is read and written unchanged to the new file. Finding no more records on the old master, the program writes a record 000008 from the transaction file, adding an employee to the new master file. With no more transaction records, the processing is now complete. We have created a new master file that reflects all deletions, updates, and additions.

Advantages and disadvantages of sequential files

Sequential files offer a low-priced means of storing and processing large quantities of data. They can use magnetic tape or disk, and their accompanying software is less complicated than that used with other file designs. Sequential files are most appropriate for batch processing programs that read or write a large number of a file's records. An added bonus is that the original ("old") master and transaction files are not altered in the update process and can be kept as backup in case the new master file is lost or damaged.

The major disadvantage of sequential files is the need to read every record in the file preceding the desired record. This process is simply too slow if only a few records in a file require updating. In addition, transaction records must be sorted into the same sequence as the old master file—an extra processing step. A final disadvantage is that the same data records appear in more than one file (a condition known as data redundancy), thus wasting storage space.

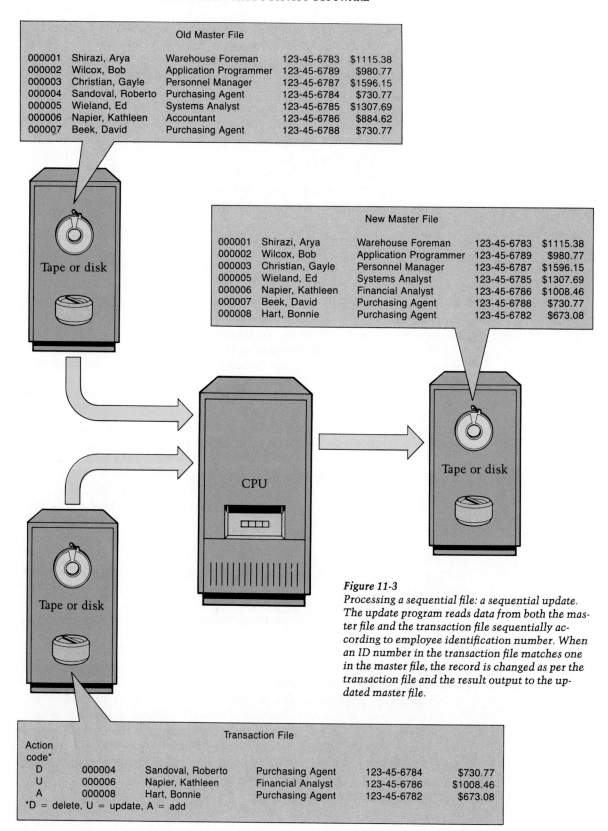

Old Master File

000001	Shirazi, Arya	Warehouse Foreman	123-45-6783	$1115.38
000002	Wilcox, Bob	Application Programmer	123-45-6789	$980.77
000003	Christian, Gayle	Personnel Manager	123-45-6787	$1596.15
000004	Sandoval, Roberto	Purchasing Agent	123-45-6784	$730.77
000005	Wieland, Ed	Systems Analyst	123-45-6785	$1307.69
000006	Napier, Kathleen	Accountant	123-45-6786	$884.62
000007	Beek, David	Purchasing Agent	123-45-6788	$730.77

Tape or disk

New Master File

000001	Shirazi, Arya	Warehouse Foreman	123-45-6783	$1115.38
000002	Wilcox, Bob	Application Programmer	123-45-6789	$980.77
000003	Christian, Gayle	Personnel Manager	123-45-6787	$1596.15
000005	Wieland, Ed	Systems Analyst	123-45-6785	$1307.69
000006	Napier, Kathleen	Financial Analyst	123-45-6786	$1008.46
000007	Beek, David	Purchasing Agent	123-45-6788	$730.77
000008	Hart, Bonnie	Purchasing Agent	123-45-6782	$673.08

Tape or disk

CPU

Tape or disk

Figure 11-3
Processing a sequential file: a sequential update. The update program reads data from both the master file and the transaction file sequentially according to employee identification number. When an ID number in the transaction file matches one in the master file, the record is changed as per the transaction file and the result output to the updated master file.

Transaction File

Action code*					
D	000004	Sandoval, Roberto	Purchasing Agent	123-45-6784	$730.77
U	000006	Napier, Kathleen	Financial Analyst	123-45-6786	$1008.46
A	000008	Hart, Bonnie	Purchasing Agent	123-45-6782	$673.08

*D = delete, U = update, A = add

Indexed sequential files

Records in an **INDEXED SEQUENTIAL FILE** are arranged in a predetermined order as in sequential files. However, an index or "road map" to the records also exists. This index is a separate, and much smaller file that is automatically established and maintained by system software.

When an application program needs a record, the system software uses the index to find out approximately where the record is stored. A file is typically broken up into groups (or segments) of 25 or 50 records, although our example in Figure 11-4 has only 3 records per group to keep matters simple. Here's how it works: If a program wants record 000005, it first searches the index, which gives 002 as the address of the record *group* containing that record. System software then goes straight to this group, and reads each record in sequence within the group until record 000005 is found. Thus, we need not read every preceding record in the file, but only those in the immediate vicinity—a great time-saver. It's like using a book index to locate the page on which you can find a particular term without having to read through the entire book to find it.

Though the name might make you think otherwise, indexed sequential files cannot use sequential media; they must be stored on direct-access storage devices. Otherwise the program could not "skip over" the unneeded record groups. By **DIRECT ACCESS**, we mean that a program can go straight to a data record, without first having to read all of the records leading up to it. While not a "true" direct-access file, since we do have to read a few records, indexed sequential files are still greatly superior to sequential files.

Figure 11-4
Indexed sequential file organization. Records follow one another in record key sequence. In addition, the starting address of groups of records is kept in an index.

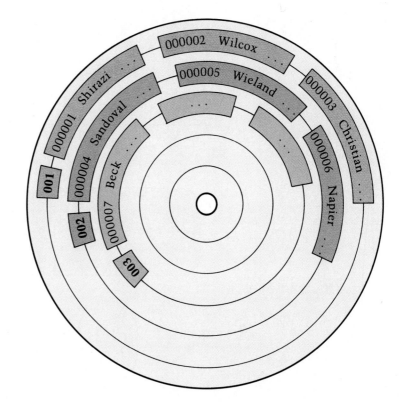

Record Key	Address of Data Segment Containing Record
000001	001
000002	001
000003	001
000004	002
000005	002
000006	002
000007	003

356

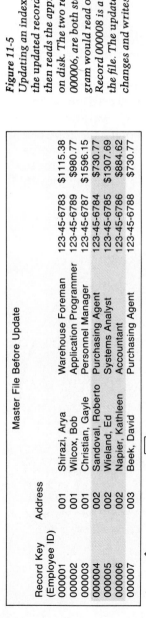

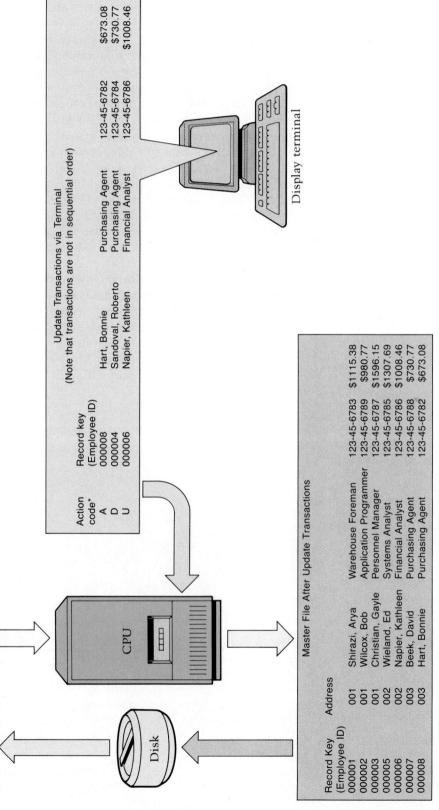

Figure 11-5
Updating an indexed sequential file. An operator enters the updated records on a display terminal. The program then reads the appropriate records from the master file on disk. The two records to be altered, 000004 and 000006, are both stored at address 002 on disk, so the program would read only the records from that address. Record 000008 is a new employee and will be added to the file. The update program makes the appropriate changes and writes the records back onto the master file.

Master File Before Update

Record Key (Employee ID)	Address			
000001	001	Shirazi, Arya	Warehouse Foreman	123-45-6783	$1115.38
000002	001	Wilcox, Bob	Application Programmer	123-45-6789	$980.77
000003	001	Christian, Gayle	Personnel Manager	123-45-6787	$1596.15
000004	002	Sandoval, Roberto	Purchasing Agent	123-45-6784	$730.77
000005	002	Wieland, Ed	Systems Analyst	123-45-6785	$1307.69
000006	002	Napier, Kathleen	Accountant	123-45-6786	$884.62
000007	003	Beek, David	Purchasing Agent	123-45-6788	$730.77

Update Transactions via Terminal
(Note that transactions are not in sequential order)

Action code*	Record key (Employee ID)			
A	000008	Hart, Bonnie	Purchasing Agent	123-45-6782	$673.08
D	000004	Sandoval, Roberto	Purchasing Agent	123-45-6784	$730.77
U	000006	Napier, Kathleen	Financial Analyst	123-45-6786	$1008.46

Display terminal

CPU

Disk

Master File After Update Transactions

Record Key (Employee ID)	Address			
000001	001	Shirazi, Arya	Warehouse Foreman	123-45-6783	$1115.38
000002	001	Wilcox, Bob	Application Programmer	123-45-6789	$980.77
000003	001	Christian, Gayle	Personnel Manager	123-45-6787	$1596.15
000005	002	Wieland, Ed	Systems Analyst	123-45-6785	$1307.69
000006	002	Napier, Kathleen	Financial Analyst	123-45-6786	$1008.46
000007	003	Beek, David	Purchasing Agent	123-45-6788	$730.77
000008	003	Hart, Bonnie	Purchasing Agent	123-45-6782	$673.08

Processing indexed sequential files

Indexed sequential files can really be processed two ways. First, they can be processed *sequentially*; that is, we can read the file in the order it was written, regardless of any index that may have been created. This is similar to playing songs on a record album in the order they were recorded, even though we could listen in some other order if we wished.

For example, let's say a personnel manager wants a list of all current employees in employee number sequence—the way they happen to be stored in the file. A simple program could read and print the records in sequential order. Useful as it may be however, this application does not make use of the direct-access nature of the file.

The direct-access potential becomes apparent if used in an *update*. Let's use Figure 11-5 to illustrate the same three changes to the master file that were incorporated in our sequential file in Figure 11-3, but now the file is an indexed sequential one. In this operation, transactions can be entered as they occur *in any order*, rather than having to save them for an occasional batch run. To get the record for a particular transaction, the program does not need to read the entire file. Instead, system software locates the address of the series that contains the desired record, and reads only those records until the record sought is found.

In small files, the time saved is not apparent. However, files can contain many thousands of records. If the desired record is in group number 900, the previous 899 groups can be skipped. If each group contains 25 records, there are 22,475 records that we do not need to read. Even if our record were last in the group, we would only have to read 24 records first. In a sequential file, however, we would have to read those 24 *plus* the 22,475 preceding them.

We might also choose to process the entire file in *index order*; that is, read each record in the order it appears in the index, not the file itself. We might access records in order of name, phone number, social security number, or any other field to create variously sequenced reports. In effect, we are reading the index sequentially and using it to find each record directly. Obviously, this also makes use of the direct-access capability. In fact, we could create different indices to the same file based on different keys. In this way, we could prepare differently sequenced lists without altering the original order of records on the file. This is equivalent to song or poetry books that offer a number of indices to the same material: by author, opening line, or subject. It is easier and more economical to build indices rather than copy the entire file into a different order.

Advantages and disadvantages of indexed sequential files

Indexed sequential files attempt to give the best of two worlds: sequential and direct access. When programs read or write a high proportion of the records in a file, indexed sequential files can be processed sequentially. When only a few records are involved, or if we desire some other order of processing, indexed sequential files offer reasonably direct access to those records. There is no restriction on the order in which these records must be processed, and there need not be duplicate records kept in multiple files.

Of course, there are always disadvantages in compromise. In this case, the "direct access" of indexed sequential files is slower than true direct access, and its "sequential processing" is slower than that provided by a true sequential file. Further, the disk hardware required by indexed sequential files is more costly than tape devices which can be used with sequential files. Another drawback is that processing most sequential files automatically results in backup copies, since old files are not disturbed when the new file is created. However, processing indexed sequential files does not, since changes are usually written directly back to the record itself, replacing any previous data it contained. Backup procedures must therefore be established and followed to avoid the risk of losing important data.

Direct-access files

The records in a true **DIRECT-ACCESS FILE**, also called a **RANDOM-ACCESS FILE**, are located in a way that is directly *related* to the record key. It differs from our previous file designs, since there is no need to read any other records first. However, like indexed sequential files, direct-access files can only be stored on direct-access storage devices (DASDs).

Direct-access files are used in many of today's business applications. They are especially suited to time-sharing and real-time programs because records can be obtained from large files quickly regardless of where the records are stored.

In the simplest direct-access file, a record's key field specifies the actual storage address of the record. For example, if the key contains five numbers, the first three might specify a disk track and the last two, the record's location on that track. A key of 21537 would indicate the 37th record on the 215th track. Locating the record would then be easy.

The problem is that this method is very hardware-dependent since the key names a specific location on the disk. We couldn't move a file to a different type of storage device without redesigning the file from scratch. Moreover, the record keys must be designed carefully, and any program using the file would have to know these keys. Having to invent a new key to point to records adds another piece of data to the record that has to be remembered—a wasteful step. Programs generally use a key that is an actual field within the record, such as an employee number. How could we use this key to show specific disk addresses as well?

Relative addressing solves this problem. **RELATIVE ADDRESSING** uses a key that does not directly name an address on the DASD but rather its position *relative* to some starting position on the disk. It's like having a group of children line up with each one remembering the child who is standing in front of them. If we move the first child elsewhere, the entire line follows. The file can be transferred anywhere we wish, with the records maintaining their relative position within the file.

In addition, a clever technique allows us to use any identifying *number* as a key: employee number, airline reservation number, student identification number. This number is then converted to the storage address through an algorithmic process (see Figure 11-6). **HASHING** is a process that transforms a key into an actual address using a formula to do the conversion. Many types of formulas can be used. One common technique divides the key by a prime number, using the remainder as the

Figure 11-6
Direct-access file organi-
zation. Records are gen-
erally distributed in a
random pattern across
the storage medium. A
formula converts the key
field to the storage ad-
dress prior to storing or
retrieving a record.

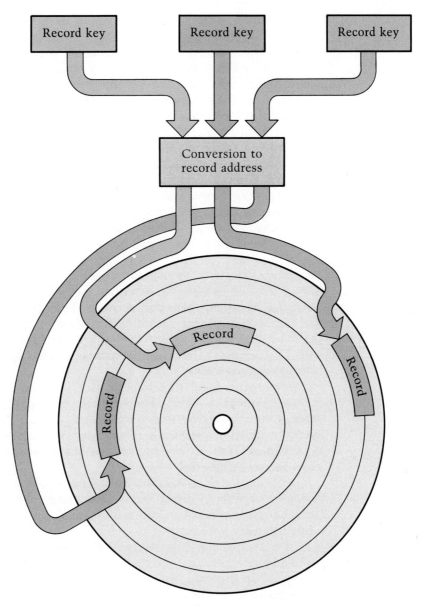

address. As you may know, a prime number can only be divided evenly by itself and by 1. Any other number produces a remainder. For hashing purposes, a prime number close to the number of records that will be kept in the file is used.

Let's assume that our program is writing a new file containing about 12,000 records. The prime number nearest to 12,000 is 12,001. Whenever our program writes a record to the file, it will first calculate an address by dividing the record's key by 12,001. If our records use stock numbers as their key, a calculation would proceed as follows:

Record key 383449709 (a stock number without dashes)
÷ 12,001 (the prime number used by the program)
= 31951 with a remainder of 5758

The remainder, 5758, is the relative address on the direct-access storage device where the program would write the record. The program does this calculation automatically. As far as we're concerned, we've typed in the stock number, and the program stored the record away. To read a record later from the same file, the program would first calculate its address using the same hashing procedure on its stock number.

Hashing formulas occasionally produce the same address for different record keys. For example, stock number 246038259 also produces a remainder of 5758. When this occurs, a *pointer* (a field containing the address of another record) is added to the record already at that address to direct future searches to an overflow area on the DASD that contains other records that "hashed" to the same address. Good hashing formulas minimize the number of times this happens, but it will still occur now and then. Fortunately for users, this procedure is automatic—they need not worry about where the records are kept.

Advantages and disadvantages of direct-access files
Direct-access files offer the fastest way to access records in nonsequential order. Many business transactions—bank account transactions, airline reservations, most data inquiries—are of this type. Other advantages (as in indexed sequential files) are that transactions need not be sorted before using them for file update, and records need not be duplicated on different files.

On the other hand, direct-access files share most of the drawbacks of indexed sequential access. They must be used on direct-access storage devices, their software is more complex, and file backup is not automatic. In addition, direct-access files need more storage space than other types of files. They are also more vulnerable to unauthorized data access and equipment failures.

In effect, direct-access files offer a trade-off between speed and cost. A system capable of direct-access processing costs more than one that isn't, but the savings in time and efficiency make those costs worthwhile for many applications.

Of course, there is no restriction to developing a direct-access file based on one access key, and then also creating index files based on some other field. In this case, we could access records directly, but could also, when needed, use slower index sequential techniques, or even sequential searches as well. Customer records for the telephone company might be keyed for direct access by phone number, but could also have indices set up to allow access (although slightly slower) by name or address.

What is a database?

Now that we've seen how data are physically stored and retrieved in files, we are ready to move on to databases. As stated earlier, a database is a collection or set of related files. Let's investigate why we should bother gathering separate files together into a database.

The advantages and drawbacks of databases

Say you're a programmer who's been asked to develop a report showing each employee's salary in relation to the range of salaries in his or her specific job classification. Unfortunately, your company keeps its data in separate files—there is no single integrated database in use. The salary data is on the payroll file. To obtain the data, you must carefully describe exactly how the file is set up, so that your program can read it.

The salary range for a particular job classification, however, is elsewhere—on the job classification file. Once again, you must describe exactly how the file is set up, but you also discover that the field linking the two files—job title—is set up differently in the two files, so you must come up with a way to match them. Only when you have completed all these steps, will you be able to *start* writing the part of your program that processes the data. Up to now, everything you have done—though it may have taken hours or days—was simply preparation for the main report. Be thankful you're not a programmer working on separate, unrelated files—especially if there is an impatient manager waiting for the report!

This example demonstrates most of the drawbacks of separate files:

- Needed data are often contained on different files, which may use different terminology to refer to similar fields, thus making it difficult to link them together.
- Files are often program-specific, with each program keeping its own set of files. This leads to DATA REDUNDANCY—the same data exists in more than one place. Not only is this wasteful of storage space, but it almost guarantees that some data will be out of date. The "wholeness," or DATA INTEGRITY of the entire data system is compromised.
- Programmers must describe files extensively within their programs before being able to read or write them. Writing and correcting these file descriptions is time-consuming, and not easily adaptable to changing reports or inquiries. DATA INDEPENDENCE, apart from its use in specific programs, does not exist.

Understandably, most programmers, information system personnel, and managers prefer databases to files. With a database, data are independent of the application programs that use them. While more work is required to initially set up a database than to create a file, once a database is established, it solves each of the problems just cited.

- *Data independence* is enhanced. Data are accessible to any program with a legitimate need for them, regardless of where the data are physically located, and regardless of the language in which the program is written.
- *Data redundancy* is minimized—data are not duplicated in different locations. As a result, *data integrity* is improved. That is, when we update a data element, we need not worry that there is a duplicate of it elsewhere that must be changed as well.
- Finally, programmers need not write and debug extensive file descriptions in order to work with data.

case in point

Maintaining data security

... According to a recent survey by Ernst & Whinney [an international accounting and consulting firm based in Cleveland], executives are most concerned about protecting their sensitive computer data from the competition. Customers were next on their list of potential threats, followed by employees, suppliers, public interest groups and foreign governments.

Those priorities represent a change, Mr. Wilson [National Director of information security services at Ernst & Whinney] said. In the past the same executives considered employees the biggest threat. "Take all the fraud and intentional incidents," he said, "and they won't begin to cause as much damage as mistakes cause everyday."

A careless employee can cripple a business inadvertently by sending sensitive data to the wrong files, entering incorrect data—or lending a secure password to a co-worker not entitled to the same computer access. The end result can be as disastrous as computer fraud or sabotage.

To guard against carelessness, companies should place a high priority on training for new employees. And to protect against improper activites, that instruction should include a clear statement on ethics and computer law and how the company will deal with employee infractions. . . .

But there is no foolproof way to guarantee the integrity of data against either intentional or accidental abuse. The best a company can do is to minimize its risks.

A significant step in that direction is to assure that responsibility for computer security rests near the top of an organization. The chief executive would do well to acknowledge that if the company is using computers, the odds are that they are being abused in some way. More than half of all companies reported that they suffered financial losses because of security problems.

Mr. Wilson suggested a step-by-step proce-dure for improving computer security, starting with making a determination of what needs to be protected.

The next step is to figure out whom you're trying to protect the data from. Competitors? Customers? Reporters? Foreign spies? Different tactics can then be developed to meet the threat, ranging from encryption to tighter screening of visitors.

Consider what would happen if the system were paralyzed for a day, or a week, by accident or intent. Is there backup, including a disaster recovery plan? What would happen if an essential data-processing employee quit in a huff or were hit by a truck?

Then look around the company and analyze the environment and the control structure that has been established.

"Senior management ought to ask themselves, 'What is really important to me?' " Mr. Wilson suggested. " 'What have I implemented to protect myself?' " If the answers are vague, they probably have a problem. Good security is implicit and clear."

. . . The security director has to have a high level of visibility, and the authority for establishing and enforcing policy. That responsibility should not be given as an afterthought or add-on to some data processing gnome who bats around bits and bytes. . . .

Mr. Wilson said senior management should then ask, "Have I established a concept of accountability for information and information control throughout the organization?" Look at the ways in which integrity is assured and checked. What controls are in place? Who has access to the system? Is access well controlled? Once a person has access, can you control what he or she does? Are the controls reasonable?

. . . The best time to begin thinking about computer security is before a problem develops, perhaps even before the organization has decided on which computer and information system to use.

A business that uses a database rather than separate files can save time and money in developing its application programs, can lower data maintenance costs and storage requirements (since the same centralized data are now accessible to all), and can more efficiently use its data since they are easier to retrieve. However, there are some disadvantages as well:

■   Data more readily accessible can also be more easily abused. Adequate security and control measures can help offset this possibility.
■   Databases require more expensive hardware and software.
■   In larger organizations, specialized personnel may have to be hired to set up and administer the database, and existing personnel will have to be trained to use it properly.

In addition, people may resist the new system simply because it is new. They may also dislike the idea of giving up control of their "personal" files. Some may have to change the way they do their work. Clearly, creating an organizational database is a complicated process, as we will see later in the chapter.

However, on balance, most organizations find that the advantages outweigh the disadvantages. The trend is toward ever-greater use of databases rather than conventional file organization.

Because of the increasing popularity of databases, prepackaged programs have become available to create and maintain databases for any size information system, from supercomputers to microcomputers. Many businesspeople are discovering the power of microcomputer-based database programs. Although such programs vary widely, they all offer the advantages we have cited, and share the general features that we will now describe.

Features of a database management system

A **DATABASE MANAGEMENT SYSTEM (DBMS)** is a program that makes it possible to create, use, and maintain a database. When using a database management system, programmers and users need not be concerned about the way data are organized or retrieved from the direct-access storage device (only rarely are other storage devices used for databases), or in which particular file the data are contained. A DBMS provides *logical* access to data, sheltering users from concern with the *physical* placement and handling of the data. Figure 11-7 shows a conceptualized view of the function of a DBMS in a modern information system.

Most medium-sized and large businesses that use databases have a **DATABASE ADMINISTRATOR** who is responsible for setting up databases, maintaining them, and helping programmers and users utilize them intelligently (see the Career box). Microcomputer users can usually create and maintain their own databases; they might hire an outside consultant to develop the initial design.

One of the key differences between a file and a database is the ability to specify how data items are related to each other. The three most frequently used structures for relating data items within a database are the hierarchical, network, and relational structures. Let's examine them briefly.

Figure 11-7
The database in the information system.

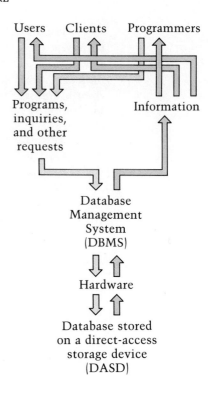

In a **HIERARCHICAL DATABASE**, the data elements are related to one another in a treelike structure that consists of "parents" and "children." A **PARENT** is merely a data element higher in the hierarchy than the child, and connected to it. A **CHILD** is a data element connected and subservient to a parent. Child data are accessed only through the parent. In a hierarchical database, which resembles a business organization tree, a parent can have more than one child, but each child can have only one parent.

Hierarchical databases

In Figure 11-8, the Item data element is the parent of the Cost, Quantity, Substitute, and Purchase Order data elements. Note that a data element can consist of more than one data item; for example, the Substitute data element consists of the item number and the item name.

Within this database, there will be an entry for each item "connected" to the four children shown. Two of the children—Substitute and Purchase Order—can have more than one occurrence per item. When an item is out of stock, for example, a replacement may be shipped, and some items can have more than one possible replacement. Similarly, an item may have been ordered from more than one supplier. When each new order was placed, an order data element would be added to describe it. Note, too, that the substitute item will then be a "parent" record for another level of the hierarchy.

Hierarchical database systems are available for any size of computer. One of the more popular systems used on mainframes is IBM's Information Management System (IMS).

Network databases

In a **NETWORK DATABASE**, data elements are related to one another as parents and children as in a hierarchical database, with access through parent records pointing to the children. However, there is one difference: a child can have more than one parent.

Figure 11-9 shows the same data as contained in the hierarchical database from Figure 11-8, with a few new data elements added on the right of the figure. The Supplier data element is parent to the Address, Contact, and Purchase Order data elements. In other words, Purchase Order now has two parents—Item and Supplier.

Figure 11-8
A hierarchical database.

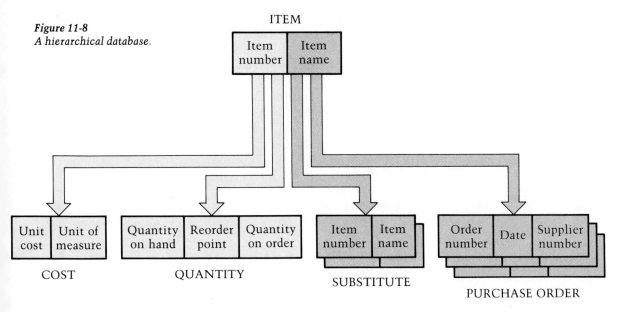

Figure 11-9
A network database.

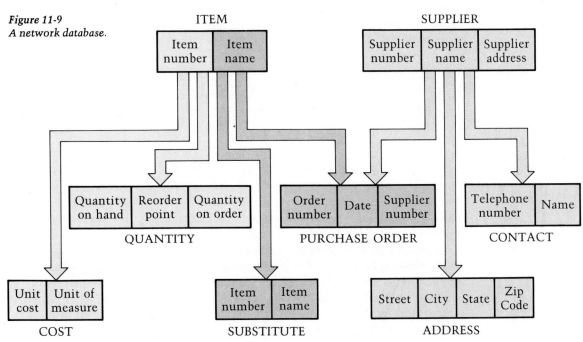

In practical terms, this means that the database management system can now deliver data two ways: by item (giving the cost, quantity, substitute, and purchase order data) or by supplier (giving the purchase order, address, and contact data). Each view of the data coexists within the database, and can be quickly utilized. This ability to access data from more than one starting point is the advantage of network databases over hierarchical databases. Network database systems exist for any size of computer. One popular system is IDMS (Integrated Database Management System), produced by Cullinet Software.

Relational databases

A **RELATIONAL DATABASE** views *all* data items as related to one another in **TABLES**, in contrast to the parent/child approach used in network and hierarchical structures. Figure 11-10 shows a relational data structure—a two-dimensional table that for a particular original item, gives the substitute item(s) and supplier.

Any number of different tables can be used in a relational database. A table might be set up showing the original item number, original item supplier number, original item supplier name, and quantity on hand. No matter how many tables are devised, the DBMS will store the data items in such a way that it can deliver the data from any table viewpoint.

In addition, the terminology of a relational database differs from other structures. The table itself is called a *relation*—a collection of rows and columns that interrelate data elements. Individual records, called **TUPLES**, form the rows; data fields, called **ATTRIBUTES**, form the columns.

Relational database systems are easier to use than hierarchical or network database systems, and are available for any size of computer. One relational database system used by mainframes is IBM's SQL/DS, which allows users to make requests for data in the English-like statements of a Structured Query Language (SQL). The major drawbacks of relational systems are their substantial hardware requirements and their slower speed for complex searches relative to other database structures.

The database at work

Regardless of the size of computer on which they may be stored, there are several common steps in creating a database: (1) surveying the data uses, (2) creating the data dictionary (or structure), (3) designing the database, and (4) implementing the database.

Surveying data uses enables us to determine what data are being used, when they are needed for making decisions, and what operations are performed upon them. Surveying data uses is generally done during the system development process (see Chapter 13). It may be as simple as a manager carefully reviewing his or her data needs in terms of reports or decisions that will be required, and then proceeding to establish the structure of the file.

Figure 11-10
Using a relational data-
base.

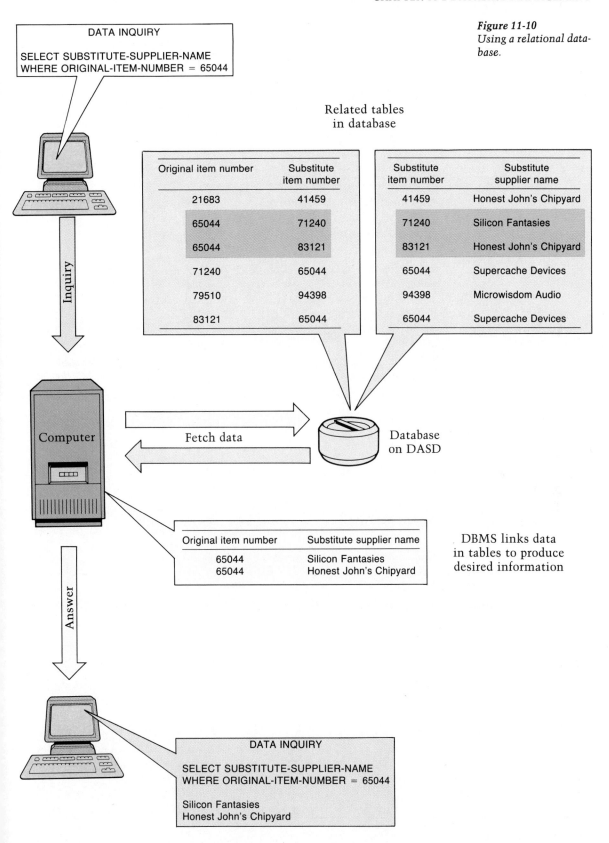

DATA INQUIRY

SELECT SUBSTITUTE-SUPPLIER-NAME
WHERE ORIGINAL-ITEM-NUMBER = 65044

Related tables
in database

Original item number	Substitute item number
21683	41459
65044	71240
65044	83121
71240	65044
79510	94398
83121	65044

Substitute item number	Substitute supplier name
41459	Honest John's Chipyard
71240	Silicon Fantasies
83121	Honest John's Chipyard
65044	Supercache Devices
94398	Microwisdom Audio
65044	Supercache Devices

Inquiry

Computer

Fetch data

Database
on DASD

Original item number	Substitute supplier name
65044	Silicon Fantasies
65044	Honest John's Chipyard

DBMS links data
in tables to produce
desired information

Answer

DATA INQUIRY

SELECT SUBSTITUTE-SUPPLIER-NAME
WHERE ORIGINAL-ITEM-NUMBER = 65044

Silicon Fantasies
Honest John's Chipyard

Comparing databases

The following is a brief comparison of five popular database management programs for IBM microcomputers.

Database	dBASE III+	Reflex	FoxBase+	Q & A	R:BASE
Company	Ashton-Tate	Borland	Fox Software	Symantec	Microrim
List price (one copy)	$695	$150	$395	$349	$725
File type	Relational	Flat file	Relational	Flat file	Relational
Memory	384K	384K	360K	512K	512K
Requires hard disk?	no	no	yes	no	yes
Supports:					
Mouse?	no	yes	no	no	yes
Menus?	yes	yes	yes	no	yes
Command line?	yes	no	yes	no	yes
Query by example?	yes	yes	no	no	yes
SQL?	no	no	no	no	yes
Natural language?	no	no	no	yes	no
Contains:					
Tutorial?	yes	no	no	yes	yes
Applications generator?	yes	no	yes	no	yes
Screen generator?	yes	no	yes	no	yes
Available for Macintosh?	yes	yes	yes	no	no

Source: Adapted from "DBMS Software Directory," *Business Software Review,* vol. 6, no. 6, Spring 1988, pp. 40–43. Reprinted with permission from *Business Software Review* copyright April 1988: ICP, Indianapolis, Indiana.

A DATA DICTIONARY, or *structure* in microcomputer systems, defines each item of data handled by a system, giving the item's name, description, format, and size, and perhaps its input source and output use. With the data dictionary in hand, we know the main characteristics of all of the different data elements a database will contain.

Once we know what data a database should contain, and how the data are used, we are in a position to design the database. We do so with a SCHEMA, a conceptual or logical view of the relationships among the data elements in the database. It is this view that separates a file from a database. Diverse data items can be related—linked by pathways in the database—as if they were contained in the same record of a file. Moreover, different users can be presented with their own tailored patterns of data items and links within the same database by using *subschemas* to describe the particular data items needed for a given application or user.

There is a difference between the schema, or *logical* description of the database, and the *physical* description of the database, or the way data are actually stored. Users need not be concerned about the physical description; software in the DBMS automatically translates any request for data based on the schema into the physical location of the data on disk.

Schemas and subschemas are written in a DATA DEFINITION LANGUAGE (DDL), which differs for each database management system. Like a programming language, a DDL has rules and procedures that must be followed if one is to successfully work with it.

With the database design complete, the schema and subschemas are input to the database management system. Physical descriptions of the data needed, such as the volume of data that the database will contain, the key fields to be used for relative addressing, and so on, are also input. The actual data can then be input to the database, where the DBMS will store it following the details of the schema and the physical descriptions. Once this demanding process has been completed, the database is ready to use. Standard report formats that will be used by the database might also be developed. Although similar procedures are followed in all databases, microcomputer databases are usually less complicated to develop than larger systems.

In much of the following discussion, we will examine these steps through the eyes of a single user, employing a micrcomputer-based database management system. We will assume that basic report needs and data uses have already been determined and that the user is about to create a new database.

File management or database management?

There are many powerful microcomputer data management programs available, yet not all of them can rightfully be called *database* management systems. Most are, in reality, FILE-MANAGEMENT SYSTEMS—only allowing one file to be opened at a time—and provide only indexed sequential access. Some of the more popular file-management systems in the mid-1980s included PFS:File, PC-FILE III, Reflex, and dBASE II. All provided nonprogrammers with powerful, although file-based, utilities. However, for most small business users, these programs supplied

Figure 11-11
Typical menu-driven database screens. (a) A pull-down menu. (b) A window menu.

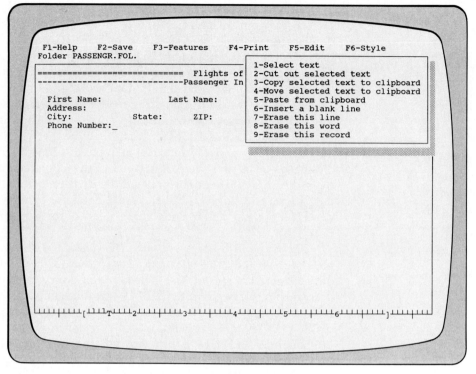

(a)

(b)

all the file-handling power they needed (or still need). True relational database management systems are usually more expensive and complicated to use. Best-selling products such as dBASE III+ and IV, R:Base 5000 and System V, and Paradox are examples of true DBMS. Even so, many users still employ these products to manage single files with accompanying indices.

Another distinction among data management systems is how users communicate with the program itself. In general, there are three methods: menus, commands, and mice.

Menu-driven programs provide users with a set of choices from which they select various operations. Figure 11-11 displays a typical program menu. Some database systems provide programming and application development languages that enable users to create and customize their own menus, as in Figure 11-12.

Command-driven programs do not offer choices on the screen but rather require users to enter commands directly to operate the program. As seen in Figure 11-13, database operations are controlled by direct command words or sentences typed onto the screen. While typed command routines are usually faster to implement, users must remember the syntax and use of the various command words. Many times, the now infamous "dot-prompt" of dBASE stared from the screen, intimidating new users as they tried to remember a particular command sequence.

Mouse-driven programs are similar to menu-driven ones, providing the user with choices on the screen in the form of words or picture *icons* (as in Figure 11-14). However, instead of typing a letter or number, the user simply moves the electronic mouse on his or her desk, which corre-

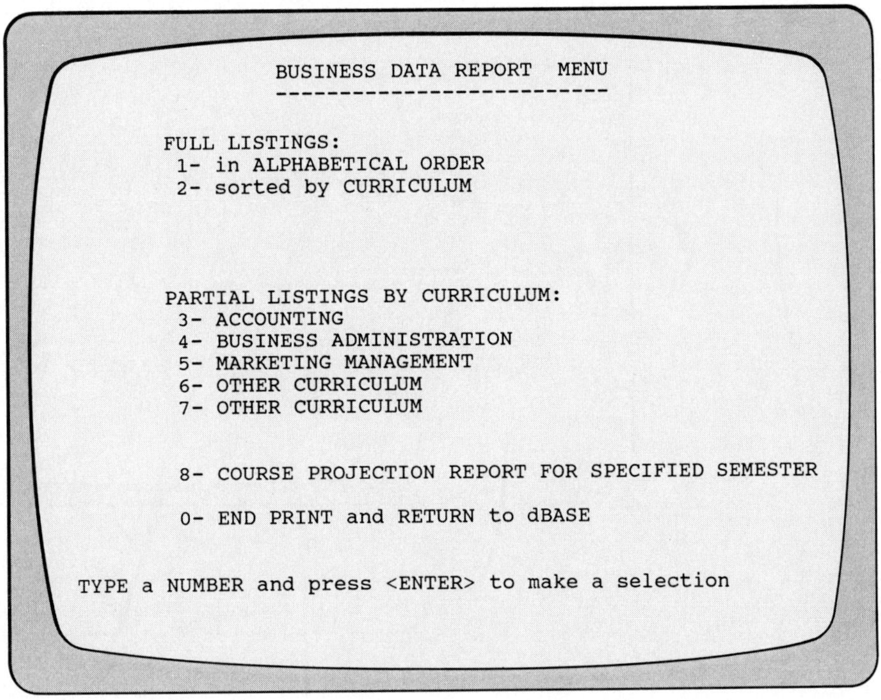

Menu-driven, command-driven, and mouse-driven programs

Figure 11-12
A customized menu for dBASE III+.

```
                    BUSINESS DATA REPORT   MENU
                    ---------------------------

        FULL LISTINGS:
          1- in ALPHABETICAL ORDER
          2- sorted by CURRICULUM




        PARTIAL LISTINGS BY CURRICULUM:
          3- ACCOUNTING
          4- BUSINESS ADMINISTRATION
          5- MARKETING MANAGEMENT
          6- OTHER CURRICULUM
          7- OTHER CURRICULUM


          8- COURSE PROJECTION REPORT FOR SPECIFIED SEMESTER

          0- END PRINT and RETURN to dBASE


     TYPE a NUMBER and press <ENTER> to make a selection
```

Figure 11-13
Some direct typed commands to control database functions.

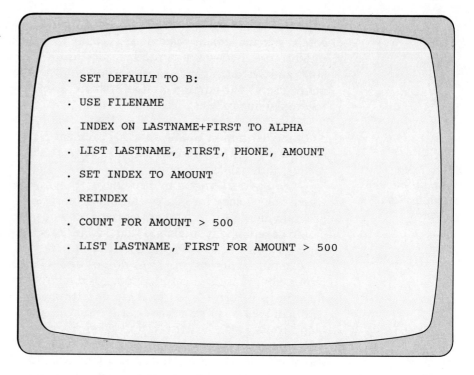

```
. SET DEFAULT TO B:

. USE FILENAME

. INDEX ON LASTNAME+FIRST TO ALPHA

. LIST LASTNAME, FIRST, PHONE, AMOUNT

. SET INDEX TO AMOUNT

. REINDEX

. COUNT FOR AMOUNT > 500

. LIST LASTNAME, FIRST FOR AMOUNT > 500
```

Figure 11-14
Microsoft's Works database offers mouse control with its menu screens.

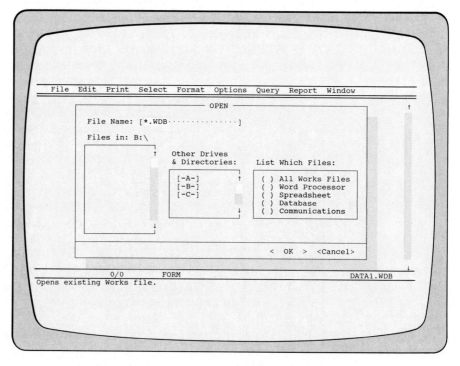

```
 File  Edit  Print  Select  Format  Options  Query  Report  Window

                            ┌─── OPEN ───┐
      File Name: [*.WDB·················]

      Files in: B:\
                         Other Drives
                         & Directories:      List Which Files:

                         [-A-]               ( ) All Works Files
                         [-B-]               ( ) Word Processor
                         [-C-]               ( ) Spreadsheet
                                             ( ) Database
                                             ( ) Communications


                                        <  OK  >  <Cancel>

          0/0          FORM                            DATA1.WDB
 Opens existing Works file.
```

spondingly moves a pointer on the screen. When the correct choice is indicated, a press of the mouse's button will activate the program. Pioneered with much success in the Apple Macintosh, mouse-driven database programs are becoming more popular on IBM-style PCs and newer OS/2 machines as well. It is clear that the mouse approach is less formidable to newer users than typing and should have greater success in the 1990s as most software expands mouse capabilities.

Combining approaches

In reality, data management programs rely on combinations of these approaches. Some programs let users select which method they prefer: dBASE's ASSIST and newer COMMAND CENTER programs and R:Base's EXPRESS mode can convert their command-driven programs into menu-driven ones. But even in menu approaches, typing is never completely eliminated. It still remains an efficient way to input data into the system, and still provides the quickest access. Even if managers use menus or mice to control operations, there will always be a portion of their time when typing is more appropriate and, in fact, required.

Creating a file structure

File structures, related to data dictionaries on larger systems, need only be created once for each file. In effect, we are designing the record form that will hold our data entries. While most programs will simply list the data fields, other programs allow the repositioning of data fields and instructions on the screen to any convenient layout for data entry, or the replication of forms already in use. Once we have designed a file structure on paper, it is a simple matter to create it in most microcomputer-based systems. We give the file a name, and then type a field name, type (character, numeric, date, or other format), and size (or width) for each data field included in the file. When specifying numeric fields, we also indicate how many decimal places should be reserved.

Let's use dBASE III+ to create a file structure called INVOICE. We want to include four fields in the record: client's name, phone number, date of invoice, and invoice amount. Note that dBASE III+, a relational database program, retains the more familiar terminology of fields and records.

Since we are in the command-driven mode, we type "CREATE INVOICE" and press <ENTER>. A screen similar to the one in Figure 11-15a appears, with the cursor awaiting our entry for the first field. We type "CLIENT" and press <ENTER>. The cursor moves to the "type" column. Now we simply press <ENTER> to retain the Char/text designation, and type 25 <ENTER> to set a width of 25 characters. The cursor proceeds to the next line, awaiting an entry for the second field, as in Figure 11-15b.

We continue to enter fields in this manner until we have completed all entries as in Figure 11-15c. Then we press <ENTER> to end the process. The file structure is complete. Most file and database management programs are similarly easy to use. In many, the structure can be modified to include new fields, delete old ones, or change names and widths.

Figure 11-15
Creating a file structure in dBASE. (a) A blank screen. (b) The screen after entry of field one. (c) Completed structure screen in dBASE III+.

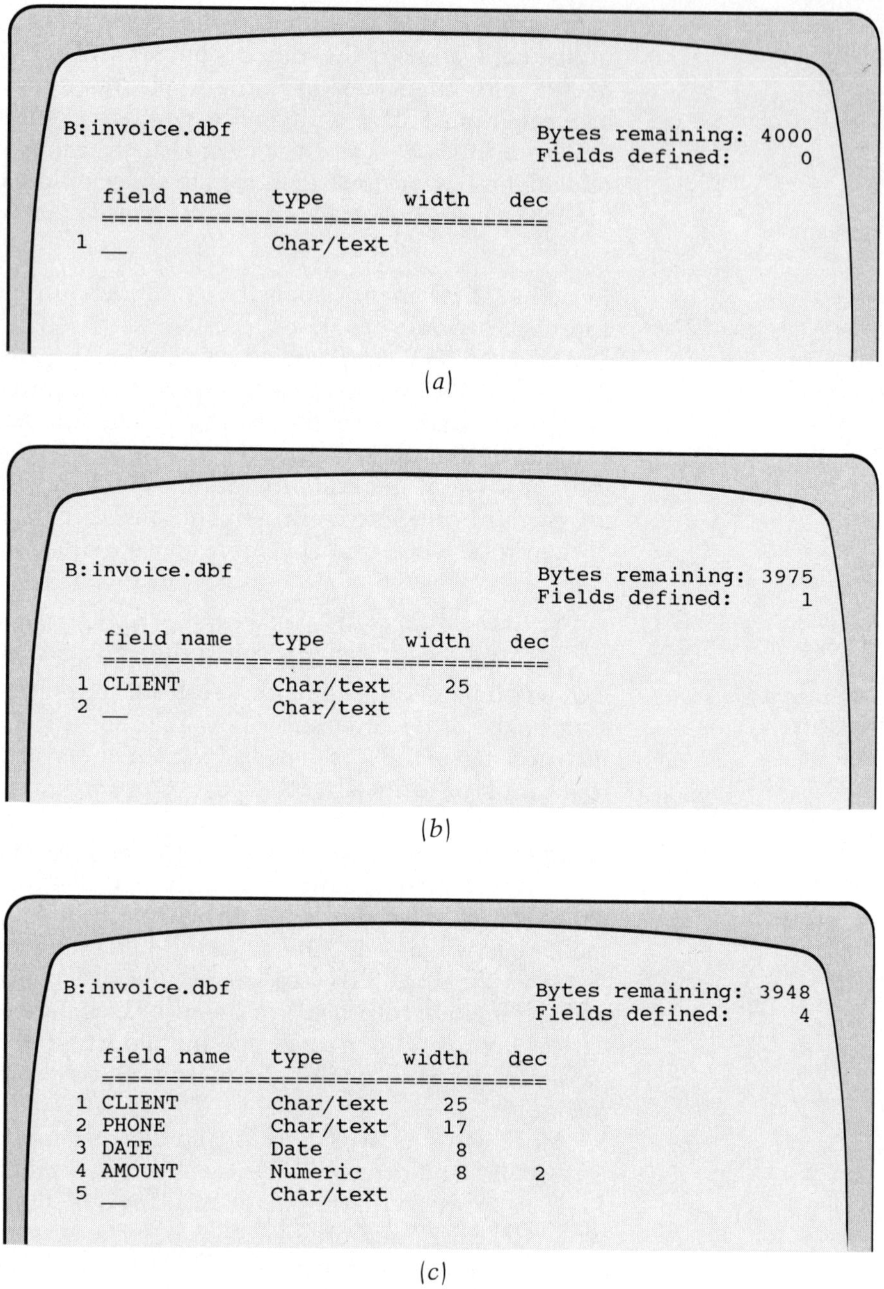

```
B:invoice.dbf                          Bytes remaining: 4000
                                       Fields defined:     0

    field name     type      width   dec
    =====================================
 1  __             Char/text
```
(a)

```
B:invoice.dbf                          Bytes remaining: 3975
                                       Fields defined:     1

    field name     type      width   dec
    =====================================
 1  CLIENT         Char/text    25
 2  __             Char/text
```
(b)

```
B:invoice.dbf                          Bytes remaining: 3948
                                       Fields defined:     4

    field name     type      width   dec
    =====================================
 1  CLIENT         Char/text    25
 2  PHONE          Char/text    17
 3  DATE           Date          8
 4  AMOUNT         Numeric       8     2
 5  __             Char/text
```
(c)

Programs like R:Base are a bit more complicated, using the relational terminology of database and tables. Figure 11-16 displays the R:Base equivalent of our invoice example using the menu EXPRESS. Here we have created a *database* named MONEY, and have defined the *table* called INVOICE, with certain *attributes*.

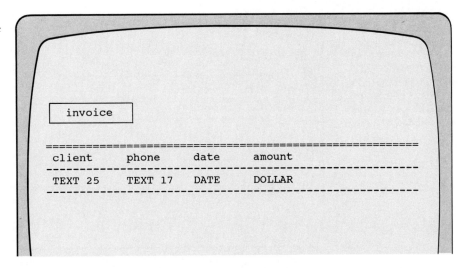

Figure 11-16
The R:base equivalent of
the same file structure.

Entering records

Once we have created a structure (or *record form* in some programs), we can enter data directly into each record by calling up a blank form as in Figure 11-17 and then typing in the appropriate data. Figure 11-17a displays a typical record as it might appear with our chosen fields in PC-FILE III. As we see, field names appear to the left of each entry, and information about each record is displayed at the top or bottom of the screen. Data are simply typed into each appropriate space to complete the form. Figure 11-17b shows a partial entry to our dBASE III+ record. Its completed form appears in Figure 11-17c. As we complete each record, a new blank form will appear on the screen.

Using the database

As a rule, databases can be used through a query language (or related techniques), or through a data manipulation language. Database management systems offer QUERY LANGUAGES for use by personnel who are not programmers. A *query* is a question posed to the database—an inquiry for some set of data. For example, purchasing agents who know nothing about computers can inquire about the current stock level of an item. Or a personnel manager might ask for a list of salespeople whose sales have already exceeded the month's quota. The commands required to get the information are fairly simple, and can be learned in an hour or two. The advantages of databases are very apparent here, because the user need not have the slightest idea of the storage medium being used for the data item, the hashing technique used, the relation of the data item to other data items, and so on. The user needs only to know what he or she is after. In addition to making inquiries with a query language, authorized users may also make changes, additions, and deletions in the database.

In recent times, microcomputer databases have offered query languages that resemble mainframe SQL—Structured Query Language, originally developed by IBM in the mid-1970s. Unfortunately, there are still too many versions of SQL to make it universal. IBM offers two: SQL/DB2 and SQL/DS. The American National Standards Institute (ANSI) released its "official" version called ANSI SQL in 1985. And, of

Figure 11-17
Entering data into a record. (a) A blank record form in PC-File III awaiting the CLIENT field entry. (b) Partially completed record form in dBASE III+. (c) A completed dBASE III+ record.

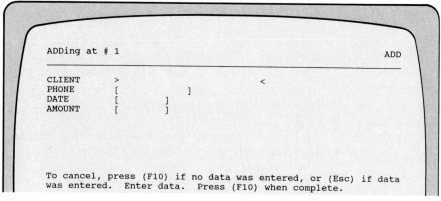

(a)

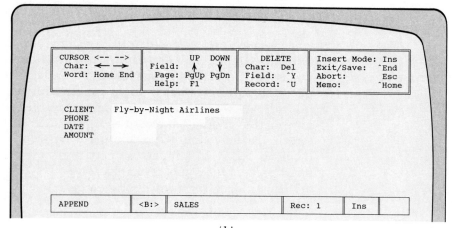

(b)

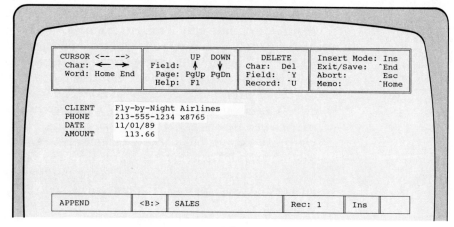

(c)

course, most software companies have created their own variation for their specific product. One of the major challenges faced by developers of database systems in the 1990s will be the selection or creation of one standard SQL to provide a truly universal and compatible method of accessing data whether on microcomputers, minicomputers, or mainframes.

Of course, queries need not be obtained solely through the use of SQL. The same effect can be obtained through interaction with menudriven programs (as we discussed earlier in the chapter) or through a technique called QBE—Query By Example. Rather than type a command, the user illustrates the desired outcome to achieve the same result.

Programmers, however, can interact with the database differently. They write their application programs in COBOL, BASIC, FORTRAN, or any other programming language the DBMS supports. In this context, the programming language is known as a *host language*. When programmers want to work with data from the database, they insert commands from a **DATA MANIPULATION LANGUAGE (DML)** into their program. These make it possible to perform any operation desired on the database. In addition, the more powerful microcomputer database systems offer their own *Applications Development Languages* for direct access by programmers or "power" users—those users skilled in the development of their own database applications. For example, dBASE III's command structure has become extremely popular in data manipulation of microcomputer databases, and is emulated by many other programs currently on the market. Figure 11-18 displays a portion of this language.

Regardless of how we choose to interact with the system, once a database structure has been created and data entered into it, we can

Figure 11-18
Some typical data manipulation language commands. These commands are usually written into an application program.

```
Edit: C:start.prg

set talk off                                                          <
set color to gR/ ,B/W,                                                <
clear                                                                 <
? '            BUSINESS STUDENT DATA - Version 881007EM'              <
set default to a:                                                     <
use STUDENT index IDENT                                               <
SET FORMAT TO SCREEN                                                  <
? '                    DEFAULT DISK set to A:'                        <
? '                    STUDENT file opened in ID ORDER'               <
?                                                                     <
? '      NOTES:  TYPE append to add new records'                      <
? '              TYPE browse to see records on one page'              <
? '              TYPE edit # to change a particular record'           <
?                                                                     <
? '      FOR PRINTED REPORTS... PRESS THE <F10> FUNCTION KEY'         <
? '      -------------------------------------------------------'    <
set function 10 to 'do reports;'                                      <
set talk on                                                          <
return                                                               <
```

manipulate its contents to retrieve information in ways that paper filing systems cannot. We can *sort* the database by any number of key fields (using indices if desired) so that information can be presented in its most useful form. We can *select*, or extract, only those records that match a specific set of criteria, such as all the clients in a particular zip code. Once we locate the desired records, we can *display* the entire set of data, or (more typically) only specific fields of interest. For example, using our database file INVOICE, we could issue the following dBASE command to find clients whose invoice exceeded $500 and list their name and invoice date:

LIST CLIENT, DATE FOR AMOUNT > 500

Imagine how much effort and time it would take a personnel clerk in a company of 500 workers to do the following: select the records of all employees 55 years of age as of July 1st and prepare a list by department, with names in alphabetical order, dates of birth, and health insurance plan codes. Then, produce mailing labels with each person's full address. A database management system would require a few sentences, or a few menu selections, to do all of it. The clerk could go on to other duties while the program carried out the instructions, producing the report within minutes (or seconds if using a mainframe)! The utility of a database system lies in its ability to respond to data requests—whether originally planned or not.

Report design

Unplanned, one-of-a-kind database queries can effectively provide immediate information to assist the decision-making process. However, queries of a repetitive nature can be designed as a formalized *report*. Like queries, reports allow users to specify what data should be selected, and how it should be presented. Reports, however, allow much more detail regarding page layout, headings, and format, and can be saved by name to be used again whenever needed. Report formats can also be modified to create additional reports, or used in combination with selection criteria to create various sets of information for different purposes. *Scheduled reports* (such as payroll) occur on a regular, planned basis. *Predictive reports* examine trends and are useful in forecasting. *Exception reports* (such as our "over quota" example) indicate conditions outside the expected norms, useful with management by exception approaches.

When designing a new report, it can be helpful to plan its layout (margins, columns, sections) on a piece of graph paper that matches the column width of the report. Some users find it more convenient to use a word processor to plan the layout. Most simply work directly with the report generator of their database system. Specifying a report to a microcomputer database system is a fairly straightforward process. In PC-FILE, for instance, you simply enter a one-line title, indicate which data fields you wish to include, and let the program worry about layout, headings, spacing, field widths, and formats.

The dBASE III+ program provides more control over how the final report will appear. Users can create headings, field widths, spacing, and allow numeric fields to be subtotaled and grouped by any sorted fields desired. Figure 11-19a shows an interactive dBASE screen leading the user through a report creation. Figure 11-19b is an example of the printed version that might result.

In most instances, the user can choose whether to send the report to a printer as hard copy, or simply to the screen for quick review. Many programs allow the report to be sent to a disk file as well, which can then be incorporated into a word processing document, or transmitted to other computers.

With the proper commands, a single report form can be used with different sets of records and different criteria, increasing its versatility. For instance, typing "REPORT FORM SALES" in dBASE III+ would print all records to the screen in the specified format called SALES. However, "REPORT FORM SALES TO PRINT" would send the report to a printer instead. "REPORT FORM SALES FOR AMOUNT > 1000" would include only those records where the amount exceeded 1000, and so on.

Maintaining the database

In large organizations, maintaining a database is a function of the database administrator. With the widespread use of microcomputers, however, it is becoming the responsibility of the users themselves to maintain their databases. By maintenance, we refer to performing such tasks as creating backup copies of the database, adding or deleting data fields in the file structure, changing field names, increasing the amount of data that the database can store, and moving the database to a different direct-access storage device.

Maintaining a database also refers to keeping it current and responsive to the needs of the user and the organization. Database management systems provide the flexibility to accomplish these tasks. Records can be edited to update data fields as conditions change. New records can be appended to files. Existing records can be deleted or extracted to other files for archiving. New subschema can be developed to allow different relations among data elements. Reports can be modified or deleted; new reports can be created. These techniques can maintain the database's usefulness for long periods of time. However, as with any system, a time may come when the database can no longer accommodate the volume of change that is needed. Then it is time to go back to the drawing board and design a new database.

Advanced functions

Database programs are constantly improving in capacity and power. Just a few short years ago, microcomputer systems were limited to thousands of records. By the late 1980s, most systems were handling billions! *Personal Computing* magazine, which named 1988 as the "Year of the Database," cited that in 1982, only 7 percent of database systems were relational. Experts predict, however, that by the early 1990s virtually every product will offer relational capabilities.

As the role of microcomputer databases grows in business, so does the necessity to offer more power to business managers and decision makers. *Ease of use* and *connectivity* are fast becoming the "buzz

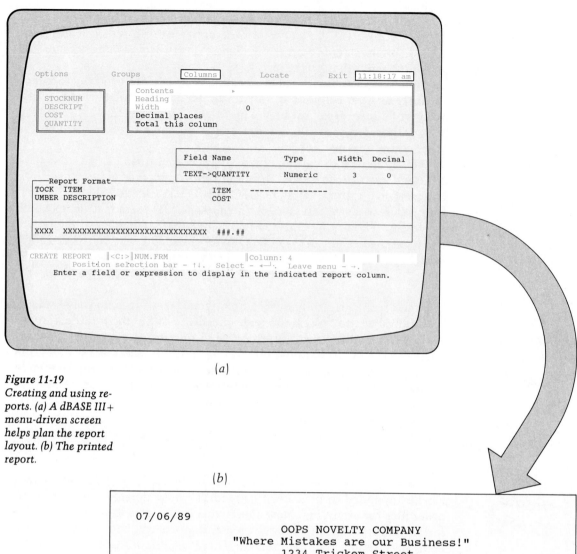

Figure 11-19
Creating and using reports. (a) A dBASE III+ menu-driven screen helps plan the report layout. (b) The printed report.

Database administrator

The database administrator is responsible for creating and maintaining databases. This involves working with systems analysts and programmers to determine the way in which applications will collect and store data, and then creating appropriate databases. Since security is a major concern in administering a database, the database administrator devises protective security measures together with the director of information processing, information resource manager, or information systems security specialist, and implements these measures on a day-to-day basis. The database administrator also sets up procedures to back up databases at regular intervals.

There is a fair amount of housekeeping to be done to keep a database up and running. The database administrator is responsible for the procedures to add and delete data from the database when valid requests are made.

The best person to educate others concerning databases is the database administrator or a qualified subordinate. It is in the best interests of an organization for programmers to know the structure of the databases and the conventions for retrieving data. Accordingly the good database administrator stresses communication with programmers and users, and must possess good interpersonal skills. Needless to say, the database administrator must also be a detail-oriented administrator. The need for technical competence and creativity comes into play most heavily during database design. The database administrator, in other words, is a well-rounded information systems professional who has specialized in databases.

Larger firms will maintain a complete staff working for the database administrator. Such a staff is in fact one of the best "ins" to becoming a database administrator in the first place. You can begin as a programmer, or even a clerk, in the database administration group, and move up as your abilities and dedication are recognized.

The other means of entry is in the small organization that may just be discovering its need for a database administrator: this individual will probably be chosen from the ranks of systems analysts who display an interest in and an aptitude for management.

Career prospects for database administrators are excellent. With file processing reduced in popularity and databases the direction the industry has taken, there is plenty of database administration to be done, and people skilled in the area are in short supply. Particularly useful would be a knowledge of telecommunications and distributed data processing.

Figure 11-20
Graphics and text can be combined on many current microcomputer databases.

words" of the 1990s. The support of Structured Query Language has become more pronounced, as has the ability of databases to be used in multiuser networks, making data accessible to more users and capable of being communicated to and from mainframes. Of course, moving from single-user to multiuser systems increases security risks to the data and requires extensive control. Password security, commonplace for larger systems, is becoming an essential item in microcomputer databases. Programs are also improving their math and file capabilities, offering accuracy to 19 digits, and allowing 32 files to be opened at one time with links possible among 200 files in the database.

Another advance is the linking of graphic images and text within a database. In 1988, we saw the expansion of Apple's HyperCard, which relates "stacks" of cards rather than files of records. *Stackware* has been developed to add video images, graphs, illustrations, photos, and sounds to normal text and data (see Figure 11-20). Connections are now being made between computer database programs and compact disk, videotape, and video disk players.

As window environments become more commonplace, the use of icons and mice will simplify many operations, combining graphic images with written text. The late 1980s saw the Apple Macintosh as a leader in graphics-oriented database. Programs like Quartz and Oracle brought the mouse-oriented windows approach to IBM database management. In the early 1990s, IBM's OS/2 Database Manager and Microsoft's Windows will provide the standards for graphics and menu operation in database design (see Figure 11-21), relying on memory in the megabyte realm, and the faster and more elaborate processors, which will greatly expand their utility.

Figure 11-21
Windows environment—the standard for IBM in the 1990s.

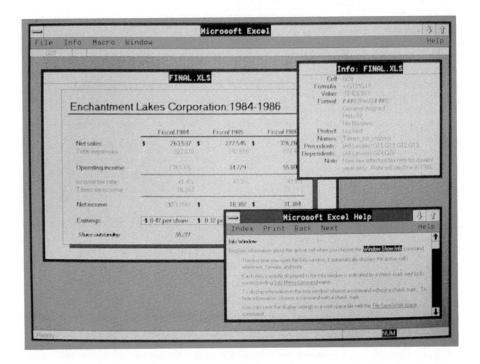

Supplementing the database

Business managers, concerned with improving efficiency, have sought to expand the usefulness of their database management systems beyond typical functions. Not surprisingly, a secondary market has grown to support and extend the functions offered by DBMSs. These include such program adjuncts as mail merge, screen generators, and report generators. Let's look at each briefly:

■ *Mail merge* is a technique that allows users to create standard forms or letters that can then be merged with the data in database files to create personalized printout. For example, we might create a standard cover letter and then "fill in the details" by selecting records and copying needed fields into their appropriate place on the form.

■ *Screen generators* greatly simplify the task of designing custom layouts of screens used for data entry. Programs like Quickcode III can significantly reduce the time it takes for power users to develop their own screen designs. Figure 11-22 compares a standard dBASE III+ layout with a customized screen. Many recent database programs incorporate screen generators as part of their improved capabilities.

■ *Report generators* assist users in the creation and design of report formats, in much the same way screen generators assist with input. Standard designs are available that can be modified to suit individual needs.

Figure 11-22
Report forms can be customized within programs or with the help of add-on programs. (a) A standard screen automatically generated by dBASE III+ places data fields in one vertical column at the left margin (the remaining fields will appear on succeeding screens). (b) The same record, rearranged with the help of Quickcode III to fit all data fields on one screen.

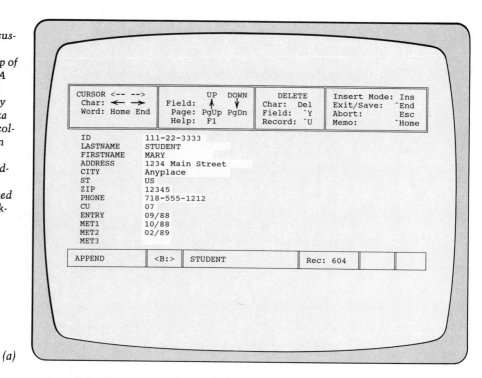

(a)

(b)

Software and people

Databases and accompanying management systems are useful only to the extent that businesspeople can organize and understand their own data needs. While newer database programs offer a "free-form" approach that is more open to unstructured queries and quick retrieval of data, it is clear that good programs are no replacement for good management. Database systems are much like automobiles—they can offer as much power and ease of use as you wish, but can't go anywhere without proper direction. It is still the human who must control the ultimate destination of the machine. Good management can thrive with the addition of a database system; poor management won't get any better.

summary

■ Data used in an information system generally fall into a data hierarchy made up of four categories. These are (from lowest to highest level) the field, record, file, and database.

■ Fields are composed of characters. A numeric field contains only numbers. An alphabetic field (or character field) contains only alphabetic characters. An alphanumeric field can contain both numbers and alphabetic characters.

■ There are three main types of file design: sequential, indexed sequential, and direct access.

■ In a sequential file, records are arranged in a predetermined order according to one or more keys contained in the record. Keys can be unique or nonunique identifiers, depending on their use. The most important key is called the primary key; supplemental keys are secondary keys.

■ Sequential files can be stored on magnetic tape or disk. They offer only sequential access to records, and are appropriate for batch processing programs that read and/or write a high proportion of the records in a file. When sequential files are used, backup copies are automatically created.

■ Disadvantages of sequential files include the need to read every record preceding the record of interest, to sort transaction records into the same sequence as the master file, and the duplication of data in multiple files.

■ Indexed sequential files also arrange records in a predetermined order, but maintain one or more indices that give the location of records. Indexed sequential files must be contained on a direct-access storage device. They offer either sequential or direct access, but are somewhat more cumbersome with either technique than a "true" sequential or direct-access file. In addition, no automatic backup copies are created.

■ Direct-access files arrange records in an order related to the record key in a way determined by program logic, most often through relative addressing. Hashing techniques are often used to transform keys into storage addresses.

■ Direct-access files offer the fastest way to read or write records in nonsequential order, but must be used on a direct-access device. Transactions need not be sorted before being used to update a file. Costs are higher than with sequential files, data are somewhat more vulnerable to unauthorized access or equipment failure, and backup copies are not automatically produced.

■ A database is a collection of related files, and offers users more flexibility than files and file-management systems. With a database, data are independent of the application programs that use them; data are accessible to any program regardless of the data location or program's language; data redundancy is minimized; data integrity is improved; and programmers need not write and debug extensive file descriptions.

■ Drawbacks of databases include the possibility of data abuse, higher hardware and software costs, and the greater amount of time and effort it takes to create and properly maintain one.

■ A database management system (DBMS) is a program that makes it possible to create, use, and maintain databases. In most medium-sized and large businesses, a database administrator is responsible for setting up databases and helping users to get the most out of them. Setting up a database involves surveying the data uses, setting up a data dictionary, and designing and implementing the database. Design is done by specifying schemas in a data definition language (DDL).

■ A database can be used through a query language or a data manipulation language. A query language is geared to managers and users, who can use English-like statements to work with data. Programmers insert statements in a data manipulation language (DML) in their programs. Programs must be written in a host language—one the DBMS supports. Users can address database management programs through commands, menus, and mouse control. QBE—Query By Example—simplifies searches in newer database programs.

■ One important difference between a file and a database is that a database can specify how data items are related to one another. A schema is used to express the logical relationship among data elements. Three structures are commonly used to relate data items within a database: hierarchical, network, and relational.

■ In a hierarchical database, data elements are related to one another as parents and children in a treelike structure. While parents can have more than one child, each child can have only one parent.

■ A network database allows children to have more than one parent.

■ Relational databases view all data items as related to one another in tables composed of tuples and attributes. They are easier to use than hierarchical or network databases, although they are slower for more complex searches.

wrap-up

Congratulations

At 4:35 P.M., Lesley entered Philip's office with her review and recommendations. The reports created by the database system, merged with the performance scores and her own evaluation of individual personalities and capabilities clearly pointed to two candidates who were more "ripe" for promotion than the others.

She placed her reports off to one side of the conference table, as Philip rose from his desk to join her. Philip knew that Lesley had enough documentation to support her recommendation, but he was more interested in her personal assessment of the situation. He could always review the data later.

"When I first examined the data," she began, "we seemed to be faced with a slight problem. Two of the candidates really deserve promotion. They're hard workers, they've been in the company for a reasonable length of time, and they're both ambitious. I am pleased with their record of accomplishment and educational background. Either one would be an asset to us in upper-level management. I fear that if we overlook one of them now, we might possibly lose a valuable manager to another company."

"Okay, we have two. What about the other three?" asked Philip.

"They have time. Steve is fairly new and needs a little more experience with the company. Susan has some minor attitude problems that need to be worked on—especially with customer relations. Roberta has had a fairly recent promotion anyway."

Lesley continued, glancing at her handwritten notes. "But, getting back to the two, I think that there is a reasonable way to retain and reward both. First, we can offer George, our warehouse manager, the opening as head of the new retail store. He's had experience with supervision, sales, and inventory. He's also quick to respond in a crisis—remember that backorder problem he resolved?—and has shown he can anticipate problems before they arise. The data show that his record is superb, and he scored the highest in that management training program we ran last year."

"Okay," replied Philip. "Then what do we do with your second candidate?"

"Well, Nina is one of our best salespeople. She knows how to work with people and is goal-oriented. The data show she's always surpassed quota by at least 10 percent each year. She's also acted as a supervisor for our newer sales staff, but never has had a real opportunity to run her own operation. I think she'd welcome the managerial slot being vacated by George. It's a higher salary than she's getting now and puts her into management rather than sales—something I know she wants."

Philip agreed with the choices and the suggestion. There was no need to look further at the pile of supporting data. It was clear that Lesley had done her work well. They agreed that Lesley would call each person in tomorrow and present the promotion offers. Philip also asked that she begin to look into developing the other three candidates for the future.

The database management system had allowed Lesley to respond quickly to Philip's personnel request, but its job was not yet over. As she gathered up the printouts and charts, Lesley realized that both George and Nina would be using the system in the very near future to help plan their staff needs and the other hirings and promotions that would follow. Then, there was still the problem of finding a replacement for Nina as supervisor of the sales force. It was time to get back to the database query program!

388

key terms

These are the key terms in alphabetical order. The numbers in parentheses refer to the page on which each term is defined.

Alphabetic field or character field (350)
Alphanumeric field (350)
Attribute (366)
Character (350)
Child (364)
Database (350)
Database administrator (363)
Database management system (DBMS) (363)
Data definition language (DDL) (369)
Data dictionary (369)
Data hierarchy (350)
Data independence (361)
Data integrity (361)
Data manipulation language (DML) (377)
Data redundancy (361)
Direct access (355)
Direct-access file (or random-access file) (358)
Field (350)
File (350)
File design (352)
File-management system (369)
Hashing (358)
Hierarchical database (364)
Indexed sequential file (355)
Key (352)
Network database (365)
Numeric field (350)
Parent (364)
QBE—Query By Example (377)
Query language (375)
Record (350)
Relational database (366)
Relative addressing (358)
Schema (369)
Sequential access (353)
Sequential file (352)
Table (366)
Tuple (366)

review questions

objective questions

True/false. *Put the letter T or F on the line next to the question.*

1. A hierarchical database allows each "child" data element only one "parent."   1 _____
2. The data element "LASTNAME" would make a good primary key field for a list of students.   2 _____
3. Fields are made up of interrelated records.   3 _____
4. Sequential files are best to use if the proportion of records to be processed in a file is low.   4 _____
5. Database security problems can be overcome by using sequential files on magnetic tape to store data.   5 _____
6. Indexed sequential files require an index file be read to determine the location of the group of records containing the desired record.   6 _____
7. A data dictionary contains the schema of the database.   7 _____
8. A secondary key must be a unique identifier for a record.   8 _____
9. A database is a set of interrelated files.   9 _____
10. Network databases are arranged in a tree-like structure.   10 _____

Multiple choice. *Put the letter of the correct answer on the line next to the question.*

1. A dentist would like to use a database to keep track of his dental patients' visits. Since he already uses a microcomputer for creating patient bills, what type of database is he likely to acquire?   1 _____
  (a) A hierarchical database.
  (b) A network database.
  (c) A relational database.
  (d) Any of the above would be acceptable.

2. Fly-By-Night Airlines needs to keep track of passenger information. What type of file design would you recommend?

   (a) Sequential file.
   (b) Indexed sequential file.
   (c) Direct-access file.
   (d) Indexed direct file.

3. With a database, users are concerned with the

   (a) Conceptual view of the database.
   (b) Physical view of the database.
   (c) File design used to store data in the database.
   (d) Both the conceptual and physical view of the database.

4. A unique identifier for a record is called a

   (a) Parent.
   (b) Child.
   (c) Primary key.
   (d) Secondary key.

5. The language for developing the schema of the database management system is

   (a) The data definition language.
   (b) The host language.
   (c) The data manipulation language.
   (d) The query language.

Fill in the blank. *Write the correct word or words in the blank to complete the sentence.*

1. The _____ shows the logical relationships between data elements in the database.

2. A _____ is a software package used to create, utilize, and maintain the database.

3. A _____ language is offered by a database management system (DBMS) to permit nonprogrammers to access the database.

4. In hierarchical and network databases, _____ data elements are superior to and connected to _____ data elements.

5. The _____ (made up of one or more characters) is the smallest usable part of the data hierarchy.

6. The use of tables to interconnect the data elements is a feature of a _____.

7. With _____ access, to read the last record in a file of 550 records requires reading all 549 preceding records.

8. One child data element can have more than one parent in a _____.

9. _____ refers to the technique used by a file to store and retrieve data from secondary storage.

10. A _____ defines each item of data handled by an information system.

short answer questions

When answering these questions, think of concrete examples to illustrate your points.

1. What are the three types of file design?
2. How do indexed sequential files differ from direct-access files?
3. What does the term *hashing* mean?
4. What is a DBMS?
5. What is a schema?
6. What is the purpose of the data dictionary?
7. What are the differences between hierarchical and network databases?
8. How are attributes and tuples similar to fields and records?

essay questions

1. What are the advantages and disadvantages of using files?
2. What are the steps needed to create a database?
3. What are the advantages and disadvantages of using databases?

Desktop publishing and graphics: art and information merge

After studying this chapter you should understand the following:

- *The importance and capabilities of desktop publishing.*
- *The concepts related to fonts, layout, and design.*
- *Current and potential business applications of desktop publishing software.*
- *How to interpret typical desktop publishing screens.*
- *The difference between typesetting and desktop publishing.*
- *The use of graphics in business.*

chapter 12

The company newsletter

"Okay, Ann," said Janis Roberts, grinning at her office assistant. "I give up! Why should we spend more money on computers?"

Ann's recent success with word processing had convinced Janis of the computer's worth to the business. As manager of Freddy Johnson's Travel Agency, Janis was always interested in new ways to cut costs and improve services.

"As you know," Ann began, "our *Trip Tips* newsletter comes out six times a year with travel hints and current bargains."

Janis did indeed know, having started it herself 2 years ago. Free copies were mailed to the agency's clients and corporate travel coordinators. Others were given to customers who walked into any of the offices around town. Janis even put them in waiting rooms of local dentists and doctors—great goodwill and advertising as well.

Ann continued, "Well, as I see it, we have three problems. First, our typesetting costs are getting out of hand. Even though typesetting looks great, it's expensive—$40 a page."

"Don't I know it," Janis agreed. "Last year, typesetting alone was over $1000—not including the printing and postage."

"Exactly," Ann replied. "But we have two other headaches. We want the newsletter to be current, but we prepare it weeks ahead to allow time for typesetting and review. Remember that last-minute special we had to insert on a typed photocopied page?"

"Do I ever," groaned Janis. "Freddy hated it!"

"Also, it's hard to change content or layout. Each change delays the newsletter and increases costs. It would be nice to be able to make changes without worrying about time or cost."

"Okay, Ann, what's the answer?"

"It's pretty easy," replied Ann, as she put some samples on the desk. "We buy desktop publishing software. We can design the newsletter right in our office, and then have it printed professionally. We save all our typesetting costs, have total control over the design, and can even add new items at the last minute!"

Janis liked what she was hearing. She also liked the samples on her desk. "Nice idea, but what does it cost?"

"Actually . . . nothing! We already have most of the equipment we need—the computer, hard disk drive, and laser printer. I figure $100 more for a mouse . . ."

"A *mouse?*" interrupted Janis.

"Not a real one," laughed Ann. "This mouse controls screen movements, and it comes with a drawing program I can use for some of the artwork. The desktop program itself runs about $700. Later on, we could add a better screen, or even a scanner for art and photographs. Of course, we can't cut our printing and mailing expenses, but the typesetting costs we save in the first year alone will more than cover the program's initial cost."

Ann paused for effect. "And then we save every year thereafter. Of course, we'll also have the program for our newspaper ads and brochures, saving even more."

"I like it! Order what you need and let's start with the next issue!" Janis thought for a moment. "And while you're at it, how about picking up some cheese for our new mouse?"

Publishing at your fingertips

The modern Gutenberg

The past five centuries have seen remarkable advances in printed communication. In 1437, Gutenberg's movable-type printing press revolutionized *mass* communication by introducing the concept of typesetting to the Western world. More recently, large-scale printing has been extended by such processes as lithography, linotype typesetting, offset printing, and phototypesetting. These processes allow duplication in large quantities and are extremely useful in the production of books, magazines, and newspapers.

The modern typewriter, developed in 1867 by Sholes, Soulé, and Glidden, similarly expanded the art of *personal* communication, enabling individual messages to be created with relative ease. Carbon paper extended the typewriter's utility by allowing several copies to be created while typing the original only once. The "cc:" placed at the bottom of many business memos reflected this now outdated concept of "carbon copy." By the 1970s, xerographic photocopiers enabled users to duplicate original documents more clearly and in reasonable quantities. Appropriately, the term "pc:" for photostatic copy (or personal copy) is now in vogue. As we have seen in Chapter 9, the modern word processor has simplified the entry and editing of typed material even further.

Yet, for the most part, typing and typesetting remained separate and distinct procedures. Typing produced originals for individual communication or quantity duplication. Typesetting was reserved for the more professional-looking requirements of books, magazines, newspapers, and brochures.

In 1985, however, these processes were effectively joined together when Paul Brainerd, president of Aldus Corporation, introduced DESK-TOP PUBLISHING—using a microcomputer to combine text and graphics into a professional-looking layout that exceeds dot-matrix or typed print and approximates typeset quality (see Figure 12-1).

As we observed in the opening example, the microcomputer can provide a cost-effective alternative to typesetting with surprisingly effective results. No wonder sales of desktop publishing software have dramatically increased among Fortune 1000 companies, where publishing costs typically consume as much as 10 percent of gross revenues.

Desktop publishing has become a hot item. According to figures compiled by the market research firm Dataquest, computer sales for desktop publishing use jumped from 4000 units in 1986 to almost 40,000 in 1987, and are projected to top 400,000 by 1990! Clearly, the last decade of this century will see more businesspeople becoming their company's own "Gutenberg"—expanding their control of the publication process through their desktop computers.

Typesetting

The traditional publishing sequence is a complicated and time-consuming process. It begins with the typing of text material on a typewriter or word processor. A printed copy is then edited to improve its clarity and

```
 These four examples are exactly the same
 except that (a) is printed on a dot-
 matrix printer. (b) is typed, (c) is
 produced with a desktop publishing
 program and laser printer, and (d) is
 typeset. Notice the resolution and
 spacing of each.
```

(a)

These four examples are exactly the same except that sample "a" was printed with a dot-matrix printer, sample "b" was typed, sample "c" was produced with a desktop publisher and printed with a laser printer, and sample "d" was typeset.

(c)

```
 These four examples are exactly the
 same except that sample "a" was printed
 with a dot-matrix printer, sample "b"
 was typed, sample "c" was produced with
 a desktop publisher and printed with a
 laser printer, and sample "d" was
 typeset.
```

(b)

These four examples are exactly the same except that sample "a" was printed with a dot matrix printer, sample "b" was typed, sample "c" was produced with a desktop publisher and printed with a laser printer, and sample "d" was typeset.

(d)

Figure 12-1
A comparison of (a) dot-matrix, (b) typed,
(c) desktop published,
and (d) typeset text.

content, and retyped if necessary. Next, it is typically sent to a copy editor who carefully reviews it for consistency of style and format. Copy-editors mark the text to indicate all changes in grammar, layout, and typestyle (see Figure 12-2). They may also make decisions concerning headings, paragraph breaks, margins, and use of underlining, boldface, and italics. Often, the marked copy is returned to the original author for review and comment. The copy-edited text is then sent to a typesetter who retypes it into a typesetting machine. Copies of the typeset material, called *galleys* (Figure 12-3), are reviewed for typographical errors, omissions, and corrected appropriately. Once approved, they are "cut and pasted" into a pleasing layout and issued as final *page proofs*. Correcting errors after they have been typeset in this manner is a tedious and costly procedure. Finally, the typeset material is printed in quantity to match the corrected page proofs. Pages are then cut and bound together in as many copies as needed.

Of course, some typesetting jobs need not follow this exhaustive procedure so closely. A one-page brochure will not involve the same complexity, personnel, and time as that required for a magazine or book. Yet, for most traditional typesetting jobs, the inability to easily modify results still remains. This is mostly due to the separate, noncompatible machines used for typing and typesetting.

The desktop publisher

Desktop publishing systems eliminate most of the problems inherent in traditional typesetting. By providing a direct link between initial entry of text and final page copy, three significant improvements are offered:

■ *They eliminate the need for retyping into galleys.* Since word processing files created by the typist control the final printing, there is no need to retype. Editing and copy-editing changes can be entered directly into the file. Errors are reduced; time and money are saved. Although

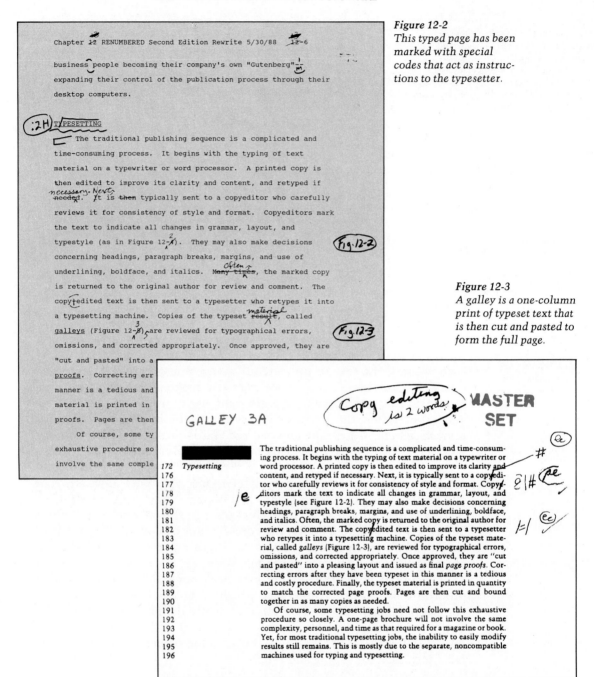

Figure 12-2
This typed page has been marked with special codes that act as instructions to the typesetter.

Figure 12-3
A galley is a one-column print of typeset text that is then cut and pasted to form the full page.

modern typesetting practices allow word processing files to be directly loaded into typesetting machines (assuming, of course, that the author has used a word processor), there is still the need to add typesetting controls to the file.

■ ***They provide direct control over design and layout.*** Most desktop systems offer WYSIWYG (what you see is what you get) capability, where users can see immediately on the screen how their changes in layout, size, or typestyle affect the document. Decisions need not wait for final page proofs.

□ *They provide flexibility for dynamic redesign and modification*. Unlike typeset pages that are static and difficult to alter, desktop publishing documents are designed to be modified with ease. The user is free to "play" with each component's position, size, and typestyle.

Features of desktop publishing

The 1980s were ripe for this new print revolution. Microcomputer hardware had become relatively powerful, inexpensive, and available to the typical business user. Not only had memory and speed dramatically improved, but computer screens and printers were now capable of displaying images and text with better resolution. More sophisticated software was introduced that made effective use of the expanded graphics, speed, and capacity of the newer microcomputers and printers.

Figure 12-4
The desktop publishing quality continuum.

Specifically, we can categorize desktop publishing into three quality levels (see Figure 12-4): *draft quality*, *publication quality*, and *professional quality*. Each higher level requires a significant increase in hardware capability, software sophistication, expense, and user expertise.

	Low Range *Draft Quality*	Mid-Range *Publication Quality*	High Range *Professional Quality*
Application	"Personal" publishing	"Business" publishing	"Corporate" publishing
Uses	Greeting cards Banners Signs Basic newsletters	Brochures Reports Newsletters Manuals	Books Magazines Newspapers High-level corporate publication
Suggested minimum hardware			
Computer	PC w/256 K	PC/XT w/640K+	AT w/1 Meg+
CPU	8088 sufficient	80286 minimum	80386
Disk drive	Floppy	Hard drive	Hard drive
Screen	Monochrome with graphics	RGB will work High-resolution EGA or VGA better	High-resolution EGA or VGA
Printer	Dot-matrix	Laser printer	Connected to typesetting equipment
Other		Mouse (suggested) Scanner (optional)	Mouse Scanner
Software	Self-contained graphics program with clip art	Word processor Spelling checker Paint program WYSIWYG page makeup package Clip art	Same as mid-range with typesetting translation programs

Draft quality

At the draft quality level, we find *personal publishing* systems, comprised of a standard microcomputer, dot-matrix printer, and software with basic text and graphics capabilities. Broderbund's Print Shop and Springboard's Newsroom are two good examples of personal publishing software. To "publish," the user selects from a menu of various typestyles, types the text, and determines basic page layout. If desired, graphics can be added with a computer version of CLIP ART—prepared artwork that is "clipped" (cut out) with scissors and then pasted onto a page. Computerized clip art images are kept on computer disk rather than in a book, and offer more flexibility than the printed variety. They are reusable, since they are copied not cut from the disk. Their size and appearance can be changed. Clip art can even be reversed (side-to-side) or inverted (upside-down). Finally, since they are not physically "pasted" anywhere, computer clip art can be moved around the screen until the user is pleased with the result. Figure 12-5 displays examples of computer clip art.

Although they have sold well in the home market, personal publishing programs are not considered serious business tools due to their low-level printing quality and inability to import text directly from word processors. Certainly, they can be used to prepare sales banners, simple signs, and in-house newsletters, but their dot-matrix output is not a reasonable alternative to professionally typeset documents.

Of course, print quality depends on hardware as well as software. Quality is a question of print resolution—the clarity with which text and graphics can be shown on paper. The 100 dpi (dots per inch) resolution of most dot-matrix printers simply cannot match typesetting resolution, which can easily exceed 2000 dpi. When we add the inconvenience of having to type material directly into such programs (especially documents of substantial length), the utility of personal publishing programs for serious business applications is diminished. However, as prototypes of the future, they opened the door, as well as people's minds, to the concept of desktop publishing.

Figure 12-5
Clip art are graphic images available on disk that can be added to text material on the screen.

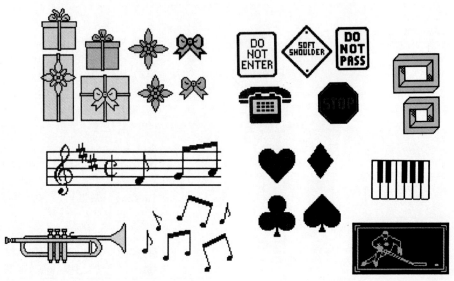

Publication quality

Apple's Macintosh computer took the first major step in removing the obstacles just discussed through its integrated word processing program—MacWrite—and graphics program—MacPaint. The "Mac" gave users their first real glimpse into serious desktop publishing. As Figure 12-6 shows, text and graphics were easily combined and manipulated to produce a pleasing layout on the high-resolution screen. Apple's Imagewriter dot-matrix printer could then reproduce the image on paper with its improved 160 dpi resolution.

By 1988, the major obstacles to serious use had been overcome with the introduction of *publication quality* systems. Faster microcomputer processors and increased storage capacity made way for sophisticated software such as Aldus's PageMaker (for the Macintosh or IBM) and Xerox's Ventura Publisher (for the IBM), the two leaders in business desktop publication. Both enabled users to take files directly from any standard word processing file, and then adjust typestyles, sizes, and layouts directly on the screen (see Figure 12-7). When used with laser printers offering 300 dpi resolution, the output was close to typeset quality. The mid-range desktop publisher had arrived.

Professional quality

Of course, 300 dpi is not 2000. Typesetting is still the choice for more demanding tasks. Not only does professional typesetting present a clean look, but it saves space. Typeset pages usually contain almost 50 percent more text than typed pages. *Professional quality* microcomputer systems were developed to bring the ease and control of microcomputer design to *high-resolution typesetting*. Such systems, costing between $30,000 and $70,000, use the microcomputer (and appropriate software) to create instructions that can directly control a typesetting machine instead of a lower-resolution printer. In this way, word-processed text can be merged with graphic images, and then transmitted directly to the typesetting machine for printing. Businesses that require substantial amounts of true typeset material may wish to invest in these high-grade systems. Most businesses, however, will find that the

Figure 12-6
The Apple Macintosh gave business its first serious look at desktop publishing's potential with Macintosh's Mac-Paint.

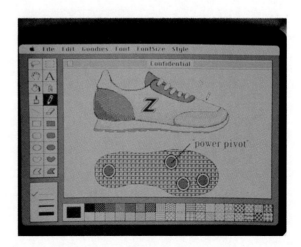

Figure 12-7
Layout screens from Xerox's Ventura Publisher and Aldus's Page-Maker: (a) Ventura in two-column book form, (b) PageMaker in a three-column newsletter.

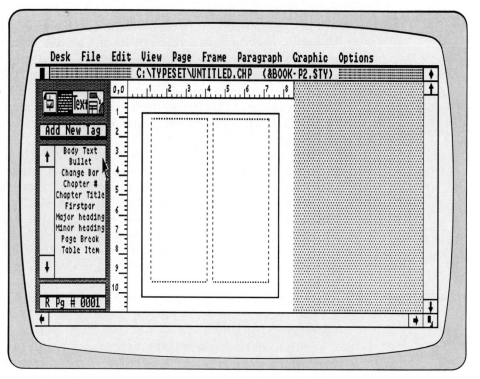

(a)

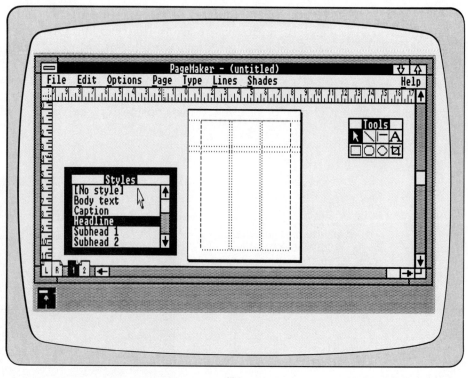

(b)

increasingly sophisticated mid-range systems will more than meet their publication requirements.

Enter the font

Typewriters offer one style and size of print at a time. Although we can augment words with CAPITALIZATION, underlining, or even **double-striking,** the typestyle remains constant. The typestyle of a particular print is called the *font*. A font is a set of characters in a particular style and size. It is designed for graphic effect or improved readability. There is an art to designing fonts and their pattern (called *text*) that are both pleasing and readable. Studies have shown that proper text design alone can increase reading speeds by almost 30 percent. As seen in Figure 12-8, standard fonts have been designed in many styles and a variety of sizes. These sizes are expressed in *points*, each point equal to 1/72 of an inch. While there are endless design variations, certain standards prevail. Fonts can have *serifs*—flat strokes to end each line—or none (called *sans serif*). Letter widths can vary to produce proportional spacing, as can the thickness of their lines. Letters that share common edges

---

FONT SAMPLES

A sampling of fonts available for your laser printer are listed here.

Helvetica	Goudy	Times Roman
Helvetica Oblique	*Goudy Italic*	*Times Italic*
Helvetica Black	**Goudy Bold**	**Times Bold**
Bookman Light	Palatino Roman	Sans Serif
Bookman Demi	*Palatino Italic*	*Sans Serif Italic*
Bookman Demi Italic	**Palatino Bold**	**Sans Serif Bold**

(a)

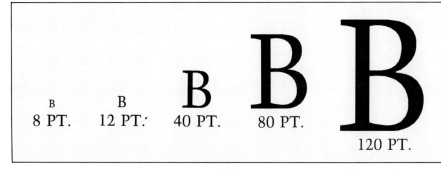

(b)

Figure 12-8
(a) A font sampler. Many of these standard fonts have been selected for their graphic impact and readability. (b) Font sizes are measured in points.

can also be placed closer together in a procedure called KERNING ("cutting-through") for easier readability, as in Figure 12-9.

Many word processors offer only one font style, but when used with dot-matrix or laser printers, provide the capability to alter it to produce expanded, compressed, boldface, or italicized print—each a different font. More advanced programs enable users to change font *size* as well, and to combine different fonts in one document.

Separate screen font programs, such as Fontasy and FanciFont, offer a variety of font styles to enhance any printed output (see Figure 12-10). In most cases, these programs allow users to input standard word processing files and then change fonts as desired.

Desktop publishing programs expand this concept by substantially increasing the size and complexity of files that can be used. They also offer a larger variety of sizes and styles of fonts, and provide direct linkage between word processing and the final document. Word processors themselves are quickly evolving into pseudo-desktop publishers. In 1988, for example, Word and WordPerfect led the transition with their capability to include graphics and layout patterns with text, in addition to expanding the array of font styles available to the user.

Bit-mapped or outlined?

In general, fonts can be handled through two different approaches. They can be *bit-mapped* or *outlined*. A BIT-MAPPED FONT is a fixed pattern of dots that displays the size, shape, and orientation of each font character. Since bit-map patterns cannot be adjusted, different sizes of the same font or simple rotations (for example, turning a letter sideways) require totally different bit-maps. Printers that use the bit-mapped approach to describe fonts, such as Hewlett-Packard's LaserJet, must have each set

Figure 12-9
Changing fonts. (a) Serif fonts have flat strokes ending each line; sans serif fonts do not. (b) Proportionally spaced font characters vary in width while constant-width fonts maintain the same size for each character. (c) Kerned letters are placed closer together than nonkerned.

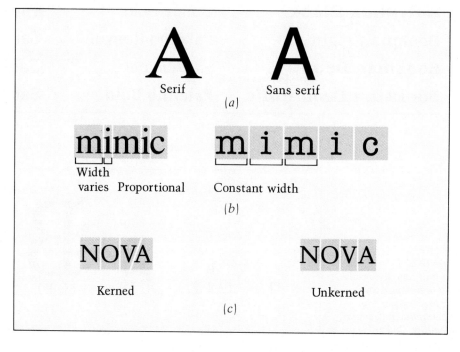

Figure 12-10
Fontasy, a word process-
ing adjunct, provides
control over typestyle
and size directly on the
screen.

of patterns loaded into their memory. This requires the software to use some form of **PRINTER CONTROL LANGUAGE (PCL)** to communicate the desired patterns of letters.

OUTLINED FONTS, on the other hand, are not patterns of dots but are mathematical models that describe the outline, or shape, of each character (see Figure 12-11). Each model can be adjusted in size and orientation to suit any purpose. It can also be modified to create variations of the same font. The flexibility of the outlining approach makes it an ideal, yet more expensive, choice for desktop publishing.

The communication of outlined fonts and layout patterns to the printer is accomplished through the use of a **PAGE DESCRIPTION LANGUAGE (PDL)** that marks changes directly in the text. Page description languages come in two forms: *code-oriented PDL*, where commands are placed directly into the text (as in traditional typesetting); and *WYSIWYG PDL*, where components are manipulated directly on the screen as they will appear in the final version. In the late 1980s, a standard page description language called *PostScript* was introduced. It allows microcomputer programs to directly communicate with appropriately

Figure 12-11
(a) Outline fonts are cre-
ated as smooth lines
based on mathematical
formulas. (b) Bit-mapped
fonts contain set patterns
of dots to form charac-
ters.

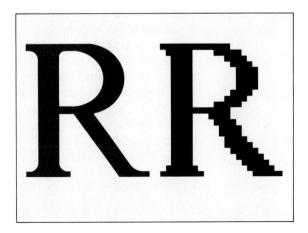

equipped printers, such as Apple's LaserWriter or the Hewlett-Packard LaserJet with add-in memory boards, without having to copy specific sets of typestyles into the printer's memory. The need to configure software to a specific printer was also eliminated. The same program commands could now work on a dot-matrix printer as easily as on a laser printer. They could also drive a professional typesetting machine.

The combination of outlined fonts and PostScript may well become the standard for desktop programs. Software need not contain an extensive collection of separate bit-mapped patterns, and users can switch among different printers. Although more expensive, the flexibility of PDL with outlined fonts greatly outweighs the PCL, bit-mapped approach. Fonts can be used in any size or orientation; new ones can be designed as well. However, both techniques remain viable alternatives for desktop publishing. Either approach will work. It's simply a matter of the application software transmitting the needed bit-maps, or the printer being able to create characters through its own outlined instructions.

Layout

Selecting a text font is only one of many considerations facing a potential desktop publisher. Thought must also be given to the design or *layout* of the entire document—no easy task.

LAYOUT concerns the interplay of text, graphics, and white space—the blank areas of the page (see Figure 12-12a). It includes such factors as paper orientation, which can be *portrait* (vertical) or *landscape* (horizontal), margins, the number and width of columns, and the space between each column (called *gutters*). Layout also includes the vertical spacing between lines, called *leading* (pronounced "ledding"), and the interrelationship among the different sizes and styles of fonts that appear on each page. Users must select font types for headings, subheadings, and text material. They must be concerned with indentations, centering, and margin justification. In addition, they must plan the location and size of graphics. Finally, users must ensure that all the chosen components work well together and that page composition remains consistent from one page to the next. To help users "see" layouts, many programs allow entire pages (or sets of pages) to be shown on the screen in reduced form. A technique called GREEKING—using lines and symbols to represent text and graphics—provides a visual interpretation of the final layout without having to first print it out. Figure 12-12b displays a "greeked" page.

While users can design layouts from scratch for any purpose, many desktop software packages include sample layout forms, or STYLE SHEETS, which have been designed by experts. Style sheets reflect careful attention to white space, proper use of fonts, and a professional interplay of all layout components. These sheets can be used as is or modified and saved as new sheets themselves. Their use significantly reduces the time needed to create documents and can improve the overall appearance of documents. A brief example may help illustrate the ease of using a desktop publisher complete with prepared style sheets.

Figure 12-12
(a) Layout consider-
ations. (b) "Greeking"
uses symbols and lines to
show text and graphics
on a reduced view
layout.

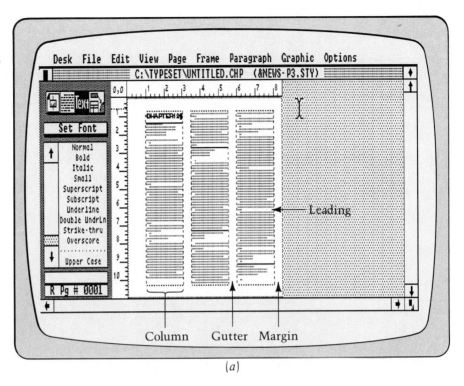

(a)

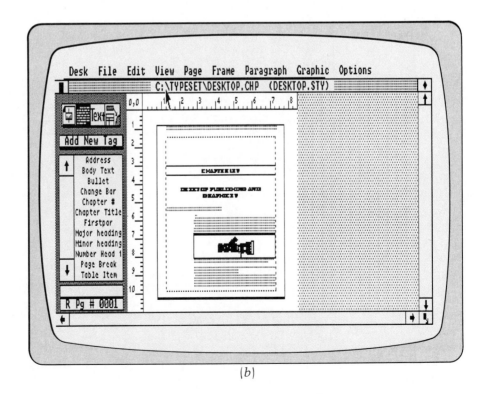

(b)

Figure 12-13
Most desktop publishing programs offer similar workscreens. Compare (a) Xerox's Ventura Publisher with (b) Aldus's PageMaker.

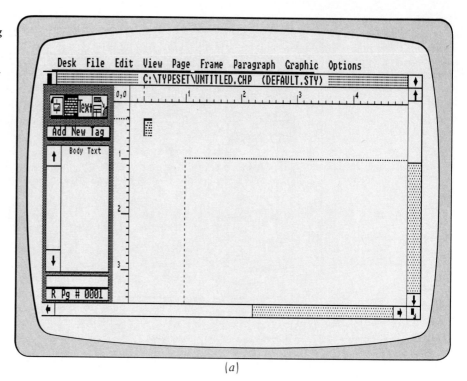

(a)

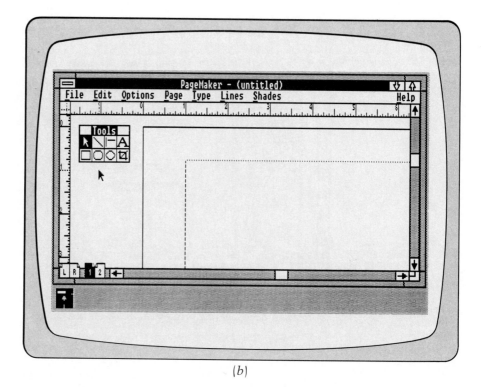

(b)

A trip through a sample publication

We'll first look at a typical modern desktop publisher—Ventura Publisher—used with medium-resolution screen. Assuming we have already installed it on our computer's hard disk, we need only type VP to begin. Within a few moments, a screen similar to Figure 12-13a appears. This is a basic workscreen, similar to most desktop publishing programs. It includes pull-down menus across the top, information boxes at the left, and the document area in the center. Note the workscreen's similarity to Aldus's PageMaker, another powerful desktop publishing program (Figure 12-13b). PageMaker, in fact, began the desktop publishing revolution on the Apple Macintosh, and now offers the same power for IBM-compatibles as well.

At this point, we move our cursor to the FILE selection by using a mouse or pressing cursor keys, and select LOAD DIFF STYLE as shown in Figure 12-14. For our example, we choose a one-column book style sheet.

With a few more menu responses, we load our text file SAMPLE, previously typed in WordPerfect as shown in Figure 12-15a. Of course, the text could have been typed on any one of a half-dozen other popular word processors, or in the desktop publisher itself. The text is immediately brought into the program and appears on the screen as in Figure 12-15b. We have magnified the page to be able to read the text and are now looking at the upper left corner.

Figure 12-14
A style sheet is selected from a menu and brought to the screen. Ruler lines can be added to help plan out the page.

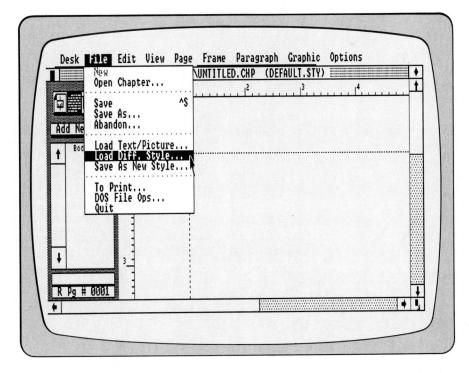

Figure 12-15
Simple text from (a) a
word processor can be
imported directly into
(b) the style sheet.

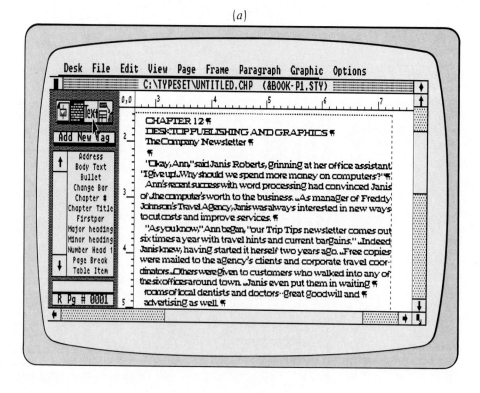

(a)

(b)

All that's left is to mark the text we wish to use for chapter headings, titles, and introduction. The fonts and sizes have been predetermined by the style sheet with *text tags* that assure uniformity throughout the document. In Figure 12-16, we have just marked the chapter title. Of course, we can also edit text on the screen, add underlining, italics, and change text tags if desired—and watch the effect of each change directly on the screen.

We can continue editing and marking text as needed throughout the text. The program will automatically move text from one page to another to match margin and layout requirements.

Finally, we can save our entire style and text back to disk, and print out the results as shown in Figure 12-17. Within a few short minutes, we have transformed our typed material into camera-ready copy! If we are unhappy with the result, we can select another style sheet and repeat the process (probably in less time than we could spell "Johannes Gutenberg").

Combining graphics

Manipulating text fonts and sizes into a pleasing layout is only one facet of desktop publishing. Many times, business users want to combine graphic images—line drawings or photographs—directly into the text material. The approach is almost as simple as using text alone.

First, existing clip art is selected, or new art is prepared with one of many available graphics editing programs (described in detail later in this chapter). Using PageMaker as an example, rectangular areas on the layout sheet, called *frames*, are created to hold the artwork as it is loaded into the program. Graphic images can now be cropped (cut down), reduced, or enlarged to suit the user's purpose (Figure 12-18) and dis-

Figure 12-16
The text can now be marked with "tags" to change its font style and size. Style sheets present options in a convenient menu.

Tag menu

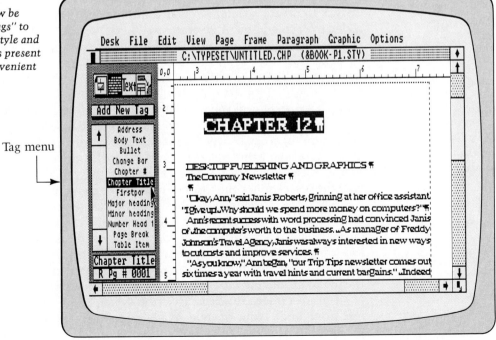

Figure 12-17
The finished page
printed on a laser
printer.

DESKTOP PUBLISHING AND GRAPHICS   ART & INFORMATION MERGE 1

CHAPTER 12

DESKTOP PUBLISHING AND GRAPHICS

The Company Newsletter

"Okay, Ann," said Janis Roberts, grinning at her office assistant. "I give up! Why should we spend more money on computers?" Ann's recent success with word processing had convinced Janis of the computer's worth to the business. As manager of Freddy

Figure 1-1 This picture has nothing to do with Ann's story, but it shows some nice artwork in desktop publishing when printed on a laser.

Johnson's Travel Agency, Janis was always interested in new ways to cut costs and improve services.

"As you know," Ann began, "our Trip Tips newsletter comes out six times a year with travel hints and current bargains." Indeed Janis knew, having started it herself two years ago. Free copies were mailed to the agency's clients and corporate travel coor-

played in their appropriate frames. Powerful desktop publishing programs like PageMaker also allow modifications of the graphic quality of images to create special effects. Captions and figure notations can be added to each graphic if desired.

Depending on the sophistication of the desktop software, text can automatically *flow around* graphic images either outside a rectangular frame or within its borders (see Figure 12-19).

The advantages and drawbacks of desktop publishers

As we have seen, desktop publishing programs are really *page composition* programs. They allow us to create text and graphics material, combine them together in any layout we choose, manipulate them for best effect, and then print out the result. Just like any other computer system, it is the joint capabilities of the computer, printer, software, and *user* that determines the professionalism of the result.

While the desktop publisher could certainly be used as a printing press to create many copies of an original, it is more appropriate to produce one master *camera-ready* copy. This master is then reproduced by less expensive, traditional approaches, such as offset printing. Although reasonable for small quantities, the laser printer, or ENGINE, would be wasted in producing multiple copies of the same page.

The advantages are clear. Desktop systems significantly increase the text, font, and layout options available to business users. They expand the flexibility of design options, provide quick turnaround time, and save the cost of typesetting. They are relatively easy to learn and apply.

Figure 12-18
(a) The original graphic
image (b) can be cropped,
(c) reduced, or (d) en-
larged as needed.

(a)

(b)

(c)

(d)

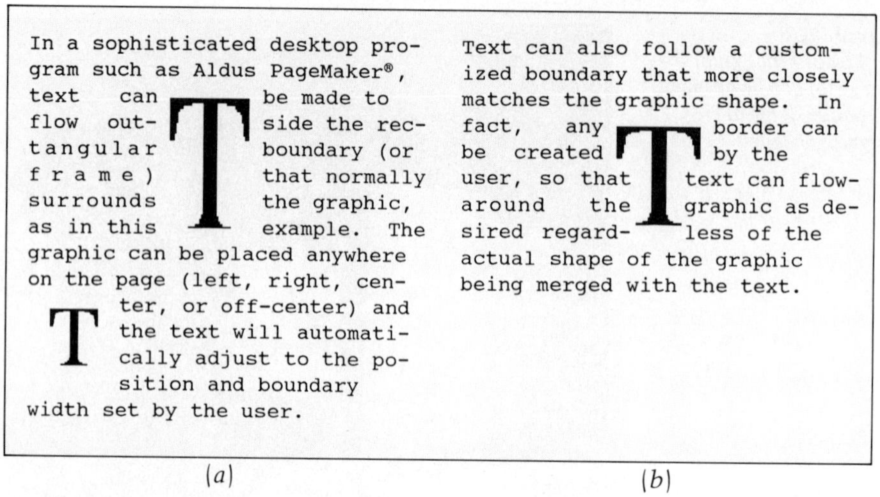

Figure 12-19
Text can flow around graphics (a) outside the graphic's rectangular frame or (b) it can be customized to flow around any shape desired.

In a sophisticated desktop program such as Aldus PageMaker®, text can be made to flow outside the rectangular frame) boundary (or that normally surrounds the graphic, as in this example. The graphic can be placed anywhere on the page (left, right, center, or off-center) and the text will automatically adjust to the position and boundary width set by the user.

Text can also follow a customized boundary that more closely matches the graphic shape. In fact, any border can be created by the user, so that text can flow around the graphic as desired regardless of the actual shape of the graphic being merged with the text.

(a)   (b)

Most importantly, they allow managers to maintain more control over the final product.

Their major disadvantages, however, cannot be overlooked. Their output quality is still inferior (though not by much) to typesetting, a reality imposed by the resolution available with today's printers and software. Desktop publishers will not replace word processing either. It is still easier to type and edit in a word processor first, and then transfer the document to the desktop publisher for final layout. In addition, desktop output is not designed to replace traditional printing for large volume duplication. It is also not appropriate for long, complex documents due to the time involved, labor cost, and the limited life of the laser printer. Color laser printers have recently appeared as a commercial reality, but printing in color is still out of reach for current software—and most budgets.

There are *hidden* disadvantages as well that must be considered. After all, publishing is not merely writing. It is a subtle combination of design, illustration, and information, which is as much an art as it is a science. The "normal" publishing process starts with the writer, but also includes an editor, proofreader, artist, layout specialist, typesetter, and printer. The typical desktop publisher attempts to combine all these talents in one person—the writer. The responsibility is awesome. Not only must the user be an expert copywriter, but must have finely developed layout design skills, an eagle eye for typographical errors, and a familiarity with syntax and word usage. Certainly, the use of word processing proofreaders, spell checkers, grammar programs, and the desktop program's ready-to-use style sheets can assist in this process. Yet, all too often, the quality of material developed in this manner falls short of professionalism, even if the result is nicely printed. Where possible, it is more reasonable to use a *team* approach for desktop publishing, drawing on those who can translate management needs into clear, highly readable, and effective presentations. Users, or even potential users, of desktop publishing would be wise to gain some experience or training in layout and design techniques as well as writing. The box Layout and Copywriting Hints, on page 422, may help you get started.

411

case in point
Is desktop publishing worth the effort?

Bring desktop publishing into an office, and publications managers can immediately toss their XActo knives, rubber cement, and typesetting bills into the nearest circular file. So goes the myth, but is do-it-yourself publishing really that simple?

Not exactly, publication managers say; first you have to put in the hours to learn your system. But once you know what you're doing, desktop publishing lives up to its billing.

"It amazed me," says Ted Hugger, a marketing manager. "I probably spent only a day or two indoctrinating myself in the program, and then I went right into our first publication."

Hugger produces catalogs and price lists, technical manuals and a quarterly newsletter. His company purchased Xerox's Ventura Publisher. "We compiled spending histories on typesetting and printing," says Hugger. "Convincing the company that desktop publishing was where we needed to go was simply a matter of looking at the numbers."

The company wanted compatibility with Microsoft Word, the ability to handle large documents, and a reasonable learning curve. Ventura met all the requirements.

While Hugger has some graphics background, he feels that Ventura's style sheets let almost anyone create presentable documents. He also took a two-day seminar from Xerox to "pick up techniques and shortcuts that might otherwise have taken me months to learn," he remarks.

Rather than buy a laser printer, he turned to a local graphics consultant. "I use Ventura's Copy All feature to save all my files to a disk, and then modem the disk's contents to the consultant, who loads it into his system and outputs it to either an Apple LaserWriter or, for a glossier look, a Linotronic 300 typesetting system," he explains.

While [his company] can now make changes down to the last minute, Hugger calls such freedom a double-edged sword. "Traditional typesetting required greater lead time, and the expense was much greater, so we didn't edit as much as we would have liked. Now, it's a different story. Because there's never an end to people's changes, you have to impose deadlines."

He also cautions against too-widespread use of desktop publishing within a company: "Do you want an engineer you're paying $50,000 to $60,000 a year formatting a document?"

Investment counselor Eric Kobren . . . produces a monthly newsletter and yearly guide to Fidelity mutual funds. Until last year, Kobren would hand hard copy to a typesetter who would then rekey it. That process drastically limited the newsletter's tables and charts. "The numbers may change at the last minute, but you can't redo a complicated graph at the last minute," he says. "I'd stay at the typesetters' until four o'clock in the morning, making changes."

. . . Kobren chose PageMaker as his desktop publisher. After playing with PageMaker for weeks . . . , Kobren rolled up his sleeves to crank out a 160-page guide. . . . "It would have taken an artist hundreds of hours to do these graphs; PageMaker whizzed right through it in two days. I imported Lotus worksheets into Window Graph, created my graphs, wrote the text in *Word*, and then merged the graphs and text into PageMaker.

Kobren now hungers for faster, high-resolution printers. . . . Another drawback, says Kobren, is that he now does more menial tasks. "People pay me hundreds of thousands of dollars for investment advice, and here I am figuring out font sizes. But on the other hand, it takes less time to do it myself than to tell a typesetter what I really want."

Source: Excerpts from the article by Marina Hirsch in *PC WORLD*, May 1988, volume 6, No. 5, pages 218–221. Reprinted by permission of PC World from Volume 6, Issue 5, May 1988, published at 501 Second Street, Suite 600, San Francisco, CA 94107.

Using desktop publishing in the office

Applying desktop publishing to business

Clearly, desktop publishing has its place in the business world. Not only can publication costs and development time be drastically reduced, but many typed documents can be greatly improved in presentation and design with little increase in human effort. The ever-increasing sales of desktop publishing software, clip art, and equipment attest to its growing applications, which can be categorized into two groups: internal and external communications.

Internal communications include such items as memos, reports, analyses, and every type of list and form imaginable—phone lists, personnel lists, inventory lists, client lists, appointment schedules, application forms, promotion forms. Each of these documents could benefit from being presented in a more readable and compact form. While not worth the cost of typesetting, these forms could certainly be developed effectively through desktop publishing.

External communications reap the rewards of desktop publishing more directly. These publications would normally be sent out for typesetting, or would certainly improve the company's image if they were. After all, how many times do clients see businesspeople in person, face-to-face? For most clients and potential customers, the presentation of the printed word is the business's calling card. At times, appearance can be just as important (if not more important) than content. External communications include business letters, invoices, brochures, newsletters, quarterly and annual reports, proposals, reports of findings, advertise-

Figure 12-20
(a) This newsletter was typed. (b) This is the same newsletter after it has been "desktopped."

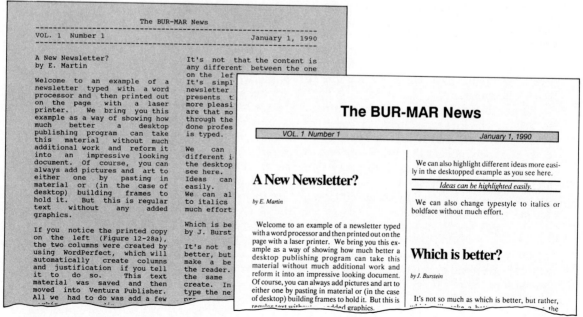

(a)   (b)

ments, as well as such mundane items as sales notices and signs. Why hand-letter signs when professional-looking layouts are possible with merely a few minutes of work at the microcomputer? Why type when you can "desktop"? Compare the impact of the typed newsletter in Figure 12-20a to the same one that has been printed by a desktop publisher (Figure 12-20b).

Expanding desktop power: enter the scanners

At times, we might wish to add original artwork or photographs to our desktop publications. Anything that is not text is called ART. Art can be subdivided into LINE ART, which contains only black lines on a white background, and CONTINUOUS-TONE ART, which contains varying tones of gray. However, the data needed to generate art cannot be entered effectively through a keyboard. Instead, optical scanners were created specifically for this purpose. As we have seen in Chapter 6, scanners digitize art—they convert the brightness patterns of the art into a corresponding numerical pattern. This pattern can then be stored on disk and later merged into desktop publishing documents.

Depending on the sophistication of the scanner and software, these images can range from simple patterns of black-and-white dots (like bit-mapped fonts or basic clip art) to highly sophisticated patterns of gray tones as in a photograph. Did you ever examine newspaper photographs closely? Newspaper photos are prepared through a clever process called HALFTONES, where different sizes and shapes of black dots create the illusion of many different shades of gray as seen in Figure 12-21. Digitizing is the computer equivalent of this process. Once the pattern of black dots on a white background is created, it can easily be printed with any number of gray tones desired. The human eye does not see the pattern, but rather a combination of blacks, grays, and whites. By restricting the number of gray tones allowed, *posterized* effects can be produced as in Figure 12-22.

Figure 12-21
(a) A photograph half-tone. (b) A close-up view of a halftone clearly reveals the pattern of dots.

Scanners (as discussed in Chapter 6) can greatly expand the graphics capabilities of desktop systems. *Movable scanners* are inexpensive add-

Figure 12-22
Posterizing is an effect achieved by restricting graytones to a small number. Aldus Page-Maker allows users to al-ter images to achieve posterized effects di-rectly on the screen.

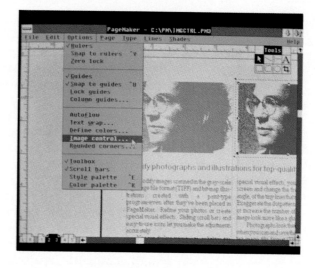

ons to existing dot-matrix printers. *Desktop scanners*, resembling small copying machines, can produce much higher quality images than the movable scanners. Because of their increased resolution, they are more useful to computer systems that employ lasers for final print. *Flatbed scanners*, the most sophisticated optical input devices, scan entire pages at once, often achieving resolutions in excess of 2000 dots per inch. These machines find application in more graphics-oriented businesses such as advertising and engineering.

Other graphics applications

Business's need for graphics does not end with the printed page. Other graphics-oriented software has been developed to respond to the need for computer-generated visual material, some of which will never appear in printed form. Instead, these visuals may be used as overhead transparencies, 35-mm slides, videotape, film, and of course, paper. The remainder of this chapter briefly examines each of these graphic forms, including *animation, analytical graphics, presentation graphics, computer-aided design,* and *graphics editors.*

Computer art for art's sake

Animation, images in motion, has developed into an effective method of communication. Many movies, from *Star Wars* to *Flight of the Navigator*, owe their existence to the ability of computers to create the illusion of reality. In business, graphic animation enables users to effectively highlight facts and demonstrate trends. Animation programs can emphasize specific facts and concepts in ways that still images cannot. They can focus attention on specific points through both color and movement, or withhold data until a dramatic point in a visual script. Output from such programs can also be saved on videotape. In this way, presentations can be designed, produced, and recorded with computers, but played back through ordinary audiovisual equipment.

Perhaps a more striking use occurs in dynamic computer SIMULA-TION, where users interact directly with the computer program and view the immediate consequences of their actions on the screen. One of the most successful microcomputer simulations has been Microsoft's Flight Simulator. Though not a business program, it allowed many desk-bound executives to vicariously experience the thrill of flight and the mishaps of crash landings, while learning geography, navigation, and cockpit instrumentation firsthand. There are easily over 100 flight simulators currently on the market, providing simulations for everything from helicopters to the F-16 supersonic jet. Graphic business-oriented simulations have been used effectively in interactive training and decision-making, providing insight into problems and situations that change according to the user's responses.

Graphs and trends

Examine the data in Figure 12-23a. How would you characterize sales? How easy was it to make a decision? Now look at the same data reflected in Figure 12-23b. It is immediately apparent that sales have increased over time. The difference between the two charts is that the columnar data in the first has been transformed with analytical graphics to create the second.

ANALYTICAL GRAPHICS are simple, low-resolution presentations of numerical data. They are typically used for in-house decision-making, and are not distributed outside the business. As we've seen in Chapter

Figure 12-23
A comparison of numer-ical data and graphics.
(a) Columnar data. (b)
The same data presented
graphically.

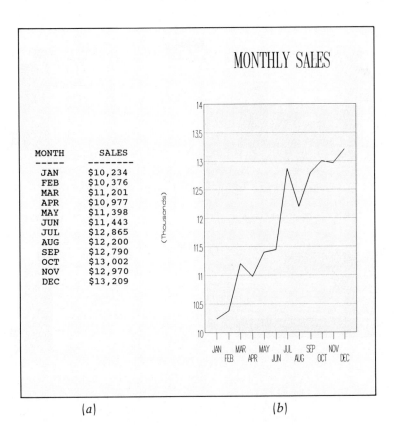

MONTH	SALES
JAN	$10,234
FEB	$10,376
MAR	$11,201
APR	$10,977
MAY	$11,398
JUN	$11,443
JUL	$12,865
AUG	$12,200
SEP	$12,790
OCT	$13,002
NOV	$12,970
DEC	$13,209

(a)   (b)

10, the more powerful spreadsheet programs (such as Lotus 1-2-3 and Microsoft Excel) integrate spreadsheets and graphics, providing the capability to produce analytical graphics directly from columnar data. Analytical graphics allow the creation of graphs, pictorial representations of data, that promote easy comparisons of data and investigations of trends. The major types of graphs include *bar graphs*, *line graphs*, and *pie charts*. Each has its own purpose and strengths:

■ **BAR GRAPHS** are useful for making visual comparisons among different values. As Figure 12-24 (created with Quattro) shows, whether they are oriented vertically (called *columns*, Figure 12-24a) or horizontally (Figure 12-24b), bar graphs make it easy to see maximum and minimum values and make comparisons among any of the values displayed. In this example, salesperson A sold the most, B sold the least. We can also see that D sold almost twice that of C. Bar graphs can include more than one set of data (Figure 12-24c) or provide *grids* (Figure 12-24d) for easier reading.

■ **LINE GRAPHS** provide visual insight into trends. They allow users to view a series of values along a time continuum. Figure 12-25a (created with Lotus 1-2-3) traces the historical pattern of sales for salesperson A. Of course, additional data and grids can be added (as in bar graphs) for comparisons and improved readability. Figure 12-25b has added salespersons B and C as well. *Area graphs* (frequency polygons) are related to line graphs but may smooth out curves and shade in the area under the line for comparison and easy reading.

Figure 12-24
Bar graphs produced with Quattro. (a) Vertical bar (column). (b) Horizontal bar. (c) Multiple data. (d) Horizontal grids added.

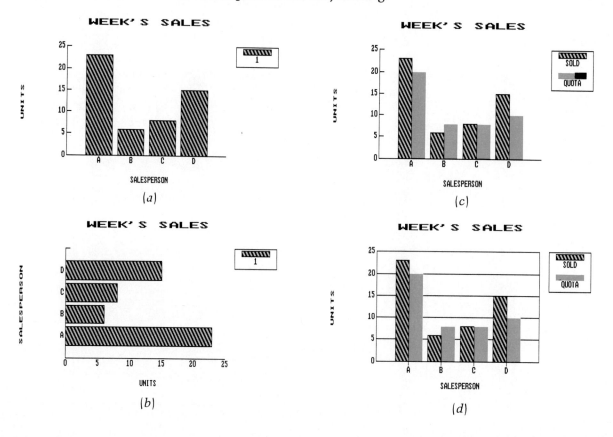

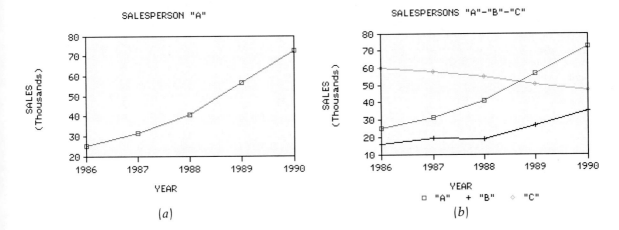

Figure 12-25
Line graphs produced
with Lotus 1-2-3. (a) One
set of data displays
trends. (b) Comparisons
can be made with two or
more sets of data.

■ **PIE CHARTS** compare the relative contributions of each value to the whole. Each value is expressed as a "piece of the pie" and can then be judged visually in relation to the size of the other pieces. Unlike bar or line graphs, however, pie charts limit their scope to one set of values at a time. Figure 12-26a (created by Excel) shows salesperson A was clearly the main contributor to sales, while D was the least. The **EXPLODED PIE CHART**, as shown in Figure 12-26b, is an enhancement that highlights data of particular interest.

Other analytic graphics include *scatter diagrams* that display the correlation between two sets of data, and *hi-lo graphs* that use vertical lines to depict differences between maximum and minimum values.

A quick graph creation
Most spreadsheet programs can create analytical graphics directly from their data. Let's follow the procedure to create a graph in Lotus 1-2-3, assuming we have already created the worksheet in Figure 12-27a. Start the graph menu by pressing /G. Next, select a graph type (TB for a BAR

Figure 12-26
Pie charts in Excel. (a) A
typical pie chart. (b) An
"exploded" pie chart for
emphasis.

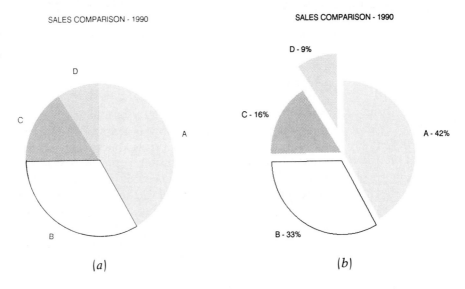

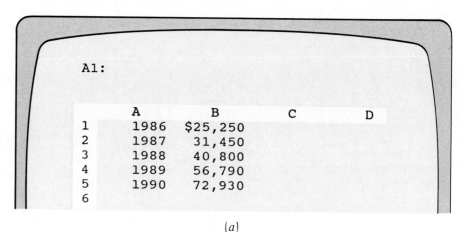

(a)

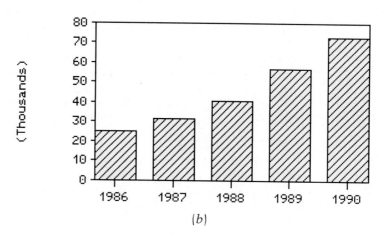

(b)

graph). Now, select the data to be shown on the horizontal (*X*) axis (with XA1.A5 <ENTER>), and the vertical (*Y*) axis (with AB1.B5 <ENTER>). The final step is to view the graph by pressing V as shown in Figure 12-27b. Less than 1 minute from start to finish! Of course, we could now add such options as titles and grids with a few more keystrokes. We could also add new data, or adjust any of the settings until completely satisfied with the display. Graph types could also be changed from bar to line or pie, with two keystrokes. How long would it take you to do that by hand? How neat would it be?

A business picture
is worth a thousand
words . . .

Not content with the simplicity of analytical graphics, software developers have extended the sophistication of such graphs to a higher art form known as **PRESENTATION GRAPHICS**. According to the market research firm Desktop Presentations, personal computer software for desktop presentations is expected to increase at an annual rate of 24 percent through 1992. Two desktop presentation programs were introduced in the late 1980s and became highly successful: Microsoft Chart and BoeingGraph, which greatly expanded the art of graphics presentation. As seen in Figure 12-28, these programs offer users an amazing palette of predesigned graph forms, fonts, and an endless variety of per-

career box
The corporate artist

For many years, businesses have relied on artistic specialists, both inside and outside the company, for assistance in the production of printed communication. Brochures, newsletters, and advertisements must be visually appealing as well as carefully worded. Copywriters and editors are concerned with the written text, but it is the graphic artist who must deal with layout and design. Although the wide-spread use of desktop publishing and presentation software will certainly tempt many corporate copywriters to try their hands at graphic layout, it will also increase the need for graphic specialists, either as corporate employees or free-lance consultants, as more businesses seek higher quality publications.

Graphic design occupations can be divided into three general classifications of applied artists with varying skill, responsibility, and compensation. All should have some background in principles of design, layout, art, mechanical drawing, and, of course, specific knowledge of computerized desktop publication systems.

At the lower level, *layout artists* design eye-catching but functional arrangements of type and illustrations; *paste-up artists* prepare the material for actual duplication, known as camera-ready "mechanicals." Desktop systems will probably combine these two functions in one person, since layout (and paste-up) will be done directly on the screen.

At the higher level, skilled artists with management aspirations may ultimately serve as *art directors*, who create, or supervise the creation of, effective visual material (such as brochures, advertisements, story boards, slides, videotape, and overhead transparencies).

Opportunities in corporate design occupations are expected to exhibit continued growth through the 1990s as businesses increase their need for communication with visual appeal.

The opportunities for free-lance layout/paste-up artists, especially those with working knowledge of desktop publishing systems, are also good. Business copywriters can create text with on-site word processing, but many will still seek outside experts to design and produce the final product. Those graphic artists who can incorporate word processing files directly into desktop publishing systems can offer their clients various design layouts, easy revision, and update capabilities faster and easier than manual methods allow.

Computer knowledge is not sufficient by itself. The successful corporate (or free-lance) artist must have appropriate artistic and design skills first, with supplemental skills in the use of a sophisticated desktop publishing program.

Figure 12-28
Microsoft Chart provides an enormous range of possibilities for presentation graphics.

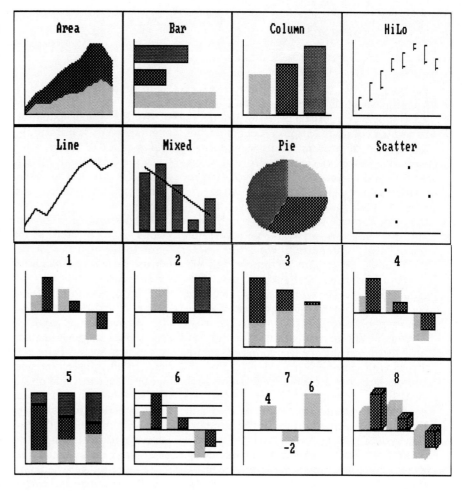

Figure 12-29
Art can be merged with graphs for more dramatic presentations.

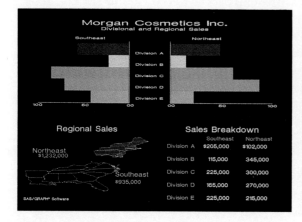
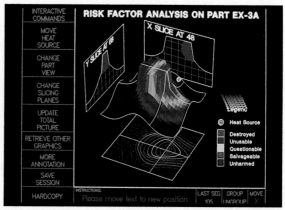

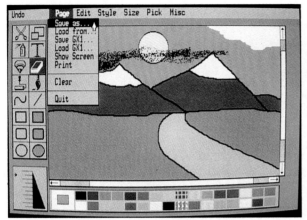

(a)

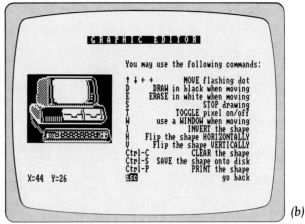

(b)

Figure 12-30
(a) Microsoft's Paint-brush pull-down menus aid selection. (b) A graphics editor in progress.

spectives and orientations. These programs also provide various fonts for titles and labels to further enhance the clarity of each graph. In addition, BoeingGraph can display data in three dimensions at once. Other presentation programs allow the addition of clip art, as in Figure 12-29, for more dramatic charts. Images created by desktop presentation programs can be saved to disk for later recall, photographed onto 35mm slides, or drawn by plotters on paper or overhead transparencies (in color if the plotter is so equipped). Of course, the images can be output to standard laser printers as well.

For users who wish to create their own graphic images, or modify others, *graphic editors*, such as Microsoft's Paintbrush are available. In such programs (see Figure 12-30), the user is presented with a visual "toolbox" of options: colors, shapes, patterns, and fonts. Typically used with a mouse, the graphic artist can select shapes, draw freehand, erase, and label, to create additional bit-mapped graphics. These can then be stored on disk, displayed, printed, or included in other graphics programs. Many desktop publishing users create their own clip art with graphic editors. They draw company emblems (called *logos*) or other art, save the results on a disk file, and then load them into a graphic frame when desired in a particular layout.

Computer-aided design (CAD)

The graphics revolution has certainly not ignored companies that rely on graphics for their success. Desktop publishing and presentation has appealed to most businesses, especially those in advertising and promotion. Yet some applications require a higher degree of graphical sophistication. Architects, automobile designers, scientists, and engineers have turned to **COMPUTER-AIDED DESIGN (CAD)** for their high-resolution needs. CAD systems are usually much more expensive than regular computer systems, requiring hardware and software capable of much higher speeds and resolution than that required by desktop publishing or presentation graphics. As Figure 12-31 shows, the results are equally impressive. Objects can be designed, modified, rotated, and viewed at any angle. The computer can also be used to create three-dimensional "solid" representations of any object or form, whether it is real or simply in the designer's mind.

Layout and copywriting tips

The use of a desktop publisher does not automatically guarantee success. It is still the human who must carefully plan the most effective wording and layouts. At our request, Alan Friedenthal, a direct marketing consultant based in New York City, offered these guidelines for improving the eloquence and impact of your printed message. Of course, all rules have their exceptions—experience and skill will tell you when to make them.

1. Always use captions to explain or enhance the meaning of photos or illustrations.
2. Never end a page of an article, letter, or story that continues onto another page, with the end of a sentence. Instead, end the page at a provocative point in the *middle* of the sentence so that the reader will be "forced" to turn the page.
3. A few words about typeface: For long blocks of copy, always use serif type. It enhances readability. Sans serif type is extremely difficult to read for long periods of time. For letters and correspondence, always use a traditional typewriter typeface—it's warmer and more reader-friendly.
4. Try to leave white space between paragraphs. Long stretches of uninterrupted copy turn off readers. The text is uninviting to read.
5. Do use subheads, **boldface**, highlighting, underscoring, dashes, and *italics*, to break up text, making it more stimulating to the reader's eye. This also allows for quick skimming of copy. A subhead in the middle or near the end of the material might get read by a skimmer who might never otherwise have read the entire text. By catching their attention, there is a good chance they will go back and read from the beginning.
6. Be careful with rule #5. If you try to emphasize everything, you'll end up emphasizing nothing.
7. Studies have shown that the human eye tends to look at a page layout in a "lazy-S" pattern. The eye starts at the upper right, moves to the left, then down to the right, and then finally across to the left.
8. A good rule of thumb regarding text size—the larger the point size, the wider the columns should be. Large type looks very awkward in a narrow column.
9. Try to avoid hyphenating words. Keep them to a minimum. If you have hyphenated words at the end of two or more successive lines, try to add, delete, or change a word, so the lines "break" better.
10. Put the words or thoughts you want remembered at the *end* of the sentence. People tend to remember the last thing they read.
11. If you must "reverse-out" type (white type on a dark background) keep the type big and the information short. NEVER reverse-out a coupon. People will not be able to fill it out. (It's surprising how many professionals violate this rule.)
12. Try to use no more than three different typefaces on a page. More than three detracts from the message and confuses the reader. Note that a change in type size should be considered a different typeface.
13. Readers tend not to read headlines that ask a question they can answer "No" to. (Not necessarily a hard and fast rule.)
14. A standard: Do not allow "widows" or "orphans" on a page. A widow is a paragraph that is missing its last line; an orphan is a line by itself.
15. Text with a justified left margin is easier to read than text with a left margin that is "ragged." Keep this in mind when "flowing" text around illustrations.

Figure 12-31
An example of a CAD
application.

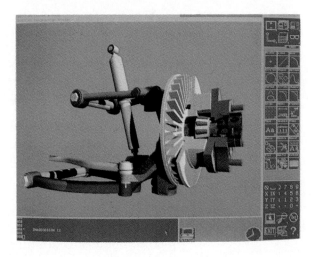

Using graphics
effectively

As in desktop publishing, computer use does not ensure effective graphics presentations. For example, color can highlight important data, such as in a computer-enhanced graphic medical display. Studies have shown that red stands out more than blue. Red-colored material tends to draw attention, while blue-colored material stays in the background. Yet, overuse of color can lead to viewer confusion. The effective use of graphics is an art that can be improved through training and practice.

SEE—a mnemonic for Simplify, Emphasize, and Equalize—expresses one approach to designing effective graphic presentations:

- *Simplify*. Keep graphics simple. Presentations that attempt to convey too many facts or ideas, or use intricate designs, only complicate the points you are trying to make.
- *Emphasize*. Place proper emphasis on those data that are most important, but don't overdo it. Careful and restrained use of color, pointers, or art can draw attention to key points in your presentation. Emphasizing everything emphasizes nothing.
- *Equalize*. There should be an equilibrium achieved among the components in a graphic—images, colors, and sizes. As in other art forms, proper balance among graphic components will encourage viewers to examine the display and draw attention to highlights; poorly planned charts will only distract from your message.

The "death of desktop"—a final thought
It is clear that the current distinctions made among word processing, desktop publishing, and presentation graphics programs will soon die out. It is likely that all three will merge into one *business presentation software* package encompassing text entry and editing, desktop publishing, and presentation graphics. Newer versions of Word, WordStar, and WordPerfect have already begun this trend by incorporating the basic font and layout capabilities of desktop publishers. Advertisements for a recent release of WordStar used the term *word publishing* to express this merger. In the near future, we can look to fully integrated text/graphics software that will simplify the publishing process.

Yet, the increased power offered by such programs places more emphasis on the artistic training and skills of potential users. Certainly, text and graphics software are wonderful tools that can significantly enhance the variety and effectiveness of business communication, and the ease with which they are produced. However, we must remember that like an artist's brush, they can just as easily produce junk as masterpieces. It is still the *human* who must creatively apply these tools and who is held accountable for their end product. The ease afforded by technology does not eliminate our responsibility for its use—in fact, it places higher demands on our skills and vigilance.

summary

■ Desktop publishing effectively joins typing and typesetting by using microcomputers to combine text and graphics into a professional-looking layout.

■ Desktop publishing can be subdivided into three quality levels: draft, publication, and professional. Higher levels offer more sophisticated techniques, higher resolution, and better printed output.

■ Typesetting is a tedious process that involves typing, editing, copy editing, and the review of galley and page proofs, before final copy can be produced.

■ Desktop publishing systems significantly improve the typesetting process by eliminating the need to retype, providing direct control over design and layout, and increasing the flexibility for redesign and modification.

■ A font is a specific style of type, which can vary in size, width, and complexity. Font size is expressed in points.

■ Fonts can be compressed, expanded, italicized, underlined, and boldfaced. They can be designed with serifs—flat strokes at the end of each edge—or sans serif. They can also be kerned for easier readability.

■ Fonts can be created by bit-mapping (a dot pattern) or outlining (a shape formula). Bit-mapped fonts require a printer control language (PCL) to communicate with the printer. Outlined fonts use a page description language (PDL), which can be code oriented or WYSIWYG (What You See Is What You Get).

■ Layout involves the composition of the completed page. It details the relationship among fonts, margins, columns, and spacing. Predesigned style sheets can be used to simplify the layout process.

■ Anything that is not text is considered to be art. Art includes line art—black lines on white, and continuous-tone art—with varying shades of gray. The process of halftoning is useful for recording gray tones.

■ Other graphic applications include animation and simulation, analytical graphics, presentation graphics, computer-aided design, and graphics editors.

■ Analytical graphics make use of simple forms such as bar graphs, line graphs, and pie charts.

■ Effective techniques for graphics production include simplicity of design, emphasis of key points, and equilibrium of components.

wrap-up

The power of the press

An eerie quiet filled Janis Roberts' office, as she and her assistant, Ann, stared expectantly at the laser printer in the corner. Any moment now, the first page of the new *Trip Tips* newsletter would quietly emerge from the laser printer into its receiving tray on top. Ann, used to the loud "rat-a-tat" clatter of her dot-matrix printer, found the laser's silence a bit unsettling. The blinking light on the front of the printer was the only indication that data were being transferred from the desktop program to the printer's memory. Ann knew that it took a few seconds for the page layout and font instructions to be completed. Even so, her eagerness to see the newsletter made the short delay seem like an eternity. For Ann, the old adage, "a watched pot never boils," had been updated to "a watched laser never prints!"

Ann's thoughts drifted back 2 days earlier when the desktop publishing software had been installed in her microcomputer. In the short time since then, Ann had learned enough from the desktop publishing tutorial supplied in the documentation to try it out on the newsletter. First, she had selected a two-column style sheet complete with fonts for masthead, headings, bylines, and articles. She especially liked the vertical lines that separated each column of text. She then copied articles from her word processing disk files directly into the style sheet and watched them appear on the screen. Next she marked off areas for headings and graphic frames, and filled the frames with drawings of planes and ships from a special clip art disk. Of course, some photographs still had to be pasted in by hand, but she had learned how to leave space for those, too. As a final precaution, Ann reviewed the page once more, adding captions, creating page numbering footers, and correcting any glaring errors in the spacing or text. The screen image looked great, but Ann couldn't wait to see the finished print. Janis' voice interrupted her thoughts.

"Here it is!" exclaimed Janis as she took the page from the printer's tray. "It's wonderful! Everything's sharp and neat. If I didn't see it myself, I'd never suspect this came from our equipment. It looks as good as typeset."

Ann was impressed, too. It looked even better than the screen led her to expect. The page looked as if it had come off a printing press. The justification and layout was as good as the $40 typeset ones.

"We're in business!" said Ann. "Now, we can add the remaining text and art. I can even design a Freddy Johnson Travel Agency logo for the masthead with my graphics editor. We have total control over the newsletter. We can change material right up to the time we have to take it to the printer for copying and folding. No more delays. No more typesetting fees!"

"And," added Janis, "no more photocopied inserts!"

key terms

These are the key terms in alphabetical order. The numbers in parentheses refer to the page on which each term is defined.

Analytical graphics (415)
Art (413)
Bar graph (416)
Bit-mapped font (400)
Clip art (396)
Computer-aided design (CAD) (421)
Continuous-tone art (413)
Desktop publishing (392)
Engine (408)
Exploded pie chart (417)
Greeking (402)
Halftone (413)
Kerning (400)
Layout (402)
Line art (413)
Line graph (416)
Outlined font (401)
Page description language (PDL) (401)
Pie chart (417)
Presentation graphics (418)
Printer control language (PCL) (401)
Simulation (415)
Style sheet (402)

review questions

objective questions

True/false. *Put the letter T or F on the line next to the question.*

1. Typesetting has greatly expanded the art of personal communication.   1 _____
2. Personal publishing is an example of the draft quality level of desktop publishing.   2 _____
3. Most businesses require the use of professional quality microcomputer systems.   3 _____
4. Fonts can be "kerned" to increase their size on the printed page.   4 _____
5. Bit-mapped fonts require the use of a page description language to communicate with the printer.   5 _____
6. Rectangular areas on the layout sheet that hold graphics are called frames.   6 _____
7. Anything that is not text is considered art.   7 _____
8. The process of converting graphic images into numerical patterns is called sampling.   8 _____
9. Scanners convert numerical data into images.   9 _____
10. Analytical graphics require a higher degree of resolution than presentation graphics.   10 _____

Multiple choice. *Put the letter of the correct answer on the line next to the question.*

1. Using microcomputers to combine text and graphics to produce printed output is known as   1 _____
    (a) Desktop presentation.
    (b) Scanning.
    (c) Optical character recognition.
    (d) Desktop publishing.
2. The resolution of most dot-matrix printers is about   2 _____
    (a) 100 dpi.
    (b) 300 dpi.
    (c) 1000 dpi.
    (d) 2000 dpi.

3. The last step in the typesetting process is
   (a) Typesetting the material.
   (b) Printing page proofs.
   (c) Copyediting the text.
   (d) Typing the text.
4. Which one of these is *not* an advantage of desktop publishing over typesetting?
   (a) The elimination of most retyping.
   (b) Improved print resolution.
   (c) Increased user control over layout.
   (d) Increased flexibility for modification.
5. A laser printer is also called
   (a) An engine.
   (b) A dot-matrix printer.
   (c) A typesetter.
   (d) A scanner.

Fill in the blank. *Write the correct word or words in the blank to complete the sentence.*

1. Graphic images available on computer disk for use with desktop systems are called _____.
2. Desktop systems that offer reasonably good resolution for laser output are referred to as _____ quality systems.
3. Font size is measured in _____.
4. Fonts can be generated through _____ or _____.
5. _____ are predesigned layouts offered with some desktop publishing programs.
6. Art that contains gray tones is called _____.
7. _____ is a process that creates printable newspaper photographs.
8. The highest resolution can be found in _____ scanners.
9. Graphics programs that allow users to immediately see the consequences of their actions are called _____ programs.
10. _____ use simple, low-resolution graphics.

short answer questions

When answering these questions, think of concrete examples to illustrate your points.

1. What is a desktop publisher?
2. What is the difference between code-oriented and WYSIWYG page description languages?
3. Name the three quality levels of desktop publishing.
4. Describe the purpose of galleys in typesetting.
5. What is a font?
6. What is a style sheet?
7. Why is line art easier to scan than continuous-tone art?

essay questions

1. Compare and contrast the three basic types of analytical graphics in terms of appearance and purpose.
2. What do we gain by using desktop publishing over typesetting? What do we give up?
3. Describe the differences between bit-mapped fonts and outlined fonts. Which is preferable in business?
4. What is the difference between desktop publishing and desktop presentation software?
5. Why do the authors feel that desktop publishing will soon "die out"?

Answers to the objective questions
True/false: 1. F; 2. T; 3. F; 4. F; 5. F; 6. T; 7. T; 8. F; 9. F; 10. F
Multiple choice: 1. d; 2. a; 3. b; 4. b; 5. a
Fill in the blank: 1. clip art; 2. publication; 3. points; 4. bit-map, outline; 5. style sheets; 6. continuous-tone art; 7. halftones; 8. flatbed; 9. simulators; 10. analytical graphics

part four

Creating business information systems

We have come a long way in this book, and in a sense have now reached the point of it all. Part One introduced basic information systems concepts, and Parts Two and Three examined in more depth the roles of hardware and productivity software in the information system. Now we turn to the information systems themselves. Chapter 13 describes how information systems are developed and changed. Next, Chapter 14 takes a look at programming and how the concepts of structured design are applied to create today's programs. Chapter 15 describes the programming languages in which software are written and the system software that enables other programs to work. Chapter 16 explores the application and design of distributed processing systems. Finally, the important topics of security, ethics, and privacy are discussed in Chapter 17.

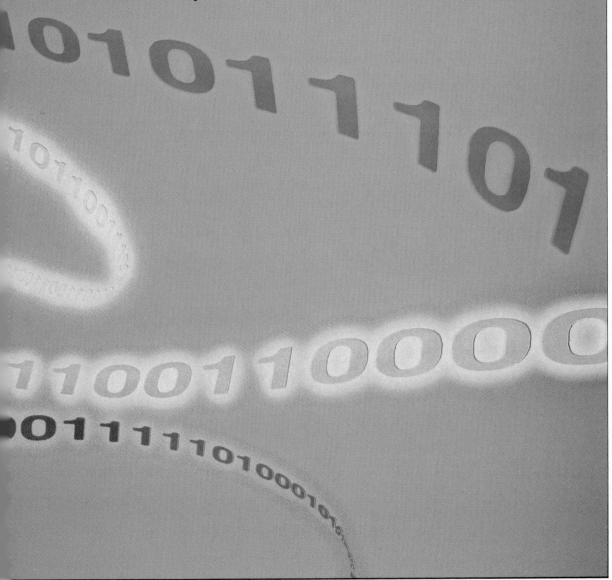

The system development process: a structured approach

After studying this chapter you should understand the following:

- *How the traditional and structured approaches to system development differ.*
- *The six steps that comprise the system development process.*
- *The main tasks of the systems analyst during the detailed investigation.*
- *The steps that are followed during the system design stage.*
- *The four methods for converting from an old to a new system.*

chapter 13

Chilled molasses

Susan Paul, vice-president of marketing at Paul's House of Electronic Wonders, entered the executive conference room next to the office of her brother—the firm's owner—Philip Paul. Ed Wieland, a systems analyst at the firm, was already there talking to Philip Paul.

"Hi Phil. Hello Ed," Susan said. "The reason I wanted the three of us to meet is to get to work solving a problem."

Philip turned to Ed. "Susan and I are worried about lost sales."

Ed picked up his pen. "What's causing sales to be lost?" he asked.

"We don't know for sure," Susan said. "That's where you come in."

"Is there any sort of pattern on the kinds of sales lost?" Ed asked.

"Low-volume customers," Philip said.

Susan nodded. "Small customers try us once or twice and then go elsewhere."

"Interesting," Ed said. "Any idea why?"

"Shipping and receiving is slower than molasses poured over a polar ice cap," Philip said.

Susan gave her brother a mock punch in the shoulder. "Opinions vary. I think the shipping and receiving department does just fine. As sales manager I personally keep my eye on them. But the purchasing department seems to let the stock levels deplete on some items, so that shipping has nothing to ship."

Ed scribbled furiously for a moment longer, and then looked up. "All right," he said. "The problem is that sales to small customers are being lost, because orders are being shipped too slowly to the satisfy the customers. You think the cause for slow shipment might be in shipping and receiving or in purchasing."

"Right," Susan said.

"There's more to the problem," Philip said.

"There usually is more," Ed said with a smile.

"We want to enter the mail-order business," Philip said.

"Mail orders mean more small customers, right?" Ed asked.

"You've got it," Susan said.

"Do I have your OK to launch a preliminary investigation of the small order problem?" Ed asked.

"I'll give the OK to you in writing today," Philip said. "And I'll notify the managers of the areas in question with a written note that you will be meeting with them soon and conducting investigations with their people, so they will not be surprised."

"Excellent," Ed said. "I would like to report back to you in 2 weeks to discuss my preliminary findings."

"That sounds fine," Philip said, as he rose to end the meeting.

Structured system development

Ed Wieland has just launched a study of one aspect of Mr. Paul's business. In this section we examine the stages in the system development process, and the structured system development techniques Ed might use. We will also observe the role of people in the system development process, and review criticisms of the structured approach.

The system development process

Recall from Chapter 2 that a SYSTEM is a set of interrelated elements working together toward a common goal. Within a business, the accounting department, personnel department, and sales department are systems—and at a higher level so is the business itself. At Paul's House of Electronic Wonders, the order-fulfillment process can be viewed as a system that crosses departmental lines, involving shipping and receiving, purchasing, and other departments.

All systems go through a process of birth, growth, maturity, decline, and perhaps rebirth. The SYSTEM DEVELOPMENT PROCESS is a method for studying and changing systems as they go through these changes. Other terms used for the same process are *structured system development process*, *system life cycle*, and *system development life cycle*.

The system development process has six stages. In order of occurrence, they are:

1. Problem recognition
2. Systems analysis
3. System design
4. System acquisition
5. System implementation
6. System maintenance

As we saw in the opening example, Paul's House of Electronic Wonders was losing small orders. The first two stages have already been encountered. The *problem recognition* stage corresponds to Susan Paul and Philip Paul realizing this. By giving Ed Wieland permission to begin studying the problem, Philip Paul launches the second stage of the process, *systems analysis*. If all goes well, the process will continue through the remaining stages, resulting in a functioning system that solves the problems.

Structured system development techniques

STRUCTURED SYSTEM DEVELOPMENT TECHNIQUES refer to a set of techniques and methods for studying and designing systems in order to make them simple to use, easy to understand, and easy to change. These techniques include a top-down approach and modular design.

Structured system development techniques evolved from earlier methods to control the haphazard analysis and design methods once common in the data processing industry. In the 1970s, people came to recognize the value of structured methods in reducing the overall costs of a system throughout its useful life.

The two main goals of the system development process are detecting errors as early as possible in the process cycle, and simplifying the maintenance or modification of the system using structured techniques. In both cases, development and maintenance costs are reduced in comparison to the earlier, less-structured methods.

In structured system development, analysts relate the parts of a system to one another following a top-down approach. With a TOP-DOWN APPROACH a solution is planned starting with an overall design at the general level, and then is broken down into the specific details of the solution. This approach is similar to the way an architect would design a building, moving from a general blueprint to specific detailed ones for each room.

The system solution is broken up into MODULES, which are self-contained subparts of a system and are easier to understand and maintain. The quality of a module depends on its level of internal cohesiveness and how closely it is coupled to other modules. A modules with high internal COHESION performs a single function which is well defined and simple, such as "verify invoice" or "prepare daily inventory totals." A module with loose external COUPLING can be taken out, modified, or replaced without substantially affecting other modules, just like a kitchen or bathroom can be remodeled without tearing down the complete house. We can think of modules as building blocks. The best types of modules are highly cohesive and loosely coupled; the worst are highly coupled low cohesion ones.

It is easier to correct errors in a system made up of modules than one that is not, because only one module may be involved and hence only one may need to be changed. Just as fixing a plumbing connection in a kitchen should not affect the pipes in the bathroom, the same applies to modifying or expanding a system—the changes can be isolated to certain modules, and the rest of the system remains unaffected, reducing the risk of damaging perfectly good working modules.

The role of people in the system development process

The *user* takes an active role with the structured approach, and is viewed as the controlling partner contributing to and eventually evaluating the stages in the system development process (see Figure 13-1). The user comes to the systems analyst with the problem, and continues to work with the information system team to analyze the problem and design, acquire, and implement the solution. The developing system is constantly checked against user needs, and can have its development halted at any stage if it deviates too far from them. The active role played by users permits the detection and correction of errors and other misunderstandings early in the system development process. The earlier an error is found and corrected, the lower the cost of doing so (see Figure 13-2). Systems that emerge from the structured approach have a strong likelihood of actually accomplishing what they are supposed to accomplish. The structured systems that result are easier for information system staff members to modify and maintain.

For *managers* of system development projects, structured methods provide useful management control techniques in the following areas:

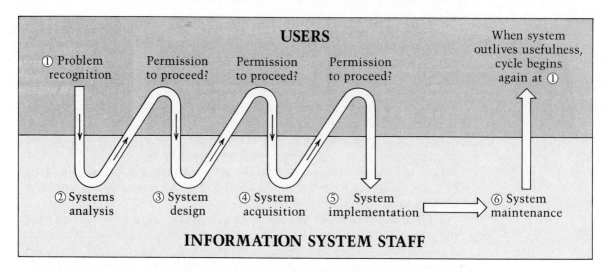

Figure 13-1
The structured approach
to the system develop-
ment process.

- Assigning analysts reasonably sized tasks.
- Assuring analysts use standard methods.
- Determining task accountability and responsibility.
- Helping limit problems caused by employee turnover.

Systems analysts prefer the structured approach with its clearly defined job tasks and accountability and offers of support services where required.

By comparison, in the less-structured approach, users initiate the system development process, but do not participate greatly in its development. As a result a system may be created that does not meet the user's needs. The user comes with a problem to the systems analyst. The systems analyst—working with other information system specialists, but in isolation from the user—eventually presents the final product to the user. Users—and sometimes analysts' own managers—are treated as outsiders whose views would only clutter up the system development process. If the user does not like the delivered system, he or she is free to reject it (often at great expense). And the manager would be responsible for the failed project.

It may seem incredible to you that a real-world business could work this way. When computers were new to businesses, however, nearly all firms followed this less-structured approach because of the promise of quick results over the short term. Some still follow this approach today, but the trend is toward the structured approach.

Criticisms of the structured approach

The structured approach to system development has not been without its critics. One perceived weakness is the amount of time initially spent analyzing and designing a flexible, easy-to-maintain project. Why not just get on with the project and worry about maintenance problems when they occur? For two decades after computers became commercially available, that is exactly what was done. Studies have proven, however, that the cost of correcting an error is higher in the maintenance stage of a problem solution than during earlier design stages.

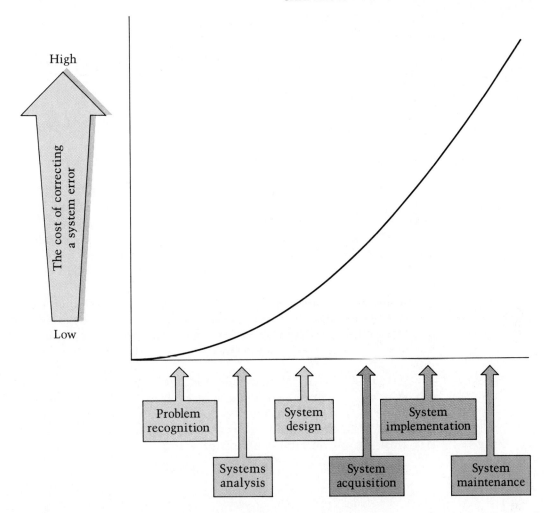

Figure 13-2
The relative cost of correcting an error in the system development process. The later an error is found in the process the more it costs to correct it.

Modifying a nonmodular system is also more expensive. For example, a payroll system that does not allow for modification when the tax laws change would probably need to be extensively rewritten or even scrapped after only 1 year. Otherwise a company using it could face legal penalties and fines for improperly withholding taxes. A well-planned and well-designed system does not guarantee perfection, but a poorly planned and designed program will most likely lead to unsatisfactory results.

Another complaint is that with the separation of tasks encouraged by structured techniques, it is difficult to see how a specific person's work fits into the overall picture. The person may not feel part of the development "team," and show only half-hearted interest toward the project.

There are cases, however, where separation of tasks is quite important, as with money-related or sensitive corporate work. Consider a project for creating a payroll program. One person may work using a small module that checks for invalid employee numbers, while another person works on the employee name and address verification routine. One person doing both these tasks could easily create fake employees and addresses.

Let's examine each phase in the system development process in detail.

Problem recognition

The first stage of the system development process, **PROBLEM RECOGNITION**, means identifying a need or opportunity that a new system could address. "Problem" as used here does not always mean that something is wrong; it can also mean a chance to expand or meet new needs. Financial incentives are usually the motivating force behind problem recognition.

In our Paul's House of Electronic Wonders example, the problem actually had two parts, one positive and one negative. The positive problem was that Philip Paul wanted his firm to expand into the mail-order business. The negative problem was that the firm was losing low-volume sales.

Most problems are recognized by either users or managers. Some, however, are identified by other people, such as the information system staff, who may be aware of new hardware or software that could better handle an organizational function, or who may realize how rusty some still-working information system has become.

Systems analysis

Once a problem has been identified, managers may feel the opportunity is attractive enough (or the problem is severe enough) that something should be done about it. They can give permission to a systems analyst or systems analysis team to investigate the problem.

The investigation takes the form of systems analysis. **SYSTEMS ANALYSIS** is a method for examining how an existing organization works in order to identify the cause of a problem. To see that the analysis remains on target, users are heavily involved in structured systems analysis; for instance, if it is a team analysis, a user will be one member of the team.

Systems analysis is usually divided into two steps:

1. The preliminary investigation
2. The detailed investigation

Each step ends with a report of the findings to users and managers. Using the report findings, the users and managers could decide to: proceed with the system development process stage, halt the project, or take a second look at the stage just completed. If the report is accepted, written confirmation should be obtained from management.

Preliminary investigation

The preliminary investigation determines the scope of the problem and gives managers information for deciding whether or not to perform the next step, detailed analysis. In comparison to the detailed investigation, the preliminary investigation is fast and cheap. The PRELIMINARY INVESTIGATION can be broken down into four steps:

1. Evaluate the user's request.
2. Determine the costs and benefits.
3. Plan the detailed investigation.
4. Draw up the project charter.

Let's examine each of these steps.

Evaluate the user's request

Evaluating the user's request means pinning down the real problem or opportunity by recognizing its true scope or nature. For example, Philip Paul thought his firm's problem was due to something amiss in the shipping and receiving department. His sister, however, attributed the problem to the purchasing department. Systems analyst Ed Wieland noted both of these beliefs, and gathered as many details as he could from both Philip and Susan. His tact and patience were rewarded not with learning the real cause of the problem, but with acquiring an overview of the existing information system and of managers' feelings about it. Ed would later go on to interview other personnel at Paul's and observe how certain activities were actually carried out, to find out the cause of the problem. Philip Paul aided Ed by notifying the appropriate managers of the upcoming study, helping to reduce the managers' concerns.

Determine the costs and benefits

The next step is determining the costs and benefits of proceeding with further development. The cost/benefit analysis involves comparing the benefits (or costs) of the existing system with the possible benefits (or costs) of a new system. It also involves a payback analysis of the new system—an analysis of the costs of the system over a period of years. Since preliminary analysis is necessarily rapid and superficial, however, these costs and benefits will only be rough approximations. The principal question is whether the new system is worth the time and money to be expended.

   The analyst should attempt to measure tangible and intangible costs of a new system, and compare them with the tangible and intangible benefits. *Tangible costs and benefits* can be measured directly in some fashion—for instance, the cost of six programmers working for a year and a half to create a new system. *Intangible costs and benefits* are important, but cannot be measured directly. For example, an enlightened paper company that satisfactorily worked out the economics of felling a virgin forest, would still have to reckon with the forest's recreational importance and beauty.

Plan the detailed investigation
The third step of the preliminary investigation is planning the detailed investigation. The approximate time necessary to carry out the detailed investigation should be determined, as well as the resources required— the salaries, office needs, information-processing support, and other day-to-day expenses to support the systems analyst or team.

The systems analyst then prepares for the project manager a PRELIMI-NARY REPORT that states the approximate costs and benefits of developing the new system, and the time and resources needed to carry out detailed analysis.

The manager must examine the information in the preliminary report carefully. Even if the cost/benefit analysis appears favorable, there may be reasons not to proceed. Other projects awaiting system design and development might have higher priority because they will ultimately deliver more to the firm.

Draw up the project charter
The fourth step involves drawing up the project charter. If the manager decides to proceed, the manager and analyst will together draw up a PRO-JECT CHARTER indicating the nature and scope of the detailed investigation to follow. Top-level management support is vital here, to help ensure that middle- and lower-level managers will take the study seriously and allow their people to participate. In addition, the charter helps middle-and lower-level managers gauge the extent of disruption the detailed investigation will cause. If, for example, their key employees will be diverted from their duties for countless interviews with analysts, the managers need to alter their own plans to allow for this. The project charter often includes the names of the project members and a timetable for completing interim steps as well as the entire project.

Two helpful planning tools for monitoring projects are the GANTT CHART and PERT DIAGRAMS which show how the various steps of a project relate to each other over time. Figure 13-3a shows a Gantt chart for the detailed investigation stage. Gantt charts can be used to model scheduling for any stage in system development. Figure 13-3b shows a PERT (short for Program Evaluation and Review Technique) diagram for the same stage.

Detailed investigation

With the preliminary investigation completed and the project charter drawn up, the systems analyst or team can begin the second step of systems analysis, the detailed investigation. The DETAILED INVESTIGATION expands upon the preliminary investigation to fully explain the nature of the problem and to offer managers possible solutions. It takes longer, is more expensive, and can be broken down into six steps:

1. Define the goal and system boundaries.
2. Collect facts.
3. Define system flow and data requirements.
4. Define system rules and policies.
5. Define system volume and timing.
6. Evaluate system performance.

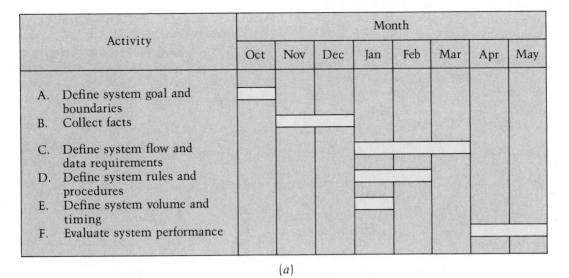

Activity	Month							
	Oct	Nov	Dec	Jan	Feb	Mar	Apr	May
A. Define system goal and boundaries								
B. Collect facts								
C. Define system flow and data requirements								
D. Define system rules and procedures								
E. Define system volume and timing								
F. Evaluate system performance								

(a)

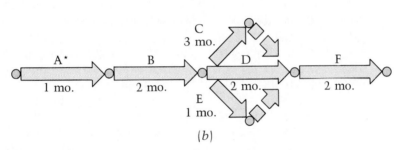

(b)

Figure 13-3
Scheduling the steps in the detailed investigation stage. (a) A simplified Gantt chart. (b) A simplified PERT diagram. (*The letters refer to the activities in the Gantt chart. The dashed lines are dummy connectors to preserve the logical consistency of the PERT diagram.)

Let's look at each of these steps separately.

Define the goal and system boundaries

In Chapter 3 we said that an organizational goal refers to the organization's purpose or objective, and that the best-understood goals were stated in clear terms. The goal for Paul's House of Electronic Wonders is to reduce the number of small orders lost. Analyst Ed Wieland should have Philip Paul translate this vague goal into clear, definite figures—say an increase of $150,000 per year in sales to small customers.

The analyst must also set limits or bounds to the scope of the problem. Setting SYSTEM BOUNDARIES delineates the scope of the system study, thus excluding unnecessary factors. Ed Wieland will set boundaries that allow investigating anything that affects the shipment of small orders, which includes the shipping and receiving and the purchasing departments. If the data he collects point in a different direction—such as the order-entry process—he will investigate that also. He is not interested, however, in any problems with the decision support system that Susan Paul uses extensively for sales analysis. Since the concern is small orders, Philip Paul defines "small order" as an order from a retail customer for less than $1000. Of course, the system studied does not exist in a vacuum. It depends on inputs from other parts of the company and produces outputs that affect those other parts of the business. It is important to view a firm within its environmental context.

Collect facts

Collecting facts refers to assembling data on how the current system works. The analyst collects facts concerning the five information system elements. Who are the people involved in an organization? What are their tasks? What data are used in the organization, including transaction and nontransaction types? Which rules and procedures are followed? What software and hardware are used? Assembling facts brings all of an analyst's interpersonal and analytical skills into play, and is one of the more difficult steps of the detailed investigation. The analyst can collect facts by:

- Assembling documents concerning the organization.
- Conducting interviews.
- Using questionnaires.
- Observing how the system works.

Which combination of techniques is used depends on the problem and the organization. For example, the corner clothing boutique would not design and circulate a questionnaire to its handful of employees, but would simply talk to them (conduct interviews). An automobile factory interested in the opinions of thousands of assembly-line workers, on the other hand, would sidestep the monumental task of interviewing them all personally by designing and circulating a good questionnaire to a small, representative sample of the employees.

Assembling documents means gathering together any written materials that relate to the way the existing system works. Here the analyst is like an archaeologist on a dig, happy to find any evidence of the lost civilization suspected of having existed there, from a lowly pottery shard to a complete book of laws. The documents an analyst assembles will provide evidence of how the system works.

Documents of interest might be organizational structure charts, procedure manuals, forms, and reports. At Paul's House of Electronic Wonders, every document concerning shipping will interest Ed Wieland. A helpful tool to keep track of these documents and their uses is the grid chart. Figure 13-4 shows an example that lists source (input)

Figure 13-4
Input/output grid chart concerning shipping and receiving at Paul's House of Electronic Wonders.

Input source documents	Output reports			
	Updated inventory	Accounts payable	Accounts receivable	Merchandise returned
Shipping label, arriving item	X			
Shipping label stub, departing item	X			
Supplier invoice		X		
Customer invoice			X	
Return slip	X	X		X

Question 1. What types of orders do you think go out the fastest?
_____ a. Small orders
_____ b. Medium-sized orders
_____ c. Large orders
_____ d. All orders go out equally fast
_____ e. Don't know

Question 2. From your department's point of view do you find the
shipping operation works well or not? Please explain.

_____

_____

_____

documents used by the shipping department, and the reports (output)
they are used to generate.

Interviews are an important source of information on how the system works. Conducting interviews requires great care; they should be
conducted in a tactful and nonthreatening fashion. Many people are
wary of analysts coming in and studying their jobs, since they feel that
their jobs may be taken away or changed. In reality, while jobs are rarely
lost, job functions may indeed change. The interview offers the first
opportunity to hint that the new system that may be developed will be
positive, helping people to do their jobs more productively and with less
frustration. In fact, most studies show few people prefer to return to old
systems if the new one has been properly designed and implemented. ✎

Questionnaires can survey a greater number of people more efficiently. Just as conducting interviews is an art, so is designing questionnaires. A questionnaire should ask questions that encourage people to
express their opinions, but not lead them down a path preplanned by the
analyst. For instance, Ed Wieland's questionnaire (Figure 13-5) for personnel at Paul's does not state that there is a problem, but seeks
unbiased answers. Findings from the questionnaires may help pinpoint
the source of shipping delays to small customers.

All of these techniques are no substitute for actually observing what
happens. A good systems analyst will *observe* people at work carrying
out their jobs, aware that his or her mere presence will cause people to
work differently (most of us tend to speed up when someone is looking
over our shoulder). Observation can spot bottlenecks or inefficiencies
that documents, interviews, and questionnaires would overlook. Once
the analyst or team has collected enough data to work with, the time has
come to analyze the data in the next steps of the detailed investigation.

Define system flow and data requirements
The detailed investigation may reveal that the existing system does not
work at all as managers or users thought it did. One way to determine
how a system really operates is to follow the actual flow of work

through the system. What happens between the time a small order comes in and the time that it goes out at Paul's? Two ways of visually presenting the flow pattern are data-flow diagrams and system flow-charts. Data requirements are collated through the use of data dictionaries.

DATA-FLOW DIAGRAMS visually trace how data move through the system. We need to see where data enter the system, at what points data are stored and processed, and where information is output. Figure 13-6 shows the symbols used in a data-flow diagram. Figure 13-7 shows a data-flow diagram Ed Wieland developed to trace the process for inventory management at Paul's. The focus of this diagram is the procedure for ordering replacement supplies. Showing the full inventory management system (including procedures for shipping orders) would take several pages of diagrams. As Figure 13-7 shows, Ed found that the inventory file (store) depended on data from marketing, management, accounting, and vendors. In turn, data flowed from the inventory file to management and vendors. Clearly inventory data affected a lot of departments at Paul's. For instance, purchasing used inventory data to determine when to order items that were getting low in inventory. The procedure seemed so reasonable that Ed's suspicions were aroused— why where there problems?

SYSTEM FLOWCHARTS visually describe the information-processing system, using symbols that give some details of the hardware used for input and output. A *flowchart* is a diagram that uses special symbols to communicate the steps (sequence, flow of data, and logic) for solving a problem. Figure 13-8 shows the symbols used in a system flowchart, and Figure 13-9 shows how Ed Wieland flowcharted the system for preparing orders for replacement supplies at Paul's. Notice this system flow-chart describes what happens in the process step 4—"prepare orders"— in the data-flow diagram in Figure 13-7.

It is important to clearly define data needs and interrelationships. One useful tool for keeping track of all the data required is the data dictionary. As briefly seen in Chapter 11, a **DATA DICTIONARY** defines each

Figure 13-6
Symbols used in a data-flow diagram.

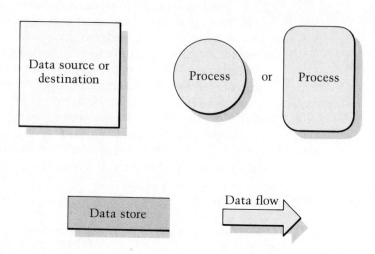

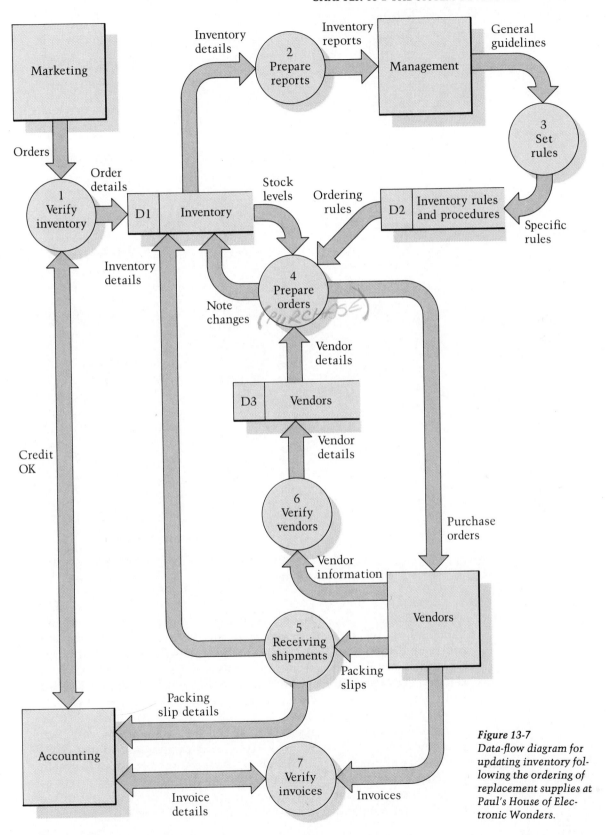

Figure 13-7
Data-flow diagram for updating inventory following the ordering of replacement supplies at Paul's House of Electronic Wonders.

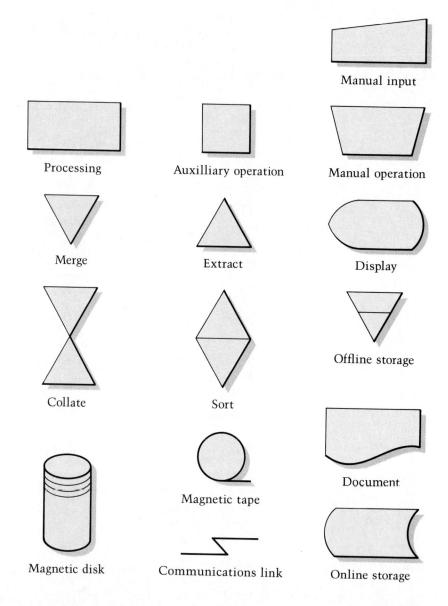

item of data and information handled by a system, giving the item's name, telling what the item is, specifying its format, giving its input source, and specifying its output use. The data will come from transaction (such as sales orders) and nontransaction (text and voice/image) sources. Developing the specifications of the nontransaction data is difficult, but necessary, to get a complete picture of the existing system.

Like other people in business, systems analysts have turned to the computer to speed up parts of the system development process. Computer-aided software engineering techniques can be used to reduce the tedium of drawing and then revising the data-flow diagrams and system flowcharts and tracking elements in data dictionaries. A **COMPUTER-AIDED SOFTWARE ENGINEERING (CASE)** package is an integrated set of system development tools which can be used in all stages of the system

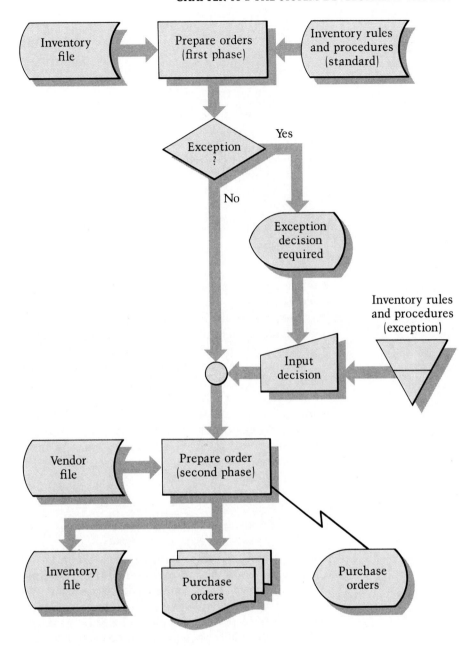

Figure 13-9
System flowchart for preparing orders of replacement supplies at Paul's House of Electronic Wonders (process bubble 4 in Figure 13-6).

design process from designing data-flow diagrams to writing computer programming code. One CASE package for the microcomputer environment is Excelerator by Index Technology.

Define system rules and policies

Many business decisions are based on overall rules or policies. Policies express what *actions* to take given a particular *condition*. Routine decisions that can be based upon quantifiable data where the specific actions are known are called *programmable decisions*. Nonroutine decisions (either unique decisions or those dependent upon qualitative data) are

		Rules							
		1	2	3	4	5	6	7	8
Conditions	If old customer	Y	Y	Y	N	N	N	Y	N
	And outstanding bills from Paul's	Y	Y	N	Y	N	Y	N	N
	Credit rating acceptable	Y	N	Y	Y	Y	N	N	N
Actions	Extend credit	X		X		X			
	Investigate further				X		X		
	Require prepayment		X					X	X

known as *nonprogrammable decisions*. A tool used to clarify specific policies for programmable decisions is the decision table. A DECISION TABLE shows what action to take given particular conditions being met. Such tables are useful for tracing complicated logic patterns by following through the possibilities for multiple decisions.

At Paul's, decision tables are used to determine whether to grant credit to certain customers (Figure 13-10). The "conditions" part of the table (known as the condition stub) labels the possible categories into which a customer falls. For example, following Column 3 down, we have an old customer with no outstanding bills owed to Paul's and an acceptable credit rating. Continuing down to the "actions" part of the table (known as the action stub), we see that Paul's would extend credit to this customer.

Define system volume and timing

The next step in the detailed investigation is to define system volume and timing. SYSTEM VOLUME is the quantity of operations of interest (usually transactions) that occur over a given period of time. Such quantitative data expressed in monetary form or dollar amounts are used in calculating cost/benefit values. For instance, Ed Wieland found through his researches that Paul's House of Electronic Wonders received an average of 68 small orders per day. The average daily total value of small orders was $10,200. And as Philip said when Ed showed him this figure, this was nothing to sneeze at.

SYSTEM TIMING refers to any time patterns or cycles that can be identified concerning the system investigation. Knowledge of these patterns assist in the planning of resources—such as employing part-time data entry personnel during peak seasons. Ed noted that small orders picked up substantially in the fall, and dropped off in the summer. He also observed that small orders were given a lower priority than larger ones, and thus were always handled late in the day.

Evaluate system performance

At this point in our detailed investigation we have defined the goal, collected facts, defined the system flow, and defined the system volume and timing. We should now be able to evaluate system performance, and identify the cause of the problem.

The systems analyst or team must now make recommendations on how to solve the problem (or realize the opportunity). The systems analyst prepares a FEASIBILITY REPORT containing the complete findings of the detailed investigation. The feasibility report, in both summary and detailed form, describes how the existing system works, details the nature of the problem with the existing system, and offers alternate solution possibilities along with the costs and benefits for each alternative (including doing nothing).

The cost/benefit figures here will be much more exact and reliable than those supplied at the end of the preliminary investigation, since they result from a much more thorough research process. Attached to the feasibility report are supplementary materials such as data-flow diagrams, decision tables, sample documents, statistics on questionnaire results, and so on.

The feasibility report is a written document, but is generally accompanied by an oral presentation to users and managers by the systems analyst. Based on the report and presentation, managers can do one of three things: study the matter further, proceed with one of the alternatives, or reject all the alternatives and make no changes in the existing system.

System design

We have now completed the problem recognition and systems analysis stages of the system development process. Assume that the managers have approved one of the alternatives to change the system put forth in the feasibility report, and let's proceed with the third stage, system design.

SYSTEM DESIGN is the process of determining, first generally and then in more detailed terms, how the new system will be set up. The system design process can be divided into four steps:

1. Logical design
2. Physical design
3. Test design
4. Design review

System design is a major effort, and at the onset must be planned and scheduled carefully. The same systems analyst or team that performed the systems analysis may continue with the system design; or a new team may be formed that includes specialists in particular design activities. In either case, design begins with determining who will perform specific design tasks, establishing a schedule, and reviewing the feasibility report.

Developing a complete system is an arduous task. This is true even if some or all the components are packaged, for decisions requiring expert judgment are still required to select and combine the right packages.

Many firms place the responsibility for system development in the hands of an information system consultant. In the case of smaller organizations or companies that lack employees of their own who are knowledgeable enough to tackle the job, this may be the only option. Giant firms also hire consultants with some frequency. They may simply have too many projects already in the works to develop another one, they may have begun the development in-house but fallen behind with project deadlines, or they too may lack employees with just the right expertise.

Enter the consultant. Ideally, this individual is up to the minute in his or her area of expertise, and has impressive experience in the area that the new system will address.

Once selected and placed on the job, the consultant works pretty much like anyone else developing a system. If in charge of the project, the consultant directs systems analysis, system design, system development, and system implementation, and will remain "on call" during system maintenance. For large or complex projects, a number of information system consultants may work as a team, each with a particular area of expertise.

Creating a new system from scratch (rather than assembling prepackaged programs) requires a fair number of noncoms as well as generals. These individuals can also be information system consultants, in the guise of systems analysts, programmers, database administrators, training specialists, and other information system professionals. Like their managerial counterparts, these consultants conduct most of their work on the premises, offering expertise that is either lacking or tied up in-house, at a high price.

How do you find work as a consultant? You have to acquire the knowledge and experience that a consultant sells. The time-honored career path is to begin work as a programmer, move up to a senior-level programmer, systems analyst, or other specialist within an organization, and then quit to become a consultant. There is great demand for consultants, since most businesses are acquiring and expanding their information systems at a breakneck pace, and do not always have just the person needed on the payroll.

Information system consultants usually work for consulting firms, which shift consultants on and off different projects as required. Some independent consultants offer their services directly to employers. Rates of pay range from double to more than quadruple the rates paid to in-house employees performing the same work. Employers are willing to pay these costs because they are desperate, and they can let the consultant go when the project is finished or if they simply do not get along.

This brings up the chief drawback of consulting: you can quickly find yourself between jobs, which tends to flatten out the inflated salary figure. Also, the pressure to produce results on the job is intense enough to eliminate some of the amenities of working life, such as reading the paper in the morning, making friends on the job, or even eating a decent lunch. On the positive side, however, consultants enjoy the challenge of remaining tops in a particular field, the chance to develop advanced systems at a high level of responsibility, and a certain glamour attached to being a maverick.

To assure a satisfactory design, user involvement remains heavy, and analysts must regularly touch base with users. In some companies a user is present on the design team.

Logical design

LOGICAL DESIGN refers to creating a conceptual model of the new system. A simple model of a system, consisting of input, processing, output, and feedback was presented in Chapter 2. In the logical design step we focus on how these four steps will interact within our *new* system.

Starting with the logical design step and continuing throughout the entire design process, data-flow diagrams, system flowcharts, and data dictionaries (useful tools to describe the *old* system) are used to design the *new* system. The system designer should develop *modules* that are both *highly cohesive* and *loosely coupled*.

Logical design begins with the "bottom line" of the new system—the information it is to *output*—which is the reason the system is required. To define the output, the analyst must determine what information the users require, how detailed it must be, and when it is needed. All three points can be best determined by asking the users themselves.

To aid in the system design process, system designers develop prototypes of the new system. **PROTOTYPING** is the creation of small working models of the system that allow designers and users an opportunity to interactively adjust the model. The design of prototypes involves the same system development steps as for full-scale systems. Knowledge gained from testing a prototype can then be applied to the full-scale system.

After the general output design is agreed upon, the analyst then works in consultation with the user to determine the *input* requirements needed to capture the necessary data to support the output. The *processing* steps (calculating, summarizing, etc.) required to transform the data are worked through. Additionally, system *feedback* steps (ways of adjusting the system based on the output) are outlined.

Physical design

With the logical or conceptual design complete, we are now ready to settle some "physical" matters about how the new system will work. In **PHYSICAL DESIGN** the physical specifications of the new system are created, using the results of the *logical design* stage as a framework. Physical design means more than just selecting hardware. Each element of the information system is examined.

▫ *People.* The number and skills of individuals required to use or operate the new system should be outlined so personnel hiring and training efforts can be coordinated.

▫ *Rules and procedures.* Any new or modified rules and procedures not previously addressed in earlier stages must be proposed.

▫ *Data.* The design of the files or databases that will store data items, and the relation of one item to another, must be determined. The sources for nontransaction data—text, voice, and video—must also be detailed.

▫ *Software.* Program requirements for either creating programs from scratch or purchasing them off the shelf must be listed.

□ *Hardware.* The performance standards for computers to run programs, and peripherals to accept input, store data and programs, output results, and communicate between devices need to organized.

All of these elements interact, and the system designer must ensure that the *total physical design* is properly constructed.

As with logical design, we start with the *output* stage. Once the basic information needed is agreed upon, the output medium must be chosen. The system designer first creates alternative sketches of reports and other output, and modifies the one chosen until the user is satisfied. The designer, for example, fills in a printer layout chart (Figure 13-11) to show how the headings and data items will physically appear on printed reports.

Next, the designer turns to *input*, and determines the medium for input data. For instance, screen display forms are used to design where input data will be displayed on a video screen as it is keyed in (Figure 13-12). Storage specifications for transaction records are also determined, using a record layout form such as that shown in Figure 13-13.

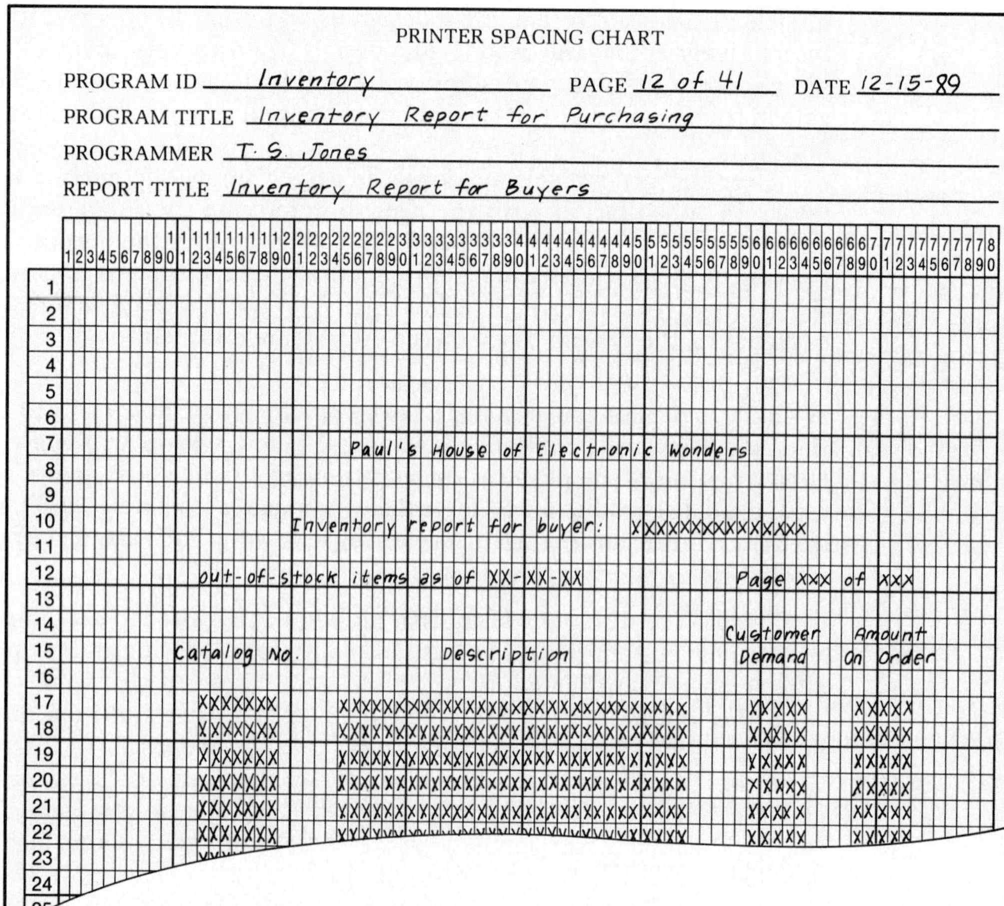
PRINTER SPACING CHART

PROGRAM ID Inventory PAGE 12 of 41 DATE 12-15-89

PROGRAM TITLE Inventory Report for Purchasing

PROGRAMMER T. S. Jones

REPORT TITLE Inventory Report for Buyers

Paul's House of Electronic Wonders

Inventory report for buyer: XXXXXXXXXXXXXXX

out-of-stock items as of XX-XX-XX Page XXX of XXX

Catalog No. Description Customer Demand Amount On Order

XXXXXXX XXXXXXXXXXXXXXXXXXXXXXXXXXXXXXXXXXXX XXXXX XXXXX

Figure 13-11
A printer layout chart.

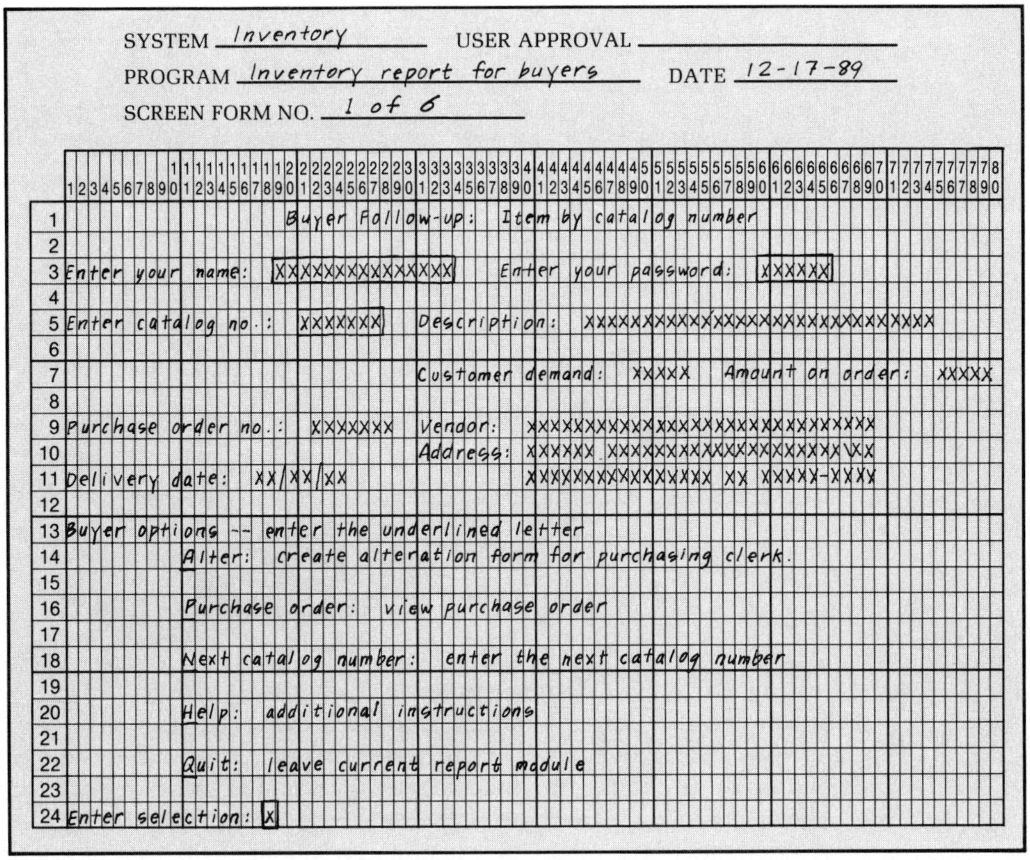

SYSTEM _Inventory_   USER APPROVAL _____
PROGRAM _Inventory report for buyers_   DATE _12-17-89_
SCREEN FORM NO. _1 of 6_

```
 1                    Buyer Follow-up:  Item by catalog number
 2
 3 Enter your name: [XXXXXXXXXXXXXXXX]    Enter your password:  [XXXXXX]
 4
 5 Enter catalog no.: [XXXXXX]    Description:  XXXXXXXXXXXXXXXXXXXXXXXXXXXXXXXXXXX
 6
 7                         Customer demand:  XXXXX    Amount on order:  XXXXX
 8
 9 Purchase order no.:  XXXXXXX   Vendor:  XXXXXXXXXXXXXXXXXXXXXXXXXXXXXXXXX
10                                Address: XXXXXX XXXXXXXXXXXXXXXXXXXXXXXX XX
11 Delivery date:  XX/XX/XX            XXXXXXXXXXXXXXXX XX XXXXX-XXXX
12
13 Buyer options -- enter the underlined letter
14        Alter:  create alteration form for purchasing clerk.
15
16        Purchase order:  view purchase order
17
18        Next catalog number:  enter the next catalog number
19
20        Help:  additional instructions
21
22        Quit:  leave current report module
23
24 Enter selection: [X]
```

Figure 13-12
A screen display form.

The *processing* mode (batch, real-time, time-sharing, or some combination) is also considered in physical design. (For more on processing modes, see Chapter 15.) Will the system perform processing as data are entered or will processing be performed periodically (hourly, weekly)? The decision reached here affects the physical design elements.

Finally, *feedback* mechanisms, such as procedures to record unusual processing, should also be designed.

We often find in physical design that the final design selected involves trade-offs in performance because of cost/benefit issues. A state-of-the-art system may not be cost-effective, while a less advanced one is a better choice. Although systems analysts do not design hardware, they must make sure that hardware required for the new system is installed at the right locations. The analyst or designer determines the *hardware requirements* of the new system and compares them with the hardware on hand.

Given the *software requirements*, programs for the system can be developed in-house or purchased. Prepackaged software exists for virtually any function and for use on any size machine (see Chapter 8).

Software written entirely in-house or modified in-house often uses structured programming, using a top-down approach and a modular design. This concept is covered in detail in Chapter 14.

Figure 13-13
A record layout form.

Employee number	Social Security Number	Last Name	First Name	M I	Job Title
1 2 3 4 5 6	7 8 9 1 1 1 1 1 1 0 1 2 3 4 5	1 1 1 1 2 2 2 2 2 2 2 2 2 2 2 3 6 7 8 9 0 1 2 3 4 5 6 7 8 9 0	3 3 3 3 3 3 3 3 3 4 1 2 3 4 5 6 7 8 9 0	4 1	4 4 4 4 4 4 4 4 5 5 5 5 5 5 5 5 5 5 6 6 6 6 6 6 6 2 3 4 5 6 7 8 9 0 1 2 3 4 5 6 7 8 9 0 1 2 3 4 5 6

Street Address	City	
6 6 6 7 7 7 7 7 7 7 7 7 8 8 8 8 8 8 8 8 9 9 7 8 9 0 1 2 3 4 5 6 7 8 9 0 1 2 3 4 5 6 7 8 9 0 1	9 9 9 9 9 9 9 1 1 1 1 1 1 1 2 3 4 5 6 7 8 9 0 0 0 0 0 0 0 0 1 2 3 4 5 6	

S t a t e	Zip + 4	Work Phone			
		AC	Telephone	Ext.	
1 1 0 0 7 8	1 1 1 1 1 1 1 1 1 1 0 1 1 1 1 1 1 1 1 1 9 0 1 2 3 4 5 6 7	1 1 1 1 1 2 8 9 0	1 1 1 1 1 1 1 2 2 2 2 2 2 2 1 2 3 4 5 6 7	1 1 1 1 2 2 3 3 8 9 0 1	

Test design

How can we determine if the new system is properly functioning? By creating a test! The designer must develop a TEST DESIGN—a plan for those tests the new system must pass in order to meet the users' approval. The plan should test for both normal and unusual operating conditions. Users can provide analysts with sample data for both types of tests. Deliberate errors should be included in test data; then, when the system actually runs data, users and analysts can check that both error and normal situations were handled properly.

Design review

Once the logical, physical, and test designs are complete, the analyst or designer produces a design report. The DESIGN REPORT includes the complete output of the system design stage. The analyst should first circulate the report to users and managers, and then conduct a formal design review. A DESIGN REVIEW is a meeting during which users, managers, and the analyst go over the system design piece by piece to make sure that such a system—if developed—will in fact meet user needs. If a system fails the design review, the managers can either direct that further efforts be dropped, or that the design be improved to correct the failure.

When the managers accept the system design, the stage is set for acquisition of the new system.

System acquisition

SYSTEM ACQUISITION refers to the creation of the new system based on the results of the design stage. At the start of system acquisition, all we have are the various specifications developed during system design; important as these are, they are only a road map to a nonexistent system. Each element of the information system—people, data, rules and procedures, software, and hardware—must be addressed during the acquisition process.

If new *hardware* is needed—whether a new optical reader, magnetic disk unit, or a complete computer system—it must be ordered. So the hardware will be available when we are ready to test and implement the new system, now is the time to initiate the ordering process—the lead time between order and delivery can be many months for some equipment.

The first step in ordering equipment involves *requesting equipment proposals* and *price quotations* from vendors, and evaluating the information vendors provide to make the best choice. Factors involved in the evaluation of equipment include cost, the amount of support and training the vendor provides, and the quality of the documentation.

Equipment—especially major equipment such as a mainframe computer—need not be purchased, but can be leased. Here again, a comparison of factors such as cost and vendor support and training can provide a basis for deciding whether to lease or buy. Computers have a way of becoming obsolete fast, and leasing does offer the flexibility of being able to dispose of equipment which is no longer useful, without the burden of ownership. Some vendors offer a combined buy-and-lease package, where a company may lease the large mainframe computer and perhaps a key peripheral or two, but purchase other peripherals needed to complete the system.

In terms of *software*, system acquisition means writing and/or testing programs for the new system. If a portion or all of the necessary programs have been purchased, then the design and writing of programs is not necessary. Testing, however, is still required to ensure that the software does what it is supposed to. Program design and writing is described in Chapters 14 and 15.

Programming of a large system can take months or even years longer than the systems analysis or system design stages. As programmers complete and document individual modules, they test them for coding errors, using data and techniques they have developed for the purpose. When all of the individual modules appear to be working, a system test is performed. Here, the test determined in advance during system design (described earlier in the section Test Design) is followed to the letter, using error-clogged data that analysts and users have specially developed to trip up the system whenever possible.

Needless to say, passing the system test is a crucial event. Many a good system has failed the first time or two around, been refined, and then passed when given another chance.

Once a system has successfully passed the system test, users and managers have a final opportunity to decide whether or not they want to implement the system. Assuming that users were active throughout the systems analysis, design, and acquisition processes, and that the test design put the new system through the paces that users believed were necessary, it is unlikely that users would reject a system at this late stage. Managers, however, might still have a reason to reject the system. Organizational priorities might have changed, or the economic picture of the business might have worsened so that additional costs associated with running the new system cannot be borne. Systems are occasionally killed at this point—or altered substantially to reflect changed conditions—even when millions of dollars have been invested in their design and development. Continual user and manager involvement with the new system is important to try to avoid this possibility in advance.

System implementation

SYSTEM IMPLEMENTATION refers to the changeover from the old system to the new. System implementation can be subdivided into the following tasks: conversion, training, and the acceptance test. Each of the information system components—people, rules and procedures, data, software, and hardware—must be accounted for during system implementation.

Conversion

Conversion entails not only putting the new software and hardware to work successfully, but also changing the data structure as required. For example, an organization's old system may use data files and the new system may require a database. The permanent data on the files must then be transferred to the database, and procedures established so that new data will be entered directly to the database.

Four methods exist for converting from the old system to a new one:

- Direct cutover or crash conversion
- Parallel conversion
- Phased conversion
- Pilot conversion

They differ in how much time each requires, and the risk each entails. Figure 13-14 compares the four methods of conversion.

In DIRECT CUTOVER CONVERSION (also known as CRASH CONVERSION) the organization stops using the old system and starts using the new one at once. Assume, for example, that analyst Ed Wieland solved the small-order problem at Paul's House of Electronic Wonders. The new system passed the system test. So Philip Paul and Ed designate September 1 as the day that the old system will be dropped and the new system used instead. The advantage here is that implementation is swift. On the other hand, if something goes wrong with the new system, the business has nothing to fall back on. This type of conversion is analogous to trading in an old car for a new car. Once you drive away with your new car there is no going back to using your old car. The risk, in other words, is great. Conversion is not often done this way.

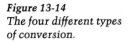

Figure 13-14
The four different types
of conversion.

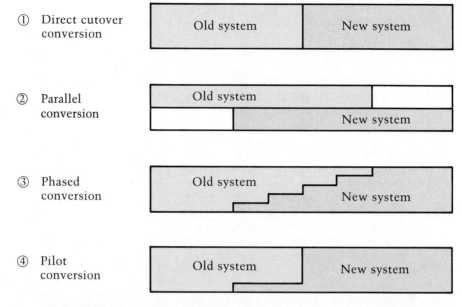

With **PARALLEL CONVERSION** the old system and the newly implemented one run side by side over a period of time. Results of the new system can then be checked against the results of the old. There are drawbacks to parallel conversion. It can cost quite a lot to run two systems simultaneously. Also, with the old system still running—the one people are comfortable with—there may be resistance to *ever* changing to the new system. However, if the new system has problems, parallel conversion minimizes the risks of prematurely depending on it.

PHASED CONVERSION gradually introduces the new system in stages over a period of time. If a given part of the new system fails, the failure can be contained, rather than spreading throughout the entire system and causing operations to halt. Phased conversion thus minimizes risk. The disadvantage is that phasing in a new system can take quite a long time.

PILOT CONVERSION introduces the new system in its entirety on a trial basis, but only to a small part of the organization. This would not work at Paul's, where only a small portion of the organization is concerned to begin with. But in a chain of stores or in a manufacturing company with a number of factories, the new system could be adopted in one and then—once the kinks are ironed out—adopted in the others as well. This minimizes risk to the total organization, but the lengthy experimental period also slows down the implementation.

Finally, we should note that a phased or pilot conversion can be performed within the context of a direct cutover or parallel conversion. When introducing the new system to a single factory in a pilot conversion, the new system can be run in parallel to the old, or a direct cutover conversion could be used. With a phased conversion, each new phase can be directly cutover into operation, or can be run in parallel with the old until the old system is dropped for that phase.

Regardless of the conversion method selected, scheduling and monitoring the conversion process requires special consideration.

By 1985, there was chaos in New Jersey. The state's Division of Motor Vehicles had awarded a contract to Price Waterhouse to modernize its management and computer operations, but the plan was ill-defined and overly ambitious, a sure recipe for disaster. When the wrong programming language was used to implement a new driver registration system, more than a million New Jersey drivers were unable to register their cars or registered them incorrectly because of computer errors. A major investigation into the mess revealed that Price Waterhouse had "professionally misjudged" the implementation. The snafu cost the state $6.5 million.

When something goes wrong in information systems, it's hard to hide. A few highly publicized fiascoes have sent shivers down many an MIS manager's back as he whispers to himself, "I'm glad that wasn't me." The following are [three] examples of such cases:

□ After nearly $5 billion spent, 7 years invested, and several major MIS casualties, Bankamerica Corp.'s foray into high technology has been nothing short of a disaster. The bank has lost tens of millions of dollars in various technological calamities, such as the failure of its Masternet, an $80 million program designed to automate the employee benefits and trust services department. The bank re-

cently scuttled the entire system (*Computerworld*, Feb. 1 [1988]).

According to the *San Francisco Examiner*, the failed attempt cost the bank $45 million as well as some important customers. It also reportedly cost Bankamerica's latest MIS chief, Louis Mertes, his job. All told, strategic MIS failures in the 1980s have helped Bankamerica slide from first place to twenty-ninth in assets of banks worldwide.

□ The Internal Revenue Service's 1985 tax processing season was a data processing nightmare, with problems leading to long delays in taxpayer refunds. . . . According to outside auditors, the problem occurred when the IRS mishandled a cutover to new mainframes and new COBOL software.

The mix-up did, however, serve to highlight the fact that the IRS systems were mismanaged and outdated. . . .

□ Beginning in 1983, Blue Cross/Blue Shield of Wisconsin attempted to convert its entire financial and claims systems. Though the company's MIS officials argue that the $600 million conversion, perhaps the largest of its kind, went off as intended, the local media in Milwaukee observed otherwise.

Blue Cross/Blue Shield contracted with Electronic Data Systems Corp. (EDS) to replace its entire DP [data processing] environ-

Training

Before users, managers, and operators can work with the new system, they have to be trained. Appropriate training courses should be devised for each group, and conducted in parallel with the end of the system development stage and the beginning of system conversion. In this way, people will be capable of using the new system as soon as it is in place; work need not grind to a halt. Many different training techniques exist. The goal of the training effort is to reassure employees who feel threatened by a new system, develop competence in using the new system, and guarantee the continued smooth operation of the organization.

Documentation is important to the training effort. Prepared as an ongoing process during the system development stage, documentation exists that is specifically targeted toward (1) users and managers, (2) operators, and (3) programmers. These materials can be used during

ment, which had grown to an unwieldy mass of confusion. Seven different claims processing systems and three different membership systems were filled with old and outdated information.

After 2 years, EDS implemented the new system, but it caused serious problems for subscribers. Claims were either not paid at all or were overpaid to the tune of tens of millions of dollars. The company lost $28 million in 1985 and nearly as much in 1986.

Furthermore, Blue Cross/Blue Shield reportedly lost more than money: 22,000 subscribers have canceled their memberships since the 1985 implementation. Both Blue Cross/Blue Shield and EDS claim that the system is now up and working as expected.

The road to ruin

The following is a checklist to follow on a surefire path to strategic disaster in MIS planning.

◻ Accept the first plan that comes across your desk, especially if it is ill-defined and overly ambitious.

◻ Allow your systems to get hopelessly outdated so that you are forced to implement massive conversions that create crisis situations within MIS.

◻ Misread your company's market—the inevitable result of miscommunication between MIS and top management.

◻ Implement MIS strategies that are inflexible and incapable of changing as the marketplace changes.

◻ Push for a centralized MIS strategy when the company is going through a major decentralization campaign.

◻ Employ technology that is overkill, much more powerful and expensive than corporate applications require.

◻ Allow top management to dismiss MIS participation in forming corporate strategy.

◻ Operate in a vacuum. Focus on technical elegance in lieu of corporate needs and direction.

◻ Depend on other sources for the integrity of your data.

◻ Rely on consulting firms without thoroughly checking references and business plans to make sure that the firm is capable of handling your project.

◻ Let fast business growth blind you to MIS needs.

Source: Glenn Rifkin and Mitch Betts, "Strategic Systems Plans Gone Awry: When the Information Blueprint Is a Lemon, Costs Can Be Staggering," *Computerworld*, 14 March 1988, pp. 1, 104–105. Copyright 1988 by CW Publishing Inc., Framingham, MA 01701. Reprinted from Computerworld.

training and, after training is completed, retained for future reference as employees gain confidence and sharpen their skills in using the new system.

Acceptance test

If a parallel, phased, or pilot conversion was performed, the moment arrives when managers must decide whether to go with the new system or continue with the old. (With a direct cutover conversion, managers who suddenly find themselves with a poorly performing new system might wish that they had such an option, but they don't—they are stuck with the new.) The last step in system implementation is the acceptance test. The ACCEPTANCE TEST is an evaluation of the new system in actual operation, using real data and doing real day-to-day work for the organization. Users and managers must evaluate the test results carefully. The

Building an information center that works

Although the information center (IC) was devised in the mid-70s by IBM to help relieve the data processing backlog . . . the concept initially was met with hostility from many data processing (DP) departments.

The information center has proved its worth, however, evolving into a broadened, generic concept, becoming the center of computing resources. . . . No matter how they are organized, however, the primary goal is always the same: providing the users with the software tools, training and support so that they can utilize the power of the computer themselves.

Solvable problems

As handy as information centers are, there are still thorns in the berry patch. Information centers must be headed by managers who periodically think through the direction [in which] their centers are heading and who have the foresight to control both the number of users and the number of supported products. Technology and user demand can be overwhelming. As one manager said, "There's so much technology out there, you can choke your department by buying too much. . . ."

Experienced managers also warn others to "watch your hardware resources." Increased use of the corporate computer system can overload it, necessitating for many companies a dedicated machine for the IC project.

Especially at the center's inception, the number of users asking for training can quickly grow, resulting in an unwieldy and frustrating backlog. Many managers deal with that problem by devising a training schedule in the very beginning, with an initial goal of one trained user per department, and then expanding from there. . . . Users must be given a realistic idea of what the system's capabilities are for their jobs and of the substantial amount of time required at the beginning of the learning process.

Two other problems often crop up which usually should not be the responsibility of the information center staff, but which it can help uncover. User department managers must monitor whether users are using information center tools as their daily work rather than as a useful augmentation. "Users become so engrossed in the process, and how much fun it is, that they are constantly doing gee-whiz things," confirms one information center manager, "and the grunt work doesn't get done any more."

The second of those problems is documentation of user-development applications and trained-user back-up. The problems arise, for

acceptance test provides a final opportunity to decide whether or not the new system solves the problem it set out to solve. If all the proper efforts were taken in its development, it should.

When the responsible managers give the green light on the new system, the old becomes history, and the new is what the organization will use for the foreseeable future. However, the system development process is not yet finished.

System maintenance

SYSTEM MAINTENANCE refers to the continuing process of keeping a system in good working order. This phase is several times longer than any

example, when just one person in a department develops the program for a vital report and then quits or is promoted to another company branch. Without documentation or a second user trained in the same application, the entire process must be started over from scratch.

Training is vital

Training continually consumes a significant amount of time and resources in an information center—it is one of the center's most important functions. Unfortunately, users don't always come into the center with a realistic notion of how much time training must take. "Data processing is an industry that learned years ago that training is a way of life—you can't survive without it," says Doug Tayler, vice president of market and business development for Deltak, Inc., the Naperville, Illinois, company which markets a variety of training products. "The end-user community, however," he continues, "is made up of people who have always viewed training as an occasional seminar for fun or development—accountants, for example, don't have to learn new technology every 6 months."

Start slowly

The first piece of advice information center managers must always stress is *start slowly*. Begin with a project you know will succeed and support it immediately.

Control and standardize microcomputer hardware and software from the very beginning, say weary IC managers. Without controls, micro acquisition can quickly run wild, causing data problems and making later plans for networking and micro-to-mainframe links impossible and/or extremely costly to implement.

Choose technically knowledgeable data processing professionals with good communication skills to staff the information center. Some information centers hire computer science graduates right after college for staff positions. A very few prefer to mix in technically knowledgeable users with a business background.

Source: Janet O'Mara, "Building an Information Center That Works," *ICP Data Processing Management* (Autumn 1984): 24–26. Reprinted with permission by Data Processing Management, Copyright © Autumn 1984: ICP, Indianapolis, Indiana.

of the previous stages. The job is not finished with the successful implementation of a system. Any information system must be properly maintained. Maintenance includes upgrading and extending the system as needed. It also involves solving problems with the system that will inevitably crop up. Rarely in a large system does one find all the bugs during earlier testing, and those that appear during normal use must be handled swiftly.

During system maintenance we reap the rewards of following the structured approach. Modules can be pulled out of the system and tinkered with or replaced without upsetting the whole system. Modules can be altered or replaced either to correct errors traced to them, or to permit new system functions, thereby adapting the system to ongoing user needs.

All elements of the information system must be addressed by system maintenance. People need continual upgrading or reinforcing of their skills. As rules and procedures of an organization change, the system must be altered accordingly. The data stored in files or databases undergo changes in structure and relationships. Software must be adjusted to changes in the data and in the rules and procedures. Hardware, too, can be altered or replaced to tune the system to greater efficiency.

At the beginning of this chapter, we stated that the system development process was a cycle. When we change a module of a system to add a new function that a user wants, we need to follow the complete system development process through each stage: problem recognition, systems analysis, system design, system acquisition, system implementation, and system maintenance.

Eventually, however, a time will come when our "new" system is truly an old system, despite our fond memories of it, and unable to do things that users demand. Then the system development process begins anew for the complete system. We are back, in other words, to the beginning.

summary

■ A system is a set of interrelated elements working toward a common goal. Any system goes through a process of birth, growth, maturity, and decline. This chain of events, or life cycle, is known as the system development process.

■ The system development process has six stages: (1) problem recognition, (2) systems analysis, (3) system design, (4) system acquisition, (5) system implementation, and (6) system maintenance. Structured system development techniques employ a top-down approach in which the user plays an active role and is viewed as the controlling partner. The system is broken down into easy-to-handle modules. The best modules exhibit high internal cohesion and loose external coupling.

■ Problem recognition means identifying a need or opportunity that a new system could address. Financial incentives, such as making more money or losing less money, are generally the motivating factor behind problem recognition.

■ Systems analysis, the next stage, is a method for examining how an existing organization works. It is done in two steps: a preliminary investigation and a detailed investigation.

■ The preliminary investigation determines the scope of the problem and gives managers a preliminary report to use in deciding whether or not to perform the detailed investigation.

■ The project charter delineates the scope of the detailed investigation. Gantt charts and PERT diagrams can be used to schedule the detailed investigation and the other stages of the system development process.

■ In the detailed investigation, analysts define the goal and system boundaries, collect facts, define system flow, define system volume and timing, and evaluate system performance. Analysis tools include data-flow diagrams, system flowcharts, data dictionaries, decision tables, questionnaires, and interviews. Computer-aided software engineering

(CASE) refers to a set of automated system development tools that can help reduce the labor spent in creating data-flow diagrams and data dictionaries. The feasibility report produced at the end of the detailed investigation presents managers with alternative suggestions for a new system that will satisfy the need or act on the opportunity.

■   If managers give the go-ahead, system design is the next stage. System design is the process of determining, in general and then more detailed terms, how the new system will be set up. The steps in system design are logical design, physical design, test design, the design report, and the design review. The data dictionary is expanded to track all the new data requirements. Prototyping permits designers to create working models of the new system for testing.

■   After a system passes the design review, the next phase is system acquisition. Here the new system is created. Hardware is purchased or built. Software packages are bought or developed and tested from scratch.

■   System implementation refers to the changeover from the old system to the new. Conversion from one system to the other must be performed; users, managers, and operators have to be trained; and an acceptance test gives managers a final opportunity to reject the new system. Assuming they do not, the new system is up and running. Conversion methods include direct cutover or crash, parallel, phased, and pilot.

■   The final stage of the system development process is system maintenance. This refers to the continuing process of keeping a system in good working order. When errors must be corrected or changes made based on new user needs, the structured approach followed in design and development pays off. Modules of a program can be removed and changed without changing the whole system.

■   Eventually, however, systems do reach a point where they are no longer acceptable. The system development process then returns to the beginning of the cycle and starts all over again.

wrap-up

The weak link in the chain

We saw at the start of the chapter that Paul's House of Electronic Wonders had a problem filling low-volume orders punctually, thereby losing sales to small-volume customers. Philip Paul also wanted to expand into the mail-order business—which meant even more small orders. Systems analyst Ed Wieland was given the job of solving the problem.

Ed and an assistant began a preliminary investigation—the first step in the systems analysis stage. They evaluated Philip's request, calculated the approximate costs and benefits of proceeding with further development, and planned how a detailed investigation would proceed. The complete preliminary investigation took 10 days.

In the report, Ed recommended that Philip drop the mail-order idea for the present, until the problem with small orders was solved. He agreed, and gave Ed permission to continue systems analysis.

The next step was the detailed investigation. Ed designed a questionnaire (we saw part of it in Figure 13-5), and circulated it to people in the shipping and receiving and purchasing departments. Using the questionnaire findings to guide him, Ed conducted over a dozen interviews with members of those departments. Both Ed and the assistant observed how the two departments did their work, and wherever Ed found a document that he could photocopy, he did.

Ed defined the data flow and system flow (as shown in Figures 13-7 and 13-9). By then he had a fairly complete picture of the order-filling process and, moreover, he had put his finger on the problem. Here is Ed's summary of the feasibility report prepared for Philip Paul:

The problem is with data flow. *When shipping and receiving ships a package, they detach part of the label on the package. These label stubs are saved until a full day's worth have accumulated. Once the loading docks close, an operator keys in the data on all of the day's label stubs using a key-to-magnetic-tape device. The tape is then taken to the computer room and used for the nightly batch processing run that updates the inventory database. In other words, inventory levels are decreased on the items that were shipped that day.*

To the purchasing department, the inventory database is the absolute truth. Purchasing receives exception reports about items that are getting dangerously low, so that it can place timely orders. Purchasing receives regularly scheduled listings summarizing the inventory, and can inquire at terminals at any time about the status of particular items. All of my investigations, Mr. Paul, could find no problem concerning the way purchasing used its database or placed orders.

The problem concerns the nightly key-to-tape procedure and the limited time between closing of the loading docks and running of the inventory update program. When push comes to shove, some data get left until the next day, or even ignored completely. Consequently, the figures that purchasing views as its database are often inaccurate, and less merchandise is actually in the warehouse than the database indicates.

Paul's has a good record with large orders because of the efficient selection of appropriate shippers, and because of the priority system followed by shipping and receiving: large orders go first. Everyone follows this rule, though I could not find it written down anywhere. If there is not enough merchandise to go around, the small orders simply wait.

Ed recommended either of two courses of action. The first was changing rules and procedures to require that all data were entered each night. This would mean hiring an additional data-entry operator, and rearranging the computer center's schedule to run the inventory program later at night. But it would not require a new system.

The other more expensive option was to use optical scanners that the shipping and receiving department already had, in order to update the inventory directly. Shipping and receiving used optical scanners to cut down on shipping mistakes—the labels on packages were scanned before shipping, to double-check that the right item was going out. The scanners, however, were not tied into the mainframe computer.

If the scanning process already in effect was used to enter the data on items shipped directly into the database—and a comparable scanning procedure followed for items received—then the nightly key-to-tape procedure could be eliminated. The nightly batch updates of the database could also be eliminated.

Though the second option was far more expensive, and would take nearly a year to design, develop, and implement, Philip Paul chose this option. Susan Paul provided him with most of the arguments for doing so. All sales—small and large—would benefit through quicker service; the shipping and receiving department would not have to do any additional work, but less; the old database could be retained and used by the purchasing department; and in all likelihood, the new system would pay back its design and development costs in under 3 years through increased sales.

"And once it's up and running," Philip said, "I intend to embark on mail orders."

key terms

These are the key terms in alphabetical order. The numbers in parentheses refer to the page on which each term is defined.

Acceptance test (457)
Cohesion (433)
Computer-aided software engineering (CASE) (444)
Coupling (433)
Data dictionary (442)
Data-flow diagram (442)
Decision table (446)
Design report (452)
Design review (452)
Detailed investigation (438)
Direct cutover or crash conversion (454)
Feasibility report (447)
Gantt chart (438)
Logical design (449)
Module (433)
Parallel conversion (455)
PERT diagram (438)
Phased conversion (455)
Physical design (449)
Pilot conversion (455)
Preliminary investigation (437)
Preliminary report (438)
Problem recognition (436)
Project charter (438)
Prototyping (449)
Structured system development techniques (432)
System (432)
System acquisition (452)
System boundary (439)
System design (447)
System development process (432)
System flowchart (442)
System implementation (454)
System maintenance (458)
System timing (446)
System volume (446)
Systems analysis (436)
Test design (452)
Top-down approach (433)

review questions

objective questions

True/false. *Put the letter T or F on the line next to the question.*

1. The system development process proceeds best with a structured bottom-up approach. 1 _____

2. Modules should have low internal cohesion and high external coupling. 2 _____

3. The system implementation stage includes system conversion and acceptance testing. 3 _____

4. Requests for proposals (or quotations) begin in the logical design process. 4 _____

5. Questionnaires are a commonly used method to collect facts during the systems analysis phase. 5 _____

6. Direct cutover is also known as crash conversion. 6 _____

7. Test design refers to preparing the standards the new system must meet in order to be accepted. 7 _____

8. The first step of the detailed investigation is to define organizational goals and system boundaries. 8 _____

9. The role of users in the system development process should be kept at a minimum. 9 _____

10. System volume and timing mean the same thing. 10 _____

Multiple choice. *Put the letter of the correct answer on the line next to the question.*

1. Which of the following is not usually used for systems analysis? 1 _____
   (a) Questionnaires.
   (b) Interviews.
   (c) Observation.
   (d) Request for quotations.

2. What is the correct order for the following stages in the system development process? 2 _____
   (a) Logical design, design review, physical design.
   (b) Physical design, design review, logical design.
   (c) Logical design, physical design, design review.
   (d) Physical design, logical design, design review.

3. What is the correct order for the following stages in the system development process?
(a) Design, acquisition, implementation, and maintenance.
(b) Acquisition, design, implementation, and maintenance.
(c) Design, acquisition, maintenance, implementation.
(d) Maintenance, acquisition, implementation, and design.

4. What is not part of the system implementation stage?
(a) Updating the new system.
(b) Acceptance testing.
(c) Training.
(d) Conversion.

5. The outcome of the systems analysis stage is the
(a) Project charter.
(b) Feasibility report.
(c) Cost/benefit report.
(d) Design alternatives report.

Fill in the blank. *Write the correct word or words in the blank to complete the sentence.*

1. Old and new systems operate simultaneously for a period of time during _____ conversion.
2. The first step in the system development process is _____.
3. A graphic method to trace the flow of data through a system is called a _____.
4. Deliberately extreme data should be used in preparing the _____ design.
5. A _____ chart is used to show the sequencing and duration of particular stages in the system development process.
6. A _____ is used to illustrate conditions and actions for decision makers.
7. The first step in the logical design stage is to determine the _____ requirements.
8. The continuing process of keeping a system in good working order is _____.
9. A _____ visually describes the system processes and includes some details about the hardware used.

10. A _____ conversion involves converting a small part of the organization to determine whether the proposed system should be adopted for the entire organization.

short answer questions

When answering these questions, think of concrete examples to illustrate your points.

1. What are the six steps in the system development process?
2. Describe the structured approach to system development.
3. What occurs during the problem recognition stage?
4. Describe the main substages of the systems analysis stage.
5. Describe the steps in the system design stage.
6. What steps occur during the system acquisition stage?
7. Describe the tasks found in the system implementation stage.
8. What are the four types of system conversion methods?
9. What is the purpose of system maintenance?

essay questions

1. Describe the six major stages of the system development process.
2. Discuss the steps involved in the systems analysis stage.
3. Why does logical design precede physical design?

Answers to the objective questions
True/false: 1. F; 2. F; 3. T; 4. F; 5. T; 6. T; 7. T; 8. T; 9. F; 10. F
Multiple choice: 1. d; 2. c; 3. a; 4. a; 5. b
Fill in the blank: 1. parallel; 2. problem recognition; 3. data-flow diagram; 4. test; 5. Gantt; 6. decision table; 7. output; 8. system maintenance; 9. system flowchart; 10. pilot

Designing software: programming for solutions

After studying this chapter you should understand the following:

- *The importance of software to all five elements of an information system.*
- *How programming fits into the system development process.*
- *Why information system users, programmers, and managers favor structured programming methods.*
- *Why and for whom programs are documented.*
- *How programs can be broken down into modules.*
- *How program steps can be outlined using flowcharts and pseudocode.*
- *The three basic logic patterns of structured programming.*

chapter 14

What's wrong with the honor roll list?

As at other schools, keeping student records up-to-date at Oakriver University is a challenge. Students, faculty members, and deans need timely and accurate records. Certain factors, however, work against this.

Fully aware of the difficulties of student recordkeeping, Alice Smith, a systems analyst, greeted the two other meeting participants and sat down at the conference table.

"I guess we all know what we're up against," Alice said.

"Basically, yes," Frank Barnes said. "Your boss and mine decided that yesterday. We have to solve the honor roll problem." Frank worked in the university's Student Records Office.

"And solve it by the end of the term," said Tom Lee. "That's a tall order!" Tom was a programmer. Both he and Alice worked for the university's Information Processing Center.

"Frank, can you summarize the problem in terms of the Student Records Office," Alice said. "Exactly what is it that you need?"

"All right," Frank said. "At present, one program does everything concerning grades. We run it at the end of each semester. It gives grade reports for each student, and prepares summary reports, such as the honor roll."

"That's all from one program?" Tom asked.

"I guess so," Frank said. "At least we run it all at once."

"That's the problem, as my boss explained it," Alice broke in. "He wants to separate the honor roll program from the program that generates grades."

Frank added, "We get so many clearances of incompletes, that some students qualify for the honor roll—but we don't find out until it has been prepared."

Alice got up, walked to the blackboard, and wrote: "Problems," and under it, "Incompletes." "Any other problems with the present system?" Alice asked.

"Yes, grades get changed occasionally, too," Frank said. "Either the professor made a mistake in the first place, or reconsiders it after talking with the student. Sometimes, too, the optical readers that take the grades from the professors' forms just plain get it wrong."

"Okay," Alice said. "Let's lump all that together as 'Corrections.' " She wrote "Corrections" on the board. "Anything else?"

"No," Frank said. "Those are the problems. That's why we can't produce the honor roll at the same time as the grade reports. To make it accurate we have to do it several weeks later, after the incompletes are in, and after we key in all the corrections. But we have to do it in time to send out the invitations to the awards ceremony!"

On the board, Alice drew a big box and labeled it "Grade Reports." Then she lopped off an end of it with the eraser, and labeled the end "Honor Roll."

Tom Lee chuckled. "That won't be done as easily as cutting off a slice of salami."

"True," Alice said. "Tom, you've worked on parts of the grade report program before, haven't you? Is it a structured program?"

"Yes, as I remember," Tom said. "It has over twenty modules."

"Modules," Alice said to Frank, "are small units of a program that do just one thing, and that follow certain conventions that make changing them easier."

"It's a batch system that runs on the mainframe," Tom said. "People with the right passwords can also make inquiries on-line with their terminals."

"I didn't quite understand that jargon," Frank said. "But it is a very complicated program. I'll vouch for that."

"Then we will have to be careful changing it," Alice said. "We'll have to follow a conservative, structured programming approach. Frank, thank you for telling us what the Student Records Office needs. Now Tom and I have got to get cracking on the details. I'll design the solution, and Tom will code and test it. We'll have to ask you more questions at certain points as we go along, to make sure we stay on target."

Programs and the information system

Computer *programs*, or *software*, consist of detailed step-by-step instructions written by **PROGRAMMERS** that a computer can interpret and act upon. *Application software* are those programs that direct the actual input, processing, and output activities for users. Although software is only one element of an information system, it has a vital relationship to all of the others.

Consider the honor roll at Oakriver University. Software affects how the *people*—the students, faculty, administrators, and staff— interact with the information system.

The software puts into effect some of the *rules and procedures* that are part of university policy, by placing them in a form that a computer can carry out. The rules state under what conditions people can gain access to information. For instance, students gain access to grades only at prespecified times, and are not allowed to change them. Faculty members use class rosters maintained at the Records Office to determine who is enrolled in their classes. These rosters are prepared according to rules governing student registration, prerequisites, class sizes, class schedules, and faculty work load.

Deans use the records data to know how many students they have and what their majors are—an example of how software affects *data*. The Oakriver University staff also use the data, and indeed it was their inability to use it at the right time that brought about a clash between what the software *actually did*, and the rules and procedures it was *supposed* to be implementing.

Software also implements rules stating how to use certain *hardware*. The university's Information Processing Center, for instance, has a printer in its computer room, to print the various reports created by the grades program as well as other programs. There is an enormous gap, however, between the desire to have the information printed, and inducing that physical object—the printer—to move its mechanical parts and spew out the printed information. This gap is bridged by software.

Even the *software* itself is affected by rules embodied in software. Tom Lee has been asked to change the grades program to produce the honor roll in a new way. He will have to follow the rules of other programs governing such matters as the type and meaning of the programming language he works in. In a nutshell, no matter which of the five information system elements we look at, software plays a crucial role.

Figure 14-1
How the program development process fits into the system development process.

Programming and problem solving

Programming and the system development process

Creating or altering a computer program, especially if it is at all complex, requires a systematic problem-solving approach. In Chapter 13, we introduced the system development process. There we noted that all systems go through a process of birth, growth, maturity, and decline. Figure 14-1 shows how the system development process and the program development process interrelate. We can identify seven steps required to solve a programming problem within the system development process:

1. Problem recognition
2. Problem definition
3. Program design
4. Program coding

5. Program testing
6. Program implementation
7. Program maintenance

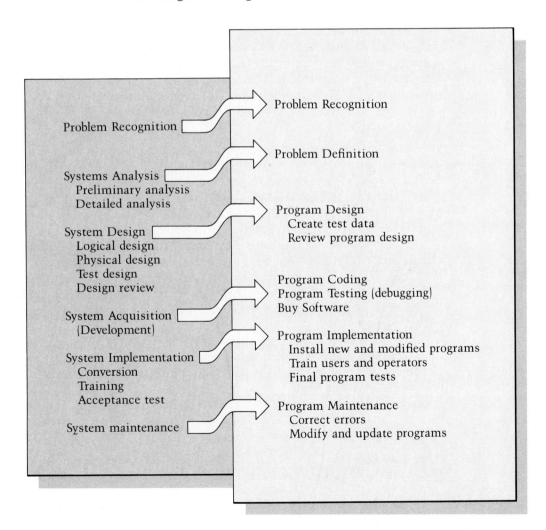

Problem Recognition

Problem Recognition

Problem Definition

Systems Analysis
    Preliminary analysis
    Detailed analysis

Program Design
    Create test data
    Review program design

System Design
    Logical design
    Physical design
    Test design
    Design review

Program Coding
Program Testing (debugging)
Buy Software

System Acquisition
    (Development)

Program Implementation
    Install new and modified programs
    Train users and operators
    Final program tests

System Implementation
    Conversion
    Training
    Acceptance test

Program Maintenance
    Correct errors
    Modify and update programs

System maintenance

The program development process

These steps comprise the **PROGRAM DEVELOPMENT PROCESS**. As with full system development process, as we move through each stage we need *checkpoints* where we ask whether we have successfully completed a step. At each checkpoint a decision must be made whether to continue the process or to return and redo the previous step. Let's take a closer look at each of the program development steps.

Problem recognition

Problem recognition is identical to the *first stage* of the system development process discussed in Chapter 13. During this stage, an organization perceives problems or opportunities and suspects a software-oriented solution might be effective. Throughout the problem recognition stage, it is important to differentiate *symptoms* from *real* problems and opportunities. Often users and less experienced analysts or programmers will leap ahead to software solutions before the problem is fully understood. Starting with this stage, the systems analyst is expected to fully document the program development process.

Problem definition

Problem definition involves specifying the exact nature of the problem. This step is part of the *systems analysis* stage where the existing information system is examined. Using the full range of techniques (see Chapter 13), the analyst will look at existing business operations and procedures in addition to programs and support documentation.

Program design

PROGRAM DESIGN involves specifying the structure of the program in detail. As with other parts of *system design*, the proposed program design moves from an overall or general *logical* solution level down to a more detailed *physical* solution (such as details unique to the selected programming language). Later in this chapter, we discuss some important techniques of program design.

An **ALGORITHM** is a set of rules that breaks down the solution into a simple procedure. Everyone uses algorithms, even if unconsciously, all the time. When doing household chores or balancing your checkbook you follow a set of rules or a routine. Programming languages are designed to express algorithms efficiently, so that a computer can carry out the steps.

Previously developed algorithms may be used for different purposes than were originally intended. For example, the algorithm for baking a lemon sponge cake can be used with only minor changes for an orange sponge cake. In the same way, some algorithms or even complete programs designed to solve one problem can also be used to solve another.

Program coding

PROGRAM CODING means translating the design into a programming language that will run on the computer. This step is part of the *system*

career box

An overview of programming careers

Computer programmers design, code, test, document, and install software of two kinds: (1) application software and (2) system software. Application programmers and programmer analysts handle application software. Systems programmers handle system software. Application programming jobs are described in the Career Box for Chapter 15.

Although each of these three types of programming has different requirements, they also have a lot in common. They all deal with the same basic concepts; differences lie in the levels of responsibility and the degree of involvement with the machine. A certain orderliness in terms of mental habits, and perhaps work habits, seems to be required to program well, along with the ability to be creative. To some extent, these two personality characteristics are opposites; the good programmer, however, unites them.

Programmers come from every conceivable background, age group, and walk of life. If one characteristic could be found that a great many share, it would be that they are "loners." This does not mean they are inept at social relationships or unwilling to take an active part in a programming team, but that they enjoy puzzling out intricate matters themselves. For all the team-oriented emphasis of contemporary structured programming, there is still plenty of opportunity to work alone. At some point, being a programmer boils down to the lonely moment of truth when you either get the machine to do what it has to do, or you fail.

To break into programming these days usually requires post-high school training—preferably an A.A. or B.S. degree in a computer-related field. Some experience with computers will certainly help you to be chosen over the mass of inexperienced people looking for programming jobs. It is sometimes possible for a person presently working for a company to become involved with programming as an outgrowth of a present job, and then to make a career switch.

Programming is a well-paid field with excellent career prospects. For the foreseeable future neither business nor government will be able to function without programmers. Each of the three types of programmer is broken down into different levels, with appropriate gradations of salary and responsibility. Most programmers join organizations as regular employees; some work as consultants. The career path out of programming is usually into systems analysis, sometimes into management, or into such other information systems careers as training and education specialist, technical writer, database administrator, and information systems auditor.

If a programmer has an area of expertise that is particularly sought after, it will be easier to find that first job, change jobs, and advance up the career ladder. Such areas include telecommunications, distributed data processing, the use of databases, and on-line as opposed to batch applications. Further career moves could include positions in management or as an independent consultant.

acquisition stage where the new system is developed or "constructed." During program coding you write the step-by-step instructions necessary to tell the computer what to do. We will see examples of program coding in Chapter 15.

Program testing

PROGRAM TESTING involves checking the program for errors and rewriting parts of the program to correct the mistakes. Like program coding, this step is considered part of the *system acquisition* stage. The process of finding and correcting errors in programs is called *debugging*. This phase of the program development cycle can be very time-consuming. Test data (developed in the design stage) are used to test the limits of the program.

Program implementation

PROGRAM IMPLEMENTATION (part of the *system implementation* stage) means using the program. A programmed solution is implemented by running the program. Sample program runs for the honor roll problem are shown in Chapter 15. If the program works, all is well. If not, the program needs further testing.

Program maintenance

PROGRAM MAINTENANCE, a part of *system maintenance*, involves correcting any undetected errors in the program and making needed changes. Programs must often be modified because the conditions affecting the original problem change. A flexibly designed program will more easily handle future modifications.

We can see how Oakriver's honor roll program in the opening example fits into the program development process. The people in the Student Records Office first *recognized* the problem of an inaccurate honor roll. When Alice, Frank, and Tom met, they began to *define* the problem. After further definition, Alice will *design* a program to solve the problem, and Tom will *code* and *test* it. The program will then be *implemented* and the staff of OU's Information Processing Center will *maintain* it. As new problems arise the program development process may begin anew.

Program documentation

Program development is more than just writing the program itself. Support materials are required. These materials, called **PROGRAM DOCUMENTATION**, consist of manuals, display screens, and sometimes audiovisual materials that tell (1) *users* how to use the program, (2) *operators* how to run it, and (3) *programmers* how to change it. Explanatory material present in the program itself and on display screens are considered part of the documentation. A major source of these program documentation materials is the system development process documents written or gathered by the system development team. Access to documentation may be restricted for system security reasons. (Security issues are discussed in Chapter 17.)

Documentation should be written clearly and simply so that it is understandable to the average user, operator, or programmer. It should contain as little jargon as possible. Documentation should be written while the program is being developed. When changes are made in a program, the documentation for the program should be reviewed, and updated where necessary.

Effective writing is always done with the audience in mind. Program documentation must also consider its audience. Users, operators, and programmers each need to know different things about a program, and separate documentation must be prepared for each group. This can mean three separate manuals; three different parts of the same manual; or some other combination, such as screen displays for users, a run manual for operators, and pseudocode for programmers.

User-oriented documentation

In the distant past of electronic computing, documentation was oriented toward aiding programmers and other members of an information system staff. Users were left to fend for themselves. Users have since come to demand good documentation, a demand reinforced by management practices.

USER-ORIENTED DOCUMENTATION includes those written documents and screen displays that assist the user in exploiting the benefits of the program. Written materials are contained in a manual; screen displays are built into the program itself. The user needs to know how to run or interact with the program, what the program can do, and what steps to take if something goes wrong.

Operator-oriented documentation

Programs that run on mainframes and minicomputers require documentation for the people who will operate the programs. The operator is distinct from the user, who may sit at a terminal thousands of miles away from the computer. OPERATOR-ORIENTED DOCUMENTATION is generally in the form of a run manual kept by the computer console. It tells how to run the program—the magnetic tapes or removable disks that must be mounted, the peripherals that need to be on-line, the type of paper for the printer, and similar considerations.

Programmer-oriented documentation

PROGRAMMER-ORIENTED DOCUMENTATION focuses on how to maintain and modify the program. Documentation for programmers responsible for maintaining and changing a program consists of the results of the structured design and the actual program code. In addition, programmers have access to user and operator documentation. Most modern programs that users work with are protected against unauthorized people changing the program. Users normally do not see the computer code in which the program was written. For example, the actual program that operates a check-writing procedure at a corporation would not be available to the people using the program to write the checks.

Buying software

Just because you have a programming problem doesn't mean you need to create your own program. Many small and medium-sized organizations, as well as most individuals who use microcomputers, don't have the resources to write their own programs. Instead, they buy the programs from software vendors. Chapters 8 through 12 discuss some of the most popular productivity software available.

When you buy software, you shift responsibility for program design, coding, and testing from yourself or your organization to the vendor. In Chapter 8, the section "Selecting Packaged Software" presents criteria for choosing software. Further, while software developers attempt to test for normal information processing requirements, errors may occur. Even if you buy, rather than write your own, you must have a clear sense of the problem you expect the software to solve, be sure you have the correct software to solve it, and make certain it is installed properly for your system.

Structured programming

The need for structured programs

Cast yourself in the role of a manager. You have decided to implement changes in your company's inventory control procedures. You contact the information processing manager and arrange to discuss the changes. At the meeting, you are shocked to hear the changes will take twice as long to reprogram as you expected. One reason for the delay is that the programmers who originally worked on the inventory control problem have left the company for other jobs, and the new programmers are having difficulties tracking the complex logic of the program. In addition, the existing program can handle only 4000 different kinds of parts used in the production process, and your future needs require a system capable of tracking twice as many. If the existing program had been written using a structured approach, modifying and maintaining the program would be greatly simplified.

In STRUCTURED PROGRAMMING, programmers use a top-down approach to break a program solution into modules. The result of the structured programming effort is a STRUCTURED PROGRAM.

The TOP-DOWN APPROACH starts with an overall design at the general level and then progresses to details of the solution. Each MODULE is a self-contained, well-defined subpart of a program that performs a single function, such as "calculate the students' grade point average" or "list the honor roll students." The modules are arranged in a hierarchy: the ones at the top give orders to other lower-level modules, which do the actual work. Use of this standard relationship among modules makes it easier to create, as well as to understand and to modify the logic of a structured program at a later time. Think of modules as the smallest unit you can manage. From your own experience, breaking down your college career into years, then terms, classes, and even into hours, is an example of the top-down approach and modules.

case in point
What's wrong with go to?

One type of logic structure that was once very common is now forbidden in structured programming. This structure is the *unconditional branch*, which directs a program to go from one part of itself to another. The mechanism for accomplishing an unconditional branch is a statement telling the program to go to some other line of code. Hence the term GO TO (or GOTO).

A branch splits a program into parts. The selection structure, for example, is a type of branch. Selection, however, involves a *conditional* branch—a test that determines which of two directions the program will take. An unconditional branch does not involve a test. It simply splits a program abruptly into parts using GO TO statements.

GO TO statements violate three principles of structured programming: modularity, linear program flow, and ease of program maintenance. The problem is that they are easily misused to patch together a poorly designed program.

Imagine yourself faced with the problem of designing a program to read a file, process the records, and write the results. It's late at night, you're tired and don't feel like spending the time to write the program correctly. Besides, you're changing jobs and won't have to worry about this program when it's time to make program maintenance changes. You've written the flowchart for the first and second process of the records when suddenly you remember that you have to write an intermediate result before you can do the second process. All you do is insert a GO TO statement into the processing step, splitting the process operation. After printing the intermediate step, you need another GO TO to return to the processing operation. One more GO TO branch is required to avoid repeating the intermediate step and reach the end of the program. The flowlines blur together. The result, as the figure shows, is a tangled mess, like a plate of spaghetti. And, in fact, programs with an abundance of GO TOs are often called spaghetti code.

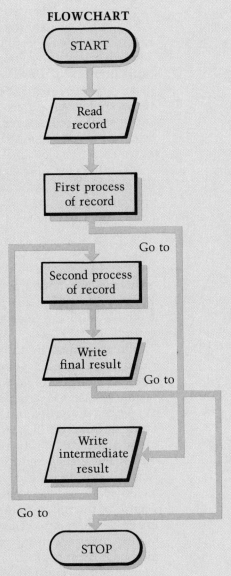

FLOWCHART

PSEUDOCODE
START
Read record
First process of record
GOTO write intermediate record
Second process of record
Write final result
GOTO stop
Write intermediate result
GOTO second process of record
STOP

Further, it is easier to correct errors in a program made up of modules, because only one module may be involved and therefore only one may need to be changed. The same applies to modifying a program or expanding its capabilities—the modifications can be isolated to certain modules, while the rest of the program remains unaffected.

Structured programming was developed to control the haphazard programming methods once common in the industry. In the 1970s, people came to recognize the value of structured methods in reducing the overall costs of a program throughout its useful life. The rise in the use of structured programming is directly related to those issues that led to the adoption of comparable methods in the *system development process.*

The two main goals of structured programming are: (1) detecting errors as early as possible in the program development process, and (2) simplifying the maintenance or modification of programs. In both cases, costs are reduced in comparison to the earlier, nonstructured methods.

How structured programming aids programmers and managers

Structured methods apply not only to the way programmers design and write programs, but also to the ways in which they do their work. These methods apply to individual programmers as well as programming teams.

Programmers prefer a structured programming approach. Structured programming defines job tasks and accountability clearly and offers support services where required. The structured programs that result are easier for programmers to modify and maintain.

Recall the problem that began this chapter. The Student Records Office at Oakriver University wanted to produce the honor roll after all other grade calculations were done. This would allow for corrected grades and grades replacing incompletes, to be considered when calculating eligibility for the honor roll.

Alice Smith, the systems analyst assigned to lead the project, and Tom Lee, the programmer, first obtained documentation for the existing grades program. They found that it was a structured program containing over twenty-five modules, designed using the top-down method. The only problem was that some of the modules were too large (containing several hundred statements) and did more than one thing. The module that created the honor roll also produced other reports. So with the aim of changing this module—but as few others as possible—Alice approached the problem afresh.

Two basic steps were necessary to create the honor roll. First, a data file had to be created. The file would contain student names and grade point averages. Second, the file had to be read and the names of those students with grade point averages of 3.5 or more extracted. This is a simplified version of the way most colleges select those eligible for an honor roll list. We are ignoring such factors as flexible grade point levels, credit hours completed, and withdrawal and incomplete policies.

For managers of programming projects, structured methods provide useful management control techniques in the following areas:

- Assigning reasonably sized tasks to programmers.
- Assuring that programmers use standard methods.
- Determining task accountability and responsibility.
- Helping limit problems caused by employee turnover.

Structured walkthroughs

One method of detecting errors in a program is to seek assistance from programming peers. A programmer peer review meeting, or STRUCTURED WALKTHROUGH, may be held at any point in a project from design through coding and testing.

The purpose of a structured walkthrough is to provide a nonthreatening environment in which to evaluate a programmer's work for errors. Besides error detection there are two other advantages of structured walkthroughs. First, by keeping others informed of an individual's efforts, time delays caused by staff turnover can be minimized; and second, potential threats to the computer program introduced either through design or accident can be detected.

Criticism and suggestions should focus on programming errors, not on programming style. Such meetings are most effective when they include the programmer working on the program, a moderator to direct the session, other programmers to "walk through" the steps of the program and record potential errors, and a representative from the user group that originally requested the program. *Managers are not present* at these meetings, to help ensure that the emphasis will be on solving problems rather than on the performance of a particular employee. The programming materials should be distributed to the peer group prior to the meeting to allow people an opportunity to review them before the session. Walkthrough sessions may last up to several hours.

Structured programming: breaking down the problem

There are many methods used in designing structured programs. The basic approach is to break a problem into its subcomponents through the process of functional decomposition. FUNCTIONAL DECOMPOSITION is the breaking down of a large task into smaller units. The goal is to create modules that contain only the activities required to perform one function.

Structured programming design does not exist in a vacuum. As part of the logical and physical design section of system design discussed in Chapter 13, the analyst or programmer will have input details (record layout, file, and database specifications), general processing requirements, and output (printer and display screen designs) details available. To trace the flow of data through the system, Alice Smith, the systems analyst, can refer to such items as the part of a data-flow diagram shown in Figure 14-2. In this diagram the student records (data) are read from a *data store* holding the student grades; honor roll students are selected in

Figure 14-2
A portion of the data-flow diagram for the student grade reporting system.

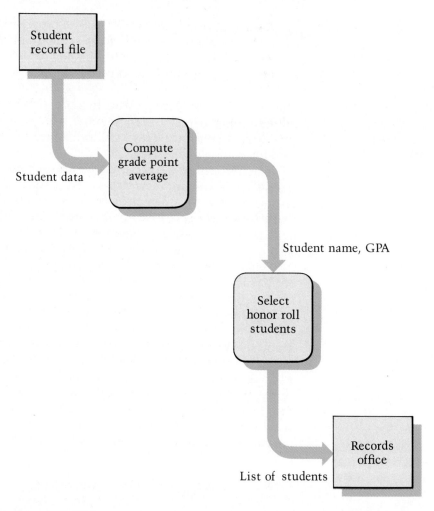

the *process bubble;* and the report is sent to the records office—the *external entity.*

Based on the system design, there are three major steps in the actual program process:

1. Creation of a **STRUCTURE CHART** that shows the hierarchical relationships between the modules of a program.
2. Development of the **INPUT-PROCESS-OUTPUT (IPO) CHARTS** that show in detail the input, processing, and output steps necessary to execute the module.
3. Writing detailed flowcharts and/or pseudocode statements. A **FLOW-CHART** is a diagram that shows how a program works in terms of sequence, movement of data, and logic. **PSEUDOCODE** is an English-like code that helps the programmer understand the steps needed to execute the program.

Once the pseudocode or the flowchart necessary to solve the problem has been formulated, it can be converted into the computer's programming language code. We learn more about this coding process in Chapter 15.

Structure charts

Program design begins with the *structure chart*. Alice Smith uses this chart to develop her understanding of how the new grades program (that is, the old grades program with a small number of the modules changed) must work, and to communicate program organization and function to others, principally Tom, the programmer.

Each program can be broken into five parts: initialization, input, processing, output, and termination. The initialization and termination steps are primarily housekeeping in nature. Alice's structure chart (Figure 14-3) starts at the top of the chart and moves down to the more specialized areas, following the top-down approach described earlier in the chapter.

Each module in the structure chart has an identification number referring to its IPO chart. The IPO chart for the honor roll program is shown later in Figure 14-6. As we move deeper into the chart, the numbers become more complex. In addition to the numbering system, the structure chart should include any other references concerning the proper flow of control and data through the program. Note that the general flow of the chart is from left to right and from top to bottom.

CONTROL MODULES at the top give orders to the other modules below. CONTROL-AND-PROCESSING MODULES perform control operations over lower-level modules and carry out processing functions. PROCESSING MODULES are at the lowest level, carrying out the orders required by the higher modules.

The main control module for the student grades report is labeled 1.0, and the subordinate control modules for initialization (start-up procedures), input, process, output, and termination are labeled 1.1, 1.2, 1.3, 1.4, and 1.5, respectively. Before the honor roll module (1.3.5.1) can be processed, the input module must be completed. Control commands (modules 1.0, 1.3, and 1.3.5) direct the activation of the honor roll selection program to create a file containing the list of the honor roll students. To produce the written report using the selected data, control is first returned to the main control module (1.0); then control is transferred to module 1.4.3.1 (through modules 1.4 and 1.4.3).

With this arrangement, the honor roll program can now be run whenever the Student Records office specifies, not as a by-product of the entire package, but "on its own."

More on modules

Some of the features that make modules so helpful in the program design process include:

■ *Performing one function.* A module should perform only a single function that can be defined in a few words, such as "calculate student grade point average." Recall from Chapter 13 that such modules are said to be *cohesive.* Each function may require several activities or steps.

■ *Independence from other modules.* For example, a processing module concerned with calculating a grade point average should have all the formulas for multiplication, addition, and division in the module, and not need to call another module to do the work. Independent modules are often called *loosely coupled* modules. Ideally a module has high internal cohesion and loose external coupling to other modules.

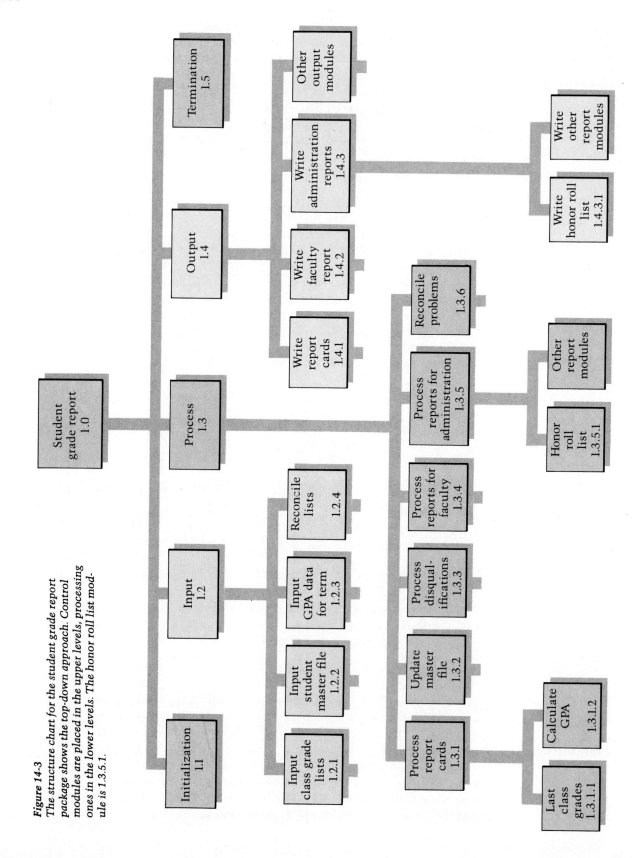

Figure 14-3
The structure chart for the student grade report package shows the top-down approach. Control modules are placed in the upper levels, processing ones in the lower levels. The honor roll list module is 1.3.5.1.

Figure 14-4
Modules have only one entrance and one exit. The flow of control, to get from one low-level module to another always requires passing through a higher-level module. Thus, module 1.3.1.2 cannot itself invoke module 1.3.2.1. Instead, when module 1.3.1.2 has finished its task, control automatically returns through 1.3.1 to 1.3. Module 1.3 can then call module 1.3.2, which can in turn call 1.3.2.1.

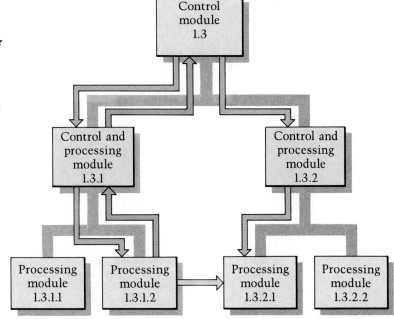

⇨ Call
⇨ Return
⇨ Incorrect flow

   ▪ *One entrance and one exit (see Figure 14-4).* There should be only one way of accessing the module from other modules and of leaving to other modules. With multiple entrances and exits, correcting or modifying the program becomes more difficult, and results might be passed to the wrong module.
   ▪ *Automatic return to the superior module.* Upon task completion, control *returns* from the lower module to the *calling* (higher-level) module which ordered the execution of the task. Lower-level modules are not allowed to call higher-level modules. For instance, module 1.3.2 in Figure 14-4 can call module 1.3.2.2, but not vice versa. The term *call* refers to a programming technique of transferring control to a SUBROU-TINE when a MAIN PROGRAM requests it. Figure 14-5 shows a main program and its subroutines. This module feature is common with many menu-driven productivity software packages.
   ▪ *Manageable size to reduce debugging problems.* Most programmers prefer to work on cohesive, loosely coupled modules that contain no more than seven activities per function and require either about 24 lines (a single screen display) or 60 lines (a page of printout).

Input-Process-Output (IPO) charts

Each module in the structure chart is expanded into an IPO chart, which shows the input requirements, basic processing steps, and overall output needs for the module. The IPO chart for module 1.3.5.1 is shown in Figure 14-6. First the input requirements are listed in order of appearance. Then, the process steps and output requirements are listed in their proper order. Every step in a module need not be laid out in an IPO chart. Very detailed steps will be handled in the flowcharting or pseudo-code-writing stages of the programming process.

Figure 14-5
How a main program and its subroutines interact.

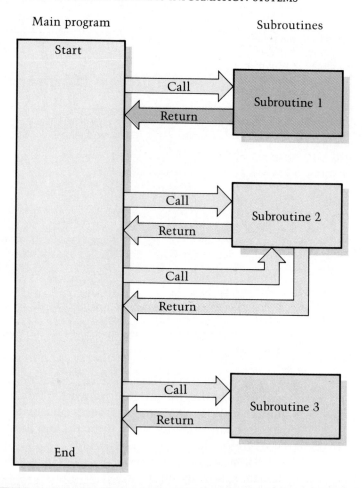

Figure 14-6
The IPO chart for the honor roll module.

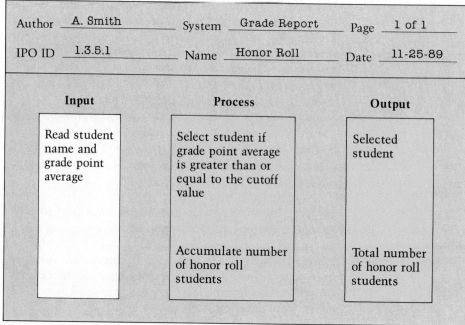

Both Alice and Tom can tell by looking at the IPO chart diagrams what the program design should be, and if it will solve the problem of the Student Records Office. Next, they can move to the specific design and programming of the required modules.

Detail development

Detailing the program logic

After the IPO charts are completed and approved the actual program can be designed. To trace the internal steps of each program design, two major methods are used: the flowchart and pseudocode.

Flowchart symbols and pseudocode phrases
Flowcharts consist of standard symbols connected by lines. The symbols can be drawn using a plastic FLOWCHART TEMPLATE. Each symbol has a different meaning. Figure 14-7 shows the meaning of the flowchart symbols, and gives the corresponding pseudocode phrase. Let's define each of the flowcharting symbols given in the figure.

The SYSTEM START/TERMINATION SYMBOL indicates the beginning or end of a program or of a subroutine within a program. The commands (usually not part of your actual program) send messages to the computer to get its attention and say that you want to start or stop.

FLOWLINES guide the reader to different parts of the flowchart. Arrows drawn on the lines help the reader follow the flowlines that link the flowchart symbols. Generally, flowcharts start in the upper left part of the page and move down the page and to the right (just like reading). The circular CONNECTORS link parts of the flowchart on the same page, while the five-sided connectors link parts on different pages. Any connectors leading the reader up the paper or to the left must use arrows to point the way.

The ANNOTATION SYMBOL represents comments or remarks that do not affect the operation of the program. Annotations explain the meaning of various programming steps (such as explaining how a complicated formula works). Comments assist future programmers in following the program if revisions need to be made.

The PREPARATION SYMBOL denotes any steps involving preliminary or preparatory functions. Examples are initializing a variable (setting it equal to 0 or some other number), or reserving data storage locations in main memory for the program's use.

The INPUT/OUTPUT SYMBOL refers to any input and output operation, such as reading in data from a keyboard, or outputting to a printer. The input/output symbol is labeled with the function and piece of equipment involved.

The PROCESS SYMBOL represents mathematical computations and data manipulation, such as calculations and summarizations. This symbol is also used when constants or variables are assigned specific values.

Operation	Flowchart symbol	Pseudocode phrase	Meaning
System interrupt (Start, Stop)		START STOP	Notes the beginning or end of a program or subroutine
Input, output		Input, get, read, print, write	All input/output operations
Process		Process, compute, calculate, initialize to a value	Process functions for arithmetic and data manipulation
Decision		IF ... THEN, or IF ... THEN ... ELSE . . . ENDIF	Decision operations for logic tests and comparisons
Preparation		Prepare, initialize	Prepare the program for later stages, set variables to a starting value (used at the beginning of FOR/ NEXT loops in BASIC)
Predefined process		CALL, subroutine	Use of a predefined function: usually a subroutine or library routine
Annotation		Comment, note, remark, annotate	These comments provide guidance to the reader of the program, but do not affect its operation
Connector	on-page off-page	Not used in pseudocode	Connector to other parts of the flowchart on the same or different pages
Flowlines		Not used in pseudocode	Shows the direction of the flow; usual flow is from top to bottom and from left to right

The DECISION SYMBOL denotes choices based upon comparisons. While the process symbol and input/output symbol have one flowline entering and exiting them, at least two flowlines must exit from a decision symbol. The exiting flowlines must be labeled (usually with a "yes" or "no"). An example of a choice might be whether to grant credit to a client. The favorable choice would be to grant credit; the unfavorable choice to deny credit.

A PREDEFINED PROCESS SYMBOL refers to a prewritten subprogram or subroutine which is called upon request. It might be a short series of mathematical formulas, for instance, calculating interest paid on a loan using different rules (simple versus compound interest).

Flowcharts have been used to advantage since the very earliest days of computing. They serve to show what a program that has not yet been written will do, so that a programmer can write code from them. They also make it possible for others to understand a program once it has been written without having to study the code in great depth.

Flowcharts, however, have certain disadvantages. For some people, a visual approach to problem solving may be confusing. The display of boxes and lines can be cluttered and difficult to trace, especially if critical steps overlap from one page to the next. Also, when changes are made in a flowchart, the entire chart may need to be redrawn. To speed up the reworking of flowcharts, software packages exist that are capable of creating and modifying flowcharts. Finally, there is a lack of standardization of some symbols. The symbols, for example, that are used to mark the beginning and end of loops that are specific to programming languages—such as FOR/NEXT loops in BASIC—are not standardized. (The rule that program design should be programming language independent is often broken in introductory programming classes.)

Pseudocode was developed to overcome some of the visual clutter associated with flowcharting. Pseudocode is not the same as programming language code (hence the "pseudo" in its name), but is a general English-like guide to solving problems. Its main advantage is that it can be written much like one talks, without complications of templates or graphics. In many work environments, pseudocode is used instead of flowcharts.

The first word in a line of pseudocode is usually an action verb written as an imperative—get, read, print, calculate, and so on. The verb is then followed by a short description of what it is acting upon—for instance, "get" might be followed by "manufacturing parts list," or "student data file."

As with flowcharts there is a lack of standardization. The command to read a data file might be written "Read data file," or "READ DATA FILE." Once a style—for either flowcharting or writing pseudocode—has been selected, stay with that format throughout the entire programming project.

Regardless of whether you use flowcharts, pseudocode, or some other design tool, the basic goals of program design are *clarity* and *simplicity*. The purpose of both flowcharts and pseudocode is to help you or someone else code a program correctly.

Program logic patterns—sequence, selection, and loops

In structured programming there are three types of logic patterns: sequence, selection, and loop. A computer program can perform any processing with one or more of these patterns. These program logic patterns are independent of the programming language used. Let's work through an example for sequence, for selection, and for two kinds of loops.

Sequence—creating an airplane ticket

A **SEQUENCE** is a set of linear steps carried out in the order of their appearance. The commands for a sequence are always action verbs such as read, calculate, print.

Consider the problem of calculating the total bill for an airplane ticket for one customer—a problem that occurs many times each day at Freddy Johnson's Travel Agency. The steps in the flowchart pattern and pseudocode lines for such a bill are shown in Figure 14-8. The sequential steps are starting, reading the ticket price, performing multiplication operations to calculate the taxes, summing the values, printing the sum, and ending the program.

PSEUDOCODE
START
Read the airline ticket price
Calculate the general tax
Calculate the security tax
Add the price and the two taxes
Print the data and the total
STOP

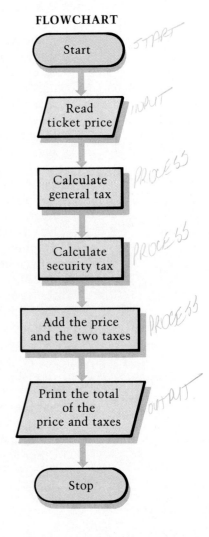

FLOWCHART

Start

Read ticket price

Calculate general tax

Calculate security tax

Add the price and the two taxes

Print the total of the price and taxes

Stop

Figure 14-8
Sequence—creating an airplane ticket.

In later examples we will show several commands within the same symbol or on the same line. The two tax calculations in Figure 14-8 could, for instance, be combined into one: "Calculate taxes."

Selection—inspecting the inspectors
SELECTION logic patterns (see Figure 14-9) use comparisons based on decisions or choices to split a program into different paths. Usually the choice is a comparison phrased in the form of a logical test. If the test proves true, then one course of action is followed; if false, another. Such selection patterns are often called IFTHENELSE logic steps. The diamond-shaped decision symbol must be labeled, showing the direction for both the true ("yes") result of the logical test and the false ("no") result.

As you can see in the figure, pseudocode indents components of the IFTHENELSE procedure to denote their subordinate role. When a choice is between doing an action and doing nothing, ELSE is placed in parentheses. This convention indicates no action is intended so a reader will not suspect a line of code has been forgotten. The ENDIF line indicates the end of the IFTHENELSE structure.

The program design in Figure 14-9 compares the quality control inspection percentages for the different inspectors who work at Global Electrical Equipment. Inspectors are supposed to take the correct action no less than 99 percent of the time. A correct action is approving an appliance that is good or rejecting one that is defective. An incorrect action is approving a defective appliance or rejecting a good one.

PSEUDOCODE
```
START
Read the inspector's NAME and PERCENTAGE
IF PERCENTAGE > = 99 THEN
        Print favorable comment
ELSE
        Print unfavorable comment
ENDIF
STOP
```

FLOWCHART

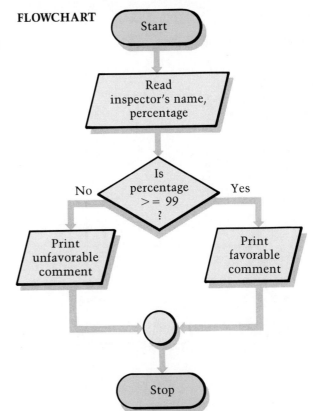

First we read in the inspector's percentage of correct actions (call this value PERCENTAGE). After PERCENTAGE is read in, a test is made. If PERCENTAGE is equal to or greater than 99, then we print a favorable statement (such as "Inspector X is meeting the standard"). If PERCENTAGE is less than 99, then we print an unfavorable comment (such as "Inspector X is not meeting the standard—take action").

DOWHILE loop—reading student records
A **LOOP** allows the program to execute repeatedly one or a series of steps. Each pass through the loop is called an *iteration*. There are two major types of loops: DOWHILE and DOUNTIL. A **DOWHILE LOOP** continues as long as a condition is true. A **DOUNTIL LOOP** keeps working until the specified condition is met. As with selection operations, notice how the pseudocode indents the processes performed inside the loop, and closes the loop with an ENDDO statement.

Figure 14-10 shows in flowchart and pseudocode form a DOWHILE loop for reading a file of student records at Oakriver University and printing the students' addresses. The DOWHILE loop requires that iter-

Figure 14-10
DOWHILE loop—reading student records.

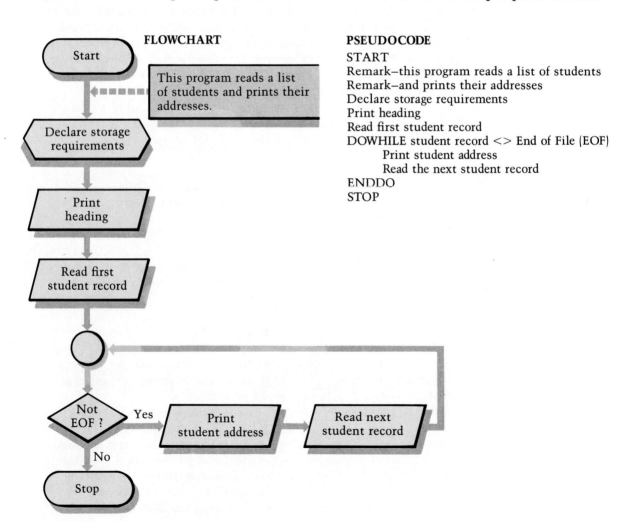

FLOWCHART

Start

This program reads a list of students and prints their addresses.

Declare storage requirements

Print heading

Read first student record

Not EOF ? — Yes → Print student address → Read next student record

No

Stop

PSEUDOCODE

START
Remark–this program reads a list of students
Remark–and prints their addresses
Declare storage requirements
Print heading
Read first student record
DOWHILE student record <> End of File (EOF)
    Print student address
    Read the next student record
ENDDO
STOP

ations (cycles through the loop) continue *while*, or as long as, a condition tests true. In this case, the condition being tested is whether or not the record just read is the last record in the file. When the condition tests false, the loop operation ends.

Before the loop is entered, the first student's record is read—an operation often called a *priming read*. The first step within the loop is a test to determine if the record just read is *not* the last one in the file (end of file or EOF). If it isn't (the test condition is true), the student's address is printed out and the next record is read for testing. When the test condition is false (the record just read *is* the last one in the file), the program leaves the loop.

Keeping track of loops: counters, trailer values, and flags

A major problem in designing loops is how to keep track of them and find a way out. In Figure 14-10, for example, if we didn't know what constituted the end of the file, we would be trapped in the loop. Three devices for keeping track of DOWHILE and DOUNTIL loop operations are counters, trailer values, and flags.

A **COUNTER** keeps track of the number of times a program has met a certain condition. Before a program enters a loop, the value of the counter is set to a specific value—usually 0 or 1—by the process of **INITIALIZATION**. Every time the program enters the loop and satisfies the condition the counter is keeping track of—the number of records in the file—the value of the counter increases.

A **TRAILER VALUE** is a nonsense value placed at the end of a data file specifically to mark the end of the file. The program in Figure 14-10, for instance, might be instructed to leave the loop when it encountered "NONAME" in the student name field, or "9999999" in the student ID field. A proper trailer value is one that will not appear under any conceivable condition. The value "-1" would be appropriate when testing for peoples' ages but not when inputting recorded temperatures in January in New York City.

A *flag* is another way to mark the end of a file. The **END-OF-FILE FLAG (EOF FLAG)** is a kind of switch set at one value—say "0" or "no" for a DOWHILE loop—before the loop starts. When the program encounters the end of the file, the switch changes value—to "1" or "yes"—and the program leaves the loop.

Nested DOUNTIL loops—student test grades

A DOUNTIL loop continues repeating an operation *until* a test is true. When the test is true, we exit from the loop. There are certain times when this technique is quite handy. The final example for loops also demonstrates nesting one loop inside another.

Figure 14-11 shows a nested DOUNTIL loop controlled by counters to read four test scores for each of thirty Oakriver University students. (The program would go on to average each student's four test scores to give a grade, but for simplicity's sake that part of the program is omitted.) For each student, we use a "row" of data with four columns, one for each test. For thirty students, therefore, we have a thirty-row, four-column set of data. On paper we would record the data as a rows-and-

Irreverent but helpful hints for novice programmers: the KISS theory of programming

Assume that your programming assignment is due next week. How can you get it finished and still keep your sanity?

An operating theory can be observed in the management of many organizations. Stated simply—in its less offensive form—it is "Keep It Short and Simple," or KISS for short. Structured programming methods help us attain this goal of simplicity. Let's review some helpful, if irreverent, hints:

□ *Allow yourself plenty of time.* Even a short program may take several hours to complete. Most computer center terminal rooms get very crowded and noisy when hordes of people rush in to complete projects.

□ *Do not code or flowchart in ink.* You're going to change your program and flowchart several times before the project is done. There is a two-way feedback process where changes in the program will lead to changes in the flowchart, and vice versa.

□ *Use variable names that make sense.* If using names with a single letter, use the first letter of the particular variable, such as "G" for "gross tax." Use the equations $N = G - D$ or NETPAY = GROSS - DEDUCT instead of $A = B - C$. If you use words for variable names, limit them to six characters, or use mnemonics (memory-jogging letter combinations). Don't forget to spell them right as well as use discretion, because a potential employer may want to see your program someday.

□ *Break the problem into small pieces.* Initialization, input, process, output, and termination—any program can be reduced to these five parts. Each part can be flowcharted, or expressed in pseudocode, on a separate sheet of paper to give you enough room. Then in your final draft, you can combine the segments. When coding your program you can follow the same process. Don't worry about fancy style—just get the program to work, and then go back and make it pretty.

□ *Write out your program before you sit down at the keyboard.* The input process will go easier, and other people waiting in the computer center to use the terminal won't glare at you as you slowly and painfully compose the first draft of your program one character at a time.

□ *Take time to learn the keyboard.* Keyboards are similar to, yet different from, traditional typewriters in a number of ways. Many people—even good typists—feel nervous when using a keyboard rather than a typewriter for the first few times. Keyboards are easier to use than typewriters, however, so don't worry if you are not a perfect typist—corrections are easy to make.

□ *Check the results.* Most problems assigned to you use test data with easy-to-find answers. This means that you can use a hand calculator to check the results.

□ *Pretend that you are a piece of data yourself and walk your way through each step of the flowchart or pseudocode and program.*

□ *Add extra print lines in various parts of your program to display the intermediate steps of the processing.* This will help you detect errors. Once your program runs successfully, you can drop these extra lines. For example, when taking an average of numbers, you should print a running total of the values as well as the final average. The printed running totals can be deleted from the final run of the program.

PSEUDOCODE
START
Remarks–this program prints a list of
Remarks–student test scores
Declare storage requirements
Print headings
Initialize row counter to 1
DOUNTIL row counter equals 31
    Read name
    Print name
    Initialize column counter to 1
    DOUNTIL column counter equals 5
        Read the test score
        Print the test score
        Increment column counter by 1
    ENDDO
    Increment row counter by 1
ENDDO
STOP

FLOWCHART

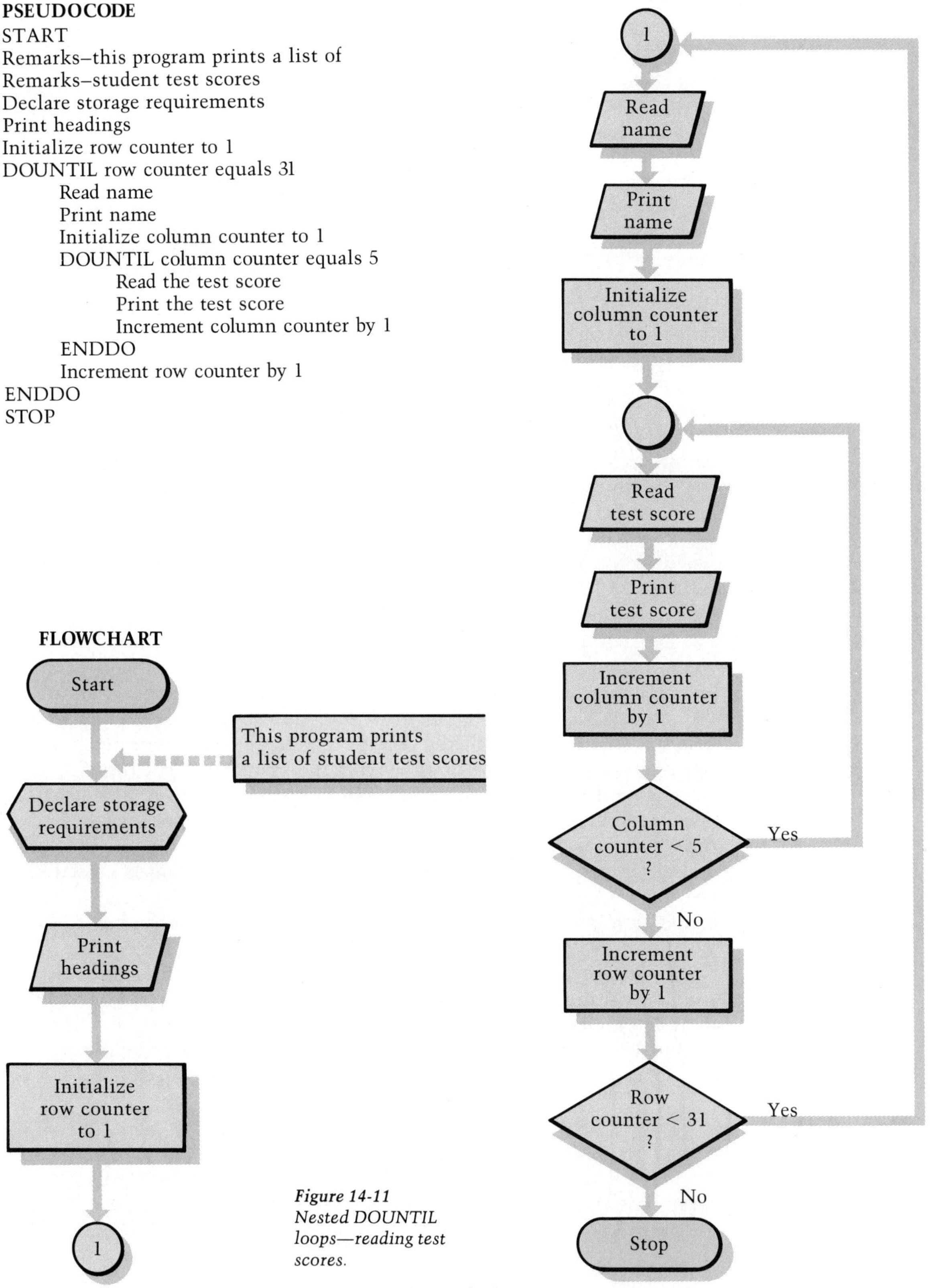

Figure 14-11
Nested DOUNTIL loops—reading test scores.

columns chart. Computer languages can follow conventions to make data stored in a computer's memory seem like such a chart.

Within the nested loop structure, the inner loop reads the scores for one student into the columns of one row, and then the outer loop advances to the next student when one student's row is filled. The inner loop is shown on the flowchart by the shorter flowline on the right, and the pseudocode that is indented. For simplicity, in the flowcharting diagram, looping operations are listed down the page.

Nested loop operations are used in many business applications. One notable example is their use in electronic spreadsheets where rows and columns of financial figures can be quickly manipulated to show the results in company profits or other areas of interest.

Putting the detail plan into action

Once we have defined the logic patterns or combination of patterns we will need in our program, and described them in a flowchart or pseudocode, we have a detail plan of what the program should be. So far as we can tell, the resulting program will solve the problem that we set out to solve. Now we are ready to put the detail plan into action. Putting it into action involves the steps of program coding and testing. Chapter 15 will explore how to write code in various languages and offer guidance on correcting errors.

Debugging procedures

DEBUGGING, the process of finding and correcting errors in programs, can take as long as the rest of the program design stages put together. One major debugging methods is desk-checking.

Typically, with DESK-CHECKING the programmer sits down with a copy of the failed program and its output and attempts to correct any errors that may have occurred. Generated with the failed program is an error report which will tell on what line, and sometimes even in what column, an error was detected. The programmer makes repeated passes through the program trying to correct the mistakes. Sometimes, even after several tries, the programmer cannot find the error. If that happens, a fellow programmer can take a look at the program. It is astounding sometimes how easy it is for someone else to look at your program and quickly spot that troublesome error. Desk-checking is a bit like writing a second draft of a term paper: you correct major and minor errors from the first draft, and might discuss it with a friend to gain valuable criticism.

Today most people write and debug programs in an interactive environment. Some call this SCREEN-CHECKING because your desk-checking in an interactive environment will not be done at a desk at all, but at a terminal, with the aid of the computer itself. A more formal type of desk-checking also occurs during a structured walkthrough.

summary

■ Five elements must work in harmony in an effective information system: people, rules and procedures, data, software, and hardware. Programs, or software, in effect codify some of the rules and procedures of an organization, placing them in a form that a computer can carry out. Software affects how people interact with the information system, how data are manipulated and used, and how the hardware of a computer system functions. In addition, software itself is affected by rules embodied in other software.

■ Programmers write software as part of the programming effort.

■ The program development process has an integral relationship with the system development process. It follows a series of steps, including problem recognition, problem definition, program design, program coding, program testing or debugging, program implementation, and program maintenance. Checkpoints within the process provide an opportunity to ask whether we have successfully completed a step.

■ Algorithms, or routines, are developed or adapted to solve parts of the problem.

■ Structured programming refers to a set of techniques for organizing and writing programs. The two main goals of structured programming are to detect errors as early as possible in the program development cycle, and to simplify the maintenance or modification of programs. In both cases, long-run total costs are reduced in comparison with earlier, nonstructured methods.

■ For programmers, creating a structured program means dividing it into modules or self-contained subparts, and relating modules to one another following a top-down approach. For managers, structured methods provide useful control techniques in assigning reasonably sized tasks to programmers, assuring that programmers use standard methods, determining task accountability and responsibility, and helping limit problems caused by employee turnover.

■ Program documentation consists of manuals, screen displays, and perhaps audiovisual materials telling users how to use the program, operators how to run it, and programmers how to change it. Documentation must be written with the audience in mind, in a clear and simple writing style. Documentation is created while the program is being developed; when the program is changed, documentation must be reviewed and changed if necessary.

■ Peer review meetings, known as structured walkthroughs, provide a nonthreatening environment for evaluating a programmer's work; managers are not present.

■ Programs are broken down into manageable modules through the process of functional decomposition. Other techniques for designing structured programs include structure charts, input-process-output (IPO) charts, and flowcharts or pseudocode.

■ Flowcharts consist of symbols joined by flowlines and connectors. Pseudocode expresses program steps with English-like expressions.

■ Modules should be independent from other modules, have only one entrance and one exit per module, perform only a single task that can be described in a few words, return automatically to the superior module upon task completion, and be a reasonable size. Control modules at the top direct the lower-level control-and-processing modules and processing modules. When the program is finally created, the main program

wrap-up

The honor roll flowchart and pseudocode

Throughout this chapter we saw how the honor roll program design was developed using the structured programming methods. Now it was up to Tom Lee to design his own flowchart to code the honor roll portion of the grades program.

Figure 14-12 shows Tom's flowchart. The second part of the figure shows the equivalent pseudocode. This presentation is a simplification, since the modules involved in our fictional honor roll program are part of the much larger grades program. Here we show them on their own in order to focus on the logic for the actual honor roll creation.

All three of the logic structures permitted by structured programming are illustrated. The structures appear as follows: sequence, a DOWHILE loop, an IFTHENELSE structure (nested inside the DOWHILE loop), and then sequence again.

The initial sequence concerns preparation steps: defining the variables and any special data storage requirements in main memory. Sometimes we do not know the exact amount of storage required, but we can estimate it. Next we print the heading for the report and initialize the counter that will keep track of the total number of students on the honor roll to 0.

The DOWHILE loop follows. It contains the major input, processing, and output steps of the program. The processing steps use an IFTHENELSE structure. If a student's grade point average is greater than or equal to 3.5 on a scale of 0 to 4, then the student's name and GPA are printed. In addition, the counter keeps track of the total number of students who made the honor roll.

When a student's GPA is below the required level (the ELSE case), nothing is printed, and the counter is not incremented. The DOWHILE loop ends after the last student record is reached.

After the program leaves the loop, a short sequence prints the closing part of the report, and the program ends. In the next chapter, we will see how Tom handles the actual computer code for the honor roll program.

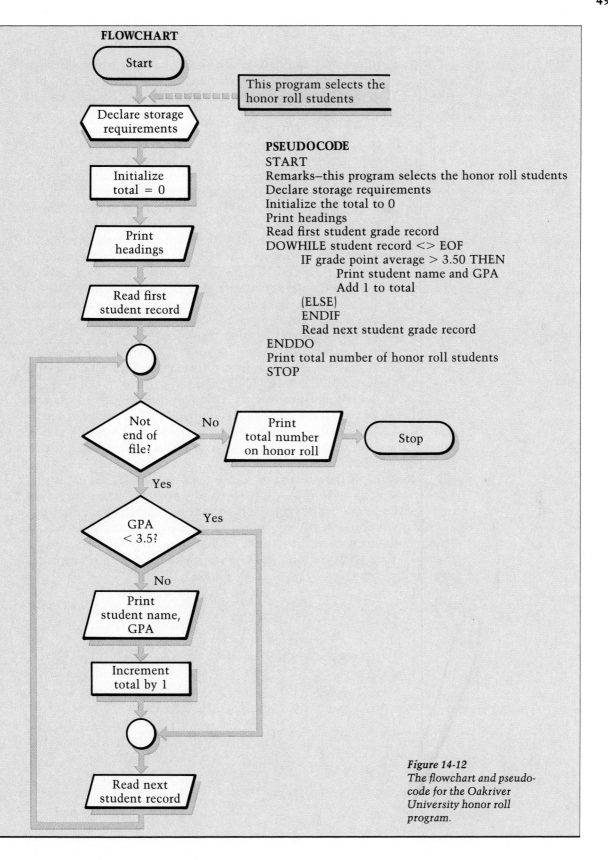

FLOWCHART

Start

This program selects the honor roll students

Declare storage requirements

Initialize total = 0

Print headings

Read first student record

Not end of file? — No → Print total number on honor roll → Stop

Yes

GPA < 3.5? — Yes →

No

Print student name, GPA

Increment total by 1

Read next student record

PSEUDOCODE
START
Remarks–this program selects the honor roll students
Declare storage requirements
Initialize the total to 0
Print headings
Read first student grade record
DOWHILE student record <> EOF
    IF grade point average > 3.50 THEN
        Print student name and GPA
        Add 1 to total
    (ELSE)
    ENDIF
    Read next student grade record
ENDDO
Print total number of honor roll students
STOP

Figure 14-12
The flowchart and pseudo-code for the Oakriver University honor roll program.

steps will control the various processing modules found in the subroutines.

■   Standard flowchart symbols (available on flowchart templates) include start/termination, annotation, preparation, input/output, process, decision, and predefined process. Flowlines and connectors link the symbols.

■   The first word in a line of pseudocode is usually an action verb such as get, read, or print. This is followed by a short description of what the verb is to act upon.

■   Whether you use flowcharts, pseudocode, or some other design tool, the goals of program design are clarity and simplicity.

■   In structured programming, there are only three types of logic patterns: sequence, selection, and loop. Any processing that a computer program has to do can be performed with one or more of these patterns. A sequence is a set of linear steps that is carried out in the order of appearance. Selection (IFTHENELSE) uses comparisons based on decisions or choices to split a program into different paths. A loop allows a program to repetitively execute one or more steps. Loops come in two varieties: DOWHILE, which iterate *while* a condition is true; and DOUNTIL, which iterate *until* a condition is true.

■   There are three devices for keeping track of the operations within a loop: counters, trailer values, and end-of-file (EOF) flags. Counters and flags must be initialized before a loop begins.

■   Once we have defined the logic patterns or combination of patterns we will need in a program, and described them in a flowchart or pseudocode, we have a detail plan of the program that can be put into action. Putting the detail plan into action involves coding and testing the program (the topic of Chapter 15).

■   Debugging is the process of finding and correcting errors in programs. It can take as long as all the rest of the program design stages put together. One major debugging method is desk-checking where the programmer sits down with a copy of the failed program and its output and attempts to correct any errors that may have occurred. When the programmer uses the computer to assist in debugging it is often called screen checking.

key terms

These are the key terms in alphabetical order. The numbers in parentheses refer to the page on which each term is defined.

Algorithm (470)
Annotation symbol (483)
Connector (483)
Control-and-processing module (479)
Control module (479)
Counter (489)
Debugging (492)
Decision symbol (485)
Desk-checking (492)
DOUNTIL loop (488)
DOWHILE loop (488)
End-of-file flag (EOF flag) (489)
Flowchart (478)
Flowchart template (483)
Flowline (483)
Functional decomposition (477)
IFTHENELSE (487)
Initialization (489)
Input/output symbol (483)
Input-process-output (IPO) chart (478)
Loop (488)
Main program (481)
Module (474)
Operator-oriented documentation (473)
Predefined process symbol (485)

Preparation symbol (483)
Processing module (479)
Process symbol (483)
Program coding (470)
Program design (470)
Program development process (470)
Program documentation (472)
Program implementation (472)
Program maintenance (472)
Programmer (468)
Programmer-oriented documentation (473)
Program testing (472)
Pseudocode (478)
Screen-checking (492)
Selection (487)
Sequence (486)
Structure chart (478)
Structured program (474)
Structured programming (474)
Structured walkthrough (477)
Subroutine (481)
System start/termination symbol (483)
Top-down approach (474)
Trailer value (489)
User-oriented documentation (473)

review questions

objective questions

True/false. *Put the letter T or F on the line next to the question.*

1 _____ 1. Structured programming helps programmers but is of little benefit to managers.

2 _____ 2. Modules should have only one entrance and exit.

3 _____ 3. Checkpoints serve to aid managers and programmers in determining progress within the programming development process.

4 _____ 4. Program maintenance is not an important issue in the program development cycle.

5 _____ 5. Modules should be as independent of each other as possible.

6 _____ 6. Pseudocode is a method for outlining program logic through the use of flowlines and a variety of visual symbols.

7 _____ 7. The selection logic structure is often called IFTHENELSE.

8 _____ 8. The (ELSE) statement in pseudocode means that nothing is to be performed during the ELSE part of an IFTHENELSE operation.

9 _____ 9. A DOWHILE loop continues as long as a condition is false.

10 _____ 10. A DOUNTIL loop performs at least one loop operation before exiting the loop.

Multiple choice. *Put the letter of the correct answer on the line next to the question.*

1 _____ 1. In creating modules one goal is to
(a) Make the modules as interdependent of each other as possible.
(b) Allow subordinate modules to call superior ones.
(c) Provide one entrance and several exits from each module.
(d) Make the modules as independent of each other as possible.

2 _____ 2. An overview of the modules required in a program solution is provided by a(n)
(a) Data-flow diagram. (c) Structure chart.
(b) Flowchart. (d) IPO chart.

3 _____ 3. Generally, structured programs compared to unstructured programs
(a) Are cheaper to design.
(b) Are cheaper over the useful life of the program.
(c) Cost more in the program maintenance stage.
(d) Permit a less disciplined approach to problem solving.

4 _____ 4. Which of the following would not be represented by a decision symbol in a flowchart?
(a) Selection. (c) DOWHILE loop.
(b) DOUNTIL loop. (d) Sequence.

5 _____ 5. With a DOWHILE loop
(a) The loop operation continues while a condition is false.
(b) It is possible never to enter the loop if the test result is false.
(c) A trailer value rather than a counter must be used as a loop control method.
(d) All of the above are correct.

Fill in the blank. *Write the correct word or words in the blank to complete the sentence.*

1. The _____ program "calls" subordinate modules called _____.

2. A _____ provides a nonthreatening environment for peer reviews.

3. The writing of the actual program is part of the _____ phase of the program development process.

4. To codify the organization's rules and procedures into a form understandable to the hardware, _____ are used.

5. The term _____ refers to a set of programming techniques used to create software that is easier to debug and maintain.

6. A DOUNTIL loop continues as long as a condition is _____.

7. Three methods _____, _____, and _____ are used for loop control.

8. A method of debugging your program while still at your computer is called _____.

9. A decision symbol requires at least _____ flowlines exiting from it.

10. The _____ line in pseudocode shows the end of the loop.

short answer questions

When answering these questions, think of concrete examples to illustrate your points.

1. What is a structured program?
2. What are the advantages of structured programming?
3. What are the steps in the program development process?
4. What is an algorithm?
5. What is the purpose of a structured walkthrough?
6. What is a structure chart?
7. Describe the three types of logic operations.
8. What purpose do nesting operations serve?
9. How do DOWHILE and DOUNTIL loops differ?
10. What is the KISS theory of programming?

essay questions

1. What benefits does structured programming provide managers and programmers?
2. Discuss the steps in the program development process.
3. Compare and contrast using flowcharting symbols versus pseudocode to create detailed program designs.

programming design exercises

Write a flowchart and pseudocode to solve the following programming problems.

1. Oakriver University's president, M. C. Laude, needs to calculate the percentage of students who are registered as business majors. Design a program to solve this problem. There are 22,000 students; 4000 of them are business majors.
2. Susan Paul needs to know the total amount of commissions earned by her salespeople for the past month. Design a program to solve her problem and use the data below to test your design.

Salesperson	Commission
Thomas Alberts	$2234
Harry Jones	$3716
Lynne Klaus	$2452
Mary Weiss	$2345
Joe Topaz	$1901

3. Dr. Clara Chips wants to give awards to the "A" students (90 percent or better) in her introductory information systems class. Design a program to determine who receives an award and use the data below to test your design.

Student name	Numeric grade	Letter grade
Eugene Alton	89	B
John Burton	78	C
Lynne Davis	70	C
Mike Franks	90	A
Cindy Smith	91	A

4. Myrtle, owner of Myrtle's Burgers, needs a program to calculate a 6 percent sales tax on items purchased at her restaurant. Each item and its cost, the subtotal, tax, and grand total must be printed out. Design a program to solve her problem and test the solution using the following order:

Super burger	@ $1.80
Large fries	@ $ .80
Small shake	@ $ .90

Answers to the objective questions
True/false: 1. F; 2. T; 3. T; 4. F; 5. T; 6. F; 7. T; 8. T; 9. F; 10. T
Multiple choice: 1. d; 2. c; 3. b; 4. d; 5. b
Fill in the blank: 1. main, subroutines; 2. structured walkthroughs; 3. program coding; 4. programs or software; 5. structured programming; 6. false; 7. counter, trailer value, end-of-file (EOF) flag; 8. screen checking; 9. two; 10. ENDDO

Harnessing the computer: programming languages and system software

After studying this chapter you should understand the following:

- *The differences between low-level, procedural, and nonprocedural programming languages.*
- *Some of the criteria used to describe and compare programming languages.*
- *The key features of BASIC, Pascal, COBOL, and FORTRAN, the four main procedural languages.*
- *Why nonprocedural languages point the way toward the future.*
- *The main features of system software including operating systems and language translators.*

chapter 15

Choosing appropriate languages

The Oakriver University campus was flooded with sun this crisp October day. Jasper Thomas, a physicist, crossed the campus toward the information-processing center. He spotted Ralph Grosse on an adjacent path and joined him. Grosse was a teacher in the foreign languages program.

The two teachers entered the Information Processing Center and found the room where the University Computer Users Committee had assembled. The committee chairperson, Miguel Abreu, referred to the written agenda and stated that the meeting would cover software, and then introduced Marty Castillo, an information-processing staff member.

Marty stood up and turned to the first of a number of flip-charts at the front of the room. "Today's topic is language," Marty said. "Computer language. As you can see from this simplified diagram, a computer language stands between you and the machine." The chart showed a drawing of a person, a drawing of a computer, and a box labeled "language" in between.

"The day will probably come quite soon when you can talk to the computer in your own language and it will do what you say," Marty said. "For now, though, we have to speak the computer's language."

"Let me apologize to those of you who already know a lot about computer languages for restating the familiar," Marty said. "It'll be new to some." Marty smiled. "Like me. I've been programming for 10 years and only know a handful of languages. And new ones are being invented all the time."

"How many computer languages are there?" Jasper asked.

"There are perhaps a thousand computer languages although only a few dozen are commonly used," Marty said.

"Why do we have to go through a selection process?" Ralph asked. "Can't we just have all the major ones?"

Several people around the room laughed.

"That's a good question!" Marty said. "But if we had all the languages, that would be like placing our new computer in the general assembly room at the United Nations. Everyone in the room could speak a different language to the computer—but they couldn't speak to each other."

Alice Smith, the systems analyst in charge of the honor roll problem, cut in. "There are some practical constraints, too," she said. "Certain languages are good for solving scientific problems, and some are pretty useless at it. Several languages are specially designed for doing things like moving data around and printing reports, which the administration needs plenty of. Using a language unsuited to a particular application ends up costing a fortune in the time it takes to write the program as well as the time it takes to run it over and over again."

"Alice has given several of the main reasons for choosing one particular computer language over another," Marty said. "Another consideration is training—it is not practical to teach students thirty different languages. Nor can experienced programmers be found to handle certain languages. In fact, some languages are widely used by colleges and other organizations, while others are as rare as aardvarks."

"So how many can we choose?" Ralph asked.

"The committee can choose as many as necessary to meet the diverse needs of the people in this room," Marty said.

"Some of us have had fairly limited exposure to computers," Jasper said. "How on earth should we know which languages to pick?"

"Ah!" Marty said. "That is what I will tell you. By considering these points." Marty flipped to a chart that ranked languages in respect to ten different attributes. He went on to explain each. This chapter will do the same.

Speaking the computer's language

*All those languages:
a programmer's
Tower of Babel*

Like the builders of the biblical Tower of Babel, we seem stricken by a multitude of languages—programming languages that is. There are hundreds of computer languages and dialects. Certainly we cannot review them all here. Instead, we will focus on just a few, approaching them from several perspectives that can be used for any language.

Proximity to the machine
One useful way to categorize a computer language is by how much attention must be paid to the workings of the computer when programming in that language. With a low-level language, you pay the most attention. With high-level (procedural and nonprocedural) languages, you pay less.

LOW-LEVEL LANGUAGES are so-named because they are very close to the computer itself. Each instruction of a low-level language corresponds to an instruction for a particular computer. The programmer has to be familiar with the inner workings of the computer, as well as with the procedures or algorithms used to solve the problem. The term *low-level* is actually somewhat misleading, since programming in these languages requires a *high level of skill*. This is analogous to driving a racing car versus a standard production model. The race car gives you more control and requires more skill to drive.

PROCEDURAL LANGUAGES use English-like statements and mathematical symbols. These *high-level* languages let programmers focus on application solution *procedures* rather than the low-level code unique to the computer. Each instruction of a procedural language is converted by system software into sequences of actual computer instructions. Using a procedural language is easier than using a low-level language; the programmer is less concerned about the inner workings of the computer, and can spend more time developing the actual solution to the problem. We will concentrate on four procedural languages: BASIC, Pascal, COBOL, and FORTRAN. In addition, the languages Ada and C will be discussed briefly.

NONPROCEDURAL LANGUAGES move even further away than procedural languages from the inner workings of the computer. *High-level* nonprocedural languages are the easiest of all to learn. With both low-level and procedural languages, the concern of a programmer is describing *how* the computer is to solve the problem. With nonprocedural languages, in contrast, we tell the computer *what* it should do, and let the software worry about *how* the computer will do it. The key drawback of most nonprocedural languages is that they are aimed at a narrow range of applications—such as generating reports—and are useless beyond that particular application. Procedural languages have a far wider range of applications; low-level languages can do anything at all that the computer can.

Several nonprocedural languages are of interest to us in this chapter: fourth-generation languages, simulation languages, and fifth-generation languages.

Which came first?
The first computer languages to be developed were low-level languages. Next, high-level procedural languages oriented toward batch processing were developed. Later, procedural languages used for interactive processing and high-level nonprocedural languages used for batch or interactive processing came along. Today, all three levels of languages are still in use. Interactive programs can be written in any level of language. In general, the higher the language level, the easier the language is for the programmer to use. (For historical details concerning the people who developed these languages see Chapter 4.)

Information system elements and language selection

The selection of programming languages to best suit an organization's needs must take into account all five information system elements. In terms of *people*, the types of reports or output desired by users may lead to selecting one language over another. The programming languages the programmers on the information system staff already know can also be a factor.

The types of *data*, the frequency of their usage, and their arrangement need close consideration when choosing a language. For instance, numeric data subjected to complex calculations need different treatment than large files of customer data.

Rules and procedures affect the programming language selected. The need for graphics for management presentations, for example, might lead to selecting a language capable of creating good visual displays.

The *hardware* available to the user has an impact as well. Some languages are particularly suited to a particular category of computer, such as mainframes. The system *software* available to translate the language is also a factor. Programs are not available to translate certain languages on some computers, or may be available only in a form of dubious efficiency.

Differences among computer languages

Choosing the right programming language for an information system is not an easy task. As we saw in the opening example concerning Oakriver University, many people in an organization have a say in language selection, especially information system managers.

Programmers may also have a measure of choice in selecting among an organization's existing languages when writing a particular program. A bank may decide that its main programming language is COBOL, but find that a few tricky operations can be done more easily in assembly language. Programmers within a given organization thus may have the chance to try different languages, and should be well aware of their characteristics.

Many of us will not be programmers, but will use programs written for us by others. To better evaluate the software we use, we also need to know how languages differ. Also, we may well find ourselves buying a

career box
Application programmer

If you decide on a career in information systems, this is probably the first job you will look for. More people work as application programmers than any other position in the computer field. It is a stepping-stone to many career opportunities in the field.

The position of application programmer, however, is by no means at the bottom of the pyramid. To become an application programmer, you must demonstrate technical aptitude (often determined in a test or technical interview) and must usually have a two-year or four-year college degree or posthigh school technical training involving computers. Companies also seek experience (so that new hires can help them out of whatever jam they're in right away). If you have programming experience—even if only a summer job, unpaid, or for a brief period—it can help separate you from the rest of the pack.

It may come as a surprise that interpersonal skills are also sought by organizations hiring application programmers. Application programmers do spend most of their time designing and coding programs to run on a machine, but they are generally organized into teams that stress cooperation, and the application programmer who shows potential can move quickly up the organizational hierarchy. Typical promotions are to programmer analyst and systems analyst—with ever-increasing managerial responsibility at each level.

What does an application programmer do? As an entry-level person, you would probably help another programmer with minor programming tasks until you become familiar with the particular system. You might be asked, for instance, to modify a simple working program that is in need of updating to meet new user needs. Perhaps after a few months, you would be asked to write a program from scratch. Since your program would have to relate to others in existence or preparation, and since you are new to the job, in all likelihood a senior-level application programmer, programmer analyst, or systems analyst would design the program for you. From the input-process-output (IPO) diagram or other diagram that this person provides, you would design and code the program, test it, write the documentation, and get it working perfectly.

To continue with our first-job scenario, once that simple program works, you would be asked to work on a larger, more important one. Soon you would become involved in the design yourself, perhaps proposing a design for review at programming team meetings. Certainly by this time—about a year after joining the firm—you would notice that you are no longer a newcomer, since you know the system. In this dynamic, ever-changing environment—where the quantity of work to be done probably exceeds the personnel on hand to do it, and the stakes for the organization are high, as is job turnover—you have every opportunity for advancement. Technical ability, competence in working on a team and in communicating with others, a good professional attitude, and a commitment to the organization—none of these qualifications would be overlooked by a competent superior and you would receive more responsibility. For instance, in large organizations it is typical for new programmers to be placed on teams working on batch processing programs. It is considered something of a plum, after you have shown your competence with the batch system, to be moved to a project designing on-line programs.

Although particular scenarios may vary from this generalized example, one thing is certain: good application programmers rarely gather cobwebs. They are rewarded with high salaries, promotions, new responsibilities, and continuing opportunities to move upward.

microcomputer and therefore be interested in the languages it can handle, or we may find our employers polling us—as at Oakriver University—to determine our language needs.

To help evaluate a language, the following ten factors should be closely examined:

- Application area.
- File-handling ability.
- Mathematical computing ability.
- Machine independence.
- Availability on microcomputers.
- Level of self-documentation.
- Quality of interactive form available.
- Allowance for structured programming.
- Total cost for a few runs.
- Total cost for many runs.

Application area refers to the general types of uses to which a computer program can be put. We can identify four broad application areas: business, government, engineering, and science. Business and government information systems usually require computer programs capable of handling large files. "Large" can mean thousands, or even millions, of records. Processing large files strains or binds the input and output capacity of an information system. U.S. government agencies have had a crucial role in fostering programming languages—by limiting bidding to those computers that can use particular languages.

Engineers and scientists need software with the capacity to manipulate complex mathematical algorithms. Therefore, languages with strong mathematical computing abilities are needed in scientific and engineering applications. Some application needs overlap—businesses or government agencies sometimes work with complex mathematical algorithms, and engineers and scientists sometimes process large files.

The second factor, *file-handling ability*, refers to the facility with which a language can manipulate large input and output data files. Data manipulation includes calculating, sorting, summarizing, and listing. Languages strong in this area can process alphabetic records with ease and have extensive report generation features. Examples of large files include the over 200 million employees' earnings and benefits records kept by the Social Security Administration. Within the topic of files and file-handling we can also look at data structures and declarations. In Chapter 11 we learned about specific file-handling methods such as sequential and direct access.

Mathematical computing ability refers to the strengths of a language in expressing calculations and in carrying them out efficiently. Languages strong in this area allow a researcher or programmer to exploit algorithms to aid in solving problems. Mathematical computing ability and file-handling ability are the main factors that define the application areas a language is suitable for.

Computer languages also differ in how they are tied to a given "brand" of computer. MACHINE INDEPENDENCE refers to how easily a program written to run using one particular make and model of computer, can be run on another. A program written in a machine independent language could, with just a few changes, be run successfully on a different computer. On the other hand, *machine dependence* refers to programs that will only work on one make or model of computer; to run the program on another would require conversion or possibly a complete rewrite. Organizations with a variety of different computers strongly prefer machine-independent languages to reduce the cost of converting and rewriting programs. Even organizations with a single computer benefit from machine independence, because when their computer becomes obsolete they will undoubtedly change to another, but will want to continue using as many of the same programs as possible.

The *availability on microcomputers* of a programming language has become important, since millions of people have access to microcomputers. Today, most of the major programming languages are available in some version for microcomputers.

The concept of SELF-DOCUMENTATION refers to how easily a program can be read and understood by a programmer or other user. Languages that allow descriptive variables—GROSSINCOME, for example, instead of G or GRI—make reading a program easier. Programs lacking in self-documentation are usually harder for a maintenance programmer to understand or modify.

The quality of the interactive form of the language is also a consideration. With INTERACTIVE PROCESSING a dialogue occurs between user requests and the computer's responses. The short time between entering commands and getting the program's response gives a feeling of immediacy to your solution. Programs that a user can *run* interactively can be written in any computer language. With many languages, programs can also be *written* on an interactive basis, with computer assistance. INTERACTIVE PROGRAMMING LANGUAGES are better than others for writing programs interactively; BASIC is one such language. ✓

The STRUCTURED PROGRAMMING method (modular design within a top-down framework for the development and execution of programs) is encouraged by some computer languages, and thwarted by others. In addition, some languages discourage the use of unconditional branches or GOTO statements, which cannot be used in structured programs.

The *total program cost* is the sum of the cost to write (a fixed cost) and the cost incurred each time the program is run (a variable cost). Factors determining total cost include the time it takes programmers to create programs in a language, the ease with which the programs can be maintained and modified, the cost and speed of the system software that translates them, and CPU processing speeds.

When performing the same functions, languages may differ greatly in both their fixed and variable costs. The goal is to *minimize* total program costs. With certain languages, it takes a long time to write programs, but they execute very quickly and are easy to maintain. These programming languages are cost-effective when used for operations that are performed thousands or millions of times over many years—they have a *low total cost for many runs*, and a *high total cost for few runs*. In other languages, programs can be written quickly but take a long time to run—they have a *low total cost for a few runs*, and a *high total cost for many*.

Interestingly, in the early years of computers, the cost of programming was cheap compared to the cost of running the program on the computer. Today the situation has been reversed: while the cost of programming has increased, the cost of computing has declined markedly. This has altered the total cost picture for the various languages.

Low-level languages for hardy programmers

Machine language

MACHINE LANGUAGE is the true language of the computer. It is the only one the central processing unit (CPU) understands. Machine language is written in binary code, consisting of combinations of the numbers 1 and 0. This code is suited to computers because it corresponds to the bipolar or on/off state of electrical components (where "on" equals 1 and "off" equals 0).

The specific machine language depends upon the CPU's design. Most mainframe computer manufacturers design a "family" of machines that use the same machine language. The language will differ, however, from one manufacturer's family to another manufacturer's family. Microcomputer manufacturers, on the other hand, often use the same microprocessors; therefore several different brands of microcomputer may have the same machine language.

When you write a program in machine language, no translation process is necessary for the machine to use it. With all of the other languages, translation is needed.

The main features of machine language are:

■ Each line of machine language refers to one operation represented by a series of 1s and 0s.
■ The first few binary digits give the operation code (or op code) which tells the computer *what operation or instruction to perform*.
■ Following the op code comes one or more operands. An operand tells the computer *what the instruction is to be carried out on*. Usually the operand shows the address of data to be operated on. An *address* is a unique location in the computer's memory.

Figure 15-1 shows a machine language instruction, with the parts of the instruction identified. For more on operation codes, operands, and addresses, see Chapter 5.

Machine language programs can be applied to any application area. If you have the patience and skill, anything written in a higher-level language—and more—can be accomplished in machine language. The file-handling and mathematical computing abilities of machine language are as great as that of the computer itself. After all, the other languages have to be converted into machine language to work. The major cost of using machine language is the expense of writing and debugging the program

Figure 15-1
Machine language instruction. The instruction adds the value of B to A, as in the equation A = A + B. The op code says to add the second value to the first value and store the answer in the first value's address. The first value, or operand A, is the variable A; the second, operand B, is variable B.

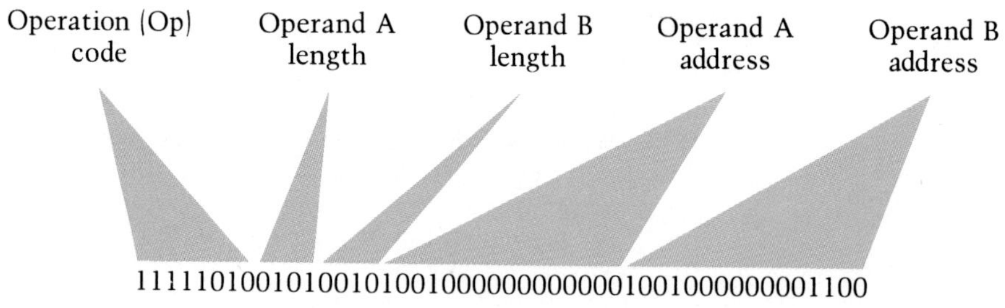

Operation (Op) code	Operand A length	Operand B length	Operand A address	Operand B address

111110100101001010010000000000000100100000000001100

code. Unless the program will be used many times, machine language is not cost-effective. This is one reason why early programming applications for business and government focused on large, repetitive batch operations, such as payroll processing. Few other operations could justify the programming expense. Today, the main use of machine language is to create system software, which allows us to work with higher-level programming languages.

Assembly language

ASSEMBLY LANGUAGE is one step removed from the machine language of the computer, and uses symbols that are easier for people to work with and remember. System software translates each assembly language instruction into one or more machine language instructions.

Like machine language, assembly language is machine dependent. Assembly language has the following features:

■ The use of mnemonics to represent machine operation codes and operands. *Mnemonics* are symbolic codes which people can remember, such as SUB for subtraction.

■ In early assembly languages, each instruction usually represented one line of machine language. Later assembly languages used *macro instructions* (similar to the macros used in productivity packages such as database management systems and spreadsheets) to generate a sequence of several machine language instructions from a single assembly language instruction.

Figure 15-2 shows an example of a line of assembly language. The op code AP means add the contents of the second storage location (VALUEB) to the contents of the first (TOTALA) and place it into the first storage location. If you compare Figure 15-2 with Figure 15-1, you can see the great leap forward for programmers that assembly language represented over machine language.

Many productivity software packages, such as Lotus 1-2-3, are written in assembly language. Of course, the assembly code is "invisible" to the spreadsheet user.

Figure 15-2
Example of assembly language code for the equation A = A + B.

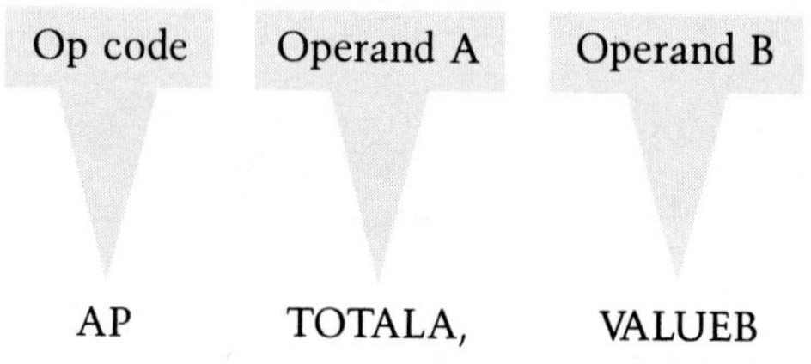

Op code	Operand A	Operand B
AP	TOTALA,	VALUEB

High-level procedural languages

The same trend that assembly language represented when compared to machine language—moving away from the way the machine runs and toward the way people think—was carried further with procedural languages. High-level procedural languages allow the programmer to focus on the procedures for problem solution, rather than on how the machine runs.

In this section we will review and evaluate four procedural languages—BASIC, Pascal, COBOL, and FORTRAN—based on the ten factors presented earlier (see Figure 15-3). A comment on the historical appearance of these languages. FORTRAN was first developed for second-generation computers, followed by COBOL. BASIC was available for third-generation machines; Pascal was first used extensively on fourth-generation computers.

We will compare the way each of the four languages handles the same program and expresses the logical structures of sequence, looping, and decision (IFTHENELSE). The program is derived from the one Tom Lee wrote for Oakriver University to solve the honor roll problem.[1] It

Figure 15-3
Summary of the features of the four main programming languages.

[1] The BASIC program was written using GW-BASIC by Microsoft Corporation. The Pascal, COBOL, and FORTRAN programs were written using a Control Data Corporation Cyber-174.

Feature	BASIC	Pascal	COBOL	FORTRAN
Application area	Business, engineering, government, science	Business, engineering, government, science	Business, government	Engineering, science
File-handling ability	Medium	Medium	High	Medium
Mathematical computing ability	High	High	Medium	High
Machine independence	Medium	Medium	Very high	High
Available on microcomputers	Almost all	Most	Some	Most
Level of self-documentation	Low	Medium	High	Low
Quality of interactive form available	Good	Good	Fair	Fair
Allowances for structured programming	Low	Very high	High	Medium
Total cost for a few runs	Low	Low	High	Low
Total cost for many runs	High	High	Medium	High

Figure 15-4
The data for the honor roll problem.

Student	Grade point average
Mary Smith	3.75
Robert Lopez	2.95
Christine Jones	2.85
Tom Toshiba	3.95
Janis Roberts	3.49
Ralph Brown	3.20
Ronald Chang	3.00
Susan O'Malley	3.50
Cathy Schwartz	3.00
Michael Ramirez	3.65

reads a list of students and their grade point averages (GPAs) on a scale of 0 to 4. From the list shown in Figure 15-4, the program selects those students with a GPA of 3.5 or more, and prints their names and GPAs for the honor roll.

BASIC

BASIC, or BEGINNER'S ALL-PURPOSE SYMBOLIC INSTRUCTION CODE, is an interactive programming language. BASIC is suited for all four application areas: business, government, engineering, and science. It has medium file-handling ability and loose data-structure rules, but is strong when used for numerical manipulation including graphics and other visual displays.

Machine independence for the present versions of BASIC is rated as medium. For the earlier versions of BASIC, machine independence was fairly low because there are a variety of "dialects" of the language. The core of the language is consistent from one version to another, but there is a lack of standardization in two areas: the commands for working with data files and for creating sophisticated output displays. A *de facto* standard was developed by Microsoft Corporation for the IBM PC and its compatibles, as well as the Apple Macintosh. Other versions include QuickBASIC, also by Microsoft, and TrueBASIC, developed by its original inventors—John G. Kemeny and Thomas Kurtz.

BASIC was one of the first languages available on microcomputers. Its level of self-documentation is low. Although structured programming methods may be used with BASIC, it also permits you to use less structure than most of the major languages. More recent versions such as TrueBASIC require the use of structured methods. BASIC, however, is one of the fastest languages in which to code and debug programs because it can be done on a thoroughly interactive basis. When few runs of the resulting program are made, the total cost is therefore relatively lower than for many other languages. However, operations requiring the manipulation of large data files—such as processing thousands of payroll checks—are not cost-effective in BASIC.

Figure 15-5 shows the honor roll program written in a version of Microsoft BASIC called GW-BASIC. As you can see, each line in BASIC begins with a line number. Following the line number is a key word, such as PRINT. After the key word is the value that word acts upon, such as the data to be printed. The REM ("Remark") lines do not affect the actual execution of the program. If used generously, these comments serve as a form of self-documentation.

Pascal

PASCAL is a structured programming language. It is useful in all four application areas. It has moderate file-handling ability and good mathematical computing ability, but Pascal has only a medium level of machine independence.

Pascal has a medium level of self-documentation and is available in an interactive form. Unique among the major languages, Pascal was designed with structured programming in mind. It forces programmers to use a modular approach, and makes it very difficult to write GOTO statements. Relative costs for both few and many runs are higher for Pascal programs than for BASIC programs. Pascal's modular approach, however, reduces the costs of modifying and maintaining a program. A Pascal program to solve the honor roll problem is shown in Figure 15-6.

Figure 15-5

The honor roll problem in BASIC. In this example as in the rest of the examples in this chapter, the data are read from a separate data file.

```
          100 REM HONOR PROGRAM
          110 REM This program prints NAMES and GPA for students
          120 REM whose GPA is 3.5 or higher.  It also prints the
          130 REM total number of honor roll students printed on report.
          140 REM VARIABLES:  N$ = Student Name    G = Grade Point Average
          150 REM             S  = Total           I = Array counter
          160 REM * * * * * MAIN PROGRAM * * * * *
          170 LET S=0
          180 OPEN "i",1,"SCORES"
          190 PRINT "      Oakriver University Honor Roll Report"
          200 PRINT
          210 PRINT "          The Honor Roll Students"
          220 PRINT
          230 PRINT "      Student Name                    GPA"
          240 PRINT
          250 FOR I = 1 TO 10
          260 IF EOF(1) THEN 320
          270 INPUT #1,N$,G
          280 IF G>3.49 THEN 290 ELSE 310
          290 PRINT USING "        \              \          #.##";N$,G
          300 LET S=S+1
          310 NEXT I
          320 CLOSE #1
          330 PRINT
          340 PRINT
          350 PRINT "     The number of honor roll students is: ";S
          360 END

          RUN
              Oakriver University Honor Roll Report

                  The Honor Roll Students

              Student Name                    GPA

              Mary Smith                      3.75
              Tom Toshiba                     3.95
              Susan O'Malley                  3.50
              Michael Ramirez                 3.65


              The number of honor roll students is:  4
```

(SEQUENCE — LOOP — SEQUENCE labels on left; IF THEN ELSE label on right)

```
        PROGRAM HONOR(INPUT/,OUTPUT,SCOREP);

        (* This program extracts the names of those students who *)
        (* have a grade-point average (GPA) greater than or equal *)
        (* to 3.50.   The name and GPA of each qualifying student, and *)
        (* the total number of the qualifying students is printed out. *)

         TYPE
             STRING = ARRAY[1..20] OF CHAR;

         VAR
             COUNT, I, J: INTEGER;
             GRADEPT: REAL;
             NAME: STRING;
             SCOREP: TEXT;
        BEGIN (* START OF PROGRAM *)
             RESET(SCOREP);
             COUNT := 0;
             WRITELN('       Oakriver University Honor Roll Report');
             WRITELN;
             WRITELN('            The Honor Roll Students');
             WRITELN;
             WRITELN('       Student Name                    GPA');
             WRITELN;
             WHILE NOT EOF (SCOREP) DO
                 BEGIN
                    FOR J := 1 TO 20 DO
                       READ(SCOREP, NAME[J]);
                    READLN(SCOREP, GRADEPT);
                    IF GRADEPT > 3.49 THEN
                       BEGIN
                          COUNT := COUNT + 1;
                          WRITE(' ':5);
                          FOR I := 1 TO 20 DO
                             WRITE(NAME[I]);
                          WRITELN(' ':10, GRADEPT :3:2);
                       END;
                 END;
             WRITELN;
             WRITELN;
             WRITELN('       The number of honor roll students is:', COUNT :3);
        END.

        RUN
```

Labels at left: SEQUENCE, LOOP, SEQUENCE

Label at right (pointing to shaded IF block): IF THEN ELSE

```
            Oakriver University Honor Roll Report

               The Honor Roll Students

         Student Name                    GPA

         Mary Smith                      3.75
         Tom Toshiba                     3.95
         Susan O'Malley                  3.50
         Michael Ramirez                 3.65


         The number of honor roll students is:  4
```

Figure 15-6
The honor roll problem
in Pascal.

COBOL

COBOL, or COMMON BUSINESS-ORIENTED LANGUAGE, is used extensively by both businesses and government agencies. Its principal strength is file-handling. COBOL can be used for both interactive processing and batch processing. It excels in payroll problems, accounting, inventory, and report-writing. By far the greater part of the application programs used in American businesses today—representing an investment worth billions of dollars—are written in COBOL. For many major corporations it is the *only* language used for business applications.

COBOL has moderately strong mathematical features to support its powerful file-handling ability, helpful for such operations as calculating payroll check amounts.

COBOL was designed to be machine-independent, a feature of great importance to large users with many different brands of computers. COBOL is available on microcomputers. With the highest level of self-documentation of any of the major languages, COBOL allows the programmer to use phrases in English (or other native tongues) to define variables. Interactive COBOL programs can be run on microcomputers, minicomputers, and mainframes. Structured programming methods can be applied to COBOL. The actual implementation of structured techniques depends upon the programmer and his or her working environment and training.

COBOL takes longer to program than other major languages; thus its relative cost for a few runs is fairly high. For running a program thousands of times, however, COBOL is very cost-effective, because it executes a program much more efficiently than the other procedural languages. COBOL is most cost-effective for programs that perform extensive input and output operations, a common trait of many business applications. And if the program is well structured, maintenance costs should be relatively low.

As Figure 15-7 indicates, there is a hierarchical arrangement to COBOL programs. From broadest to narrowest, the hierarchy is as follows: program, division, section, paragraph, and sentence. Notice that each sentence of COBOL ends with a period.

FORTRAN

FORTRAN, or FORMULA TRANSLATION, is a programming language designed chiefly for applications in science and engineering. Moderately proficient for file-handling, particularly for numerical files, FORTRAN's real strength is in "number-crunching" complex mathematical algorithms. FORTRAN is moderately machine independent, and is available on microcomputers. It has a low level of self-documentation, and is available in interactive forms. Early FORTRAN programmers were notorious in their use of GOTO statements, but the language can be used with structured programming methods. The relative cost for using FORTRAN is just slightly higher than for using BASIC.

Figure 15-8 shows the honor roll problem in FORTRAN. Observe how the data are incorporated into the program. Notice how the statement numbers are used for input, output, and loop control.

Figure 15-7
The honor roll problem in COBOL.

```
        IDENTIFICATION DIVISION.

        PROGRAM-ID.             PROGRAM-SCORE.
        AUTHOR.                 TOM LEE.
        INSTALLATION.           ORISC.
        DATE-WRITTEN.           JANUARY-12, 1990.

        ENVIRONMENT DIVISION.

        CONFIGURATION SECTION.
        SOURCE-COMPUTER.    CYBER-174.
        OBJECT-COMPUTER.    CYBER-174.
        INPUT-OUTPUT SECTION.
        FILE-CONTROL.
            SELECT RECORDS-IN ASSIGN TO SCORES, USE "RT=Z".
            SELECT PRINT-OUT ASSIGN TO OUTPUT.

        DATA DIVISION.

        FILE SECTION.
        FD  RECORDS-IN
            LABEL RECORDS ARE OMITTED.
        01  IN-RECORD           PIC X(72).
        FD  PRINT-OUT
            LABEL RECORDS ARE OMITTED.
        01  PRINT-LINE          PIC X(72).
        WORKING-STORAGE SECTION.
        77  STUDENT-COUNT       PIC 9(3)        VALUE ZEROES.
        01  FLAG.
            05  END-OF-FILE-FLAG PIC X          VALUE "N".
            05  NO-MORE-DATA    PIC X           VALUE "Y".
        01  STUDENT-RECORD.
            05  NAME-RD         PIC X(20).
            05  GRADE-PT        PIC 9V99.
            05  FILLER          PIC X(49).
        01  HDG.
            05  FILLER          PIC X(5)        VALUE SPACES.
            05  FILLER          PIC X(9)        VALUE "OAKRIVER ".
            05  FILLER          PIC X(11)       VALUE "UNIVERSITY ".
            05  FILLER          PIC X(17)       VALUE "HONOR ROLL REPORT".
            05  FILLER          PIC X(30)       VALUE SPACES.
        01  HDG-1.
            05  FILLER          PIC X(10)       VALUE SPACES.
            05  FILLER          PIC X(15)       VALUE "THE HONOR ROLL ".
            05  FILLER          PIC X(8)        VALUE "STUDENTS".
            05  FILLER          PIC X(39)       VALUE SPACES.
        01  HDG-2.
            05  FILLER          PIC X(5)        VALUE SPACES.
            05  FILLER          PIC X(12)       VALUE "STUDENT NAME".
            05  FILLER          PIC X(18)       VALUE SPACES.
            05  FILLER          PIC X(3)        VALUE "GPA".
            05  FILLER          PIC X(34)       VALUE SPACES.
        01  HDG-3.
            05  FILLER          PIC X(72)       VALUE SPACES.
        01  STUDENT-LINE.
            05  FILLER          PIC X(5)        VALUE SPACES.
            05  NAME-LN         PIC X(20).
            05  FILLER          PIC X(10)       VALUE SPACES.
            05  GRADE           PIC 9.99.
            05  FILLER          PIC X(33)       VALUE SPACES.
        01  TOTAL-LINE.
            05  FILLER          PIC X(5)        VALUE SPACES.
            05  FILLER          PIC X(14)       VALUE "THE NUMBER OF ".
            05  FILLER          PIC X(11)       VALUE "HONOR ROLL ".
            05  FILLER          PIC X(12)       VALUE "STUDENTS IS:".
            05  STUDENT-NUMBER  PIC ZZ9.
            05  FILLER          PIC X(27)       VALUE SPACES.
```

```
                    PROCEDURE DIVISION.

                    MAIN-PROGRAM.
                        PERFORM START-PROCESS.
                        PERFORM DECISION-FOR-HONOR-ROLL
                           UNTIL END-OF-FILE-FLAG = "Y".
                        PERFORM WRAPITUP.
                        STOP RUN.
                    START-PROCESS.
                        OPEN INPUT RECORDS-IN OUTPUT PRINT-OUT.
                        MOVE SPACES TO STUDENT-LINE.
   SEQUENCE            WRITE PRINT-LINE FROM HDG AFTER ADVANCING 2 LINES.
                        WRITE PRINT-LINE FROM HDG-1 AFTER ADVANCING 2 LINES.
                        WRITE PRINT-LINE FROM HDG-2 AFTER ADVANCING 2 LINES.
                        WRITE PRINT-LINE FROM HDG-3 AFTER ADVANCING 1 LINES.
                    DECISION-FOR-HONOR-ROLL.
                        READ RECORDS-IN INTO STUDENT-RECORD
                           AT END MOVE NO-MORE-DATA TO END-OF-FILE-FLAG.
                        MOVE NAME-RD TO NAME-LN.
   LOOP                MOVE GRADE-PT TO GRADE.
                        IF (GRADE-PT > 3.49)                              IF THEN ELSE
                          WRITE PRINT-LINE FROM STUDENT-LINE
                          AFTER ADVANCING 1 LINE ADD 1 TO STUDENT-COUNT.
                        MOVE STUDENT-COUNT TO STUDENT-NUMBER.
                    WRAPITUP.
   SEQUENCE            WRITE PRINT-LINE FROM TOTAL-LINE AFTER ADVANCING 3 LINES.
                        CLOSE RECORDS-IN, PRINT-OUT.

                    RUN

                        OAKRIVER UNIVERSITY HONOR ROLL REPORT

                           THE HONOR ROLL STUDENTS

                        STUDENT NAME                    GPA

                        MARY SMITH                      3.75
                        TOM TOSHIBA                     3.95
                        SUSAN O'MALLEY                  3.50
                        MICHAEL RAMIREZ                 3.65


                        THE NUMBER OF HONOR ROLL STUDENTS IS:    4
```

Additional procedural languages

There are a variety of other procedural languages available today. Two of the newest languages are Ada and C.

Ada

ADA incorporates features of both structured programming and software engineering methods. In many respects Ada is similar to Pascal. The major difference is that Ada incorporates within itself SOFTWARE ENGINEERING methods for automating program creation and maintenance especially through the use of modular program-building algorithms. Software engineering speeds up program design.

Major applications using Ada include weapons systems control programs where reliability is demanded. The language is heavily supported by the U.S. Department of Defense—any computers it purchases must

```
                    PROGRAM HONORF(INPUT,OUTPUT,SCOREF,TAPE60=INPUT,TAPE61=SCOREF)
        C   THIS PROGRAM EXTRACTS THE NAMES OF THOSE STUDENTS WHO
        C   HAVE A GRADE-POINT AVERAGE (GPA) GREATER THAN OR EQUAL
        C   TO 3.50.    THE NAME AND GPA OF EACH QUALIFYING STUDENT, AND
        C   THE TOTAL NUMBER OF THE QUALIFYING STUDENTS IS PRINTED OUT.
                    CHARACTER * 20 NAME(10)
                    REAL GPA(10)
                    INTEGER COUNT
                    COUNT = 0
                        PRINT *,'      OAKRIVER UNIVERSITY HONOR ROLL REPORT'
                        PRINT *,' '
                        PRINT *,'            THE HONOR ROLL STUDENTS'
                        PRINT *,' '
                        PRINT *,'    .STUDENT NAME                         GPA'
                        PRINT *,' '
                    DO 70 I = 1, 10
                        READ(61,40) NAME(I), GPA(I)
        40          FORMAT(A20,F4.2)
                    IF (GPA(I) .GE. 3.5) THEN
                        PRINT 50, NAME(I), GPA(I)
        50          FORMAT(5X,A20,10X,F4.2)        IF THEN ELSE
                        COUNT = COUNT + 1
                    END IF
        70  CONTINUE
                    PRINT 80, COUNT
        80  FORMAT(//,5X,'THE NUMBER OF HONOR ROLL STUDENTS IS:',I3)
                    END

        RUN

            OAKRIVER UNIVERSITY HONOR ROLL REPORT

                THE HONOR ROLL STUDENTS

            STUDENT NAME                         GPA

            MARY SMITH                           3.75
            TOM TOSHIBA                          3.95
            SUSAN O'MALLEY                       3.50
            MICHAEL RAMIREZ                      3.65


            THE NUMBER OF HONOR ROLL STUDENTS IS:   4
```

SEQUENCE

LOOP

SEQUENCE

Figure 15-8
The honor roll problem in FORTRAN.

be able to support Ada. Business applications include manufacturing process control and production management. Efforts are underway to replace both COBOL and FORTRAN with Ada. Proponents claim Ada successfully weds the file-handling powers of COBOL with the mathematical computing abilities of FORTRAN. Ada is designed to be machine independent. A version of Ada should soon be available on larger microcomputers. Ada has moderate self-documentation, and it can be used to write interactive programs. Like Pascal, Ada not only allows, but requires the use of structured programming methods.

While Ada has not been subjected to the economic scrutiny of the other programming languages, the total cost picture should be about the same as for Pascal. Whether Ada will compete successfully against other languages remains to be seen. Relatively few programmers are familiar with Ada, and businesses and government agencies have invested billions of dollars in COBOL programs that would have to be rewritten if Ada became standard.

C

One language is called simply c, so-named because it was developed from a language called *B*. C has features of both procedural and low-level languages, and resembles Pascal in its structure. It is a modular language used primarily by programmers to write application software packages and system software for users. In fact, C has begun to replace assembly language for this purpose because it is relatively machine independent. Available on microcomputers, this language has been used to create sophisticated business and word processing packages. C shows promise for becoming a popular programming language.

High-level nonprocedural languages

The purpose of a high-level nonprocedural language is to do a particular type of work. The focus within an application area is much narrower than with a procedural language. For example, the procedural language FORTRAN can tackle nearly any type of mathematical or engineering problem. A nonprocedural simulation programming language, in contrast, can address only a narrow range of such problems—building and testing models. Within this range, however, the nonprocedural language is very powerful, and is also easier to learn. Nonprocedural languages are part of the recent trend to develop programs that can be used easily, are documented clearly, describe problems in a user's own terms, and often actively assist a user in solving problems through an interactive dialogue. With some nonprocedural languages, a programmer is not required at all, since the user can work with the language directly without extensive training.

We will describe three types of nonprocedural languages: fourth-generation languages, simulation languages, and fifth-generation languages.

Fourth-generation languages

FOURTH-GENERATION LANGUAGES are business-oriented nonprocedural languages designed to link with databases. Most fourth-generation languages incorporate features for input and output screen design, report formats, database design, maintenance, inquiry, and security features. With a fourth-generation language the amount of coding is substantially reduced, though the programs allow less programmer flexibility. The most popular fourth-generation language is RPG III (short for *Report Generator*), developed for IBM's small mainframe computers. Other languages include FORTH, NOMAD2, EASYTRIEVE, GIS, MARK IV/REPORTER, Powerhouse, and SQL (System Query Language).

Simulation languages

SIMULATION LANGUAGES use mathematical or logical formulas to model real-world events and to predict the possible consequences of those events. For instance, the behavior of a new airplane engine can be modeled and tested by a computer program before any version of the engine is actually built. If an engineer has basic specifications for what seems to be a good engine design—maximum thrust generated, weight, fuel-consumption rate, and so on—he or she can "test" this would-be engine under thousands of computer-simulated environmental conditions. This is, of course, much easier and less expensive than building the engine, mounting it on a test plane, and finding after some months that it fails under certain conditions. With a program written in a simulation language, months of work can be condensed into minutes, and the model refined and tuned to ever-greater perfection. Then the physical prototype can be built and—once it passes tests in an actual laboratory—mounted on a plane and tested more.

Business applications of simulation languages include modeling production and other management problems. The user describes the general constraints of the problem, such as the materials, wages, worker skills, and other factors in the business system. The simulation program then translates the general model into machine language the computer can understand. Once again, the advantage is that simulating something makes it possible to find out that it either won't work or will work before actually implementing it.

Examples of simulation languages include DYNAMO, GPSS (General Purpose System Simulator), and SIMSCRIPT. These languages are often taught and applied in management science courses.

Fifth-generation languages

FIFTH-GENERATION LANGUAGE programs are used to express complex logical versus computational operations in a form understandable to the computer. Fifth-generation languages are used extensively in the area of artificial intelligence. **ARTIFICIAL INTELLIGENCE (AI)** refers to efforts to capture the way humans think and learn and apply it to the computer. Today, AI efforts are exploiting parallel processing where large numbers of processors (CPUs) work simultaneously on solving pieces of a problem. Other applications for fifth-generation languages include robotics.

One type of fifth-generation language is a **LIST-PROCESSING LANGUAGE**, which as the name says, processes data in the form of lists. Generally, the logical order of data in the list can be changed without physically moving the data. List-processing languages are valuable for research. An example of a list-processing language is **LISP (LIST PROCESSING)**. One of the most important applications of LISP is the development of artificial intelligence programs. LISP is an unstructured, interactive language, and is available on some microcomputers.

LOGO (which means "word" in Greek) was derived from LISP during the 1960s. LOGO was meant to be so user-friendly that it would be fun to use. Relying upon simple words for commands, LOGO allows the programmer to communicate with the computer in a free-form, unstructured style. LOGO is a very popular language for children and adults alike. This interactive language is available on microcomputers, and is extensively used in schools to familiarize children with computers.

Another type of fifth-generation language is PROLOG (PROGRAMMING IN LOGIC), where logical statements are invoked through a series of descriptive clauses. This language is used in the development of a number of expert systems used in business, medicine, and science.

Toward natural language

The long-term trend in programming languages is toward languages that are easier for the average person to use. This means that new nonprocedural languages will be developed, and existing procedural languages will be refined. As computers continue to become cheaper, faster, and more accessible to the average person, user languages can be expected to impose ever-fewer demands.

Many prewritten software packages, such as dBASE III+ and Lotus 1-2-3, provide their own "languages" through the use of "macro" instructions (see Chapters 10 and 11). (Of course the actual code—invisible to the user—for most packages is written in assembly language or C.)

Ideally, people should be able to talk to the computer as they do to each other—in a NATURAL LANGUAGE such as Chinese, English, or Greek. Nonprocedural languages will resemble natural languages more and more closely. Applications already exist where spoken commands activate a computer program, and then provide the necessary input data. So far, the repertoire of commands for such applications is fairly limited, much like the verbs in a computer program; but the systems can take account of individual variations in speech and get the right command much of the time. Is it farfetched to speculate that these may be the humble beginnings of a process that will end with the use of natural languages as computer languages? Perhaps someday Tom Lee could request the Oakriver University computer to handle the honor roll problem for him—in writing or verbally—like this:

> *Please print a list of the names and grade point averages of all students who had a GPA of 3.5 or more last term. Give me the number of such students as well.*

When this type of request becomes possible, we will have reached the end of our developmental odyssey that started with machine language. When computers can be "programmed" in a natural language, then computer languages will be a topic of interest only to software designers.

System software

SYSTEM SOFTWARE is prewritten software that links application software to the computer hardware. It does its job with little direction from the user. The most important type of system software, the OPERATING SYSTEM, supervises and directs the hardware as well as all other software components of the information system. PROCESS PROGRAMS, another type of system software, are subordinate to the operating system and

case in point

Big lessons from a small shop

Nestled among Detroit's multibillion-dollar giants is a $340 million machine tool builder with the unlikely name of Lamb Technicon. It's a thriving company, having sold production systems to all major U.S. automakers and to companies in fifteen foreign countries. From this small company comes a startling approach to building systems, one that may provide lessons for its bigger brethren.

"We do very little software maintenance here at Lamb," beams Ted Linder, VP of MIS, a post Lamb upgraded from director just for him in recognition of his accomplishments. "In fact, we rewrite our applications every year."

Linder's approach has practical merit. Applications built afresh are more coherent than "spaghetti programming," the labyrinth of go-to commands that tends to result from continual upgrades. When an application is rebuilt, it's easier for users to find data in that application. To realize his rewrite strategy, Linder has discarded COBOL in favor of Software AG's Natural 4GL.

"Natural is so easy to use that my staff can spend up to 75 percent of their time on applications design and only 25 percent on implementation and maintenance," says Linder. Most shops spend about 70 percent of their time on maintenance, although some shops equal Linder's performance using COBOL.

MIS at Lamb finds Natural is easier for its programmers. The problem with upgrading COBOL, Linder maintains, is that it tends to collect "fingerprints," the programmer's idiosyncrasies that color the work.

Natural allows end users an easy way to access applications, giving them options in the form of multiple command formats to search for data, as opposed to COBOL, which is limited by a single command format. More information can be gained with fewer steps using a 4GL.

Clearly, throwing out applications yearly places enormous demands on a small staff. Jim Domsick, senior program analyst, coordinates the project teams (known locally as "Bad Boys Inc." and "The Mob") that farm the yearly improvements.

"It's two months of hell," says Domsick about implementation, which begins in November.

Earlier in the year, project teams are assembled from the major operating departments and MIS personnel. With the exception of accounts receivable, every application will get thrown out and rewritten. Domsick stresses the importance of attitude in determining the success of Lamb's information strategy. "We need dynamic personalities—the kind that can make decisions. People need a corporate rather than a parochial mindset."

Source: Adapted from Michael Puttre, "Big Lessons from a Small Shop," *InformationWEEK,* 22 February 1988, 28. © 1988 by CMP Publication, Inc., 600 Community Drive, Manhasset, NY 11030. Reprinted with permission from InformationWEEK.

Figure 15-9
The place of system soft-
ware in the information
system.

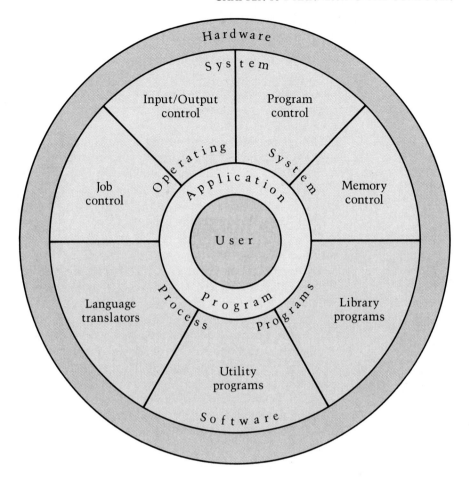

perform specific functions that a user requests, such as translating an application program into machine language. Process programs consist of language translators, utility programs, and library programs.

As Figure 15-9 suggests, we can imagine the system software as sitting between your application program and the computer hardware. You, the user, occupy the innermost ring. The second ring is your application program. The application program interacts with the system software components shown in the next ring. The operating system programs are shown in the top half of the system software ring. Dependent on the operating system software are the process programs, shown in the lower half of the ring. The system software components, in turn, deal with the hardware, the outermost component, which does the work.

The operating system

In the truest sense, the operating system is in charge of the computer. You may have bought the computer yourself, plugged it in, and turned it on; you may also have selected and installed the operating system. To get any work done, however, you will have to go through the boss—the operating system. The main component programs of the operating system handle:

- Job control
- Input/output control
- Program control
- Memory control

Fortunately the operating system is as much servant as master. The operating system performs the formidable job of integrating the elements of a computer system into an effective, cohesive unit.

Job control program

That portion of an operating system known as the JOB CONTROL PROGRAM prepares an application program and its data (known collectively as a *job*) to be run. The preparations include checking for valid account numbers and passwords (for security), assigning input/output devices, setting limits such as how long the program should run and how much it should print, monitoring account usage, and determining job priorities.

Input/output control program

An INPUT/OUTPUT CONTROL PROGRAM supervises the transfer of data from input devices to main memory, and from main memory to output devices. It helps overcome the challenges associated with mediating differences between input, output, communication, and processing speeds. Input and output devices read and write data much more slowly than the computer's central processing unit processes the data. It is not uncommon to see a computer sitting inactive while it waits for an input or output operation to be completed. The first commercially available computers were inactive much of the day, while peripheral devices crept along at a relative snail's pace. Today's input/output devices are much faster; high-speed printers can produce over 50,000 lines of print per minute. Computers can handle *millions* of operations per *second*.

Program control programs

The PROGRAM CONTROL PROGRAMS handle the movement of programs (or parts of programs) into main memory so that the computer can execute the program instructions. With early computers, program management was not an issue, since the computer ran only one program at a time, and all of the program was in main memory at once. Today, there are a number of different ways of running programs, most of which entail running more than one program at the same time. The program manager sorts this all out so the user is not even aware that the computer is also being used for other jobs at the same time.

The three major processing modes are batch processing, time-sharing, and real-time processing. A given operating system is designed to handle one or more of these modes. Any mainframe or minicomputer is capable of running a program in any of the modes, provided it has the correct operating system.

In addition to the three processing modes, we will describe two execution techniques: multiprogramming and multiprocessing. These techniques are operating-system dependent, and can be used to run programs in any of the three modes (batch, time-sharing, or real-time).

With *batch processing*, data are collected over a period of time and processed as a group. Figure 15-10a shows the batch processing concept.

In *time-sharing processing* the computer alternates between several operations. This allows several users to run programs at the same time, on the same computer, by assigning each user a *time slice* or tiny bit of computer time. During each time slice the computer carries out part of the user's program. When one user's time slice is used up, the system moves on to the next user, and then the next, eventually returning to the first—giving each user the illusion he or she has exclusive use of the computer. Time-sharing can be used to support *interactive processing*. Figure 15-10b shows the time-sharing concept.

With *real-time processing*, the computer processes data rapidly enough that the results can be used to influence a process that is still taking place (Figure 15-10c). Like time-sharing, real-time processing is generally interactive, and usually involves more than one user of the computer. The principal difference is speed: with a real-time system, the response must be immediate. With time-sharing, the loss of a few seconds is not so crucial.

Real-time systems are used in space navigation. Banks and credit card companies also use real-time systems to check customer balances that may well be changing simultaneously because of another transaction. This level of service could never be offered with batch processing.

Through some of the techniques we have already described in this chapter, today's computers give the illusion that they perform a number of things at the same time. The fact remains, however, that even the most sophisticated CPU only executes one instruction at a time. One instruction at a time, however, need not mean one program at a time. The earliest computers did handle only one program at a time, but in the early 1960s, the concept of multiprogramming was introduced. MULTI-PROGRAMMING refers to the concurrent execution of more than one program at a time. Instructions of one program are executed, then instructions of the next program, then instructions of a third program, and so on. The operating system's program control software directs the CPU telling it which program to deal with and when.

Multiprocessing is not a variant of multiprogramming, but a different concept that is often confused with it. In MULTIPROCESSING, two or more CPUs execute instructions at the same time. The instructions may be from different programs or from the same program. Multi*programming*, in contrast, handles two or more programs at the same time within a *single* central processing unit.

Multiprocessing configurations vary. Sometimes several computers take on tasks on an egalitarian basis, as if on the principle that "two heads are better than one." Another configuration consists of a larger computer that handles most of the main operations, and subordinate computers that deal with less important tasks, such as editing input or handling the maintenance of files. Both of these configurations (see Figure 15-11) are common for scientific and business applications that require more power than a single computer can deliver.

Memory control program
Keeping track of a program's location in the computer's main memory and secondary storage is the job of the MEMORY CONTROL PROGRAM.

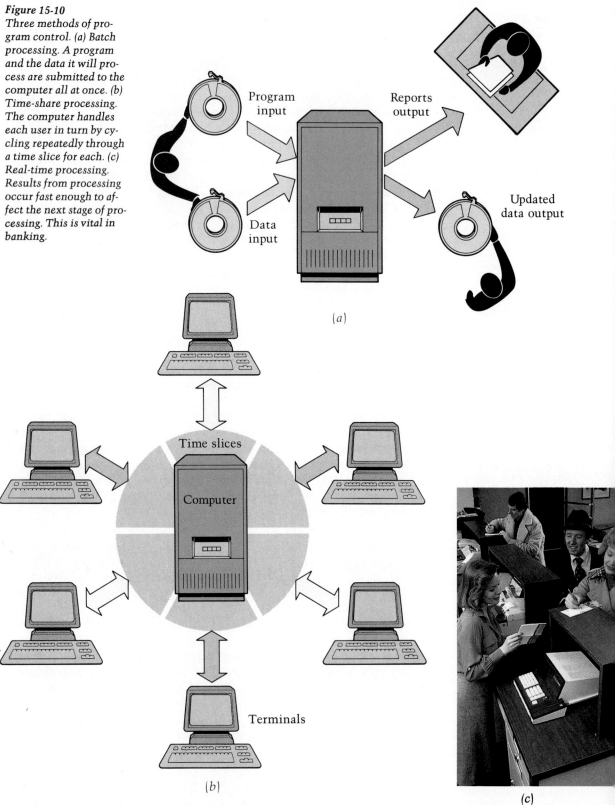

Figure 15-10
Three methods of program control. (a) Batch processing. A program and the data it will process are submitted to the computer all at once. (b) Time-share processing. The computer handles each user in turn by cycling repeatedly through a time slice for each. (c) Real-time processing. Results from processing occur fast enough to affect the next stage of processing. This is vital in banking.

Program input

Reports output

Data input

Updated data output

(a)

Time slices

Computer

Terminals

(b)

(c)

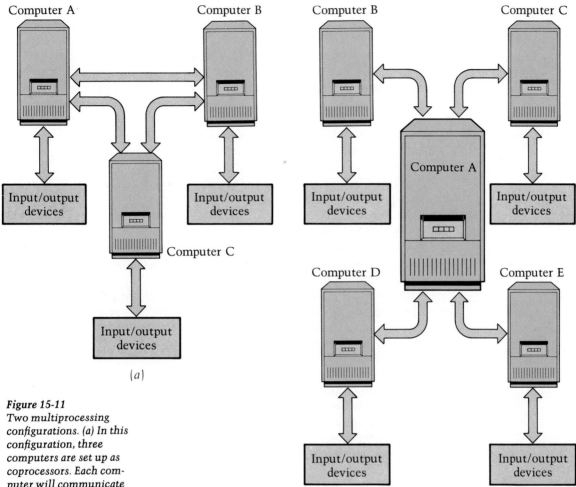

Computer A   Computer B   Computer B   Computer C

Input/output devices   Input/output devices   Input/output devices   Computer A   Input/output devices

Computer C

Input/output devices

Computer D   Computer E

(a)

Input/output devices   Input/output devices

(b)

Figure 15-11
Two multiprocessing configurations. (a) In this configuration, three computers are set up as coprocessors. Each computer will communicate with the others and be able to access the others' main storage. (b) In this configuration, one main computer does computations and delegates other tasks to subordinate computers.

The memory control program writes parts of the application programs being run as well as parts of the operating system that are not needed for the moment onto a secondary storage device. When software that is on secondary storage is needed in main memory, it is read in and something else is kicked out onto secondary storage to make room.

Now that we have completed our look at the operating system, let's examine those subordinate system software components that the operating system calls upon as required: process programs. We will review the three main types of process programs here—language translators, utility programs, and library programs.

Process programs

Language translators
Consider the problem of conversing with someone who speaks a different language. We are faced with four options. First, we could learn the other person's language; second, the other person could learn our's; third, we could both learn a third language; or fourth, we could hire a

translator. Suppose the other person could not learn your language or a common language, and you could not devote the effort to learning another language. The only viable option is to use a translator. The same situation exists when working with computer languages. When you write a program in any language except machine language, it must be translated into machine language in order to run on the computer. LAN-GUAGE TRANSLATORS translate procedural, nonprocedural, or assembly languages into machine language. In addition, they check for and identify errors that may be present in the program being translated.

There are three types of language translators: compilers, interpreters, and assemblers. We will describe each in turn.

A COMPILER translates a complete program written in a high-level language into machine language (see Figure 15-12). Compilers are used to translate COBOL, FORTRAN, Pascal, and some versions of BASIC, such as QuickBASIC and TrueBASIC.

Before compiling, your program is known as a *source program*. Using a compiler, the source program goes through three main steps: compile, link-edit, and execution (or GO).

During the compile step your source program is treated as if it were data. If any errors in syntax or logic are encountered, the process stops and a list of error messages is generated. The result of successful completion of the compile step is an *object program*.

During the link-edit process the object program is merged with pre-written object programs, which might include, for example, a routine for calculating square roots. Usually this process passes without any problems. The combined object programs are called the *load program*.

The load program is what the CPU actually processes when the program is executed. During execution the data to be processed are taken into the CPU. If no data errors are detected the program will execute successfully.

Like compilers, interpreters translate a program written in a high-level language into machine language. Unlike compilers, however, INTERPRETERS perform the translation one instruction at a time, and then execute the resulting machine language instructions immediately. On most microcomputers it is an interpreter that translates BASIC into machine language.

An ASSEMBLER translates a program written in assembly language into machine language. Apart from the fact that it deals with a low-level language rather than a high-level language, and thus has less of a gap to bridge in translation, an assembler operates the same way as a compiler.

Utility programs

Computers must do some types of processing over and over again. A UTILITY PROGRAM performs such general-purpose repetitive processing for the information system. The operating system calls upon utility programs when it needs them; the user can also call upon them, through job control statements. Examples of utility programs include text-editing programs, diagnostic programs, inter-peripheral file transfers, and sort/merge programs.

FLOWCHART

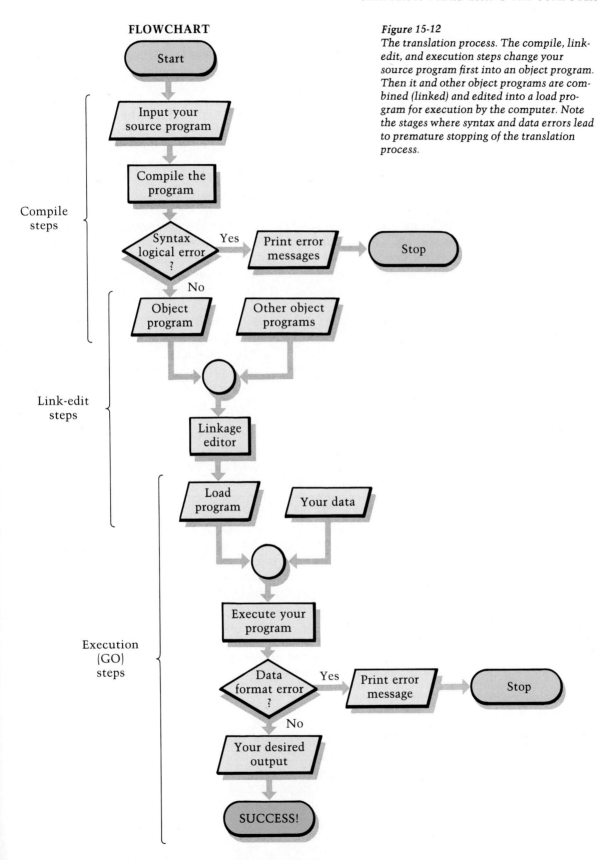

Figure 15-12
The translation process. The compile, link-edit, and execution steps change your source program first into an object program. Then it and other object programs are combined (linked) and edited into a load program for execution by the computer. Note the stages where syntax and data errors lead to premature stopping of the translation process.

Library programs
Prewritten programs for general use stored in object code on a direct-access device are known as **LIBRARY PROGRAMS**. Examples of library programs include routines to calculate square roots and to generate lists of random numbers.

System software for microcomputers

Microcomputers have operating systems that perform the same general functions as larger computers. One key difference lies in the fact that most microcomputers are used by only one person; therefore, considerations of sharing resources with others do not usually apply.

The second important distinction between microcomputer operating systems and the operating systems for mainframes and minicomputers is that microcomputer operating systems work with more than one brand of microcomputer. Operating systems for mainframes and minis, however, are usually confined to machines by the same manufacturer. Operating systems will work on more than one brand of microcomputer because most are designed to run on a specific brand of microprocessor chip, and different manufacturers of microcomputers use the same microprocessor chips.

The IBM PC (Personal Computer), introduced in 1981, popularized the operating system **MS-DOS (MICROSOFT-DISK OPERATING SYSTEM)**. (The version that runs on the IBM PC is called PC-DOS). Due to the popularity of the IBM PC, and the fact that many other computer manufacturers have since designed their hardware and software to be PC-compatible, the use of MS-DOS has become widespread today.

OS/2 (OPERATING SYSTEM/2), also by Microsoft, serves as the operating system for the IBM PS/2 line of personal computers. OS/2's features include greater memory control, the ability to manage several simultaneous users, and the ability to support the use of SQL (System Query Language), a fourth-generation language.

In the history of computers, serious attempts have surfaced from time to time to make one intelligible to another. The UNIX operating system has emerged as one such attempt. Bell Laboratories developed **UNIX** as an operating system capable of running on many different computers, including the minicomputers that Bell Labs used for its own research. The operating system became popular on various machines in-house, and soon began to spread outside of Bell Labs. Various UNIX versions are now used on microcomputers, minicomputers, mainframes, and supercomputers alike, a unique characteristic that makes UNIX a possible contender for the operating system of the future. A number of UNIX-like operating systems, and systems that add other features to UNIX itself, have also appeared.

summary

■   One useful way to categorize the many different programming languages is by how much attention must be paid to the workings of the computer when programming in the language. With a low-level language, the most attention must be paid. With a high-level procedural language, less is paid, and therefore more can be concentrated on solving the problem at hand. High-level nonprocedural languages are furthest from the workings of the machine and are designed to make solving a narrow range of problems easier. Historically, languages developed in the same order, from low-level to nonprocedural. All three levels are in use today.

■ The selection of a programming language within an information system depends upon the existing hardware, people, rules and procedures, programs, and data. Usually the individual programmer has little say over what languages are picked. It is useful, however, for programmers to know the characteristics of the main languages, for they may have a choice of which to use for a given application. A knowledge of programming language characteristics can make those of us who are not programmers more informed users and purchasers of software.

■ Ten characteristics can be used both to describe a language and to compare one to another. These are application area, file-handling ability, mathematical computing ability, machine independence, availability on microcomputers, level of self-documentation, quality of interactive form available (both for interactive processing and interactive programming), allowance for structured programming, total cost for a few runs, and total cost for many runs. Total program cost includes the cost of writing the program, the cost incurred each time it is run, and the cost of maintaining it.

■ Machine language is the true language of the computer. Programs written in any other language must be translated into machine language by system software to run. Machine language consists of strings of 1s and 0s. Assembly language, also a low-level language, is one step removed from machine language.

■ Procedural languages use English-like statements and mathematical symbols, allowing the programmer to focus on problem-solving procedures rather than the inner workings of the machine. Among the procedural languages, BASIC is one of the first languages that many people learn. Pascal is a language designed with structured programming in mind. COBOL must be ranked as the prime language of business, if only because at this point in history most programs for American corporations are coded in COBOL. FORTRAN is another venerable language with essentially the opposite characteristics that make it useful for technical applications.

■ Other procedural languages include Ada and C. A special characteristic of Ada is that it incorporates software engineering methods that speed program design.

■ Within a fairly narrow application range, nonprocedural languages are both powerful and easy to learn. Included in this category are fourth-generation business-oriented languages—especially report generators that link to databases—simulation languages, and fifth-generation languages.

■ Fifth-generation languages have been used in artificial intelligence (AI) research including robotics. They include list-processing languages such as LISP. LOGO, also a list-processing language, is used extensively in schools from the earliest grades on. PROLOG is another fifth-generation language.

■   Nonprocedural languages point the way toward the future: the replacement of computer languages by the natural languages that we speak every day.

■   System software helps application software use the computer. The most important type of system software, the operating system, supervises and directs the hardware as well as all other software components of an information system. The operating system is made up of four parts: the job control, input/output control, program control, and memory control programs.

■   The job control program prepares an application program, or job, to be run. The input/output control mediates between the faster speed of the computer and the slower input/output devices.

■   The program control program handles the movement of software into main memory so that the computer can run it.

■   Three common processing modes in which programs are run are batch, time-sharing, and real-time. With batch processing data are collected over a period of time and processed as a group. Time-sharing processing allows several users to run programs at the same time by assigning each a time slice. With real-time processing the computer processes data rapidly enough for the results of processing to influence a process that is still taking place. Both time-sharing and real-time processing permit interactive processing.

■   Multiprogramming refers to the concurrent execution of more than one program at a time. In multiprocessing, two or more central processing units execute instructions at the same time.

■   The memory control program keeps track of a program's location either in primary or secondary storage.

■   Process programs are system software components that an operating system calls upon as required, often at a user's request. These include language translators, utility programs, and library programs.

■   Language translators include compilers, interpreters, and assemblers. Compilers convert entire source programs into object programs in a single process. Interpreters translate a program one line at a time. Assemblers translate assembly language programs.

■   Utility programs include text-editing programs, diagnostic programs, inter-peripheral file-transfer programs, and sort/merge programs.

■   Library programs are prewritten programs available for users of an information system.

■   Microcomputer operating systems perform the same general functions as those of mainframes and minicomputers. There are differences, however: many microcomputers are used by only one person, and microcomputer operating systems work with more than one brand of microcomputer. Popular microcomputer operating systems are MS-DOS, OS/2, and UNIX.

wrap-up

Oakriver University picks the top ten

Miguel Abreu, the committee chair, thanked Marty Castillo, Alice Smith, and the other information-processing center staff for their helpful presentation and their patience in answering the many questions posed by members of the University Computer Users Committee.

"Now it's your turn," Miguel said to the committee members. "What language needs do you see for your particular schools?"

Elizabeth Slater, who taught in the Information Resource Management Department of the School of Business, spoke first. "The Business School needs several different programming languages," Elizabeth said. "For our introductory computer courses, most instructors teach BASIC, although a few prefer Pascal. The main language for more advanced courses is COBOL and a fourth-generation language. In addition, several instructors use simulation languages for classes in areas like finance, human resources, marketing and production management."

"Naturally our needs differ," Daniel Powers said. "In the School of Engineering, we use C, Pascal, FORTRAN, and assembly language extensively. It turns out that many defense contractors are hiring our graduates and need engineers with experience in using Ada. So we have to teach Ada, too."

Ralph Grosse spoke up. "What you presented about those very high-level natural languages was enlightening. I know my colleagues in the Foreign Languages Department would be interested in using some of them for research."

Bobby-Joe Peters, the representative from Administrative Services, joined the discussion. "We really don't have a language selection problem," he said. "The administration will continue to use COBOL for virtually all of its large-scale programming needs. The cost of changing languages now would be simply too great."

After every interested committee member had spoken, Miguel Abreu asked the committee to rank the desired languages. As the "output" of today's meeting, the top ten languages would be chosen. More languages could be added later if funds permitted and interest was strong.

The top ten languages were BASIC, C, COBOL, FORTRAN, Pascal, Ada, LISP, PROLOG, a fourth-generation language, and assembly language.

"Now that we have resolved the language problem for the present," Miguel said, "our meeting next Wednesday will cover additional fourth-generation languages and prewritten software packages."

key terms

These are the key terms in alphabetical order. The numbers in parentheses refer to the page on which each term is defined.

Ada (515)
Artificial intelligence (AI) (518)
Assembler (526)
Assembly language (508)
BASIC (Beginner's All-Purpose Symbolic Instruction Code) (510)
C (517)
COBOL (COmmon Business-Oriented Language) (513)
Compiler (526)
Fifth-generation language (518)
FORTRAN (FORmula TRANslation) (513)
Fourth-generation language (517)
Input/output control program (522)
Interactive processing (506)
Interactive programming languages (506)
Interpreter (526)
Job control program (522)
Language translator (526)
Library program (528)
LISP (LISt Processing) (518)
List-processing language (518)
LOGO (518)
Low-level language (502)
Machine independence (505)
Machine language (507)
Memory control program (523)
MS-DOS (Microsoft-Disk Operating System) (528)
Multiprocessing (523)
Multiprogramming (523)
Natural language (519)
Nonprocedural language (502)
Operating system (519)
OS/2 (Operating System/2) (528)
Pascal (511)
Procedural language (502)
Process programs (519)
Program control program (522)
PROLOG (PROgramming in LOGic) (519)
Self-documentation (506)
Simulation language (518)
Software engineering (515)
Structured programming (506)
System software (519)
UNIX (528)
Utility program (526)

review questions

objective questions

True/false. *Put the letter T or F on the line next to the question.*

1. COBOL has the ability to handle large files.   1 _____

2. BASIC has a high level of machine independence.   2 _____

3. The level of self-documentation for COBOL is low compared to other major languages.   3 _____

4. The total cost for many runs of a program is higher for FORTRAN than for COBOL.   4 _____

5. The total cost for a few runs of a program is higher for BASIC than for COBOL.   5 _____

6. A language translator is part of the operating system.   6 _____

7. LISP is an example of a simulation language.   7 _____

8. Pascal is noted for its requirements for structured programming techniques.   8 _____

9. An interpreter is a language translator that translates the source program as a single unit.   9 _____

10. Fourth-generation languages are primarily used for business-oriented applications.   10 _____

Multiple choice. *Put the letter of the correct answer on the line next to the question.*

1. Which languages are available on microcomputers today—BASIC, COBOL, FORTRAN, or Pascal?   1 _____
  (a) BASIC and Pascal.
  (b) BASIC and FORTRAN.
  (c) BASIC, FORTRAN, and COBOL.
  (d) All four languages are available.

2. Razor-Thin Lasers markets shaving devices. Their accounting department needs a new payroll program. The program must be well documented, and usable on several different computers. Which language would you recommend?   2 _____
  (a) BASIC.   (c) Pascal.
  (b) COBOL.   (d) FORTRAN.

3. Professor Genie Splitter needs a "quick and dirty" program to perform some calculations on the DNA configuration for a "new" animal. What language would she be *unlikely* to use?
    (a) FORTRAN.   (c) Pascal.
    (b) C.   (d) COBOL.

4. Easy Money Loan shop often has to change locations on extremely short notice. They need a programming language capable of calculating simple (but extremely high) interest payments using a number of different computers. What language would you recommend?
    (a) FORTRAN.
    (b) Pascal.
    (c) BASIC.
    (d) None of the above.

5. Two examples of low-level, highly machine-dependent languages are:
    (a) COBOL and FORTRAN.
    (b) BASIC and assembly.
    (c) Machine and assembly.
    (d) BASIC and machine.

Fill in the blank. *Write the correct word or words in the blank to complete the sentence.*

1. A _____ language is used to model real-world events.

2. The programming language, _____, is a procedural structured language that makes extensive use of software engineering techniques.

3. A language translator that translates one program line at a time is called a(n) _____.

4. A(n) _____ program is a translated program written in machine code.

5. The term _____ refers to the ability of two or more computers linked together to execute simultaneously two or more instructions.

6. The _____ helps the application software use the computer.

7. The term _____ refers to how "English-like" the program code reads to people.

8. The _____ control program portion of an operating system prepares an application program and its data to be run.

9. A(n) _____ translates assembly language programs.

10. The term _____ refers to the ability to process two or more programs concurrently within the computer.

short answer questions

When answering these questions, think of concrete examples to illustrate your points.

1. What languages are best for business applications?
2. What are the major weaknesses of BASIC?
3. What are the major distinguishing features of COBOL?
4. What are the major strengths of Pascal?
5. What is a natural language?
6. What are the four major parts of the operating systems?
7. What are the three major types of processing programs?
8. Differentiate among the different types of language translators.
9. Describe how a compilable program is processed for execution.

essay questions

1. Compare and contrast BASIC and Pascal.
2. Compare and contrast COBOL and FORTRAN.
3. In your business, or in an area of interest at school, which languages would be frequently used? Why?

Answers to the objective questions
True/false: 1. T; 2. F; 3. F; 4. T; 5. F; 6. F; 7. F; 8. T; 9. F; 10. T
Multiple choice: 1. d; 2. b; 3. d; 4. d (COBOL); 5. c
Fill in the blank: 1. simulation; 2. Ada; 3. interpreter; 4. object; 5. multiprocessing; 6. system software; 7. self-documentation; 8. job; 9. assembler; 10. multiprogramming

Distributed processing: linking the world

After studying this chapter you should understand the following:

- *How distributed processing differs from centralized processing.*
- *What types of applications lend themselves to distributed processing.*
- *The features of data communications networks.*
- *The different types of network topologies.*
- *The types of media used for data communications.*
- *Characteristics of message or data transmission.*

chapter 16

Connections great and small

Something George Roberts saw in the Global Electrical Equipment newsletter startled him. The same computer that had given him performance data on his inspectors was in constant touch with Paris, Hong Kong, and Madrid. Several space satellites were used in the linkup. The only weak part of the link, the article concluded, was that data took a few seconds to go halfway around the world.

George already knew something about data communications. After all, he was an engineer. He knew data communications involved hooking up computers and peripherals over distances, generally using the telephone system, in order to get work done. He also knew that data could be sent and received globally by satellite, but he hadn't been aware that it happened at this facility.

A voice cut into his thoughts. "George, my micro is down," Sylvia Fischer said. "Can I use yours?"

"Sure," George said. "Ward's got it in his office."

"Will it read my disks?"

"That's a good question," George said. "Let's go see."

George had an idea as he and Sylvia walked down the hall. "Sylvia, how many micros do we have around here anyway?"

"In this plant? I don't know—several dozen, I think."

"Do you know what we should do?" George asked. "We should link them together. Because now we're working in the dark ages, with everybody using different programs and different microcomputers as if we were reinventing the wheel. We should be able to share data and even connect to the mainframe."

George paused and pointed to the computer room. "Do you know where the machines are that the mainframe is hooked up to? Madrid, Hong Kong, Paris. If that machine can bounce signals off satellites," he said, "shouldn't we be able to run a few cables under the floor here in the plant to let our micros communicate?"

"Let's find out," Sylvia said.

Distributed processing

The evolution of distributed processing systems

Centralized processing

Early in the history of computers, an organization had a computer and that was that. Anybody who wanted to use the computer would bring their data in a batch to the computer center, and later would go back to pick up their output. There were no other options. This is known as CENTRALIZED PROCESSING. Still in existence, today's centralized processing networks also support real-time and time-sharing (Figure 16-1a).

There are valid reasons for some centralization of computing. Consider situations where sales transactions are best managed in conjunction with a single database. With ON-LINE TRANSACTION PROCESSING (OLTP), real-time transaction updates can be performed via the network upon the corporation's database. And, of course, it is no longer necessary to physically trek to the central computer—the data communications network will do that for you.

The demand for OLTP has sparked interest in fault tolerant computers. FAULT TOLERANT COMPUTERS have special hardware and system software features that make them highly resistant to failure. These machines are popular in situations where they are expected to be in constant use. Stock brokerages, which compete in the worldwide marketplace, have acquired many of these computers. Of course, OLTP and fault tolerant computers can be used with the two types of processing described next.

Decentralized processing

As computers became cheaper and more accessible, and as users became frustrated with bottlenecks at the centralized computer, organizations began to increase the number of computers. These computers functioned independently of the first, central computer. Organizations that operated in a decentralized way tended to adopt this DECENTRALIZED PROCESSING approach (Figure 16-1b). Each computer was part of its own information system, with the local managers in control of hardware, software, and data. Despite the hands-on computer power, communication within an organization was stifled, as was control of resources. Computing was scattered among mainframes at corporate headquarters, minicomputers within departments, and microcomputers "owned" by individual end-users.

Distributed processing

Distributed processing seeks a middle path between the centralized and decentralized approaches. DISTRIBUTED PROCESSING spreads information-processing capabilities throughout an organization (Figure 16-1c).

Computers, perhaps of various sizes, are used at different points in the organization, and are linked together for data communications. This

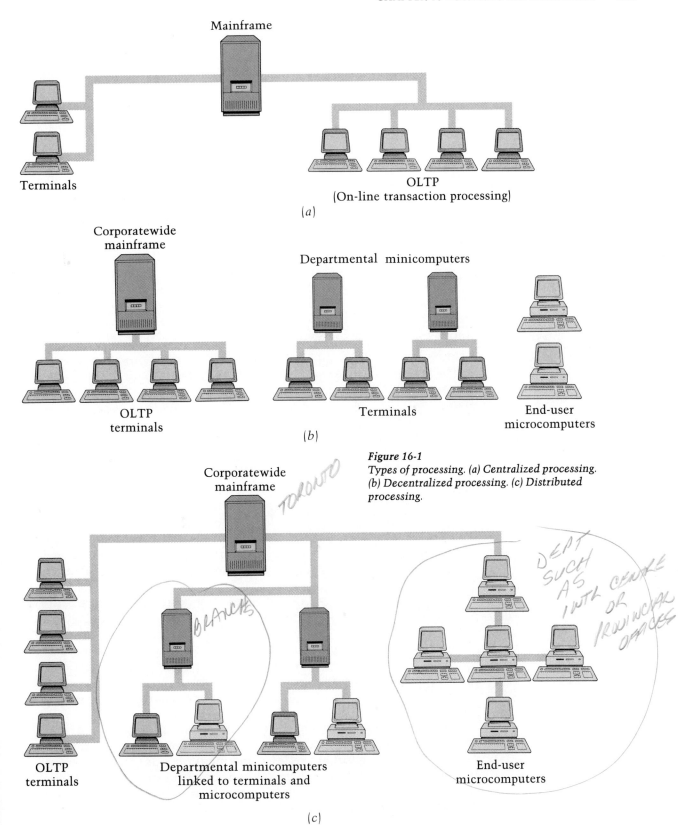

Mainframe

Terminals

OLTP
(On-line transaction processing)

(a)

Corporatewide
mainframe

Departmental minicomputers

OLTP
terminals

Terminals

End-user
microcomputers

(b)

Corporatewide
mainframe

TORONTO

Figure 16-1
Types of processing. (a) Centralized processing.
(b) Decentralized processing. (c) Distributed
processing.

BRANCHES

DEPT
SUCH
AS
INTL CENTRE
OR
PROVINCIAL
OFFICES

OLTP
terminals

Departmental minicomputers
linked to terminals and
microcomputers

End-user
microcomputers

(c)

linkage makes it possible to centralize control of computer resources, to share important data companywide, and to provide backup in case of computer failure. With this approach users in local offices also have access to their own computers to get work done, and do not have to rely on a centralized system.

In most corporations, distributed processing has led to a three-tier division of computing responsibilities:

- **CORPORATEWIDE COMPUTING** is the highest level, where computing services for the entire organization are performed. Preparing budget projections, for instance, requires company data from many departments or regional offices.
- **DEPARTMENTAL COMPUTING** provides mid-level computing services. The purchasing department, for instance, can use its own computers to track suppliers' delivery schedules.
- **END-USER COMPUTING** permits individual or small groups of users to run software using appropriate data that meet their decision-making needs. For example, a marketing representative can use data from the company database to create presentation graphics for a sales presentation. Using a *local area network,* the presentation material can be transmitted to colleagues for their comments.

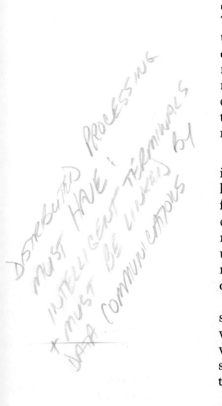

None of the three approaches is perfect. The advantage of centralized processing is that it makes efficient use of the computer rather than letting it sit idle. This efficiency is obtained at the cost of reducing user flexibility, however. A modified form of centralized processing quite common today, places terminals in the hands of users, and links the terminals to the centralized computer in a hierarchy. This is not distributed processing unless the terminals are so intelligent (or are in fact microcomputers) that they are doing substantial processing on their own.

With decentralized processing it is often difficult to maintain and share data on an organizationwide basis because the procedures, hardware, software, and database at each location may not be compatible with those at other locations. Thus an organization with a decentralized system should try to use compatible hardware and software to facilitate the exchange of data.

Distributed processing does attempt to coordinate hardware, software, and databases. Downward-spiraling hardware costs, coupled with software that is steadily becoming easier to use, suggest that the current trend to place computers at many points within an organization will continue. Linking computers together through data communications, for true distributed processing rather than merely decentralized processing, can help ease the problems of compatibility, control, and exchanging data.

The most sophisticated businesses and organizations use data communications networks—either connecting computers together for distributed processing, or, at the least, linking terminals to a centralized computer. Networks have changed the way businesses handle day-to-day operations. Let's look at data communications and networks that support these processing methods.

Information systems and data communications networks today

How do we send messages to another person? For the *sender* to pass a *message* to another person the sender must *encode* (package) the message in a form that can be *transmitted* (delivered). The received message must be in an encoded form that can be *decoded* and understood by the *recipient*. Miscommunication can occur at any one of these steps. For computers to communicate and share data or programs these same steps must be followed and potential pitfalls avoided.

Before looking at how computers and peripherals are joined into powerful systems, let's define data communications and networks.

■ DATA COMMUNICATIONS are the transmission, reception, and validation of data. With data communications, processing is performed by a computer system at some distance from the user. The distance may be great, such as from the West Coast to the East Coast, or small, such as between two floors of the same building. Even smaller yet, the links between a computer and its peripherals is also data communications. Other terms for data communications include *teleprocessing*, *telematics*, and *telecommunications*. To avoid confusion we will stick to the term *data communications* for this chapter.

■ NETWORKS are a combination of computers and peripherals linked together for the purpose of data communications.

The specific configuration of data communications equipment in an information system is determined by the other elements in the system, most importantly the needs of *people*—users, clients, and staff—who depend on it. People determine the *rules and procedures* for data communications and define the *data* to be processed. The *hardware* requires appropriate communications *software* if it is to work at all.

Data communications networks can be simple or complex, large or small. The idea behind any data communications system, however, is simple: the different hardware elements of an information system are linked together by some medium. Data travel from one point to another within the system and are processed. Even a microcomputer, which has its keyboard, disk drives, and display screen built into a single cabinet with the computer, links the different components through an internal data communications medium. The microcomputer is not a true data communications network since everything is right there in one spot.

Many types of applications are served by data communications networks. A computer in a police squad car can be linked to the police department's central dispatch computer. A commodities trader in Chicago can use a data communications network to obtain financial data from around the world. Spaceships and their ground stations are linked in data communications networks responsible for bringing back human beings and equipment intact. Figure 16-2 shows some applications.

Figure 16-2
Some uses of data communications. (a) Over-the-counter stock prices are maintained in a single, coast-to-coast network by NASDAQ (National Association of Securities Dealers Automated Quotations). (b) Commercial data communications companies make a variety of services—electronic mail, conferencing, news wires, travel information, and business data—available to both home and business subscribers.

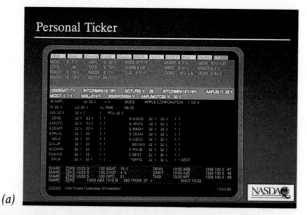

(a)

(b)

Microcomputers can use data communications networks. In fact, many users converse with each other across the nation via electronic bulletin boards. An *electronic bulletin board* is a computer-maintained list of messages that can be posted and read by different computers. Users exchange views and information on topics that interest them and "post" them on the bulletin board. These microcomputer users can carry on private dialogs with strangers in distant cities. Their link to the world of data communications networks is a plain old telephone.

Data communications networks and the information system

Data communications networks have changed the way businesses operate. If businesses used to get along just fine without data communications networks, why can't they now? Some do get along without them. Many others, however, have found that they are much better off *with* them. Organizations use networks for three reasons: organizational control, economic considerations, and geographic factors.

Organizational control—the way in which responsibilities are distributed within the organization—affects a business's approach to data communications networks. A tightly controlled, centralized organization usually constructs a network to match, with corporate headquarters in command of the network. At the other extreme, a loosely organized company may prefer a decentralized structure.

Economic considerations involve economies of scale. In general, the more a computer is used, the cheaper each transaction becomes. Also, networking a computer system means that more users can retrieve data from databases and use hardware to which they would not otherwise have access. The organization benefits by the time saved between the capture of data and the availability of the information derived from data. For example, stock market activity in London can be instantly transmitted to brokers all over the world, allowing analysts to make informed decisions on whether to buy or sell a particular security.

The compelling geographic reason for data communications networks is that businesses today often carry out their functions over large territories. A firm like Global Electrical Equipment must link together its many offices and manufacturing facilities for its own best self-interest. The more the scattered facilities communicate, the better the firm as a whole operates.

Given these organizational control, economic, and geographic considerations, it is easy to see why no "perfect" data communications network exists that can meet all the needs of every organization. Information systems that perform data communications must balance the same five elements as other information systems: the people, rules and procedures, data, software, and hardware. In this chapter we are concerned with the hardware necessary for data communications networks.

Hardware
The information system element, hardware, can be divided into local user hardware, the host processor, and communications devices. These three hardware types are shown in Figure 16-3.

LOCAL USER HARDWARE can consist of one or more peripheral devices, such as display terminals, printers, and secondary storage units. Local user hardware can also consist of a computer of any size. The function of local user hardware is to transmit data to a computer elsewhere in the data communications network for processing, or to receive data from this other computer. If local user hardware is itself a computer, it can also be used to perform local information processing independently of the network.

The HOST PROCESSOR is the computer to which the local user hardware is connected, and which does the actual processing of data. In some networks, a computer can serve simultaneously as a host processor for distant users, and a local processor for nearby users. Networks may have more than one host processor, or do without the host, as we will see when we discuss network topologies (forms) later in the chapter.

The COMMUNICATIONS DEVICES link the local user hardware with the host processor. There are two types of communications devices: switching equipment and media. Communications switching equipment serves as the intermediary between local user hardware and data communications media, and between the host processor and data communications media. Data communications media handle the actual transmission of data between local user hardware and the host processor.

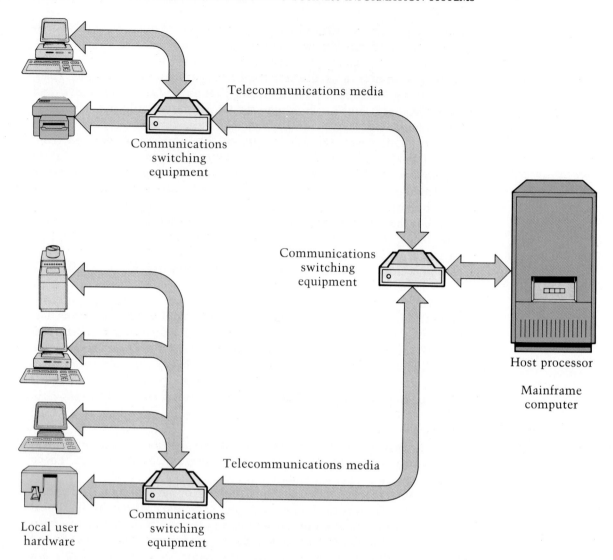

Figure 16-3
The relationship among local user hardware, communications devices, and the host computer.

Supporting all types of processing

Data communications networks can help support time-sharing, real-time processing, batch processing, or a combination of the three. Consider how Global Electrical Equipment links together its powerful computers into a vast network. At the same time one computer is answering inquiries from local user hardware on a time-sharing basis, another might be guiding one or two batch application programs while it waits for database queries. A third computer might give top priority to a real-time test it is monitoring but still be communicating with the other computers when not tied up with the test.

Linking local microcomputers to host computers

Microcomputers can serve as local links between users and host computers. Host computers may be mainframes, minicomputers, or other microcomputers. With a **MICRO-TO-MAINFRAME LINK**, the microcomputer can serve as a terminal with all processing being performed by the host computer, or it can be used for processing. The physical link requires the installation of special add-on "boards" and system software. We refer to a microcomputer as being in the **TERMINAL EMULATION MODE** when it is linked to a minicomputer or mainframe computer and is used as a terminal, not for processing. In the *non*emulation mode, a user can *download* a small portion of the data contained in the mainframe computer system's database, manipulate the data locally, and then *upload* the results to the host computer system.

MICRO-TO-MICRO LINKS are hardware and software that permit a microcomputer user access to files and programs stored on a different microcomputer. With micro-to-micro links, not all microcomputers are equal. A **FILE SERVER** is a microcomputer that controls the major hard disk containing the shared database and programs.

The price of data communications networks
For all its advantages, there are some drawbacks associated with data communications networks. Data are vulnerable to loss during transmission over data communications media. The cost of using data communications media can be quite high, and must be balanced against the benefits gained. Data communications networks involve more equipment than a locally contained information system; the more equipment one uses, the greater the possibility of equipment failure and consequent disruption. On the other hand, a distributed system with equipment spread out in different sites may be more capable of recovering from a local disaster.

Finally, when data are placed on-line in a network, sensitive data can sometimes be viewed, and even changed, by people who have no right to do so. Chapter 17 will discuss security issues at greater length.

Network topologies

Data communications networks come in a variety of forms, called topologies. The **NETWORK TOPOLOGY** is the logical and physical arrangement of the communications hardware, computers, and other peripherals. The particular form an organization uses reflects the structure and size of the organization, the applications for which it requires data communications, and the data communications technology available to it.

Star network
With a **STAR NETWORK** (Figure 16-4a) a central computer is connected to remote peripherals or other computers, which are not connected to each other. If terminals form the points of the star, this is a "liberated" form of centralized processing—one computer does everything but users at least get their own terminals. If microcomputers or other computers are used as points of the star, this is a form of distributed processing in which the central computer clearly remains in command.

An example of a star network with computers at the points is a department store with several branches. The main department store has the central computer—a mainframe—at the center of the star pattern. The central computer performs most processing for all the stores, such

Figure 16-4
(a) A star network. (b) A hierarchical network.

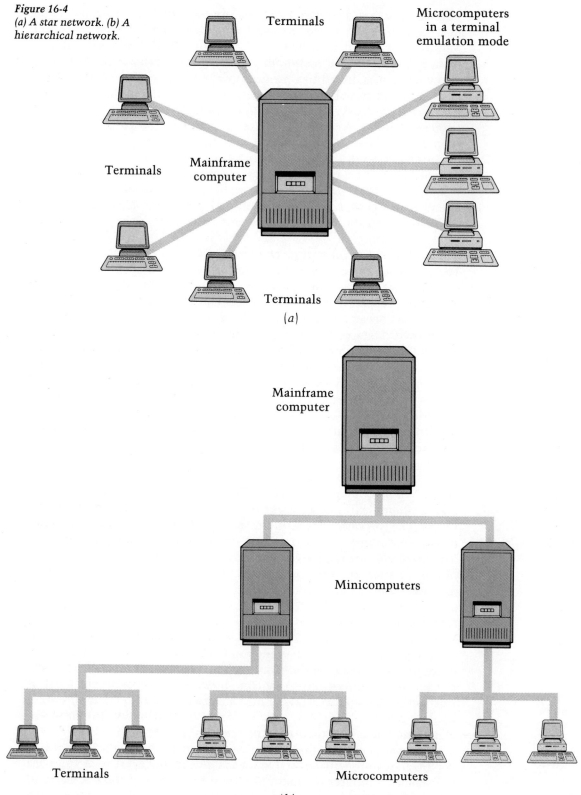

as keeping personnel records up to date, writing paychecks, verifying credit card purchases, and analyzing sales trends. Each branch has a minicomputer of its own to keep track of sales data, which are communicated to the central computer and processed there. The local computers keep track of matters such as scheduling personnel for their particular branch, without the involvement of the main computer. Star networks are a common topology for local area networks used in a microcomputer environment, where programs and data may be shared.

Hierarchical network

The HIERARCHICAL NETWORK (Figure 16-4b) has a main computer at its top, the most important level in terms of control. Communication links spread downward and outward much like the roots of a tree. At each branching point is a computer; the further down the hierarchy, the smaller the computer. The main computer at the top of the hierarchy is in command of everything, with successively subordinate tasks performed at each lower level.

This type of structure might be used by a large organization that must retain central control of the information system yet needs to delegate substantial computing power to individual departments or offices within the organization. Corporate headquarters would have the computer at the top, with the manufacturing, marketing, and research divisions receiving the subordinate but substantial computers at the next level down. Within each corporate division, a further distribution of computer power could be made. In the manufacturing division, for example, the computer could assist and coordinate the computers at the next lower level that controlled the production line, processed quality-control test results, and updated the inventory.

Bus network

A BUS NETWORK (see Figure 16-5a) uses a single line to link computers and peripherals. Much as a transit bus line has many stops along a bidirectional line, data are picked up by the network and then dropped off at the proper destination. There is no host computer. Again, a number of local area networks use this topology.

Ring network

A RING NETWORK links computers into a loop, as shown in Figure 16-5b. The loop has no central computer; instead, all of the computers are equal and communicate with one another. As an example, several mainframes might be hooked together in a loop for a large insurance firm. Users could perform the processing they needed at a particular computer, and could also communicate through that computer with any of the others in the loop when necessary. One mainframe might handle administrative details, another life insurance, another health insurance, and another automobile insurance. If the computer at the life insurance processing center had any free time while the computer processing health insurance forms was overburdened, the computer with the extra time could share the other's load. In a local area network a series of microcomputers can be placed in a ring.

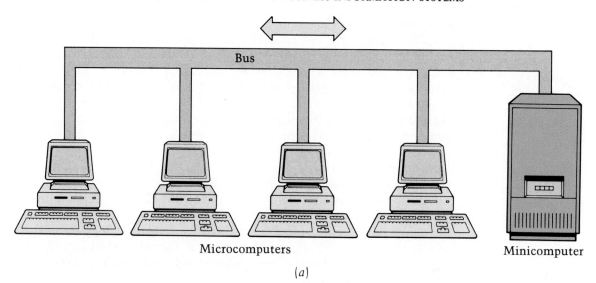

Bus

Microcomputers

Minicomputer

(a)

Figure 16-5
(a) A bus network. (b) A ring network.

Terminals

Mainframe or minicomputers

Terminals

(b)

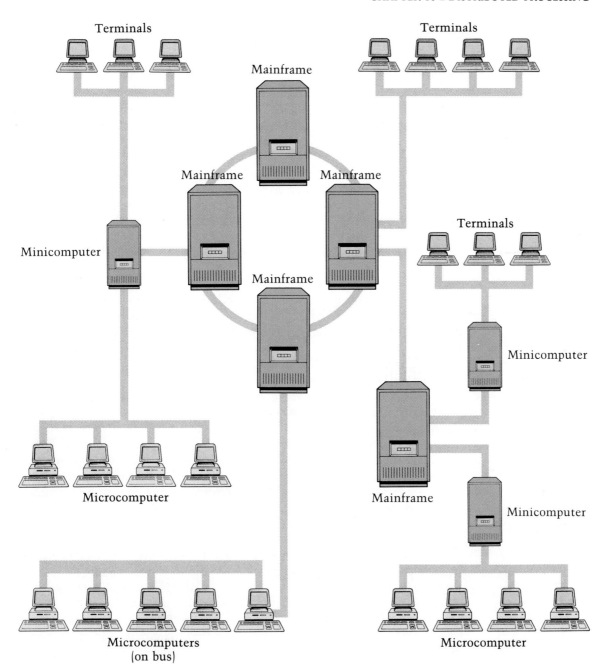

Figure 16-6
A mixed network.

Mixed network

A **MIXED NETWORK** uses a combination of the four approaches. In the example shown in Figure 16-6, the network has a combination of the star (left), bus (bottom), ring (middle), and hierarchical (right) configurations. Other combinations are, of course, possible. Often, several ring networks are joined together, with each serving as the point of a star network, or as a level in a hierarchical network.

Data communications media

Networks require the transmission of data via data communications media. In this section we will describe the different types of media, and then look at media capacity and the directions that data travel.

Types of media

A **DATA COMMUNICATIONS MEDIUM** is the physical link by means of which data are transmitted from one part of the network to another. The particular medium chosen for a given connection depends upon such factors as distance, volume of data, and security needs. The main media available are twisted-wire pairs, coaxial cables, fiber-optic cables, and microwave systems. Figure 16-7 shows these different media.

Twisted-wire pairs

TWISTED-WIRE PAIRS consist of two parallel copper wires. Although the wires are no longer twisted around one another, the original name has remained in our vocabulary. The oldest type of medium, twisted-wire pairs have the advantage of still being the backbone of the telephone system, and are thus readily available.

Twisted-wire pairs have only a limited capacity for transmitting data, however, as we will see later. When twisted-wire pairs are bound together into the heavier cables that make up the telephone lines visible aboveground in most parts of the country, they are subject to "crosstalk"—messages crossing from one twisted-wire pair to another. You have probably experienced it at one time or another when talking on the phone and hearing another conversation faintly in addition to your own. Crosstalk is a nuisance during phone conversations; it is more serious for data communications, because it can garble data.

Coaxial cables

Overcoming some of the limitations of wire pairs, **COAXIAL CABLES** consist of one conducting wire surrounded by an insulator, which is in turn encased in a second conductor. A group of coaxial cables is bound together into cables. Transmission capacity is considerably greater than for wire pairs, and crosstalk is minimized. The major drawback of coaxial cables is that they are more expensive than wire pairs and are not as extensively used. Coaxial cables are often employed to link high-speed peripherals to nearby computers, to link telephone switching centers together, and for other high-volume applications. The simplicity of coaxial cables is shown by their use in linking VCRs to television sets.

Fiber-optic cables

FIBER-OPTIC CABLES involve a completely different technology. Tiny fibers of glass transmit data as light-beam signals generated by lasers. Fiber-optic cables are so small that far greater numbers can be bound together into a cable than with twisted wire or coaxial cables. Fiber-optic cables have the greatest transmission capacity of any data commu-

(a)

(b)

(c)

(d)

Figure 16-7
Data communications media. (a) Twisted-wire pairs—a telephone switching center. (b) A microwave station. (c) Cross section of a coaxial cable. (d) Fiber-optic cable.

nications medium. Although a recent discovery, fiber-optic cables have begun to replace coaxial cables for data transmission as well as for transmitting voice and television signals.

Microwave systems
MICROWAVE SYSTEMS use high-frequency electromagnetic waves to send messages through air or space to microwave receiving stations. Microwave systems have a greater transmission capacity than coaxial cables or wire pairs. No cables are involved at all. Earthbound or terrestrial microwave systems send signals through the atmosphere between repeater stations. The stations must be within "line of sight" of each other, and hence are placed close enough together—no more than 30 miles apart—

case in point
McDonald's serves up global ISDN strategy

The company that pioneered Big Macs, drive-thru windows, Chicken McNuggets, and headsets for counter help is pushing into another frontier: Integrated Services Digital Network (ISDN). McDonald's is the first business in the world to incorporate the full voice and data features of ISDN into its daily operations.

That's only the beginning. The company's goal is to rope all of its 10,000 stores into one network. Each of those stores around the world will feed sales and marketing information back to headquarters instantaneously. From that flow of information, McDonald's will be able to make faster, more informed decisions on what products to sell and how to sell them. . . .

But that worldwide network is 10 years off. Its beginnings, however, are evident in simplified access over inexpensive telephone wire, one of the benefits of ISDN.

The ISDN strategy works like this: A professor at Hamburger University, McDonald's training ground for managers, wants to discuss how last month's promotional campaigns affected sales. He calls the Chicago regional sales manager in Oak Brook, Ill., a mile away. Both the professor and the sales manager can access the month's sales figure as they discuss them over the phone. Both the voice and the data flow over the same phone line. Without ISDN, achieving this simultaneous flow of data and voice is difficult. Each office would require a cluster of outlets and a knot of extra wires. . . .

"With ISDN we will have one network in and one network out and you can cross over and share databases with all of them without an extensive amount of work," says Bonnie Kos, vice president of facilities and systems at McDonald's.

The benefits are myriad. Details of a promotional campaign can be sent via data channels anywhere in the world. And the store managers can inform their regional sales offices of how the promotion is working immediately. The store managers and their regional bosses can access each other's files to check sales or inventory. They can share databases from anywhere in the world. New employees can be trained by computer on-site.

Without ISDN, McDonald's believes, it couldn't erect such a network. ISDN, which is nothing more than a set of interface protocols, gives corporations a blueprint for linking computer and communication devices. The standards include signaling protocol, interface standards, and bandwidth allocation.

"We are growing rapidly and that poses a serious challenge for our information systems," Kos says. "This system is designed to keep things simple as we grow. We want to free up store managers for the more important job of serving the customer."

An ISDN network uses relatively inexpensive twisted-pair cabling, dramatically lowering the cost of wiring buildings and offices. . . .

ISDN is nothing if not inconspicuous. Next to every desktop in McDonald's new office building in Oak Brook, Ill., is one access outlet that can receive and carry integrated voice, data, image, and message signals on standard twisted-pair wire.

Those features unique to ISDN—like electronic directory, calling number identification, and message-waiting and retrieval—link together phone and computer. Electronic directory allows users to look up company telephone numbers and place calls at the touch of a button. . . .

Source: Richard Layne and Cassimir J. Medford, "McDonald's Serves Up Global ISDN Strategy," *InformationWEEK*, 15 February 1988, 36–37. © 1988 by CMP Publication, Inc., 600 Community Drive, Manhasset, NY 11030. Reprinted with permission from InformationWEEK.

that the curve of the earth does not interrupt this line of sight. The terrain must also be free of intervening tall buildings and hills; in fact, the microwave stations themselves are often placed on top of such features to reduce the number of stations required. Dust and humidity can also interfere with data transmission.

Microwave systems using communications satellites overcome the distance limits of the terrestrial systems. Communications satellites are placed in a geosynchronous orbit in space, which means that the satellite remains in place over a given geographic area of the earth, since its speed allows it to exactly match the earth's rotation. Microwaves are then transmitted from an earth station to the satellite 36,200 kilometers (22,500 miles) away, and then from the satellite to another earth station. A signal from one earth station to another will take about ¼ second—a considerable propagation delay for some real-time processing systems. In contrast, to move a signal the 3945 kilometers (2450 miles) from New York to Los Angeles via land-based lines takes less than 2/100ths of a second. To reach further points, the signal can be bounced between additional satellite and earth stations. Terrestrial and satellite-based microwave systems are widely used for long-distance telephone calls.

Media capacity and mode

Data communications media are evaluated not only in terms of their physical nature but also (as we have already touched on) in terms of their capacity and the directions in which the transmission can travel.

Media capacity: bandwidth

A given communications medium has a bandwidth associated with it. BANDWIDTH, or width of the frequency band, refers to the capacity of a medium. The bandwidth determines how much data can be sent within a given amount of time. The general unit of measurement for bandwidths is the BAUD RATE, the number of bits per second (bps) or signals that can be transmitted on a line. The more data that can be transmitted per second, the faster the medium, much as a wide highway can handle more traffic than narrow city streets.

The three bandwidths commonly associated with data communications media are narrowband, voice-grade, and wideband. Figure 16-8 shows which apply to the media just discussed.

NARROWBAND, or SUB-VOICE-GRADE, MEDIA transmit data at rates of 40 to 300 bps. These media are used to transmit to and from low-speed data terminals. Teletype and telegraph systems use narrowband.

Figure 16-8
Capacities and common applications of data communications media.

Type	Capacity	Application
Twisted-wire pairs	Narrowband to voice grade	User to teleprocessing system
Coaxial cables	Voice grade to wideband	Linking high-speed devices
Microwave systems	Wideband	Long-distance links
Fiber-optic cables	Wideband	Long-distance links

552

career box

Telecommunications manager

Managing the often extensive data communications activities of today's organizations is an important and demanding job. Unknown in the early days of computing, the position of telecommunications manager has become vital to the life of many corporations, government agencies, and nonprofit institutions.

Data communications is a field that is evolving so rapidly that no one can predict with certainty where it will go. Telecommunications is constantly growing, however, as is the need for personnel capable of taking charge of it. The telecommunications manager reports to the organization's information resource manager or director of information systems (these positions are described in the Career boxes of Chapters 3 and 6, respectively). In turn, the telecommunications manager is responsible for coordinating specialists in telecommunications. In a larger organization, these will include telecommunications programmers, who develop the systems, and the hardware-oriented telecommunications technicians, who install and repair the electronic equipment. Smaller organizations will consolidate these positions.

The telecommunications manager is responsible for managing all telecommunications activities within an organization. This includes planning the systems, implementing them, and seeing that they work, with the help of the appropriate specialists. The networks involved can be far-flung multinational arrangements, local area networks, or both.

In an area as new as this one, entry is best made by being able to demonstrate expertise. That is, if you know a lot about telecommunications, and are able to pick up hands-on experience as an analyst, programmer, or technician, you are on your way. In a field where there is a great need for personnel, and few people available with appropriate experience, it is possible to rise quickly to become an "expert."

As in any information system job, people skills are important, because you will have to keep your own technical team working smoothly, as well as interact effectively with other managers in the organization in order to best determine and meet their telecommunications needs.

VOICE-GRADE MEDIA, characteristic of the telephone system, transmit data at rates ranging from 300 to 9600 bps. Specially conditioned lines that boost the signal power at certain intervals are necessary to obtain the higher speeds. Applications include connections between terminals and the central processing unit for data-entry and inquiry systems.

WIDEBAND MEDIA transmit data at the fastest speeds of all, ranging from 19,200 to more than 800,000,000 bps (with fiber-optic cables). Wideband media are used as links from one computer to another.

The greater the bandwidth, the faster a single message can be sent over the medium. Or, wide bandwidths can be subdivided into narrower channels to permit sending *more* messages at the same time. For example, a number of transmissions at the voice-grade rate can be made simultaneously using a subdivided wideband medium.

Media mode: direction of transmission
Now that we have seen the different types of media, and classified the speeds at which data may be transmitted over them, one more consider-

ation remains: in which direction can data travel. Data can be sent in one direction only; in both directions, but only one way at a time; or in both directions simultaneously. Figure 16-9 illustrates simplex, half-duplex, and full-duplex transmission between a terminal and a computer.

SIMPLEX TRANSMISSION, like a one-way street, allows for transmission in only one direction. The direction might be, for example, from a computer to a peripheral device, with no response possible, or desired, back to the computer. Commercial radio and television use simplex transmission—signals go out from a transmitter to receivers, but not back the other way.

HALF-DUPLEX TRANSMISSION allows transmission in one direction at a time. Once a message has been received and the line cleared, then a message can go back the other way. Telegraph and two-way radio communications follow this mode. Half-duplex transmission is frequently adequate for links between terminals and a computer. It is similar to a one-way bridge where the oncoming traffic takes turns crossing in either direction when the way is clear.

Figure 16-9
Simplex, half-duplex, and full-duplex trans-mission.

Simplex line allows only one-way travel.

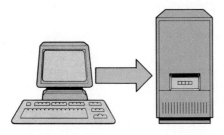

Half-duplex lines allow two-way communication, but only one way at a time.

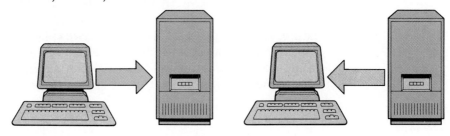

Full-duplex lines permit simultaneous two-way communication.

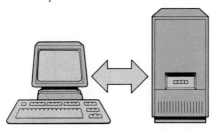

FULL-DUPLEX TRANSMISSION (also known as **DUPLEX TRANSMISSION**) allows for simultaneous, bi-directional traffic. The most powerful mode, full-duplex transmission is used by most computer-to-computer links and some terminal-to-computer links. Telephone communication, in which both parties can talk at the same time, is an example of full-duplex transmission.

Data communications conventions

Although the concept of data communications is not difficult to understand, an examination of the field quickly gets into technicalities that are difficult, or at least specialized. This section deals with several such technicalities.

Following certain data communications conventions make life easier. The ones we will cover here are the conversion of digital to analog signals, transmission codes used, asynchronous versus synchronous transmission, and certain rules of the house known as protocols.

Digital to analog and back

Digital computers generate digital signals, which show an abrupt on-off pattern (Figure 16-10). In contrast, many data communications media—most notably, a fair percentage of telephone lines—accept only analog signals, which show rounded wave patterns. To transmit digital signals over analog data communications media requires that the original signal be translated from digital to analog patterns. This process is called modulation. **MODULATION** converts the digital signal into a form that can be carried over analog lines. Likewise, the signal must be converted back to digital form at the receiving end, a process known as **DEMODULATION**.

A **MODEM** (Figure 16-11) performs the tasks of modulation and demodulation. The term *modem* is derived from *modulation-demodulation*. Some modems are electronic boards placed inside the computer's cabinet, while others are external self-contained units attached to the computer that uses them. If the modem is external, a modular telephone jack is plugged into it. In contrast, the earliest type of modem (and one

*Figure 16-10
Digital and analog signals.*

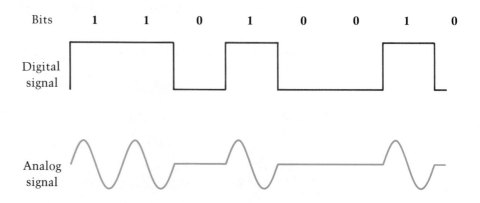

Figure 16-11
A modem and its accompanying communication software.

still in use), an *acoustic coupler*, can use any telephone receiver on a temporary basis by creating sound signals. The acoustic coupler then handles the conversion from the digital "talk" of the device to the telephone line's analog, or from the telephone line's analog to the device's digital. This type of device permits people traveling on the road to link portable terminals to their central information system, even from a phone booth, automobile telephone, or pay phone aboard a commercial flight. Microcomputer communications software packages for use with modems include Crosstalk, Kermit, and Smartcom. Most modems for microcomputers give you the option of transmitting or receiving at 1200, 2400, or up to 9600 bps.

Certain telecommunications media, including some telephone lines, can transmit digital signals. In these situations a modem is unnecessary. Instead, a line interface unit links a device or computer to a telecommunications network.

Regardless of whether they are analog or digital, signals are subject to noise and distortion. To counteract the loss of signal integrity because of a weakening signal over distance, analog telecommunications media use amplifiers to regenerate the signal. Digital systems use repeaters for the same purpose.

Asynchronous and synchronous transmission

Devices send and receive data at different speeds. Peripheral devices are much slower than computers, and vary widely from one another in speed. In addition, devices with a keyboard, such as a display terminal, do not send data steadily but in spurts that correspond to the person's thought processes as he or she keys in the data.

To assure that devices can send and receive data despite these speed differences, the sending and receiving devices need to agree completely on what constitutes a byte. They will then know when a byte ends and the next begins.

There are two conventions followed for doing this. ASYNCHRONOUS TRANSMISSION sends one byte at a time. So that the receiving device will recognize the series of bits as a byte, a start bit precedes the byte, and a stop bit follows it. In other words, the sending device in effect shouts "Ready!" before sending a data byte, then sends the byte, and finally shouts "That's all for this one!" Therefore bytes do not have to be sent at regular intervals, since the receiving device can always tell what it's dealing with. The actual coding patterns for the binary digits that represent each byte are displayed in Chapter 5, Inside the Computer.

ASYNCHRONOUS MODE

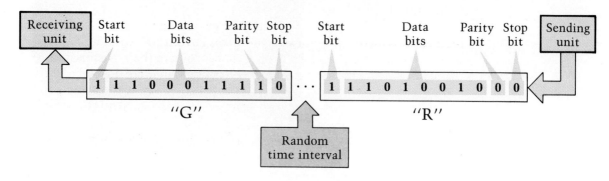

SYNCHRONOUS MODE

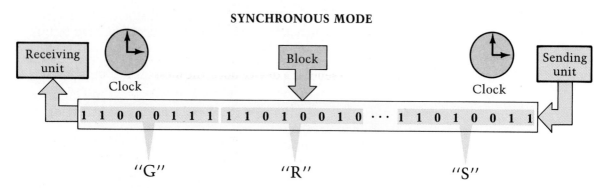

Figure 16-12
In asynchronous transmission, data is transmitted a byte at a time. Each byte is preceded by a start bit and followed by a stop bit. In synchronous transmission, groups of bytes are transmitted in a block. The receiving and sending devices are synchronized so each can recognize where one byte ends and another begins. Here we see how the word "GREETINGS" would be transmitted in both modes using ASCII-8.

SYNCHRONOUS TRANSMISSION uses another approach to solve the same problem. Here bytes are sent in blocks, or groups of bytes, between devices that are "in synch"—that is, timed to match one another precisely. Clock mechanisms at both the sending and receiving end coordinate the signal timing. Special signals flag the start and end of the transmission, much like start and stop bits. But within the transmission, the receiving device itself separates one byte from another through the timing coordinated with the sender.

Synchronous transmission is often used to link high-speed peripherals such as magnetic disk units to computers, or one computer to another. Because of the necessary timing mechanisms, synchronous transmission systems cost more initially, but will save money in high-volume applications. Figure 16-12 illustrates asynchronous and synchronous transmission.

Protocols

Imagine driving on a busy highway where there were no traffic regulations. It would be a scary and dangerous experience. The fact that most everyone follows traffic regulations makes orderly transportation possible. The same is true with data communications networks. We can follow all of the conventions described so far and still have chaos. We would not know where data was coming from and going to. We would have head-on collisions, traffic jams, and little chance to perform data communications of meaningful data. The sender and receiver have to follow the same protocols.

PROTOCOLS are rules and procedures governing the use of data communications media. Specifically, protocols govern how to choose among users competing for system resources, coordinate the transmission of messages, and check for errors in the transmission. For instance, both the sending and receiving modems must both be set at the same baud rate. Protocols are built into the system software that controls data communications networks.

Although protocols operate with little or no human intervention, information system personnel and users do ultimately have control over the protocols followed. For example, protocols exist that allow high-priority users not to wait their turn to send a message but to cut in ahead of everybody else.

Protocols follow one of three methods to determine which device to allow to transmit at a given time. These methods are known as polling, contention, and packet switching.

With POLLING, the computer in charge periodically asks each device if it has a message to send. If a device does, the message is sent. The computer then goes on to ask the next device if it has a message to send. Eventually, in round-robin fashion, the computer will come back to ask the first device again.

CONTENTION takes the opposite approach, with the device asking the computer if the medium is free for transmission. If it is free, the message is sent. If another device is using the medium, the protocol requires that the peripheral wait. One common method used to manage a contention protocol is through a technique called TOKEN PASSING. A token is a set of 8 bits (usually 11111111) that permits access to the network. When a terminal has received the token, it can transmit its message to the appropriate receiving device. The token then passes to the next terminal, and so on, granting each in turn access to the network.

CSMA/CD (CARRIER SENSE MULTIPLE ACCESS/COLLISION DETECTION) is another contention protocol. Devices send messages as needed. There is a risk messages will be sent at the same time, resulting in a collision and a garbled transmission. The collision detection feature will order retransmission.

Polling usually works best when terminals are in frequent use, and contention when they are infrequently used.

The third protocol, packet switching, is used in mixed networks. In PACKET SWITCHING messages are broken into standard-sized units called packets. *Packet switching* methods rely on the *X.25 standard* developed by the CCITT (an international standards body within the United Nations). Each packet can then be transmitted from the sending to the receiving device along a different communications path and the whole message reassembled at the receiving station. The advantage of packet switching is that it makes possible the most efficient use of the network—if one line is too crowded, the message, or part of it, can be sent along another line.

Protocols also check the parity bits appended to transmitted bytes for errors. When an error is detected, the protocol dictates that the byte (for asynchronous transmission) or block (for synchronous transmission) containing the error be sent again, in the hope that it will come through error-free. If the error is still present, the protocol follows predetermined procedures.

Data communications and computer equipment manufacturers, software designers, and users are still debating over protocols. At present no standard protocol exists that allows all devices to communicate with one another.

Communications processors

In a data communications network there is a trade-off between access to a computer and the economics of providing that access. At one extreme, every user would have his or her own direct line to the computer. At the other extreme, all users would have to share one line and take their turn in the queue.

With the first extreme, the data communications links would be expensive to provide, and so many users would want to use the computer at the same time that the computer would become overloaded. For the stand-in-line extreme, long waiting times are guaranteed.

Compromises are therefore the order of the day. Historically, the first compromise was the multidrop line. Later came communications processors.

MULTIDROP LINES link devices together like the beads on a chain, and allow them to contend for use of the shared line to a computer (see Figure 16-13). This was an early technique used to link terminals and printers to a computer. The main drawback is that while one user is on the line, the others have to sit back and wait.

Figure 16-13
Multidrop lines string terminals together onto a shared line.

To develop more efficient ways of serving multiple users, COMMUNICATIONS PROCESSORS were created. These handle the switching and coordination of messages and data. Four major types of communications

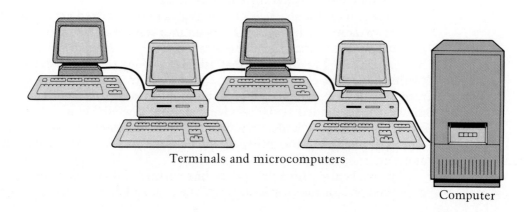

Terminals and microcomputers

Computer

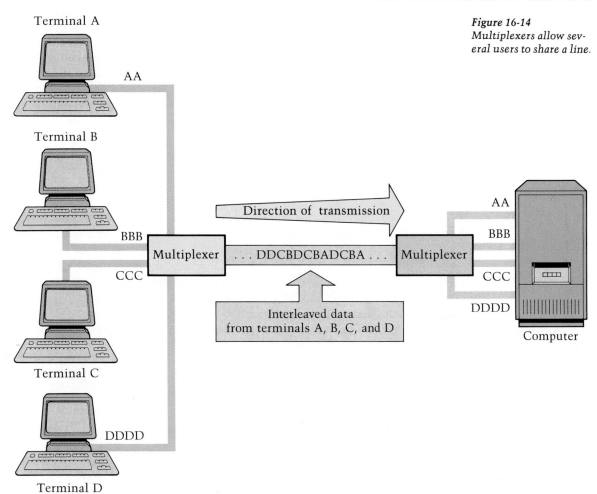

Figure 16-14
Multiplexers allow several users to share a line.

processors are multiplexers, concentrators, front-end processors, and message-switchers.

Multiplexers

MULTIPLEXERS (sometimes spelled "multiplexors" and abbreviated MUXs) allow multiple users simultaneously to share a common data communications medium. Figure 16-14 shows an example. The earliest and least sophisticated of communications processors, a multiplexer interleaves, or layers together, simultaneous messages and data for users of the transmission line. This type of transmission method allows a number of users to communicate with the computer at the same time. Two multiplexers are required: one at the transmitting end combines the messages, and one at the receiving end separates them.

Concentrators

Like multiplexers, CONCENTRATORS combine incoming and outgoing messages into a more compact unit. Concentrators are more complex devices, however, and can be programmed to edit data, compress data, convert between differing byte encoding formats, and check for errors, for both incoming and outgoing data.

Front-end processors

FRONT-END PROCESSORS (Figure 16-15) are usually located near a computer that receives data from peripheral devices or from other computers. Front-end processors are generally minicomputers that relieve the larger computer of overseeing input and output. Besides doing everything that a concentrator can, a front-end processor can be programmed to do more, such as checking for reasonableness of incoming data values, and message switching.

A close relative, the *back-end processor*, is a computer used to link the larger computer to a database stored on a direct-access storage device. A back-end processor relieves the front-end processor of this task.

Message-switchers

While multiplexers, concentrators, and front-end processors are capable of coordinating messages from different sources, some systems demand the power of a dedicated message-switcher. A MESSAGE-SWITCHER helps route messages from many incoming data communications media into the front-end processor, and may even reroute transmissions that can't be handled immediately to less heavily used front-end processors. Modern information systems often make use of combinations of multiplexers, concentrators, front-end processors, and message-switchers.

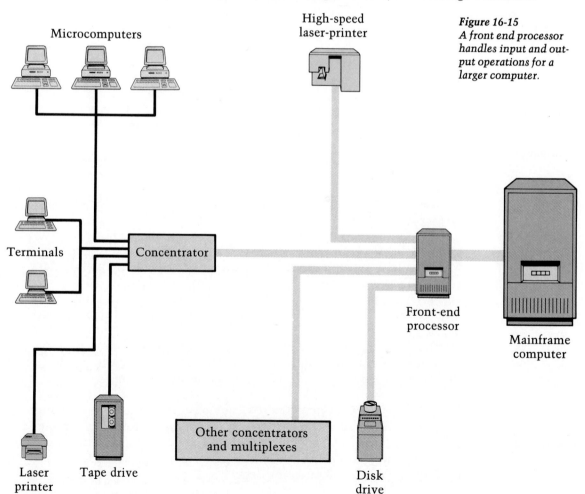

Figure 16-15
A front end processor handles input and output operations for a larger computer.

Ownership and control

As with other information system resources, money changes hands when data communications media are used. Media can be purchased outright for an information system, or leased. Some leased media are accompanied by extra services. We will describe each of these possibilities, and then close this section with a description of very-short-distance data communications networks called local area networks that can be owned.

Private and common carrier networks

Data communications networks can use private telecommunications media, which are purchased by the information system for its exclusive use. This is expensive and generally limited to large data communications networks. Alternatively, data communications networks can lease telecommunications media provided by a common carrier. A **COMMON CARRIER** provides communication services for the public to virtually anywhere, abiding by published regulations and rates. Telephone and telegraph companies are examples of common carriers. A data communications network may use a combination of services provided privately and by common carriers. Usually each country regulates the level of competition (if any) and service within its borders. In the United States common carriers are regulated by the FCC (Federal Communications Commission) and state public utility commissions. Depending upon the volume of traffic, common carriers can provide *switched lines*—where access is through standard dialing methods—or *nonswitched* (*leased* or *dedicated*) *lines*.

Integrating PBXs and the ISDN concept

An organization still needs to link its telephone or data lines to the private or common carrier. Most companies use a form of private branch exchange. A **PRIVATE BRANCH EXCHANGE (PBX)** is a switching center that connects a group of private users' telephone equipment to a smaller number of outside telephone lines to the local telephone company. Newer PBXs use digital technology that can handle both voice and data communications.

Through the efforts of a number of common carriers in many countries as well as most computer hardware manufacturers, international standards for network *connectivity* have been proposed. The most important proposal—**INTEGRATED SERVICES DIGITAL NETWORK (ISDN)**—is a set of international standards developed to integrate both voice and data within either private or public networks through the use of digital (instead of analog) lines and switches. These standards are expected to be adopted over the next 10 to 20 years as companies upgrade their equipment. Besides ISDN, two other standards are being negotiated—*electronic data interchange (EDI)* and *open systems interconnect (OSI)*.

Information systems can lease data communications media through a **VALUE-ADDED NETWORK (VAN)**. VANs not only provide the media that an information system needs, but offer extra services, such as electronic mail/message systems and data security measures (hence the "value-added" in the name). They also charge higher rates. VANs offer communications processors, the use of large databases, and even sophisticated computers that can be tapped into. You pay only for the services used. VAN operators generally do not own the data communications media that they lease out; rather, they lease them in turn from common carriers. Some VANs offer so many services that they are called super-VANs.

LOCAL AREA NETWORKS (LANs)—sometimes simply called local networks—provide offices with the capability of data communications in a smaller setting. Remember we said at the start of the chapter that data communications does not need to span a great distance. LANs don't. Usually a LAN includes a single office, or a set of offices. The data communications media are owned rather than leased. Generally fiber-optic cables or coaxial cables are used. As with any other information system, a LAN can also be connected to outside data communications facilities. With outside connections users have access to a vast pool of information contained in public databases, such as the Dow Jones Retrieval Systems. Figure 16-16 shows an example of a LAN.

The two types of LANs that use coaxial cable technology are called baseband and broadband. **BASEBAND NETWORKS** use a single channel multidrop line. **BROADBAND NETWORKS** use the same physical cable technology as cable television; however, the micro-to-network links are more expensive than for baseband systems.

LANs are increasingly being used to hook together microcomputers. The same thought that occurred to George Roberts in the example at the beginning of the chapter has occurred to many other microcomputer users: Why have so many machines in close proximity been unable to communicate with one another? The price tag on interface hardware offered by microcomputer manufacturers to permit attachment to a network has dropped steadily, at the same time as the equipment has improved in reliability.

Microcomputers linked together in a LAN can share peripheral devices such as sophisticated printers and secondary storage systems, making it possible to justify devices that a single microcomputer user might not be able to afford. Another advantage of a LAN is that microcomputer users can share data that are kept up to date on one of the machines (the *file server*). For example, if the current database is contained on a single hard disk, to which all of the microcomputers in a LAN have access, the problem of each microcomputer maintaining its own copy (some of which are sure to be out of date) is resolved. Microcomputer users in a LAN can also communicate with one another by means of electronic mail/message systems, saving flurries of telephone calls and "while you were out" messages.

Creating a LAN has proved more complex for some microcomputer users than they initially expected. For instance, certain hardware can only be connected in a LAN if the computers and peripheral devices are

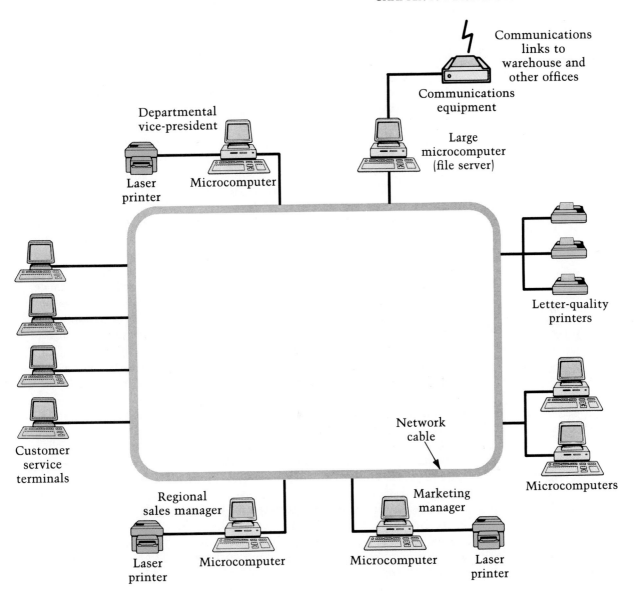

Figure 16-16
An example of a local area network (LAN). All the computing equipment in a branch office is linked together in a LAN, which in turn is linked to other offices through communications equipment.

made by the same manufacturer. In other cases, machines of different makes can be joined. In a rapidly evolving field, the promises of microcomputer manufacturers about how easy their machines are to interconnect have not always corresponded to reality. Nevertheless, this is a burgeoning area of activity that seems certain to have a major impact on the future of microcomputers, just as LANs used for larger machines are also increasing in popularity.

A **WIDE AREA NETWORK (WAN)** uses the technology of LANs, but over a larger geographic area. A number of universities and corporate offices use technologies such as broadband to link all the computers across an entire campus or throughout an office complex.

Today, *global networks* combine LANs and WANs with larger-scale networks, literally giving desktop users the world at their fingertips.

summary

▪ Early in the history of computers an organization had a computer and that was that. People came to it and used it. This is known as centralized processing. Decentralized processing, in which computing facilities are scattered throughout an organization, often without any plan, arose partly in response to difficulties in accessing the central computer. Distributed processing seeks to place computers of various sizes throughout an organization *with* a plan, and to link them together through data communications networks. In a distributed system computing can involve corporatewide, departmental, and end-user computing.

▪ Real-time, batch, and time-sharing processing can be supported in either centralized, decentralized, or distributed systems. Another trend has been the introduction of on-line transaction processing (OLTP) and fault tolerant computers.

▪ Processing can be performed by a computer system at a distance from the user. The distance may be great, but need not be. To allow for such processing, data communications transmit data over distances. A network is a combination of devices linked together for data communications; the devices can be both computers and peripherals.

▪ Micro-to-mainframe links are facilitated either when micros are switched to the terminal emulation mode or perform processing locally. Micro-to-micro links connect microcomputers to a file server (the microcomputer that manages shared data and programs).

▪ Data communications networks permit processing applications, most of them motivated by organizational, economic, and geographic considerations. In short, data communications helps firms—particularly those that cover or deal with a wide area—operate more efficiently and save money.

▪ Information systems that perform data communications must balance the same five elements involved in any information system: people, rules and procedures, data, software, and hardware.

▪ Within data communications networks the host processor performs the actual computing. Local user hardware hooks into the host processor through the use of communications devices.

▪ Despite the advantages of data communications, there are some drawbacks: high cost, more equipment with the possibility of failing, and the possibility of others tampering with your data.

▪ Network topologies (forms) include star, hierarchical, ring, bus, and mixed networks.

▪ The main types of data communications media are twisted-wire pairs, coaxial cable, fiber-optic cable, and microwave systems (using either land-based or geosynchronous orbiting satellites).

▪ Bandwidth (often called baud rate) refers to the capacity of a medium—how much data can be sent over it in a given amount of time. The three bandwidths commonly associated with data communications media are narrowband or sub-voice-grade, voice-grade, and wideband.

■   Simplex transmission permits data to be sent in only one direction; half-duplex—in both directions but not at the same time; and duplex or full-duplex—in both directions simultaneously.

■   Digital signals used by computers must be transformed to analog signals to be transmitted over ordinary phone lines. Modulation converts digital signals to analog signals; demodulation reverses the process. The devices that accomplish this process are called modems. Acoustic couplers are portable modems that can be used with most telephones.

■   In asynchronous transmission, one byte is sent at a time. In synchronous transmission bytes are sent in blocks synchronized by a clock mechanism.

■   Protocols are rules and procedures governing the use of data communications media. These include polling, contention, token passing, CSMA/CD (carrier sense multiple access/collision detection), and packet switching.

■   The multidrop line was an early hardware technique for allowing more than one user to use the network at the same time. Communications processors followed; these are more sophisticated, and include multiplexers, concentrators, front-end processors, and message-switchers.

■   Data communications media can be purchased outright or leased from a common carrier. Some firms offer value-added networks (VANs), which provide extra services in addition to the media. An organization gains telephone and data communications through its private branch exchange or PBX. Integrated services digital networks (ISDNs) are standards to fully link telecommunication devices. For data communications within a very limited area—such as the same office—local area networks (LANs) can fill the bill. Two types of coaxial cable-based LANs are baseband and broadband networks. Wide area networks (WANs) use LAN technology to link users over citywide or campuswide networks.

Global go home

The new data communications network that George Roberts and Sylvia Fischer persuaded Global Electrical Equipment to install had been in place now for a full month.

There were forty-three micros in the plant. Of these, twenty-six were in the local area network (LAN). The network form that George, Sylvia, and the other managers had arrived at was a combination of ring and star. All the micros were linked in a ring; in addition each was linked to the mainframe in a star.

Seventeen microcomputers weren't part of the LAN because of equipment incompatibility in some cases, and because of people who simply did not want to share data in other cases. As an engineer, George had enjoyed finding out about cables, transmission methods, and the like. Fiber-optic cabling now ran under the floor, joining the twenty-six microcomputers and the mainframe. Full-duplex transmission was used. The cables handled digital signals, so modems were not needed.

The mainframe turned out to already have several front-end processors in use. Global's computer center staff reprogrammed one of the front-end processors so that the new microcomputer network could use it to gain access to the mainframe.

Global owned the LAN—no leased media or telephone lines were involved. George and his quality-control inspectors out on the line communicated constantly using their micros. For example, the inspectors recorded the serial number of every device inspected and their findings and relayed this data to George's machine, where a program processed the data, did some totaling, stored the data on George's hard disk, and produced a report.

George also *enjoyed* data communications. He looked at his watch. It was 3:30 P.M., and a Friday. The data sent in by his employees today showed that everyone had done a full day's quota of inspections already: the whole week had been well above quota. George swiveled in his chair, turned on the micro, and typed in the codes that signaled to the data communications system that whatever he typed next would be displayed on the microcomputers out on the line.

"GO HOME, GANG, IT'S BEEN A GREAT WEEK," George typed.

The first response came. "YOU SERIOUS, BOSS?" flashed on the screen of George's microcomputer.

"WOULD I LIE TO YOU?" he typed back.

Deciding he did not want to wait around for the answers to that question, he turned off his computer, locked his desk, put on his jacket, and left for the weekend.

key terms

Asynchronous transmission (555)
Bandwidth (551)
Baseband network (562)
Baud rate (551)
Broadband network (562)
Bus network (545)
CSMA/CD (Carrier sense multiple access/collision detection) (557)
Centralized processing (536)
Coaxial cable (548)
Common carrier (561)
Communications devices (541)
Communications processor (558)
Concentrator (559)
Contention (557)
Corporatewide computing (538)
Data communications (539)
Data communications medium (548)
Decentralized processing (536)
Demodulation (554)
Departmental computing (538)
Distributed processing (536)
End-user computing (538)
Fault tolerant computer (536)
Fiber-optic cable (548)
File server (543)
Front-end processor (560)
Full-duplex, or duplex, transmission (554)
Half-duplex transmission (553)
Hierarchical network (545)
Host processor (541)
Integrated services digital network (ISDN) (561)

Local area network (LAN) (562)
Local user hardware (541)
Message-switcher (560)
Micro-to-mainframe link (542)
Micro-to-micro link (543)
Microwave system (549)
Mixed network (547)
Modem (554)
Modulation (554)
Multidrop line (558)
Multiplexer (559)
Narrowband, or sub-voice-grade, medium (551)
Network (539)
Network topology (543)
On-line transaction processing (OLTP) (536)
Packet switching (557)
Polling (557)
Private branch exchange (PBX) (561)
Protocol (557)
Ring network (545)
Simplex transmission (553)
Star network (543)
Synchronous transmission (556)
Terminal emulation mode (543)
Token passing (557)
Twisted-wire pairs (548)
Value-added network (VAN) (562)
Voice-grade medium (552)
Wide area network (WAN) (563)
Wideband medium (552)

review questions

objective questions

True/false. *Put the letter T or F on the line next to the question.*

1 _____ 1. Twisted-wire pairs are affected by "cross-talk."

2 _____ 2. A star network is usually associated with centralized data communications systems.

3 _____ 3. Time-sharing networks allow users to gain access to more computing power than they could otherwise afford.

4 _____ 4. On-line transaction processing is possible only with centralized computer systems.

5 _____ 5. A data communications link which requires you to use a modem to link your terminal into the system does not require a modem for the host processor.

6 _____ 6. A multiplexer is used to link high-speed disk drives to the host computer.

7 _____ 7. End-user computing is a major advantage of centralized processing.

8 _____ 8. A VAN provides communications processing to network users.

9 _____ 9. Mixed networks are the most common type of network.

10 _____ 10. One of the major disadvantages of data communications networks are their vulnerability to unauthorized use.

Multiple choice. *Put the letter of the correct answer on the line next to the question.*

1 _____ 1. A company where computing power and data are shared among the various user departments would most likely have which data communications network.

(a) Decentralized.
(b) Distributed.
(c) Centralized.
(d) None of the above.

2 _____ 2. Some contention protocols use _____ to manage which sending unit should have access to the network.

(a) Polling.
(b) Token passing.
(c) Packet switching.
(d) Multiplexing.

3 _____ 3. A _____ transmission line permits simultaneous bi-directional sending of data or messages.

(a) Duplex.
(b) Half-duplex.
(c) Simplex.
(d) Half-simplex.

4 _____ 4. The most powerful type of communications processor is the

(a) Message switcher.
(b) Multiplexer.
(c) Concentrator.
(d) Front-end processor.

5 _____ 5. The transmission of randomly spaced bytes is a feature of

(a) Synchronous transmission.
(b) Packet switching.
(c) Analog signals.
(d) Asynchronous transmission.

Fill in the blank. *Write the correct word or words in the blank to complete the sentence.*

1. A _____ is used to convert data from a digital to an analog form and back again.

2. An organization where managers in the headquarters office desire a great deal of control over outlying operating divisions would impose a _____ data communications network.

3. A _____ network can serve to link several equal host processors.

4. A _____, made up of tiny glass fibers, can be used for _____ band transmissions.

5. A _____ provides data communications facilities to any paying customer.

6. A _____ usually links several users in the same office.

7. The acronym VAN stands for _____.

8. To use _____ transmission requires that the sending and receiving units be coordinated.

9. Simultaneous two-way transmissions are permitted with _____ links.

10. The breaking and later recombining of messages into easily transmitted units is called _____.

short answer questions

When answering these questions, think of concrete examples to illustrate your points.

1. What are the differences between centralized and decentralized processing?

2. What are the advantages and disadvantages of wire pair and microwave transmission lines?

3. What is meant by the term *bandwidth*? Describe the three major types.

4. What are the types of communications processors? How do they differ in functions performed?

5. What is the difference between asynchronous and synchronous transmission?

6. How do centralized and distributed networks differ?

7. Describe the different network topologies.

8. What is a common carrier?

9. Describe the function of a value-added network.

10. What is a LAN?

11. What are two disadvantages of data communications networks?

essay questions

1. How does organizational structure affect a data communications network used in an information system?

2. What kinds of modems and communications processors would Global Electric Equipment and Oakriver University make use of?

3. What are the advantages and disadvantages of data communications?

Answers to the objective questions

True/false: **1.** T; **2.** T; **3.** T; **4.** F; **5.** F; **6.** F; **7.** F; **8.** T; **9.** T; **10.** T
Multiple choice: **1.** b; **2.** b; **3.** a; **4.** d; **5.** d
Fill in the blank: **1.** modem; **2.** centralized; **3.** ring; **4.** fiber-optic cable, wide; **5.** common carrier; **6.** local area network (LAN); **7.** value-added network (VAN); **8.** synchronous; **9.** full-duplex or duplex; **10.** packet switching

System control: data integrity, security, and privacy

After studying this chapter you should understand the following:

- *Why system controls are needed for today's information systems.*
- *How control techniques can be applied to the five elements of an information system.*
- *How accounting and auditing methods are used as information system controls.*
- *Some of the issues and legislation concerning the right to privacy.*

chapter 17

Suspicion

"It's a funny thing," Ed Wieland said to Vincent Kent. "I was performing a little audit on the system yesterday. You know, just to see what resources were being used. And one person was making heavy use of your inventory database the whole time."

"Why do you find it strange?" asked Vincent, the database administrator at Paul's House of Electronic Wonders.

"I thought nothing of it at the time," Ed said. "But by coincidence, I had to talk to the purchasing manager right after I'd performed my little audit. So I walked all the way through the purchasing department to get to his office. Well, the whole department was in a meeting. The manager, too. All the terminals were off. So who was using that database?"

Vincent stared at the opposite wall of his office. "A few people in other departments are allowed to look at it," he said, "though they rarely do."

"That's what I thought," Ed said. "Were you folks doing maintenance or something on the database?"

"Yesterday? No, we had other fires to put out."

"Interesting," Ed said.

As a systems analyst, Ed's mind was trained to mistrust superficial appearances and to look behind them. He returned to the computer room, sat down at a monitor, and invoked a real-time program to determine which computer resources were presently being used. Over a dozen users were on-line. Ed made a few queries to the program, and found that two users were retrieving data from the inventory database.

Ed got up and walked briskly to the purchasing department. Once there, he slowed down and tried to note what everyone was doing as he headed toward the purchasing manager's office. Only one terminal was on, and a purchasing agent was working at it. OK, Ed thought, it could be the manager.

Ed knocked on the manager's door. When he got no response, he opened it. The manager wasn't there. Back in his own office, Ed came to a decision. His gnawing suspicion that someone was eavesdropping into the computer system at Paul's wouldn't go away.

Ed picked up the phone and dialed Philip Paul. Ed briefly explained his suspicions.

"Who might conceivably be interested in what's stored in our inventory database?" Ed Wieland asked.

"Competitors," Philip said promptly. "We're in the middle of a price war right now. I can name at least four companies that would love to see us go under."

"Interesting," Ed said. "Mr. Paul, I would like your permission to evaluate the controls used on that database. I would like to do so on a kind of emergency basis, and maybe add some equipment that we don't have, so that if somebody's eavesdropping we can catch him at it."

"You're on," Philip Paul said.

The need for system control

INFORMATION SYSTEM CONTROLS strive to monitor and ensure the proper operation of all five information system elements: people, rules and procedures, data, software, and hardware. Controls help to ensure the integrity of the data, the security of the information system, and the privacy of users and clients of the information system.

DATA INTEGRITY (as we have seen in Chapter 11) refers to the accuracy of the data and its consistency throughout a database. For an information system to output accurate reports, the input to the system and the steps in processing the input must be monitored. Sometimes the consequences of inaccurate output can be disastrous. If, for example, a computerized government forecast predicted substantial commodity shortages and other serious economic problems in the near future, various U.S. government agencies, private industry, and the governments of other countries could react in panic. Yet, the forecast might have resulted from a miskeyed decimal point.

Security is also an important consideration where computers are involved. SECURITY refers to the methods used to protect the five elements of the information system. Let's say that an industrial spy is able to learn how a competitor's database is structured. Most database management systems do not keep a log of requests for data that do not change the data. So the spy who knew his or her way around the database could make inquiries that would yield valuable trade secrets, even whole files full of them.

PRIVACY refers to the protection of individuals and organizations from unauthorized access to or abuse of data concerning them. Privacy is not always easy to come by in a computerized society. Incidents such as this one have really taken place: A man applies for a life insurance policy, and is turned down when an investigator discovers in a database that the man was once arrested for auto theft. The database does not indicate the outcome of the case, but the investigator rejects the life insurance application anyway. The truth of the case is that the man was accidentally arrested for stealing his own car. His car was in fact stolen, but by someone else, and the police entered data on the theft into a database. Later the car was recovered in another police jurisdiction, but its recovery was not recorded in the first jurisdiction's database. So when the owner was driving his recovered car back in his home jurisdiction, he was erroneously arrested for the theft. The arrest report was sent to several other databases run by the state and federal agencies, one of which the insurance investigator consulted. The fact that it was all a mistake, however, was not recorded.

Even the people entrusted with operating an information system can sometimes give in to temptation. A COMPUTER CRIME occurs when a person uses a computer for illegal purposes (Figure 17-1). In one instance a programmer at a bank embezzled money from peoples' accounts by diverting fractions of cents from their accounts into his own.

Figure 17-1
Watch out for computer crime!

Attitudes toward white-collar crimes of any sort—computer crimes included—used to be rather permissive. Whereas a street criminal would be jailed, the white-collar criminal was often merely reprimanded or allowed to make restitution. Thus the potential gains were, from the criminal's point of view, worth risking the punishment. Many companies were reluctant to prosecute because publicity surrounding the case would be bad for the company image. Photographs of programmer-embezzlers on the evening news would not fit with a bank's image as protector of its customers' hard-earned money.

Today attitudes have changed. Companies are more likely to push for prosecution of such white-collar crimes as embezzlement, tampering with confidential data, and fraud. Additionally, institutions are moving to minimize the risks of losing money from computer-based theft, through some of the security measures we will examine in this chapter.

Despite the tougher attitude by information system owners and the judicial system, convictions for computer-based crimes are hard to come by for three reasons:

1. Computer crimes are difficult to detect.
2. If a crime has been detected, pinning it on a particular culprit is even harder.
3. If a person is brought to trial, proving the case—given its technical complexity—to the satisfaction of the jury is the most difficult.

To counter computer crimes, federal law enforcement officials can turn to the **COMPUTER FRAUD AND ABUSE ACT** (1986). This law makes it a federal crime to illegally access, use, and/or destroy the data contained in computer systems owned by the federal government, used in interstate or foreign commerce, or containing medical records. Stiff penalties, including fines and prison sentences, can be imposed on people convicted under this act.

This legislation came about, in part, because of abuses by a tiny minority within that dedicated community known as hackers. **HACKERS** are individuals who enjoy the challenge of testing the operating limits of their computer system. Most hackers limit their activities to their own equipment and software. Occasionally though, some will attempt to access other individuals' or organizations' information systems—that's when the trouble starts. What may be perceived as a challenge by a few may be viewed as an illegal act by many others.

In addition to deliberate abuse of a system, accidental abuse can occur. Personnel can accidentally erase or alter company records, forget to prepare backup copies that are needed when a system crashes, or commit blunders in operating the hardware.

Controlling an information system

In Chapter 3 we saw that managers organize people and other resources to achieve some organizational goal. One goal should be to run an information system that is accurate, secure from internal and external threats, and does not violate privacy. This section will describe the repertoire of control possibilities available to managers. They should not be added as an afterthought; they should be built into the system as part of the system development process (see Chapter 13).

Which controls are actually used will depend upon the managers and the situation. The same principle applies to running an information system as to running other parts of an organization: the involvement of top-level managers makes the creation and implementation of procedures—in this case control systems—easier.

Controls for people

Controls for people begin with proper training of the user and information system staff in how to interact with the particular part of the information system that affects them. Two important controls for people are separation of tasks and standardization of work.

Separation of tasks

SEPARATION OF TASKS is the division of tasks and responsibilities among a number of different people. There are good reasons for doing so. Everyone has heard a story that runs something like this: A trustworthy bookkeeper always helps the boss by doing the accounting and writing the checks. So trustworthy is this individual that he or she is always first in the office, last to leave, and never takes a day off unless the entire office shuts down. One day, however, the boss comes to work and finds the bookkeeper has vanished without a trace, along with funds embezzled gradually over the years.

What went wrong? There was no separation of tasks. Whenever financial or other sensitive matters are processed by an information system, extra care must be taken. No one person should be responsible for handling the data input, the processing, and the output distribution. For instance, the person who writes a payroll program should not also be the operator responsible for feeding blank checks to the printer, or the person who distributes the printed checks. The temptation may be too great to resist. In fact, some companies contract with an outside service to do payroll checks for the information-processing staff, while letting the information-processing staff produce the checks for the rest of the company's employees.

Workers in financial areas should be required to take regularly scheduled vacations and other days off. In addition, people should be rotated from task to task, rather than indefinitely assigned to perform the same job. This will minimize the chance of illegal cooperation among several people. Sensitive information is distributed on a *need-to-know* basis.

Hiring presumably honest people in the first place can preclude many of these problems. After all *bribery* is still a frequently used method to gain unauthorized access. Controls here include careful screening of a potential employee's resume and checking out references.

Rewarding employees with adequate salaries, formal recognition, and plain old praise can forestall many problems. Employee grievances should be given serious attention. A worker who feels part of a caring organization will be far less likely to abuse the information system or any other part of the organization.

The penalties for abusing an information system should be made known to users and information system staff. These could range from dismissal from a job to civil or criminal legal action. In addition to their existence on the books, the penalties must also be enforced: Managers must stand behind them.

For example, computer users at San Jose State University in California must sign a form that contains this statement:

> I certify that the requested account(s) will be used only for related course work, that the proposed use of the SJSU computing services is justified by the program of the California State University and College system. I further understand that the unauthorized use of SJSU computing facilities is a violation of Penal Code 502 and therefore punishable by a fine not exceeding $5,000.00 and/or imprisonment not exceeding three years, and that the account will be canceled.

Standardization of work

STANDARDIZATION OF WORK means assuring that people have clearly defined tasks. Different employees performing the same type of task should perform it in approximately the same manner. For instance, in data-entry operations, clerks should follow written conventions as to what data are input, when, and in what format. In program design, programmers follow the conventions of structured programming, breaking programs into modules and organizing the modules in a top-down structure. Structured programming methods serve as the work standard for programmers. Likewise, rules for structured system development serve as the work standard for those involved in that process.

Controls for rules and procedures

The rules and procedures of an organization, and the way in which they are developed, should always reflect a concern for control techniques. Two areas of particular concern are written procedures or standards and exception procedures.

Written procedures or standards

Closely tied to the standardization of work are WRITTEN PROCEDURES or STANDARDS, which explicitly state the proper steps needed to complete a task. Most people need clear direction in their work. Written standards—that are also enforced—help people understand what their tasks are. These rules and procedures are recorded in a standards manual. Standards should be well thought out and written in a manner that users can understand. This is not an easy job and larger organizations use writers who specialize in describing standards. Both normal and exceptional operating conditions should be included in the standards. Any changes in procedures are worked out in meetings between users and information system representatives. It is important for users to feel that their opinions are solicited, rather than merely tolerated. The changes to be made should be implemented gradually to give users enough time to adjust to the new procedures. Of course, occasionally a procedural change has to be made quickly, say to plug a security breach. There may be no time to meet with users in such a case—especially if one of the users is suspected of being the security problem.

An example of a written standard is the checkout procedure a tape librarian follows. When you ask to remove a magnetic tape from the library, the librarian would consult the standards manual to determine if that particular tape can be checked out, whether or not you qualify to do so, and whether you can only read the data on the tape or are also allowed to change the data.

Other standards include the proper disposal of manuals, documents, and other materials. Passwords should not be written down on the ubiquitous Post-it™ and then stuck to the terminal screen.

Exception procedures

EXCEPTION PROCEDURES—which are also written down—specify what an organization should do when standard operating procedures cannot be followed or do not apply. Exception procedures ensure flexibility. A rigid system that cannot handle unusual situations will not satisfy users or clients.

One useful exception procedure is the one that an organization follows when its computer is not working. Another concerns how to stop the repeated creation of an inaccurate bill for a customer. If the amount of a purchase was entered into the system incorrectly, a customer could be incorrectly billed over and over before the problem is resolved, unless an exception procedure exists for correcting the error. When feasible, exception procedures should be incorporated into the standards manual. Some organizations require that a log be kept when exception procedures are used, to give the organization a written record of what was done.

Controls for data

Data controls affect who is able to view and alter data, and also evaluate the integrity of the data as it moves through the system. The purpose of data controls is to ensure that data are neither misused nor subjected to unauthorized alteration or destruction. Even the transfer of data across national boundaries is a data control issue.

Data quality assurance

DATA QUALITY ASSURANCE is the evaluation of data integrity—from initial collection through input, processing, storage, and output. Maintaining a high standard of data integrity is one of the most challenging—and most important—tasks of information system control.

Just as people have a tendency to believe what they read in books merely because it appears in print, so do people have a tendency to believe computer output because it was produced by such wonderfully complex and futuristic machines. By now, however, you are aware that what computers produce is only as good as what a program that somebody wrote could do with the data that were given to the computer. A classic phrase in information processing is "Garbage in, garbage out" (GIGO). Data quality assurance tries to ensure that garbage doesn't come out, by checking that the data are accurate at their source and are kept accurate through the different stages of their use.

Various methods exist for checking the integrity of data. VERIFICATION involves checking data by keying them in a second time and, where discrepancies are found, correcting them. The chances are extremely small that a data-entry operator will make the same entry error twice. VALIDATION uses the computer itself, or an intelligent terminal, to see whether or not the data entered lie within reasonable limits or have certain sought-after characteristics. For example, a program could safely reject a social security number that contains a letter, a supplier code that is a negative number, an order placed in the last century, or a date like February 30th.

CONTROL TOTALS are another technique of finding errors. Typically, a clerk manually compiles a total of monetary amounts (checks, bills) in a batch of source documents to be entered. An intelligent terminal or computer compiles its own total during entry, and when all data are in, the two figures should match.

For example, Paul's House of Electronic Wonders carefully controls the printing of payroll checks. Each check run through the printer must be accounted for, including any checks damaged by the printer before or during printing. Various subtotals are accumulated during check printing, and compared against the figures expected by the accounting office. With these controls in place, one type of ploy, known as "salami slicing," could not be used at Paul's. Programmers have sometimes shaved pennies off payroll deductions on employees' checks, accumulated the tiny amounts until they grew large enough, and printed them on blank damaged checks made out to nonexistent employees. At Paul's, both the subtotals and the check control procedure would catch this ruse.

CHECK DIGITS offer another type of control, applying a formula to check the digits of identifiers that follow a specific scheme, such as Universal Product Codes, International Standard Book Numbers, or customer numbers in a well-designed database. Credit cards have one of the digits serve as the check digit (the specific digit varies). Data that do not follow a predetermined pattern—such as names or sums of money—can be checked using other types of formulas.

Another data check was discussed in Chapter 5—the parity bit. *Parity bits* are especially useful in detecting data that are garbled during transmission between computers or between different components of the same computer. Like most of these checks, parity bits cannot tell how to correct the problem, but they can alert users that a problem exists.

Data security measures

DATA SECURITY refers to the protection and care of data. Accidental or deliberate misuse of data can have serious consequences. For instance, the rise of distributed data processing has given many people with a microcomputer and an electronic spreadsheet the opportunity to retrieve data from the company database. Sometimes the data are inadvertently changed through the use of incorrect or inappropriate formulas with the spreadsheet. At other times simply nudging an electronic mouse during spreadsheet operations can accidentally change data in the wrong cell. If the altered, incorrect data are stored in the database, they will erase the original, correct data. Certain companies have a policy of barring use of electronic mice during spreadsheet operations.

Two data security measures can protect a database: access restriction and backup procedures. These issues were also addressed in Chapter 11. Access restriction can be achieved through carefully designed and administered password procedures. Employees can be assigned passwords that restrict them to viewing only the portion of a database that concerns them, on a need-to-know basis, and that may or may not allow them to alter data there. Figure 17-2 shows an example. Passwords can also be used with file systems.

Passwords must be changed frequently to prevent former users of the system, such as disgruntled ex-employees, from reentering the database or file. Also, there are some computer enthusiasts who delight in cracking passwords purely for the challenge. Allowing any given password to mature to a ripe vintage increases the odds that someone is going to crack the code.

Backup procedures provide a copy of the data as they should be—or the means of reconstructing such a copy—in case the original is damaged or destroyed. Some database management systems will keep a journal of changes to the database. In addition, the database in its entirety is copied at predetermined intervals. With a copy of the database in some previous version, together with a record of all the changes to the database from that version to the present time, an organization can reconstruct its database.

When data are transmitted, the possibility of eavesdropping arises. EAVESDROPPING involves tapping into an electronic signal. The "line" may be tapped at any point in the telecommunications link. Microwave signals can be intercepted and read, as can data traveling via cable. Eavesdroppers can even intercept your log-off signals that indicate to the host computer that you are finished using your terminal or computer, and then send back to you the normal response to a log-off— while keeping the line to the host computer wide open and continuing to communicate with it for the eavesdroppers' own purposes.

One way to foil eavesdroppers is through encryption. ENCRYPTION is the coding or scrambling of data, messages, or programs. Only the sender and receiver know the particular coding technique used, thus lock-

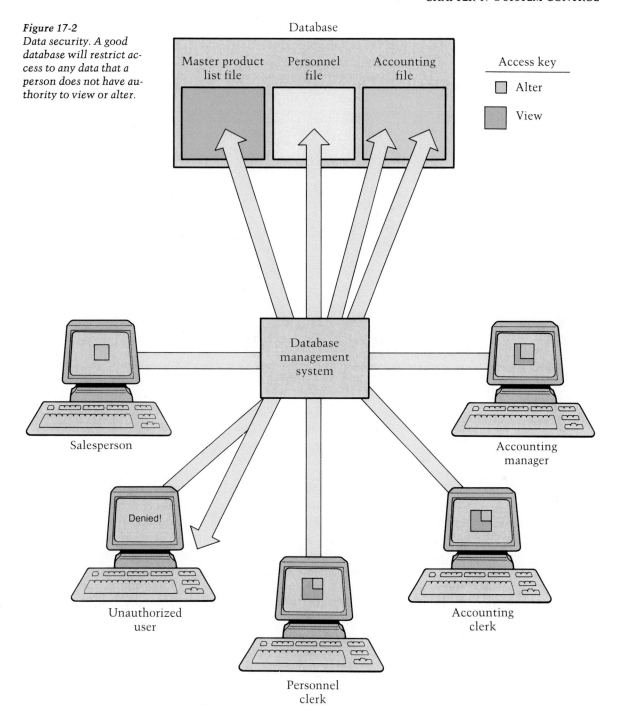

Figure 17-3
An encrypted message.
The encryption code
used here is a fairly sim-
ple one that involves
substituting one charac-
ter for another. Much
more complex, and more
difficult to crack, codes
exist.

Encrypted message: _RQ_E#G1_Y5G9$GE–9!GI4RC#M
Encryption code:

Original character	Coded character	Original character	Coded character
(blank)	G	Q	Z
A	_	R	!
B	1	S	#
C	Y	T	>
D	2	U	9
E	C	V	)
F	I	W	Q
G	U	X	(
H	*	Y	E
I	4	Z	%
J	A	!	M
K	5	#	(blank)
L	R	(	J
M	K	)	X
N	N	,	<
O	–	.	'
P	$		

Decoded message: ALWAYS BACK UP YOUR FILES!

ing out any attempts by a third party to decipher a well-designed code. Figure 17-3 shows how a message might be coded for transmission and decoded upon receipt.

Transnational data flows

TRANSNATIONAL DATA FLOWS refer to the transfer of useful data across national boundaries. Business organizations no longer exist exclusively within national borders. Home offices may be in one country, and marketing and manufacturing scattered in many others. Most countries limit the items that can be exported. What about data? If information has value, what controls should limit the transfer of information? Should "confidential" marketing data gathered in one country be transmitted back to a corporate headquarters? Some countries, such as Sweden, say "No." What about the transfer of technological or industrial process codes acquired when two companies merge? This issue promises to raise interesting questions regarding national economic self-interest and defense security issues. The challenge to managers of multinational firms will be great.

Controls for software

Software controls refer to methods that regulate the development, accessing, and maintenance of programs. We will explore three major threats to software control—breaches of security, piracy, and computer viruses.

Software security measures

Just as data can be altered, so too can programs. **SOFTWARE SECURITY** measures attempt to protect the programs from misuse or tampering.

Misuse can occur when a minor maintenance change is sloppily done, thus throwing off the program. Tampering results from people deliberately changing a program to their advantage, such as making the program allow them to get at data that they are not authorized to view.

Concern for security should begin when software development begins. Careful application of structured design and programming techniques can help avoid careless programming. Access to software under development, in use, or being maintained should be governed by log-on procedures, particularly a well-devised scheme of secret passwords that are periodically changed. When passwords are changed, if certain programmers no longer have a right to one, they don't get a new one.

Copies of software should be kept in both the source program form (before the program is translated) and the object program form (after the program has been translated into machine language).

Once a program is in use—especially if, like a payroll program, it will be heavily used for a long time with occasional maintenance changes—it should be periodically audited to guarantee that it is doing what it is supposed to. The backup programs and the versions used for daily processing should be compared with one another on a line-by-line basis and evaluated by special test data. If discrepancies appear, they should be carefully evaluated.

Another means of protecting programs is preventing people from getting at them in the first place. The media that contain programs should be kept in a safe place, such as a fireproof vault. Backup copies should be stored off-site. Various storage companies will keep both data and program copies in underground sites, such as renovated mine shafts. In addition, encryption (described earlier) can be used to render software unintelligible to those who don't know the code. Using these techniques, the integrity of programs can be assessed and reassessed throughout their lives.

Threats to program integrity include:

■ *Logic bombs*—programs that are activated randomly or when a specific logical action occurs. In one case, a disgruntled programmer placed a logic bomb inside his company's personnel management program that would destroy the file if his record were deleted. In another case, a programmer used a logic bomb to activate a computer virus (see the box on Computer Viruses).

■ *Superzapping*—normally used to restart a system after it "crashes," this program can also be used to access any part of the system. In the wrong hands, this tool can be used to gain access to any software in the system.

■ *Backdoors*—programs that allow authorized programmers access to restricted parts of a program by bypassing most security measures. Since most backdoors have lower security, an unauthorized user can easily gain access to rewrite or destroy the program.

Piracy

As we saw in Chapter 8, a large industry exists dedicated to creating prepackaged software for all sizes of computers. Substantial investments are made by the producers of prepackaged software, who seek to recover

Virus found in commercial software

A computer virus has infected a commercially available personal computer product for what is believed to be the first time, calling into question the safety and reliability of software sold in retail stores.

The startling development, discovered in software available from a major software company, has led one software company to change the way it manufactures software and is likely to force other companies to do the same.

Computer viruses are small, mischievous programs that are created by computer hackers as practical jokes or as acts of vandalism. They can be spread inadvertently, infecting other software.

Although the virus discovered last week in FreeHand, a Macintosh design program from Aldus Corp. of Seattle, was a harmless "message of peace," a more destructive virus could have wiped out expensive computer data or years of work.

And it's possible that software produced by companies such as Lotus Development Corp., Apple Computer Inc. of Cupertino, and Ashton-Tate may be infected by the virus.

The viruses are secretly inserted into computer programs, attach themselves to disks they come into contact with, and then pop up unexpectedly with a message or to erase computer information.

Until this incident, personal computer viruses were thought to be hidden only on noncommercial software—programs available for free or minimal cost, often distributed on computerized bulletin boards—or on software disks shared by computer users to swap programs.

Computer experts had said viruses could be avoided if users didn't use freely distributed software and instead used only off-the-shelf programs.

But the infection of the Aldus software shows that isn't the case.

The "message of peace" virus, which originated at a Canadian publication called *MacMag*, was a short message designed to pop up on Apple Macintosh computers. It was distributed by many bulletin boards in a program that purported to be a new listing of products made by Apple.

The virus was inadvertently passed to Aldus by Marc Canter, president of MacroMind Inc. of Chicago, which makes training disks for Aldus.

When Canter was traveling in Canada, he was given an infected disk that contained a

their costs and turn a profit through sales. Frustrating this goal is SOFTWARE PIRACY, or the unauthorized duplication of software that can be obtained legally only through purchase. Buyers of prepackaged software often sign contracts stipulating that they will not copy the software (except for a backup), pass it on to someone else, or sell it. Nevertheless a lot of prepackaged software exists that—if it was purchased at all—was not purchased from the manufacturer.

For example, considerable trading of software takes place among home computer users. To make it harder to copy a floppy disk and give it to a friend, software manufacturers try many techniques. One method is to scramble the tracks used for the program. A person trying to use standard disk copy methods to copy a floppy disk with scrambled tracks would be unable to do so. Some microcomputer users, however, have systems capable of exactly duplicating the bit patterns on a disk, one bit at a time, without trying to unscramble the track patterns. This overcomes the intended control technique.

A more advanced antipiracy technique is to scatter special bits on

program called Mr. Potato Head, which lets a Macintosh user play with a computerized version of the toy character. Canter ran the Mr. Potato Head program only once, he said.

Unbeknownst to him, his computer was infected with the virus. When Canter used the same computer to work on training software for Aldus, the disk destined for Aldus also became infected.

Without either Canter or Aldus realizing what they had done, the computer virus was copied onto disks that were sold to consumers. When the consumers used the disks, their computers became infected.

The virus is thought to be harmless now, since it was designed to pop up on Macintosh screens on March 2, the anniversary of the introduction of the Apple Macintosh SE and Macintosh II. "The time bomb already went off," said Donn Parker, a computer security specialist at SRI in Menlo Park.

Although *MacMag* and computer experts said that the peace virus was harmless, Canter said it forced his Macintosh II computer to shut down and caused him to lose some computer information. "My system crashed," Canter said. "I was really angry."

Canter fears that more of his customers may have been infected with the virus. MacroMind's clients include Microsoft Corp., Lotus Development Corp., Apple Computer Inc., and Ashton-Tate.

Microsoft Corp. has determined that none of its software has been infected with the virus, a company spokeswoman said. Apple and Lotus could not be reached for comment. Ashton-Tate declined to comment on whether its software was infected.

Aldus would not disclose how many copies of FreeHand are infected but admits a disk duplicating machine copied the infected disk for three days. Half the infected disks have been distributed to retail outlets; the remainder are in Aldus' warehouse.

Aldus will replace the infected disks with new, uninfected disks to any FreeHand buyer who requests it, according to Aldus spokeswoman Laury Bryant. The company will also replace the infected disks in its warehouse.

Source: Jim Bartimo, *San Jose Mercury News*, 14 March, 1988. Reprinted with permission from the San Jose Mercury News.

the floppy disk with a weak magnetic charge between 0 and 1. These deliberate imperfections are not a problem when the disk is used with the program; however, when the disk is copied, the computer will write the weak bits as either normal-strength 1s or normal-strength 0s. Thus when the operating system of the computer performing the illegal copying operation discovers that the copy and the original do not agree, it stops copying.

To reduce the pressure to "pirate" software many microcomputer-based software application companies offer SITE LICENSES that allow the organization to make or obtain sufficient legal single-user copies or networkable versions for a negotiated fee. A number of software vendors have stopped making copy-protected software because legal users, who wished to copy the software onto their hard drives to gain faster access, bridled at the need to insert the original disk into a floppy drive each time they used the package.

Another approach to countering the incentive for piracy is to drastically reduce the price of the software. We have seen another approach in

Chapter 8. Called *shareware*, users can freely obtain the software, then if they like it, pay the software developer for the "use" of the software.

Computer viruses

A recent threat to information systems is the introduction of computer viruses onto secondary storage media. A COMPUTER VIRUS is a tiny program that can attach to the operating system's codes that are normally passed onto secondary storage media when disks are formatted or copied. They are extremely difficult to detect, in part because perpetrators of such acts often code in a TIME BOMB or date-dependent code that will activate the virus well after it has been passed along to other unsuspecting victims. Antidotes for viruses exist in the form of computer software that can detect and "kill" or disable them.

Controls for hardware

Hardware controls ensure that authorized people have access to the equipment needed to perform their jobs, and that unauthorized people do not. All types of hardware need controls: input and output devices, computers, secondary storage devices, and communications hardware.

Physical security measures

PHYSICAL SECURITY refers to the protection of the hardware and storage media used in information systems from theft, vandalism, and misuse. With the rise of the microcomputer and distributed data processing, physical security has become more complex than it was even a few years ago, when the computer center was guarded like Fort Knox and the problem was thereby largely solved.

Microcomputers can be picked up and carried away. So can their peripheral devices, floppy disks, and other removable storage media (Figure 17-4). To prevent theft, equipment can be bolted into place and connected to a central alarm system. Identification tags affixed to the equipment can make it easier to recover if stolen. To help prevent vandalism and misuse, the area containing the equipment can be monitored by closed-circuit cameras during normal operating hours and by special motion detectors after these hours. Misuse can also be thwarted by using locks that require a key to gain access to the microcomputer's on-off switch. Many businesses have electronically controlled entrances for their employees.

Larger computer centers—the classic Fort Knox situation—generally have elaborate physical security procedures (see Figure 17-5). Access to the computer room is controlled either by a security guard or by a device that reads an employee badge and decides whether or not the person should be admitted. In either case, the person's name and entry date and time can be logged for future reference. After hours, motion detectors can be used to sense intruders. To protect against fire, special fire-suppressant (Halon) gas can be released into the computer room at a concentration lethal to the fire but safe for people. Another precaution is selecting a site that minimizes the risk of damage from earthquakes, floods, or other natural disasters.

To protect against electrical disturbances, the computer and its peripherals must be properly grounded and equipped with devices that protect the hardware from the sudden surges in power that electrical

Figure 17-4
Small computer parts can be easily lost or stolen.

Figure 17-5
Physical security measures at a large computer center.

utilities do on occasion deliver. Backup batteries can provide sufficient power to continue running the system at a reduced level of services, or to gain valuable time to store data before shutting down. These protection devices and batteries provide for an uninterruptible power supply (UPS) system.

Fireproof vaults are used to store removable disk packs and magnetic tapes within the computer center. Disks and tapes must then be logged in and out by the media librarian.

case in point
Computer crisis

Chicago—Welcome to the era of the electronic disaster.

The fire that gutted a small but critical telephone-switching station outside Chicago earlier last month virtually shut down United Stationers Inc., an office-products wholesaler with $730 million in annual sales. It knocked out all but a handful of lines linking the company's offices and customers to its central computer in Forest Park, Ill.

Without those links, customers couldn't place orders, salesmen couldn't check inventory and clerks couldn't find pencils and other supplies in the company's vast warehouses.

So it went with many companies. The damage to Illinois Bell's "hub" in Hinsdale also meant banks in Chicago's western suburbs couldn't process checks, order cash, or wire money through the Federal Reserve System. Air-traffic controllers outside Chicago and those at O'Hare International Airport couldn't transmit data to each other. Bekins Co.'s dispatchers were cut off from the company's moving vans nationwide and from its mainframe computer in Glendale.

Although serious disruptions are rare, they are becoming more common as computers spread. . . .

Most businesses are ill-prepared to cope with electronic disasters, computer and communications specialists say. That's partly because computers have crept gradually into companies, leaving many top executives unaware of their strategic importance.

Nevertheless, a growing number of companies—led by major financial institutions, which would be hardest hit by a disruption—are taking precautions. . . .

BankAmerica Corp. of San Francisco has designed its computer network so that if an earthquake destroyed its data-processing center in Los Angeles, it could shift most daily operations to a parallel center in San Francisco. It also could call on a new computer complex in Concord, which normally develops only programs.

Other companies are signing on with so-called disaster-recovery firms, buying what amounts to disaster insurance. For a monthly fee that ranges from $1500 to 25,000, companies get the right to pay an additional fee to use backup computer centers and networks if catastrophe strikes. . . .

The two largest disaster-recovery companies are Comdisco Disaster Recovery Services Inc., a unit of Comdisco Inc. of Rosemont,

No matter how thorough the security measures, accidents do still happen. In one case, an electrician installed a lightning rod at a building under construction and, seeking a ground, found a large metallic object that looked suitable. When the building was completed, the metallic object turned out to be the media vault. Some weeks after the new computer center was opened, a bolt of lightning struck the computer center during a thunderstorm. The lightning rod did its job and passed the massive electrical charge directly to its ground—thereby destroying all of the data contained on the disks and tapes.

Dual processing
There are many organizations that effectively come to a halt when their computers stop working. To prevent such a disaster, some companies use dual processing. DUAL PROCESSING uses redundant equipment to provide a means of preventing equipment failures from jeopardizing important projects. When one hardware component fails, the system simply switches to another. Redundancy in hardware is quite common in the aerospace industry. For example, a space shuttle has five on-board com-

Ill., and Sungard Recovery Services, a unit of Sungard Data Systems Inc. of Wayne, Pa. They have nearly 1500 clients between them, including Chase Manhattan Corp., First Chicago Corp., Pepsico Inc., and Harlequin Enterprises Inc., the publisher of romance novels.

Their services are expensive—but can pay off in an emergency, as United Stationers learned. . . .

On May 9, when company engineers realized there was a problem, they first tried to get around the Hinsdale switching plant by routing calls through their headquarters in nearby Des Plaines. The attempt failed, and at 7 A.M. United Stationers called Comdisco to declare an emergency.

Their call set in motion a carefully crafted disaster plan. Within hours, United Stationers dispatched a thirty-one-man team, with backup data tapes, to a Comdisco computer facility in Carlstadt, N.J. Meanwhile, it turned its employee cafeteria at headquarters in Des Plaines into a computerized "war room," pulling extra telephone and computer lines out of the ceiling.

By the next day, United Stationers had reconstituted its entire computer network around the borrowed mainframe in New Jersey, with sales personnel and other employees working on personal computers in the Des Plaines cafeteria.

When Heritage Bank in Woodridge, Ill., lost its links to the computer it uses in downtown Chicago, tellers were forced to check accounts, update balances and process loan payments by hand. The cumbersome process tripled transaction times, says President Thomas H. Hackett. It also increased the bank's exposure to fraud because tellers had time to check transactions only of more than $500.

But the bank's problems lasted only three days. Had they extended through its busiest period, on Friday and Saturday, "We probably would have had a mutiny on our hands," Hackett says. "We truly are a creature of the electronic age."

puters: four to perform the flight operations and one to monitor the other four. Any of the five computers is capable of doing the job unaided, but the redundant computers minimize the chances of the ship being left computerless. For business organizations the same technique can be, and frequently is, used. There also are firms that for a retainer will provide backup computing and peripherals (including telecommunications equipment) to keep an organization's vital functions continually working.

Distributed processing security

Today, one rarely has to walk into a computer room to gain access to the computers that are running there. Strong walls and armed security guards have no effect on abuse via telecommunication links. Access can easily be gained using a microcomputer and a modem connected to the central computer via a telecommunications link (Figure 17-6). An information system must try to balance the needs of legitimate off-site users against the security needs of the system. The system needs to discourage MASQUERADING, or unauthorized users passing themselves off as authorized users. The perpetrator manages to obtain a legitimate user's account number and password. Clever masqueraders can sometimes steal just the account number, and then arrive at the password by mental deduction based on what they know about the person whose account number they have stolen—trying out his or her birthdate, the names of family members, and so on, until the right password is hit upon. A variation of masquerading, called *piggy-backing*, involves waiting for a legitimate user to log in successfully and then sneaking onto the line and cutting off the legal user—without the computer detecting the switch.

A common control method is to permit only two or three attempts at a password before a user is locked out. The person must then reenter the account number. A log of the attempts may be kept by the system.

Another control technique is the automatic callback. With the **AUTOMATIC CALLBACK**, once a user logs on, the host computer attempts to call back the user at his or her regular terminal number, to make sure that this is in fact the terminal that just logged on. A masquerader at a different telephone number will not be connected, as the computer will not have a record of the unauthorized number.

The most common type of masquerading at universities is when illegal users sit down and use terminals that have been left logged on by careless students or faculty members. Automatic disconnect devices exist that will turn off such terminals after a given period of time if the user fails to log off.

Masquerading is done by a wide range of people—government spies after national secrets, corporate spies after corporate secrets, nosy people, or individuals interested in cracking a system just for for the sake of doing so without any particular malice in mind. Indeed, some masqueraders are not out to steal anything beyond the computer's time for carrying out certain processing operations.

Figure 17-6
Distributed processing is a great benefit for many organizations, but it also leaves them vulnerable to the theft of valuable data and information.

Accounting and auditing

Both accounting and auditing procedures are utilized by modern information systems for control purposes. We will examine some of the ways that they are used.

Accounting and the information system

Accounting procedures are applied as control measures to monitor use of information resources, to control who uses the system, and to bill users for their use of the system.

RESOURCE UTILIZATION PROCEDURES attempt to pinpoint and modify patterns of an information system's resources. The operating systems of larger computers maintain statistics on the extent of use of the computer and peripheral devices, and the frequency of data access. Based on such information the information system staff can rearrange peripheral devices to spread the load, phase out old equipment, order new equipment, identify an underutilized database, and so on. By changing the rate structure for computer use, managers can change the pattern of use. By substantially lowering the evening rates, they might encourage night time use of the computer center by departments unable to afford prime time. An organization's managers can fine-tune and direct the operation of the entire information system using similar techniques. For example, effective user education, coupled with a high-caliber database administration staff, could encourage users to scrap their proprietary files that cause an organization so much grief through inconsistent data and high storage costs, and use the company database instead.

The operating system's job control program determines who can use the system in the first place. It checks for valid passwords and account numbers, limits the types of operations that particular users can perform, and often keeps a log of exactly who is using the system and for what purpose. The job control program also keeps the books, recording each user's time spent on the computer and the specific resources used, so that the information system staff can bill the user on the basis of these records. The operating system does not set policy in such matters, but carries out decisions made by managers of the organization.

Auditing techniques

The principal means of monitoring the use and abuse of the information system is through the auditing process. An AUDIT is an examination of the information system to test the effectiveness of its various control procedures. Originally limited to business accounts, auditing has now expanded to include such nonaccounting concerns as performing detailed reviews of the software used in processing, checking how well the data security measures work, and monitoring user requests for sensitive data. The job of information system auditor exists in most larger organizations today, which usually maintain a department of such individuals.

Auditors inspect everything, from the source materials for data input, through the intermediate results, to the final output of a system. Usually auditors do not analyze all of the data that flow through a sys-

The computer detective and the auditor

There is a growing demand for personnel capable of protecting information systems from intrusion and other disasters. Whether serving in an "enforcement" role as a computer detective or in a "preventive" role as an auditor, an inquiring mind is definitely a must. The first excerpt looks at a true detective story; the second discusses how auditors can help prevent unnecessary exposure to risk without strangling the flow of information to authorized users.

A bold raid on computer security*
For months the computer intruder moved like an invisible man—until one day Clifford Stoll . . . a systems manager at California's Lawrence Berkeley Laboratory, knew something was amiss when one of the computers in his care revealed that an electronic trespasser was trying to use the lab's machines without providing a billing address. . . . Stoll launched a novel experiment. Instead of shutting out the interloper, he allowed him to roam at will through the system while carefully recording his every keystroke.

Thus began a game of cat and mouse that led Stoll and half a dozen investigative agencies far beyond the Berkeley campus. For ten months, they followed the hacker as he wended his way through the networks that link U.S. military and industrial computers all over the world. By the time the hacker was tracked to a ground-floor apartment in Han-

nover, West Germany, he had accomplished perhaps the most extensive breach of U.S. computer security to date. While no top secrets appear to have been uncovered, the incident shows how easy it can be to go fishing for sensitive information via phone lines and personal computers.

The case . . . , which identified the suspect as a 24-year-old computer-science student with the pseudonym Mathias Speer. . . . [T]he young hacker used the Lawrence Lab computer as a gateway to Internet, a U.S. government-owned network that connects some 20,000 computers handling scientific research and unclassified military work. While Speer used fairly standard techniques for cracking passwords, he showed uncommon persistence. He attacked some 450 different computers and gained access to more than 30.

The intruder's appetite for military data is what eventually did him in. To trick him into staying connected long enough to effect a telephone trace, Stoll dangled an irresistible lure: a file of bogus Star Wars information titled SDI Network Project. The sting worked. The hacker stayed on the line for more than an hour, greedily loading the phony data into his home computer. (The information was booby-trapped as well, containing an address in Berkeley for more information on the fictitious project.) West German authorities, working with the FBI, traced the call to the

tem, but take a sample and study it intensively. Auditors generally focus on the most valuable parts of an organization: its money, materials, and sensitive data.

A time-honored auditing technique applied to information systems is that of tracing an audit trail. An **AUDIT TRAIL** consists of the physical or visible documentation of the steps that money, documents, or data follow through the organization. The trail can trace who made what decisions from the initial stages to final action. Authorized signatures can also be checked. When a problem is spotted, it should be able to be traced back to its source and corrected there. The specifics of the audit trail technique have changed over the years—progressing from auditing *around* the computer, to auditing *through* the computer, and, most recently, to auditing *with* the computer.

Hannover apartment, questioned its occupant, and later confiscated his machine.

The intrusions came to an abrupt halt, but the mystery persists. . . . Three months after Speer took the Star Wars bait, the lab received a request for more information on the bogus project. Postmarked Pittsburgh, it was signed by a reputed arms dealer with ties to Saudi Arabia. How could he have got the address? The only way, lab officials insist, was to have been in cahoots—or at least in contact—with the Hannover hacker.

Confessions of an EDP auditor†

Wherever there is a computer running today in a large, efficient organization, an EDP auditor (EDPA) or information systems auditor is also there at work. Here is how one auditor describes his job:

I am an EDP auditor. People generally see the EDPA as a computer room busybody, a sort of electronic Mary Worth, who searches diligently for even the most minor infraction. They don't realize that EDPAs must have programming knowledge, an understanding of computer operations, the ability to report uncomfortable truths to upper management,

and the ability to provide computerized support and advice to financial auditors. The EDPA has to keep abreast of federal regulations and be aware of innovations in hardware and software technology within the industry. . . .

Since the EDP audit function is fairly new, it is rare to find detailed job descriptions for it. But in one form or another, all of the descriptions I have seen usually come down to two items—verifying controls and identifying exposures.

So what the EDPA does, essentially, is look for the possibility of loss and the degree of risk involved. If the risk is low and the chance of loss is low, odds are that management will elect to accept the risk. Most of the time, the EDPA will find low-loss and low-risk exposures, but will still report them to management. It is up to management to decide what action will be taken. . . .

The EDPA is not the answer to all of management's fears, nor is he an insurance policy against loss or fraud. . . . Management must realize that EDPAs cannot find and solve 100 percent of their company's problems, but they can help reduce the possibility of loss.

*Source: Philip Elmer-DeWitt, "A Bold Raid on Computer Security." Reported by Rhea Schoenthal/Bonn and Dennis Wyss/San Francisco, Time, 2 May 1988. Copyright 1988 Time Inc. All rights reserved. Reprinted by permission from TIME.
†Source: Dale F. Farmer, "Confessions of an EDP Auditor," Datamation, July 1983. Excerpted from DATAMATION, © (1983) Cahners Publishing Company.

Originally, auditors assumed that if what went into a computer system was correct, and what came out of it was correct, the processing must also have been correct. This became known as auditing *around* the computer because the processing stage was left unexamined. Unfortunately, final results can be correct—or look correct—even though errors have occurred along the way, or unscrupulous people have diverted leftover change to their own pockets.

Aware of this problem, auditors moved to auditing *through* the computer. This means that the input and processing steps are closely examined; if they are found to be correct, the output is also assumed to be correct. Test data are created and run through the system to verify the data's accuracy. Unfortunately, this approach too has its limits.

The limits are apparent with time-sharing and real-time systems.

Tracing an audit trail here is almost impossible without the active participation of the computer software itself—hence the concept of auditing *with* the computer. Distributed data processing further complicates the picture, with scattered users sharing a database, sending electronic messages hither and yon, and each processing the data in different ways. Fortunately, there is software that can perform audits for the complex circumstances under which today's computers operate. Auditing software packages can operate simultaneously with the programs, user queries, and real-time transactions that are being audited. Indeed, with the larger and more sophisticated computer systems, auditing is a continuous operation, performed concurrently with other operations.

Privacy and ethics

Protecting the right to privacy

In our discussion of control techniques so far in this chapter, we have focused primarily on matters of accuracy and security. Let's now shift our focus to the matter of privacy.

In the dictionary, "privacy" is defined as being apart from other people and protected from observation or unauthorized intrusion. With the widespread presence of modern information systems that maintain large databases and telecommunications links to other databases, "intrusion" can take on new dimensions. Specifically, because data are collected about us, maintained in databases, traded from one organization to another, and put to various uses, our privacy may be violated. In these circumstances, protecting our privacy means protecting ourselves from unauthorized access to, or abuse of, data concerning us. Two areas of concern are the gathering of inaccurate or false information, and the abuse of data (whether it is accurate or inaccurate) once they are gathered.

Some information systems have enormous capacities, and quite a few imposing files and databases are maintained by government agencies as well as by private organizations. Many people are not pleased with this situation. The federal government alone maintains billions of records about its citizens. Add to that the databases maintained by local governments and private organizations, and the total becomes even more impressive.

Assuring privacy is a major problem facing managers of information systems. Several factors must be taken into account. Managers need to decide what legitimate rights (if any) government agencies and private organizations have to data that the organization maintains. A company like Paul's House of Electronic Wonders, for instance, would not supply data to outsiders, except to institutions requesting legitimate credit checks and to the government at certain preestablished "exit points" for the data, such as employee withholding tax statements. If audited by the Internal Revenue Service, Paul's would have to supply the information requested. None of these uses necessarily violates the privacy of personnel, but inaccurate information could be proliferated.

Managers also need to address the rights of individuals and organizations to examine the data maintained about them, and to correct data that are legitimately maintained but inaccurate. For example, any employee at Paul's can examine his or her personnel file. If data about the person are found to be wrong—such as listing the wrong college degree, or attributing a prison record to the wrong person—they can be corrected in the personnel file and in the relevant database.

Many people have been concerned about actual and possible abuses of data, and proliferation of inaccurate data. The "Big Brother is watching" feeling does not sit well with residents of a democracy. Accordingly citizens have pressed for protective legislation. Laws governing the use of databases have been enacted by a number of countries, provinces, and states. National legislation in the United States, all stemming from the early 1970s, includes the Fair Credit Reporting Act, the Freedom of Information Act, the Education Privacy Act, and the Privacy Act.

The **FAIR CREDIT REPORTING ACT (1970)** gives individuals the right to examine credit records maintained by private organizations. If you apply for a charge card, for instance, and are denied it on the basis of your credit history, you have the right to inspect your records kept by the agency that denied the credit. The service costs a small fee. You also have the right to inspect your records if granted credit. If you claim the records are wrong, the credit agency is required by this law to investigate the truthfulness of your claim.

The **FREEDOM OF INFORMATION ACT (1970)** gives individuals, as well as organizations, the right to inspect data concerning them that are maintained by agencies of the federal government. In addition, the law opens up for your scrutiny some of the files concerning how these agencies are run. Information obtained under this act is in the news quite frequently, sometimes indicating that statements made by government officials are inconsistent with data with which they were familiar.

The **EDUCATION PRIVACY ACT (1974)** protects the privacy of students concerning grades and other types of evaluation data maintained by schools. Any public or private school that receives direct or indirect aid from the federal government must abide by this act, which stipulates that students or guardians can view their records and challenge inaccuracies, and that schools may not release the records to others without permission of the students or guardians.

Finally, the **PRIVACY ACT (1974)** offers protection to individuals and organizations from data-gathering abuses by the federal government. The law states that data gathered by a federal agency must have a specific and authorized purpose, and that people can see the data gathered about them, learn how they are used, and have the opportunity to correct any erroneous data. In effect, this law expands upon the Freedom of Information Act. In addition to its provisions concerning the government, the act set up the Privacy Protection Study Commission to review privacy questions involving private organizations. This commission has made several recommendations for national legislation regulating the use of data by private organizations.

Since their passage, these laws have been modified to take into account the ever-greater pervasiveness of data about individuals in private and government databases. The most recent modification, the ELECTRONIC COMMUNICATIONS PRIVACY ACT (1986), was enacted to broaden the scope and enforcement powers of the Privacy Act of 1974.

Many states and localities have also passed similar legislation. These days, even though "Big Brother" is in fact not only watching, but recording what he sees in databases, individuals do have some weapons to fight back with, and may even succeed in keeping a certain amount of data all to themselves.

Computer ethics

The term *ethics* means "standards of conduct and moral judgment," or "what you would do if no one is looking, and no one would find out." To establish standards of moral judgment codes of ethics can be developed. CODES OF ETHICS are sets of professional standards and guidelines developed by professional associations. Figure 17-7 displays the "Standards of Conduct" subscribed to by members of the Data Processing Management Association.

COMPUTER ETHICS are the standards used by people in the information-processing industry. Ethical conduct means more than simply avoiding illegal behavior; it also refers to conduct that falls between those choices that are clearly right or wrong. Contrary to the image of freewheeling hackers, recent studies show the vast majority of information-processing personnel apply as high or higher ethical standards to their work as does the general population.

summary

■ Information system controls serve to monitor and ensure the proper operation of all five information system elements. Controls help to assure the integrity of the data, the security of the information system, and the privacy of users and clients of the information system. Controls also help prevent computer crime. To counter computer-based abuses by criminals, federal law enforcement officials can turn to the Computer Fraud and Abuse Act (1986). Hackers are individuals who enjoy the challenge of testing the operating limits of their computer system.

■ Controls for people include separation of tasks and the standardization of work. Separation of tasks divides tasks and responsibilities among different employees, so that no one person controls financial or other important matters. Standardization of work helps assure a measure of consistency by clearly defining tasks.

■ Controls for rules and procedures include written procedures or standards and exception procedures. Written procedures or standards codify tasks so that employees can understand them. Exception procedures, which specify what an organization should do when standard operating procedures can't be followed, ensure flexibility.

■ Controlling data means assuring the quality of the data and assuring that the data are secure. Data quality assurance concerns evaluating data integrity from initial collection through input, processing, storage, and output. Various means of checking data integrity exist, including verification, validation, control totals, check digits, and parity bits. Data security measures protect data from accidental or deliberate misuse.

Figure 17-7
Code of Ethics for the
Data Processing Manage-
ment Association.

Standards of Conduct

These standards expand on the Code of Ethics by providing specific statements of behavior in support of each element of the Code. They are not objectives to be strived for, they are rules that no true professional will violate. It is first of all expected that an information processing professional will abide by the appropriate laws of their country and community. The following standards address tenets that apply to the profession.

In recognition of my obligation to management I shall:

- Keep my personal knowledge up-to-date and insure that proper expertise is available when needed.
- Share my knowledge with others and present factual and objective information to management to the best of my ability.
- Accept full responsibility for work that I perform.
- Not misuse the authority entrusted to me.
- Not misrepresent or withhold information concerning the capabilities of equipment, software or systems.
- Not take advantage of the lack of knowledge or inexperience on the part of others.

In recognition of my obligation to my fellow members and the profession I shall:

- Be honest in all my professional relationships.
- Take appropriate action in regard to any illegal or unethical practices that come to my attention. However, I will bring charges against any person only when I have reasonable basis for believing in the truth of the allegations and without regard to personal interest.
- Endeavor to share my special knowledge.
- Cooperate with others in achieving understanding and in identifying problems.
- Not use or take credit for the work of others without specific acknowledgment and authorization.
- Not take advantage of the lack of knowledge or inexperience on the part of others for personal gain.

In recognition of my obligation to society I shall:

- Protect the privacy and confidentiality of all information entrusted to me.
- Use my skill and knowledge to inform the public in all areas of my expertise.
- To the best of my ability, insure that the products of my work are used in a socially responsible way.
- Support, respect and abide by the appropriate local, state, provincial and federal laws.
- Never misrepresent or withhold information that is germane to a problem or situation of public concern nor will I allow any such known information to remain unchallenged.
- Not use knowledge of a confidential or personal nature in any unauthorized manner or to achieve personal gain.

In recognition of my obligation to my employer I shall:

- Make every effort to ensure that I have the most current knowledge and that the proper expertise is available when needed.
- Avoid conflict of interest and insure that my employer is aware of any potential conflicts.
- Present a fair, honest, and objective viewpoint.
- Protect the proper interests of my employer at all times.
- Protect the privacy and confidentiality of all information entrusted to me.
- Not misrepresent or withhold information that is germane to the situation.
- Not attempt to use the resources of my employer for personal gain or for any purpose without proper approval.
- Not exploit the weakness of a computer system for personal gain or personal satisfaction.

Reprinted by permission Data Processing Management Association Inc.

These measures include restricting access to data through the use of passwords, making backup copies of important data, and using encryption to foil eavesdropping during data transmission.

■   Transnational data flows refer to the transfer of useful data across national boundaries.

■   Software controls refer to methods regulating the way programs are developed, accessed, and maintained. Software security measures include the use of structured design and development techniques throughout the software development process and periodic auditing of programs. Other software security measures are the same as those for data—passwords, backup copies, and encryption. To control software piracy, there are various techniques that make it difficult to copy programs. Another means to counter piracy is to issue site licenses, where for a negotiated fee the organization can make or obtain sufficient legal single-user copies or networkable versions.

■   Computer viruses are tiny programs that can attach to the operating system's codes that are normally passed onto secondary storage media when disks are formatted or copied. Some perpetrators write time bombs to activate the virus well after the virus has been passed along.

■   Hardware controls ensure that authorized people have access to the equipment needed to perform their jobs and that unauthorized people do not. Physical security measures protect the hardware and storage media from theft, vandalism, and misuse. Such protection involves not only physically securing the hardware, but foiling unauthorized users who, by masquerading as authentic users, can enter a system via telecommunications links. One technique for controlling masquerading is the automatic callback. Dual processing provides redundant processing capability in case the primary hardware fails.

■   Both accounting and auditing procedures are employed by modern information systems for control purposes. Resource utilization procedures monitor the usage of information resources, control who uses the system, and bills users. Auditing inspects everything from the source materials for data input, through the intermediate results, to the final output. An audit trail consists of the physical or visible documentation of the steps that money, documents, or data follow through an organization. Auditors use auditing software packages to help them perform their tasks with today's complex computer systems.

■   Privacy refers to protection from unauthorized access to, or abuse of, data concerning individuals or organizations. Managers of an organization need to decide what data (if any) should be released to government agencies or private organizations. Managers must also establish procedures to allow individuals to inspect the data maintained about them, and to correct data that are inaccurate. Legislation that backs up the individual's right to privacy includes the Fair Credit Reporting Act (1970), the Freedom of Information Act (1970), the Education Privacy Act (1974), and the Privacy Act (1974). The Electronic Communications Privacy Act (1986) was enacted to broaden the scope and enforcement powers of the Privacy Act.

■   Computer ethics are the standards used by people in the information-processing industry. Codes of ethics are sets of professional standards and guidelines developed by professional associations.

wrap-up

Suspicion confirmed

Suspecting that someone was illegally examining data from the inventory database at Paul's House of Electronic Wonders, Ed Wieland got the go-ahead from Philip Paul to investigate.

For an entire morning Ed sat at a monitor in the computer room writing down the user identification numbers of the people who were using the inventory database. All of the numbers were valid, of course; otherwise the system would not have let the people use the database. Similarly, all of the users clearly knew their passwords.

Passwords were not recorded anywhere, but a list of valid user identification numbers was kept in the computer room. Ed noticed that no one outside of the purchasing department and the shipping and receiving department ever used the database. Ed made a few tours of these areas, and again found one more user logged on than he could actually see using a terminal. The missing person was the manager of the purchasing department.

Ed did not discuss his investigation with the purchasing manager. Instead, he advised Philip Paul to give a directive to the information-processing center ordering that all passwords for all databases be changed the next day. For individual users, the loss of a familiar password, and the few moments required to think up a new one, would be only a minor nuisance.

Philip issued the directive, and the next day Ed again sat at his monitor in the computer room. The person who had been using the manager's I.D. and password to retrieve data from the inventory database had disappeared!

Pleased with his success, Ed went to talk to Philip.

"Well done, Ed," Philip Paul said. "I just wish we could have caught him."

If he'd been in-house, we would have," Ed said. "I'm pretty sure no one who works here was involved. Someone must have been using a phone line to get in from outside."

"I can see where with a bit of snooping someone from outside could come up with a valid I.D.," Philip said. "But knowing the password puzzles me."

"A computer thief can often psych it out based on what he or she knows about the particular user. I don't know myself what the password was. But if you try names of kids, schools, hometowns, and dogs long enough, the odds are good for hitting it."

"Ed," Philip said, "how do we keep this from happening again?"

"First, Mr. Paul, you should ask the database administrator to do a complete audit of the database. We need to see if the thief just looked at data or changed them. After taking care of that situation, I think we need a regulation that passwords get changed once a month."

"That's all right by me," Philip said.

"And I would like to install an automatic callback system," Ed said. "It would be a new form of protection that just might shut out intruders. The way it works is that when someone logs on, the computer calls them back immediately at the terminal they're assigned to. If they're not there, then they can't get into the system at all."

"Wonderful," Philip Paul said. "Let's hope that will be the end of our data theft."

key terms

These are the key terms in alphabetical order. The numbers in parentheses refer to the page on which each term is defined.

Audit (589)
Audit trail (590)
Automatic callback (588)
Check digit (577)
Codes of ethics (594)
Computer crime (572)
Computer ethics (594)
Computer Fraud and Abuse Act (1986) (573)
Computer virus (584)
Control totals (577)
Data integrity (572)
Data quality assurance (577)
Data security (578)
Dual processing (586)
Eavesdropping (578)
Education Privacy Act (1974) (593)
Electronic Communications Privacy Act (1986) (594)
Encryption (578)
Exception procedures (576)
Fair Credit Reporting Act (1970) (593)
Freedom of Information Act (1970) (593)
Hacker (573)
Information system controls (572)
Masquerading (587)
Physical security (584)
Privacy (572)
Privacy Act (1974) (593)
Resource utilization procedures (589)
Security (572)
Separation of tasks (574)
Site license (583)
Software piracy (582)
Software security (580)
Standardization of work (575)
Time bomb (584)
Transnational data flow (580)
Validation (577)
Verification (577)
Written procedures or standards (576)

review questions

objective questions

True/false. *Put the letter T or F on the line next to the question.*

1. Computer crime occurs when a person uses a computer for illegal purposes.   1 _____

2. Information system controls only serve to monitor the integrity of data.   2 _____

3. The check digit in the Universal Product Code is an example of a control total.   3 _____

4. Integrity refers to the security of the data.   4 _____

5. Permitting one worker to handle many operations in a sensitive area is a violation of the separation-of-tasks principle.   5 _____

6. Information systems should not account for exception procedures.   6 _____

7. Security refers to the steps taken to protect the information system.   7 _____

8. The Fair Credit Reporting Act (1970) gives people the right to inspect credit reports about them maintained by public agencies.   8 _____

9. Verification involves checking data by keying them in a second time and correcting any discrepancies between the two versions.   9 _____

10. With the rise in the use of microcomputers the privacy issue has become less important.   10 _____

Multiple choice. *Put the letter of the correct answer on the line next to the question.*

1. Access to data gathered by federal agencies concerning individuals and organizations is made possible by the   1 _____
   (a) Fair Credit Reporting Act (1970).
   (b) Freedom of Information Act (1970).
   (c) Education Privacy Act (1974).
   (d) Electronic Communications Privacy Act (1986)

2. Dual processing is primarily a control for   2 _____
   (a) People.   (c) Software.
   (b) Rules and procedures.   (d) Hardware.

3 _____ 3. Determining if a data value is within an acceptable range is accomplished by
  (a) Verification.   (c) Check digits
  (b) Validation.   (d) Control totals.

4 _____ 4. Illegal users can fool the computer into thinking they are legitimate users through
  (a) Eavesdropping.   (c) Masquerading.
  (b) Disencryption.   (d) Wiretapping.

5 _____ 5. Protection of individuals and organizations from data gathering abuses of federal agencies is addressed in the
  (a) Fair Credit Reporting Act (1970).
  (b) Freedom of Information Act (1970).
  (c) Education Privacy Act (1974).
  (d) Privacy Act (1974).

Fill in the blank. *Write the correct word or words in the blank to complete the sentence.*

1. The process of tracing the steps money or items follow through an organization is known as a(n) _____.
2. When auditors check the input and processing steps and assume the output is correct they are auditing _____ the computer.
3. Manuals for users, programmers, and systems analysts are examples of _____.
4. The extra digit on a Universal Product Code is an example of a _____.
5. Maintaining data integrity and restricting unauthorized access to data are issues of _____.
6. The term _____ procedure refers to monitoring and adjusting the patterns of information system usage.
7. Listening into transmissions is an example of _____.
8. Data accuracy means the same as _____.
9. Intrusion into your personal records is usually considered a violation of your _____.
10. The coding of data for privacy during transmission is known as _____.

short answer questions

When answering these questions, think of concrete examples to illustrate your points.

1. What are two examples of controls affecting people in the information system?
2. How can information-processing centers reduce the risk of threats to physical security?
3. What means are used to audit on-line real-time systems?
4. What methods are used for data quality assurance?
5. What are some telecommunications security measures?
6. Why do information systems require exception procedures?
7. Comment on the risks of not separating tasks.
8. What are some examples of software controls?
9. What is meant by the term *computer ethics*?
10. How does a computer virus work?

essay questions

1. Discuss the need to balance maintaining information security while giving users the opportunity to use the system.
2. What are the major information security controls at your work or school?
3. Discuss whether government agencies should have unrestricted access to data gathered about you and held in private databases.

Answers to the objective questions
True/false: 1. T; 2. F; 3. F; 4. F; 5. T; 6. F; 7. T; 8. F; 9. T; 10. F
Multiple choice: 1. b; 2. d; 3. b; 4. c; 5. d
Fill in the blank: 1. audit trail; 2. through; 3. standards or written procedures; 4. check digit; 5. data control; 6. resource utilization; 7. eavesdropping; 8. data integrity; 9. right to privacy; 10. encryption

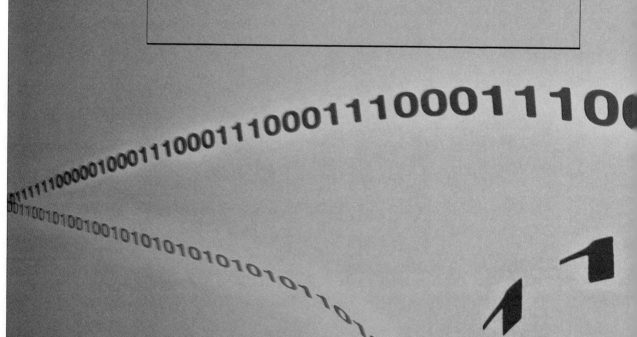

part five

Social issues

We come to the closing section of this textbook. In Part Four we explored information systems in detail. Where do we go from here? Well, in Chapter 18 we examine some of the present and anticipated impacts that computers have on our lives.

18 Computers and the future: impact and issues

Computers and the future: impacts and issues

After studying this chapter you should understand the following:

- *Some of the main ways computers and information systems have affected people.*
- *The characteristics and limitations of robots.*
- *Contemporary issues concerning rules and procedures, data, software, and hardware.*
- *The main possibilities for the evolution of computers and information systems.*

chapter 18

The cutting edge

The future had entered the Roberts family's life with a bang. In less than a year Janis had gone from being a travel agent who knew little about computers, to becoming the mainstay of the information-processing staff at Freddy Johnson's Travel Agency, with several computer courses under her belt.

In the example at the beginning of Chapter 2, we saw Freddy Johnson's Travel Agency planning its computerization process, and at the end of Chapter 2 we described how the system worked after 3 months in operation. The results were promising. Freddy, the owner, was enthusiastic. Although bugs were still being ironed out of the system, people were still getting used to it, and all the votes were by no means in, neither Janis nor Freddy had reason to be pessimistic. Janis had advanced personally at an unprecedented rate, with two promotions within a year and a reputation within the firm as the computer expert. Her assistant, Ann, was already branching out into word processing and desktop publishing. Everything Janis heard from the agency's branch managers and the travel agents themselves suggested that the new system was making it easier for them to work more efficiently, as well as enabling them to offer clients an increased level of service.

George Roberts was also being propelled into the future at Global Electrical Equipment. He was called into his manager's office one morning and told that in 2 months half of his employees would no longer be human. Seven people were being replaced by robots.

His engineer's mind greeted the new development with enthusiasm. From a managerial vantage point, too, he recognized what Global's directors were doing. The assembly-line operations at Global's different plants were enormous. Robots had been used for years for simple operations such as spot welding. But in his department, the directors wanted to carry out an experiment that was risky but had great potential impact. By replacing half of his inspectors with robots, George would compare how well they performed against the human inspectors. The results could determine the future of quality-control operations throughout the huge company.

Global's expansion into the use of robots was at the cutting edge of technology. Robots capable of telling whether an appliance such as a toaster worked right were something new. Managing them would be something new as well. And the results would ripple through the industry.

As a manager, George was also responsible for the professional, and to a degree, the personal well-being of his employees. His excitement over the robots did not last even a full minute before he felt the same panic he knew his employees would feel. Automation phased out jobs! People read it in the paper often enough, and now seven of his employees were going to experience it. It would be George's responsibility to sort out the human consequences. George spent several anguished days trying to explore different options, following formal company policy as well as his knowledge of what might be done informally. He would work out a complete plan and then take it to his boss for approval. Then he would break the news to his employees. But what could he tell them?

Social issues and the information system

Each major technological innovation since the dawn of history has had a major effect on society, transforming or at the least modifying, the way people live. The automobile reshaped the American landscape, creating suburbs, causing cities first to decline and then to regenerate in new form, changing social and leisure patterns, creating unmatched levels of air pollution, and threading concrete ribbons from coast to coast. You can make up a similar list of the effects of the telephone, the airplane, television, video cassette recorders, radios, electricity, or the atomic bomb. For even more fundamental catalysts of change, go further back in history and consider the taming of fire or the invention of the wheel.

But what about the computer? In its half a century or so of modern existence, it has changed the way business does business, made space exploration possible, created whole new industries and occupations, and nurtured a vast educational enterprise dedicated to imparting computer proficiency. It has dramatically altered the role information plays in business and other organizations. Any other technology, profession, or product that you would care to name has probably been computer-ized: automobiles, home appliances, telephones, medicine, weapons, banking, aeronautics. Chapter 1 outlined a number of such applications, some of them surprising. Little computer chips defrost our refrigera-tors, run the watches on our wrists, and may soon provide guidance to artificial organs implanted in our bodies.

Yet the computer revolution has only begun. Trying to predict its course is like trying to chart the course of an ocean liner based on its first few movements out of port. We don't really know where the ship is headed. Worse, the computer revolution is like a ship with no captain.

People

There are several conflicting views on the impact of computers and information systems on people. Three basic schools of thought exist.

The first view holds that computers have been of great benefit to our society, helping to usher in a new golden age in which people can use computers to lighten their burdens and brighten their lives. Advances in health care, the sciences, and even the arts, have been fostered by the computer, and a computerized business community is better able to turn a profit, benefiting everyone.

The second school of thought is less rosy. According to this view, the addictive use of, and belief in, the power of computers has led us well along the path toward a regimented society. Models of our near future are offered by George Orwell's novel *1984* (though its title refers to a year now past), with its citizens dominated by thought-control police, and by the cold, brutal technocracy depicted in Aldous Huxley's *Brave New World*. Thanks to the computer, millions of jobs have been lost; government databases hold our deepest secrets; and damage has been done to the environment. Worst of all, one of the many errors with which computer systems are rife could lead the United States or the

Soviet Union into thinking the other had launched an attack (as in the fictional movie *War Games*), and so to launch the "counterattack" in earnest that could end life on this planet.

As you can probably see, neither of these two viewpoints is quite right; yet neither is quite wrong either. A third school of thought exists. It holds that the net effect of computers upon human society will be essentially neutral. Society has absorbed many profound changes in the past without losing its bearings. With computerization, some people will gain, others will lose, but the total effect will not fundamentally change the direction of society. The question for society then becomes how to redistribute the "gains" of some members to those other members who lose. Translated into more specific terms, society's problem becomes one of how to retrain people thrown out of their jobs by automation or by the need for higher levels of education to use new and unfamiliar technology. Let's look at some of the areas that are relevant to the three viewpoints: automation and robotics, job replacement, and job displacement.

Automation and robotics
AUTOMATION refers to the replacement of human control of a process by a machine. Automation may be used to make an existing product more cheaply, rapidly, or safely, or to create a new or refined product to replace an existing one. For example, the use of automation in the production of manufactured goods allows greater control over the quality of a product. In the electronics industry automated testing machines serve to speed up the testing process and to scan incredibly small microcircuit elements that would be difficult or impossible for humans to test.

Most of us work or will have to work to earn a living, and some working people fear the loss of their jobs to robots. A ROBOT is a machine capable of coordinating its movements itself by reacting to changes in its environment. In other words, a robot has sensing devices and a built-in program to direct its movements based on the different input signals or conditions sensed. ROBOTICS refers to the study and application of robots.

Their glamorous and threatening public image notwithstanding, the robots of today are capable of handling many dangerous, boring, and dirty jobs (see Figure 18-1). Robots are used in manufacturing for a wide variety of tasks such as welding, lifting, and painting. Large robots are capable of maneuvering an automobile body while performing welding operations on that body. Small, dexterous robots can assemble tiny electric motors.

Some robots are capable of walking and talking to people, and are packaged in a shape with trunk, limbs, and "head" to make their humanlike qualities more obvious. There are kits to build your own robot capable of doing routine household chores, such as bringing you a cup of coffee. More significantly, however, robots can perform many hazardous tasks. For example, the bomb squad of the New York City Police Department uses a remote-controlled robot to investigate suitcases or packages that may contain a bomb. The robot picks up and

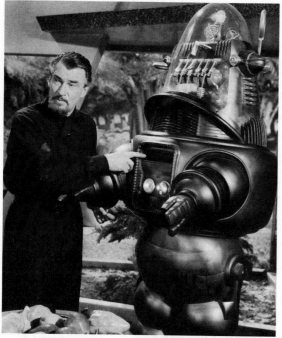

(a)

(b)

Figure 18-1
*Robots in our lives don't
always fit the image pre-
sented in fiction. (a) The
classic image—Robbie
the Robot from the 1955
science fiction movie
The Forbidden Planet.*
(b) A walking robot. (c) A
small robot being devel-
oped to help severely
handicapped people feed
themselves. (d) A large
robot used to weld auto-
mobiles. (e) A robot used
by the New York City
Police Bomb Squad. (f) A
robot used to teach medi-
cal students to conduct
cardiopulmonary resus-
citation. The robot's
"body functions" appear
on the television screen.

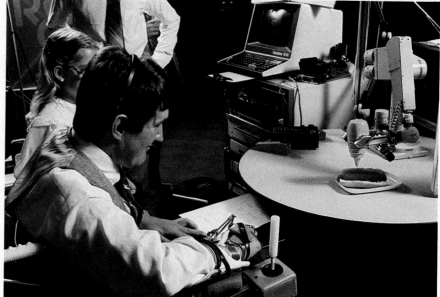

(c)

places the suspected explosive in a truck with a specially sealed and reinforced cargo area; the truck is then driven outside of the city where the
bomb is removed and defused.

Robots are also used in industry to handle radioactive substances
while the humans in charge watch from a safe, sealed-off distance. Their
science fiction billing aside, robots are basically very dumb and do not
live up to their reputations. For the types of applications we have men-

(e)

(d)

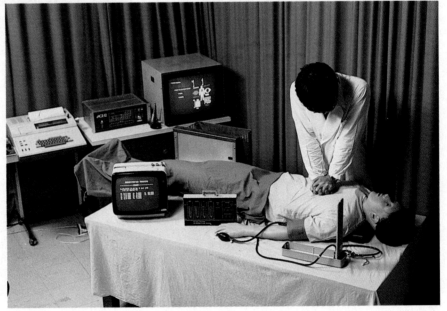

(f)

tioned, however, robots are being increasingly used, and are subtly transforming manufacturing and other industrial processes (see the following box).

Job replacement and job displacement
JOB REPLACEMENT occurs when a job held by a person is taken over by a robot or other machine programmed to perform the same task. People

The robotic dairy

Amsterdam

The milkmaid, that smiling symbol of wholesome country goodness, is already an endangered species. If a group of Dutch agricultural engineers called "Farm 2000" gets its way, she will be gone for good. They have produced the first fully automated dairy, in which cows are caringly milked, monitored and generally made a fuss of by an impersonal-looking array of computer-controlled arms and electronic sensors, with not a rosy cheek in sight.

A prototype of the system was unveiled at an agricultural-engineering conference in Paris. . . . The robot-cowshed consists of a set of stalls in which cows are both fed and milked. When a cow enters a stall, ultrasound sensors automatically scan its teats and find out where and how large they are. That information is used to produce an image of the teats in the central computer, which serves to guide a robot arm.

This arm then attaches teat cups to the cow. A conventional vacuum system, like those used in today's less sophisticated automatic milkers, coaxes the milk from the carefree cow. Once the suction has begun, the robot, which can attend to several animals at once, is then free to start work on another cow.

This does not all happen willy-nilly. Mr. Wim Rossing, the project's engineer at the Institute of Agricultural Engineering in Wageningen, insists that the robot will keep milking only if it thinks the time is right. It makes decisions after considering information from a range of monitors and sensors that measure everything from the yield, temperature and composition of the milk to the cows' movements and general state of health. Mastitis, for example, can be diagnosed from the milk's conductivity.

The robot can also find out if the cow is in its fertile period or not. It does this by measuring the amount the cow has been moving around—all the cows have counters on their legs which record their movements—and measuring its temperature. The computer spots cows in oestrus with an accuracy of 93 percent.

The cows might be forgiven for feeling rather alienated by all this—but the central computer does contrive to treat them all as individuals. Each cow is identified by a miniaturized transmitter worn on its neck, and information about it received during a milking is automatically compared with records. When measurements vary too widely from their expected values, the computer singles out that particular cow for investigation or treatment.

The computer also provides tailor-made meals for its bovine guest. When a cow steps into the stall its favored menu is identified from the information contained in its collar-mounted transmitter. A carefully balanced helping of weighed forage is mixed with the right amounts of various concentrated foods. The meal is dumped in a small bunker which is guided along a rail to the appropriate stall; there the mixture is dished up to the waiting cow.

Combining the use of feeding boxes with milking stalls lets the cows be milked several times a day, at the most opportune moments. During an 11-week trial period some 20 cows were milked in such a shed. The cows, which turned up for food an average of 5.4 times a day, were content to be milked four times a day. The greater number of milkings (cows are usually milked twice daily) stimulated the cows' capacities for production; average yield . . . was 14 percent higher.

The frequent milkings, says Mr Rossing, do not improve only the milk yields; they also improve the cow's well-being. Cows milked twice a day are sometimes compelled to stagger around with their udders filled to near bursting point. Emptier udders reduce the chances of cows injuring themselves.

. . . [The institute hopes to] cooperate in the production of a cost-effective model to be fully tested at the end of 1989. . . .

Source: "Automatic Dairies: Cold but Comfortable Farm," *The Economist* 23 April 1988, p. 94. Reprinted with permission.

trained to weld an automobile chassis on an assembly line, for instance, may find themselves replaced by robots that can do the job much more rapidly and safely. If their skill cannot be transferred to another operation or to another factory, these workers will have to be trained in a new skill (quite possibly at a lower salary).

If no such retraining program is available for them, or if they cannot find another job after attending such a program, then they will join the unemployment rolls. Automation does have its casualties; it would be unrealistic to say otherwise. Society's job is to face up to rather than ignore the situation, and provide training and employment opportunities for those who lose their jobs.

JOB DISPLACEMENT occurs when the skills necessary to perform a job change. For example, in a typing pool the ability to type accurately was once paramount. Correcting mistakes on hard copy is difficult and time-consuming. When word processing systems entered the picture, accuracy became less important, since correcting mistakes became much easier. As a result, less capable typists could do the work. This has displaced some "classical" typists; others have learned to use the new equipment, and continue to thrive in the office environment.

Job replacement and job displacement occur even within the computer field itself. Repair personnel once worked on large circuits with testing meters and soldering irons. Now they run diagnostic programs and replace whole chips or boards rather than tinker with them. Most repair personnel who were used to doing things the old way were also capable of doing them the new way, since the new way is less demanding. Many voluntarily retrained for other areas of the computer field, however, since they found the new work too repetitive and lacking in challenge.

Some labor force analysts fear that extensive use of computers will lead to a two-tier society. According to this view, a few skilled managers at the top levels of organizations would direct the work of a vast number of far less skilled people. The middle- and lower-level management roles would be considerably reduced in scope. The effect would be to drastically reduce chances for upward mobility. Since moving toward the top is a prime goal for many people, this would have far-reaching personal and social consequences.

Even professionals would not be exempt. Engineers, scientists, physicians, attorneys, and teachers would have to struggle to keep up with changes in their fields. Without continuous reeducation (in some cases required by accrediting organizations), professionals would face the risk of becoming technologically outdated in their fields, and would watch their status and earnings fall while more information-proficient colleagues advanced.

Job enhancement

We have presented quite a few negative factors thus far. Fortunately, they do not make up the whole picture. On the positive side, JOB ENHANCEMENT can occur by making existing jobs far easier and more enjoyable. Surveys by our business students over the past 5 years indicate that most computer users would not think of running their businesses without computer assistance. New occupations can be created.

For example, a vast industry currently exists to produce, sell, and support a product that hadn't even been invented a dozen years ago—the microcomputer. Besides the vast industrial base that produces the machines and their components, the nation is peppered with computer stores (Figure 18-2), and literally thousands of software companies turn out products for the micros. In addition, there is a heavy demand for teachers to train users of these new systems, technical writers to describe them, and repairpeople to fix them.

The main effect of computers on the working world, however, has been made by mainframes and minicomputers. In North America, Western Europe, and Japan virtually every business of any size has been computerized. Considerable resistance was initially experienced, and the transitional period from operating without a computer to operating *well* with a computer sometimes lasted up to a decade. With many billions of lines of computer code presently in place in American businesses, and the trials of conversion for the most part past, management knows that things work better. Most employees will agree.

Ask someone who survived the computerization of a bank whether he or she would rather check a balance the old way—by consulting outdated ledgers, making phone calls, and guessing—or by using the computer terminal. Few would want to turn the clock back. Most jobs that entail clerical operations are easier today with computers than they were before computers arrived on the scene, taking some of the drudgery out of work.

The electronic cottage

With the rise of distributed information systems and microcomputers, the age of the electronic cottage has begun, allowing people to perform many types of jobs without leaving their homes (Figure 18-3). Working

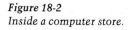

Figure 18-2
Inside a computer store.

Figure 18-3
Life in the electronic
cottage.

as an employee at your home through a telephone link between your microcomputer or display terminal and the company office is known as TELECOMMUTING. Although only a fraction of the American work force telecommutes today, the number is growing. Analysts wonder if the effects of the automobile might be reversed by telecommuting. The automobile made it possible for people to live at great distances from their jobs. Telecommuting places the job right in the home. Just one of the results of this trend is to allow working parents more time with their children.

Historically, cottage industries flourished just before the start of the Industrial Revolution, and fostered a piecework orientation that often led to exploitation of workers and an assurance that they could never rise from poverty. Some people wonder if in moving the clock forward with telecommuting, we are really turning it backward. It is not a simple question.

Rules and
procedures

The creation and rapid expansion of communication networks for information systems allow us to move, analyze, and respond to data more quickly. People can make fast decisions—sometimes even the wrong ones.

For instance, with a manual accounting system or a semi-automated system, checks on the people using the system occur over a period of time. If a blunder is committed somewhere along the way, the odds are great that it will be caught before it reaches the world at large. With an automated system, however, the traditional checks may not operate.

One company went out of business because its automated accounting system was programmed to send out checks against incoming bills, but was not programmed to send out bills to those who owed the company money. Eventually the checks the company wrote bounced, as there was no money in the bank to cover them. The company went under.

In the early days of computerization it was not uncommon for the representatives of a business to blame poor service on the machine. That should never be an excuse now. Most people realize that they, rather than the machines, run businesses. If you are ever told that a request can't be answered because "the computer can't handle it," that means the company simply doesn't want to deal with your request and give you the proper service, or that their software was poorly designed without

Figure 18-4
Electronic banking at home.

the foresight to alter data or procedures. Complain, or at the least ask, "Who's in charge here, your managers or your machine?"

The rise of distributed information systems has in fact led to greater responsiveness in handling exceptional conditions. When booking an airline ticket we have come to rely not only on the standardized service that gets us a seat on the right flight, but on attention to special conditions such as our requirement for vegetarian, kosher, salt-free, or low-cholesterol meals. Individual service is alive and well in the computer age—when the machines are programmed correctly.

Those of us who do not telecommute can still utilize certain information services in our home. For example, you can pay your bills or shift money from one account to another (but alas, not make cash withdrawals) using your home microcomputer (Figure 18-4). You can also query databases, check the latest stock quotations, reserve hotel rooms, and check the weather, without setting one foot out in the rain.

Data

The growth of large, centralized databases and the rise of microcomputers have raised issues of security. Using a modem and a telecommunications link, a determined outsider (or insider) may be able to gain access to confidential data contained in a database, and even to alter or destroy the data. Consider the impact of a competitor copying customer files and leaving the original in scrambled form, which has in fact occurred.

Another area of concern is the increasing use of home computers to tie into systems to handle banking transactions. In general, of course, this is a convenient new service. However, dishonest but clever individuals may figure out ways to steal money from the bank or from other people's accounts, all from the convenience of their own home. Crooks too may telecommute. It is also possible to sit down at another customer's terminal and, if you know the password, to transfer money from his or her account to yours; could the first user recover the loss here? In addition, banks send billions of dollars back and forth via telecommunications links, and as we saw in Chapter 17, telecommunications links can be tapped.

With today's reliance on databases, the risk exists of inaccurate data being introduced to a database and then transferred to other databases *ad infinitum* before the error is found. For example, there have been incidents where people have deliberately fabricated false data on others—such as not having paid back loans that they did pay back, or having served prison terms—and placed the data in the records maintained in a database. The false information is usually not detected until the person affected is turned down as a bad credit or insurance risk and realizes something is amiss. As the section Protecting the Right to Privacy in Chapter 17 discussed, legislation exists to enable people to examine and challenge data contained about them in a database.

Software

A common complaint about software is that it is oversold by the maker. You can perhaps understand why when you consider that there are over 30,000 different software packages available for microcomputers. From the vendor's point of view, it is difficult to stand out from the pack without promising the moon.

From the user's point of view, it is very difficult to determine which package is right for a particular job. Once you have acquired a given software package, another murky area is entered: If software fails to work properly, or to live up to promises of the moon, who is liable for your business loss? It is not easy to go to court and prove that a program didn't do what it promised to do. To this day, most people don't even understand what a program is, let alone the difference between a good one and a bad one.

The software firms themselves do not have an easy time. Suppose you were offered something worth $300 for a quarter or less—would you take it? Most people would. That is about how much it costs for the floppy disk needed to copy someone's software package. The loss of sales revenues to the creators and sellers is a major problem, running into the tens of millions of dollars per year. This problem often stifles software developers' interest in creating new products. One method of countering such "program borrowing" is to manufacture the software using the more expensive process of "burning" the software onto a read-only memory (ROM) chip; the purchaser pays more for this protection of the vendor.

Factors of buying and selling aside, there is concern about the power that software has over our lives. All sizable modern weapon systems are computerized, as are the satellite surveillance systems that would detect incoming missiles. In other words, these systems are supervised by computer hardware, which is in turn supervised by software, which one hopes is in turn supervised by a human being.

A human's involvement is important because software is usually full of errors. Anyone who has ever written a program knows how far from perfect it was. Vendors regularly ship software with an average of 2 to 3 lines of incorrect code per 100 lines of code. What if the programs used to run our national defense system are also filled with this level of errors? The fact is that much of the code has never been, and can never be, tested under real-life conditions. The decision time for the life and death choices to be made by the U.S. or Soviet heads of state before pressing the button has been dramatically shortened, to less than 6 minutes after the detection of submarine-launched missiles. This does not leave a whole lot of margin for ironing out software bugs.

Hardware

It has been said that computers constitute a clean industry. The once-quiet towns of the Santa Clara Valley of California—informally known throughout the world as Silicon Valley—welcomed the semiconductor firms with their absence of industry's traditional belching smokestacks, their need for workers, and their contributions to the tax rolls. This valley of great wealth, the center of the semiconductor or "chip" industry, has become an industrial disaster area, through the quiet but deadly percolation of chemicals into the groundwater. Ironically, these chemicals were not just dumped irresponsibly but were placed in underground tanks, following the best disposal method of the time, in an attempt to avoid the problems that have occurred anyway.

In addition, recent studies have shown that a number of the chemicals used in the production of silicon chips have been improperly handled. Some production-line workers have allegedly developed severe health problems due to the chemical processes involved.

There has been little methodical investigation into the health and safety of people who use display screens. As has happened often enough with other new inventions or technologies, there is a tendency to first use something extensively, and then after the damage has been done, to stop and think about whether it was such a good idea. It has become virtually the office norm to work with a terminal, and data-entry operators spend the entire workday looking at them. Visual problems can result, just as they can from watching television for hours on end. The human eye tries to "resolve" what it sees into a crisp image, a process continually frustrated by staring at a blurry image (blurry when compared, say, to print) that cannot be resolved. Display screens also emit a low level of electromagnetic radiation; as yet, no one knows whether it will have any long-term effects.

The physical act of sitting at a terminal is no easy job, either; it can lead to a variety of chronic aches and pains. According to Bernardina Wilcox of the Lauderdale-Wilcox Physical Rehabilitation Center in Anaheim, California, "Persons who operate video display terminals have a high rate of back stress and back injury."[1] In 1988, legislation was enacted in New York's Suffolk County mandating work conditions for video display users.

Future trends: the shape of tomorrow

At the 1939 World's Fair in New York City, a number of experts were asked to predict what the most important inventions of the near future would be. They completely missed two of the most significant inventions: the atomic bomb and electronic computers. Making predictions definitely has its limits. Like weather forecasting used to be (before

[1]Walt Murray, Knight-Ridder News Service, taken from *San Jose Mercury-News,* 18 November 1984.

computers), predictions are as often wrong as right. But let's take a chance anyway.

People

It is difficult to say who will be the real winners or losers of the information age. Flexibility seems to be the most important characteristic of people best able to adjust to the changes brought on by computers. Generally speaking, people who are well educated but not overly specialized can adjust easily. Someone who enters the work force today should expect to need retraining every few years, and perhaps even a career change every 10 to 15 years.

Two groups of people will face serious difficulties: the less educated, and the educated who cannot or will not adapt to change. Some of the major career growth areas today are in fields that didn't even exist 20 years ago. Figure 18-5 projects into the future job growth for six computer-related occupations.

Not all information system-related jobs are expected to grow over the next few years. One category in particular is expected to decline—data-entry operators, numbering 320,000 in 1982, are projected to number only 286,000 in 1995.

The increasing reliance by managers in all industries on computerized decision support systems (DSSs) has led to speculation that these systems might change the role of managers. In a sense, by ceding to computers the authority to make certain kinds of routine decisions, some low- and middle-level managers may be putting themselves out of business. The effects are not likely to be so drastic, however. DSSs should enhance the quality of information available to managers and ease of access to it. The systems will not be able to use that information to make decisions. Managers will still be needed for that.

The same may not be true for blue-collar workers. In the future we can expect robots—dubbed the "steel-collar" work force—to have an increasing impact on the human work force. Japan will probably continue to be the major producer as well as user of robots. The United States and Western European countries will also produce tremendous quantities of these machines (see Figure 18-6). Robots are now used primarily in the manufacturing of automobiles, trucks, and electronic

Figure 18-5
Jobs in 1995. Predicted job growth in the United States for six computer-related occupations. (Source for 1987 figures: Occupational Outlook Handbook, U.S. Department of Labor Bureau of Statistics, April 1988, Bulletin 2300. Source for predicted employment: "Employment Projections for 1995," U.S. Department of Labor Bureau of Statistics, March 1984, Bulletin 2197.)

Occupation	Employment in 1987	Predicted employment in 1995
Computer operators	263,000	371,000
Computer programmers	479,000	471,000*
Computer service technicians	69,000	108,000
Computer system analysts	331,000	471,000
Office machine repair persons	56,000	95,000
Peripheral EDP equipment operators	46,000	80,000

*Note the number of computer programmers working in 1987 already exceeds the predicted level. The rate of increase for this occupation is expected to continue into the 1990's.

616

case in point
Multinational information systems

. . . On the congested data highways of multinational corporations, the problems of getting the right data in the right amount to the right people at the right time are multiplying daily as global markets emerge. "It's a battleground," say Ron Ponder, senior vp of information systems at Federal Express, Memphis. Last year, the $3.2 billion company dramatically increased its overseas operations to the point where it now services 89 countries and employs nearly 5000 workers (10 percent of its work force) outside of the United States.

The problems are amplified if you are a large multinational with diverse product families, such as 185-year-old E. I. du Pont de Nemours & Co. The chemical giant generates a third of its $27 billion in revenue overseas, employing 35,000 people abroad in some 150 plants and offices. "When remote corporate clients as far apart as Rio, Tokyo, or Rome get 'gobbledygook' on their PCs, the situation is especially frustrating," says Lee Foote, manager of Du Pont's Electronic Data Interchange Section at Wilmington, Del. "There are many misconceptions about what this right stuff—information—actually is."

If Europe's instrument makers, Japan's machine tool producers, America's automakers, and the thousands of other manufacturers and service companies worldwide are to survive in this new era of globalization—a time when no supplier is too distant, no customer too foreign—they must rid themselves of the informational chaos endemic to international operations. But how? The answers may be the following: enlightened management, effective use of information technology tools and standards, such as electronic data interchange (EDI) and structured query language (SQL), and enterprisewide alliances.

Although many will insist that computers and information are inseparable, data spewed out by legions of mainframes should not be confused with information. "Properly structured data will result in information, but only in the minds of individuals and under certain contexts and time frames," Du Pont's Foote explains. IS [information system] groups that

don't understand this distinction and haven't found out what data client organizations really need will simply print everything out. And the result? Data overload.

User managers—division and department heads who bear functional (as opposed to IS) titles—are already attempting to protect themselves from a torrent of useless data (not just from their own systems organizations) by erecting specially designed software screens and filters. These programs take the form of preference profiles, which rank incoming data and voice messages by order of importance. Such programs are the forerunners of future expert systems and currently are being embedded in computer networks so that they function automatically.

For their part, IS managers are embracing EDI and SQL as the means by which to create information. EDI describes a standardized way of using computers to transmit and receive business documents, such as purchase orders. SQL, on the other hand, is a standard means of accessing database management systems that are shared by different architectures.

Du Pont's customers in the United States and elsewhere, for example, can use EDI to conduct more of their business chores with the company electronically. "Any company that's tried EDI has become an apostle of effective data management," Foote says, "but getting the message over has been tough." He says his section had to sell the EDI concept both to top management at Du Pont and to information technology vendors.

"We've pretty much had to educate the vendors, lead them by the nose," echoes George Higgins, a colleague of Foote's and a data resource management (DRM) consultant for Du Pont. Higgins stresses that too many vendors forget that technology is simply a means to an end, not an end in itself. "You've got to show them what the end state is," Higgins feels, "that for example, you've got this database in Geneva and another in Wilmington that you want to link together if the right technical means can be found."

Source: Ralph Emmett Carlyle, "Managing IS at Multinationals," *Datamation*, 1 March, pp. 54–56, 1988. Excerpted from DATAMATION, © 1988 by Cahners Publishing Company.

Figure 18-6
Annual robot production
estimated for 1990 for
the major Western coun-
tries. (Source: "The Ro-
botics Industry," U.S.
Department of Com-
merce, April 1983, p. 20.)

Rank	Country	1990 (est.)
1	Japan	57,500
2	United States	31,300
3	West Germany	12,000
4	United Kingdom	21,500
5	Sweden	5,000
6	Italy	3,500
7	France	3,000
8	Norway	2,000
All other countries		4,200
Total worldwide		140,000

equipment. The main duties of robots had been simple machining and welding tasks. Increasingly, robots are expected to carry out more sophisticated tasks, with their main job being the assembly of machined and welded parts.

The effect of robots on people employed in manufacturing could be devastating. A study by the Rand Corporation forecasts that the percentage of people employed in manufacturing jobs might decline from about 20 percent of the work force in the early 1980s to 2 percent by the year 2000. Naturally, someone has to make, control, and repair the robots, which opens up new jobs. But analysts have predicted that for each job created by the robotics industry, five will be lost. If job loss of this magnitude occurs, severe social and economic disruptions could result. As stated earlier in the chapter, the issue of providing retraining and new jobs must be faced.

Rules and procedures

Will rules become more or less rigid in the future? Who will make the rules? Certain signs seem to indicate that rules will become less rigid, allowing people greater flexibility over their lives. For instance, telecommuting has relaxed the rules pertaining to where and when some people work. On the other hand, information systems can now keep track of exactly how you spend your time, and can compare your job efficiency with that of other workers using hard data rather than your supervisor's imperfect knowledge. This would seem to point toward less flexibility. As with any crystal ball gazing, no one really knows for sure.

Data

Every day more and more data about us are being compiled. Databases keep records on our buying habits, health problems, family life, and other matters. There has even been talk of setting up a national centralized database that would contain all of the information concerning individuals that is presently maintained by different governmental agencies, so that all of the agencies could share it. Using a password and an identifier such as your social security number, various agencies and people would be able to access confidential data concerning you, whether they needed it or not. Needless to say, there has been considerable resistance to the idea of a national database.

Issues of centralization aside, data will be managed differently in the future. Database management systems are expected to become cheaper, faster, and easier to use. The systems should be better able to limit unauthorized access, while at the same time increasing the ease of use by the proper personnel. Database languages will become more powerful, yet simpler to use. Inquiries will be made in the languages that we speak—or languages close to them.

Software

Program development will become more automated with computer-assisted programming tools. These tools will reduce the amount of time programmers need to spend debugging the actual program, and free up time to spend on program design. They will also force programmers to use structured techniques more consistently in all stages of program development. Hopefully future software will contain fewer errors than present-day software, thus offering greater reliability. Programs will be further integrated into hardware through the use of the various types of firmware.

As with database languages, programming languages may continue the trend toward natural languages. Data inquiry languages will permit the user to converse with the hardware in a pattern which the system "learns"—that is, records, analyzes, and retains—to help structure future data inquiry sessions. Expert systems will become available in a wide variety of fields, and will be addressed to users of different skill levels. For example, expert systems in medicine that use nontechnical terminology may be used to interview patients directly. A physician can then perform an examination or interview and also consult the results of analysis by the expert system, in order to better reach a diagnosis and determine the right course of treatment.

Software is already big business. The emphasis of computer systems has shifted from hardware being virtually the sole focus of investment, to a point where software is nearly as important (see Figure 18-7). In the future, this trend is expected to accelerate. The overall size of the software and computer-support industry is expected to grow substantially in the 1990s.

Figure 18-7
Projected worldwide sales by U.S. computer companies for 1990. (Source: Estimate given for 1990 using the 15 percent compounded annual rate suggested in "The Computer Industry," U.S. Department of Commerce, April 1983, p. 15.)

Equipment	Sales (in billions of dollars), 1990
Mainframes	43.4
Minicomputers	38.8
Microcomputers	6.1
Peripherals	32.7
Software/services	68.4
Total	189.4

Hardware

How will we communicate with the computers of the future? In all likelihood, it will be different from the way we do now. Communication will be based less upon traditional key entry of data and more upon source data automation. Machines capable of reading vast quantities of text or manuscript material will be available to many users. In addition, more reliable and flexible voice-recognition systems will be available for the business market.

Figure 18-7 gives projections for computer hardware sales in 1990. Although the breakdown into the familiar categories of mainframes, minicomputers, and microcomputers remains, we should expect significant changes. Several new technologies are presently in the works that may give rise to a new breed of machine, or radically transform the existing breeds. The main projects in computer circuitry presently underway include:

- The further development of silicon chip semiconductors using VERY-LARGE-SCALE INTEGRATION (VLSI), including 16 megabit chips.
- The substitution of MICROLASERS for the circuitry in today's computers, possibly leading to the creation of optical rather than electronic computers.
- The substitution of BIOCHIPS, which utilize molecular structures and processes developed using biotechnology, for the electronic components of today's machines.
- The further development of JOSEPHSON JUNCTIONS, which exploit the electrical properties of low-temperature *superconducting* switches. These circuits, named after their inventor Brian Josephson, offer extremely fast memory access.
- The widespread commercialization of PARALLEL PROCESSING COMPUTERS where thousands of processors work in concert to solve a problem.
- Further on the horizon we might envision "high-temperature" superconducting components for computers, the use of mechanical elements on silicon chips, the commercialization of conductive plastic compounds, or the use of ordinary house wiring to carry communication signals "piggybacked" onto the alternating current.

Regardless of the specific technology that will be used, the computers of the future are certain to shrink in size. As we have seen, smaller means faster when it comes to electrical circuits, since electricity has to traverse a smaller distance with smaller components. At the speed of electricity, shrinking a chip by another fraction of an inch might not seem to matter much; yet it does when electricity must repeatedly traverse the same distance many millions of times. So we can expect to be working with both smaller and faster machines in the future.

One present trend with computers should continue: they will become less visible as they are incorporated into more products at home and at work. Computers will be used for process control not only in factories and offices, but at home, monitoring and controlling heating, air conditioning, and security systems. The electronic components contained in automobiles will continue to increase in sophistication, but

Getting started in the computer field

How do you get started in the computer field? The first step is to learn something more about computers. There are two ways to do this: (1) through formal education and (2) through on-the-job training. Once you have decided on a career in information systems you should keep up with the field by reading books and magazines on the subject and taking refresher courses.

Formal education

Formal education does not guarantee entry to the computer field, but it helps. Almost all new systems analysts are expected to have a bachelor's degree. For programmers, a bachelor's degree certainly helps, but more than half of starting programmers have only a high school degree and some training in a 2-year college program. To obtain formal training, there are several different routes you can take.

First, you could attend a community or 2-year college and take the introductory information systems courses. If the job you want requires more than a 2-year degree, you would want to transfer your credits to a 4-year institution and get a bachelor's degree.

Second, you could also take a 4-year course of study and major in an information systems program. The names of programs and the degrees they offer vary, but they fall into two main categories: information systems or computer science.

An *information systems program* corresponds to the general business-related approach that we have followed in this book. An information systems program emphasizes the processing of data to produce information that will be used by a general business or a government employer. Courses will cover the fundamentals of computing, one or more programming languages, the system development process, distributed data processing and database concepts, as well as offering electives in advanced topics.

The *computer science program* follows a slightly different route. The curriculum is more technical than that for information systems, and less oriented toward achieving practical business applications. Computer science also covers the fundamentals of computing, a programming language or two, system development, and other areas covered in this book. More emphasis is given, however, to software and hardware design.

will remain essentially invisible to the driver. Microprocessors will record the status of a car's systems, including keeping a record of when the car has been misused. Smaller, cheaper, and more powerful microprocessors will be incorporated into many items that they have not yet reached, including artificial hearts and other organs. Some experts have suggested that a notebook-sized computer capable of taking input directly from handwriting or drawing on its surface with a stylus will become commonplace by the turn of the century.

You may witness the birth of the first computers that really think. ARTIFICIAL INTELLIGENCE, which refers to efforts to capture the way humans think and learn as applied to the computer through computer programs, has been a field of lively investigation for years. Today's computers run very fast but only do one thing at a time: their "stunt," in other words, is rapid computations. Everyone knows people can do more without even trying. People reason, learn, and make decisions based upon partial or ambiguous data. People can do more than one

Both programs provide a good foundation in computers and information systems, and offer a degree that will meet the "must be college-educated" requirement of a potential employer. Business employers will probably find an information systems degree more relevant, however. If you wish to design software, the computer science degree is usually preferable.

Our comments here have been general; while they probably apply to your school, they may not. Ask your instructor about the programs available at your school.

On-the-job-training

There is another route. Computers exploded onto the scene long before computer science or information systems courses existed. People learned from others, and taught themselves, on the job. How can you receive on-the-job training today?

By getting a bachelor's degree in information systems or computer science and impressing a potential employer, you may get an entry-level job. This first job is itself viewed by the employer as training, despite the fact that you have already been trained in school.

The training is in applying your general knowledge of information systems to what the employer wants you to do.

Some larger employers have in-house training programs that you will be enrolled in; most, however, hand you a stack of manuals, let you ask questions, and bring you on board on a sort of apprenticeship basis for about a year.

Those same employers with the formal in-house training programs may also hire you without a degree, and provide you with training. This is the second on-the-job training possibility.

The third type of on-the-job training is that picked up by people who already have a job. If your work entails the use of computers, the opportunity probably exists to learn more about them on the job. It is common for users to become fascinated by the systems that serve them, and cross over into the technical side and become involved in designing those systems. It is also common for clerical employees without any formal computer training to become proficient enough in their use of a microcomputer so that they will quit their jobs and find other jobs on the basis of their computer knowledge.

thing at a time, and can deal with unknowns. The long-awaited FIFTH-GENERATION COMPUTERS being developed both in the United States and Japan may unveil machinery that can more closely do what humans do—that is, think. Perhaps, however, this will take a few more computer generations.

summary

■ The computer revolution has only begun, and different observers hold conflicting opinions about its impact upon society. People have been affected by automation and robotics, job replacement, and job displacement. Automation refers to the replacement of human control of a process by a machine. Robots today handle many dangerous, boring, and dirty jobs. Job replacement occurs when a job held by a person is taken over by a machine; job displacement when the skills necessary to perform a job change. Computers have been responsible for both.

■ On the brighter side, computers have also been associated with job enhancement. Some existing jobs have been made easier, and whole new occupations have been created. In addition, some observers claim that with the rise of distributed information systems and microcomputers, the age of the electronic cottage has begun, with people telecommuting to work via a home terminal or microcomputer.

■ Computerization has affected the rules and procedures by which businesses operate, speeding up operations and, if anything, making rules more flexible.

■ Centralized databases raise issues of the security and accuracy of data maintained about us.

■ Social issues involving software include, for the user, questions about the reliability of programs; and for the vendor, loss of revenues to software piracy. Another software issue involving all of us, is the reliance of our national defense system on software that can't be tested under live conditions.

■ Social issues involving hardware include possible environmental damage associated with the manufacture of silicon chips, and possible health hazards associated with the prolonged use of display screens.

■ Some people are expected to gain by the increasing use of computers, others to lose. Well-educated but not overly specialized people will probably adjust best. Robots will play an increasing role in the workplace.

■ Certain trends—toward telecommuting, for example—suggest that rules and procedures, at least for working patterns, may become more flexible. Other trends—for example, the ability of information systems to keep accurate track of an employee's work patterns—point in the opposite direction.

■ Database management systems will be cheaper, faster, and easier to use. The potential concentration of data about individuals in a national database, however, raises concerns about privacy.

■ Software design will become more automated through the use of computer-assisted programming tools, and programming languages may continue the trend toward natural languages. Expert systems will become available in a wide variety of fields.

■ To communicate with computers of the future we will rely more on source data automation and voice-recognition systems.

■ Computers of the future are certain to shrink in size still more, and to become faster. Current technologies leading in this direction include very-large-scale integration (VLSI) of electronic chips; microlaser-based optical circuitry; biochips; Josephson junctions; and widespread use of parallel processing computers.

■ We can expect increased use of computers in familiar settings such as the home and car.

■ Although the gap between the capabilities of computers and human thought is still vast, artificial intelligence has made strides in recent years. Fifth-generation computers may come very close to thinking like humans. And we may witness the birth of such computers.

wrap-up

The pluses and the minuses

At the behemoth Global Electrical Equipment—where George Roberts found himself heading a pilot application project that used robots as quality-control inspectors—the situation was highly charged. The robots had been on the job for a month, and the human situation was George's first concern.

George had encouraged the corporation to offer the seven displaced inspectors alternative jobs. Global had done so, offering quality-control inspection jobs at different plants. Three employees took the jobs, moving away from Oakriver to do so. The remaining employees did not want to leave Oakriver, and George negotiated a promise from management to give them priority for transfers to comparably ranked inspection positions on the assembly line. George knew well, however, that all of his people hated assembly-line work. That was why they had moved to quality control in the first place. However, the offer was the best George could manage; two employees took it, and two left in a huff.

So, out of George's fifteen employees, three had had to leave Oakriver, two to transfer to jobs they disliked, two had left to seek work elsewhere, and the remaining eight not replaced by robots could read the writing on the wall—if the experiment succeeded, the same fate awaited them. Worse, it awaited most of the quality-control inspectors throughout this plant and at other locations. Global's personnel department hired a retraining consultant, to determine whether inspectors replaced by robots could make lateral moves to other acceptable positions.

On the positive side, George rather liked the machines. He had enrolled in a course at the Automated Intelligence Institute at Oakriver University, and was beginning to understand what made robots tick. These robots had limbs, but there any resemblance to human beings ceased. They were stationary machines, with articulated "arms" able to manipulate and test a small appliance once it reached their range of operation on the assembly line. One advantage even the human coworkers had to concede was that the robots had their test instruments built right into them. This was a hard act to follow. On the other hand, the programs that controlled the robots could not cover all test situations; when a robot encountered an appliance with doubtful but not definitely negative test results, it placed the appliance to the side and called in a human inspector.

All things considered, the experiment dictated by Global's directors probably would pan out. The robots worked about 25 percent faster than people, with comparable or lower error rates. In addition, they took no lunch nor coffee breaks, and did not attempt to unionize—yet! George had not seen cost figures, but he was certain that over the long run the robots were substantially cheaper than people, needing no deductions for social security, vacations, medical insurance, and so on. Global seemed headed into the future on a track that would increase its profit margin, drop its prices, and help it remain competitive with other highly automated firms in the United States and abroad.

key terms

These are the key terms in alphabetical order. The numbers in parentheses refer to the page on which each term is defined.

Artificial intelligence (620)
Automation (605)
Biochip (619)
Fifth-generation computer (621)
Job displacement (609)
Job enhancement (609)
Job replacement (607)
Josephson junction (619)
Microlaser (619)
Parallel processing computer (619)
Robot (605)
Robotics (605)
Telecommuting (611)
Very-large-scale integration (VLSI) (619)

review questions

objective questions

True/false. *Put the letter T or F on the line next to the question.*

1. Automation refers to the replacement of human control of a process by a robot. 1 _____

2. Robotics is the study and application of robots. 2 _____

3. Job replacement occurs when a job held by a person is taken over by a robot or other machine. 3 _____

4. There are nearly 5000 computer programs available for microcomputers. 4 _____

5. Artificial intelligence is still 30 to 50 years away. 5 _____

6. Telecommuting may make it possible to reduce automobile travel by office workers. 6 _____

7. Professionals will be exempt from the impact of computers. 7 _____

8. Josephson junctions use superheated circuits to speed switching times. 8 _____

9. The electronic cottage is a form of telecommuting. 9 _____

10. Very-large-scale integration (VLSI) increases switching speeds on silicon chip circuitry. 10 _____

Multiple choice. *Put the letter of the correct answer on the line next to the question.*

1. The major producers of robots are 1 _____
 (a) Japan and the United States.
 (b) Japan and West Germany.
 (c) The Soviet Union and the United States.
 (d) The United States and Western Europe.

2. Which of the following job areas in information processing will grow the least over the next several years? 2 _____
 (a) Systems analysts.
 (b) Data-entry operators.
 (c) Computer programmers.
 (d) Computer operators.

3. Many processors working in concert to solve a problem is a feature of
  (a) Josephson junctions.
  (b) Artificial intelligence.
  (c) Robotics.
  (d) Parallel processing conputers.
4. Job displacement
  (a) Means the same as job replacement.
  (b) Is not a major concern among workers.
  (c) Occurs when the skills necessary to perform a job change.
  (d) Occurs when a job a person holds is lost to a robot or other machine.
5. Job enhancement means
  (a) Making some existing jobs easier.
  (b) Creating new occupations.
  (c) Creating new industries.
  (d) All of the above.

Fill in the blank. *Write the correct word or words in the blank to complete the sentence.*

1. The ability to work far from the office environment is known as _____.
2. The study of robots and their applications is _____.
3. A _____ may use organic molecules to store data in future computers.
4. Optical computers may use _____ to replace electronic circuitry.
5. A change in the skills required to perform a job refers to _____.
6. The _____ computers are hoped to be capable of thinking like people.
7. The _____ recalls how people worked at home in the era before the Industrial Revolution.
8. To pack great numbers of electronic components onto silicon chips, _____ is used.
9. The country of _____ produces the largest number of robots.
10. The term _____ refers to the ability of machines to think like people.

short answer questions

When answering these questions, think of concrete examples to illustrate your points.

1. What is the difference between job replacement and job displacement?
2. What industries have been created in the information age?
3. Do professionals face threats to their livelihoods from the rise of computers?
4. What is the study of robotics?
5. What impact might the electronic cottage have on society?
6. What hardware advances are expected in the coming years?
7. What is meant by the term *fifth-generation*?
8. What impact may future developments have upon rules and procedures?

essay questions

1. Who is likely to gain from projected changes in software and hardware?
2. Have computers made jobs you have held easier or more difficult?
3. Have computers had an impact upon your personal life?

Answers to the objective questions
True/false: 1. F; 2. T; 3. T; 4. F; 5. F; 6. T; 7. F; 8. F; 9. T; 10. T
Multiple choice: 1. a; 2. b; 3. d; 4. c; 5. a
Fill in the blank: 1. telecommuting; 2. robotics; 3. biochips; 4. microlasers; 5. job displacement; 6. fifth-generation; 7. electronic cottage; 8. very-large-scale integration (VLSI); 9. Japan; 10. artificial intelligence

appendix

An introduction to programming in BASIC

SECTION ONE: BASIC—Getting started
SECTION TWO: BASIC—Speeding up the process
SECTION THREE: BASIC—More techniques
BASIC Glossary and index

This appendix presents the fundamentals of the BASIC programming language. A major reason for learning a programming language in an introductory course is to gain self-confidence in working with computers. You can achieve some level of competence in programming, as well as a better understanding of the programming process, by designing and writing your own program, testing it, and correcting your mistakes. Creating a successfully executing program is a satisfying and rewarding process.

We will use the structured programming methods discussed in Chapter 14 as an aid in explaining the programming process. Once you have completed this appendix, you should have a solid beginner's knowledge of structured programming, and the ability to write simple working programs that do a variety of things.

After studying this appendix, you should understand the following:

- *How to use structured methods to design a program written in BASIC.*
- *How to create problem solutions that combine sequences, decisions, and loops.*
- *How to use some techniques to help avoid errors and to diagnose those that do occur in your programs.*
- *How to document your program design properly using internal program comments, flowcharts, and pseudocode.*
- *How to create programs that produce easy-to-read output.*

SECTION ONE

BASIC—Getting started

The program development process

Creating or altering a program, especially if it is at all complex, requires a systematic problem-solving approach. The *program development process* (introduced in the "Programming and Problem Solving" section of Chapter 14) gives us some insight into writing programs. The program development process itself is a component of the *system development process* presented in Chapter 13. Within the program development process we will use the techniques for *program design, program coding, program testing,* and *program implementation.*

We will apply the principles of structured programming to the problems presented in this appendix. The programs will be designed using a top-down modular approach, coupled with internal and external documentation to create programs that are easily followed and that can easily be modified. Our main focus will be on using structured programming methods in the area of detailed design—flowcharts and pseudocode.

Flowcharts and pseudocode

Designing the details of the program solution can be accomplished by various methods. The two that we will work with are flowcharts and pseudocode. A FLOWCHART is a diagram that shows how a program works in terms of sequence, movement of data, and logic. PSEUDOCODE is an English-like code that helps the programmer understand the steps needed to execute the program. While less impressive visually than flowcharts, pseudocode is easier to produce because we can write it using a word-processing package. Flowcharts and pseudocode accompany selected programs in this appendix.

Over the years people have come to agree which flowchart symbols should represent particular functions. Figure A1-1 illustrates the most commonly used flowchart symbols and their corresponding pseudocode phrases. Moving from left to right in the figure, you can see the desired operation, the flowchart symbol, the corresponding pseudocode phrase, and the meaning of the operation.

As shown in Chapter 14, structured programming employs three basic logic patterns:

■ SEQUENCE—a set of linear steps to be carried out in the order of their appearance.
■ SELECTION—comparisons based on decisions or choices to split the program into different paths.
■ LOOP—repetitive execution of one or more steps. There are two types of loops, DOWHILE (which continues *while* the test is true) and DOUNTIL (which repeats *until* the test is true).

Figure A1-2 expresses the basic logic patterns in both flowcharts and pseudocode. When you design programs, be sure to follow carefully any rules your instructor gives you concerning flowcharting and preparing pseudocode.

Program documentation

PROGRAM DOCUMENTATION helps the programmer (or supervisor) to understand the program. Documentation for student-oriented projects can consist of the following components:

1. A description of the problem and its significance. The description can include the variables used and their characteristics. Additionally, a written narrative describing the steps required to solve the problem can be placed in this part.
2. A description of any new or unusual programming procedures.
3. A description of the hardware used. This includes the central processor and the necessary peripheral equipment.
4. A description of the software used. Usually this is just the programming language itself and any special canned software you may have used.
5. A statement of the total programming time required to solve the problem and write the report.
6. Flowcharts or pseudocode as needed to display accurately the programming steps and patterns of the program.

Figure A1-1
Flowchart symbols and
pseudocode phrases.

Operation	Flowchart symbol	Pseudocode phrase	Meaning
System interrupt (Start, Stop)		START STOP	Notes the beginning or end of a program or subroutine
Input, output	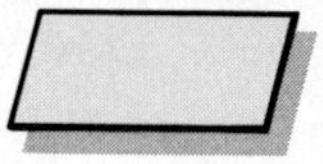	Input, get, read, print, write	All input/output operations
Process		Process, compute, calculate, initialize to a value	Process functions for arithmetic and data manipulation
Decision	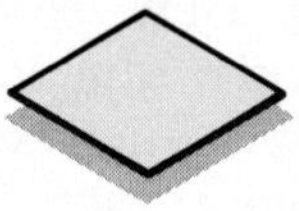	IF ... THEN, or IF ... THEN ... ELSE . . . ENDIF	Decision operations for logic tests and comparisons
Preparation		Prepare, initialize	Prepare the program for later stages, set variables to a starting value (used at the beginning of FOR/ NEXT loops in BASIC)
Predefined process		CALL, subroutine	Use of a predefined function: usually a subroutine or library routine
Annotation		Comment, note, remark, annotate	These comments provide guidance to the reader of the program, but do not affect its operation
Connector	  on-page	Not used in pseudocode	Connector to other parts of the flowchart on the same or different pages
	off-page		
Flowlines	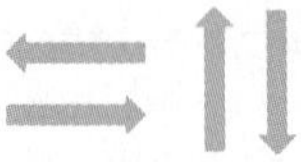	Not used in pseudocode	Shows the direction of the flow; usual flow is from top to bottom and from left to right

Figure A1-2
The logic patterns used in structured programming: sequence, selection, and loop. Both flowchart and pseudocode are shown. (a) Sequence. (b) Selection (IF/THEN/ELSE). (c) Loop.

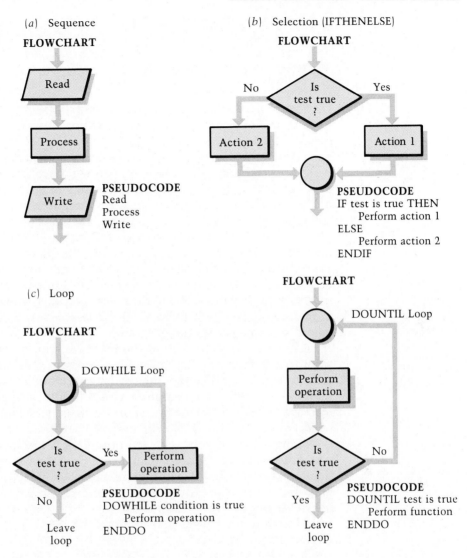

The BASIC programming language

Once we have worked out the logic of a problem using a flowchart or pseudocode, we can write and test a program to solve it. The programs will be written in BASIC (BEGINNER'S ALL-PURPOSE SYMBOLIC INSTRUCTION CODE). In the following sections, we will use programs to help explain the details of BASIC.

BASIC was developed by John G. Kemeny and Thomas Kurtz, while they were mathematics professors at Dartmouth College in the 1960s. It was designed with the novice programmer in mind. BASIC is used for a wide variety of applications in business, the scientific community, and government. Its merits relative to other languages are discussed in Chapter 15. One note of caution, there are a number of slightly different although similar versions of BASIC. We use the version of *interpreted* BASIC used with IBM and IBM-compatible microcomputers. *Therefore, the code presented in this appendix might need to be modified to work on your computer.*

Where to begin with BASIC

Let's get started. The first step in learning to use BASIC is to learn how to turn on your computer correctly. If you have not already done so, carefully read the computer instruction manual or the instructions posted at your computer lab to find the on/off switch.

Once your machine warms up, you will have to get the attention of the operating system (the programs that supervise the overall operations of the computer). Depending on your computer, the operating system may require you to perform a number of steps before you can actually get down to the business of writing or using programs. Some sample preliminary start-up procedures are shown in Figure A1-3. You tell the operating system what to do through a set of commands called SYSTEM COMMANDS. These system commands (also shown in Figure A1-3) communicate important orders to the computer, such as when you want the program you have written to be run. The other system commands help you to save and later recall programs.

After you have turned on the machine, you must tell it that you want to use the BASIC programming language. Notice again in Figure A1-3 how the BASIC programming language can be accessed using different computers. The computer will tell you through either a direct message or a change in the format of the display terminal that it is ready to accept instructions you write in the BASIC programming language.

Many systems require you to provide a name for your program if you wish to save it. How you name your programs depends on each particular system. Usually the program name can be up to eight characters long and must start with an alphabetic character. Check with your instructor about your system.

After you finish with your program, BE SURE TO SAVE IT! IT IS A GOOD IDEA TO SAVE YOUR PROGRAM OFTEN AS YOU WORK AND CERTAINLY FOR SAFE-KEEPING BEFORE YOU RUN IT. When you are keying in your program, it is stored in the CPU. Unless you save your program either on disk or on tape, the program will vanish when you turn off your computer or terminal. Then you will have to retype it all over again!

A line of BASIC

BASIC can be executed in two ways: direct and deferred. A *direct command* is executed by the computer after it is typed and the Enter key is pressed. *Deferred commands* make up a BASIC program. They are a list of steps the computer will follow when the system command *RUN* is given.

Now we are ready to try out our first line of BASIC. We simply want to print out a name. The following line prints what is enclosed within the quotation marks.

```
500   PRINT "My name is Jerry." [enter]
```

To tell your computer to run, or execute the PRINT command displayed

	Computer Systems				
	IBM PS/2 or IBM PC with Microsoft	*Hewlett-Packard 3000*	*Computers using the CP/M operating system*	*Apple II*	*Digital Equipment*
Start-up procedures:					
Power switch	Right side	Right rear	Varies	Left rear	Left rear
System response	A>	:	A>	]	Varies by model
Calling BASIC	BASICA or GWBASIC for compatibles	BASIC	MBASIC	No call required, begin typing	BASIC and system responds with READY, begin typing
System commands:					
Starting a new program called AGE	NEW Now begin typing after the OK appears	NAME AGE Now begin typing after the > appears	NAME "AGE" Now begin typing after the OK appears	NEW	NEW AGE
Listing a program	LIST	LIST	LIST	LIST	LIST
Listing lines 100-140	LIST 100-140	LIST 100-140	LIST 100-140	LIST 100-140	LIST 100-140
Running a program	RUN	RUN	RUN	RUN	RUN
Saving a new program	SAVE "AGE	SAVE	SAVE "AGE"	SAVE	SAVE
Recalling a saved old program	LOAD "AGE	GET AGE	LOAD "AGE"	LOAD AGE	OLD AGE
Saving a recalled program	SAVE "AGE	SAVE AGE	SAVE "AGE"	SAVE AGE	SAVE
Deleting a program	KILL "AGE.BAS	PURGE AGE	KILL"AGE"	DELETE AGE	UNSAVE AGE
Closing a programming session:					
You enter	SYSTEM	EXIT	SYSTEM	Nothing	BYE or GOODBYE
System response	A>	:	A>	Nothing	Varies with model
Additional user entry	None	:BYE	None	None	Varies with model
Finished	Turn power off	Turn power off	Turn power off	Turn power off	Turn power off

Figure A1-3
Important system information: start-up procedures, system commands, and closing procedures for selected systems.

on the above line, type the system command RUN and press the Enter key. When our sample line is executed by the computer, the output (response) will look like this when displayed:

```
RUN
My name is Jerry.
```

The letter "M" in this phrase will appear in the first column on your display terminal or on the printed output.

Each line of a program begins with a LINE NUMBER (500 will be used throughout as a typical line number). The line number is followed by a space and then a BASIC statement. At the end of each BASIC statement, it is necessary to depress the Enter key (sometimes indicated by an arrow pointing down and to the left). When we show the formats of BASIC statements, we will omit the [enter] at the end of each program line.

A short program

To better understand the concepts used in programming in BASIC let's look at a short program that will read a person's name, hourly salary, and hours worked this week. We will calculate the person's gross weekly pay. A heading line is used to label the output clearly and make the program easy to read. Finally, we will print out the person's name, hourly salary, hours, and gross pay. Figure A1-4 shows the program flowchart and pseudocode design, plus the list of the BASIC statements and the results of running the program.

Figure A1-4
The payroll problem:
flowchart, pseudocode,
list and run.

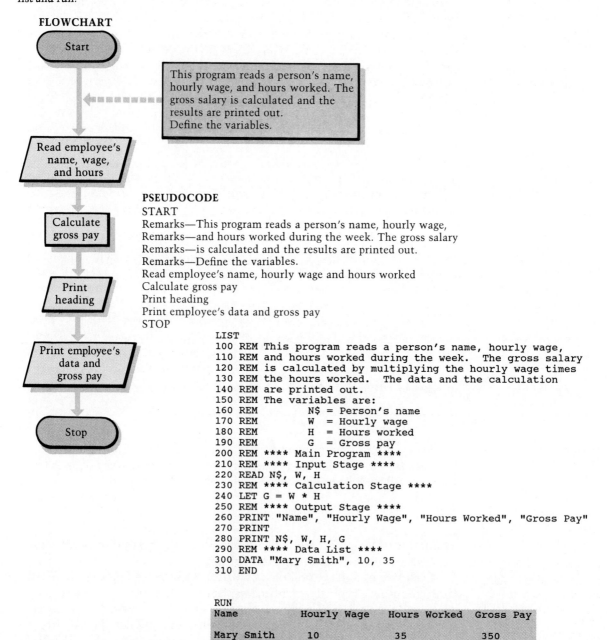

FLOWCHART

Start

This program reads a person's name, hourly wage, and hours worked. The gross salary is calculated and the results are printed out.
Define the variables.

Read employee's name, wage, and hours

Calculate gross pay

Print heading

Print employee's data and gross pay

Stop

PSEUDOCODE
START
Remarks—This program reads a person's name, hourly wage,
Remarks—and hours worked during the week. The gross salary
Remarks—is calculated and the results are printed out.
Remarks—Define the variables.
Read employee's name, hourly wage and hours worked
Calculate gross pay
Print heading
Print employee's data and gross pay
STOP

```
LIST
100 REM This program reads a person's name, hourly wage,
110 REM and hours worked during the week.  The gross salary
120 REM is calculated by multiplying the hourly wage times
130 REM the hours worked.  The data and the calculation
140 REM are printed out.
150 REM The variables are:
160 REM         N$ = Person's name
170 REM         W  = Hourly wage
180 REM         H  = Hours worked
190 REM         G  = Gross pay
200 REM **** Main Program ****
210 REM **** Input Stage ****
220 READ N$, W, H
230 REM **** Calculation Stage ****
240 LET G = W * H
250 REM **** Output Stage ****
260 PRINT "Name", "Hourly Wage", "Hours Worked", "Gross Pay"
270 PRINT
280 PRINT N$, W, H, G
290 REM **** Data List ****
300 DATA "Mary Smith", 10, 35
310 END
```

```
RUN
```

Name	Hourly Wage	Hours Worked	Gross Pay
Mary Smith	10	35	350

The line numbers allowed for BASIC range from 1 to 9999 on most computers (some accommodate higher numbers). BASIC programs begin executing the program starting with the lowest line number and, unless ordered otherwise, proceed sequentially to the highest number. For clarity, depress the space bar to leave a space after the line number. For programming ease many people start their line numbers at 100 and increase them in increments of 10 (100, 110, 120, and so forth). Incrementing by 10 each time allows you to add lines later between the ones you have already written without throwing off the sequence. Most systems will allow you to renumber the lines when you clean up your program before running and listing the final copy.

If you make a mistake keying in a character, you can always correct it. When just starting out, it might be easier to retype the line completely. Later you will have time to learn how to edit the lines you have written. If you want to erase a complete line of BASIC, simply type the line number press the Enter key and the line will be erased from memory. Depending on your system, to delete a character you can use the backspace key, a delete key, a cursor key, or the control key and H key simultaneously.

Reserved words

BASIC has a number of RESERVED WORDS, that have a special meaning to the interpreter or compiler and can only be used as intended. Be sure to spell them correctly and use them properly. The BASIC reserved words are listed in Figure A1-5.

Character set

In BASIC we use a CHARACTER SET consisting of upper- and lowercase letters, the decimal numbers 0 to 9, and special symbols. We shall explain these symbols as we encounter them.

Constants

Two types of values are used in BASIC: constants and variables. CONSTANTS do not change during execution. There are two types of constants of interest to us: character strings and numeric constants. CHARACTER STRING CONSTANTS (also called *string constants* or *literals*) are enclosed in quotation marks. Examples include:

```
"a"
"Greetings"
"My name is Jerry"
"67-435-23"
```

Character string constants can contain up to 255 characters.

Figure A1-5
Selected reserved words in BASIC. Reserved words include all BASIC commands, statements, function names, and operator names. Reserved words cannot be used as variable names.

ABS	DIM	IF	NEXT	RND	TAN
AND	ELSE	IMAGE	OR	SGN	THEN
ATN	END	INPUT	PRINT	SIN	TIMER
CLEAR	EXP	INT	RANDOMIZE	SQR	TO
CLS	FOR	LET	READ	STEP	USING
COS	GOSUB	LOG	REM	STOP	WEND
DATA	GOTO	LPRINT	RETURN	TAB	WHILE

NUMERIC CONSTANTS can be integers, real numbers with decimal places, or real numbers written in floating-point form. These include:

4434	an integer
24.455	a real number in decimal form
2.4455E + 2	the floating-point or "scientific-notation" form where 2.4455×10^2 equals 244.55

Most of the problems in this appendix will deal with numbers in decimal form.

Numeric and character variables

While some programs use only constants, most problems involve variables as well. A VARIABLE is a symbol that can take on different values, either numeric or alphabetic. Two major types of variables are used in BASIC:

1. **NUMERIC VARIABLES.** These are represented by a single alphabetic character, such as A, Y, or W; by an alphabetic character combined with a number, such as A1, E3, or X7; or (in some systems) by combinations of up to 40 alphabetic characters and numbers, such as WEIGHT25, TEST1, or FIRSTENCOUNTER.

2. **CHARACTER STRING VARIABLES.** These are represented by combinations of letters, symbols, and numbers ending with a $. The $ tells the computer that the variable is a character string. Examples include H$, X1$, or THISISMYNAME$. Character string variables can represent a single character or several words (up to a total length of 255 characters).

Some systems will not accept variable names that are longer than one letter plus one number and the $ symbol. Check to see if yours is such a system.

The reason we need to identify character strings differently from numbers is that the computer stores each type of value in a different way. If the computer accidentally encounters an alphabetic value where a numeric value is expected, a data format error message is generated—after all, how could you take the square root of your name?

Simple statements

We will now look at the most commonly used BASIC statements. Where possible the relevant statements used in the payroll problem are used as examples (refer to Figure A1-4).

REM statement

REM is a nonexecutable command for writing remarks or comments. The general form of the REM statement is

500 REM *remark*

For example, look over the first lines from the payroll program:

```
100 REM This program reads a person's name, hourly wage,
110 REM and hours worked during the week.  The gross salary
120 REM is calculated by multiplying the hourly wage times
130 REM the hours worked.  The data and the calculation
140 REM are printed out.
150 REM The variables are:
160 REM          N$ = Person's name
170 REM          W  = Hourly wage
180 REM          H  = Hours worked
190 REM          G  = Gross pay
```

Comment statements, which appear in a listing of a program, help the programmer or other people understand what the program is all about. Sometimes the date on which the program was last modified and the programmers' names are given in the REM statements. Often a brief description of the variable names, formulas, and other features of the program are provided. Additional REM statements are frequently interspersed throughout the program to delineate the various modules for input, processing, and output, as well as to make the program *list* more readable to the programmer. However, the computer does not need REM statements to *execute* the program, nor do REM statements appear in the output when the program is run.

LET statement (Assignment statement)

To perform processing upon data, we must first get the data into the program. The data values must be assigned to variables. There are three ways in which a BASIC program accepts data: (1) by using a LET statement, (2) by using a READ statement, and (3) by using an INPUT statement. READ and INPUT statements will be discussed in the next sections.

The **LET** statement is used to assign values to different variables. It is commonly called the **ASSIGNMENT STATEMENT**. The assignment operator in BASIC is the equal sign (=). The general form of the LET statement is

500 LET *variable = expression*

or without even keying LET

500 *variable = expression*

THE EQUAL SIGN DOES NOT CARRY THE SAME MEANING AS IN ALGEBRA! On the left side of the equal sign is one variable, and on the right of the sign the expression can range from simply another variable or a constant to a complicated mathematical formula. The value of the expression on the right is assigned or placed into the variable on the left.

In the payroll example line 240 demonstrates a LET statement.

```
230 REM **** Calculation Stage ****
240 LET G = W * H
```

In this case the variable for the hourly wage (W) is multiplied (*) by the variable for the hours worked (H) and assigned to the variable for the gross pay (G).

The expression to the right of the equal sign can be either a constant, a variable, or some combination of constants and variables. Both numeric and string constants and variables can be used in LET statements. Some examples of LET statements are given in the table:

LET statement	Meaning
200 LET X = 6	The numeric constant 6 is assigned to the numeric variable X.
400 LET N$ = "Hot"	The character string constant "Hot" is assigned to the character string variable N$.
500 LET H = A + B	The sum of numeric variables A and B is assigned to the numeric variable H.
700 LET X = X + 1	The current value of X is incremented by 1.
1000 LET G$ = M$	The contents of the character string variable M$ is assigned to the character string variable G$.

Mathematical expressions in LET statements in BASIC follow the same precedence (order of operation) rules you have learned in math classes. Figure A1-6 shows the arithmetic operators used with LET statements. Exponentiation (indicated by the symbols ** or ^) has the highest precedence, and so is performed first if present. The next highest are division (/) and multiplication (*), followed by addition (+) and subtraction (−). If two operators of equal precedence are present, they are performed in order from left to right.

Parentheses are used for clarity or to change the precedence. Expressions are solved inside the innermost parentheses first, working out-

Figure A1-6
Hierarchy of mathematical operators and examples in BASIC from highest to lowest.

Operation	Algebraic form	BASIC form	Example
( ) or [ ]	$[(A + B)(A − B)]/C$	100 LET X = ((A + B)*(A − B))/C	$((7 + 2) * (7 − 2))/4 = 11.25$
Exponentiation	A^x	200 LET Z = A^X 200 LET Z = A**X	$3 \wedge 2 = 9$
Multiplication	$(A)(B)$ or $A \times B$	300 N = A*B	$7 * 2 = 14$
Division (real numbers)	A/B	400 P = A/B	$7/2 = 3.5$
Addition	$A + B$	500 R = A + B	$7 + 2 = 9$
Subtraction	$A − B$	600 Q = A − B	$7 − 2 = 5$

ward. Both the left and right parentheses must be used. For example, just as 1 + 2/3 is not the same as (1 + 2)/3, the expression A + B/C will give different results than (A + B)/C. A helpful mnemonic device is the sentence *"Please excuse my dear Aunt Sally."*

An important rule: A legal LET statement must have *only one variable to the left of the equal sign.* Freely translated, this means "place the value on the right of the equal sign into the memory location named by the variable on the left side." This is a legal statement:

```
200 LET Z = ((A + B) * (A - B))/C
```

These are illegal statements:

```
300 LET 6 = W      Numeric constant on left side of = sign.
400 LET X^D = A    Two variables on left side of = sign.
```

Simplifying the LET command
Most BASIC packages allow you to write LET statements in a shorthand style, by dropping the word LET from the statement. The statement

```
240 LET G = W * H
```

can be rewritten as

```
240 G = W * H
```

Two other useful commands are CLEAR and CLS. The CLEAR statement sets all numeric values to zero and all character strings to "null." It is written as

```
500 CLEAR
```

The CLEAR command works pretty much like the "clear" key on your calculator—it erases from your computer's main memory any stored variable data associated with your program. The CLEAR statement is usually the first non-REM statement in your program.

The CLS statement clears any image on your display screen. It is written as

```
500 CLS
```

The CLS command is often used in interactive programs.

READ/DATA statements

The READ statement tells the computer to assign data contained within a DATA statement to specific variables. The general form for the READ statement is

```
500 READ variable(s)
```

Because READ statements require DATA statements, they are often linked together as READ/DATA statements. DATA statements are non-executable—they simply hold data values called constants. The general form for the DATA statement is

```
500 DATA constant(s)
```

Since data are prespecified, the computer need only search until it finds the first available data (stored on the DATA line).

In the payroll problem line 220 reads the data contained on line 300.

```
210 REM **** Input Stage ****
220 READ N$, W, H
   .
   .
   .
290 REM **** Data List ****
300 DATA "Mary Smith", 10, 35
```

Figure A1-7 shows another example of a program using READ/DATA statements. It reads in Ms. Barker's data and prints them out.

The structure of the READ line requires that each variable be separated by a comma. The DATA line also follows certain rules. All data items on a line must be separated by commas. There is no comma after the last data item on the data line. Character strings must be enclosed by quotation marks on most systems. Whenever there are commas, or leading or trailing blanks (careful: using commas in this way may generate errors on some systems) in a data item, it must be enclosed in quotation marks; for example:

Figure A1-7
Program using READ/DATA.

```
LIST
100 REM  This a program using READ/DATA commands.
110 REM  The variables are:
120 REM          N$ = Student name
130 REM          A  = Student age
140 REM          M$ = Student major
150 REM          Y$ = Year in school
160 REM          C$ = Home city
170 REM ***** Main Program *****
180 REM ***** Input Stage  *****
190 READ N$, A, M$, Y$, C$
200 REM ***** Output Stage *****
210 PRINT "Student Data Report"
220 PRINT
230 PRINT "Student name   ----- "; N$
240 PRINT "Student age  ------- "; A
250 PRINT "Student major  ----- "; M$
260 PRINT "Year in school ----- "; Y$
270 PRINT "Home city  --------- "; C$
280 PRINT
290 PRINT
300 PRINT "End of Program"
310 REM ***** Data List *****
320 DATA "Cassandra Barker",25,"Business","Senior","Montreal"
330 END
```

```
RUN
Student Data Report

Student name   -----   Cassandra Barker
Student age  -------    25
Student major  -----   Business
Year in school -----   Senior
Home city  ---------   Montreal


End of Program
```

```
2000 DATA "Lansing, Michigan"
```

Here are several more examples of READ and DATA statements. The first example shows how to read two numeric variables:

```
100 READ A, B
910 DATA 12.3, 23
```

The values of the constants 12.3 and 23 are stored in the spots reserved for variables A and B:

A	B	←Variables
12.3	23	←Values

The second example reads in a combination of numeric and character strings:

```
200 READ E, G$, S$, T
1000 DATA 45.76, "Tony Andress", "Male", 23
```

The values stored in the computer's memory are

E	G$	S$	T	←Variables
45.76	Tony Andress	Male	23	←Values

After a value is stored for a variable using a READ statement, the value can be changed later by executing a second READ statement. The old value is replaced by the new data. To illustrate, let's read two variables (N$ and A) twice. The first READ line (200) assigns the string Sue and the number 12.4 to the variables. The second READ line (230) then assigns Donna and 56.1 to the respective variables, "erasing" the earlier data in the computer's memory.

```
200 READ N$, A
210 PRINT N$, A
220 PRINT
230 READ N$, A
240 PRINT N$, A
900 DATA "Sue", 12.4
910 DATA "Donna", -56.1
9999 END
```

```
RUN
Sue          12.4

Donna        -56.1
```

Beginning students often have problems with errors concerning READ/DATA statements. The three most common errors are:

- Data format or type mismatch errors
- Attempting to read nonexistent data
- Incorrect values for the data

A data format, or type mismatch error, is a syntax error that occurs when the computer cannot match the data with the type specified in the READ statement (as when character string data are read into a real number variable location). Consider the following:

```
350 READ N$, A
900 DATA "John Smith", "Terance Davis"
```

Running a program with these lines would generate a syntax error message (usually: Syntax Error line 900) because "A" is a real variable whereas "Terance Davis" is a character string.

The second problem concerns trying to read more data than actually exist in your DATA statements:

```
560 READ B, T, W4
1000 DATA 442.3, 41
```

The attempt to read the third number fails, resulting in an "Out of DATA in 560" message.

Finally, if you enter the wrong data in the DATA statement, you will have the wrong values stored for the variable. (For example, when you enter the number 12 instead of 102.) This condition is the most dangerous because NO ERROR MESSAGE IS PROVIDED!

INPUT statement

With the INPUT statement the data will be entered as the program is executed. The general form of the INPUT statement is

500 INPUT *variable(s)*

or

500 INPUT *"prompt" variables*

where a prompt will be displayed to assist the user. Prompts are brief instructions that tell a person when to input.

When the system comes to an INPUT statement, the computer will display a question mark on the screen, then pause and wait for your response (usually from your keyboard). The INPUT statement can be used for keying in responses requiring numeric data, alphanumeric data, or a combination of the two.

When using INPUT a prompt should be used to instruct the user as to what to do. Prompts should be written to guide the users, not confuse them.

Here is an example of an INPUT statement with a prompt:

```
150 INPUT "What is your name"; N$
```

It would produce this prompt when the program is run:

```
What is your name?_      (The cursor would be flashing here.)
```

The person at the keyboard would type in his or her name and then press the Enter key to continue with whatever the program does next.

```
What is your name? Tobias Hamilton
```

INPUT statements can be utilized in a variety of ways. In the simplest case, you can use an INPUT statement to input a single variable:

```
250 INPUT F
```

As a response the computer will output:

```
?
```

In response to the question mark, you type in a real number. You can input both a numeric variable and a character string variable in this way:

```
350 INPUT K, K$
?
```

In response to the question mark, you type in a real number, then a comma followed by the character string (which on most systems is not enclosed within quotation marks). For example, you might type:

```
? 241.9, "Tobias Hamilton"
```

These two examples underscore the need to accompany input statements with prompts. To let the user know how to respond to the question mark, you should include screen prompts in the program. For example, the prompt can be displayed using a PRINT statement:

```
450 PRINT "In response to the question,"
460 PRINT "type in two numbers separated by a comma."
470 PRINT "When you are done, press the Enter key."
480 INPUT A, B
```

would produce this output:

```
In response to the question,
type in two numbers separated by a comma.
When you are done, press the Enter key.
? 424.0, 47
```

Or, recalling the first example, a prompt can also be incorporated onto a single line. For example,

```
150 INPUT "What is your name"; N$
What is your name? Tobias Hamilton
```

Input statements using prompts with semicolons permit you to type the data onto the same line as the prompt. The question mark need not be typed into the prompt because the INPUT command automatically displays a question mark. Replacing the semicolon with a comma in line 150 suppresses the automatic question mark.

Type mismatch errors in entry are usually detected automatically by the computer. An error message typically written as REDO FROM START will appear when you try to assign a character string value to a numeric variable. Unfortunately, in some cases, forgetting to fully answer the prompt or entering incorrect data might not be detected.

INPUT and READ/DATA statements can be used in the same program. For example, you might use READ/DATA statements to enter raw data into the program. Your responses to INPUT commands might then determine what processing operations should be performed on the data. You could use READ/DATA, for example, to enter a series of numbers, and the INPUT response to indicate whether you want to take an average of the numbers or find and display the highest number read in.

PRINT statement

The **PRINT** and **LPRINT** statements control the type and format of output at both the display terminal and the printer. PRINT and LPRINT statements can be used to print character strings, numeric values, constants, or combinations of all three (technically called *parameters*). On many microcomputer systems, the LPRINT statement is used to direct output exclusively to the printer. On those types of systems, the PRINT statement affects only the display screen. The general form of the PRINT and LPRINT statements are

500 PRINT *list of parameters*

or

500 LPRINT *list of parameters*

In the payroll problem the PRINT lines are used to print a heading (line 260), to skip a line (line 270), and to print the data and the calculation (line 280).

```
250 REM **** Output Stage ****
260 PRINT "Name", "Hourly Wage", "Hours Worked", "Gross Pay"
270 PRINT
280 PRINT N$, W, H, G
```

When this program is run, the PRINT statements will direct the results to the computer screen. By pressing the Shift and Print Screen (PrtSc) keys on most computers, the entire screen can be copied to the printer to provide you with a hard copy.

There are many times programmers wish to direct results to the printer as part of the program instructions. To accomplish this, they can add LPRINT lines to their program. For instance, we can insert LPRINT statements to send the person's name and gross pay to the printer as well.

```
250 REM **** Output Stage ****
260 PRINT "Name", "Hourly Wage", "Hours Worked", "Gross Pay"
265 LPRINT "Name", "Gross Pay"
270 PRINT
275 LPRINT
280 PRINT N$, W, H, G
285 LPRINT N$, G
```

Let's look at some examples of PRINT and LPRINT. To print a constant or literal expression, enclose what you want printed in quotation marks ("). The first character, number, or blank after the opening quotation mark is printed in the first column. Here is an example of a BASIC PRINT statement and the resulting output:

```
100 PRINT "This is a literal statement."
This is a literal statement.
```

To skip a line, simply key in the word PRINT after the line number. This will print or display a blank line, which can help make your output more readable. An example is

```
200 PRINT
```

To skip two lines you could type

```
200 LPRINT:LPRINT
```

The colon (:) between the LPRINTs tells the BASIC program the command to the right of the colon is on the "next" line. This command can be used to reduce the length of your program on the display screen. *Warning:* Using the colon in complicated parts of your program should be avoided.

To print the value of a single variable, name the variable in your PRINT statement. Here is an example that prints the variable X, which currently has a value of 23.45:

```
300 PRINT X
 23.45
```

Note: The value 23.45 is printed starting in the second column. This is because the first column is reserved for the sign ("+" or "−"), which in this case is "+" and is implied but not printed.

Commas and semicolons, separating the variables and literals, can be used to control the placement of the output on a line. Most printers and screens are divided into five zones, although the number varies from system to system. The use of commas activates the default feature (assumptions made by the computer) for single-line placement of output in these zones. Usually the zones are 13 or 14 columns wide with a space after each zone. The examples in this book use 14-column zones with one space between each. Because the zones are only 14 columns wide, long character strings such as peoples' names or street addresses can create unwieldy-looking results using this method of spacing output. With 14-column zones and a one-space separation the zones start in columns 1, 16, 31, 46, and 61. With a 13-column format the zones start in columns 1, 15, 29, 43, and 57.

Let's see how we can print five numeric constants using zones (of course, character string constants and numeric or string variables may be handled in the same way). Here is a statement to print the values 13.5, −67, 46, 487, and 24.3. The output is shown on the line below the PRINT statement.

```
400 PRINT 13.5, -67, 46, 487, 24.3
 13.5          -67           46              487           24.3
```

Another example of zones would be a student's name and several pieces of data concerning her. We want to print out her name, age, major in school, year in school, and place of birth. The actual data are: Cassandra Barker, 25, Business, Senior, Montreal. Because Ms. Barker's name is too long for a 14-column print zone, we must use two print zones to hold it. As a result the output is printed on two lines:

```
500 PRINT "Cassandra Barker", 25, "Business", "Senior", "Montreal"
Cassandra Barker              25              Business      Senior
Montreal
```

If we must fit all the data into the first five print zones, we would need to abbreviate her first name:

```
C. Barker       25            Business      Senior          Montreal
```

Semicolons in a PRINT line override the print zone default procedure. In general, if you mix literals and variables in the same output line, you can achieve a more readable and attractive display using semicolons instead of commas. Here's an example using semicolons to display Ms. Barker's data on a printer:

```
600 LPRINT "Cassandra Barker"; 25; "Business"; "Senior"; "Montreal"
    Cassandra Barker   25   Business Senior Montreal
```

Note that with some systems, to achieve properly spaced output using semicolons, you have to add a space to the string constant. In other words,

```
700 PRINT "Cassandra Barker "; 25; "Business "; "Senior "; "Montreal"
```

The five numeric constants shown earlier could be printed close together, with a column skipped between each variable, with this statement (not counting the sign):

```
800 LPRINT 13.5; -67; 46; 487; 24.3
    13.5 -67   46   487   24.3
```

Our final example shows a combination of constants and variables. Notice that with this format it is necessary to insert extra spaces (by enclosing spaces within quotation marks) before or after the letters in the constant expression to create the desired attractive output display. In this example the value of N$ is Penny Brown and the value of S is 83,

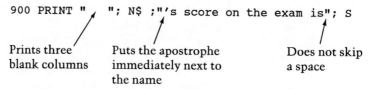

```
900 PRINT "   "; N$ ;"'s score on the exam is"; S
```

Prints three blank columns   Puts the apostrophe immediately next to the name   Does not skip a space

The output from this statement is

```
    Penny Brown's score on the exam is 83
```

Later in this appendix we will learn about additional features we can combine with the PRINT and LPRINT commands.

END statement

The **END** statement is not required for most BASIC programs, but it is good practice to use it. An example of an END statement is

```
9999 END
```

On a few systems if you forget an END statement, it will be impossible to save your program for later use. Even though the system used to create the programs given in this appendix does not require this statement, it has been included, since forgetting it on a different system could be fatal to your program.

The END statement should always have the highest line number of any statement in the program. People commonly assign the END statement a line number of 9999, well above any line number you are likely to use. *A word of caution:* If the line number for your END statement is lower than the numbers of some of the other lines, the higher numbered lines could be permanently lost when you attempt to save your program on some systems.

wrap-up program

Calculate a customer's bill

This program requires you to use a READ/ DATA combination. It calculates the bill for a single customer. The total cost is calculated as the product of the item quantity and the item cost. Then the output is printed in a clear format. Figure A1-8 illustrates a possi- ble solution to this problem. Observe how the character strings are read in and then dis- played in the output. The cost calculation is shown in line 290 and is blocked off by REM statements. Use the following data. *Note:* Zip code is a string variable.

Customer and Address: Bits and Bytes 67 Main Street Last Chance Nevada 89133	Item Name: Microprocessor Item Quantity: 1500 Item Price: $ 6.85

FLOWCHART

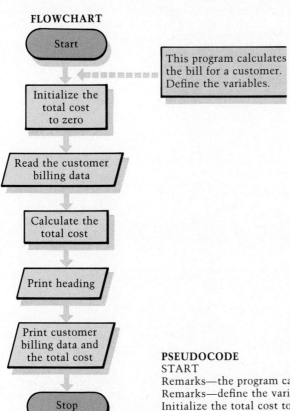

Figure A1-8
Flowchart, pseudocode, list and run for the Sec- tion One wrap-up pro- gram.

PSEUDOCODE
START
Remarks—the program calculates the bill for a customer
Remarks—define the variables
Initialize the total cost to zero
Read the customer billing data
Calculate the total cost
Print heading
Print the customer billing data and the total cost
STOP

wrap-up
program

Figure A1-8
(continued)

```
LIST
100 REM   This program will bill one customer.
110 REM   First we will assign the company a name,
120 REM   then we will enter the data from data statements.
130 REM   The variables are:
140 REM       N$ = The name of the company
150 REM       A$ = The street address of the company
160 REM       C$ = The city of the company
170 REM       S$ = The state of the company
180 REM       I$ = The name of the item the customer wants
190 REM       Z$ = The zip code of the customer
200 REM       Q  = The quantity of the item
210 REM       T  = The total cost of the order
220 REM       C  = The cost of the item order
230 REM **** Main Program ****
240 REM **** Initialize Variable ****
250 LET T = 0
260 REM **** Input Stage ****
270 READ N$, A$, C$, S$, Z$, I$, Q, C
280 REM **** Process Stage ****
290 LET T = C * Q
300 REM **** Output Stage ****
310 LPRINT "This program calculates the bill for one customer."
320 LPRINT
330 LPRINT "Customer and Address:"
340 LPRINT
350 LPRINT N$
360 LPRINT A$
370 LPRINT C$; " "; S$; "  "; Z$
380 LPRINT
390 LPRINT
400 LPRINT "Purchase data:"
410 LPRINT
420 LPRINT "Item: "; I$
430 LPRINT "Quantity:"; Q
440 LPRINT "Cost: $"; C
450 LPRINT "The total cost of the order: $"; T
460 LPRINT
470 LPRINT
480 LPRINT "End of Program."
490 REM **** Data List ****
500 DATA "Bits and Bytes", "67 Main Street"
510 DATA "Last Chance", "Nevada", "89133"
520 DATA "Microprocessor", 1500, 6.85
530 END
Ok
```

```
This program calculates the bill for one customer.

Customer and Address:

Bits and Bytes
67 Main Street
Last Chance Nevada  89133


Purchase data:

Item: Microprocessor
Quantity: 1500
Cost: $ 6.85
The total cost of the order: $ 10275


End of Program.
```

key terms

These are the key terms in alphabetical order. The numbers in parentheses refer to the page on which each term is defined.

Assignment statement (A-11)
BASIC (Beginner's All-purpose Symbolic Instruction Code) (A-5)
Character set (A-9)
Character string constant (A-9)
Character string variable (A-10)
CLEAR (A-13)
CLS (A-13)
Constant (A-9)
DATA (A-13)
END (A-20)
Flowchart (A-3)
INPUT (A-16)
LET (A-11)
Line number (A-7)
Loop (A-3)
LPRINT (A-18)
Numeric constant (A-10)
Numeric variable (A-10)
PRINT (A-18)
Program documentation (A-3)
Pseudocode (A-3)
READ (A-13)
REM (A-10)
Reserved word (A-9)
Selection (A-3)
Sequence (A-3)
System command (A-6)
Variable (A-10)

review questions

objective questions

Multiple choice. *Put the letter of the correct answer on the line next to the question.*

1. For character strings, which of the following is not a valid variable name?   1 _____
   (a) N$
   (b) NAME$
   (c) N
   (d) N1$
2. Which LET statement is incorrect?   2 _____
   (a) 100 LET W + 10 = Z
   (b) 200 LET Q = W - 12.4
   (c) 300 N$ = M$
   (d) 400 Z = (10*X)^2
3. If W = 9, what value will X be assigned in the following?   3 _____
   660 LET X = ((3 + W)^2 + W^.5)
   (a) 28.5
   (b) 87
   (c) 147
   (d) 148.5
4. Which operation will be performed first?   4 _____
   (a) Exponentiation
   (b) Multiplication
   (c) Addition
   (d) Subtraction
5. Which statement can be used to assign values to a variable.   5 _____
   (a) The READ statement.
   (b) The INPUT statement.
   (c) The LET statement.
   (d) All of the above answers are correct.

review questions

short answer questions

1. What is the reason we might use semicolons in PRINT statements?
2. When would an INPUT statement be preferred over READ statements?
3. Write the READ statement to read the following data.

NAME	WEIGHT (KG.)	HEIGHT (CM.)
Tom Herbert	85	190
Linda Jones	50	160
Del Torres	75	180

4. Write a PRINT statement to print out the data in question 3.
5. Given that 2.2 pounds = 1 kilogram, write a LET statement to convert the kilogram weights to pounds in question 3.

programming exercises

1. Write a program to read and print your name, weight, and age.
2. The Testing Office at Oakriver University has administered 500 advanced-standing tests; 150 failed the test. Write a program to find out what percentage passed.
3. Write a program to solve the following. Larry Dumas is a passenger on Fly-By-Night Airlines flight 131 from Los Angeles to New York. His ticket costs $150. There is a 6 percent sales tax and a 1.5 percent airport security tax. Both taxes are assessed against the price of the ticket. Write a program to input the ticket price, calculate the separate taxes, and print the subtotals and total bill. Be sure to label your answer.
4. Read in the following data, and convert Ms. Jones's height and weight to inches and pounds respectively.

	Kgs.	Cms.
Linda Jones	50	160

Remember that 1 kilogram = 2.2 pounds, and 1 centimeter = 0.3937 inches.

Answers to the objective questions

Multiple choice: 1. c; 2. a; 3. c; 4. a; 5. d
Short answer: 1. We use semicolons in a PRINT statement to override the print zones to create better-looking output. 2. INPUT statements are preferred over DATA statements when the exact data are not known at the time of program creation—as in interactive programming.
3. 200 READ N$, W, H
4. 400 PRINT N$ W, H
or 400 LPRINT N$, W, H
5. LET P = W * 2.2

SECTION TWO

BASIC—Speeding up the process

Up to this point we have looked at programs that execute in a sequential manner. Many programming problems, however, require making choices (selection), repeating steps again and again (looping), and creating easy to read output. In this section we will learn how to create programs using selection and looping procedures. We will discuss the IF/THEN/ELSE statements for selection and looping, the GOSUB/RETURN statements for subroutines, and how to create attractive output through the use of PRINT TAB AND PRINT USING statements.

Selection procedures

The IF/THEN/ELSE statements

IF/THEN/ELSE statements are used for decisions. Often we refer to these statements together as the IF/THEN statement or the IF/THEN/ELSE statement. The IF/THEN/ELSE statement is used for a wide variety of selection procedures as well as loop control operations.

The general form of the IF/THEN/ELSE statement is

$$500 \text{ IF } \begin{Bmatrix} expression \\ is\ true \end{Bmatrix} \text{ THEN } \begin{Bmatrix} perform\ an \\ operation \end{Bmatrix} \text{ ELSE } \begin{Bmatrix} perform\ another \\ operation \end{Bmatrix}$$

"Perform an operation" can be either a BASIC expression or a line number. If the operation is a BASIC expression, it is executed directly and the program continues at the following line. If a line number is provided, the program branches to that line number and execution of the program continues from there.

In the following example, students (denoted by the variable N$) who are eligible for an award if they earned a grade (denoted by the variable G) of "B" or better (equal to or greater than a score of 80) in their senior seminar will have their names printed out with the phrase "AWARD WINNER." Non-award winners will have only their names printed out.

```
100 IF G >= 80 THEN PRINT N$,"AWARD WINNER" ELSE PRINT N$
```

If ELSE is not available on your system, the statement can be rewritten using two IF/THEN statements:

```
100 IF G >= 80 THEN PRINT N$,"AWARD WINNER"
110 IF G < 80  THEN PRINT N$
```

following the general form:

$$500 \text{ IF } \begin{Bmatrix} expression \\ is\ true \end{Bmatrix} \text{ THEN } \begin{Bmatrix} perform\ one \\ operation \end{Bmatrix}$$

IF/THEN/ELSE statements can even be nested within one another; that is, an IF/THEN/ELSE statement can be one of the operations to perform.

Within the IF/THEN/ELSE statement, the expression is tested using either relational or logical operators. A RELATIONAL OPERATOR compares two values. One numeric value is compared against another numeric value, or a character string value is compared with another character string value. The inequality symbols ($<$, $<=$, $>$, $>=$) and the equality and nonequality symbols ($=$, $<>$) are known as relational operators.

Since numbers can be arranged from smallest to largest, they can be compared with each other. For example, 2 is less than 6 ($2 < 6$) and 21 is greater than 14 ($21 > 14$). Similarly, character strings can be ordered by alphabetizing them. So "ab" is less than "ba" ("ab" $<$ "ba") and "cat" is greater than "bird" ("cat" $>$ "bird"). In addition, lowercase letters are given higher values than uppercase letters so that "bird" is greater than "CAT" ("bird" $>$ "CAT").

LOGICAL OPERATORS (AND, OR) test on a true/false basis. Logical operators are called BOOLEAN OPERATORS and are often used to combine two or more relational operators into compound relations. Figure A2-1 shows a number of relational and logical operators.

Figure A2-1
Relational and logical
operators used with IF/
THEN/ELSE statements.

Expression	*Symbol*	*Meaning when the test is true*
Less than	<	The value is less than the test condition.
Less than or equal to	<=	The value is less than or equal to the test condition.
Equal to	=	The value is exactly equal to the test condition.
Greater than or equal to	>=	The value is greater than or equal to the test condition.
Greater than	>	The value is greater than the test condition.
Not equal to	<>	The value is not equal to the test condition.
Logical OR	OR	At least one condition in the test must be met.
Logical AND	AND	All conditions in the test must be met.

Here are some examples using relational and logical operators to demonstrate their use. In the following statement:

```
100  IF A < B THEN PRINT "Hello" ELSE PRINT "Goodbye"
```

if A is less than B, then "Hello" is printed, while if A is greater than or equal to B, "Goodbye" is printed. Compare this with the example

```
200  IF C >= 450 THEN LET D = K^2 ELSE LET D = K^3
```

If C is greater than or equal to 450, then $D = K^2$, while if C is less than 450, then $D = K^3$.

For the example

```
300  IF N$ = "last name" THEN 1210 ELSE 230
```

N$ must equal "last name" exactly ("Last Name" and "LAST NAME" are not acceptable). So if N$ does equal "last name" then the program continues executing at line 1210; otherwise it continues at 230.

Another example of branching in an IF/THEN/ELSE statement is

```
400  IF E$ = "END OF DATA" THEN 900
```

This means that if the string variable E$ equals "END OF DATA", then the program will go to line 900. This is useful to end programs in certain situations. For example, line 900 could contain the END statement.

For nonequality, we have

```
500  IF HOME$ <> "APT" THEN PRINT NAME$
```

If a person's home is not an apartment (abbreviated "APT"), then that person's name is printed.

The following examples illustrate compound relational statements. In the statement

```
600  IF AGE < 21 OR HEIGHT > 65 THEN PRINT STUDENT$
```

FLOWCHART

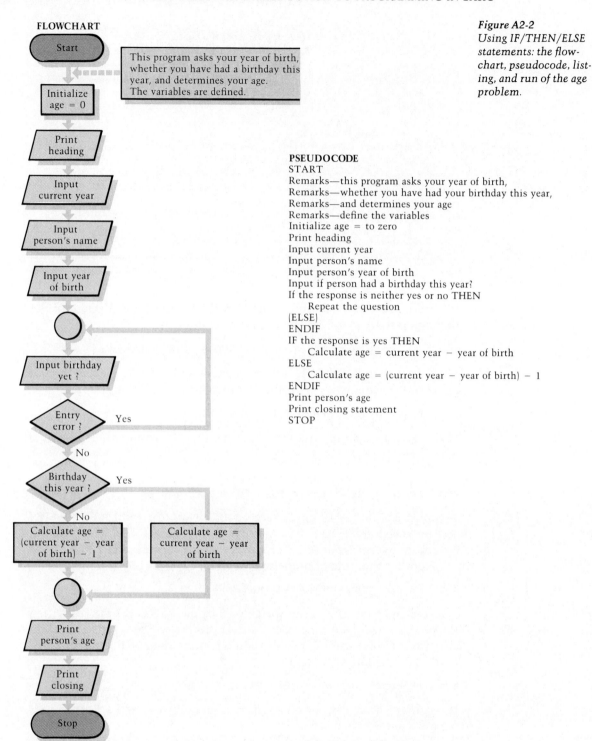

Figure A2-2
Using IF/THEN/ELSE statements: the flowchart, pseudocode, listing, and run of the age problem.

This program asks your year of birth, whether you have had a birthday this year, and determines your age. The variables are defined.

PSEUDOCODE
START
Remarks—this program asks your year of birth,
Remarks—whether you have had your birthday this year,
Remarks—and determines your age
Remarks—define the variables
Initialize age = to zero
Print heading
Input current year
Input person's name
Input person's year of birth
Input if person had a birthday this year?
If the response is neither yes or no THEN
    Repeat the question
(ELSE)
ENDIF
IF the response is yes THEN
    Calculate age = current year − year of birth
ELSE
    Calculate age = (current year − year of birth) − 1
ENDIF
Print person's age
Print closing statement
STOP

```
LIST
100 REM  This program will ask your name and what year
110 REM  you were born in.  Then the program will calculate
120 REM your age.
130 REM The variables are:
140 REM     N$ = Your name
150 REM     A$ = Birthday this year
160 REM     Y  = Your year of birth
170 REM     A  = Your age
180 REM     C  = Current year
190 REM **** Main Program ****
200 REM **** Initialize Variable ****
210 LET A = 0
220 REM **** Input Stage ****
230 PRINT
240 PRINT "This program will ask your name and year of birth,"
250 PRINT "then it will print your age."
260 PRINT
270 PRINT "What year is it";
280 INPUT C
290 PRINT
300 INPUT "What is your name? ", N$
310 PRINT
320 PRINT "Well, ";N$;", in what year were you born";
330 INPUT Y
340 PRINT
350 PRINT "Answer yes or no:  Have you had your birthday this year";
360 INPUT A$
370 REM  The next line catches errors in answering the question
380 REM  and sends the user back to line 350 to reask the question
390 IF A$ <> "yes" AND A$ <> "no" THEN 350
400 REM **** Process Stage ****
410 IF A$ = "yes" THEN LET A = C - Y
420 IF A$ = "no" THEN LET A = C - Y - 1
430 REM **** Output Stage ****
440 PRINT
450 PRINT
460 PRINT "My goodness, ";N$;", you are"; A;"years old!"
470 PRINT
480 PRINT
490 PRINT "End of program."
500 END


RUN
```

```
This program will ask your name and year of birth,
then it will print your age.

What year is it? 1989

What is your name? Mike

Well, Mike, in what year were you born? 1968

Answer yes or no:  Have you had your birthday this year? N
Answer yes or no:  Have you had your birthday this year? no


My goodness, Mike, you are 20 years old!


End of program.
```

A person could either be less than 21 years old or taller than 65 inches, or meet both conditions to be listed.

In the next example,

```
700   IF AGE > 25 AND SEX$ = "Female" THEN LET C = C + 1
      ELSE LET N = N + 1
```

we accumulate the number of people in two possible categories. Category C records the total number of people who meet *both* conditions of being over the age of 25 *and* female. Category N records the total number of people who do not meet the conditions (all males as well as females 25 years old and younger). *Notice:* The last part of line 700 (ELSE LET N = N + 1) appears just below the IF command. This alignment is accomplished by repetitively depressing the space bar after the number 1 in the expression allowing the line to "wrap around" to the next line on the screen.

Applying IF/THEN/ELSE statements

To illustrate an interactive program we will create one that calculates your age given your name and year of birth. We do need to use an IF/THEN statement to determine whether or not you have already had a birthday this year. As shown in Figure A2-2, three IF/THEN statements are used. The first (line number 390) determines whether you have correctly answered if you have already had a birthday this year. (You literally must type "yes" or "no" in lowercase letters.) This compound relational IF statement directs the program to repeat the question if an error occurred. Depending upon your answer, one of the next two IF statements (lines 410 or 420) will calculate your age.

Using subroutines: the GOSUB/ RETURN statements

Another important control structure is the subroutine. Subroutines are self-contained modules used to perform special functions. They are outside of the main flow of the program. The use of subroutines is an important part of the structured approach to programming. They help organize large programs so that the logic used is easier to follow and modify if necessary. They are also effective when a similar procedure must be used at different points in the program. The procedure is written as a subroutine that is called when needed by the main program. Several subroutines can be used in the same program, and they can even be nested; that is, one subroutine can be written inside another.

To call a subroutine in BASIC, the GOSUB statement is used. The RETURN statement is later used to close the subroutine and direct control back to the next command following the GOSUB statement. The general form of the GOSUB and RETURN statements are

500 GOSUB *line number at start of subroutine*

and

1500 RETURN

The structure of a subroutine is as follows:

```
600 GOSUB 3000
610 REM The main program resumes at this line.
    .
    .
    .

2980 REM line 2990 halts execution
2990 END
3000 REM This is the beginning of the subroutine
    .
    .
    .

3500 REM line 3510 returns program control to the main program
     (in this case line 610)
3510 RETURN
    .
    .
    .

9999 END
```

The GOSUB statement (line 600) contains the line number where the subroutine begins. In this case the program flow is directed to line 3000. The computer processes the subroutine until it encounters the RETURN statement (line 3510), which sends control to the line following the specific GOSUB statement that sent it to the subroutine (line 610). The main program then continues to execute until the END statement is encountered. More than one GOSUB statement can be used to access the same subroutine. With some versions of BASIC the END statement can only be used once as the last line of the program. In those cases, a STOP statement should be used instead of END to terminate the program prior to the beginning of the subroutine. This prevents accidental entry into the subroutine procedure.

Looping procedures

With many programming problems we need to repeat the same task several times. Procedures are repeated by using loops. There are two main types of loops: (1) the number of repetitions is known, and (2) the number of repetitions is unknown.

When the number of repetitions is known, we can set the loop by use of a counter. When the number of repetitions is unknown, we must tell the computer when to stop processing the loop by using a trailer value, or sentinel value, at the end of the data to be processed. We will discuss each situation in turn.

Figure A2-3
How a counter is used in a loop.

PSEUDOCODE
START
Remarks—this program uses a counter for loop control to read
Remarks—and print, and add up and print the sum of six numbers
Remarks—define the variables
Initialize the counter and total
Print headings
DOUNTIL counter = 6
    Read the number
    Print the number
    Accumulate the number
    Add 1 to the counter
ENDDO
Print total of the numbers
STOP

Using a counter

The value of a loop COUNTER changes by a fixed amount with each iteration (pass through) of the loop. When the counter reaches a predetermined value, the loop is exited. Three steps are involved:

1. Initializing the counter
2. Incrementing the counter
3. Testing the counter for the end of the loop

A sample program is shown in Figure A2-3. Initializing refers to setting the starting value of the counter. Most counters are initialized at 1 or 0. We increment the counter each time we pass through the loop. For example, if a counter is set to 1 and it is incremented by 1 each time through the loop, the values will go from 1 to 2 to 3 to 4, and so forth. Each time the loop is executed, the counter value is tested to see whether it is time to exit the loop. Usually we test to see if the counter exceeds a certain value. If the test is false, we stay in the loop for another repetition. If the test is true, we exit the loop and continue the program.

    Until the test is true, a GOTO statement is used in line 360 to direct the looping flow to line 290. The GOTO statement is an unconditional branch that directs the program flow to a specific line number. The general form of the GOTO statement is

500 GOTO *another line*

The line "400 GOTO 300", for example, directs the flow back to line 300.

Using a trailer value

A loop that tests for a TRAILER VALUE is often used during input operations to tell the program when to stop processing input data. We often call this trailer value a sentinel value or test value. Usually a trailer value is not used in the same loop with a counter test. A GOTO statement is used to close the loop when a trailer value is used.

    Figure A2-4 shows how to write a simple summation program that reads and adds six numbers by using a loop with a trailer value. The IF/THEN statement in line 270 of the program has an implied or hidden GOTO statement.

FLOWCHART

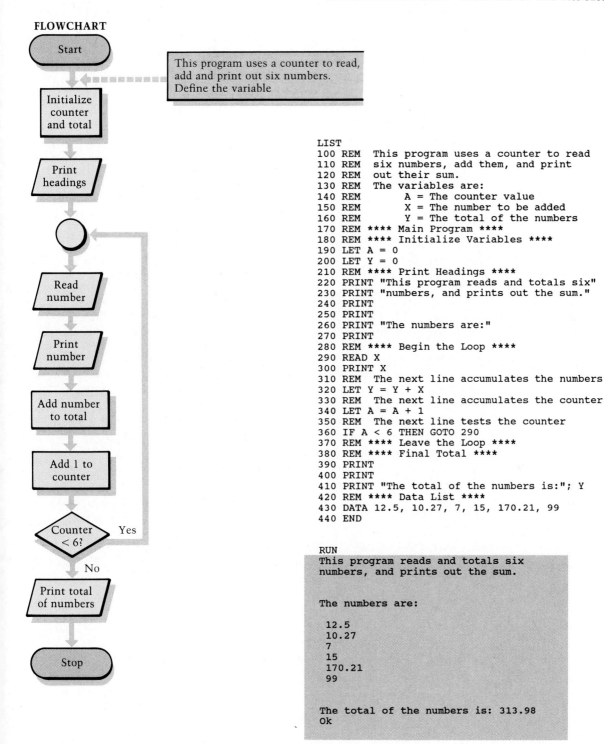

This program uses a counter to read, add and print out six numbers. Define the variable

```
LIST
100 REM   This program uses a counter to read
110 REM   six numbers, add them, and print
120 REM   out their sum.
130 REM   The variables are:
140 REM        A = The counter value
150 REM        X = The number to be added
160 REM        Y = The total of the numbers
170 REM **** Main Program ****
180 REM **** Initialize Variables ****
190 LET A = 0
200 LET Y = 0
210 REM **** Print Headings ****
220 PRINT "This program reads and totals six"
230 PRINT "numbers, and prints out the sum."
240 PRINT
250 PRINT
260 PRINT "The numbers are:"
270 PRINT
280 REM **** Begin the Loop ****
290 READ X
300 PRINT X
310 REM   The next line accumulates the numbers
320 LET Y = Y + X
330 REM   The next line accumulates the counter
340 LET A = A + 1
350 REM   The next line tests the counter
360 IF A < 6 THEN GOTO 290
370 REM **** Leave the Loop ****
380 REM **** Final Total ****
390 PRINT
400 PRINT
410 PRINT "The total of the numbers is:"; Y
420 REM **** Data List ****
430 DATA 12.5, 10.27, 7, 15, 170.21, 99
440 END
```

```
RUN
This program reads and totals six
numbers, and prints out the sum.

The numbers are:

 12.5
 10.27
 7
 15
 170.21
 99


The total of the numbers is: 313.98
Ok
```

Figure A2-4
How a trailer value is
used in a loop.

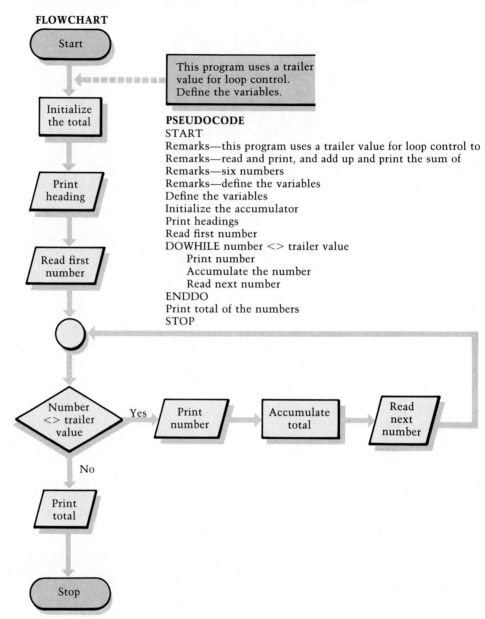

FLOWCHART

This program uses a trailer value for loop control. Define the variables.

PSEUDOCODE
START
Remarks—this program uses a trailer value for loop control to
Remarks—read and print, and add up and print the sum of
Remarks—six numbers
Remarks—define the variables
Define the variables
Initialize the accumulator
Print headings
Read first number
DOWHILE number <> trailer value
    Print number
    Accumulate the number
    Read next number
ENDDO
Print total of the numbers
STOP

```
LIST
100 REM   This program uses a loop tested with a trailer value
110 REM   to read six numbers, add them, and print out their sum.
120 REM   The variables are:
130 REM        X = The number to be added
140 REM        Y = The total of the numbers
150 REM **** Main Program ****
160 REM **** Initialize the Accumulator ****
170 LET Y = 0
180 REM **** Print Headings ****
190 PRINT "This program reads and totals six "
200 PRINT "numbers, and prints out the sum."
210 PRINT
220 PRINT
230 PRINT "The numbers are:"
240 PRINT
250 REM **** Begin the Loop ****
260 READ X
270 IF X=-9999 THEN 340
280 PRINT X
290 REM   The next line accumulates the numbers
300 LET Y = Y + X
310 REM   The GOTO command returns the program flow
320 REM   to the READ statement in line 260
330 GOTO 260
340 REM **** Leave the Loop ****
350 REM **** Final Total ****
360 PRINT
370 PRINT
380 PRINT "The total of the numbers is:"; Y
390 REM **** Data List ****
400 DATA 12.5, 10.27, 7, 15, 170.21, 99, -9999
410 END
```

```
RUN
This program reads and totals six
numbers, and prints out the sum.


The numbers are:

 12.5
 10.27
 7
 15
 170.21
 99


The total of the numbers is: 313.98
```

If you use a trailer value to end a loop containing a read operation, dummy values must be placed in the data statement, otherwise the program will abort with an out-of-data error message. For example, in the program

```
100 READ X$, A, B
110 IF X$ = "END OF DATA" THEN 300
    .
    .
    .

290 GOTO 100
300 REM Continue with the rest of the program.
    .
    .
    .

900 DATA "END OF DATA"
```

the line 900 needs to be rewritten:

```
900 DATA "END OF DATA", 0, 0
```

Sometimes a loop uses a trailer value when the data are first read in. Within this loop an accumulator statement records the number of iterations of the loop. In that way any later counter-controlled loops can use the final accumulated value as the test value for the end of the loop.

GOSUB versus GOTO statements

We need to distinguish between the functions performed by GOSUB and GOTO statements. Compare the use of a line number with a GOSUB in an IF/THEN statement. The statement

```
500   IF X = 1 THEN GOTO 700
```

means if X equals 1, then branch to line 700, and the flow of the program continues from line 700 to the end to the program. However, for the statement

```
500   IF X = 1 THEN GOSUB 700
510   (next instruction)
```

the program branches to the subroutine that starts at line 700, but when its RETURN statement is executed, the program continues execution at the next line (510).

GOTO statements have been rightly criticized by programming professionals because they allow the development of sloppy programming habits and work against the principles of structured programming. *GOTO statements are not recommended for any purpose other than closing or exiting a loop.*

Creating attractive output

The PRINT TAB and LPRINT TAB statements

The **PRINT TAB** and **LPRINT TAB** statements position output on a line in much the same manner as the tab operation on a typewriter. The general form of the PRINT TAB statement is

500 PRINT TAB*(expression); what to print*

The reserved words PRINT TAB tell the computer that a special output operation is being ordered. The expression within the parentheses indicates the column number where the tabbing function ends. The number can be represented by a constant, as in PRINT TAB(23), or by a variable, as in LPRINT TAB(N − 1). The next column to the right of the tab number holds the first character of the value to be printed. Always follow the PRINT TAB*(expression)* in a series by a semicolon. Commas in PRINT TAB statements override the tabbing function. The following line of code illustrates use of the PRINT TAB statement:

```
500 PRINT TAB(14); "Name = "; N$ ; TAB(40); "Age in years ="; A
```

This line prints out the following result:

```
             Name = Thomas Jones    Age in years = 27
```

| 13 Blank | 14th | 40th |
| Spaces | Column | Column |

Notice how the line containing the PRINT TAB statement can refer to several different tabbing operations. (*Caution:* On some systems printing begins one column after the tabbed column—that is, PRINT TAB(14) may mean begin printing in the 15th column instead of the 14th.)

PRINT TAB statements can be used to create designs for such items as computer-generated greeting cards and pictures. Figure A2-5 shows a program to create a pattern in the shape of an hourglass.

The PRINT USING and LPRINT USING statements

The **PRINT USING** and **LPRINT USING** statements format output and are useful methods for creating attractive output. Unfortunately these are not standard commands. Some computer systems have PRINT USING options (Apple Macintosh, IBM, Microsoft, HP, DEC, and several that use CP/M as their operating system) while others do not (most notably early Apple models). The general form of the PRINT USING statement is

490 *Format control expression*
500 PRINT USING (*line number of IMAGE or formal control expressions*), (*what to print*)
500 PRINT USING (*formal control or expressions*), (*what to print*)

```
LIST
100 REM   This program uses PRINT TAB statements to create a
110 REM    picture of an hourglass
120 REM   The variable is:
130 REM         G = The loop counter and TAB variable
140 REM **** Main Program ****
150 REM **** Print the top edge of the hourglass ****
160 PRINT ":=======================:"
170 REM **** Using a DOUNTIL loop to print the top half of the hourglass ****
180 LET G = 1
190 PRINT " :"; TAB(2 + G); "*"; TAB(23 - G); "*"; TAB(23); ":"
200 LET G = G + 1
210 IF G <= 10 THEN GOTO 190
220 REM **** Using a DOUNTIL loop to print the bottom half of the hourglass ****
230 LET G = 1
240 PRINT " :"; TAB(12 - G); "*"; TAB(13 + G); "*"; TAB(23); ":"
250 LET G = G + 1
260 IF G <= 9 THEN GOTO 240
270 REM **** Print the bottom edge of the hourglass ****
280 PRINT ":=======================:"
290 END
```

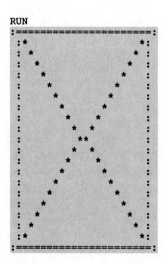

Figure A2-5
Using PRINT TAB statements to create the design of an hourglass.

IMAGE or format control expressions may be incorporated into the PRINT USING line or located in a separate line elsewhere in the program (usually before the PRINT USING line). Image statements provide a "mask" or template showing how the output will appear. Image statements vary in format and syntax. Examples of PRINT USING operations and the IMAGE statements for some of the computer systems you might be using are shown in Figure A2-6. For additional ways of formatting output with PRINT USING and LPRINT USING, or if your computer is not on the list, consult your programming manual or ask your instructor for assistance.

Figure A2-6
PRINT USING opera-
tions for several different
computer systems. The
example requires us to
print a person's name
(N$) and grade point av-
erage (A) in the columns
shown. In addition, skip
a line and print the term
(T$) as shown. Note that
specifications for PRINT
USING may be different
for your computer—con-
sult your manual or ask
your instructor.

```
Column      00000000011111111112222222223
number      12345678901234567890123456789 0

Example:
                    Thomas Roberts      3.21

            For term ending:    Spring 90


For most systems (IBM-PC, Macintosh, DEC, CP/M):

300 LET E$ = "         \                  \      #.##"
310 LET F$ = "For term ending:   \          \"
320 PRINT USING E$; N$, A
330 PRINT
340 PRINT USING F$; T$

        or

400 PRINT USING "        \                  \      #.##"; N$; A
410 PRINT
420 PRINT USING "For term ending:   \          \"; T$


For Hewlett-Packard-3000 systems:

200 PRINT USING 210 N$, A
210 IMAGE 5X, 15A, 4X, D.DD
220 PRINT
230 PRINT USING 240 T$
240 IMAGE "For term ending:", 3X, 9A
```

wrap-up program

Presenting the team report

The Oakriver University baseball team has 12 nonpitchers. This program reads in each player and then calculates and prints each player's name, at-bats, hits, and each player's batting average, as well as the team batting average. For any player batting over .325, print next to the player's average, "all-star." The suggested solution is shown in Figure A2-7.

Player	At-Bats	Hits	Player	At-Bats	Hits
Bill Edwards	123	43	John Young	49	15
Ronald Trout	131	30	Kevin Kline	79	26
David Freud	85	22	Wally Johnson	106	29
Bobby Dalton	21	6	Don Lopez	103	29
Reggie Tsang	101	31	Gene Kline	52	15
Ernie Tobin	119	27	Allan Long	98	25

FLOWCHART

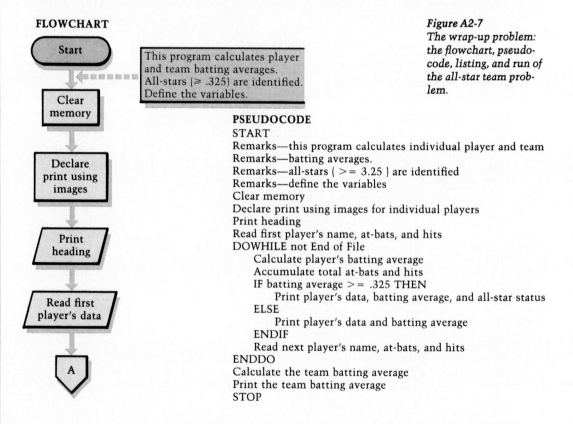

Figure A2-7
The wrap-up problem: the flowchart, pseudo-code, listing, and run of the all-star team problem.

PSEUDOCODE
START
Remarks—this program calculates individual player and team
Remarks—batting averages.
Remarks—all-stars (>= 3.25) are identified
Remarks—define the variables
Clear memory
Declare print using images for individual players
Print heading
Read first player's name, at-bats, and hits
DOWHILE not End of File
    Calculate player's batting average
    Accumulate total at-bats and hits
    IF batting average >= .325 THEN
        Print player's data, batting average, and all-star status
    ELSE
        Print player's data and batting average
    ENDIF
    Read next player's name, at-bats, and hits
ENDDO
Calculate the team batting average
Print the team batting average
STOP

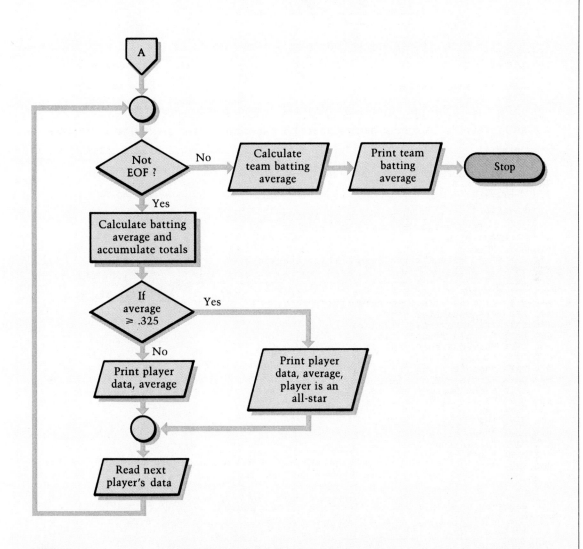

```
LIST
100 REM This program calculates individual player and team
110 REM batting averages.
120 REM All-stars ( average >= .325 ) are identified.
130 REM The variables are:
140 REM        P$ =  The player name
150 REM        B  =  The number of times at bat
160 REM        H  =  The number of hits
170 REM        A  =  The player batting average
180 REM        N  =  The number of players
190 REM        T1 =  The total number of "at-bats"
200 REM        T2 =  The total number of hits
210 REM        T3 =  The team batting average
220 REM        A$ =  The "print image" for All-Stars
230 REM        N$ =  The "print image" for non All-Stars
```

wrap-up program

```
240 REM **** Clear Memory and Define Print Images ****
250 CLEAR
260 LET A$ = "    \                    \    ###      ###      .###     All-star"
270 LET N$ = "    \                    \    ###      ###      .###"
280 REM **** Main Program ****
290 PRINT
300 PRINT "     Oakriver University Baseball Team's Batting Report"
310 PRINT
320 PRINT TAB(4); "Player's Name"; TAB(23); "At-bats"; TAB(34); "Hits"; TAB(42);
        "Average"
330 PRINT "----------------------------------------------------------------"
340 READ P$, B, H
350 IF P$ <> "EOF" THEN 360 ELSE 420
360    A = H / B
370    T1 = T1 + B
380    T2 = T2 + H
390    IF A >= .325 THEN PRINT USING A$; P$, B, H, A
           ELSE PRINT USING N$; P$, B, H, A
400    READ P$, B, H
410 GOTO 350
420 REM **** Calculate the Team Batting Average ****
430 T3 = T2 / T1
440 PRINT "    ----------------    ------    -----    ------ "
450 PRINT USING "    Team Results           ####      ###      .###"; T1, T2, T3
460    IF A(I) >= .325 THEN PRINT P$(I), A(I)
470 REM **** Data List ****
480 DATA "Bill Edwards", 123, 43
490 DATA "Ronald Trout", 131, 30
500 DATA "David Freud", 85, 22
510 DATA "Bobby Dalton", 21, 6
520 DATA "Reggie Tsang", 101, 31
530 DATA "Ernie Tobin", 119, 27
540 DATA "John Young", 49, 15
550 DATA "Kevin Kline", 79, 26
560 DATA "Wally Johnson", 106, 29
570 DATA "Don Lopez", 103, 29
580 DATA "Gene Kline", 52, 15
590 DATA "Allan Long", 98, 25
600 DATA "EOF", 0, 0
610 END

RUN
```

```
     Oakriver University Baseball Team's Batting Report

    Player's Name       At-bats    Hits    Average
    ----------------------------------------------------------------
    Bill Edwards          123       43      .350     All-star
    Ronald Trout          131       30      .229
    David Freud            85       22      .259
    Bobby Dalton           21        6      .286
    Reggie Tsang          101       31      .307
    Ernie Tobin           119       27      .227
    John Young             49       15      .306
    Kevin Kline            79       26      .329     All-star
    Wally Johnson         106       29      .274
    Don Lopez             103       29      .282
    Gene Kline             52       15      .288
    Allan Long             98       25      .255
    ----------------    ------    -----    ------
    Team Results         1067      298      .279
```

key terms

These are the key terms in alphabetical order. The numbers in parentheses refer to the page on which each term is defined.

Counter (A-32)
GOSUB/RETURN (A-30)
GOTO (A-32)
IF/THEN/ELSE (A-25)
IMAGE (A-38)
Logical operator or Boolean operator (A-26)
LPRINT TAB (A-37)
LPRINT USING (A-37)
PRINT TAB (A-37)
PRINT USING (A-37)
Relational operator (A-26)
STOP (A-31)
Trailer value (A-32)

review questions

short answer questions

1. What is wrong with this line of BASIC?

```
200 IF N = "New York" THEN PRINT "Big Apple"
```

2. Write a line of BASIC to test if X is greater or equal to Y; and if so, to print your name.
3. Given the following lines, write a DATA statement to activate the trailer value and leave the loop.

```
300 READ N$, W, E, R, T$, Y
310 IF N$ = "END-OF-FILE" THEN 500
```

4. Write a line of BASIC to test whether a person is aged 21 or over and is a sophomore at college, and if so print the person's name.
5. How many lines of data would be used to thoroughly test question 4? Write them.
6. Which of the following are not valid IF/THEN/ELSE statements?

```
(a) 500 IF N$ = '34' THEN LET Z = N$^2
        ELSE X = X^2

(b) 600 IF W = "LAST" AND X <> 10
        THEN LET X = Z   ELSE X = Y

(c) 700 IF R < 23 OR R < 45 THEN
        PRINT "OUT OF RANGE"

(d) 800 IF P = 23.45 THEN GOSUB 5000
    810 IF P < 23.45 THEN GOSUB 6000
```

7. Why is the STOP statement used in programs containing subroutines?
8. To what line does the RETURN statement direct the program flow?
9. How many times will the letter "A" be printed?

```
100 LET X = 0
110 PRINT "A"
120 LET X = X + 1
130 IF X < 7 THEN 110
140 END
```

10. Rewrite the BASIC code in question 9 to demonstrate using a trailer value.
11. Why are semicolons used in PRINT TAB statements rather than commas?
12. What are the advantages of working with PRINT USING?
13. What are the disadvantages of working with PRINT USING?

review questions

14. Write the following line using a PRINT TAB statement.

```
           Name              Job Class               Weekly Salary
      Gene Tomaselli     Marketing Training            $600.00
```

15. Reproduce the lines in question 14 using PRINT USING.

programming exercises

1. Susan Paul needs the total of the commissions earned by her salespeople for the past month. Devise a solution and use the data below to test your solution.

Salesperson	Commission
Thomas Alberts	$2234
Harry Jones	$3716
Leon Klaus	$2452
Milt Weiss	$2345
Joe Topaz	$1901

2. Dr. Clara Chips wants to give an award to those students who earned A's (90 percent) in her introductory information systems class. Design a program solution to determine who receives an award. Use the data below to test your design.

Student name	Numeric grade	Letter grade
Eugene Alton	89	B
John Burton	78	C
Lynne Davis	70	C
Mike Francis	90	A
Cindy Smith	91	A

3. Myrtle, owner of Myrtle's Burgers, needs a program to calculate a 5 percent sales tax on items purchased at her restaurant. (*Optional:* Use the relevant tax for your local area.) Each item and its cost, the subtotal, tax and grand total must be printed out. Use an INPUT command to ask if the order is "for here or to go?" If it is "for here," use the subroutine to calculate the sales tax. To test the program, use the following order:

Item	Price
Superburger	$2.80
Large fries	$1.00
Small shake	$0.90

4. Paul's House of Electronic Wonders (PHEW) is sending out invoices to three customers. The data include customer name, item purchased, the cost, the quantity purchased, and the discount. For each invoice, calculate both the nondiscounted subtotal and the discounted total. Compute the total of all three invoices.

Customer	Item	Cost	Qty	Discount (decimal)
Quick Office	Computer	$400	350	0.20
Handichips	Memory chips	$ 1	2000	0.10
The Chipshack	Cables	$ 10	500	0.15

5. Paul's House of Electronic Wonders has hired you to write part of an accounts payable program to determine how much money PHEW owes the following six suppliers. Read in the data. Then, calculate the nondiscount balance, the difference between the current balance and the balance still in the discount period. Print these fields for each vendor.

Calculate and print out the totals for the current, discount, and nondiscount balances. What percentage of the total current balance is nondiscount?

Vendor name	Current balance	Discount balance
Quick Chips	$11,500	$ 8,000
Octopus Cable	$16,500	$14,500
Shanghai Mod.	$ 5,550	$ 3,535
JCN Inc.	$20,160	$18,500
Orient Elec.	$ 3,500	$ 2,850
Applepie Co.	$44,700	$41,340

6. Use PRINT TAB statements to reproduce the following rectangle.

7. Use PRINT TAB statements to reproduce the following picture.

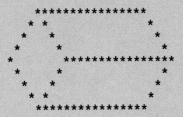

8. Use PRINT TAB and PRINT USING statements to create a greeting card for a friend.

Answers to the short answer questions

1. N should be N$.
2. `200 IF X >= Y THEN PRINT "JERRY"`
3. `900 DATA "END-OF-FILE", 0, 0, 0, "X", 0`
4. `1000 IF A >=21 AND C$ = "SOPHOMORE"`
   `     THEN PRINT N$`
5. `2000 DATA "TOM", 20, "JUNIOR"`
   `2010 DATA "SUE", 21, "SENIOR"`
   `2020 DATA "RALPH", 20, "SOPHOMORE"`
   `2030 DATA "LINDA", 21, "SOPHOMORE"`
   `2040 DATA "CINDY", 22, "SOPHOMORE"`
6. **(a)** The LET statement is attempting to take the square of a character string and the value 34 is enclosed in single quotation marks. **(b)** The numeric variable W is set equal to a character string. **(c)** The inequality symbol for R < 45 is incorrect (should be R > 45) or the test R < 23 is redundant. **(d)** This one is correct.
7. The STOP statement is used to prevent accidentally entering the subroutine.
8. The RETURN statement directs the program flow back to the line immediately following the GOSUB statement.
9. 7 times.
10. `100 READ X`
    `110 IF X = 1 GOTO 150`
    `120 PRINT "A"`
    `130 GO TO 100`
    `140 DATA 0, 0, 0, 0, 0, 0, 0, 1`
    `150 END`
11. We use semicolons because commas override (cancel out) the tabbing function.
12. The advantage of working with PRINT USING is the ability to create better looking—less computer-like output.
13. The disadvantage of working with PRINT USING is the lack of standardization between different computer systems. In addition some systems do not have this feature.
14. `110 PRINT N$; TAB(18); J$; TAB(37);`
    `    "$";S`
15. *Note:* Your answer may be different!
    `250 X$ =`
    `    "\          \ \ \ $###.##"`
    `300 PRINT USING X$; N$; J$; S`

SECTION THREE

BASIC—More techniques

To continue the discussion of loops, this section introduces easier loop handling through the use of the FOR/NEXT and WHILE/WEND statements. We then move on to discuss how to set up and process arrays of data. Array processing is done with loops. Next the applications concerning predefined functions are discussed. At the end of the section, the wrap-up program demonstrates array processing to carry out a common operation in business—sorting data.

FOR/NEXT statements

We can take our understanding of counters used in loops one step further. The difficulties with loops using counters are knowing where to place the initialization, incrementation (or decrementation), and testing steps within the program. BASIC provides us with a convenient way to avoid these problems by using the paired FOR/NEXT statements to facilitate looping. FOR/NEXT operations reduce the time and energy spent in programming.

The general form of FOR/NEXT statements is

500 FOR I = J TO K STEP L
   procedure inside the loop
550 NEXT I

where

I represents the loop counter
J represents the starting value of the counter
K represents the ending value of the counter
L represents the amount to increment (decrement) each iteration of the counter

The beginning and stopping points for the counter are usually whole numbers. Incrementation loops start with a lower number and stop at a higher one. Decrementation loops follow the opposite approach, from highest to lowest.

Consider a simple example. Figure A3-1 shows the flowchart, pseudocode, and program using a FOR/NEXT loop to print the word "Greetings" five times. In this example, the FOR statement begins counting with the number 1 and goes through the loop five times one digit at a time.

To flowchart a FOR/NEXT loop, we perform five steps (refer to Figure A3-1):

1.   At the beginning of the flowchart we use the hexagonal symbol for preparation: ⬡. Within the beginning symbol, we place the FOR statement and make note of the initial value, increment (or decrement) amount, and test value for the counter.

2.   We flowchart the processing steps within the loop in the usual fashion (see examples earlier in the appendix).

3.   At the end of the loop, we use the decision symbol: ◇.

Within the decision symbol we write NEXT followed by the loop counter variable and a question mark. Two flow lines exit from this decision symbol.

4.   The first flow line is used when there is another loop iteration to perform. It is labeled "Yes" and drawn to the left out of the NEXT symbol, and links up to the middle of the preparation symbol. Be sure to use arrows to indicate the direction of the flow line.

5.   The second flow line shows the exit from the loop. This exit line, labeled "No," leads down or to the right from the decision symbol.

In contrast to the "complexity" of flowcharting, pseudocode for a FOR/NEXT command shows the two command lines flanking the operation you wish to repeat.

FOR I = J TO K STEP L

   (*procedure goes here*)

NEXT I

FLOWCHART

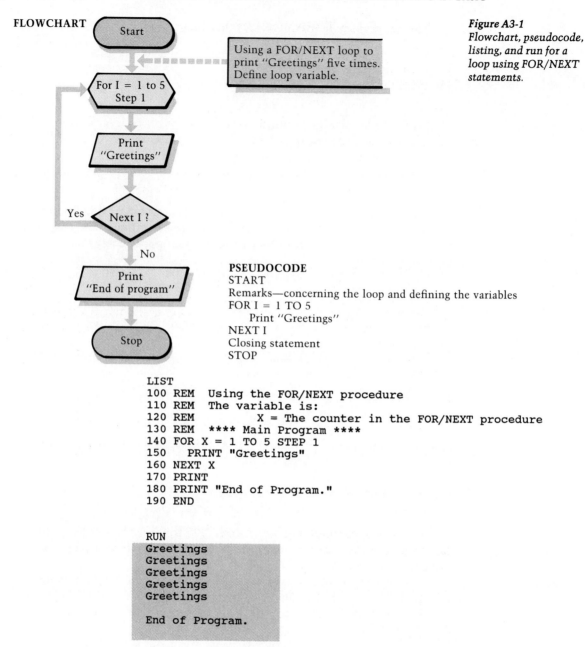

Figure A3-1
*Flowchart, pseudocode,
listing, and run for a
loop using FOR/NEXT
statements.*

Using a FOR/NEXT loop to
print "Greetings" five times.
Define loop variable.

PSEUDOCODE
START
Remarks—concerning the loop and defining the variables
FOR I = 1 TO 5
    Print "Greetings"
NEXT I
Closing statement
STOP

```
LIST
100 REM  Using the FOR/NEXT procedure
110 REM  The variable is:
120 REM         X = The counter in the FOR/NEXT procedure
130 REM  **** Main Program ****
140 FOR X = 1 TO 5 STEP 1
150    PRINT "Greetings"
160 NEXT X
170 PRINT
180 PRINT "End of Program."
190 END
```

```
RUN
Greetings
Greetings
Greetings
Greetings
Greetings

End of Program.
```

There are other accepted ways to create flowcharts and write pseudo-code for FOR/NEXT loops. Your instructor may suggest or require an alternative.

**FOR/NEXT loop
control**

A loop is controlled by a counter variable which determines the number of times the loop is executed. Counter variables can be set to numbers or other variables. As we look at some examples of loop control, we can also see how the results look printed out.

The first example shows a loop that increases by 1 with each iteration:

```
100 REM A simple loop
110 FOR I = 1 TO 6 STEP 1
120     PRINT "Hello"
140 NEXT I
150 END
```

The output looks like this:

```
RUN
Hello
Hello
Hello
Hello
Hello
Hello
```

When the increment is 1, the explicit STEP command can be omitted.

The second FOR/NEXT example demonstrates a loop that has a step value other than 1—in this case incrementing by a decimal value. This technique is useful for accounting programs involving interest payments, depreciation, mortgage problems, and other business applications.

```
200 REM Using fractional steps
210 FOR P = 1 TO 3 STEP .5
220     PRINT "P ="; P
230 NEXT P
240 END
```

```
RUN
P = 1
P = 1.5
P = 2
P = 2.5
P = 3
```

The third example illustrates decrementation. We begin with a larger number as our starting value and decrease the value by 4 each time until we reach 0.

```
300 REM Moving backward--decrementation
310 FOR K = 20 TO 0 STEP -4
320     PRINT "K ="; K
330 NEXT K
340 END
```

```
RUN
K = 20
K = 16
K = 12
K = 8
K = 4
K = 0
```

Our fourth example shows the proper way to direct the flow when using IF/THEN/ELSE statements within a loop. In addition, it uses variables instead of constants to set the counter range. Depending on the results of the test, either the number or its squared value is printed out.

```
400 REM Using an IF/THEN/ELSE Statement inside a loop,
410 REM and using variables for loop control.
420 LET K = 1
430 LET L = 5
440 FOR S = K TO L
450     READ X
460     IF X < 100 THEN PRINT "X ="; X
470     ELSE PRINT "X SQUARED ="; X 2
480 NEXT S
490 DATA 30, 110, 99, 100, 101
500 END

RUN
X = 30
X SQUARED = 12100
X = 99
X SQUARED = 10000
X SQUARED = 10201
```

The program flow is eventually directed to the line containing the NEXT statement. The flow should never be sent to the line with the FOR statement because an error message would be generated. Since the logical structure used in the fourth example is more complex than the previous three, the flowchart and pseudocode are shown in Figure A3-2.

Programs can have more than one FOR/NEXT loop. FOR/NEXT loops can follow each other consecutively through the program. Figure A3-3 illustrates two consecutive loops. Notice that the same variable (I in this case) can be used as a counter more than once in the same program. However, the letter chosen as the counter variable for a loop cannot be used to represent another variable within that loop.

Nested FOR/NEXT loops

FOR/NEXT loops (like any other type of loop) can also be nested one within another. An example of such NESTED LOOPS is given in Figure A3-4. Nested loops may even contain three, four, or more embedded loops inside each other. Different machines have different maximum levels for nesting. The flowchart and pseudocode show that the inner loop is wholly within the outer loop.

How many times do the inner loops execute? Look at Figure A3-4. The outer loop (FOR I = 1 TO 5) executes five times. With each iteration of the outer loop, the inner loop (FOR J = 2 TO 6) is executed five times: (J = 2, J = 3, J = 4, J = 5, J = 6). For the whole program, the inner loop is executed 25 times (5 × 5).

Notes on debugging

Each FOR statement requires a NEXT statement at the end of the loop. If you forget the NEXT statement, a "FOR without NEXT" error message will result. Similarly, if you have a NEXT statement but forget a FOR statement, a "NEXT without FOR" error message will result.

Do not overlap nested loops! The inner loops must be located completely within the outer loop. If you overlap them, the program will fail to run. An example of an improperly created nested loop, and how to correct it, is shown in Figure A3-5. Avoid using IF/THEN/ELSE statements to redirect flow in and out of the loop, or to skip to the FOR line. Properly prepared flowcharts and pseudocode will help prevent such errors.

Figure A3-2
Flowchart and pseudo-
code for using an
IF/THEN/ELSE
statement inside a
FOR/NEXT loop.

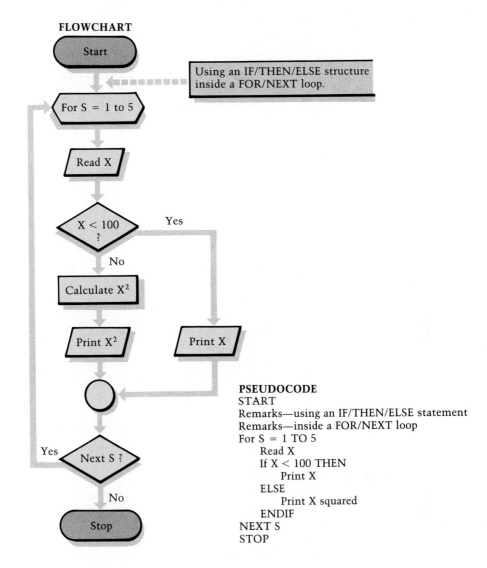

FLOWCHART

Using an IF/THEN/ELSE structure inside a FOR/NEXT loop.

PSEUDOCODE
START
Remarks—using an IF/THEN/ELSE statement
Remarks—inside a FOR/NEXT loop
For S = 1 TO 5
    Read X
    If X < 100 THEN
        Print X
    ELSE
        Print X squared
    ENDIF
NEXT S
STOP

Figure A3-3
Example of two consecutive FOR/NEXT loops in a program.

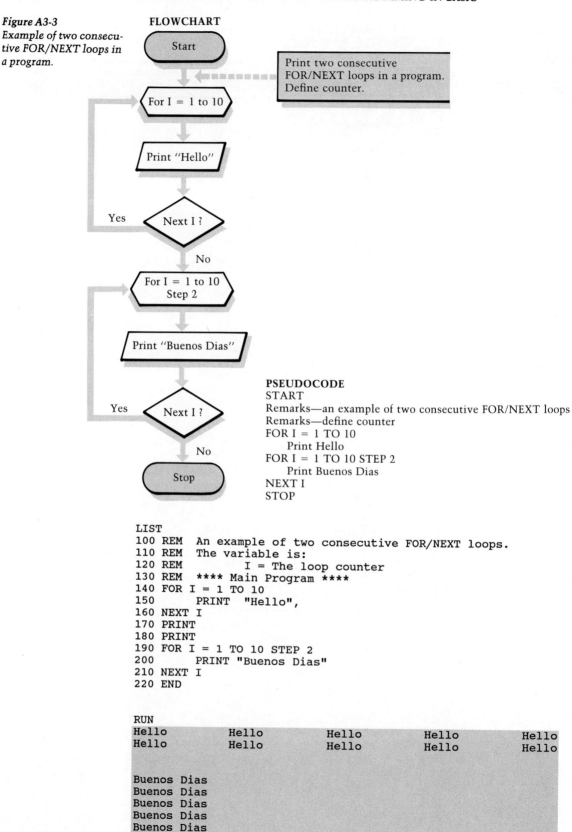

FLOWCHART

Print two consecutive FOR/NEXT loops in a program. Define counter.

PSEUDOCODE
```
START
Remarks—an example of two consecutive FOR/NEXT loops
Remarks—define counter
FOR I = 1 TO 10
     Print Hello
FOR I = 1 TO 10 STEP 2
     Print Buenos Dias
NEXT I
STOP
```

```
LIST
100 REM   An example of two consecutive FOR/NEXT loops.
110 REM   The variable is:
120 REM         I = The loop counter
130 REM   **** Main Program ****
140 FOR I = 1 TO 10
150      PRINT  "Hello",
160 NEXT I
170 PRINT
180 PRINT
190 FOR I = 1 TO 10 STEP 2
200      PRINT "Buenos Dias"
210 NEXT I
220 END
```

```
RUN
Hello          Hello          Hello          Hello          Hello
Hello          Hello          Hello          Hello          Hello


Buenos Dias
Buenos Dias
Buenos Dias
Buenos Dias
Buenos Dias
```

Figure A3-4
Example of a nested
FOR/NEXT loop.

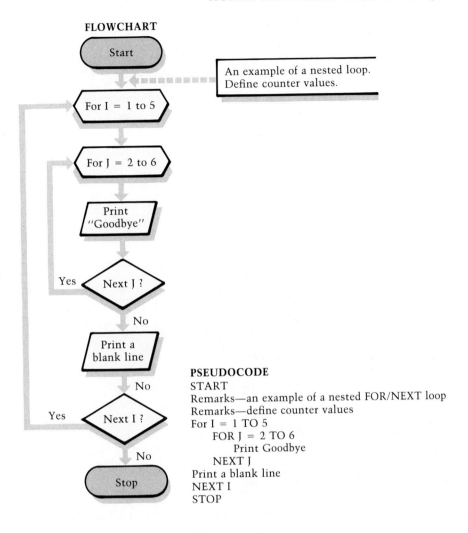

FLOWCHART

An example of a nested loop.
Define counter values.

PSEUDOCODE
START
Remarks—an example of a nested FOR/NEXT loop
Remarks—define counter values
For I = 1 TO 5
    FOR J = 2 TO 6
        Print Goodbye
    NEXT J
Print a blank line
NEXT I
STOP

```
LIST
100 REM  An example of a nested loop
110 REM  The variables are:
120 REM         I = The outer loop counter
130 REM         J = The inner loop counter
140 REM  **** Main Program ****
150 FOR I = 1 TO 5
160    FOR J = 2 TO 6
170       PRINT "Goodbye",
180    NEXT J
190    PRINT
200 NEXT I
210 END
```

```
RUN
Goodbye      Goodbye      Goodbye      Goodbye      Goodbye

Goodbye      Goodbye      Goodbye      Goodbye      Goodbye

Goodbye      Goodbye      Goodbye      Goodbye      Goodbye

Goodbye      Goodbye      Goodbye      Goodbye      Goodbye

Goodbye      Goodbye      Goodbye      Goodbye      Goodbye
```

Figure A3-5
Example of an improperly nested loop and how to correct it.

```
LIST
100 REM   An example of an incorrectly nested loop
110 REM   The variables are:
120 REM              I = The outer loop counter
130 REM              J = The inner loop counter
140 REM **** Main Program ****
150 FOR I = 1 TO 5
160    FOR J = 1 TO 4
170       PRINT "I ="; I, "J ="; J
180    NEXT I
190 NEXT J
200 END


RUN
NEXT without FOR in 190



LIST
100 REM   An example of a correctly nested loop
110 REM   The variables are:
120 REM              I = The outer loop counter
130 REM              J = The inner loop counter
140 REM **** Main Program ****
150 FOR I = 1 TO 5
160    FOR J = 1 TO 4
170       PRINT "I ="; I, "J ="; J
180    NEXT J
190 NEXT I
200 END


RUN
I = 1          J = 1
I = 1          J = 2
I = 1          J = 3
I = 1          J = 4
I = 2          J = 1
I = 2          J = 2
I = 2          J = 3
I = 2          J = 4
I = 3          J = 1
I = 3          J = 2
I = 3          J = 3
I = 3          J = 4
I = 4          J = 1
I = 4          J = 2
I = 4          J = 3
I = 4          J = 4
I = 5          J = 1
I = 5          J = 2
I = 5          J = 3
I = 5          J = 4
```

WHILE/WEND: another looping method

A number of microcomputers, notably those using Microsoft BASIC (such as the IBM PC and its compatibles) and Apple computers, permit the use of an extended looping procedure with **WHILE/WEND** statements. The general form is

500 WHILE expression is true
      perform loop operation
550 WEND

This loop executes while the expression is true. When the program encounters the WEND statement, the loop iteration begins again starting with the test of the numeric expression at the top of the loop. If the test is false, program control is passed to the first executable statement after the WEND statement. WHILE/WEND permits the programmer to make direct use of the DOWHILE looping logic (shown in Chapter 14 and Appendix A-1) which is preferred in structured programming. Figure A3-6 illustrates the use of a WHILE/WEND loop to find the sum of six numbers. A sentinel value (test value) of -9999 is used to indicate the end of data, and so end processing. When X is set to -9999 in line 310, the test $X <> -9999$ in line 280 fails, and the loop is exited.

Arrays and subscripted variables

Now that you know about loops, it is time to learn how lists or tables of data can be processed using arrays. The connection here is that arrays are generally processed using loops.

An **ARRAY** is a collection of related data. In an array a single variable name is assigned to hold the data for an entire list or table. For a list, the variable name represents a one-dimensional array. Tables are two-dimensional arrays. We shall look at both one- and two-dimensional arrays.

Each location in an array where data are stored is identified by a unique label or subscript. The variable is thus known as a **SUBSCRIPTED VARIABLE**.

The general form for an element in a **ONE-DIMENSIONAL ARRAY** is

variable (location in array)

For example, if the array X has 100 numeric elements, they range from X(1) to X(100). If array Y$ has 25 character elements, they range from Y$(1) to Y$(25). *Note:* Some systems will set the initial array location at 0. Thus a 101-element array would range from X(0) to X(100). The subscripted variable X(1) in this case is the second element in the array.

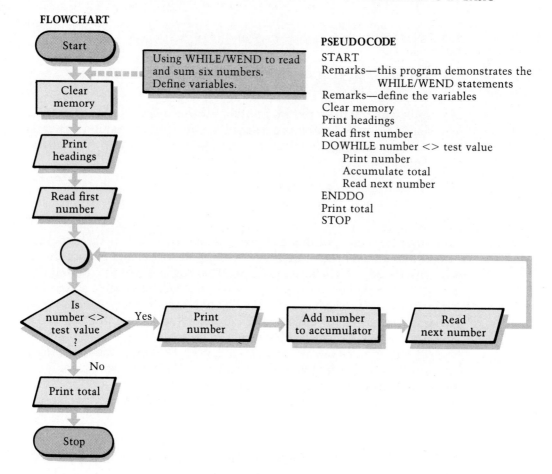

FLOWCHART

PSEUDOCODE

Using WHILE/WEND to read and sum six numbers. Define variables.

```
START
Remarks—this program demonstrates the
            WHILE/WEND statements
Remarks—define the variables
Clear memory
Print headings
Read first number
DOWHILE number <> test value
    Print number
    Accumulate total
    Read next number
ENDDO
Print total
STOP
```

Figure A3-6
How WHILE/WEND
statements are used in a
loop.

```
LIST
100 REM   This program uses WHILE/WEND statements to read
110 REM   six numbers, add them, and print out their sum.
120 REM   The variables are:
130 REM          X = The number to be added
140 REM          Y = The total of the numbers
150 REM **** Main Program ****
160 REM **** Initialize Accumulator ****
170 LET Y = 0
180 REM **** Print Headings ****
190 PRINT   "This program uses WHILE/WEND statements to read"
200 PRINT   "six numbers, add them, and print their sum."
210 PRINT
220 PRINT
230 PRINT "The Numbers:"
240 PRINT
```

```
250 REM **** Read the First Value ****
260 READ X
270 REM **** The WHILE/WEND loop ****
280 WHILE X <> -9999
290     PRINT USING "  ###.##"; X
300     LET Y = Y + X
310     READ X
320 WEND
330 REM **** Print the Total ****
340 PRINT
350 PRINT USING "The total of the numbers is: ###.##"; Y
360 DATA 12.5, 10.27, 7, 15, 170.21, 99, -9999
370 END
```

```
RUN
This program uses WHILE/WEND statements to read
six numbers, add them, and print their sum.

The Numbers:

    12.50
    10.27
     7.00
    15.00
   170.21
    99.00

The total of the numbers is: 313.98
```

With most systems default procedures permit you to store up to 11 data elements. Thus you must declare your storage requirements using the DIM statement when you have arrays with more than 11 values. In addition, if you create subscripted variables—such as a variable representing the sum of two subscripted variables—be sure to dimension them.

For a **TWO-DIMENSIONAL ARRAY** the general form for a subscripted variable is

variable(row, column)

Thus the array element Z(20,12) is in row 20 and column 12. Remember that the rows are declared first and the columns second.

In BASIC we use the DIM statement (short for DIMENSION) to declare the data array list or table. The DIM statement reserves storage for array variables. The general form of the DIM statement is

500 DIM *variable(maximum subscripts)*

The values chosen must be integers. They must be large enough to reserve enough storage to hold all of your data elements. Although the values can be larger than the number of data elements, if they are smaller, the program will fail to run.

Here are some examples of valid DIM statements.

FLOWCHART

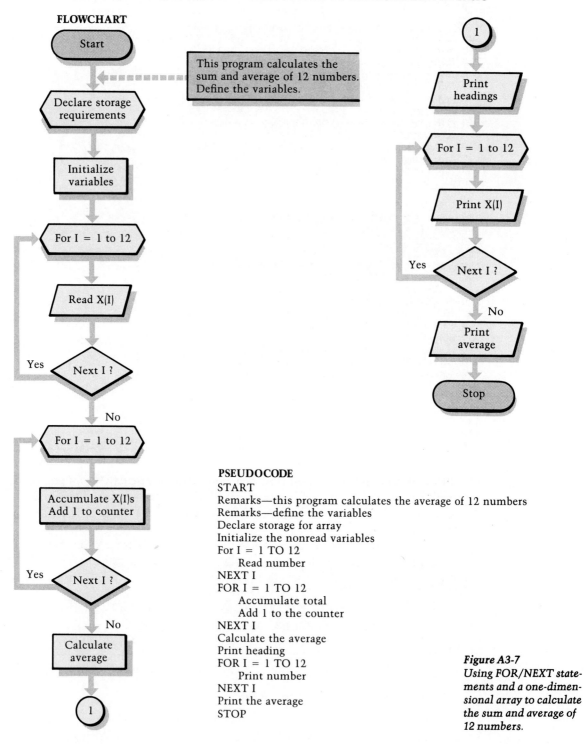

PSEUDOCODE
START
Remarks—this program calculates the average of 12 numbers
Remarks—define the variables
Declare storage for array
Initialize the nonread variables
For I = 1 TO 12
    Read number
NEXT I
FOR I = 1 TO 12
    Accumulate total
    Add 1 to the counter
NEXT I
Calculate the average
Print heading
FOR I = 1 TO 12
    Print number
NEXT I
Print the average
STOP

Figure A3-7
Using FOR/NEXT state-
ments and a one-dimen-
sional array to calculate
the sum and average of
12 numbers.

```
LIST
100 REM   This program uses arrays and FOR/NEXT statements to
110 REM   read twelve numbers, add them, and then average them.
120 REM   The variables are:
130 REM      A = The average
140 REM      C = The number of values of x
150 REM      X = The array of numbers to be added
160 REM      Y = The total of the numbers
170 REM      I = The loop counter
180 REM   **** Main Program ****
190 REM   **** Declare array storage ****
200 DIM X(12)
210 REM   **** Initialize Variables ****
220 LET A = 0
230 LET C = 0
240 LET Y = 0
250 REM   **** Input Stage ****
260 FOR I = 1 TO 12
270    READ  X(I)
280 NEXT I
290 REM   **** Process Stage ****
300 FOR I = 1 TO 12
310    LET Y = Y + X(I)
320    LET C = C + 1
330 NEXT I
340 REM   **** Calculate Average ****
350 LET A = Y/C
360 REM   **** Output Stage ****
370 PRINT "This program uses an array and FOR/NEXT statements to"
380 PRINT "read 12 numbers and calculate their average"
390 PRINT
400 PRINT "The numbers:"
410 PRINT
420 FOR I = 1 TO 12
430    PRINT X(I);
440 NEXT I
450 PRINT
460 PRINT
470 PRINT USING "The average of the numbers is: ###"; A
480 REM **** Data List ****
490 DATA 12, 4, 16, 10, 7, 13, 18, 2, 10, 11, 9, 8
500 END
```

```
RUN
This program uses an array and FOR/NEXT statements to
read 12 numbers and calculate their average

The numbers:

 12   4   16   10   7   13   18   2   10   11   9   8

The average of the numbers is:   10
```

Line in BASIC	Explanation
`100 DIM A(125)`	Reserves 125 locations for a one-dimensional array.
`200 DIM B(20,15)`	Reserves 20 rows and 15 columns containing 300 locations for a two-dimensional array.
`300 DIM C$(20)`	Reserves 20 rows in a one-dimensional array containing string variables. (Depending on the system, a row might store an entire character string element or just a single character.)
`400 DIM D$(33,25)`	Reserves 33 rows and 25 columns for character strings in a two-dimensional array. (Depending on the system, the column value could refer to characters in a string variable or to the number of string variables in a row.)
`500 DIM E(R)`	Dimension can be a variable name. The value R must be defined in a previous LET statement (for example: `100 LET R = 100`

To help you to know what to avoid, here are some examples of invalid DIM statements:

Invalid DIM statement	Explanation
`600 DIM F(12.3)`	Dimension is not an integer value.

`700 DIM G(10)`
`710 FOR I = 1 TO 20`
`720 READ G(I)`
`730 NEXT I`
	Dimension is too low a value for the loop, rewrite line 700 as 700 DIM G(20)

Note: Arrays of 10 items or less need not be DIMensioned.

Using arrays permits us to exploit the modular features of structured programming in our BASIC programs. This exploitation is made possible because a value assigned to an array location during the input stage can be recalled for the process and output steps without rereading the data.

To show this point more clearly we will sum a list of twelve numbers and calculate their average. Figure A3-7 shows the program. Notice how the input process and output stages are separated into three loops. The DIM statement is set to 12 to accommodate the number of data values. The average is the sum of all the values divided by the number of values.

Predefined functions

There are a number of predefined functions useful for business applications. A **PREDEFINED** or **LIBRARY FUNCTION** is "built into" the BASIC compiler or interpreter. Predefined functions permit you to use a short code word to call up a prewritten subroutine. To find the square root of a variable X, we can use the predefined function **SQR(X)**.

```
100 Let A = SQR(X)
```

Several predefined functions are shown in Figure A3-8. Many functions are used in business statistics and operations research. In addition to the square root function just shown, let's take a look at INT(X) and RND.

The **INT(X)** function (integer) returns an integer value for any number X. It returns the largest whole number that is less than or equal to the original number. For positive numbers the INT function truncates (lops off) the fraction or decimal part; so INT(3.98) is 3. With negative numbers the value is the next lower whole number; thus INT(-4.55) is -5. The following program in Figure A3-9 shows how INT works.

We can also use INT(X) to round numbers. The general methods for rounding to a whole number and rounding to two decimal places are

```
500 LET R = INT(X + .5)
510 LET H = INT(100*X + .5)/100
```

For the number 23.494 we get the whole number 23 using line 500 and to two decimal places 23.49 using line 510, since INT(23.494 + .5) = 23 and INT(2349.4 + .5)/100 = 23.49.

The **RND** function (randomize) can be applied to several business areas such as simulation and sampling that require random numbers. We might also use it to build the element of chance into computer games or to select students randomly for oral presentations. On some systems a variable such as X is required, and it is necessary to write RND(X). The RND function normally is used to generate a series of random numbers between 0 and 1. Since we usually need numbers that

Figure A3-8
Representative predefined numeric functions.

Function	Meaning
ABS(X)	The absolute value of X
ATN(X)	The arctangent of X in radians
COS(X)	The cosine of X in radians
EXP(X)	e raised to the X power
INT(X)	The integer value of X
LOG(X)	The natural logarithm of X
RND	A random number between 0 and 1
SIN(X)	The sine of X in radians
SQR(X)	The square root of X
TAN(X)	The tangent of X in radians

Figure A3-9
How the INT(X) function works.

```
LIST
100 REM  An example of how the INT(X) function works
110 PRINT "Using the INT(X) function."
120 PRINT
130 PRINT " Original       Integer"
140 PRINT "   Value         Value"
150 PRINT
160 FOR H = 1 TO 8
170 READ T
180 PRINT USING " ####.###         ####" ; T; INT(T)
190 NEXT H
200 DATA 123, -12.05, 224.901, -240.5
210 DATA 544, 2, 23.494, 2923.2
```

```
RUN
Using the INT(X) function.

 Original          Integer
   Value            Value

  123.000             123
  -12.050             -13
  224.901             224
 -240.500            -241
  544.000             544
    2.000               2
   23.494              23
 2923.200            2923
```

cover a far wider range, we can modify these values. We will take a look at two possibilities.

1. Unspecified randomization, which creates a random number between the values of 0 and 1. This is accomplished through the use of the function RND.

2. Specifying the desired range. The random number needs to be converted into a value in the desired range. The general form N*RND sets up a range from 0 to N. So 5*RND will range from 0 to 4.999999. Notice that the value N = 5 is not included (it is an upper bound). Another way of creating integer values uses the INT function. We can write this as INT(N*RND). This time INT(5*RND) returns any one of the integers 0, 1, 2, 3 or 4. Since the function INT is used, the numbers are truncated and 5 is not included. If we wanted integers from 1 to 5, we could have used INT(5*RND + 1).

The following programs illustrate each case. In the first example five random numbers are obtained between 0 and 1.

```
LIST
100 REM Creating 5 random numbers between 0 and 1
110 FOR I = 1 to 5
120       PRINT RND
130 NEXT I
140 END
```

```
RUN
 .1213501
 .651861
 .8688611
 .7297625
 .798853
```

The second example shows how to obtain five random integers from 1 to 5 by converting a random number into an integer. The function used is INT(N*RND + 1), with N equal to 5.

```
LIST
200 REM Creating 5 random numbers between 1 and 5
210 FOR I = 1 TO 5
220     PRINT INT(5*RND + 1)
230 NEXT I
240 END

RUN
 1
 4
 5
 3
 4
```

Most computers will use a standard starting point called a "seed" number to create a set of random numbers. Since the algorithm is known, we really are creating pseudorandom numbers. Each time the RND function is used, the same set of numbers is generated. To overcome this drawback (certainly to relieve boredom in games, if nothing else), you can specify a nonstandard randomization feature. Place on a line before the RND function one of the following randomization statements:

500 RANDOMIZE

or

500 RANDOMIZE TIMER

Either of these statements will generate fresh numbers. RANDOMIZE permits you to select a starting number, and RANDOMIZE TIMER uses a value present in the computer's clock as the starting "seed" number.

wrap-up program

Sorting a list

A common problem in business is the sorting of data. Sorting operations are applications of arrays. Our wrap-up program shows how to sort numbers. We use a sorting technique known as a **BUBBLE SORT**. The bubble sort is slow, but fairly easy to understand. Values that are out of order are switched. Recall that if we read data into a storage location that is already occupied (whether in an array or not), the original value will be replaced by the new value. To avoid losing the original value, a special temporary holding location is used to save a copy of it.

Figure A3-10 shows how the bubble sort works by sorting ten numbers from smallest to largest. The idea behind a bubble sort is to compare pairs of numbers successively, exchanging them if they are in the wrong order. In Figure A3-10 we order the numbers from smallest to largest. The comparisons are made in line 400. For example, if A(1) <= A(2), then the next line executed is line 410, and the inside loop now compares A(2) and A(3). But if A(1) > A(2), the two numbers are out of order and must be switched by using the rest of the statements contained on line 400. A temporary storage location is required. The value stored in A(1) is temporarily stored in T, A(1) is set equal to A(2), and then A(2) is set equal to T. Notice that if we had not used the temporary variable T, the original value of A(1) would have been lost.

At the first completion of the inside loop, the largest number is stored in A(10). The next time through the loop, the next largest number is stored in A(9), and so on until the numbers are sorted from smallest to largest. The smaller numbers appear to "bubble up."

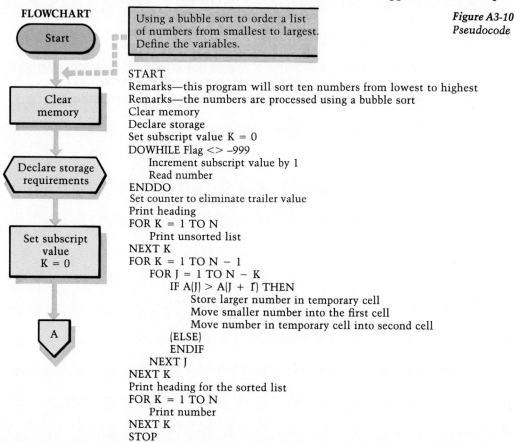

FLOWCHART

Start

Clear memory

Declare storage requirements

Set subscript value K = 0

A

Using a bubble sort to order a list of numbers from smallest to largest. Define the variables.

Figure A3-10
Pseudocode

```
START
Remarks—this program will sort ten numbers from lowest to highest
Remarks—the numbers are processed using a bubble sort
Clear memory
Declare storage
Set subscript value K = 0
DOWHILE Flag <> –999
    Increment subscript value by 1
    Read number
ENDDO
Set counter to eliminate trailer value
Print heading
FOR K = 1 TO N
    Print unsorted list
NEXT K
FOR K = 1 TO N – 1
    FOR J = 1 TO N – K
        IF A(J) > A(J + 1) THEN
            Store larger number in temporary cell
            Move smaller number into the first cell
            Move number in temporary cell into second cell
        (ELSE)
        ENDIF
    NEXT J
NEXT K
Print heading for the sorted list
FOR K = 1 TO N
    Print number
NEXT K
STOP
```

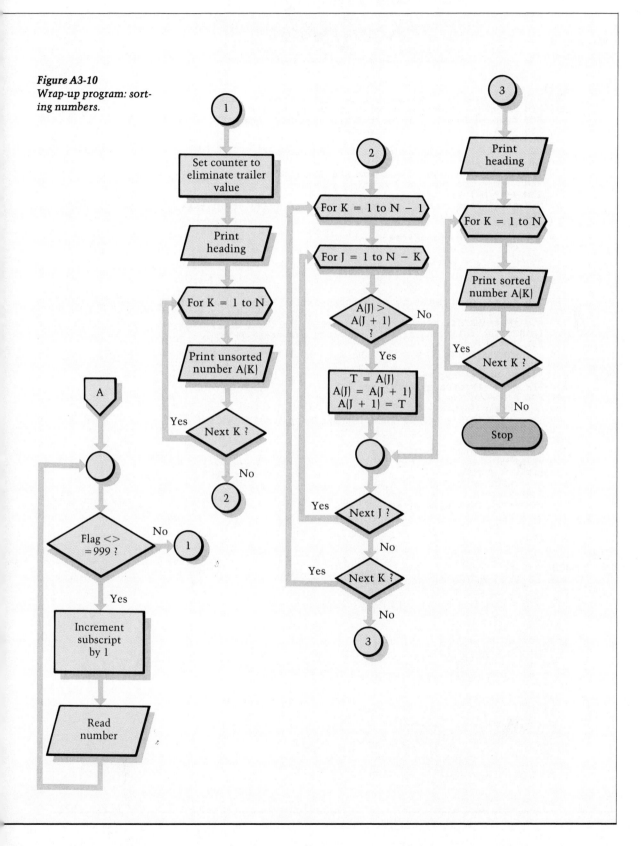

Figure A3-10
Wrap-up program: sorting numbers.

wrap-up
program

```
LIST
100 REM This program uses the bubble sort method to sort
110 REM an unspecified amount of numbers (up to 50)
120 REM from smallest to largest.  The variables are:
130 REM    A = The value to be sorted
140 REM    J = The inner loop counter
150 REM    K = The outer loop counter and subscript variable
160 REM        for the DOWHILE loop
170 REM    N = The upper limit for the FOR/NEXT statement
180 REM    T = The temporary holding location for swapping
190 REM **** Main Program ****
200 REM **** Clear memory and declare storage array at 50 ****
210 CLEAR
220 DIM A(50)
230 REM **** Input Stage ****
240 K = 0
250 WHILE A(K) <> -999
260    LET K = K + 1
270    READ A(K)
280 WEND
290 REM ***** Set counter to eliminate trailer value at end of list *****
300 N = K - 1
310 REM ***** PRINT UNSORTED LIST *****
320 PRINT "The following are the unsorted numbers:":PRINT
330 FOR K = 1 TO N
340    PRINT A(K);
350 NEXT K
360 PRINT: PRINT: PRINT
370 REM ***** PROCESS STAGE *****
380 FOR K = 1 TO N - 1
390    FOR J = 1 TO N - K
400       IF A(J) > A(J+1) THEN T=A(J): A(J)=A(J+1): A(J+1)=T
410    NEXT J
420 NEXT K
430 REM ***** OUTPUT STAGE *****
440 PRINT "The sorted list:":PRINT
450 FOR K = 1 TO N
460    PRINT USING " ###"; A(K)
470 NEXT K
480 REM ***** DATA LIST *****
490 DATA 75, 46, 11, 36, 6, 78, 19, 54, 21, 75
500 DATA -999
510 END


RUN
The following are the unsorted numbers:

 75  46  11  36  6  78  19  54  21  75


The sorted list:

   6
  11
  19
  21
  36
  46
  54
  75
  75
  78
```

key terms

These are the key terms in alphabetical order. The numbers in parentheses refer to the page on which each term is defined.

Array (A-55)
Bubble sort (A-64)
DIM (A-57)
FOR/NEXT (A-46)
INT(X) (A-61)
Nested loop (A-50)
One-dimensional array (A-55)
Predefined or library function (A-61)
RANDOMIZE (A-63)
RND (A-61)
SQR(X) (A-61)
Subscripted variable (A-55)
TIMER (A-63)
Two-dimensional array (A-57)
WHILE/WEND (A-55)

review questions

short answer questions

1. Determine if there are any errors in the following sets of FOR/NEXT statements.

(a)
```
100 FOR I = 1 TO 15
110   READ C
120   IF C = 100 THEN 100
130   PRINT C
140 NEXT I
```
(b)
```
200 FOR G = 3 TO 36 STEP 3
210   READ N$(I)
220   PRINT N$(I)
240 NEXT I
```
(c)
```
300 FOR K = 2 TO 20 STEP -1
310   PRINT X(K)
320 NEXT K
```
(d)
```
400 FOR R = 1 TO 10
410   READ X
420   PRINT X
430   LET Z = Z + X
440   PRINT Z
450 NEXT R
```
(e)
```
500 FOR A = 4 TO 20
510 FOR Y = 2 TO 30
520   PRINT A*Y
530 NEXT A
540 NEXT Y
```

2. What are the differences between a FOR/NEXT loop and a WHILE/WEND loop?

3. What is an array? What is a subscripted variable?

4. How does using an array affect the structure of your program?

5. What is a bubble sort? How does it work?

6. Write a FOR/NEXT loop to decrement by 4 from 40 to X where X is set equal to 20 in a LET statement placed before the loop. In this loop print your name.

7. Write lines of code to create:
   (a) Random numbers between 1 and 8
   (b) Random integers between 4 and 15

8. Write a line of code to round 12.49999 to the nearest 1/1000th.

9. Write a line of code to round the square root of 10 to two decimal places.

10. Write a line of code to take the square root of your age. Use it in a short program.

review questions

programming exercises

1. George Roberts supervises 15 quality-control inspectors at Global Electric's Small Appliance Division factory. Inspectors must examine 30 appliances per hour and correctly classify 29 out of the 30, for an error rate of 3.3 percent. From the following sample data, write a program to determine which of the 15 are performing satisfactorily. What is the overall inspection rate? What would you recommend?

Inspector name	Average number of inspections per hour	Average number of incorrect choices per hour
S. Thomas	34	1
R. Baker	35	0
G. Miller	25	3
M. Tanaka	31	2
W. Chou	29	1
I. Halpern	38	1
L. Swartz	31	0
J. Edwards	30	2
M. Elliot	29	0
E. Gorman	24	1
G. Werton	32	2
H. Warrick	33	1
K. Smith	31	1
W. Hernandez	30	0
O. Parsons	28	0

2. Using the following data list, write a program to sort the people by age from oldest to youngest.

Name	Age in years
Terri Roberts	34
Jennifer Lee	23
Leon Lawson	19
Sally Field	43
Ernst Halard	21
Hope Jones	26
Mitch Manor	23
Bobby Carver	24

3. The graduate business school of Oakriver University has hired you to create a program to select graduates for the M.B.A. program. Admission is based upon a combined total of a student's grade-point average (GPA) and graduate management aptitude test (GMAT) score. The combined total is found by multiplying the GPA by 200 and adding it to the GMAT score. The minimum combined score is 1150. On the final report:

First list each student's data, including name, GPA, GMAT, combined score, and admission status.

Second list just the names of the people who were admitted.

Finally show the number of people who were admitted and their average GPAs and GMATs.

The table provides the data.

Name	GPA	GMAT
1. Alice Jones	3.12	345
2. Thomas Robertson	2.56	563
3. Tim Martinez	3.06	583
4. Janis Roberts	3.56	576
5. Orestes Fox	3.01	547
6. Electra Adamson	2.34	463
7. Susan Smith	3.29	492
8. Albert Torrez	3.16	524
9. Tina Osaka	3.45	445
10. Hubert Wong	2.68	522
11. Francis Weiss	3.29	552
12. Barbara Miller	2.98	487
13. Sally O'Brien	3.30	640
14. Lynne Claudette	3.89	714
15. Penny Smith	2.88	453

4. Write a program to toss a coin. Let 1 = a head and 0 = a tail. Print out the results of the first 20 attempts. What percentage was tails? Note: percentage = (number of tails/20) * 100.

5. Let's have some fun! Consider a real growth industry—genetic technology. Try building your own creature. Dr. Genie Splitter has a grant to create a new kind of "creature." The double-helix DNA has four components: adenine, cytosine, guanine, and thymine. Adenine only binds with thymine; and cytosine with guanine. Label the components using the letters A, C, G, and T, respectively.

6. The Oakriver University football team has just completed its latest season. The alumni are happy and the coach has not been fired yet. As the team statistician, you will have

work to do. For each game print out the name of the opponent, the score, whether Oakriver University won or lost, and the absolute difference between the two scores. Next calculate the sum of the points Oakriver University scored and calculate the average. Then do the same for its opponents. Finally, calculate the average winning margins and losing margins for Oakriver University for the season. Should the coach keep his job?

Opponents	Score for Oakriver	Score for opponent
Egmont College	34	28
Big State University	14	24
Even Bigger State University	23	20
Abraham Grant Tech	45	10
College of the Big Spenders	23	44
Semipro State University	3	63
University of Techies	22	22
Oakriver Institute of Technology	10	13
Alpha Omega Classics University	42	17
Seaside Polytechnic University	34	23
MBA University	42	32

7. Both SQR(X) and INT(X) can be used in calculating the economic order quantity (EOQ), a common business application. Paul's House of Electronic Wonders needs to analyze its inventory needs. As the staff inventory analyst, you must determine the economic order quantity for the following items. Use the equation for the EOQ:

$$Q = \sqrt{\frac{2 \times (\text{Annual demand}) \times (\text{Ordering cost})}{(\text{Holding cost}) \times (\text{Unit cost})}}$$

Q = amount of the item to order

Annual demand = estimated annual demand for the item

Ordering cost = cost of placing an individual order, including office expenses such as Telex, typing, and personnel costs; usually between $50 and $100 per order.

Holding cost = cost per monetary unit for holding the item in storage, including insurance, borrowing costs, storage space, obsolescence, and other factors; usually between 20 and 40 percent per monetary unit (generally so many cents on the dollar).

Unit cost = price of a single unit of the item, a case, dozen, gross, or other amount.

The data are as follows:

Item name	Annual demand	Ordering cost	Holding cost	Unit cost
Memory chip	10,000	70	0.30	2
Printer cable	500	50	0.25	10
Printer	1,200	60	0.30	600
IRM computer	3,000	100	0.30	1,000
Testing switch	100	60	0.25	3
Applebetty computer	4,000	60	0.30	500

Answers to the short answer questions

1. (a) Line 120 incorrectly directs the flow to line 100 instead of line 140. (b) G should be changed to I. (c) The 2 and the 20 in line 300 are in the wrong order for decrementation. (d) is correct. (e) NEXT A and NEXT Y have been reversed.
2. FOR/NEXT statements use counters for loop control, whereas WHILE/WEND statements use a DOWHILE loop test. 3. An array is an ordered list or table of numbers. A subscripted variable is a data element identified by a unique label.
4. Arrays permit you to perform input, processing, and output operations in separate modules in a program. 5. A bubble sort is a procedure for reordering values into a new sequence. It performs the sort procedure by comparing pairs of values and exchanging them if they are in the wrong order.
6.
```
100 LET X = 20
110 FOR I = 40 TO X STEP -4
120    PRINT "JERRY"
130 NEXT I
```
7. (a) `400 LET X = INT(8*RND + 1)`
(b) `500 LET Z = INT(12*RND + 4)`
8.
```
100 READ X
110 LET V = INT(1000*X + .5)/1000
120 DATA 12.49999
```
9.
```
190 INPUT X
200 LET T = INT(100*(SQR(X) + .5)/100
```
10.
```
200 INPUT "WHAT IS YOUR AGE", A
210 LET S = SQR(A)
220 PRINT USING
    "The square root is: #.##", S
230 END
```

BASIC
glossary and index

The page number of each term is shown in parentheses. An example of each BASIC statement is shown.

AND A logical operator used when all conditions must be met in order to perform an operation. (A-26)

```
600 IF X > 6 AND W < 9 THEN PRINT Y
```

ARRAY A collection of related data in list or table form. (A-55)

ASSIGNMENT STATEMENT Refers to the LET statement in BASIC that assigns values to variables using the equals sign (=). *See* LET statement. (A-11)

BASIC (BEGINNERS' ALL PURPOSE SYMBOLIC INSTRUCTION CODE) Interactive programming language developed by John G. Kemeny and Thomas Kurtz with the novice programmer in mind. (A-5)

BOOLEAN OPERATOR *See* Logical operator. (A-26)

BUBBLE SORT A technique for sorting data where pairs of values are tested and the reordered values "bubble-up" the list. (A-64)

CHARACTER SET Upper- and lowercase alphabetic letters, the decimal numbers 0 to 9, and special symbols, used in BASIC. (A-9)

CHARACTER STRING CONSTANTS Also called string constants or literals, they are combinations of letters, symbols and numbers enclosed in quotation marks. (A-9)

CHARACTER STRING VARIABLES Combinations of letters, symbols and numbers represented by a $ at the end of the variable name (F$, MAJOR$). (A-10)

CLEAR Statement that sets all numeric variable values to zero and all character string variable values to null in main memory. (A-13)

```
600 CLEAR
```

CLS Statement that erases the existing image on the display screen but does not affect what is stored in main memory. (A-13)

```
600 CLS
```

CONSTANT A value that does not change during execution. (A-9)

COUNTER Variable used to increase or decrease a variable by a fixed amount—often used in loop control. (A-32)

DATA Nonexecutable statement that stores data in the program. Each data item must be separated by a comma. (A-13)

```
600 DATA "Tom Smith", 12.5, 45
```

DIM A reserved word that declares the number of row and column elements in an array. On some systems DIM declares the maximum number of characters in a string variable. (A-57)

```
600 DIM X(100, 24), W$(100)
```

ELSE *See* IF/THEN/ELSE. (A-25)

END The last statement in a BASIC program. (A-20)

```
600 END
```

FLOWCHART Diagram that shows how a program works in terms of sequence, movement of data and logic. (A-3)

FOR/NEXT Paired statement for loop control. (A-46)

```
600 FOR I = 1 TO 10 STEP 2

    operation within the loop

650 NEXT I
```

GOSUB Statement used in BASIC to access a subroutine. *See also* RETURN statement. (A-30)

```
600 GOSUB 3000
```

GOTO Statement used to direct the program to a specific line number. May be used to close a loop but is strongly discouraged in structured programming. (A-32)

```
600 GOTO 200
```

IF/THEN   A conditional statement used for selection and looping operations. (A-25)

```
600 IF Q = 6 THEN LET W = Q*R
```

IF/THEN/ELSE   A more advanced conditional statement used for selection and looping operations. (A-25)

```
600 IF T = 9 THEN PRINT A$
    ELSE PRINT B$
```

IMAGE   A statement of some systems used for creating attractive output. To be activated the IMAGE statement number must be called by a PRINT USING statement. (A-38)

```
650 IMAGE "\     \ #####.##"
```

INPUT   A statement that ensures that the data entered by the user, as the program is executed, is assigned to a variable. (A-16)

```
600 INPUT B$, T
```

INT(X)   Command that truncates a number to the whole integer less than or equal to the number. (A-61)

LET   Commonly called an assignment statement, it gives values to different variables. (A-11)

```
600 LET R = 12 * E
```

LINE NUMBER   Appears at the beginning of each line of a program. Unless directed otherwise by your program, these numbers are executed in sequence from lowest to highest. (A-7)

LOGICAL OPERATOR   Boolean operator such as OR and AND used in IF/THEN/ELSE statements. (A-26)

LOOP   Allows the program to execute repeatedly one or a series of steps. Two major types of loops in BASIC are FOR/NEXT and WHILE/WEND. (A-3)

LPRINT   Statement used on some microcomputers to direct output only to the printer. (A-18)

```
600 LPRINT "jumped over the dog."
```

LPRINT TAB   Statement for placing output into certain columns much like the tab operations on a typewriter. (A-37)

```
600 LPRINT TAB(23); W$; TAB(35); H
```

LPRINT USING   Statement that directs output onto a user-designed format. The format can be incorporated into the LPRINT USING; or created using an IMAGE statement, which is then called by the LPRINT USING statement. (A-37)

```
600 LPRINT USING "\     \ ##.#"; X$,W
```

NESTED LOOP   A loop or several loops completely inside another loop. (A-50)

NEXT   *See* FOR/NEXT. (A-46)

NUMERIC CONSTANTS   Can be integers, real numbers with decimal places, or real numbers written in exponential form. (A-10)

NUMERIC VARIABLES   Real numbers represented by an alphabetic character or an alphabetic character combined with a number. In some systems they may be up to 40 characters (R, TESTSCORE). (A-10)

ONE-DIMENSIONAL ARRAY   Data displayed in a list form. (A-55)

OR   Logical operator that tests true when one or more conditions is true. (A-26)

```
600 IF W > 1 OR K < 6 THEN PRINT Z
```

PREDEFINED OR LIBRARY FUNCTION   A function that is built into the BASIC compiler or interpreter. *See* for example INT, SQR, or RND. (A-61)

PRINT   A statement that controls the type and format of output at both the display terminal and printer. (A-18)

```
600 PRINT "jumped over the dog."
```

PRINT TAB   Statement for placing output into certain columns much like the tab operations on a typewriter. (A-37)

```
600 PRINT TAB(23); W$; TAB(35); H
```

PRINT USING   Statement that directs output onto a user-designed format. The format can be incorporated into the PRINT USING; or created using an IMAGE statement, and called by the PRINT USING statement. (A-37)

```
600 PRINT USING "\     \ ##.#"; X$,W
```

PROGRAM DOCUMENTATION Manuals, display screens, and other materials that tell users how to use the program, operators how to run it, and programmers how to change it. (A-3)

PSEUDOCODE An English-like code to help the programmer understand the steps needed to execute the program. (A-3)

RANDOMIZE Statement used to tell the computer to generate a fresh list of random numbers. (A-63)

600 **RANDOMIZE**

READ Statement that assigns data from a DATA statement to a particular value. (A-13)

600 **READ** W, A$, J

RELATIONAL OPERATOR Operators <, <=, =, >=, >, and <> used in IF/THEN/ELSE statements. (A-26)

REM Nonexecutable statement for writing remarks or comments and storing them within the program. (A-10)

600 **REM** This is a REM statement

RESERVED WORD A word that has precise meaning in BASIC. It must be correctly spelled and used only for its assigned purpose and not as a variable. (A-9)

RETURN A statement in BASIC used to close the subroutine and direct control back to the main program. *See* GOSUB. (A-30)

600 **RETURN**

RND(X) Predefined function for randomizing numbers. (A-61)

SELECTION Logic patterns that use comparisons based on decisions or choice to split a program into different paths. (A-3)

SEQUENCE Set of linear steps to be carried out in the order of their appearance. (A-3)

SQR(X) Predefined function for finding the square root of a number. (A-61)

STEP Statement used with FOR/NEXT statements for incrementing and decrementing. (A-47)

600 FOR I = 3 TO 45 **STEP** 3

STOP Statement that immediately halts the execution of a program. (A-31)

600 **STOP**

SUBSCRIPTED VARIABLE A variable representing an array in which each value is uniquely identified—N(N, Y). (A-55)

SYSTEM COMMANDS The commands we use to communicate with the computer's operating system (RUN, LIST, SAVE, and LOAD). (A-6)

THEN *See* IF/THEN and IF/THEN/ELSE. (A-25)

TIMER Reserved word when used with RANDOMIZE will generate random numbers using the computer's clock. (A-63)

600 RANDOMIZE **TIMER**

TRAILER VALUE A nonsense value placed at the end of a data file to close a loop. (A-32)

TWO-DIMENSIONAL ARRAY A way of displaying data by locating it in a row and column format. (A-57)

VARIABLE A symbol which can take on different values. (A-10)

WHILE/WEND Statements used to create a DOWHILE loop structure. (A-55)

600 **WHILE** F <> X

　　　operation within the loop

650 **WEND**

Glossary of key terms

ABACUS First mechanical contrivance used for calculations. (102)

ACCEPTANCE TEST Last test before the new information system is fully implemented. (457)

ACCESS TIME Time necessary to retrieve a data item from secondary storage and place it into main memory. (211)

ACCOUNTING PACKAGES Prewritten programs ranging from simple bookkeeping and check-register programs to complex packages. (255)

ACTIVE CELL In an electronic spreadsheet, the cell where the highlight is currently positioned, into which the user can enter data. (321)

ADA A procedural language named for Lady Ada Augusta, Countess of Lovelace and developed for the U.S. Department of Defense. It uses structured programming and software engineering to speed up program design. (515)

ADDRESS A unique location in main memory. (140)

AIKEN, HOWARD The developer of the Mark I. (107)

ALGORITHM Set of rules that break down the solution to a programming problem into a simple, repetitive procedure. (470)

ALPHABETIC FIELD A field that only contains alphabetic characters. (350)

ALPHANUMERIC FIELD A field that contains alphabetic characters, numbers, and symbols. (350)

ALU *See* Arithmetic/logic unit.

ANALYTICAL GRAPHICS Simple, low-resolution pictorial representations of numerical data. (415)

ANALYTIC ENGINE Steam-driven device invented by Charles Babbage that had all the parts of a modern computer but was never successfully completed. (105)

ANNOTATION SYMBOL Represents comments or remarks on the flowchart that do not affect the operation of the program. (483)

APPLE I The first commercially successful microcomputer. It was designed by Steven Wozniak and Stephen Jobs. (119)

APPLICATION SOFTWARE Programs that direct the actual input, processing and output activities for users. (45)

ARGUMENT The part of a spreadsheet's built-in function that identifies data on which the function will work (value, cell, or range). (327)

ARITHMETIC/LOGIC UNIT (ALU) Part of the CPU that performs calculations and logical operations as directed by the control unit. (50, 138)

ART Anything that is not text, usually graphic images, which exist as line art or continuous tone art. (413)

ARTIFICIAL INTELLIGENCE (AI) Efforts to capture the way humans think and learn applied to the computer. (124, 518, 628)

ASCII (AMERICAN STANDARD CODE FOR INFORMATION INTERCHANGE) Assigns a specific bit pattern to each of the decimal numbers 0 through 9, lowercase and uppercase alphabet, and commonly used symbols. (147)

ASSEMBLER System software that translates a program from assembly language into machine language. (526)

ASSEMBLY LANGUAGE Low-level language using mnemonic symbols instead of 1s and 0s. (113, 508)

ASYNCHRONOUS TRANSMISSION Sending data one byte at a time. (555)

ATANASOFF-BERRY COMPUTER (ABC) The first electronic computer developed from 1937 to 1942 by Dr. John V. Atanasoff and Clifford E. Berry. (108)

ATANASOFF, JOHN V. AND CLIFFORD E. BERRY Developers of the Atanasoff-Berry Computer (ABC). (108)

ATTRIBUTE The relational database equivalent of a data field. (366)

AUDIO OUTPUT DEVICE Allows the user to listen to the computer. (200)

AUDIT Examination of the information system to test the effectiveness of its various control procedures. (589)

AUDIT TRAIL Physical or visible documentation of the steps data follow through an organization's information system. (590)

AUTOMATIC CALLBACK Control technique whereby the computer calls back the user in an attempt to foil masqueraders. (588)

AUTOMATION The replacement of human control of a process by a machine. (605)

BABBAGE, CHARLES (1792–1871) British mathematician who invented the difference engine and later worked on the analytic engine. (103)

BACKUS, JOHN Developer of the FORTRAN programming language. (116)

BANDWIDTH The capacity of a communications medium. (551)

BAR CODE READER An optical scanner that reads data coded as lines of varying width. (189)

BAR GRAPH A pictorial representation of data that uses rectangular bars oriented horizontally or vertically. (416)

BASEBAND NETWORK A LAN that uses a single channel multidrop line. (562)

BASIC (Beginner's All Purpose Symbolic Instruction Code) Interactive programming language developed by John G. Kemeny and Thomas Kurtz with the novice programmer in mind. (118, 510)

BATCH PROCESSING This occurs when data are collected over a period of time and processed as a group. (11)

BAUD RATE Number of bits per second transmitted through a communications medium. (551)

BERNOULLI BOX Removable disk cartridge sometimes used with microcomputers. (217)

BINARY CODED DECIMAL (BCD) A coding scheme to represent decimal numbers and characters in binary. (147)

BINARY DIGIT See BIT.

BINARY (BASE 2) NUMBER SYSTEM Number system that computers use, utilizing only the numerals 1 and 0. (45, 146)

BIOCHIP Electronic component that utilizes molecular structures and processes. (619)

BIT (from Binary Digit) Refers to a 1 or a 0. (45, 146)

BIT-MAPPED FONT A fixed pattern of dots that displays the size, shape and orientation of a specific character. (400)

BLOCKING FACTOR Numbers of records contained in a block on a magnetic tape. (224)

BOILER PLATING A word processing technique in which previously typed paragraphs are merged to form a new document. (227)

BROADBAND NETWORK A LAN that uses cable-TV style technology for network links. (562)

BUBBLE MEMORY Primary storage using tiny, movable magnetic bubbles implanted in thin film on a garnet wafer. (229)

BUFFER Internal storage area used to balance the transfer of data between hardware components with different transmission speeds. (141, 225)

BUILT-IN FUNCTION One of many spreadsheet formulas supplied within the program that performs a standard statistical, logical, or mathematical calculation. (327)

BUS NETWORK A single line linking computers and peripherals. (545)

BYTE Binary character made up of adjacent bits that the computer stores and processes as one unit. (45, 147)

C A procedural language used to create application and system software. (517)

CAD See Computer-aided design.

CAI See Computer-assisted instruction.

CALCULATING Performing mathematical functions on data such as addition, subtraction, multiplication, division, and exponentiation. (15)

CAM See Computer-aided manufacturing.

CANNED PROGRAM See Prewritten software.

CARRIER SENSE MULTIPLE ACCESS/COLLISION DETECTION See CSMA/CD.

CELL The intersection of a spreadsheet row and column, which can contain a value, label, or formula. (312)

CENTRALIZED PROCESSING All data processing is done at one central computer center. (536)

CENTRAL PROCESSING UNIT (CPU) Part of the computer that contains the control unit and the arithmetic/logic unit and carries out the instructions of the software. (50, 138)

CHARACTER Individual letters, numbers or symbols that make up a field. (44, 350)

CHARACTER PRINTER Peripheral that prints one character at a time. (194)

CHARGE-COUPLED DEVICE Very fast semiconductor storage using tiny storage cells to hold charges. (229)

CHECK BIT See Parity bit.

CHECK DIGITS Data integrity control that checks data against predetermined patterns. (577)

CHILD A data element in an hierarchical or network database that is beneath a "parent" and connected to it. (364)

CIRCULAR REFERENCE An error in spreadsheet design where a formula in one cell actually refers to itself. (326)

CLASSIFYING Grouping of data by certain characteristics. (16)

CLIENTS Those people for whom users provide a service. (41)

CLIP ART Prepared artwork, normally kept on disk files, that can be added as graphic images in desktop publishing layouts. (396)

COAXIAL CABLES Communications medium of insulated wire pairs bound together into cables. (548)

COBOL (COmmon Business Oriented Language) Procedural language strong in file processing and used extensively today by businesses and government agencies. (116, 513)

CODES OF ETHICS Standards and guidelines set by professional organizations. (594)

COHESION Describes a module that performs a single function that is well-defined and therefore has loose cohesion. (433)

COLUMN In spreadsheets, a vertical collection of cells extending from the top of the spreadsheet to the bottom—usually represented by one or more letters in the cell address. (312)

COMMON CARRIER A company that furnishes communication services for the public. (561)

COMMUNICATING Transmitting data or information from one place to another. (16)

COMMUNICATIONS DEVICES Hardware linking the local user hardware with the host computer. (58, 541)

COMMUNICATIONS MEDIUM See Data communications medium.

COMMUNICATIONS PROCESSORS Devices that handle the switching and coordination of messages and data and include multiplexers, concentrators, front-end processors, and message switchers. (558)

COMPARING Determining whether two items are the same or different. (15)

COMPILER Language translator that converts a complete program written in a specific procedural language into machine language. (526)

COMPUTER Very-high-speed electronic device that can accept data and instructions, use the instructions to perform logical and mathematical operations on the data, and report the results of the processing. (6, 46, 138)

COMPUTER-AIDED DESIGN (CAD) Computer systems that facilitate design of a product. (20, 251, 421)

COMPUTER-AIDED MANUFACTURING (CAM) Using computers to direct actual production or assembly processes. (21, 257)

COMPUTER-AIDED SOFTWARE ENGINEERING (CASE) Integrated set of system development tools which can be used in all stages of the system design process. (444)

COMPUTER-ASSISTED INSTRUCTION (CAI) Software used to teach material to a student or other user, generally on an interactive basis. (260)

COMPUTER CRIME Use of a computer for illegal purposes. (572)

COMPUTER ETHICS Standards used by people in the information-processing industry. (594)

COMPUTER FRAUD AND ABUSE ACT (1986) Federal law that makes it illegal to access, use, or destroy data contained in a federal, interstate, foreign commerce, or medical database. (573)

COMPUTER NETWORK See Networks.

COMPUTER-OUTPUT MICROFILM (COM) System that can produce up to 50,000 lines per minute of output onto microfilm from the computer using a high speed camera. (201)

COMPUTER SIMULATION Programs that model real-world events and attempt to predict possible consequences of those events. (21)

COMPUTER VIRUS Tiny program that can attach to the operating system's codes and are passed onto secondary storage media. (584)

COMPUTER WORD An expression made up of one or more consecutive bytes. (149)

CONCENTRATOR Device that combines incoming and outgoing messages into a more compact unit and can also be programmed to edit data, compress data, con-

vert between ASCII and EBCDIC, and check for errors. (559)

CONNECTORS Circular connectors link parts of a flowchart that are on the same page; five-sided connectors link parts that are on different pages. (483)

CONTENTION Opposite of polling, a protocol where the peripheral device asks the computer if the medium is free for transmission. CSMA/CD (Carrier Sense Multiple Access/Collision Detection) and token passing are two examples of contention. (557)

CONTENTS LINE A line located at the top or bottom of spreadsheet screens that identifies the active cell and displays its contents. (320)

CONTINUOUS TONE ART Graphic images that contain varying shades of gray ranging from white to black. (413)

CONTROL MODULE The top module that gives orders to other modules in the program. (479)

CONTROL-AND-PROCESSING MODULE This middle module performs control operations over lower-level modules and carries out processing functions. (479)

CONTROL TOTALS Technique for checking the integrity of the data. (577)

CONTROL UNIT Part of the CPU that directs the arithmetic/logic unit that performs the input, processing, and output of data. (50, 138)

CORPORATEWIDE COMPUTING Where computing services for the entire organization are performed. (538)

COUNTER A variable that changes by a fixed value each time it is encountered in a program; often used in loop control. (489)

COUPLING Describes how easily a program module can be removed and modified. (433)

CPU See Central processing unit.

CRASH CONVERSION See Direct-cutover conversion.

CRT See Display terminal.

CRT-BASED WORD PROCESSOR Computer that displays a text document file directly on a screen

(CRT) for text entry and editing. (273)

CSMA/CD (Carrier Sense Multiple Access/Collision Detection) A contention protocol with the feature of ordering retransmission if there is a garbled transmission. (557)

CUBE See Workpad.

CURSOR The movable, sometimes blinking symbol on the display screen that shows you where you are. (180)

CYLINDERS A conceptual "slice" of a disk made up of vertical stacks of tracks and a way of storing data on a disk that speeds up seek time. (218)

DAISY-WHEEL PRINTER Character printer that produces letter-quality output using a print element that spins to the appropriate character. It is slower than most other types of impact printers. (194)

DASD See Direct Access Storage Device.

DATA Facts from which information may be drawn. (7)

DATABASE A set of interrelated files. (44, 350)

DATABASE ADMINISTRATOR Person responsible for setting up databases, maintaining them, and helping programmers and users to utilize them properly. (363)

DATABASE MANAGEMENT SYSTEM (DBMS) Software that allows users with different application needs to create, access, modify, and maintain databases. (247, 363)

DATA CELL See Magnetic strip cartridge system.

DATA COMMUNICATIONS The transmission, reception, and validation of data. (539)

DATA COMMUNICATIONS MEDIUM Physical link by which data are transmitted. (548)

DATA DEFINITION LANGUAGE (DDL) The language used in schemas and subschemas for a database. (369)

DATA DICTIONARY Definitions of each item of data and information handled by a system that give format, input source, and output use. (369, 442)

DATA ENTRY The process of getting facts into a form that the computer can interpret. (174)

DATA-FLOW DIAGRAM A visual way to trace how data move through the system. (442)

DATA HIERARCHY The classification of data from lowest to highest level: field, record, file, and database. (43, 350)

DATA INDEPENDENCE A condition that exists in a database or file when data are accessible to any legitimate program regardless of the data's physical location, or the program's language. (361)

DATA INTEGRITY The accuracy of the data throughout the system. (361, 572)

DATA MANIPULATION LANGUAGE (DML) The commands programmers use when performing operations on a database. (377)

DATA QUALITY ASSURANCE The process of evaluating data integrity throughout the system. (577)

DATA REDUNDANCY When the same data exist in more than one place in a database or file. (361)

DATA SECURITY The protection and care of data. (578)

DATA-TRANSFER TIME Time it takes to transfer the data from a location either to the computer for reading or from the computer to the disk for writing. (217)

DBMS *See* Database management system.

DDL *See* Data definition language.

DEBUGGING The process of finding and correcting errors in programs. (492)

DECENTRALIZED PROCESSING Several computers functioning independently of others within the same organization. (536)

DECIMAL (BASE 10) NUMBER SYSTEM The number system we are all familiar with; it uses the numerals 0 through 9. (163)

DECISION SUPPORT SYSTEM (DSS) System that managers can use easily and that provides highly refined information to help in making nonroutine decisions. (86)

DECISION SYMBOL Denotes choices based upon comparisons. (485)

DECISION TABLE Shows what action to take given particular conditions. (446)

DECODER The part of the control unit that reads the instruction code and sets circuitry for the operation. (140)

DEDICATED WORD PROCESSOR A computer that has been programmed and equipped with a special keyboard to perform only word processing tasks. (273)

DEFAULT SETTING The "normal" computer data set-up; used by a computer program that defines a usual operating condition or hardware configuration. (265)

DELETION The process by which text is removed from a document. (274)

DEMAND REPORT A report that is generated only when requested, and generally concerns a specific topic of interest to a manager. (76)

DEMODULATION Converting the analog signal back to digital at the receiving modem. (554)

DEPARTMENTAL COMPUTING Mid-level computing. (538)

DESIGN REPORT Complete output of the system design stage. (452)

DESIGN REVIEW A meeting at which user, managers, and the systems analyst go over the system design. (452)

DESK-CHECKING Debugging technique where the programmer sits down with a copy of the failed program and its output and attempts to correct any errors that may have occurred. (492)

DESKTOP PUBLISHING Using a microcomputer to combine text and graphics into a professional-looking layout that approximates typeset quality. (254, 392)

DESKTOP SCANNER Resembling a small copy machine, it has applications in advertising and engineering. (188)

DESTRUCTIVE WRITE Writing new material into a storage location and erasing the old material in the process. (142)

DETAILED INVESTIGATION The second step of the system development process that details the nature of the problem and offers possible solutions. (438)

DIFFERENCE ENGINE Mechanical device invented by Charles Babbage for generating tables of squares, cubes, and other functions but was never completed. (104)

DIRECT ACCESS Ability to retrieve or write a given record without first having to process all the records leading up to it. (212, 355)

DIRECT-ACCESS FILE OR RANDOM-ACCESS FILE File that locates the address of a record using a key. (358)

DIRECT-ACCESS STORAGE DEVICE (DASD) Another name for a magnetic disk unit. (213)

DIRECT CUTOVER CONVERSION Also known as crash conversion, it refers to implementing the new system all at once and dropping the old system at the same time. (454)

DISK OR DISKETTE *See* Floppy disk.

DISK CARTRIDGE One or two hard disks placed in a sealed disk cartridge. (214)

DISK PACK A number of disk platters stacked vertically as a unit. (214)

DISPLAY SCREEN An output element for producing "soft copy" a person can view. Part of a display terminal. (57)

DISPLAY TERMINAL Also known as a CRT (cathode-ray tube) or VDT (video display terminal), this peripheral has an input device, display screen, and a screen control unit to link the two. (177)

DISTRIBUTED PROCESSING System that shares computing power among several different computers via data communications throughout an organizations network. (536)

DML *See* Data manipulation language.

DOCUMENTATION Materials that explain to users how to use the program, operators how to run it, and programmers how to change it. (476)

DOCUMENT READER An optical scanner that can read all forms of printed matter. (186)

DOT-MATRIX PRINTER A common type of character printer that uses tiny pins in a cluster to print a letter, number or symbol. (194)

DOUNTIL LOOP Program process that continues until a specified condition is met. (488)

DOWHILE LOOP Program process that continues as long as a condition is true. (488)

DSS *See* Decision support system.

DUAL PROCESSING Using redundant equipment in case of equipment failures which would jeopardize important projects. (586)

DUMB TERMINAL Display terminal with no information-processing capabilities. (179)

DUPLEX TRANSMISSION *See* Full-duplex transmission.

EAVESDROPPING Illegal interception of data sent via a data communications link. (578)

EBCDIC (EXTENDED BINARY CODED DECIMAL INTERCHANGE CODE) Assignment of a bit pattern to each of the decimal numbers 0 through 9, lower- and uppercase alphabet, and commonly used special symbols. (147)

EDITING The manipulation of text into a more useful and understandable form. (295)

EDSAC (ELECTRONIC DELAY STORAGE AUTOMATIC COMPUTER) The prototype for today's computers, it used the stored program concept. (109)

EDUCATION PRIVACY ACT (1974) Protects the privacy of students concerning grades and other evaluation data maintained by schools. (593)

ELECTROMECHANICAL ACCOUNTING MACHINE (EAM) Machine that used electrical impulses to activate mechanical elements and used punch card technology to process data. (106)

ELECTRONIC BULLETIN BOARD Computer-maintained list of messages that can be posted and read by different computers. (250)

ELECTRONIC COMMUNICATIONS PRIVACY ACT (1986) Broadens the scope of the Privacy Act of 1974. (594)

ELECTRONIC COMPUTER Uses only electrical switches and circuitry to carry out processing or computing functions. (108)

ELECTRONIC MAIL *See* Electronic Mail/Message System.

ELECTRONIC MAIL/MESSAGE SYSTEM (EMMS) OR E-MAIL Allows people to send memos, messages, facsimiles, illustrations, and so on by electronic means. (81, 248)

ELECTRONIC MOUSE Palm-sized device that can be moved across a flat surface in order to move a pointer on the display screen. (177)

ELECTRONIC SPREADSHEET A type of software that offers the user a financial worksheet with rows and columns and an easy way to change figures around within the worksheet. (244, 313)

ELECTRONIC THESAURUS A word processing adjunct program that suggests synonyms for selected words in the document. (301)

E-MAIL *See* Electronic Mail/Message System.

EMBEDDED SYMBOLS Special characters placed on a computer screen by some word processing programs to indicate character changes. (286)

EMMS *See* Electronic Mail/Message System.

ENCRYPTION Coding or scrambling of data, messages, or programs in order to foil eavesdroppers. (578)

END-OF-FILE (EOF) FLAG A kind of switch set to mark the end of a program loop. (489)

END-USER COMPUTING Individual and small groups of users. (538)

ENGINE Another term for a laser printer—specifically, the main component of the printing mechanism. (408)

ENIAC (ELECTRONIC NUMERICAL INTEGRATOR AND CALCULATOR) Built between 1943 and 1946 by John W. Mauchley and J. Presper Eckert, it was used by the U.S. army for calculating ballistics tables. (108)

ENVIRONMENT The external factors that affect the system. (38)

EPROM (ERASABLE PROGRAMMABLE READ-ONLY MEMORY) PROM's that may be reprogrammed by the user. (155)

ERASABLE PROGRAMMABLE READ-ONLY MEMORY *See* EPROM.

EXCEPTION PROCEDURES Rules and procedures used when standard operating procedures cannot be followed. (43, 576)

EXCEPTION REPORT A scheduled or special report that highlights significant changes from whatever conditions are usual. (76)

EXECUTION CYCLE The performance of one computer operation. (144)

EXPERT SYSTEM Software that tries to imitate human experts by giving technical advice in forms closely resembling the user's language. These packages are subsets of a decision support system. (87)

EXPLODED PIE CHART An enhancement of a pie chart that separates pieces in order to highlight data of particular interest. (417)

EXTERNAL STORAGE *See* Secondary storage.

FAIR CREDIT REPORTING ACT (1970) A law that gives individuals the right to examine credit records maintained about them by private organizations. (593)

FAULT TOLERANT COMPUTERS Special computers highly resistant to failure. (536)

FAX OR FACSIMILE TRANSMISSION MACHINES Devices that allow text or art to be sent electronically from one location to another via a telephone line. (189)

FEASIBILITY REPORT The complete findings of the systems analyst's detailed investigation. (447)

FEEDBACK This process allows a system to regulate itself by treating the effect of its output on the environment as new input. (39)

FERRO-ELECTRIC RAM Nonvolatile memory using a ceramic film over a silicon chip. (231)

FIBER-OPTIC CABLE Communications medium using ultra-thin glass filaments that transmit data with light-beam signals generated by lasers. (548)

FIELD A single data element such as name, age, or social security number that is treated as a unit. (44, 350)

FIFTH-GENERATION COMPUTER Newest computer technology now being developed in the United States and Japan. (621)

FIFTH-GENERATION LANGUAGE A language used to express complex logical versus computational operations in a form the computer can interpret. (518)

FILE A set of related records. (44, 350)

FILE DESIGN Techniques used to store and retrieve data. Three main types of file design are: sequential, indexed sequential, and direct-access. (352)

FILE-MANAGEMENT SYSTEM (FMS) A data filing program that allows only one file to be open at a time. (369)

FILE SERVER A microcomputer that controls the shared database and programs in a micro-to-micro link. (543)

FINANCE PACKAGES Software for forecasting, credit checking or modeling the outcomes of various investment decisions. (256)

FIRMWARE Programs permanently recorded on ROM OR PROM chips—a blend of hardware and software. (52, 155)

FIRST-GENERATION COMPUTERS (1951–1958) Much faster than earlier electromechanical devices, these machines used vacuum tubes for internal processing. (111)

FIXED-LENGTH WORDS Computer words that contain a specific number of bytes, making parallel arithmetic possible. (149)

FLAG See End-of-File Flag.

FLEXIBLE MANUFACTURING SYSTEM (FMS) An approach using computer-directed machinery throughout the production process. (21)

FLOPPY DISK OR DISKETTE Flexible plastic disk covered with magnetic material commonly used for storage on all types of computers. (215)

FLOWCHART Diagram that shows how a program works in terms of sequence, movement of data, and logic. (478)

FLOWCHART TEMPLATE Guide for drawing flowchart symbols. (483)

FLOWLINES Lines with arrows that link the symbols on a flowchart and help the reader follow the information flow. (483)

FMS See Flexible Manufacturing System.

FORMATTING Organizing of data on a disk surface. (218)

FORMULA In spreadsheets, a mathematical statement placed in a cell to relate values in one or more cells. (324)

FORTRAN (FORmula TRANslator) A science-oriented procedural programming language developed at IBM by John Backus and introduced in 1957. (116, 513)

FOURTH-GENERATION COMPUTERS (1971–?), This computer is distinguished from the third-generation model by the development of the microprocessor. (119)

FOURTH-GENERATION LANGUAGE Business-oriented nonprocedural languages designed to link with databases. (517)

FREEDOM OF INFORMATION ACT (1970) Gives individuals, as well as organizations, the right to inspect data concerning them that are maintained by agencies of the federal government. (593)

FRONT-END PROCESSOR A minicomputer that oversees input and output operations for a host computer. (560)

FULL-DUPLEX OR DUPLEX TRANSMISSION Simultaneous, bi-directional transmissions. (554)

FUNCTIONAL DECOMPOSITION A method used to break a problem into its subcomponents and used in structured programming for creating modules. (477)

GANTT CHART A helpful planning tool that shows how various steps of a project relate to each other over time. (438)

GATES, BILL A software designer whose Microsoft Corporation produced the MS-DOS and OS/2 operating systems that control processing in IBM's microcomputer lines. (124)

GENERAL-PURPOSE DIGITAL COMPUTER The main type of computer in use today, it can be used for a variety of large and small business, engineering, and scientific applications. (46)

GIGABYTE OR G A billion bytes. (210)

GRAMMAR CHECKERS Adjunct programs that identify errors in basic punctuation and syntax of word processing documents. (303)

GRAPHICS PACKAGE Software that allows the construction and output of pictorial information. (250)

GRAPHICS SCANNER An optical scanner that can digitize art and other graphic patterns. (187)

GRAPHICS TABLET OR DIGITIZER Electrically wired surfaces upon which a user can draw diagrams for entry as data. (177)

GREEKING Used in desktop publishing, it provides a reduced visual representation of a page layout. (402)

HACKER Individual who enjoys the challenge of testing the operating limits of a computer system. (573)

HALF-DUPLEX TRANSMISSION Transmission in one direction at a time as found, for example, in telegraphs and two-way radios. (553)

HALFTONE A procedure for printing photographs where different sizes and shapes of black dots create the illusion of various shades of gray. (413)

HARD COPY Computer printout on paper, punched cards, microfiche, labels, forms, or reprographics machine output. (57)

HARD DISKS Rigid or metal disks inside a magnetic disk unit. (214)

HARDWARE Physical equipment used in an information system. (46)

HASHING Technique that transforms a key into an actual address. (358)

HEXADECIMAL (BASE 16) NUMBER SYSTEM A number system sometimes used on computers to reduce the space required; it consists of the numerals 0 through 15. (167)

HIERARCHICAL DATABASE The arrangement of data elements to one another as "parents" and "children" following a treelike structure and where each "child" can have only one "parent." (364)

HIERARCHICAL NETWORK This structure has a main computer at its top with communication links spread downward and outward with the main computer in command. (545)

HIGHLIGHTING The use of increased screen brightness to indicate a range of text or values. (286)

HIGH-SPEED PAGE PRINTER This printer usually uses laser technology to produce a page of output at one time. (197)

HOLLERITH, HERMAN (1860-1929) Statistician who developed a tabulating machine using a punch card system. (105)

HOME MANAGEMENT SOFTWARE Performs convenience-oriented services such as checkbook balancing, recipe recall, and shopping-list generation. (261)

HOPPER, GRACE A major developer of COBOL and considered by many to be the world's second computer programmer (after Lady Ada, Countess of Lovelace). (116)

HORIZONTAL SOFTWARE Prewritten, general-use programs that can be applied to many businesses (i.e., word processing). (243)

HOST PROCESSOR The computer to which the local user hardware is connected and that does the actual processing. (541)

IBM PC A microcomputer offered by IBM in 1981 and also called the Personal Computer, it legitimized the role of microcomputers in the workplace. (119)

IBM 360 Most significant third-generation computer, it served both scientific and business users. (117)

IC See Integrated circuit.

ICONS Pictorial representations of operations the computer can carry out. (181)

IFTHENELSE Another name for selection logic patterns shown in the diamond-shaped flowchart symbols on a flowchart. (487)

IMPACT PRINTER Peripheral whose printing mechanism physically contacts the paper. (194)

INDEXED SEQUENTIAL FILE Files arranged in a predetermined order but with a separate index file for finding records. (355)

INDEXING In word processing, a process in which an alphabetical list of selected words and their page references is prepared. (303)

INFERENCE ENGINE A component of expert system software for carrying out logical reasonings (as differentiated from data calculations.) (88)

INFORMATION Knowledge communicated in a timely, accurate, and understandable fashion. (7)

INFORMATION RESOURCE MANAGEMENT SYSTEM (IRMS) System which coordinates the total acquisition, flow, storage, and distribution of data and information in an organization and which uses not only transaction data but data from written text and voice/image communications. (90)

INFORMATION SYSTEM A set of interrelated elements working together to produce information. (10, 40)

INFORMATION SYSTEM CONTROLS Features that monitor and ensure the proper operation of all five information-system elements. (572)

INFORMATION SYSTEM STAFF The personnel who support the users with assistance in developing and maintaining the system. (41)

INITIALIZATION Setting a counter to a certain value before a program enters a loop. (489)

INK-JET PRINTER Nonimpact printer that uses electrically charged ink droplets sprayed between two electrically charged plates. (197)

INPUT The stage where data enter the information system from the environment. (11, 39, 174)

INPUT DEVICE Hardware that transmits data and software to the computer for processing. (56)

INPUT/OUTPUT CONTROL PROGRAM Part of the operating system program that supervises the transfer of data from input devices to main memory, and from main memory to output devices. (522)

INPUT/OUTPUT SYMBOL Represents any input or output operation on a flowchart and is labeled with the function and equipment used. (483)

INPUT-PROCESS-OUTPUT (IPO) CHARTS Diagrams that show in detail the input, processing, and output steps necessary to execute the module. (478)

INPUT STORAGE Part of main memory that holds data that have been read from an input device. (141)

INSERT/INSERTION A procedure that allows new text to be added to a document without destroying old text material. (274)

INSTALLATION PROGRAM A set of options included with most programs that allows a user to match the program to specific hardware, or configure the program for specific needs. (265)

INSTRUCTION CYCLE Time in which the CPU fetches an instruction, selects an op code, and interprets the operand. (144)

INTEGRATED CIRCUIT (IC) Combines transistors and circuitry into one unit etched onto a silicon chip. The IC was the major technological breakthrough for third-generation computers. (116)

INTEGRATED SERVICES DIGITAL NETWORK (ISDN) Set of international standards to integrate voice and data through the use of digital lines and switches. (561)

INTEGRATED SOFTWARE PACKAGES Prewritten software that contains features such as electronic spreadsheets, database management, and graphics. (251)

INTELLIGENT TERMINAL OR SMART TERMINAL A display terminal that can perform some processing on its own. (178)

INTERACTIVE PROCESSING Whereby the user can make requests to the computer and receive responses as though sharing a dialogue. (506)

INTERACTIVE PROGRAMMING LANGUAGES Languages such as BASIC that are better than others for writing programs interactively with the computer helping the programmer. (506)

INTERBLOCK GAP Space between "blocks" of records on a magnetic tape allowing the tape to reach operational speed. (224)

INTERPRETER Language translator that translates a program one line at a time. (526)

INTERRECORD GAP Space left between each record on a magnetic tape allowing the tape to reach operational speed. (224)

INVERSE VIDEO A reversal of foreground and background colors used to highlight text on a computer screen. (286)

IRMS *See* Information Resource Management System.

JACQUARD, JOSEPH-MARIE (1752–1834) Inventor of the Jacquard loom. (103)

JACQUARD LOOM A machine that used a punch card reading system to weave certain patterns. Forms of this machine are still in use today. Most important, it developed the means of controlling a machine by a variable program. (103)

JOB CONTROL PROGRAM Part of the operating system that prepares an application program and its data (a job) to be run. (522)

JOB DISPLACEMENT This occurs when the skills necessary to perform a job change. (609)

JOB ENHANCEMENT Making a job easier and more enjoyable. (609)

JOB REPLACEMENT When a job held by a person is taken over by a robot or machine programmed to perform the same task. (607)

JOSEPHSON JUNCTIONS Named after Brian Josephson, these circuits use supercooled temperatures and offer extremely fast memory access. (619)

JUSTIFICATION In word processing, the alignment of text so that it falls exactly on the margin; typically refers to full justification where text is aligned on both left and right margins. (274)

K Kilobit (1024 or 2^{10} bits). (155)

KEMENY, JOHN G. AND THOMAS KURTZ Co-developers of the BASIC programming language. (118)

KERNING Placing letters with common edges closer together for easier readability and space-saving. (400)

KEY A field that orders a sequential file and that uniquely identifies a record. (352)

KEYBOARD Typewriter-like sets of keys used for entering numeric and alphabetic data and are the most common input device. (57, 177)

KILOBYTE OR K Just over one thousand bytes. (1024 or 2^{10} bytes). (45)

KNOWLEDGE BASE OR RULE SET Part of the knowledge system that tells the inference engine how to reason in a particular business environment. (88)

KNOWLEDGE SYSTEM A component of an expert system that contains the knowledge base or rule set, transaction databases, productivity software, and analytical models. (88)

LABEL In spreadsheets, a combination of typewritten characters used to display non-numeric data. (322)

LAN *See* Local Area Network.

LANGUAGE TRANSLATORS System software that translates procedural nonprocedural, or assembly languages into machine language. (526)

LARGE-SCALE INTEGRATION (LSI) Process of placing thousands of integrated circuits onto a single silicon chip. (119)

LASER PRINTER Printer that uses low-intensity laser beams for printing an entire page of high-quality output at high speed. (197)

LAYOUT In desktop publishing, a page arrangement interplay of text, graphics, and white space. (402)

LIBRARY PROGRAM Prewritten software usually stored on a direct-access device for general use. (528)

LIGHT PEN Pencil-like light-sensitive rod that can be pointed at a display screen to perform input functions or draw diagrams. (177)

LINE ART Graphic images that contain only black lines on a white background. (413)

LINE GRAPH A pictorial representation of data using lines to connect a series of values along a time continuum. (416)

LINE PRINTER Peripheral that prints an entire line at once. (194)

LISP A list-processing language which is being used in the development of artificial intelligence programs. (518)

LIST-PROCESSING LANGUAGE A nonprocedural language that processes data in the form of lists. (518)

LOCAL AREA NETWORK (LAN) Also known as local network, it provides offices with the capability of data communications in a smaller setting. (562)

LOCAL USER HARDWARE One or more peripheral devices (even a computer) having a data communications link to the host computer. (541)

LOGICAL DESIGN Determining the logical or conceptual model of input, output and feedback requirements for the new system. (449)

LOGIC GATE One of the main components of the ALU, it performs comparisons. (141)

LOGO A nonprocedural language derived from LISP during the 1960s and used extensively in schools. (518)

LOOP When a program repetitively executes one or a series of steps. Two major types of loops are DOWHILE and DOUNTIL. (488)

LOVELACE, LADY ADA AUGUSTA, THE COUNTESS OF (1816–1852) A brilliant mathematician who worked with Charles Babbage on the analytic engine's machine instructions, thus becoming the world's first programmer. (105)

LOW-LEVEL LANGUAGE A computer language in which each instruction corresponds to an instruction for a particular computer. (502)

LSI *See* Large-Scale Integration.

MACHINE CYCLE The time required to carry out one operation inside the CPU. (144)

MACHINE INDEPENDENCE How easily a program written to run using one particular make and model of computer can be run on another. (505)

MACHINE LANGUAGE The only language the central processing unit understands; it consists of 1s and 0s. (113, 507)

MACRO A list of computer instructions that can be activated with one preset keystroke. (337)

MAGNETIC DISK An input, output, and secondary storage medium from the third generation still used today. (213)

MAGNETIC DISK UNIT Peripheral device that can send, receive and store data at high rates of speed and is sometimes called a direct-access storage device. (57, 212)

MAGNETIC-INK CHARACTER RECOGNITION (MICR) A system of letters, numbers and symbols imprinted with a special iron-oxide ink, used primarily in banking. (190)

MAGNETIC-STRIP CARTRIDGE SYSTEM OR DATA CELL One of the most common types of mass storage media. (226)

MAGNETIC STRIP READERS Devices that read data encoded on the backs of credit and bank debit cards. (190)

MAGNETIC TAPE Rapid, high-capacity secondary storage media. (220)

MAGNETIC TAPE CASSETTES Secondary storage media sometimes used on microcomputers instead of disks. (223)

MAGNETIC TAPE UNIT Also known as a tape drive, this common secondary storage device can send, receive, and store large amounts of data at high rates of speed. (57, 222)

MAIL MERGE In word processing, a technique that combines previously prepared form letters with specific data to produce personalized documents. (278)

MAIN MEMORY OR PRIMARY STORAGE UNIT Part of the computer that stores data and instructions that have been input and are waiting to be processed, and stores the results of processing until they are released to output devices or to secondary storage. (50, 138)

MAIN PROGRAM The overall program that directs subroutines. (481)

MAINFRAME COMPUTERS Computers that range over a wide spectrum of processing speeds and capabilities and are used by business, government, science, engineering, and education in a variety of applications. (53)

MANAGEMENT INFORMATION SYSTEM (MIS) An information system designed to aid in the performance of management functions. It processes the transactions of an organization's day-to-day operations, and creates information in the form of reports. (84)

MANAGEMENT-ORIENTED SOFTWARE Programs for the areas of personnel management, operations management, forecasting, facilities maintenance, and resource management. (256)

MARK I Also known as Automatic Sequence Controlled Calculator was an electromechanical computer invented by Dr. Howard Aiken. (107)

MASQUERADING Unauthorized users passing themselves off as authorized users. (587)

MASS STORAGE DEVICES Magnetic strip cartridges or data cells, multiple-disk-drive-systems, optical disk systems and videotape systems on which enormous quantities of data can be stored. (225)

MATH GATE One of the three main components of the arithmetic/logic unit, it performs basic calculations. (141)

MAUCHLY, JOHN W., AND J. PRESPER ECKERT Co-developers of ENIAC. (108)

MEGABYTE OR M One million bytes. (45)

MEMORY CONTROL PROGRAM Part of the operating system that keeps track of a program's location in main memory and secondary storage. (525)

MENU A series of choices concerning the use of the program. (242)

MENU MACROS Automated customized lists of options in a spreadsheet created by a macro. (337)

MESSAGE SWITCHER Data communications device that routes messages from many incoming telecommunications media into the front-end processor. (560)

MICROCOMPUTER Smallest type of computer and that usually has its CPU upon a single chip, it is also known as a personal computer. (52)

MICROLASERS Possible future optical substitute for electronic circuitry in computers. (619)

MICROPROCESSOR The control and arithmetic/logic unit of the computer and some main memory etched onto a single chip. First produced commercially by Texas Instruments Corporation in 1971, it paved the way for the development of the microcomputer. (51, 119, 150)

MICROSECONDS Millionths of a second—the speed at which second-generation computers could perform arithmetic and logical operations. (114)

MICRO-TO-MAINFRAME LINK When the microcomputer serves as a terminal to the host computer. (542)

MICRO-TO-MICRO LINK Hardware and software that permits a microcomputer user access to files and programs stored on a different microcomputer. (543)

MICROWAVE SYSTEM A communications medium that uses high-frequency electromagnetic waves through space to microwave receiving stations. (549)

MILLISECONDS Thousandths of a second—the speed at which first-generation computers could make calculations. (111)

MINICOMPUTER Larger, faster and with more memory capacity than the typical microcomputer, it is frequently used to support scientific and engineering tasks. (53)

MIS *See* Management Information System.

MIXED NETWORK Also known as an unconstrained network, it uses a combination of the four approaches: star, ring, hierarchical, and bus. (547)

MODEM Communications hardware that performs the task of

modulation and demodulation. (554)

MODULATION Converting digital signals by means of a modem into a form that can be carried over analog lines. (554)

MODULE A self-contained, well-defined subpart of a structured program that performs a single function. (433, 474)

MS-DOS (MICROSOFT-DISK OPERATING SYSTEM) An operating system that has become standard for most microcomputers. (528)

MULTIDROP LINE Links multiple devices on a shared data communications line. (558)

MULTIPLE-DISK-DRIVE SYSTEM Mass storage that teams up magnetic disk units and is used for large-scale real-time applications such as travel reservation systems and credit card validation systems. (226)

MULTIPLEXERS OR MULTIPLEXORS Devices that allow multiple users to share a common data communications medium. (559)

MULTIPROCESSING Two or more CPUs executing instructions at the same time from the same or different programs. (523)

MULTIPROGRAMMING Concurrent execution of more than one program at a time. (523)

NANOSECONDS Billionths of a second—the speed at which some third-generation computers can operate. (117)

NARROWBAND OR SUB-VOICE GRADE MEDIUM This communications medium transmits to and from low-speed data terminals such as teletypewriter and telegraph systems. (551)

NATURAL LANGUAGE Our speaking languages such as Chinese, English, or Greek. (519)

NETWORK Computers linked together with communications devices. (58, 539)

NETWORK DATABASE A database similar to an hierarchical database but one in which each "child" can have more than one "parent." (365)

NETWORK TOPOLOGY Logical and physical arrangement of the communications hardware, com-

puters and other peripherals. (543)

NIBBLE OR NYBBLE Half of a byte—usually 4 bits. (147)

NONDESTRUCTIVE READ The ability to look at or copy the data in a storage address without destroying it. (142)

NONIMPACT PRINTER A peripheral whose print mechanism does not contact the paper in order to print. Thermal, ink-jet, and laser are three main nonimpact types of printers. (196)

NONPROCEDURAL LANGUAGES Computer languages even farther away from the inner workings of the computer than low-level and procedural languages and include fourth-generation, simulation, and fifth-generation languages. (502)

NUMERIC FIELD A field that contains only numbers such as an employee number. (350)

NYBBLE See Nibble.

OCTAL (BASE 8) NUMBER SYSTEM A numbering system sometimes used on computers that is based on eight numerals (0 through 7). (165)

OFF-LINE STORAGE Storage not under the direct control of the computer. (57, 212)

OFF-THE-SHELF PROGRAM See Prewritten software.

ON-LINE STORAGE Data and software that the computer can directly access. (57, 212)

ON-LINE TRANSACTION PROCESSING (OLTP) Real-time updating of a company's database. (536)

OP CODE OR OPERATION CODE The part of machine instructions that tells the computer what operation to perform. (140)

OPERAND Machine instructions that give the address of the data that are to be operated on. (140)

OPERATING SYSTEM A type of system software that supervises and directs all of the other software components plus the computer hardware. The main components of the operating system include the job, input/output, program, and memory control programs. (45, 521)

OPERATOR-ORIENTED DOCUMENTATION Paperwork consisting of a run manual which describes how to run the program and which peripherals should be on-line, and so on. (473)

OPTICAL CARD SYSTEM Cards the size of a credit card that can store millions of bytes of data. (229)

OPTICAL CHARACTER READER (OCR) This peripheral can detect printed letters and numbers as well as marks. (186)

OPTICAL DISK SYSTEM Type of archival mass storage also known as a laser disk system. (227)

OPTICAL MARK READER (OMR) This peripheral senses marks on special paper forms. (185)

OPTICAL SCANNER This peripheral uses visible light or lasers to read characters, numbers or patterns. (57, 185)

OS/2 (OPERATING SYSTEM/2) Operating system used on IBM PS/2 microcomputers. (528)

OUTLINED FONT A mathematical model that describes the shape of each character. (401)

OUTPUT Communicates the results of processing. Output is often in a form people can read: permanent copy on paper or temporary form as on a display terminal, and sometimes on permanent machine-readable storage (magnetic disk or magnetic tape). (19, 39, 175)

OUTPUT DEVICE Hardware that can produce information in a form that people can read, or that is machine-readable. (56)

OUTPUT STORAGE Holds the processed information to be transmitted to an output device at a slower speed. (141)

PACKAGED SOFTWARE See Prewritten software.

PACKET-SWITCHING Protocol found in multiply connected networks that allows the most efficient use of the network. (557)

PAGE DESCRIPTION LANGUAGE (PDL) A set of instructions used to communicate outlined fonts and layout patterns from a word processor or desktop publisher to a printer. (401)

PARALLEL ARITHMETIC Performing calculations on all digits of a number (or computer word) simultaneously. (149)

PARALLEL CONVERSION Implementation of the new system while running the old system side by side over a period of time. (455)

PARALLEL PROCESSING COMPUTERS Computers with many processors that can carry out many instructions at the same time. (124, 619)

PARENT A data element in a hierarchical or network database that is above the "child" and connected to it. (364)

PARITY BIT OR CHECK BIT A protective bit added to a byte and used to spot cases of garbled bytes. (148)

PASCAL A structured programming language developed by Niklaus Wirth and named after the French inventor and mathematician Blaise Pascal. (122, 511)

PASCAL, BLAISE (1623–1662) French mathematician who invented the mechanical calculator, the Pascaline. (102)

PASCALINE The first mechanical calculator, invented by Blaise Pascal, it could add and subtract. (102)

PERIPHERAL EQUIPMENT Input, output, storage, and communications devices that are attached to the computer. (11)

PERT DIAGRAM Helpful planning tool for monitoring a project. (438)

PHASED CONVERSION Gradually implementing the new system in stages over a period of time. (455)

PHYSICAL DESIGN Determining specifications of the new system using the results of the logical design stage including the hardware and software requirements of a system. (449)

PHYSICAL SECURITY Protection of the hardware and storage media from theft, vandalism, and misuse. (584)

PICOSECONDS Trillionths of a second—the speed at which some of today's fastest computers can be measured. (120)

PIE CHART A circular pictorial representation of data that compares the relative contribution of each value (shown as a pie slice) to the total. (417)

PILOT CONVERSION Implementing the new system in its entirety on a trial basis but only to a small part of the organization. (455)

PIXEL (Picture Element) The smallest element of a display screen assigned color and intensity. (179)

PLOTTER A device that can output computer graphics. (198)

POINT-OF-ACTIVITY (POA) TERMINAL Input units located where a specific activity occurs, to capture data at their source. (184)

POINT-OF-SALE (POS) TERMINAL An input device that combines a cash register with a computer terminal linked to an information system. (28, 184)

POLLING Protocol where the computer checks each device periodically to see if it has a message to send. (557)

POSITION IDENTIFIERS In word processing, numbers shown on the screen that help users keep track of their position in the document—typically page, line, and column. (284)

PREDEFINED PROCESS SYMBOL Indicates a prewritten subprogram or subroutine which is called upon request. (485)

PREDICTIVE REPORT Report based upon specific data that attempts to identify future trends but does not show much detail. (76)

PRELIMINARY INVESTIGATION The first step in systems analysis includes evaluating the user's request, determining costs and benefits, and planning the detailed analysis. (437)

PRELIMINARY REPORT Report prepared by the systems analyst upon completion of the preliminary investigation. It states approximate cost or benefits of developing a new system and the time and resources to carry out detailed analysis. (438)

PREPARATION SYMBOL Denotes any steps that involve prelimi-

nary or preparatory function such as initializing a variable. (483)

PRESENTATION GRAPHICS An extended form of analytical graphics that employ better resolution and may combine sophisticated art. (418)

PREWRITTEN SOFTWARE Programs that were written and tested by someone else. (240)

PRIMARY STORAGE See Main memory.

PRINTER Device that produces hard or permanent copy. (57)

PRINTER CONTROL LANGUAGE (PCL) A set of instructions used to communicate bit-mapped fonts and layout settings from a word processor or desktop publisher to a printer. (401)

PRINTING Producing a hard copy on paper. (277)

PRIVACY The protection of individuals and organizations from unauthorized access to or abuse of data concerning them. (572)

PRIVACY ACT (1974) Offers protection to individuals and organizations from data-gathering abuses by the federal government. (593)

PRIVATE BRANCH EXCHANGE (PBX) A switching center that connects a group of user's telephone equipment to a smaller number of outside telephone lines. (561)

PROBLEM RECOGNITION The first and most important step of the system development process involves identifying a need or opportunity. (436)

PROCEDURAL LANGUAGES High-level, computer languages that use English-like statements and mathematical symbols and include: BASIC, Pascal, COBOL, and FORTRAN. (502)

PROCESS PROGRAM A type of system software subordinate to the operating system that performs specific functions such as translating an application program into machine language. (521)

PROCESS SYMBOL Represents mathematical computations and data manipulation. (483)

PROCESSING The stage in which raw data are manipulated to produce the desired information. Performed either manually or by computer, processing can consist of one or more action(s) including: calculating, comparing, communicating, sorting, summarizing, selecting, storing, and recalling. (11, 39)

PROCESSING MODULE The lowest level of modules in structured program design which carry out the orders required by the higher modules. (479)

PRODUCTIVITY SOFTWARE Prewritten, pretested, ready-to-run software packages from outside suppliers. (46)

PROGRAM See Software.

PROGRAM CODING Translating the program design into a programming language that will run on the computer. (470)

PROGRAM CONTROL PROGRAM Part of the operating system that handles the movement of programs (or parts of programs) into main memory. (522)

PROGRAM DESIGN Specifying the structure of the program in detail. (470)

PROGRAM DEVELOPMENT PROCESS Seven steps needed to solve a programming problem: problem recognition, problem definition, program design, coding, testing, implementation, and maintenance. (470)

PROGRAM DOCUMENTATION Manuals, display screens, and other materials that tell users how to use the program, operators how to run it, and programmers how to change it. (472)

PROGRAM IMPLEMENTATION The actual use of the new program. (472)

PROGRAMMABLE READ-ONLY MEMORY (PROM) A chip that holds procedures that cannot be erased. (52, 155)

PROGRAM MAINTENANCE Correcting any undetected errors and making needed changes. (472)

PROGRAM STORAGE Holds instructions from system and application programs which enter the CPU. (141)

PROGRAM TESTING Checking the program for errors and rewriting parts of the program to correct the mistakes. (472)

PROGRAMMER Person who writes computer programs or software. (468)

PROGRAMMER-ORIENTED DOCUMENTATION Paperwork that focuses on how to maintain and modify the program. (473)

PROGRAMMING Process of designing and writing programs or software. (45)

PROJECT CHARTER Drawn up by the manager of the project and the systems analyst, it outlines the scope of the detailed investigation that is to follow. (438)

PROLOG A fifth-generation nonprocedural language where logical statements are invoked through a series of descriptive clauses. (519)

PROM See Programmable read-only memory.

PROTOCOLS Rules and procedures governing the use of data communications media. (557)

PROTOTYPING Creating small working models of the system to test and adjust for flaws. (449)

PSEUDOCODE An English-like code to help the programmer understand the steps needed to execute the program. (478)

PUBLIC-DOMAIN SOFTWARE Software that is not copyrighted and therefore available for use and distribution without a fee. (264)

PUBLICLY-SUPPORTED SOFTWARE See Shareware.

PULL-DOWN MENU An option list that appears from the top of a computer screen when activated by the user. (284)

QBE (QUERY BY EXAMPLE) Technique whereby the user illustrates the desired outcome instead of using a query. (377)

QUERY LANGUAGE A way to access the database designed for use by personnel who are not programmers. (375)

RAM See Random access memory.

RANDOM-ACCESS FILE See Direct-access file.

RANDOM ACCESS MEMORY (RAM) The mainstay of main memory which can access any address without referring to any adjacent locations. (51, 154)

RANGE In spreadsheets, a rectangular-shaped group of cells ranging in size from one cell to the entire spreadsheet; usually indicated from the upper left cell address to the lower right. (327)

READ-ONLY MEMORY (ROM) CHIP Chip on which programs have been permanently encoded, sometimes called firmware. (51, 155)

REAL-TIME PROCESSING Processing data rapidly enough so that the results can be used to influence a process that is still taking place. (13)

RECALLING Bringing data from secondary storage. (19)

RECORD In database management, a set of one or more fields concerning one individual or case. (44, 350)

REEL-TO-REEL MAGNETIC TAPE Secondary storage media used with large computers. The data are recorded one byte at a time spreading the bits across the width of the tape. (222)

REFORMATTING Rearranging word processing text on a computer screen to fall within set margins. (274)

REGISTER High-speed temporary storage unit used in the control unit and the ALU of the CPU. (142)

RELATIONAL DATABASE All data items are viewed as related to one another, in table form. (366)

RELATIVE ADDRESSING This key uses a field of a record and converts it to an address through an algorithmic process. (358)

RESOURCE UTILIZATION PROCEDURES Tracking and modifying patterns of an information system's resources and using them in the most effective way. (589)

RESPONSE TIME Time between making an inquiry or request and the start of the response. (211)

RETRIEVE Copy from secondary storage into the computer's main memory for subsequent display or use by a program. (275)

RING NETWORK Computers linked in a loop with no central computer in control. (545)

ROBOT Machine capable of coordinating its movements itself by reacting to changes in the environment. (121, 605)

ROBOTICS The study and application of robots. (121, 605)

ROM *See* Read-only memory.

ROW In spreadsheets, a horizontal line of cells extending from one end of the spreadsheet to the other; represented by a whole positive number. (312)

RULER LINE In word processing, a line that defines the horizontal typing area and provides visual references to margins, typing columns, and tabs. (284)

RULES AND PROCEDURES Written and unwritten guidelines that help guide an organizations' operations. (43)

RULE SET *See* Knowledge base.

SAVE Copy from the computer's main memory into secondary storage. (275)

SCHEDULED LISTING The most common type of report, created on a regular basis. (76)

SCHEMA Conceptual or logical view of the relationships among the data elements in the database. (369)

SCREEN-CHECKING Debugging a program with the aid of the computer itself while sitting at the terminal. (492)

SCROLLING Moving a screen window vertically or horizontally to view different sections of a word processing document or spreadsheet. (180, 280)

SEARCH In word processing, a procedure by which a character string can be located within a document. (275)

SEARCH AND REPLACE In word processing, a procedure by which a specific letter, word, or phrase is located in a document and replaced with another. (275)

SEARCH TIME Time it takes for the data to spin under the head for writing or reading the disk or the tape. (217)

SECONDARY, OR EXTERNAL, STORAGE DEVICES Devices that record and store data and programs on a machine readable medium for later use. (57, 210)

SECOND-GENERATION COMPUTERS (1958–1964) Computers that used transistors instead of vacuum tubes, magnetic cores instead of drums. (114)

SECTORS Pie-shaped sections radiating out from the center of the disk. (218)

SECURITY Methods used to protect the five elements of the information system. (572)

SEEK TIME Time required to position the read/write head over the correct part of the disk. (217)

SELECTING Extracting from data those items with certain characteristics. (19)

SELECTION Logic patterns that use comparisons based on decisions or choices to split a program into different paths. (487)

SELF-DOCUMENTATION How easily a program can be read and understood by a programmer or other user. (510)

SEMICONDUCTOR Compound that has both conductive and insulative properties such as transistors and integrated circuits. (114)

SEPARATION OF TASKS Division of tasks and responsibilities among a number of different people in the interest of security. (574)

SEQUENCE Set of linear steps to be carried out in the order of their appearance and always an action verb such as read, calculate, print. (490)

SEQUENTIAL ACCESS The necessity of reading every record in a file leading up to a desired record. (212, 353)

SEQUENTIAL FILE Records arranged in a predetermined way and ordered by a field known as a key. (352)

SERIAL ARITHMETIC Performing of calculations digit-by-digit rather than on the entire number at once. (149)

SHAREWARE Software whose author allows you to freely copy and distribute it, but requires a fee to be paid once the user has decided to keep it. Also known as publicly supported or user-supported software. (264)

SHOCKLEY, WILLIAM, JOHN BARDEEN AND WALTER H. BRATTAIN Inventors of the transistor at Bell Telephone Laboratories in 1948. (114)

SILICON CHIP A piece of glass upon which integrated electronic circuitry can be etched. (50, 116, 150)

SIMPLEX TRANSMISSION One-way transmission, as found in commercial radio or television. (553)

SIMULATION A modeling technique in which users can see the immediate consequences of their actions on a computer screen or printout. (416)

SIMULATION LANGUAGE Uses mathematical or logical formulas to model real-world events, and to predict the possible consequences of those events. (518)

SITE LICENSE Sold by software companies so an organization may make a number of legal copies for its own use. (583)

SMART TERMINAL *See* Intelligent terminal.

SOFT COPY Temporary information displayed on a terminal. (57)

SOFTWARE OR PROGRAMS General name for lists of detailed instructions written in a language the computer can interpret. (11, 45)

SOFTWARE ENGINEERING Automated program-creation and maintenance methods that use modular program building algorithms. (515)

SOFTWARE PIRACY Unauthorized duplication of software. (582)

SOFTWARE SECURITY Measures to protect programs from misuse or tampering. (580)

SORTING Arranging data into some desired order. (16)

SOURCE DATA AUTOMATION The use of machine-readable documents for data entry. (175)

SOURCE DOCUMENT An original business form such as a sales-order form, time card, or the like, containing transaction data. (11)

SPEECH RECOGNITION DEVICE Translates the human voice into signals for use as input media. (192)

SPELLING CHECKER An adjunct program in word processing that locates and identifies potential misspellings in text by comparing words to a predetermined dictionary. (300)

SPREADSHEET A presentation of data arranged in columns and rows; *see also* Electronic spreadsheet. (312)

STANDARDIZATION OF WORK Clear definition of tasks so they are performed in approximately the same way each time. (575)

STANDARD OPERATING PROCEDURES (SOP) Rules and procedures of an organization in normal situations. (43)

STAR NETWORK A central computer connected to remote peripherals or other computers which are not connected to each other. (543)

STATUS LINE In word processing, a line of text at the top or bottom of the screen that presents useful data about current conditions such as cursor position and document identification. (281)

STORAGE HIERARCHY Pyramidal view of storage with the fastest and most expensive computer storage at the top of the pyramid and with slower, less expensive, and roomier secondary storage at the bottom. (210)

STORED PROGRAM CONCEPT Proposed by mathematician John von Neumann, it sped up the time it took to change a program. (109)

STORING Placing data into secondary storage for later recall. (19)

STRUCTURE CHART Diagram that shows the hierarchical relationships between the modules of a program. (478)

STRUCTURED PROGRAM Program written using structured program methods and techniques including modules and the top-down approach. (474)

STRUCTURED PROGRAMMING A top-down framework for developing structured programs. (474, 506)

STRUCTURED SYSTEM DEVELOPMENT TECHNIQUES Methods for studying and designing systems in order to make them simple to use, easier to understand, and easy to change. (432)

STRUCTURED WALKTHROUGH Review meeting of programming peers to evaluate a programmer's work for errors and at which no managers are present. (477)

STYLE CHECKERS Adjunct word processing programs that identify clichés and poor word usage, and rate the document's readability and sentence length. (304)

STYLE SHEET A predesigned layout form in desktop publishing that simplifies page creation. (402)

SUBROUTINE A module of a program which can be called by the main program. (481)

SUBSYSTEMS Systems contained within a larger system or supersystem. (38)

SUMMARIZING Reducing data to an easily understood format. (19)

SUPERCOMPUTER Biggest and fastest of computers, it executes hundreds of millions of calculations a second. (54)

SUPERSYSTEM Two or more smaller systems. (38)

SYNCHRONOUS TRANSMISSION Sending of blocks, or groups of bytes. (556)

SYSTEM Set of interrelated elements working together to produce a common goal. (10, 38)

SYSTEM ACQUISITION Creation of a new system based on the results of the system design stage. (452)

SYSTEM BOUNDARIES These must be set by the systems analyst in order to delineate the scope of the problem. (439)

SYSTEM DESIGN Process of determining, in general, then more detailed terms, the way the new system will be set up. (447)

SYSTEM DEVELOPMENT PROCESS A method for studying and changing systems. (60, 432)

SYSTEM FLOWCHART Visual representation of the information processing system using symbols that give details of the hardware used for input and output. (442)

SYSTEM IMPLEMENTATION Process of changeover from old to new system including conversion, training, and acceptance testing. (454)

SYSTEM MAINTENANCE Continuing process of keeping a system in good working order. (458)

SYSTEM SOFTWARE Programs that link application software to the computer hardware. (45, 519)

SYSTEM START/TERMINATION SYMBOL Indicates the beginning or end of a program or a subroutine within a program. (483)

SYSTEM TIMING Any time-identified patterns or cycles that can be discerned concerning the operations (usually transactions) under investigation. (446)

SYSTEM VOLUME Quantity of operations that occur over a given period of time. (446)

SYSTEMS ANALYSIS A method for examining how an existing system works in order to determine the cause of the problem. (436)

SYSTEMS ANALYST Person who studies and develops information systems that meet the needs of users and clients. (63)

TABLE In relational databases, a two-dimensional representation that contains all data in the form of tuples and attributes. (366)

TABULATING MACHINE Device invented by Herman Hollerith in the 1880s that used punch cards. (106)

TAPE DRIVE *See* Magnetic tape unit.

TELECOMMUNICATIONS *See* Data communications.

TELECOMMUNICATIONS MEDIUM *See* Data communications medium.

TELECOMMUTING Working at home through a link between a microcomputer or display terminal and the office. (83, 611)

TELECONFERENCING Using a computer network to link people in different locations in a meeting. (81)

TELEPROCESSING *See* Data communications.

TEMPLATE A spreadsheet that contains formulas, headings and formats, but no data. (315)

TERABYTE OR T Trillion bytes. (210)

TERMINAL Input/output device that can send data to, or receive information from, a computer through a telecommunications link. (177)

TERMINAL EMULATION MODE A microcomputer linked to a host computer and used as a terminal for micro-to-mainframe links. (543)

TEST DESIGN A plan for the tests that the system must pass in order to meet the user's approval. (452)

TEXT BLOCK In word processing, a large portion of text in a document that can include words, sentences, or paragraphs. (291)

TEXT DATA Facts found in written sources—reports, documents, articles from magazines or journals and other printed media. (7)

TEXT ENTRY In word processing, keying in characters from the keyboard into a document contained in the computer for subsequent display and use. (273)

TEXT ENTRY AREA In word processing, the area of the screen that displays text material, which will later be printed on paper. (285)

THERMAL PRINTER This nonimpact printer uses treated paper that responds to a heated printing element. (197)

THIRD-GENERATION COMPUTER (1964–1971) Machine characterized by the use of the integrated circuit and by the speeding of calculations to nanoseconds. (116)

THREE-DIMENSIONAL SCANNER A peripheral that can look at objects in terms of their width, length, and depth. (190)

TIME BOMB A date-dependent code that activates a destructive computer program. (584)

TIME-SHARING PROCESSING Processing during which the computer alternates between several operations and allows many users to share, at the same time, the same computer. (12)

TOKEN PASSING A method used to manage a contention protocol. A token is a set of 8 bits (usually 11111111) that permits access to the network and is passed to the next terminal granting each, in turn, access to the network. (557)

TOP-DOWN APPROACH Method that relates system or programming modules by starting at a general level and proceeding to the details. (433, 474)

TRACK Concentric ring of magnetized bits on disk media. (218)

TRAILER VALUE Nonsense value placed at the end of a data file to close a loop. (489)

TRANSACTION DATA Facts gathered from routine day-to-day operations. (7)

TRANSISTOR Solid-state semiconductor invented by Shockley, Bardeen, and Brattain in 1948 that replaced the vacuum tube. (114)

TRANSNATIONAL DATA FLOW Transfer of useful data across national boundaries. (580)

TUPLE The relational database equivalent to a database record. (366)

TWISTED WIRE PAIRS Two parallel copper wires, the backbone of the telephone system. (548)

TYPE-AHEAD BUFFER A temporary memory area that holds keystrokes from the keyboard and feeds them into the computer. (273)

TYPEOVER The word processing mode of operation in which new text can be typed directly over old text material, replacing it character for character. (274)

UNIVAC I (UNIVERSAL AUTOMATIC COMPUTER) Available in 1951, it was the first commercially produced computer. (112)

UNIVERSAL PRODUCT CODE (UPC) Data coded as lines (bars) or varying width and found on almost all prepackaged goods. (189)

UNIX An operating system developed by Bell Laboratories that has become popular for many different types of computers. (528)

USER INTERFACE A component of expert system software that includes easy-to-follow menus, readable display screens, and high-quality printed output. (88)

USER-FRIENDLY OUTPUT Output that is uncomputerlike such as a business letter or multicolor graphics. (177)

USER-ORIENTED DOCUMENTATION Written documents and screen displays that assist the user in exploiting the benefits of the program. (473)

USERS People who employ the information system to provide services for their clients. (41)

UTILITY PROGRAM Part of system software that performs general-purpose repetitive processing. (528)

VACUUM TUBES Devices used in first-generation computers for internal processing. (111)

VALIDATION A control in the computer or an intelligent terminal that checks to see that the data are reasonable. (577)

VALUE A numeric entry upon which mathematical calculations can be performed. (322)

VALUE-ADDED NETWORK (VAN) Company that leases data communications media, databases, and sophisticated computers. (562)

VARIABLE-LENGTH WORD Common on microcomputers and other small computers; computer words of varying length minimize wasted main storage. (150)

VERIFICATION Checking data by keying them in a second time. (577)

VERTICAL SOFTWARE Prewritten programs that are useful to one specific industry. (243)

VERY-LARGE-SCALE INTEGRATION (VLSI) Process of placing millions of IC's on a single silicon chip. (120, 619)

VIDEOTAPE SYSTEM Mass storage that uses the videotapes similar to those used in home entertainment to record bytes of data. (223)

VLSI *See* Very-large-scale integration.

VOICE-GRADE MEDIUM Communications medium that transmits data at a higher speed than narrowband media. (552)

VOICE/IMAGE DATA Facts gleaned from telecommunications media from both inside and outside the organization. (7)

VON NEUMANN, JOHN Mathematician who conceived the stored program concept. (109)

WATSON, THOMAS, SR. The first president of IBM. (108)

WIDE AREA NETWORK (WAN) LAN technology used over a large geographic area. (563)

WIDEBAND MEDIUM A communications medium that transmits over the widest range of frequencies. (552)

WINDOW Smaller subdivision of a computer screen containing instructions or data that allow users to work on more than one document or file at a time. (180, 284)

WIRE PAIRS *See* Twisted wire pairs.

WIRTH, NIKLAUS Developer of the Pascal programming language named in honor of Blaise Pascal. (122)

WORD PROCESSING The creation, adjustment, and printing of text material. (272)

WORD PROCESSING SOFTWARE Pre-written programs for entering, modifying, arranging and printing test material. (244)

WORD PROCESSING SYSTEM Allows people to compose, edit, and store text using a computer. (81)

WORD WRAP In word processing, a technique that automatically moves whole words onto the next line if they do not fit within the right margin. (274)

WORKING STORAGE Holds the results of work in progress, such as intermediate answers to mathematical computations the computer is carrying out. (141)

WORKPAD A three-dimensional spreadsheet that organizes cells into columns, rows and pages. (341)

WORM (WRITE-ONCE, READ-MANY) Optical disk technology that resembles a compact disk. (227)

WOZNIAK, STEPHEN AND STEVEN JOBS Designers of the Apple I, the first commercially successful microcomputer, and founders of Apple Computer Corporation in 1977. (119)

WRITTEN PROCEDURES OR STANDARDS Statements of the proper steps needed to complete a task. (576)

Credits

PHOTO CREDITS

Chapter 1

Fig. 1-1a: Tom Tracy, b: Courtesy McDonnell Douglas, c: Roger Tully, d: Courtesy Eastman Kodak Co., e: Courtesy Radio Shack/Tandy Corp., f: Courtesy IBM Fig. 1-5: Courtesy IBM Fig. 1-11c: Courtesy United Airlines Fig. 1-12: Courtesy IBM Fig. 1-13: Courtesy Ford Motor Co. Fig. 1-14: Charlton Photos Fig. 1-15: Courtesy Harris Corp. Fig. 1-16: Courtesy Bureau of Mines, Fig. 1-17a: Courtesy Southern Calif. Edison, b: Courtesy Electric Power Research Inst., c: Courtesy Aydin Controls Fig. 1-18a: Courtesy Assoc. of Am. Railroads, b: Courtesy BART Fig. 1-19a: Charles Feil/FPG, b: Courtesy United Airlines Fig. 1-20: Courtesy Harnesfeger Fig. 1-21: Courtesy Ralph's Grocery

Chapter 2

Page 49a, b: Courtesy Lotus Corp, c: Courtesy Aldus Corp. Fig. 2-9a: Courtesy Motorola, b: Courtesy National Semiconductor Fig. 2-10a: Courtesy Apple Computer, b: Courtesy Motorola Fig. 2-12, 2-13: Courtesy Unisys Fig 2-15: Courtesy Cray Computers Fig. 2-16a: Courtesy Unisys, b: Courtesy Kurzweil Computer Products Fig. 2-17a: Courtesy IBM, b: Courtesy HP Fig. 2-18a: Courtesy IBM, b: Courtesy Sperry, c: Courtesy Radio Shack/Tandy Corp. Fig. 2-19a: Courtesy 3M, b: Courtesy BASF Fig. 2-20a: Courtesy Hayes Microcomputers, b: Courtesy M/A-Com Inc., c: Courtesy GTE Spacenet, d: Courtesy HP, e: Courtesy McDonnel Douglas

Chapter 3

Fig. 3-2: Henley & Savage/The Stock Market Fig. 3-3: Courtesy Hewlett-Packard Co. Fig. 3-4, 3-11a: Courtesy IBM, b: Courtesy AT&T, c: Courtesy Contel Fig. 3-12: Courtesy Toshiba Fig. 3-13: Courtesy IBM Fig. 3-14: Tom Campbell/FPG Fig. 3-15: Courtesy Apple Computer, Inc. Fig. 3-16: Chris Jones/The Stock Market

Chapter 4

Fig. 4-1: Eve Arnold/Magnum Fig. 4-2a, b, 4-3: Courtesy IBM Fig. 4-4a: Historical Pictures Service, Inc., b: Historical Pictures Service, Inc. Fig. 4-5, 4-6a, b, 4-7: Courtesy IBM Fig. 4-8: Wide World Photos Fig. 4-9a, b, c: Courtesy Iowa State University Fig. 4-10a, b, c: Courtesy Unisys Corporation Fig. 4-11: Historical Picture Service, Inc. Fig. 4-12: Courtesy IBM Fig. 4-13: Courtesy Unisys Corporation Fig. 4-14: Courtesy IBM Fig. 4-16a, b: Courtesy AT&T Archives Fig. 4-17, 4-18: Courtesy IBM Fig. 4-19: Courtesy U.S. Navy Fig. 4-20: Courtesy AT&T Archives Fig. 4-21: Courtesy IBM Fig. 4-22: Courtesy True Basic, Inc. Fig. 4-23: Courtesy Intel Corporation Fig. 4-24a, b, c: Courtesy Apple Computer, Inc. Fig. 4-25a: Courtesy Unisys Corporation, b: Courtesy Harris Corporation, c: Courtesy Hewlett-Packard Co. Fig. 4-26: Courtesy Cincinnati Milicron Fig. 4-27b: Courtesy Thinking Machines Corporation Fig. 4-28: Courtesy NASA

Chapter 5

Fig. 5-10a, e, h: Courtesy Motorola, Inc., b: Courtesy Ford Motor Company, c, d, f, g: Courtesy National Semiconductor Corp, i: Courtesy McDonnel Douglas Corporation Fig. 5-11: Courtesy Motorola Inc.

Chapter 6

Fig. 6-2a: Courtesy Radio Shack, a division of Tandy Corporation, b: Courtesy Apple Computer, Inc., c: Courtesy Hewlett-Packard Co., d: Courtesy TRW, Inc. Fig. 6-3a: Courtesy IBM, b: Courtesy Hewlett-Packard Company Fig. 6-4: Courtesy Microsoft Corporation Fig. 6-5a, b: Courtesy IBM Fig. 6-6a: Courtesy Radio Shack, a division Tandy Corporation, b: Courtesy Gilbarco Fig. 6-7: Courtesy Hewlett-Packard Co. Fig. 6-8a: Courtesy Eastman Kodak Company, b: Courtesy Unisys Corporation, c: Courtesy Hewlett-Packard Company Fig. 6-9: Reprinted by permission of San José State University Fig. 6-10a: Courtesy Caere Corp. Fig. 6-11a: Courtesy Houston Instrument, a Division of AMETEK, b: Courtesy Apple Computer Fig. 6-12: Courtesy Pitney Bowes, photograph by Gary Gladstone Fig. 6-13a: Courtesy Hewlett-Packard Co., b: Courtesy Ralph's Grocery Company Fig. 6-14a: Courtesy Unisys Corporation Fig. 6-15: Courtesy IBM Fig. 6-16: Courtesy Harris Corpora-tion Fig. 6-17: Courtesy GE's MR Development Center Fig. 6-18: Courtesy IBM Fig. 6-19a: Courtesy Apple Computer, Inc. c, 6-20a, b: Courtesy DataProducts Corp. Fig. 6-21: Courtesy Hewlett-Packard Company Fig. 6-22: Courtesy IBM Fig. 6-23a: Courtesy Hewlett-Packard Company, b: Courtesy IBM Fig. 6-24: © 1987 Cynthia M. Kurtz, b, c, d, e: Digital Art/Westlight Fig. 6-25a: Courtesy Versatec, b: Courtesy Houston Instrument, a Division of AMETEK Fig. 6-26a: Courtesy Texas Instruments, b: Courtesy Digital Equipment Corporation

Chapter 7

Fig. 7-2: Courtesy IBM Fig. 7-3: Courtesy Seagate Fig. 7-4: Courtesy IBM Fig. 7-5: Courtesy BASF Corporation Information Systems Fig. 7-6: Courtesy Sperry Corporation Fig. 7-7: Courtesy Data Storage Products Group, Control Data Corporation Fig. 7-9: Courtesy Apple Computer, Inc. Fig. 7-10: Iomega Corporation Fig. 7-14a: Courtesy IBM, b: Courtesy Unisys Corporation, c: Courtesy Hewlett-Packard Company Fig. 7-16: Adapted with permission from Honeywell Test Instruments Division Fig. 7-18: Courtesy IBM Fig. 7-19: Courtesy 3M Fig. 7-20: Courtesy Bell Laboratories

Chapter 8

Fig. 8-1: Courtesy Lotus Corporation Fig. 8-3: Courtesy Hewlett-Packard Company Fig. 8-6a: Courtesy IBM, b: Courtesy Microsoft Corporation Fig. 8-7: Courtesy Computervision a division of Prime Computer, Inc., Bedford, Mass. Fig. 8-10: Courtesy Xerox Corporation Fig. 8-12: Courtesy General Motors Corporation Fig. 8-13a, b, c, 8-14a, b: © Teri Stratford 1988 Fig. 8-15a, b, 8-16: Courtesy IBM

Chapter 9

Fig. 9-1, 9-2: Courtesy IBM Fig. 9-3: Courtesy Smith Corona Fig. 9-4: Courtesy IBM Fig. 9-6: Courtesy Apple Computer, Inc. Fig. 9-9: Courtesy Xerox Corporation Fig. 9-12: Courtesy Ashton-Tate Fig. 9-13a: Courtesy WordPerfect Corporation Fig. 9-15: Courtesy IBM Fig. 9-16: © Teri Stratford 1988 Fig. 9-17: Courtesy Apple Computer, Inc. Fig.

9-18: Courtesy WordPerfect Corporation **Fig. 9-24:** Courtesy WordPerfect Corporation

Chapter 10
Fig. 10-3: © Teri Stratford 1988 **Fig. 10-4, 10-8a:** Courtesy Lotus Corporation **Fig. 10-8b:** Courtesy Microsoft Corporation, **c:** © Teri Stratford 1988 **Fig. 10-12:** Courtesy Apple Computer, Inc. **Fig. 10-18:** © Teri Stratford 1988 **Fig. 10-23:** Courtesy Funk Software **Fig. 10-24:** Courtesy Microsoft Corporation **Fig. 10-25c:** Teri Stratford 1988

Chapter 11
Fig. 11-20: Courtesy Apple Computer, Inc. **Fig. 11-21:** Courtesy Microsoft Corporation

Chapter 12
Fig. 12-6: Courtesy Apple Computer, Inc. **Fig. 12-18:** Image © 1988 Aldus Corporation. All rights reserved **Fig. 12-21a, b:** Courtesy Unisys Corporation, **b:** **Fig. 12-22:** Courtesy Aldus Corporation **Fig. 12-28:** Microsoft ® Chart © copyright Microsoft Corporation 1984–1987. Reprinted with permission from Microsoft Corporation **Fig. 12-29:** (left) Courtesy SAS Institute, Inc., (right) Courtesy Computer Associates International, Inc. **Fig. 12-30a:** © Teri Stratford 1988 **Fig. 12-31:** Courtesy Computervision, a division of Prime Computer, Inc., Bedford, Mass.

Chapter 16
Fig. 16-2a: Courtesy National Association of Securities Dealers, Inc., **b:** Courtesy Fairchild Industries **Fig. 16-7a:** Courtesy DSC Communications Corporation, **b:** Courtesy M/A-COM, Inc., **c, d:** Courtesy AT&T

Bell Laboratories **Fig. 16-11:** Courtesy Hayes Microcomputer, Products, Inc.

Chapter 17
Fig. 17-1: A. Tannenbaum/Sygma **Fig. 17-4:** Brownie Harris/The Stock Market **Fig. 17-5:** Courtesy General Motors Corporation **Fig. 17-6:** Courtesy Gabe Palmer/The Stock Market

Chapter 18
Fig. 18-1a: Lester Glassner/Neal Peters, **b:** J. P. Laffont/Sygma, **c:** D. Goldberg/Sygma, **d:** Courtesy General Motors Corporation, **e:** Giovanni/Photoreporters, **f:** Malcom S. Kirk/Peter Arnold, Inc. **Fig. 18-2:** Gabe Palmer/The Stock Market **Fig. 18-3:** John Maher/The Stock Market **Fig. 18-4:** Richard Kalvar/Magnum

TRADEMARKS

Ashton-Tate, Assist, Command Center, dBASE II, dBASE III+, Framework, and Multimate are registered trademarks of Ashton-Tate.
@Liberty is a trademark of SoftLogic Solutions.
BoeingCalc is a registered trademark of the Boeing Co.
Chuck Yeager's Advanced Flight Trainer is a trademark of Electronics Arts.
Crosstalk is a registered trademark of Crosstalk Communication.
Dollars & Sense is a registered trademark of Monogram.
Easytrieve is a registered trademark of Panasophic Co.
Enable is a trademark of The Software Group.
Excell, Flight Simulator, Multiplan, Paintbrush, Windows, Word, and Works are registered trademarks of Microsoft Corp.
Excelerator is a registered trademark of Index Technology.
Express, R:Base 5000, and R:Base System V are registered trademarks of Microrim Corp.
FoxBase+ is a registered trademark of Fox Corp.
Gato is a registered trademark of Spectrum HoloByte.
Hypercard is a registered trademark of Apple Corp.

IBM and PC-DOS are registered trademarks of International Business Machines Corp.
Joe Spreadsheet is a registered trademark of Holt, Rinehart and Winston.
Lotus 1-2-3, Hal, and VisiCalc are registered trademarks of Lotus Development Corp.
MacWrite and MacPaint are registered trademarks of Claris Corp.
Managing Your Money is a registered trademark of MECA, Inc.
Mark IV-Reporter is a registered trademark of Informatics Corp.
Newsroom is a registered trademark of Springboard Software Inc.
Nomad II is a registered trademark of D & B Computing Services.
Note-It and SQZ! are trademarks of Turner Hall Publishing.
Oracle is a registered trademark of Oracle Corp.
Pagemaker is a registered trademark of Aldus Corp.
PC-Calc, PC-File III, and PC-Style are registered trademarks of Buttonware, Inc.
Perfect Calc is a registered trademark of Thorn EMI Computer Software, Inc.
PFS:First Choice and PFS:Plan are registered trademarks of the Software Publishing Corp.
POWERHOUSE is a registered trademark of COGNOS Corp.

Q&A is a registered trademark of Symantec Corp.
Quattro, Reflex, and Paradox are registered trademarks of Borland International.
QuickBASIC is a registered trademark of Microsoft Corp.
Quickcode III is a registered trademark of Fox & Geller.
RPGIII, GIS, and SQL are trademarks of International Business Machines Corp.
SmartCOM II is a registered trademark of Hayes Microcomputer Products Inc.
Sideways is a registered trademark of Funk Software.
SuperCalc is a registered trademark of Computer Associates International.
Symphony is a trademark of Lotus Development Corp.
Truebasic is a registered trademark of Truebasic Inc.
Unix and ISDN are registered trademarks of AT&T.
Ventura Publisher is a registered trademark of Xerox Corp.
VP-Planner is a registered trademark of Paperback Software Corp.
WordPerfect is a registered trademark of WordPerfect Corp.
WordStar is a registered trademark of MicroPro International Corp.

Index